Methods of Educational & Social Science Research

METHODS OF
Educational
Social Science
Research

AN INTEGRATED APPROACH

David R. Krathwohl
Syracuse University

SECOND EDITION

 LONGMAN

An imprint of Addison Wesley Longman, Inc.

New York • Reading, Massachusetts • Menlo Park, California • Harlow, England
Don Mills, Ontario • Sydney • Mexico City • Madrid • Amsterdam

Acquisitions Editor: Virginia L. Blanford
Sponsoring Editor: Art Pomponio
Associate Editor: Arianne J. Weber
Developmental Manager: Arlene Bessenoff
Marketing Manager: Renee Ortbals
Project Coordination and Text Design: Ruttle, Shaw & Wetherill, Inc.
Cover Designer: Kay Petronio
Cover Photo: © 1997 PhotoDisc
Art Studios: Burmar Technical Corporation; Ruttle, Shaw & Wetherill, Inc.
Electronic Production Manager: Christine Pearson
Manufacturing Manager: Willie Lane
Electronic Page Makeup: Ruttle, Shaw & Wetherill, Inc.
Printer and Binder: The Maple-Vail Book Manufacturing Group
Cover Printer: The Lehigh Press, Inc.

Library of Congress Cataloging-in-Publication Data

Krathwohl, David R.
    Methods of educational and social science research : an integrated
approach / by David R. Krathwohl. — 2nd ed.
        p.   cm.
    Includes bibliographical references and index.
    ISBN 0–8013–2029–1
    1. Social sciences—Research—Methodology.   2. Social sciences—
Statistical methods.   I. Title.
H62.K6793   1997
300'.72—dc21   97–20165
                                                                CIP

Copyright © 1998 by Addison-Wesley Educational Publishers, Inc.

0–8013–2029–1

    45678910—MA—0099

To
Charles and Minnie
Marie, Sarah, and William
Helen Jean
Chris, David, Jim, Kate, Kristin, and Ruth
Becca, Elizabeth, Jamie, Keith, and Sarah
Five generations that have so greatly enriched my life

Contents

Preface for the Instructor

Goals of the Text and Changes in This Edition

We have long lacked an integrating framework in research. The first edition of this book presented an important one that improves our understanding of the research process. Its importance continues in this edition, which does more than bring the material up to date. It is designed to better serve master's level students, while continuing to meet the needs of doctoral level ones. Although the goals have not changed, some have received increased emphasis, and there are other changes as well. The goals are that:

Readers should understand science as a social process through which findings become accepted as knowledge. The importance of understanding science as a social process is continued; this topic both opens the core of the text (Chapter 3, From Findings to Knowledge) and closes it (Chapter 25, The Macrosystem of Educational and Social Science Research).

Readers should comprehend how the criteria by which research is judged flow from the knowledge development process with implications for how research is done and reported. The text continues to be integrated by the chain of reasoning, the foundational concepts of internal and external validity, and the framework of which the chain and validities all are a part. Causation and internal validity have been combined into a single chapter because the former identifies the basis for inferring the latter. External validity and sampling are also discussed in one chapter because they have a similar relationship. Combining these previously separate chapters increases integration and facilitates learning and recall.

Readers should understand the chain of reasoning as a conceptualization of the fundamental logic underlying the presentation of data in support of a generalization—realizing also, however, that the order of steps in actually doing a study may be different and that the goal of some research is to describe rather than to present generalizations. This goal and its treatment are unchanged.

Readers should acquire the background needed to read, analyze, and understand research using a variety of approaches, as well as know the hallmarks of methods necessary to evaluate them. They should find methods that comfortably fit them personally and that they will want to master as they do research. Students need a broad understanding of methods—their logic, their strengths and weaknesses, and their complementarity. A broad understanding can also promote greater understanding and respect for each other's research. This edition uses the continuum of research methods, introduced in Chapter 2, to organize Sections 4 through 6, which treat basic research methods. Anchored by quantitative and qualitative approaches, with adaptations of both approaches in between, the continuum provides a broad treatment that helps readers realize they need not be confined to one approach. They can synthesize and creatively adapt methods. This point is further emphasized in Chapter 24, which suggests combinations of research approaches or their adaptations are often required to develop the best study feasible. Such diversity of choices enhances the richness with which future researchers will pursue problems. Although the qualitative-quantitative continuum is used as an organizing framework for instructional purposes, the complementarity of the different methods is stressed, rather than examining them as opposing points of view about how research should be done.

Section Four provides a significantly fuller treatment of qualitative research than the first edition. Its discussion has been expanded from one to five chapters—an introductory chapter followed by four tracing the qualitative research process. This provides a more balanced presentation with quantitative methods and, I believe, is one of the most complete treatments of qualitative methods in any current comprehensive text.

The discussion of meta-analysis has been expanded to chapter length and shown as a quantitative method in its own right. A substantial treatment of research by practitioners has been added in the description of action research in the evaluation chapter.

Readers should understand that the responsibility for ethical research is fundamentally theirs and that value choices are involved in research, beginning with the choice of problem. The topic of ethics has been made more central by placing it before the chapters on research approaches, instead of in the final section of the book as in the first edition. Ethical questions are further discussed within the methods chapters as appropriate.

Readers entering doctoral programs or planning on doing a master's thesis or long paper should be able to prepare their research proposal. The Appendix, on writing a research proposal, is new and should be helpful to doctoral students preparing dissertation proposals and master's students doing theses. It includes material on writing formats applicable to research reports. This section, although based on this book's approach, is adapted from the author's *How to Prepare a Research Proposal*, third edition; the latter is designed for proposals submitted for funding.

Other changes in this edition: References to the Internet have been added. It is rapidly becoming an important resource for facilitating the research process. This topic will gain greater importance with each new edition. The two contrasting examples of research, previously Chapter 2, have become Chapter 1 in this edition, so students immediately form a concrete idea of what research is and how it can be approached in different ways. Answers to the application problems now appear at the end of each chapter, rather than at the back of the book. More accessible after the problem has been tried, they now become a more integral part of the presentation of content. The volume has been slimmed down by eliminating material treated in advanced statistics courses and some less common kinds of research.

Unique Aspects of the Text

As you no doubt realize from the foregoing material, this text has several unique aspects. Some examples are:

- The chain of reasoning as a model of the logic of research reports (Chapter 4)
- The concentration on knowledge of the types of indexes and their advantages and weaknesses in the chapter on the literature search, information that is necessary for successful reference use; most such chapters conclude by listing specific materials any good librarian could help students to find (Chapter 6)
- Discussion of the complexities of the terms *cause* and *effect* not typically realized (Chapter 7)
- Definitions of internal and external validity that reorganize and extend the scope of the Campbell and Stanley and the Cook and Campbell conceptualizations and that define these validities in ways that better conform to the way the terms are usually used (Chapters 7 and 8)
- Sampling described in terms of principles that, once understood, make clear how the major sampling plans flow from them (Chapters 8 and 16)
- The framework surrounding external and internal validity, which makes explicit other decisions involved in the design of both qualitative and quantitative studies (Chapter 9)
- A comprehensive treatment of research ethics that goes beyond institutional review boards to discuss the researcher's individual responsibility (Chapter 10)
- Discussion of measurement validity from the standpoint of the new Test Standards being adopted by the APA, AERA and NCME. They make construct validity the overall validity umbrella and add evidence not considered in previous versions of the standards (Chapter 18)
- Discussion of the many possible trade-offs involved in all studies that frequently go unrecognized, yet affect the study's quality (Sections Four, Five, and Six and Chapter 24)
- A treatment of statistics that provides an understanding of their nature and logic; concentrating on the forest instead of the trees with verbal and graphic descriptions, it has a minimum of formulas and computation (Chapters 17 and 19)
- Examination of how well science works (Chapter 25)

Using This Book in Instruction

This book, by providing a panorama of choices, allows instructors to adapt the content to the needs of the students. I consider the following a core around which to build: Chapter 3, From Findings to Knowledge; Chapter 4, The Research Chain of Reasoning; Chapter 7, Causal Inference and Internal Validity; Chapter 8, Sampling, Representation, and External Validity; Chapter 9, Research Criteria to Optimize and Constaints to Observe; Chapter 10, Ethical Standards and Legal Constraints; Chapter 11, Qualitative Research Methods; Chapter 16, Survey Research and Questionnaires; Chapter 20, Experimental Methods and Experimental Design; and Chapter 25, The Macrosystem of Educational and Social Science Research.

The choice of chapters to assign beyond this depends on the makeup of the class (for example, if you have many practitioners, include Chapter 23 and emphasize action research). Instructors of one-semester courses may find it necessary to emphasize one or the other of the research approaches to give students more than just a once-over-lightly feel for research.

Those teaching doctoral courses might find it helpful to start with the problem finding and literature review chapters and the appendix on proposal writing to get students started on their dissertation proposals. For a two-semester course, an approach that I have found works well, is to start with students doing a small qualitative project (Section Four) and then move to the foundational skills and concepts material (Sections Two and Three) as appropriate, using the previous work to illustrate it. This gives students an immediate feel for research that one can build on.

Be sure to request the Instructor's Manual, which has been adapted for this edition by Dr. Jane McGraw, who built on the first edition's version prepared by Dr. Richard Kenny. It provides some teaching suggestions, some supplementary materials, chapter objectives, and suggested test items.

A Request

I have requested students to send me their comments and suggestions, I very much hope you will as well. The changes in this edition are in response to suggestions made about the first one. Your reactions are absolutely key to determining how best to make this text fit what is needed. So please e-mail your comments and suggestions for this *Research Text*'s 2nd *edition to:* ResTxt2e@aol.com.

Acknowledgments

Alex Haley, author of *Roots* says, "Whenever you see a turtle on top of a fence post, you know he had a lot of help getting there." I am, for sure, like that turtle! The first edition's lengthy list of acknowledgments makes clear the help necessary to produce a text such as this. Although there are many changes, this edition is built on the solid base of the first, and my debt to those individuals continues in this one.

In addition, I am most grateful to Dr. Ginny Blanford and Dr. Arthur Pomponio who, as Addison Wesley Longman's Education Editors, have made great suggestions, have been very supportive, and have steered the production of this edition on a steady course toward improvement through a period of publishing merger and reorganization. I am grateful to Mrs. Bridgett Dougherty of Ruttle, Shaw & Wetherill for cheerfully seeing the many manuscript changes through production. Many substantial changes resulted from the efforts of Ms. Arlene Bessenoff, as Developmental manager, who, with her assistant Mr. Michael Spurlock, provided an excellent set of reviews of early drafts as well as helpful developmental editing by Ms. Barbara Conover.

Those reviewers to whom I owe such a special debt of thanks for their remarkably thoughtful and insightful comments and suggestions are: Robert Calfee, Stanford University; Carolyn Dickman, Radford University; Stephen Jenkins, Georgia Southern University; James Johnson, Pennsylvania State University; Golam Mannan, Indiana University Purdue University Indianapolis; Jane McGraw, California State Polytechnic University; Pietro Pascale, Youngstown State University; A. William Place, University of Dayton; John Rogan, Western Montana College; Leslie Riggin, Florida State University; and Joan Stark, University of Michigan. The text was markedly improved by their suggestions. I am especially appreciative of the extensive time and effort they expended, some giving far more than could reasonably be expected. I can't single out the latter since identifying information was removed from my copies. They know who they are, however, and I hope they will take this as a personal "Thank you so *very* much!"

D. R. K.

Preface for the Student

Intellectual mastery is rewarding. It is particularly so when you recognize the cumulative power of learning, that learning one thing permits you to go on to something that before was out of reach. It gives you increasing self-confidence in your abilities.

After Jerome Bruner

What This Book Covers

"You've got to know the territory!" sings Professor Harold Hill in *The Music Man.* He's right, it does help you get where you are going. So that you'll know the "territory," following is a road map of the book's sections in the form of the questions answered by its chapters.

Section One shows that you already have some knowledge of social science research on which to build and presents several important basic concepts. It answers such questions as: Chapter 1—How well can I critique two contrasting research studies? Chapter 2—What is the qualitative-to-quantitative continuum of research methods? Chapter 3—How do findings from a research study become accepted as knowledge? Chapter 4—What is the chain of reasoning, and how is it a useful, universal model for planning, analyzing, implementing, and critiquing research?

Section Two deals with two foundational research skills. Chapter 5 addresses the question: What are good research problems, and how do I find them? Chapter 6 answers the question: How do I find and use past research in the development of my problem?

Section Three, using the chain of reasoning as a base, explores foundational research concepts such as: Chapter 7—What really is meant by cause and effect, and on what evidence do we infer causation? (We call this the linking power—LP—of a study, or the internal validity that links cause to effect.) Chapter 8—What are the basic principles of sampling that allow generalization from a study's sample to a population? (Similarly, we call this the generalizing power—GP—, or external validity of a study.) Chapter 9—How do these criteria fit into a larger framework of goals to be optimized and constraints to be observed? Chapter 10—What ethical problems are encountered in research, and what is the researcher expected to do about them?

Sections Four through Six illustrate the continuum of research approaches. Section Four starts at the qualitative end with Chapter 11's general question: What is qualitative research? Next, successive chapters trace the qualitative research process: Chapter 12—How does one go about fieldwork to gather qualitative data, especially through observation? Chapter 13—How does one gather qualitative data through interviews? Chapter 14—How does one analyze qualitative data? Chapter 15—How does one draw conclusions from qualitative data and prepare a research report?

Section Five's Chapter 16 presents the first of three examples of the qualitative/quantitative middle (the other two are in Section Seven) and answers: What is survey research and how does it involve both quantitative and qualitative methods?

Section Six develops the quantitative end of the continuum beginning with three chapters on the tools used: Chapter 17—How do I describe in numbers as well as words? Chapter 18—What is the logic used in inferential statistics? Chapter 19—How do I translate a concept or a construct into good instrumentation? Indeed, what are the characteristics of good measures? Then two chapters show these tools in use: Chapter 20—What are the principles of experimental design, and how are they exemplified in sample designs? Chapter 21—How does meta-analysis synthesize the multiple studies of a phenomenon into a single result, and how is it a research method in its own right?

Section Seven presents the two other examples of research fields that occupy the qualitative/quantitative middle: Chapter 22—How are quantitative and qualitative methods used in history? Chapter 23—How are they used in evaluation, and what is action research and how do professionals use it to improve their practice?

Section Eight takes a step backward to view the research system in perspective: Chapter 24—How are two or more research methods often better than one for attacking many problems? In designing research, why is there always a problem of trade-offs, of "wanting to have one's cake and eat it too"? And, finally, Chapter 25—How well does the research system work? Does the system do what it is supposed to? What are its strengths and weaknesses?

The Appendix provides guidance for writing a research proposal for a doctoral dissertation or a master's level thesis or paper. In addition, it provides examples of APA style headings and references for papers, research reports, and proposals.

The book is written in an informal style. As a student, Jim Ellsworth, wrote to me, "It is intended to avoid the traditional 'droning lecture on paper' style exhibited by all too many authors" and "to treat the reader as a colleague, which is both appropriate and important for an upper-level text."

Abundant Help for Learning

You learn better if you can fit what you are learning into a scheme that organizes the material into its proper places. Early on, therefore, the substance of Chapters 3, 4, and 7 to 9 are synthesized into a useful framework that integrates the book.

Starting with a discussion of how science works, it describes the chain of reasoning and the criteria by which research is judged that flow from it (see the diagram on the inside front cover as a handy reference). All chapters describing a link in the chain of reasoning open with a spotlight on the part of the chain that shows you where the chapter fits in the framework. Especially if you are a doctoral or master's student doing a proposal for a dissertation, thesis, or long paper, read the Appendix early. Then it, too, becomes an organizer with slots into which you will fit successive pieces of the text as they are mastered.

Many students make the mistake of assuming that once they have read something they have processed it well enough to recall it. That may be true for a few, but most of us need to process more deeply, deeply enough to embed new material in the network of things we have already learned. Doing so makes it "yours." It creates chunks out of individual pieces that are connected so that recalling one helps us to remember others. Experts and novices "chunk" material differently. Read Chase and Simon's (1973) excellent example of the differences on page 89 under the heading "Talk to the Specialists in the Field." Then read the section on the preceding page under the heading "Organize the Material You Have Read" to see how experts build chunks.

How can you effectively chunk material? Use the features that appear in each chapter designed to help you learn. These all contribute to the deeper processing of material that results in chunking. Arranged in the order in which they appear in the chapter, and with an indication of how they will help you, they include the following items.

Learning Aids at the Beginning of the Chapter

An *Overview* section tells you what to anticipate in the chapter. Research shows that learning is facilitated by advance organizers that help you anticipate what you are about to learn. In doing this, the overview provides a scaffolding around which to mentally organize the material as well as to help you set your own priorities. Next, a *Chapter Table of Contents* section shows the organization of the chapter in greater detail. By examining it, you can anticipate where the material is going and the length of sections and thus process it more efficiently. Then, an *Introduction* sets the material to come in context and provides more detail.

Learning Aids in the Body of the Chapter

Summaries after major points or sections are set off from the text by stars, different type, and indentation from the margin. (See the examples on the next two pages. To see a sample in the text, turn to page 27.) They briefly restate the previous material, often slightly differently, so you'll have to think about it—that is, process it—to see that it is the same (for example, the one on page xxiii). Such processing of the material as you read is especially important to being able to recall it and making it "yours." To further facilitate this, periodically summarize *in writing* the material you have read and compare your summaries with those placed throughout the text. Writing does more than simply make a record, it helps you process the material as you choose and organize what you put down. Your summary may be better than the one provided, but where there are significant differences, reread the material to sort out and evaluate those differences.

✦ *Thinking about material as you read is important. Summarizing periodically in writing and comparing your summaries with those in the text will help you process the material and make it part of what you know.*

Learning Aids at the End of the Chapter

Six useful learning aids are found at the end of each chapter. A *Summary* section supplements the starred summaries and highlights the chapter's important material. Check it to find anything you missed. A *Look Ahead* section helps you anticipate how the material you have just read ties into what comes next. An *Additional Reading* section provides suggestions for reading more about a topic or perhaps finding an alternative presentation of a point or concept.

Examine each chapter's *Important Terms* section to see what you can recall about each term and why it is significant. If you miss some, look them up in the Glossary in the back of the book. Glossary terms appear in **bold** type when they are first significantly discussed in the text. (The Glossary follows the Appendix at the end of the book. Use it to refresh your understanding of terms or to look up new ones. Definitions are often phrased differently from the text. A page reference leads you to where the term is discussed.)

Application Problems and their answers should be considered part of the chapter's text. Try them and then check your answers against those given at the end of the chapter. Your answer may be better than the printed one, but be sure you understand the reasonableness of the given answer.

Application Exercise sections begin with Chapter 5 (see page 96), and their purpose is to carry you through the book, learning on your own research problem. You are asked to choose a problem and then to develop it further by applying the content of each successive chapter. This not only helps you learn the material but also, for doctoral students, can result in completing the first draft of a proposal for your dissertation. This has helped many of my students advance from ABDs ("all but dissertation" status) into doctorates. *Doctoral students especially should read the Appendix very early in the course for advice, and refer to it again periodically as they develop their proposals.*

Particularly for those aided by visual presentations, the addendum to Chapter 5 (beginning on page 98) introduces a way to organize your notes on the chapter's content differently from outlining. It is especially useful in helping you think through and see the relationships between what you are learning and what you have already learned.

✦ *Using the variety of learning aids built into the text will help you to more deeply process the material and thereby better remember it.*

Special Learning Aids in the Research Methods Chapters

Special features in the chapters describing particular research approaches highlight important aspects for researchers and for research consumers:

- *Hallmark* sections. How do you know when a research method has been used well or on what aspects to concentrate when you use it? All research methods chapters have sections describing the hallmarks of quality so that you'll recognize good work when you see it. Like the guild hallmarks of the Middle Ages, they help ensure the excellence of the product.
- *Tips* sections. These sections describe how to use the method to create a stronger study. Many describe additional characteristics to those summarized for research consumers in the hallmarks section. Sometimes tips and hallmarks are combined.

◆ *Hallmark sections (signals of research quality) and tips sections (actions that improve research quality) supplement the chapter summaries in the chapters discussing research methods.*

A Request

To improve this book, I need to hear your suggestions and to learn of any problems that you encounter. Were your answers to problems better than ours? Tell me about them. Please send your e-mail regarding this *Research Text*'s 2nd edition to: ResTxt2e@aol.com. Thank you!

D. R. K.

SECTION ONE

The Nature of Research

This section is intended to help you become comfortable with the notion of what research is and its variety of methods. It explores how research findings come to assume the status of knowledge and the structure that permits them to do so.

- Chapter 1 introduces you to the nature and goals of social and behavioral research. Starting off with examples of two studies, it helps you recognize that you have a good knowledge base to build on.
- Chapter 2 shows the wide variety of methods that are employed in the social and behavioral sciences.
- Chapter 3 examines how the findings of a research study become knowledge.
- Chapter 4 describes a valuable general model of a study—the chain of reasoning—that we will use throughout the book.

Although this book opens with two research studies purposely chosen to illustrate contrasting research orientations, in the very next chapter we note there are other research approaches. Indeed, we explain that while for purposes of explanation these two can be considered the end points of a continuum, there are many research types in between, each with its unique characteristics. This allows researchers to choose research approaches best suited to their problems and skills.

The conceptualization of a continuum is carried further and reinforced in the middle of the book where both the continuum's ends are explored in depth (Sections Four and Six), and one of many possible in-between points, survey research, is similarly extensively examined (Section Five). Section Seven describes methods used in two other in-between-on-the-continuum examples of common research fields, history and evaluation/action research.

The book closes, bringing this point full circle, by emphasizing that many problems are best investigated, and many researchers best served, by using a hybrid approach that appropriately combines parts of different research methods (Chapter 24).

CHAPTER 1

An Introduction to Two Contrasting Research Styles

We are a scientific civilisation; that means a civilisation in which knowledge and its integrity are crucial. Science is only a Latin word for knowledge.

Jacob Bronowski, *The Ascent of Man*

I believe that human life is ours to study.... With a few exceptions, only students in our century have managed to hold it steadily in view ... without piety or the necessity to treat traditional issues. Only in modern times have university students been systematically trained to examine all levels of social life meticulously.

Goffman, 1983, p. 17 as found in Lofland (1995)

OVERVIEW

For centuries researchers used the relatively dull edge of experience to attack social problems, and discerning observers and perceptive thinkers made some progress. In the twentieth century, however, increased attention was given to methods of investigation. The result has been a keener blade of sophisticated research methods involving the collection and analysis of both verbal and numerical data. With these methods we have begun laying bare fundamental explanations of individual and group behavior.

This chapter reprints the text of two research studies illustrating two of a number of different ways of approaching research. As you read them, you will sense their strengths and weaknesses and realize that certain studies may be more amenable to one approach than another. This chapter also provides an opportunity to try your skill at analyzing studies and show how much you already know about social and behavioral science research. Though you may miss certain aspects on your first read-through, you will be surprised at how many you recognize when they are pointed out. One function of this book is to make this kind of knowledge come more readily to mind in an integrated form.

CHAPTER CONTENTS

Social and Behavioral Science:
Important but Historically Young

"Mom, why is Grandpa so suspicious of everyone these days? He seems always to feel that folks are trying to hide something from him, that they are out to get him. I'm sure not! And that stuff about not wanting him around, where did he get that idea? He used to be so easygoing! I don't understand what's going on!"

"I wish I knew, son, but I don't. I've noticed the change, too, and it's got me worried."

Zimbardo and associates (1981) thought they understood what was occurring in cases like this. They did an experiment to test their hunch. Researchers call such hunches that guide studies **hypotheses.** Research hypotheses are surmises that a particular relationship or condition exists. Their hypothesis was that individuals who are gradually growing deaf don't realize it. Deafness changes their perception of the world, which they interpret as increasingly hostile. Testing that hypothesis was an attempt to provide evidence supporting the experimenters' explanation of this phenomenon. Such testing is a common goal in research. Researchers call this confirmation process, the gathering of supporting evidence, **validation.** It is one of many important roles served by research.

The problems that accompany aging are only a few of the many such problems that have been speculated about since time began. How do you and I learn? Why do we act differently in a group from the way we act when we are alone? Why do we choose different ways to organize our governments, economies, and social groups? These fascinating questions have evoked many answers. Only in the twentieth century, however, did we begin to investigate social and behavioral questions by using systematic observation and measurement methods, standardized tests, sophisticated coding schemes for analyzing verbal and observational data, carefully constructed questionnaires, individual and group interview techniques, and large masses of data. Although our progress has become increasingly rapid in the past few decades as we have gained experience, many people believe it is still much too slow, especially if we consider the social problems that it might relieve. One hope is that with improved methods and well-trained researchers, progress will accelerate. This book is intended as a step in that direction.

Physical and biological phenomena have been scientifically studied for several centuries. Hence one might think their research methods have become stable; yet, they are still continually evolving. So it is not surprising that, since scientific study of societal and individual problems is new in the twentieth century, its methods are undergoing change and development even as this book is written. In part because of their recent evolution, however, these methods are still close to the layperson's perspective. It does not require a lifetime of work to understand their underlying rationale. The methods result from straightforward application of logical reasoning and will fit easily into your typical pattern of thinking once you have mastered the terminology—research, like all other fields, has its own jargon. Especially watch out for special definitions of common terms that have a particular meaning in the context of research. For instance, the problem of "mortality" means persons dropped out of the study, not that they died.

Just the words *statistical methods* can create fear in people uncomfortable with mathematical equations and calculations. But, we can develop a conceptual understanding of a statistic's purpose and its usage, just as we can for any other research method. Correct usage of statistics in specific situations may still be daunting. Today, however, computation is usually done by computer programs, and learning statistical computation is often not necessary for understanding and interpreting the statistics themselves. Although you may have to stretch a bit to comprehend complex statistical procedures beyond the scope of this book, such as canonical correlation or ridge regression, you can get help by placing a request on one of the listservs or bulletin boards maintained by professional associations on the Internet.

Your common sense will be a sound guide for most of what you will learn from this book. You don't believe it? The personal demonstration in the next section should ease any concerns you may have about your ability to master this material.

Two Illustrative Studies

There is no better way to understand what is meant by "research" and to sense the fact that social sciences use a variety of research methods than to start with examples of two contrasting but equally important methods of doing research.

The First Example
- Uses **quantitative methods**
- Measures and statistics describe phenomena
- Is a tightly designed experiment in which events are controlled by the researcher
- Employs deductive logic to predict the results from the proposed explanation (hypothesis)
- Validates an explanation and demonstrates a relationship

The Second Example
- Uses **qualitative methods**
- Verbal descriptions portray phenomena
- Consists of unstructured interviews in which subjects, expressing their own thoughts, explore the topic with the researcher
- Employs inductive logic to find an explanation
- Develops an explanation for a perceived relationship

This chapter contrasts two methods of data collection and analysis, which, as you will see in the next chapter, can be viewed as the opposite ends of a continuum of research methods. But, *research methods and research fields not only borrow from both ends of the continuum, but also add important and useful aspects of their own.* This is shown in the discussions of survey, historical, evaluation, and action research (Sections Five and Seven of this book). Further, many researchers use both qualitative and quantitative methods in the same study in complementary fashion to develop their case better. It is true that quantitative and qualitative methods each have their own tradition, supporters, and literature, and so the distinction is useful for instructional purposes. But, for most of us, making too much of it can get in the way of seeing all methods as contributors to a panorama of tools from which to select to accomplish best one's research purposes.

Almost without regard to method, however, untrained readers show amazing skill in critiquing important aspects of a study. Training will make you sensitive to even more aspects and, most important, will give you a framework to retain the important points in your memory. Read the following study critically, making notes on its strengths and weaknesses.

A Quantitative Experimental Study[1]

Induced Hearing Deficit Generates Experimental Paranoia

Philip G. Zimbardo
Susan M. Andersen
Stanford University
Loren G. Kabat
State University of New York, Stony Brook

Abstract. The development of paranoid reactions was investigated in normal people experiencing a temporary loss of hearing. In a social setting, subjects made partially deaf by hypnotic suggestion, but kept unaware of the source of their deafness, became more paranoid as indicated on a variety of assessment measures. The results support a hypothesized cognitive-social mechanism for the clinically observed relationship between paranoia and deafness in the elderly.

1. Clinical observation has uncovered a relationship between deafness and psychopathology (*1–3*). In particular, when deafness occurs later in life and the hearing loss is relatively gradual, paranoid reactions are often observed (*4–14*). Delusions of persecution and other paranoid symptoms, first noted by Kraepelin (*6*) in 1915, seem especially prevalent among the hard-of-hearing elderly (*7–9*). Audiometric assessment of hospitalized, elderly patients (with age and other selection factors controlled statistically) has revealed a significantly greater degree of deafness among those diagnosed as paranoid than among those with affective disorders (*10–12*).

2. Maher (*15*) suggested that one process by which deafness may lead to paranoid reactions involves an initial lack of awareness of the hearing defect by the person, as well as by interacting others. Paranoid thinking then emerges as a cognitive attempt to explain the perceptual anomaly (*16*) of not being able to hear what people in one's presence are apparently saying. Judging them to be whispering, one may ask, "about what?" or "why me?" Denial by others that they are whispering may be interpreted by the hard-of-hearing person as a lie since it is so clearly discrepant with observed evidence. Frustration and anger over such injustices may gradually result in a more profound expression of hostility.

3. Observers, without access to the perceptual data base of the person experiencing the hearing disorder, judge these responses to be bizarre instances of thought pathology. As a consequence, others may exclude the hard-of-hearing person, whose suspiciousness and delusions about their alleged plots become upsetting (*17*). Over time, social relationships deteriorate, and the individual experiences both isolation and loss of the corrective social feedback essential for modifying false beliefs (*18, 19*). Within a self-validating, autistic system, delusions of persecution go unchecked (*20*). As such, they eventually become resistant to contrary information from any external source (*21*). In this analysis, paranoia is sometimes an end product of an initially rational search to explain a perceptual discontinuity, in this case, being deaf without knowing it.

4. We now report an experimental investigation of the development of paranoid reactions in normal subjects with a temporary functional loss of hearing. Across a variety of assessment measures, including standard personality tests, self-reports, and judgments of their behavior by others in the situation, these subjects became significantly more paranoid than did subjects in two control conditions. The effect was transient and limited to the test environment [by the specificity of the instructions, by extensive post-experimental interviews (debriefing procedures), and by the healthy "premorbid" status of each participant]. Nevertheless, qualitative observations and objective data offer support for the role of deafness-without-awareness as a causal factor in triggering paranoid reactions. Although the subjects were young and had normal hearing, these results have obvious bearing on a possible cognitive-social mechanism by which deafness may eventuate in paranoia among the middle-aged and elderly.

5. Participants were 18 college males selected from large introductory classes. In the selection process, each student (i) demonstrated that he was highly hypnotizable according to the Harvard Group Scale of Hypnotic Susceptibility (*22*) and the Stanford Scale of Hypnotic Susceptibility, form C (*23*); (ii) evidenced posthypnotic amnesia; (iii) passed a test of hypnotically induced partial deafness; (iv) scored within the normal range on measures of psychopathology; and (v) attended at least one of two hypnosis training sessions before the experiment.

6. Six participants were randomly assigned to the experimental treatment in which partial deafness, without awareness of its source, was hypnotically induced. The remaining participants were randomly assigned to one of two control groups. In one of these groups, partial deafness with awareness of its source was induced to demonstrate the importance of the knowledge that one's difficulty in understanding others is caused by deafness. In the other control group, a posthypnotic suggestion unrelated to deafness was experienced (a compulsion to scratch an itchy ear) along with amnesia for it, to establish whether merely carrying out a posthypnotic suggestion with amnesia might be sufficient to yield the predicted results. Taken together, these two groups provide controls for experimental demand characteristics, subject selection traits (hypnotic susceptibility), and the rational basis for the experienced sensory anomaly (*24*).

7. During group training sessions, each subject was instructed in self-hypnosis and completed consent and medical history forms, a number of Minnesota Multiphasic Personality Inventory (MMPI) scales (*25*), and our clinically derived paranoia scale (*26*). In the experimental session, subjects were hypnotized, after which they listened through earphones to deep relaxation music and then heard taped instructions for one of the three treatments. The use of coded tapes randomly selected in advance by one of the researchers (L.K.) made it possible for the hypnotist (P.Z.), experimenter (S.A.), observers, and confederates to be ignorant of the treatment assignment of the subjects. All subjects were given the suggestion to begin experiencing the changed state when they saw the posthypnotic cue ("FOCUS") projected on a viewing screen in the laboratory. In order to make the task socially realistic and to conceal the purpose of the experiment, each subject was led to believe he was participating, along with two others (who were confederates), in a study of the effects of hypnotic training procedures on creative problem solving. Because of the hearing defect that subjects were to experience, all instructions and tasks were projected automatically by timed slides, the first of which was the posthypnotic cue. While working on a preliminary anagram task,

the two confederates engaged in a well-rehearsed, standard conversation designed to establish their commonality, to offer test probes for the subject's deafness, and to provide verbal content that might be misperceived as antagonistic. They recall a party they had both attended, laughed at an incident mentioned, made a funny face, and eventually decided to work together, finally asking the subject if he also wanted to work with them.

8. The instructions had previously suggested that group effort on such tasks is usually superior to solitary responding. The subject's behavior was videotaped, observed directly by two judges from behind a one-way mirror, and scored independently by the confederates immediately after the session. After this conversation, the three participants were asked to develop stories about pairs of people in ambiguous relationships [Thematic Apperception Test (TAT)]. On the first task, they had the option of working together or of working alone. Thus, an interdependence among confederates and the subject was created [important in the natural etiology of paranoia (*17, 19, 21*)], which centered around developing a common creative solution. On the second TAT task, participants had to work alone.

9. After these tasks were completed, each confederate was instructed by the slides to go to a different laboratory room while the subject stayed in the room to complete evaluation forms, including the MMPI and others. Extensive debriefing followed (*27*), and to remove any tension or confusion, each subject was rehypnotized by the experimenter and told to recall all the events experienced during the session. Subjects were reevaluated in a 1-month follow-up.

10. Major results are summarized in Table 1, which presents group means and one-tailed *t*-test values derived from a single a priori planned comparison that contrasted the experimental group with the two control groups taken together (*28*). This analysis followed standard analysis of variance tests. As predicted, the experience of being partially deaf, without being aware of its source, created significant changes in cognitive, emotional, and behavioral functioning. Compared with the control groups, subjects in the deafness-without-awareness treatment became more paranoid, as shown on an MMPI paranoia scale of Horn (*25*, p. 283) and on our clinically derived paranoia scale (*26*). Experimental subjects also had significantly elevated scores on the MMPI grandiosity scale of Watson and Klett (*25*, p. 287)—one aspect of paranoid thinking. Experimental subjects perceived themselves as more irritated,

agitated, hostile, and unfriendly than control subjects did and were perceived as such by confederates ignorant of the treatment. When invited to work with confederates on the TAT task, only one of six experimental subjects elected to do so; in contrast, 9 of 12 control subjects preferred to affiliate ($z = 4.32$, $P < .001$).

11. The TAT stories generated by the subjects were assessed in two ways. Subjects' own ratings of the creativity of their stories indicated that experimental subjects judged their stories to be significantly less creative than did subjects in either of the control groups. Second, the stories were scored (reliably by two judges) for the extent to which subjects evaluated TAT characters. An evaluative-judgmental outlook toward other people is a hallmark of paranoia. The experimental subjects used significantly more evaluative language, both positive and negative (for example, right–wrong, good–bad) ($t = 2.86$, $P < .01$) than controls did. In addition, they differed significantly ($z = 5.00$, $P < .001$) from the controls in their greater use of positive evaluative language. Experimental subjects reported feeling no more suspicious than did control subjects. These last two findings weaken the possible criticism that the results were based simply on anger induced by the experimental manipulation.

12. Both groups experiencing a hearing deficit reported, as expected, that their hearing was not keen, but reported no other sensory difficulties. Those who were partially deaf without being aware of the source of the deafness did experience greater confusion, which is likely to have motivated an active search for an appropriate explanation. Over time, however, if their delusional systems were allowed to become more coherent and systematized, the paranoid reaction would be less likely to involve confusion. Ultimately, there is so much confidence in the proposed paranoid explanatory system that alternative scenarios are rejected.

13. Despite the artificiality of our laboratory procedure, functionally analogous predicaments occur in everyday life. People's hearing does deteriorate without their realizing it. Indeed, the onset of deafness among the elderly is sometimes actively denied because recognizing a hearing deficit may be tantamount to acknowledging a greater defect—old age. Perhaps self-deception about one's hearing deficit may even be sufficient, in some circumstances, to yield a similar response, namely, a search for a more personally acceptable alternative that finds fault in others rather than in oneself. When there is no social or cultural support for the chosen explanation and

TABLE 1 *Mean Scores on Dependent Measures Distinguishing Experimental from Control Subjects*

Dependent measures	Treatment				
		Control			
	Deafness without awareness (N = 6)	Deafness with awareness (N = 6)	Posthypnotic suggestions (N = 6)	t(15)	P
Paranoia measures*					
MMPI–Paranoia	1.50	.33	−.17	1.838	<.05
MMPI–Grandiosity	1.33	−.83	−1.00	1.922	<.05
Paranoia clinical interview form	.30	−.09	−.28	3.667	<.005
TAT					
Affective evaluation	83.35	16.65	33.50	2.858	<.01
Self-assessed creativity	42.83	68.33	73.33	3.436	<.005
Self-rated feelings					
Creative	34.17	55.83	65.83	2.493	<.05
Confused	73.33	39.17	35.00	2.521	<.05
Relaxed	43.33	81.67	78.33	2.855	<.01
Agitated	73.33	14.17	15.33	6.586	<.001
Irritated	70.00	25.00	7.00	6.000	<.001
Friendly	26.67	53.33	56.67	2.195	<.05
Hostile	38.33	13.33	13.33	2.047	<.05
Judges' ratings					
Confused	40.83	27.08	17.67	1.470	<.10
Relaxed	34.17	54.59	65.42	2.839	<.01
Agitated	51.25	24.59	13.75	3.107	<.005
Irritated	45.84	18.92	11.25	3.299	<.005
Friendly	23.34	48.34	65.00	3.385	<.005
Hostile	18.75	5.00	1.67	2.220	<.05

*These measures were taken before and after the experimental session; reported means represent difference scores (after minus before).

the actor is relatively powerless, others may judge him or her to be irrational and suffering from a mental disorder. Although our subjects were young and had normal hearing, these findings have obvious bearing on a possible cognitive-social mechanism by which deafness may lead to paranoia among the middle-aged and elderly.

REFERENCES AND NOTES

1. B. Pritzker, *Schweiz. Med. Wochenschr.* **7**, 165 (1938).
2. F. Houston and A. B. Royse, *J. Ment. Sci.* **100**, 990 (1954).
3. M. Vernon, *J. Speech Hear. Res.* **12**, 541 (1969).
4. K. Z. Altshuler, *Am. J. Psychiatry* **127**, 11 and 1521 (1971).
5. Personal communication from J. D. Rainer (14 July 1980), who has studied the psychiatric effects of deafness for the past 25 years at the New York State Psychiatric Institute.
6. E. Kraepelin, *Psychiatrie* **8**, 1441 (1915).
7. D. W. K. Kay, *Br. J. Hosp. Med.* **8**, 369 (1972).
8. F. Post, *Persistent Persecutory States of the Elderly* (Pergamon, London, 1966).
9. H. A. McCelland, M. Roth, H. Neubauer, R. F. Garside, *Excerpta Med., Int. Congr. Ser.* **4**, 2955 (1968).
10. A. F. Cooper, R. F. Garside, D. W. K. Kay, *Br. J. Psychiatry* **129**, 532 (1976).
11. A. F. Cooper, A. R. Curry, D. W. K. Kay, R. F. Garside, M. Roth, *Lancet* (**1974-II**, 7885 (1974).
12. A. F. Cooper and R. Porter, *J. Psychosom. Res.* **20**, 107 (1976).

13. A. F. Cooper, *Br. J. Psychiatry* **129,** 216 (1976).
14. D. W. K. Kay, A. F. Cooper, R. F. Garside, M. Roth, *ibid.* **129,** 207 (1976).
15. B. Maher, in *Thought and Feeling,* H. London and R. E. Nisbett, Eds. (Aldine, Chicago, 1974), pp. 85–103.
16. G. Reed, *The Psychology of Anomalous Experience* (Houghton Mifflin, Boston, 1974).
17. E. M. Lemert, *Sociometry* **25,** 2 (1962).
18. L. Festinger, *Hum. Relat.* **7,** 117 (1954).
19. N. A. Cameron, in *Comprehensive Textbook of Psychiatry,* A. M. Freedman and H. I. Kaplan, Eds. (Williams & Wilkins, Baltimore, 1967), pp. 665–675.
20. A. Beck, in *Thought and Feeling.* H. London and R. E. Nisbett, Eds. (Aldine, Chicago, 1974), pp. 127–140.
21. W. W. Meisner, *The Paranoid Process* (Jason Aronson, New York, 1978).
22. R. E. Shor and E. C. Orne, *Harvard Group Scale of Hypnotic Susceptibility, Form A* (Consulting Psychologists Press. Palo Alto, Calif., 1962).
23. A. M. Weitzenhoffer and E. R. Hilgard, *Stanford Hypnotic Susceptibility Scale, Form C* (Consulting Psychologists Press, Palo Alto, Calif., 1962).
24. A fuller presentation of procedures is available by request.
25. W. G. Dahlstrom, G. S. Welsh, L. F. Dahlstrom, *An MMPI Handbook,* vol. 2. *Research Applications* (Univ. of Minnesota Press, Minneapolis, 1975).
26. We derived this scale specifically for this study: it consisted of 15 self-declarative statements responded to on 7-point rating scales. The scale was drawn from a clinical study of paranoia *(14)*.
27. L. Ross, M. R. Lepper, M. Hubbard, *J. Pers. Soc. Psychol. 35,* 817 (1977)
28. W. L. Hays, *Statistics for Psychologists* (Holt, Rinehart & Winston. New York, 1965), p. 465.
29. This report is dedicated to Neal E. Miller as part of a commemoration by his former students of his inspired science teaching. We wish to acknowledge the expert and reliable research assistance of Harry Coin, Dave Willer, Bob Sick, James Glanzer, Jill Fonaas, Laurie Plautz, Lisa Carrol, and Sarah Garlan. We thank Joan Linsenmeier and David Rosenhan for critical editing of the manuscript.

Analysis

What did you think of this study? Did you find in it things that concerned you? Were there things in it that you felt especially good about? When this study was discussed with several classes, students listed these strengths and weaknesses:

Strengths

- There is an excellent explanation of the relationship of deafness to paranoia, both shown to be conditions of aging.
- Three different measures of paranoia were used just in case one might be considered suspect by a reader.
- Hypnosis was cleverly employed to substitute available subjects for ones who could not ethically be used. The researchers just couldn't let elderly subjects go deaf and not tell them!
- There was an excellent use of groups to eliminate possible alternative explanations. One eliminated posthypnotic suggestion as the cause since the group with the itchy ear did not show paranoia. The group that knew it was partly deaf showed that the phenomenon occurred only without knowledge of deafness. These two groups were like the experimental group in every way but one—they did not have unrecognized deafness. They are called "control groups" and permit the researcher to eliminate alternative explanations; that is, they control for those explanations.

- Random assignment of the subjects to the groups meant that, on average, the groups were comparable in the relevant characteristics that might otherwise bias the experiment. For example, if one group were more anxious than the other, it might have performed differently. Even though anxiety was not measured and equated over the groups, random assignment will, on average, have that effect.
- None of the individuals who had contact with the subjects or who were responsible for making observations of the development of paranoia— hypnotist, researcher, observers, and confederates—knew to which treatment any given subject had been assigned. They couldn't have biased the results to come out "right" even if they had wanted to. In research terms, the observers were kept blind to the treatment.
- The first instructions to subjects were tape recordings; thus they were treated identically before being given different treatments. Later, instructions for different treatments, given by automatically projected timed slides, served the same purpose without calling attention to the diminished hearing of two of the three groups.
- The confederates engaged in a well-rehearsed standard conversation so that all subjects were exposed to the same possibilities of misperceiving antagonistic parts of the "script."
- Subjects were extensively debriefed after the study to make sure that there were no negative consequences of their participation. They were followed up a month later to provide further reassurance that there were no lingering problems.

Weaknesses
- Six persons in each group is a very small sample size.
- Only the subjects who were most susceptible to hypnosis were chosen. Such subjects might in some way be "different" and therefore bias the result.
- The subjects were not drawn from the population to which the results were to be generalized, the elderly; all were male and all were college students.
- The length of time the hypnotized condition existed was not given.
- Reliability and validity data were not given for the researchers' own "clinically derived" paranoia scale, so we cannot be certain that it is a valid instrument. By contrast, data on published instruments are publicly available. (They did give a reference, however, so we could presumably get such data.)
- Subjects knew it was an experimental setting and it was also an unusual one. They may have reacted accordingly.
- The researcher had to deceive the subjects.
- Hypnosis, an unusual procedure more associated with show business than with science, was used with no explanation or defense.
- There was no assurance that the paranoia created under the experimental conditions was the same as that affecting the elderly.
- Confederates had the opportunity to learn which subjects were partly deaf since their conversation included probes for the partial deafness to assure that it was maintained.

How did your lists compare? You might not have identified all the strengths and weaknesses. Remember that my lists are a compilation of the common responses across several classes. No doubt when you recognized an item not on your list, you said to yourself, "Oh, I should have put that down, too!" Remember that this is in fact a sophisticated behavioral science experiment in which many readers, without previous training in research methods, can either identify strengths and weaknesses or recognize them when pointed out. Furthermore, although these weaknesses and strengths were found in an experiment, most are relevant to other research methods as well.

This example suggests that you have a solid base of knowledge on which this book can build. That is not a surprise; Einhorn and Hogarth (1986) point out that in everyday life individuals use systematic rules for assessing cause as well as in science. We will further explore such rules in Chapter 7.

A Qualitative Research Study

Having examined a quantitative study, let us now look at qualitative methodology. Although both quantitative and qualititative methods can be used to explore, quantitative methods are more often used to test an explanation. Qualitative methods are particularly useful in constructing them. This is shown in our next study. Hoffmann-Riem (1986) studied how families who adopt a child construct "the sense of a common bond" that is perceived to exist in biologically related families. Although the report has been abridged for reproduction, nothing essential has been omitted.[2]

Adoptive Parenting and the Norm of Family Emotionality

Christa Hoffmann-Riem
University of Hamburg

Abstract: This paper is concerned with the construction of "the sense of a common bond" in adoptive families. [1] First, I clarify how adoptive families construct this sense in relation to biological families. Second, by examining features of adoptive family life, I suggest a new way of understanding non-adoptive families. Presuppositions about "normal" family relationships dominate the start of adoptive family life. As seen from the actors' perspective, "emotional normalization" is a crucial indica-

NOTE: I appreciate Shulamit Reinharz' careful editing, and thank her for helping me share some of my research findings with an American audience. Address correspondence to: Institut für Soziologie, Universität Hamburg, Sedanstrasse 19, 2000 Hamburg 13, West Germany.
[2] From "Adoptive Parenting and the Norm of Family Emotionality" by Christa Hoffmann-Riem, 1986, *Qualitative Sociology, 9,* pp. 162–177. Reprinted by permission. (The complete original list of references is reprinted for the purposes of Chapter 7. Paragraph numbers added.)

tor of successful adoptive family life. I outline how involuntarily childless couples try to accomplish normality when applying for a child, and how achieving the assumed normality of non-adoptive families continues after adoption.

Methodological Assumptions and the Technique of the Narrative Interview

1. The fundamental processes which underlie the symbolic structuring of kinship and parenthood are usually invisible. Examining a special case (i.e., adoptive families) may help render these processes accessible if an appropriate method is used. Unfortunately, the sociological literature on adoption reflects the prevailing methodological orientation of the discipline, the pre-structuring of data collection by a set of hypotheses and their operationalization in a standard interview. The researcher who works with pre-structured categories will find only that which he or she has previously considered. An exception to this general trend is the work of David Kirk (1964) which draws on his own experiences as an adoptive father.

2. My study starts with the methodological assumption that basic structures of family life can be disclosed only if informants are given the opportunity to present their experiences in a manner I call "autonomous." Studies based on biographical documents like letters, e.g., Sorosky, Barron & Pannor (1979) or the detailed case study of an adoptive family (Huth, 1983) are the closest to my work. . . .

3. My research method, the "narrative interview," was drawn from the work of Fritz Schuetze (1977; see also Labov and Waletzky, 1967 and Kallmeyer and Schuetze, 1977), who recommends a strict division of the interview into two parts. The first or main part consists of the story told by the narrator without interruptions by the researcher; the second part consists of questions carefully put by the researcher in response to information already presented by the interviewee. . . .

4. My introductory question was formulated in the hopes of uncovering the whole history of the adoption, beginning with the decision to make an application for a child and ending with the development of their family life. After a number of introductory remarks emphasizing that the adoptive parents should tell their story the way they wanted, they were asked: "Can you still remember what it was like when you applied for a child?" I did not select a specific beginning, e.g., involuntary

childlessness, for a chain of adoption events. Rather, the couples began to recapitulate the beginning of their adoption story as they saw it (e.g., childlessness) or started with the process of application and then came to recognize that something was missing. This prompted them to return to that "missing link" in the chain (childlessness) in order to enable me to have a proper understanding of their story. I interviewed couples and generally, the adoptive parents gave a combined account as a couple rather than two separate accounts. On the average, telling the story took about two hours. All interviews were recorded on tape and transcribed verbatim.

Sampling

5. The selection of informants was guided by the idea that ability to communicate should have priority over the representativeness of the subjects. Representative sampling would have been possible only if I had been able to use the data of the adoption agency in Hamburg. I rejected this idea since it would have associated me with the agency and possibly revived negative experiences (e.g., dependency, control) or positive associations (e.g., getting a child). Fifteen couples who participated in regular discussion group meetings of adoptive parents were selected. Most members of these discussion groups were middle class, similar to most applicants for adoption. The procedures to define class membership and a comparison of class membership between the sample and a universe of applicants for one year are presented in detail elsewhere (Hoffmann-Riem [1984], pp. 17–19, 42–45, 314, 328). I had taken part in the meetings of one group for several months to get some insight into the social world of adoptive parents. I presented my research design to the members of another discussion group and asked them to support the project.[2] I legitimized my research by referring to the fact that I needed to know more about the practical purposes, application process and the image of adoptive families. Almost all of the members were interested in participating as a means of informing the public (and the adoption agency) about adoptive family life. . . .

Data Interpretation

6. . . . My concern was not with the idiosyncracies of a single case but with the commonalities of all the cases. To begin, I outlined the rough chronology of events reflected in the story: (1) the couple's motivation for adoption, (2) the process of applying for a child, (3) the development of the parent-child relationship. Since each of these categories contained a wealth of information, I further differentiated within them. First I sought the shared properties of all the cases. Then I used specific data from each of the interviews to illustrate variety. For example, to analyze the "motivation process" I first showed how the desire for a child is based on conceptions of the "normal" adult role. Then I examined more closely the alternatives to being a parent envisioned by childless couples, how the desire for a child is integrated into male and female role definitions, and how the prospective child is instrumentalized for the adult role.

7. I started by comparing cases that differed widely from one another ("strategy maximizing differences") in order to develop polar types. Then my analysis of the narratives in terms of their similarities allowed the range between the poles to be filled in.

8. My data interpretation is confined strictly to a reconstruction of what the research subjects themselves presented as their experiences. . . . I attempt to reflect the actor's perspective throughout the paper even if it is not explicitly stated in each sentence.

The Desire for a Child

9. On the basis of very detailed adoption stories, I came to recognize that the majority of data can be subsumed under the concept of "constructing normality." [This idea had not been on my mind when I started the research.] . . . Before elaborating the adoptive parents' work to establish a "normal" parent-child relationship, I shall briefly outline the starting point of adoption—the desire for a child—as a chain of normalization processes.

10. The Federal Republic of Germany has the world's largest birth rate. Viewed against this background, narrative interviews with adoptive parents reveal that children are still very important in biographical planning for some West German adults. All the adoption stories begin with "We wanted a child." Considering the consequences of this desire, it is particularly worthy of note that no explanation is given. Seen from the narrator's per-

spective, no further clarification of the remark was necessary.

11. The motivational story preceding the decision to adopt is divided into sequences: a shift from what the couples defined as the "normal" starting point of marriage, to deviation and then, finally, to an attempt to reconstruct normality. Among these couples marriage was entered into with the aim of establishing a family. But like other couples, realization of the desire for a child was postponed until the household had been set up. As long as they practiced birth control, the couple experienced itself as being in harmony with the institutionalized pattern of the family life cycle. The unquestioned (or only slightly questioned) confidence in their joint reproductive ability made married life appear congruent with their own biographical planning for children. This enormous confidence paved the way for a crisis among these families and presumably the ten to fifteen per cent of married couples who unwillingly remain childless in West Germany.

12. Planning the transition from the phase of household establishment to the realization of a family is the step that progressively leads the couple away from feeling "normal." Biographical denormalization begins with the couple's first suspicions. When a certain level of fear is reached, medical help is sought so that the plan of family establishment, once regarded as something they could achieve on their own, might be pursued. Many of the narratives express the suffering the couples endured during the medical procedures. They turned to the medical option in order to rescue their original biographical plans, yet it was that very system that forced them to recognize the impossibility or improbability of its realization. A sequence of short, temporally connected sentences provides an idea of the extent to which the narrators feel rushed as they go from doctor to doctor in an effort to prevent the threat of childlessness.

Adoptive Mother: We thought that we would like to have children.
Adoptive Father: And since that did not work although we were trying hard—my wife was under medical treatment and I went to see a doctor—, and since it was extremely improbable that we would get children of our own, we started to think of adoption. . . . But first we have been in the university clinics for a long treatment, and a very, very good and sensible doctor was in charge of us, and we submitted to

a *lot* of treatment to get an own child and be it convulsively [sic]. You know, then they increase the doses of hormones you get from one treatment to the next, and finally we came to the point that if there would be a pregnancy the probability was one to ten for twins and one to hundred for triplets, and that was already a critical limit. . . . And my wife had to go to the clinic every day to be checked if there weren't any negative side-effects. And then we always had to get there at a special date dependent on the cycle, for example Sunday night at 10 or Sunday morning at 9.

Adoptive Mother: Yes, whenever ovulation was expected.

Adoptive Father: And the doctor rushed to the clinic to wait for the right moment. Believe me, I could write a *book* about all those events in the hospital.

Adoptive Mother: We were cared for very well, but finally we said to ourselves: Oh God, what are we doing here, why all this trouble?

13. Their "desperate" utilization of all the technological reproductive means available to them suggests that the definition of the family as a group of genealogically related persons is still firmly in place. It takes the couple a long time to accept the idea that being a "flesh and blood" relation is not the only way of constituting a family. Narrative interviews with adoptive parents reveal a great deal about the significance of kinship, i.e., the desire for establishing genealogical families who belong together. It takes the experience of missing parental autonomy and the suffering it causes to illustrate the way the biological family is an essential part of the normal biographical planning of many adults.

14. When medical procedures no longer justify the couples' hopes for a birth, the pattern of normality is redefined. The interviews reflect the couples' shift from being rushed to and fro to a new initiative of action: "And then we thought: let's adopt a child."

Adopting a Child: From Strangeness to Familiarity

15. Adoption does not coincide with the actors' concept of a "normal" family. Therefore, once the adoption has been carried out the normality of parental role fulfillment has yet to be reached. One

means for constructing "normal" parent-child relationships is through an emotional bond. The parents define this as something that has to be worked at. While waiting for a child the applicants experience a high degree of insecurity concerning their prospective roles as parents. Experiences as prospective adoptive parents are framed by suppositions concerning the "normal" case. For example, the anxious question: "Will I be able to love a child that is not my own?" crops up in several interviews. The question illustrates how prospective parents worry about the quality of their future family life. Since the principle of biological filiation is violated, the parents fear that a quality constitutive of family life—the emotional bond—may also be adversely affected. The fact that prospective adoptive parents are so concerned about the affective bond shows how deeply the emotional parent-child relationship is accepted. When the principle of filiation is in effect, the emotional bond appears almost automatic.

16. When the status passage from applicant to parent is achieved, the emotional quality of the parent-child relationship becomes a point of overwhelming significance. This was reflected in every narrative interview. The conditions of developing an emotional relationship differ substantially: in some cases only a few moments or hours were needed for the couple to feel attracted to a baby; but in the case of an older child, it may take years to overcome the sense of unfamiliarity. The beginning of family life may be full of happiness or irritation. Even allowing for these differences, every narrative interview arrives at some kind of statement of relationship: "And then an intensive relationship (quickly/slowly) developed between myself and the child."

17. For adoptive parents this process signifies the attainment of a goal. It means conformity with a central norm of family life. However, the structure of the parents' narrative shows that this statement is not the final presentation of the relational quality. It is followed by another key statement which reveals how adoptive parents organize their experiences in relation to the "normal" case. In the majority of narrative interviews, the following sentiment is expressed: "It is as if it were our own child."

18. Since without any interviewer guidance the majority of adoptive parents recapitulate events using this endpoint, we can assume that it refers to highly relevant experiences of family life. I am suggesting that the "achieved relationship" brings adoptive parents in line with the "normal" case. Only by evaluating their own experiences in the "primary framework" of the biological family [3] can adoptive parents ensure that the new quality of their relationship is communicated without misunderstanding. "It is like one's own child"—that is how adoptive parents indicate to themselves and others that the normality of family life has been accomplished.

19. Almost every narrative reflects the point at which the adoptive parents no longer need to typify their boy or girl as an *adopted* child. Whereas for a short or a long period they may have observed an emotional distance between themselves and the child because of its adoption status, ultimately they experience an emotional identification. This is a turning point in symbolic interaction with the child—the turning point from adoptive child to child. One could call this turning point the moment of emotional normalization. Emotional normalization means overcoming the strangeness of a child that is my child to be. The case of adoption presents an interesting coincidence of "The Stranger" and "The Homecomer" (Schuetz, 1972). The problem of every stranger who has to approach a new social world is accentuated in the case of adoption because the adoption stranger is expected to become a familiar person. The stranger as the homecomer who has not been at home before— that is the frame in which the interview data could be analyzed. In the following section I will describe how the chances of overcoming strangeness differ enormously, depending on the age of the child. The baby is the homecomer with minor strangeness, whereas the older child is the stranger with minor homecoming properties. Consequently, quite different trajectories of emotional normalization shall be outlined here.

Emotional Normalization When Taking in a Baby

20. "I've grown so fond of the child so quickly" was commonly expressed during the twenty-one interviews done with parents who adopted a child younger than seven months. Their emotional bond with the child developed unburdened by the difficulties of its long "prehistory." Attachment evolved as a matter of course, as if the process had unfolded "automatically."

Adoptive Mother:. . . he was simply so tiny and so . . . and so in need of help that you

automatically direct your affection toward the child and that happens . . . immediately. . . . [4]

Since the development of an emotional relationship is seen as occurring automatically, the narrative recapitulation of events does not usually involve long reflections on how the result was brought about. The new quality of the parent-child relationship is regarded as normal and the parents no longer analyze it from a reflexive distance ("I don't think about it any more"). Some see the declining preoccupation with one's own special status of family as evidence of unquestionably belonging together. In the words of Alfred Schuetz and Thomas Luckmann (1979), one could call this the development of a new "natural attitude."

21. The baby's physical dependence in itself produces an enormous density of parental interaction. Their involvement leads to a situation in which the child, at an extremely dependent life stage, quietly turns into the little being who seems familiar to them. His/her physical growth and first efforts to communicate reveal traces of their parental influence. A number of recent studies in developmental psychology have attempted to outline in detail the process of the emerging parent-child relationship. These investigations discovered a surprisingly wide-ranging repertoire of interactive behavior which a baby of only a few weeks can initiate and sustain (Stern, 1980; Schaffer, 1980). Smiling, movements of eyes, hands and feet, the turning of its head, and finally, the first prevocal sounds—these media of expression are the active bonding part of the child to which the parents react "automatically." They are what Stern (1980, p. 24) calls "infant-elicited behavior." In parental care the child unfolds its communicative abilities and radiates the charm of a small partner.

22. Adoptive parents of very young babies quickly come to believe that the principle of biological filiation is almost irrelevant for an emotional relationship. Here is an example:

Adoptive Father: What is it that really builds up the relationship? I'm not sure if it is really built up because the child has been /eh/ borne for nine months. Isn't it rather built up because /eh/ when it is still very small you have to feed it six times a day and to put on its nappies and to care for it and . . . you have to play with it and you observe its reactions to . . . to you own/eh/ remarks and aura . . . I think that

/eh/ this is much more important than bearing the child for nine months during pregnancy. . . .

23. According to the narrative interviews, pregnancy and birth can be renounced as binding experiences if adoptive parents are able to utilize the plasticity of the child in its most formative developmental phase [5] and if they can superimpose social familiarity on biological strangeness. The turning point from adoptive child to child is then reached. This emotional normalization is reflected in almost every interview concerning a very young adopted child.

> *Adoptive Father:* . . . We take it for granted that we feel this way,
> *Adoptive Mother:* Yes, it's your own child, and that's it
> *Adoptive Father:* you adapt yourself to it; it's your own child.
> *Adoptive Mother: It is your own* child, and that's it, it is . . . /eh/ now and again you also forget that it is adopted, it's incredible how much you forget.

Late Adoptions

24. The narratives concerning late adoptions make it clear that the trajectory of emotional normalization includes a process of self-communication, especially on the part of the adoptive mother. It may take months or years before so-called motherly emotions for the child are directly recognized as such, since attention initially focuses on coming to terms with other immediate problems. The narrative interviews relating to a late start in family life illustrate that emotionality is often not discovered in the ongoing interaction process but is grasped retrospectively. To give an example: one adoptive mother infers from the sadness she feels when her daughter has to stay in hospital that the emotional bond must be more developed than she had assumed. The fact that her daughter shows a deeper attachment to her than she had expected reinforces the new feeling of belonging together. Another adoptive mother observes with relief that she now defends the child more against people outside of the family or that she has more sympathy for her child when it is ill or has been injured than she had in the beginning. It may take months or years before an adoptive mother is able to appreciate that she

had "caught up with" the attitudes of biological parents.

Conclusion

25. The constitution of the adoptive family has been discussed in terms of the emotional work invested in parent-child relationships. The turning point from adoptive child to child is a source of relief and happiness, a sign of family authenticity. It is also a point of danger. Adoptive parents can indulge themselves in the feeling of normality to such an extent that they neglect to handle the structural difference characteristic of their family on a cognitive level. They may act as if they were the biological family, and reject the idea that they are not. [6]

26. Adoptive family life is family life with double parenthood. Emotional normalization is only a partial solution to the problems arising from the structural peculiarities of the adoptive family. Structuring the "awareness context" (Glaser & Strauss, 1965) towards the child and towards relatives, friends, and strangers is the work that remains after the emotional bond has been established.

27. Emotional normalization has been described as a process worked at by adoptive parents to minimize the difference between their own type of family and "normal" families. The process of overcoming strangeness in the adoptive family affords some insight into the conditions needed for the constitution of any family. The difficulties in constructing family reality without the principle of filiation, and without a common history of early socialization suggest that the conditions of the "healthy" personality as outlined by Erikson must be understood in terms of specific types of families. The child has to experience certain interactive relationships and the parents must initiate and sustain them in order to establish familiarity. The greater the number of developmental phases that the child has gone through before the common history of the adoptive family, the more divergent are the systems of relevance of adoptive parents and child. Hence emotional normalization may not be established for a long time or at all.

28. This research may be useful for adoptive parents, applicant couples, and agencies who deal with adoptive family life. It should alert agencies to the different burdens they put on parents when placing a baby or a five-year-old child. Beyond the field of adoption, the findings might have some relevance for the growing number of step-parent–child relationships where familiarity also has to be accomplished. Finally, the concept of emotional normalization might contribute to an understanding not only of parent-child relationships but other types of family interactions as well.

NOTES

1. A detailed analysis is presented in Hoffmann-Riem, Das adoptierte Kind—Familienleben mit doppelter Elternschaft (*The Adopted Child: Family Life with Double Parenthood*), Munich: Fink, 1984.
2. Twenty-three adoptive parents had adopted one child, four of them had also one biological child, two others had two or three biological children. Seven other adoptive parents had adopted two children, two of them also had one or two biological children. Among the eight cases with a combination of adoptive and biological children, there were only two where the adoptive child came first. For further information concerning the exact age see Hoffmann-Riem (1984), p. 327.
3. To use an analytical term of Goffman's (1974), the biological family is taken as a "primary framework" for determining the quality of relationship in the adoptive family.
4. All interview material is translated from German by the author.
5. One extreme statement about this dependency is Alfred Portmann's characterization of the dependence of the infant's first year as the prolongation of the fetal period ("extrauterines Fruhjahr"): A. Portmann, Die Biologie und das neue Bild vom Menschen, Bern, 1942, p. 21.
6. David Kirk conceptualized the adoptive family's alternatives as "rejection-of-difference" and "acknowledgment-of-difference" in his influential study *Shared Fate* (1964).

REFERENCES

Arbeitsgruppe Bielefelder Soziologen (eds.) 1973 Alltagswissen, Interaktion und gesellschaftliche Wirklichkeit, Vol. 2. Rowohlt.

Douglas, Mary 1970 Natural Symbols: Explorations in Cosmology, London.

Glaser, Barney G., and Strauss, Anselm 1967 The Discovery of Grounded Theory, Chicago: Aldine.

Goffman, Erving 1974 Frame Analysis, New York.

Goffman, Erving 1959 The Presentation of Self in Everyday Life, Garden City: Doubleday.

Hoffmann-Riem, Christa 1980 "Die Sozialforschung einer interpretativen Soziologie—der Datengewinn. Kölner Zeitschrift für Soziologie und Sozialpsychologie, 22:339–372.

Hoffmann-Riem, Christa 1984 Das adoptierte Kind—Familienleben mit doppelter Elternschaft, Munich: Fink.

Huth, Wolfgang 1983 Adoption und Familiendynamik, Frankfurt/Main: Fachbuchhändlung für Psychologie.

Kallmeyer, Werner, and Schuetze, Fritz 1977 "Zur Konstitution von Kommunikationsschemat der Sachverhaltsdarstelling." In: Dirk Wegner (ed.), Gesprächsanalysen, Hamburg.

Kirk, David 1964 Shared Fate, New York: Free Press.

Labov, William, and Waletzky, Joshua 1967 "Narrative Analysis: Oral Versions of Personal Experience." In J. Helm (ed.), Essays on the Verbal and Visual Arts. Proceedings of the Annual Spring Meeting, Seattle. University of Washington Press.

Portmann, Alfred 1942 Die Biologie und das neue Bild vom Menschen, Bern.

Schaffer, Rudolph 1980 Mothering, Cambridge, Mass.: Harvard University Press.

Schuetz, Alfred 1972–3 Collected Papers, Vols. I and II. The Hague: Nijhoff.

Schuetz, Alfred and Luckmann, Thomas 1979 Strukturen der Lebenswelt, Vol. 1, Frankfurt/Main: Suhrkamp.

Schuetze, Fritz 1977 "Die Tecknik des narrativen Interviews in Interaktionsfeldstudien." Arbeitsberichte und Forschungsmaterialien der Fakultät für Soziologie der Universität Bielefeld, 1: 1–62.

Sorosky, Arthur D., Baran, Annette, and Pannor, Reuben 1979 The Adoption Triangle, Garden City: Doubleday.

Stern, Daniel 1980 The First Relationship: Infant and Mother. Cambridge, Mass.: Harvard University Press.

Tyrell, Hartmann 1978 "Die Familie als 'Urinstitution': Neuerliche spekulative Überlegungen zu einer alten Frage." Kölner Zeitschrift für Soziologie und Sozialpsychologie, 30: 611–651.

Tyrell, Hartmann 1979 "Familie und gesellschaftliche Differenzierung." In: Helge Pross (ed.), Familie—wohin? Reinbeck: Rowohlt.

There are clearly distinct differences in the two methods, each with its own strengths and weaknesses. Finding the strengths and weaknesses in the qualitative study is this chapter's application exercise. The exercises at the end of each chapter are an important part of the instruction offered by this book. It's a good idea to work them through even if your instructor doesn't require you to do so. You will find that they highlight important aspects you may have missed or not understood in the chapter itself. Once you have constructed your answer, compare it with those in the "Answers to Application Problems" section at the end of each chapter. In the first four chapters it immediately follows the Application Problems section, but don't deprive yourself of important learning by reading the answer before trying to answer the problem.

SUMMARY

Your experience with the two studies you have just examined shows you have a basic sense of what constitutes good research. What you need is to sharpen those skills and find a framework that will make such critiques easier and more comprehensive. Learning is like Velcro and without a framework you do not have a complete fastener.[3] This book will provide you with an undergirding of basic concepts in a framework that integrates many of them so they are better fastened. Then even as methods evolve you will be able to grasp and appreciate improvements readily as they occur. Further, you will be able to read research with an understanding and critical eye and, with careful study, can learn enough to begin to conduct your own research.

A Look Ahead

It is important to note that researchers do not have to choose between the two approaches illustrated in these examples. They may employ a hybrid, combining those aspects of each that best fit their research problem and match their skills and adding other important aspects. The next chapter demonstrates some of this variety of possibilities as it develops a continuum of approaches anchored at the ends by these two and then describes some of the diversity of other kinds of research, most of which are best characterized as being somewhere between the extremes.

IMPORTANT TERMS

Hypotheses
Qualitative research

Quantitative research
Validation

APPLICATION PROBLEM

As you did for the Zimbardo study, critique the Hoffmann-Riem research and note its strengths and weaknesses. *Compare your critique with that in the section for application problem answers beginning on page 20.* As with the Zimbardo study, when you read this critique you will probably find yourself saying, "I should have thought of that" or "That occurred to me too, but I didn't tie it down."

Be sure to first write out your own answer to this and similar problems at the ends of chapters. Answering in your own mind and then reading the given answer does not provide as significant an encounter with the material to be learned as does writing the answer. Writing enforces clarity of thought.

---

[3] Analogy adapted from Wurman (1989) p. 132.

ANSWER TO THE APPLICATION PROBLEM

Strengths

- The explanation makes sense; that is, the account that couples experience a progression from trying to have their own child to seeking a medical solution to adopting a child is plausible. Further, the explanation of the process of emotional normalization also has intuitive appeal—that once a child has been adopted, an emotional attachment develops similar to that of a biological family.

- The research was presented to the couples in a manner that would encourage cooperation, saying that the purpose was to inform the public (and adoption agencies) about adoptive life.

- The choice of couples from existing support groups aided communication. The researcher could safely assume that since these couples were accustomed to discussing their problems and experiences about adoption, they would more readily discuss them with an interviewer.

- Hoffmann-Riem recorded and transcribed the interviews. Recording could have a negative effect on an interview, but given the apparent cooperativeness of the subjects, it appears that it did not. Combined with the investigator's own observations, it provided an accurate and detailed record of each interview.

- The interviews were open-ended. In the first part, the couples were encouraged to "tell their story" without interruption. In the second part, Hoffmann-Riem used their comments to probe further. She was open to their accounts and did not attempt to lead or direct the discussion.

- The adoptive parents were interviewed as couples. This could be seen as both a strength and a weakness. Its strong point is that both members could fill in details, add to each other's comments, and so enrich the information.

- Hoffmann-Riem began the study with only a general idea of what she might discover. She was able to let the couples tell their stories and to let her conclusions develop inductively, to "emerge from the data." She was less likely to be blinded by her preconceptions and miss an important point.

- Her sample could be considered representative of adoptive parents in general as most were members of the middle class, the segment of West German society that adopted most.

Weaknesses

- The data collected consisted entirely of narrative (words). There was no way to analyze it statistically. Another investigator could, presumably, interpret it differently.

- Since Hoffmann-Riem provides only small samples of her data, there is no way to verify her conclusions.

- There was no control on researcher expectancy effect, that is, no guarantee that Hoffmann-Riem was not leading or directing the interviews in some way (even subconsciously, perhaps) toward predetermined conclusions.

- The interview technique relied on self-reporting by the couples. The investigator had no real check on whether or not what they said was truly what they felt or believed. Further self-reports may limit information to whatever is comfortable or reflects favorably.

- The couples were interviewed together. A possible weakness in this approach is that one of the couple might dominate the interview or bias the spouse's answers. Separate interviews might provide different information.

- The sample could be viewed as unrepresentative because the couples were all members of a particular support group. Adoptive parents who participate in such groups may well have different attitudes from those who do not. Also, the support group itself could lead to changes in their views that would not otherwise have occurred.

- Fifteen couples is a small sample on which to base generalizations to all adoptive couples, although such sample sizes are not atypical in this kind of research. Further, the researcher drew the interviewees from only two support groups rather than sampling several such groups.

- Though Hoffmann-Riem did refer to prior research to justify her choice of methods, she might also have used it to help support her conclusions.

- Accuracy of translation is often a problem where two languages are involved. Perhaps this is not an issue in this instance because of the researcher's apparently excellent command of English. Back-translation into the original language by someone not familiar with the study permits comparison with the original statements for accuracy. This method is often used to check on the accuracy of translation of a test or measuring instrument.

CHAPTER 2

The Variety
of Research Methods

Science is a very human form of knowledge. . . . Every judgment in science
stands on the edge of error and is personal. Science is a tribute to what we can
know although we are fallible.

Jacob Bronowski, *The Ascent of Man*

OVERVIEW

The two studies of Chapter 1 give some substance to the nature of research but
clearly are contrasting ways of going about it. This chapter pursues those differences more deeply and shows how they help to define a continuum of methods
from quantitative to qualitative. Survey research, it points out, occupies a place
between them. The chapter then describes other methods, noting how they relate
to the roles of description, explanation, and validation. Creative efforts to describe social phenomena, to explain them, and to validate those explanations have
led to the development of a social science with broad scope and a variety of research methods.

CHAPTER CONTENTS

Contrasting the Two Approaches

Each of the two studies in Chapter 1 typifies to a significant degree a different research approach: the Zimbardo study a quantitative, deductive approach, the Hoffmann-Riem study a qualitative, inductive approach. But, it is often difficult to classify a study as either qualitative or quantitative. For example, suppose instead of measures, Zimbardo's observers had interviewed the subjects to determine whether paranoia developed in the subject during the social interaction, writing up case studies on each one and then analyzing this material for generalities. That study is still designed around the testing of a hypothesis, a characteristic we usually associate with the quantitative approach, but the analysis of verbatim transcripts is usually associated with the qualitative approach. So it would have been much more difficult to characterize the study; but what is important is whether the research methods were appropriate and properly used. Characterizing the approach employed as one of the common research methods mainly facilitates this judgment and helps us master the methods in the first place. *Such characterization is not at all important to this book otherwise.* Although there are some researchers who seek to rigidify the differences and develop "schools" of qualitative and quantitative methodology, use of these terms in this book is primarily for purposes of learning investigative approaches and providing a spectrum of methods so the variety of research may be more easily conceptualized. In this respect, the terms quantitative and qualitative are useful shorthand for a number of distinctions, which may be characterized as follows:

- *The explanation guides the development of the quantitative study, whereas the explanation grows out of the data in the qualitative study.* Note the difference between the starting point of Zimbardo's experiment, beginning with a hypothesis and seeking to verify it, and the starting point of Hoffmann-Riem's. She was exploring, seeking to inductively develop an explanation from her data—the goal of most qualitative research. She wanted to learn how the process looked to adoptive parents. In interviewing them, she found that most of the behavior could be understood as "constructing normality," working to establish "normal" parent-child relationships. This proved a useful framework in which to understand "belonging together emotionally." But the notion of "constructing normality" emerged from her data as she listened to parents talk about their experiences. It was not an explanation she had thought of when she entered the study. Researchers with this point of view prefer to listen to, or observe, natural behavior and then to construct their understanding of it. This orientation is typical of those using qualitative research methods.

By contrast, in quantitative research, a proposition is being validated,[1] that is, data are being gathered that would support the hypothesized condition or relationship. In Zimbardo's study this is validation of the hypothesis that unrealized deafness leads to paranoia. Hypotheses are derived from observation or prior investigation, and deductively determine the nature of the study because they are translated into measures and/or observation scales and treatments that make up the study's **design.** Zimbardo and associates deductively constructed a study to provide data that would demonstrate the hypothesized relationship, if it were true, and that would rule out reasonable alternative explanations. This is typical of those using quantitative research methods.

- *Related to the first point is that in the quantitative approach, the creative work of research precedes actually doing the study but in the qualitative, it takes place after entry into the field.* The creative work of an experiment goes into its careful design before the data are collected. Most of the work that comes after data collection follows as a result of the design. (That is, if the study turns out as expected. If it doesn't, there is a lot of creativity in analysis, just as in qualitative studies.) By contrast, in Hoffmann-Riem, once the subjects were chosen and the interview's starting point had been carefully considered, most of the creative work followed the data collection—sorting the interview statements into meaningful categories and trying to make sense of them.

- *The quantitative researcher is concerned with an objective reality that is "out there to be discovered." The qualitative researcher is concerned with how individuals perceive their world and sees reality as an interpretation of these perceptions constructed by each individual.* This pair of studies is unique in that the explanation advanced grows out of the perceptions of the subjects in each study. This is worth emphasizing because it makes the point that social phenomena, in this case perceptions, can be examined by a variety of methods. Although they both deal with perceptions, there are fundamental differences between the two methods. In the quantitative approach, the perception of social isolation was created and expected to cause paranoid behavior. The presence of this particular outcome was then confirmed three different ways. An overt behavioral outcome is the focus of the study.

---

[1]If you have already studied inferential statistics, you may be balking at the idea of "validation" or "confirmation" of a hypothesis, since you have been taught studies can only disconfirm hypotheses. True enough, but as enough studies fail to disconfirm, we increasingly act as though the hypothesis has been confirmed—indeed, often after a single study. Read the Bronowski quotation at the start of Chapter 3; it is analogous to this situation and states this problem well. Further, increasingly, statisticians (e.g., Cohen, 1990) are arguing against significance tests and this up-or-down reasoning; they favor using effect sizes and confidence intervals, which avoid this problem. Put aside your concerns; further understanding will come with succeeding chapters.

If you don't understand this footnote; that's fine, you weren't bothered in the first place. It's just for those who were.

By contrast, in the qualitative approach, the focus is on the covert process of interpreting the world by an adopting family as it perceives itself taking on the characteristics of a "normal" family. The perceptions result from their normal everyday behavior. Further, in studying the process of "normalization," Hoffmann-Riem is seeking to *view the adopting family's world as her informants perceive it—a constructed reality.* Even though you and I may argue that the necessity of having a normal family is all in their minds, nevertheless, those perceptions have a real influence on them and their behavior. They make up the data of Hoffmann-Riem's study, and it is out of a collection of them that she derives her explanation.

- *Quantitative studies describe behaviors with measures or observation scales (or both), whereas qualitative studies describe behaviors in words.* The Zimbardo study is full of measures: the Harvard Group Scale of Hypnotic Susceptibility, the Stanford Scale of Hypnotic Susceptibility, the Minnesota Multiphasic Personality Inventory, the Thematic Apperception Test, and a clinically derived paranoia scale. By contrast, in Hoffmann-Riem, there are no measures; all description is in words. We have descriptions but no measure of the extent to which these parents consider it important to achieve a "normal" family relationship. There is also no tally or count to indicate how well they succeed in comparison with biological parents. Further, unless differences are large, it is harder with words than with scores to discriminate one level from another. On the other hand, no numbers can as eloquently convey meaning as does Hoffmann-Riem's "It is your *own* child, and that's it, it is . . . /eh/now and again you also forget it is adopted, it's incredible how much you forget." "Normality" is described in words. Description in words results in a longer report but can conjure up vivid images that scores lack unless they are accompanied by qualitative data. Each approach has its advantages.

- *The quantitative study focused on a cause-and-effect relationship between two variables, while the qualitative study emphasized the description of the development of a process.* One of the essential differences between the two methods is what they are seeking. The Zimbardo study is asking if the unnoticed increasing deafness is the cause of the paranoia, a cause-and-effect relationship, whereas the qualitative study is interested in the wholistic process of how an adopting family establishes the sense of a common bond. The former looks for a single kind of behavioral outcome, paranoia, resulting from a single causative factor, unnoticed deafness. Although not confined to the interaction of two variables, quantitative methods nonetheless seek to simplify the interaction to relatively few variables so that it is clear what is influenced by what variables. By contrast, there are a variety of variables involved in different adopting families in the relationships among the parents, adopted child, and possible siblings.

In an experiment, the most common kind of quantitative study, the researcher controls the application of whatever is hypothesized to cause an effect. That application is called a **treatment**; it is any potential cause controlled by an investigator. The investigator controls who receives what levels of treatment, under what circumstances, and when. In Zimbardo's study, the experimental treatment made the subjects temporarily deaf by telling them, while hypnotized, that when they woke up, they would not be able to hear well enough to understand the conversation around them. An alternative treatment resulted in an itchy ear. Experiments may have multiple treatments, as the Zimbardo study did, and may examine how the treatments interact with characteristics of the subjects or the conditions under which the study was carried out (or both).

Researchers also use the term **independent variable** to refer to something they believe may be a cause. It is a broad term. Besides including treatments, it encompasses potential causes such as social status or class, variables not under the control of the investigator. If a cause is named an independent variable, it follows that we would call the effect the **dependent variable.** So, in the Zimbardo study, paranoia's (the dependent variable's) appearance is dependent on the presence of partial deafness and social interaction (the two independent variables, which together cause the paranoia).

In the qualitative approach, behavior is studied in its natural setting rather than in a laboratory or experimental one. Not only do researchers not introduce treatments, but they take pains to disturb the normal course of events as little as possible. Usually, the researcher is not focusing on a single variable or a single behavioral outcome but is studying the process as it naturally occurs—in Hoffmann-Riem's case, the process of "naturalization."

A Continuum of Research Approaches

Perhaps you can sense now there are at least two different approaches to research: (1) starting with hunches or hypotheses and seeking to validate them or (2) gathering data describing situations of interest and letting the explanations emerge. As a pedagogic device, we can show the differences in these two approaches and their methods on a continuum, like that shown in Figure 2.1.

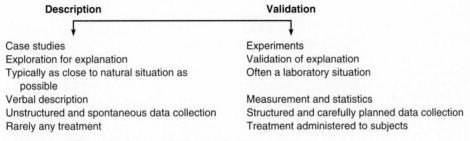

Description	Validation
Case studies	Experiments
Exploration for explanation	Validation of explanation
Typically as close to natural situation as possible	Often a laboratory situation
Verbal description	Measurement and statistics
Unstructured and spontaneous data collection	Structured and carefully planned data collection
Rarely any treatment	Treatment administered to subjects

FIGURE 2.1 The qualitative-quantitative continuum.

At the left of this continuum is the qualitative research approach, which provides descriptions of a case, a group, a situation, or an event, in what is often called a *case study.* Qualitative researchers typically begin their interviews and/or observations with a target of interest, but they are open to whatever emerges of significance and change their data collection accordingly. They work in natural situations and seek explanations that provide the best understanding of what was observed. The description is in words, picturing not only what happened, but also qualifying the description with adjectives and adverbs to portray it more clearly.

By contrast, the approach on the right is the quantitative research approach, deductively preplanned and designed around one or more hypotheses with data that are numbers representing quantities of whatever was measured. A hypothesis specifies the variables of interest and the relationship(s) between them.

A variety of methods span the continuum and, depending on the particular configuration, can be considered either qualitative or quantitative. Survey research is an example of one such method, so in Figure 2.2 we now introduce a middle column into our continuum. Survey research can be either quantitative, as when one of the big polling organizations does pre-election questionnaire studies of a political campaign, or qualitative, as in Hoffmann-Riem's study. It usually attempts to provide an understanding of the group of people surveyed. Respondents to the survey are typically a carefully chosen sample, representative of some population. Thus survey researchers usually provide some careful rationale for the persons selected for study.

Although we have set up a continuum of methods for illustrative purposes, and, among others, we will study in some detail qualitative survey and experimental methods, research is a creative act we cannot and should not fix into firm categories. To further keep you from thinking too rigidly about these approaches, let's consider another approach somewhere between the extremes; it is quantitative in that it deals with measures but is exploratory in orientation. Sometimes, like the researcher searching for schizophrenia cures who tries all kinds of substances to see if they work, behavioral science researchers try a variety of test items with only a vague notion that they may work. The hypothesis, if we can consider it as such, is that something in this mass of items ought to relate, for example, to specific mental illnesses. They find that, for instance, persons diagnosed

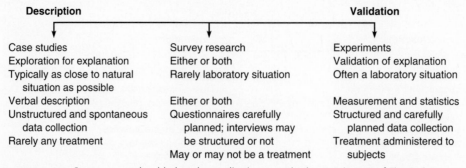

Description		Validation
Case studies	Survey research	Experiments
Exploration for explanation	Either or both	Validation of explanation
Typically as close to natural situation as possible	Rarely laboratory situation	Often a laboratory situation
Verbal description	Either or both	Measurement and statistics
Unstructured and spontaneous data collection	Questionnaires carefully planned; interviews may be structured or not	Structured and carefully planned data collection
Rarely any treatment	May or may not be a treatment	Treatment administered to subjects

FIGURE 2.2 Survey research added to the qualitative-quantitative continuum of Figure 2.1.

as schizophrenics answer a number of items differently from normal persons. The researchers then score just those items and employ that score to help diagnose schizophrenia. Even without an explanation of why the items work, merely being able to show that they do is enough to produce useful research. The Minnesota Multiphasic Inventory, one of the most successful psychometric instruments, was constructed this way, and scores have been developed for a number of mental disorders. Similarly the Strong-Campbell Vocational Interest Inventory (Strong, Campbell, and Hansen, 1981) uses as part of its mathematician scale the fact that persons interested in mathematics show an unusual interest in music—even though there is no explanation for it. It is another similarly constructed instrument that has proven highly useful in vocational counseling.

As still another example, Hoffmann-Riem's methods are somewhere between survey research and qualitative research. Although her data-collection methods are qualitative, she is clearly trying to represent the views of adoptive parents, a group of people to whom she expects her data to generalize. She believes, of course, that her subjects are typical, but we have to accept this on faith. Instead of ensuring that her sample represents adoptive parents, she uses a convenience sample. A survey researcher would have used sampling methods that provide an undergirding for such faith.

We will use this continuum of methods to organize the presentation of the different approaches, methods, and fields of research covered in this book. The ones chosen help define both the ends of the continuum and points in between (survey, history, evaluation, and action research). Emphasizing the fact that it is, continuum makes clear that there are other examples along it that could have been the subject of study. The intent is to illustrate the continuum well enough so that you can place other combinations of methods in the context of what you have studied, and can usefully combine elements from different points as appropriate for whatever research you wish to do.

Research, however, is a creative act; don't confine your thinking about it to specific approaches. Researchers creatively combine the elements of methods in any way that makes the best sense for the study they want to do. Their only limits are their own imagination and the necessity of presenting their findings convincingly. The research question to be answered really determines the method.

◆ *To facilitate understanding, we can place methods of research on a continuum from qualitative to quantitative orientations.*

◆ *Quantitative approaches are characterized by a deductive approach with preplanning and structuring, by validation of hypotheses, by describing in numbers, and by using measures.*

◆ *Qualitative approaches are characterized by an inductive approach, beginning without structure but structuring the study as it proceeds, by exploring to find what is significant in the situation, by trying to understand and explain it, by working in a natural situation, and by description in words.*

◆ *Many research studies use aspects of one or the other or both approaches as best befits their study, creatively adapting approaches to achieve their goals.*

Categories of Research Studies

Another reason for not being rigid about qualitative and quantitative approaches is that the names we give categories of research, while sometimes indicating that a study typifies some aspects of one of these approaches, may also specify a method, a content or subject matter, a design, or combinations of these. To help you know what to anticipate from a name, a brief description of some research categories, in alphabetical order, follows. Most of the categories are treated in greater detail in later chapters.

Action Research

Action research, a topic of Chapter 23, is intended to result in the solution or improvement of a practical problem. It may be used to determine whether a practice or process works, or how to adapt it so it does. Particularly in professions—education, social work, and library science, for example—it is considered a useful approach to solving practical everyday problems. The research is often carried out by the persons facing a problem or considering adopting a practice. Usually they have help and guidance from a researcher, but sometimes they do it on their own. They themselves are the intended consumers of the research, though they may write it up to help others facing similar situations.

Research findings are often not used unless they are trusted and "made real." Action research builds such trust through an "ownership" of the findings that is difficult to achieve when a study is experienced vicariously. The category is broad and includes research in a variety of subject matters, approaches, designs, and research methods.

Classification Schemes and Theory Building

The biological taxonomy of plants and animals provides a useful way of classifying new living things and showing their relation to previously known ones. Similarly, a classification of educational objectives has provided a set of useful handles for describing educational goals and relating them to one another (Bloom, 1956; Krathwohl, Bloom, and Masia, 1964; Anderson and Sosniak, 1994). Such classification schemes follow two rules (Bailey, 1994). The categories formed must include all instances of the phenomena, and they must be mutually exclusive—no cases equally fit two categories (Kipnis, 1997). They typically include well-chosen examples that show the scheme's usefulness instead of an empirical base of data when they are set forth. Their value is usually tested not by prediction but by their usefulness in organizing and describing phenomena and events.

Similarly, theories describe the way in which variables are related in certain situations. Because they often integrate previously disparate facts and findings, they are especially treasured. They are also sometimes advanced on the basis of speculation, which follows acute observation and study. Piaget

(1952), for instance, having observed a number of children, set forth a scheme describing their cognitive development. Skinner (1957), after much experimentation and observation, set forth a theory about how people learn verbal behavior. Further, he used only empirically verifiable descriptions that could be sensed directly rather than describing mental behavior that would have to be inferred.[2] Both theories markedly exceeded the data available when they were set forth. But both proved useful as they were subjected to experiments for validation and as the practical implications were teased out for application to school learning. Piaget's studies identified the most appropriate time for students to develop certain skills. Skinner's led to the development of programmed teaching materials, especially as they have been adapted to computer-based instruction. The category name indicates only that such schemes develop out of an inductive qualitative approach, but there is no clear design or research method, and any content is fair game.

Evaluation Studies

The category name, evaluation, mainly tells you the study was designed to answer an applied question regarding value or worth—the effectiveness or worth of some kind of treatment, how well units, persons, or programs are working, comparing programs against one another or against some standard (for example, a 95 percent graduation rate). As you will learn in Chapter 23, evaluation studies may use the quantitative or qualitative approach, use any design or method, and cover any subject matter or content.

Experimentation

Experimentation is discussed in Chapter 20. Although the category title tells nothing about the nature of the subject matter, experimentation typically follows a quantitative approach, has a design with a treatment, and provides a comparison of one or more treated with untreated conditions either over time or between groups. It generally uses measures, but interviews and/or observations can also be the main source of data. For example, in some now considered classic experiments on the relative effects of authoritarian, democratic, and no leadership conditions, observations showed more hostility and submissiveness under authoritarian conditions, more creativity and friendliness under democratic conditions, and about equal effectiveness in productivity (White and Lippitt, 1960).

---

[2]We will discuss this matter further in Chapter 18, but I think you can sense that there is a difference between stating that a child is intelligent, which is a characteristic you cannot determine through the five senses, and stating that a child is good at finding figures that are hidden in the details of a picture, which you can directly observe.

Historical Research

The designation *historical research,* covered in Chapter 22, tells you most about a characteristic of the subject matter—it is the past. It tells little about the qualitative or quantitative approach, design, or method since a variety could be used. Because the data of history are whatever has been left behind as records, choice of method must often defer to the kind of evidence the historian can uncover. This makes surveys and experimentation unlikely choices. Historical research has also the problem of authenticity. The German newspaper that paid large sums for what it believed was Hitler's diary was not alone in being duped by evidence that is not what it appears to be. Important skills for historical research include ways of authenticating evidence.

Longitudinal Studies

Longitudinal studies use the panorama of techniques to gather data over time and determine the pattern of changes. Many new parents in the United States turn to the work of Gesell, Ilg, Learned, and Ames (1943) to determine whether their child is developing normally. Gesell and colleagues followed newborn babies, noting changes in growth and determining what stages represented a normal pattern. Because longitudinal studies require long-term preplanning, they follow a quantitative approach, though they may gather and analyze data qualitatively at various developmental stages. Their content is usually growth and change of human beings. Though not covered in detail, the treatment of time series designs in Chapter 20 covers the fundamentals.

Meta-analysis

Meta-analysis, the subject of Chapter 21, began simply as a way of combining statistical results from a number of quantitative studies into a single finding, the size of the effect resulting from some cause. It combines studies of the same phenomenon done under different circumstances with different measures of the effect of some variable or condition. These variations in studies, which would seem to be a weakness of the method, have become a strength as meta-analysis has developed into a method of investigation in its own right. By grouping studies involving similar circumstances or variables, researchers uncover those under which a relationship holds, how it changes under other conditions, and/or how it is affected by other variables. Its data are other quantitative studies. The method can be used with any subject matter with enough existing studies.

Model Building

Economists are perhaps the best-known model builders. They describe the relationships among such things as the supply of money, the growth of government debt, the level of interest rates, and the expansion of the economy. Using data describing past events, they predict what should have occurred at some point in time. They then assess whether their model provides an accurate description of what did occur. Figure 2.3 is an example. Davis (1985) developed a model to predict adult earnings. His model assumed earnings are determined in three ways. One is the direct effect of the status of one's parents (line C). Parental status also directly affects educational attainment (line A). Educational attainment affects earnings directly (line B) and indirectly by opening opportunities in occupations with prestige and thereby earnings (lines D and E). The researcher tests such a model by inserting data into the model in these relationships and determining how well earnings are predicted.

Modeling is increasingly being used in other social science fields. It follows a quantitative approach, has a clear design, uses statistical methods, and can be applied to any subject matter that can be measured.

Survey Research

Survey research studies, discussed in Chapter 16, as the name implies, include a sampling plan and so have a design. When focused on answering a specific question, as is usual, they use the deductive orientation of the quantitative approach, but data collection and analysis may resemble either quantitative or qualitative approaches. Survey research is a method often used in other studies such as evaluation and longitudinal studies, so the category name tells nothing about subject matter.

Single-Subject Studies

A variation on longitudinal studies, the category name, single-subject studies, mainly designates following one person, instead of a group, over time; it tells little else. Obviously, such studies may have the characteristics of a longitudinal study, but they can also be a short-term experiment. For example, a child who demonstrates aberrant behavior when a food dye is added to his or her food returns to normal when the dye is removed and then acts up again when it is reintroduced. In other instances, the study may qualitatively chronicle the treatment

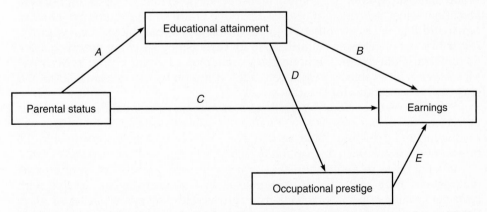

FIGURE 2.3 Example of structural modeling. (Adapted from J. A. Davis, *The Logic of Causal Order*, p. 17. Copyright © 1985 Sage Publications, Inc. Reprinted by permission of Sage Publications, Inc.)

of a particular condition, as do many clinical case studies. Again, the treatment of time series designs in Chapter 20 covers the fundamentals.

The Roles and Outcomes of Research

We have already noted that research sometimes explains phenomena and sometimes validates propositions, but basic to both of these roles is the role of exploring and describing phenomena. Research's three main roles are creative exploration and description, creative explanation, and creative validation. Notice that the word *creative* is used with each of these outcomes. Research is often taught as though the steps were pedestrian and routine, like a paint-by-numbers picture. Not true! All good research involves some element of **creativity.**

Some researchers mainly describe—as did Whyte (1993) when he told what life was like for a group of lower-class men in Boston. Some seek precise description, as when sample surveys estimate voter preferences to predict elections. Description frequently leads to explanation, as in Hoffmann-Riem's description of "normalization," implying that it is a way for these families to be part of "mainstream" society. Seeking explanations or causes is heavily emphasized in social science research. Reasonable fit of an explanation to the evidence in a single study is usually not totally convincing; we frequently want more evidence, confirmation, and validation. Validation is illustrated in Zimbardo's research, the development of evidence to support the explanation of why paranoia may be prevalent in the elderly. Note, however, that evidence does not always support; it may lead to modification or even negation of a particular explanation.

Exploration and Description

Poking around where others haven't, trying something to see what happens, bringing fresh eyes to old situations—all these can discover new situations and relationships. In Chapter 1's Hoffmann-Riem study, we have seen creative **exploration** and **description.** She could have stopped there, merely reporting her conversations—just describing. Purely descriptive studies often illuminate parts of our world that we might otherwise not encounter. Anthropologists make primitive tribes and developing countries real for us; sociologists study groups outside the cultural mainstream, the homeless or religious cults, for example. Margaret Mead (1928), for example, wrote about adolescence in the Polynesian Islands and suggested implications for Western society.

What is **creative** about description? Not making up something; rather, it is perceiving important aspects of a situation (possibly those missed by others) and organizing and presenting them so richly and vividly that they come alive in the theater of the mind. Such description makes the obscure real and understandable.

Inventiveness in description also occurs when researchers define and name phenomena in an immediately meaningful way. Kounin (1970) did this with *momentum,* an apt term borrowed from physics to convey an aspect of good teaching—maintaining the pace of classroom activity rather than getting bogged down in details. Binet (1912), developing what he called an "intelligence test," introduced this important and much disputed attribute into psychology. Defining an attribute and inventing a way to recognize it through measurement or observation effectively add to our store of useful terms and concepts.

Unfortunately the exploration that precedes research is rarely published so it tends to go unrecognized except as one infers what had to precede the write-up of results. Pursuit of multiple leads in the literature that are blind alleys or yield no new ideas, the many pilot studies using oneself as subject or a few friends, the various provisional trials to determine what works and what doesn't—these and many other aspects of research go unreported and therefore unseen. Provisional trials preceding the invention of physical objects are often saved in museums. Except for saving the occasional laboratory apparatus or unless details are embodied in biographies or discussions of how a particular study came about, there is no physical record of exploration in the social and behavioral sciences.

Although unreported, regardless of method, appropriate exploration is critical to a good final product. Exploration should probably be separated out as a fourth important research role. Because it is so rarely reported, however, and is often a first step in description, it is combined with it here. It is sometimes a predecessor to finding an explanation as well as to finding the best way to proceed in validation. While important to creative problem finding at the outset, exploration also often occurs toward a study's end. After data have been analyzed for anticipated findings, they are reanalyzed and/or augmented for further nuggets of information.

Explanation

Explanation is the second important role of research. We have seen how explanation logically followed description in Hoffmann-Riem's study of adopting parents, in which she creatively synthesized her interviews into an understanding of how adoption creates a normal family. Explanation also often follows recognition that a certain behavior follows another, as when Dollard and Doob (1939) associated frustration with aggression. For example, the unsocialized child, failing to take a desired toy from a playmate, hits him instead.

Explanation, by helping us understand situations well enough to predict what will happen, allows us to take steps to change projected outcomes. Kounin, Friesen, and Norton (1966), examining many classroom videotapes, noted that equally emotionally disturbed children disrupted classes of some teachers but not others. Why? Videotapes showed maintaining class momentum (referred to earlier) and making smooth transitions between activities appeared where no outbreaks took place. Clearly, this finding has important implications for handling emotionally disturbed children in normal classrooms.

Validation

Validation or testing of the explanation is the third important role of research—a role apparent in Chapter 1's Zimbardo study. Though this study is more creative than most, it is but one of thousands of such investigations. Studies designed as experiments help determine whether predictions based on an explanation will prove accurate. They uncover incorrect explanations, oversights, one-time occurrences, limitations or restrictions, and other flaws. Scientists who expect behavioral and social science research to be like that of the physical and biological sciences consider validation as a major role.

We have discussed these roles as if they were sequential; that is, exploration and description lead to explanation and then to validation, and indeed this is a fruitful sequence many findings follow. In real life, however, research isn't necessarily that orderly; a lucky hunch may allow one to show something works without prior exploration, description, or explanation—the explanation is left to be filled in later.

> ✦ *Three critical roles and results of research are explanation and description of social and behavioral phenomena, explanation of how and why they occur, and validation of the explanations. In good research, all three contain an element of creativity. Creative exploration frequently precedes these roles but may also follow them.*

Comparison of Roles of Various Research Approaches

What are the relative emphases on the descriptive, explanatory, and validation roles of the variety of research categories? Because of their diverse use, many are difficult to categorize. Though it markedly oversimplifies the realities of their use, Figure 2.4 indicates by the darkness of the rectangles the common or typical roles for a few selected methods in which such emphases seem better established. The methods are arranged roughly on our continuum from qualitative to quantitative, which runs vertically instead of horizontally in this dia-

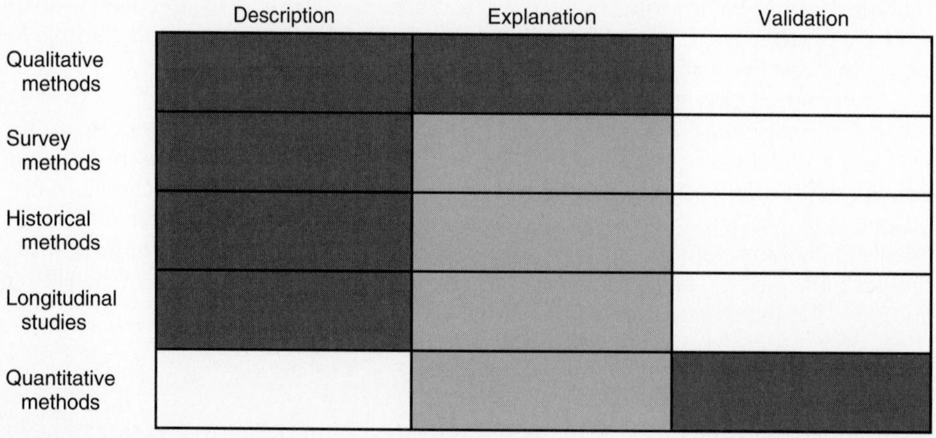

FIGURE 2.4 Relative role emphases of selected research categories; the darker the rectangle, the greater the emphasis of the category on that role.

gram. In general, the heaviest shades at the qualitative end are for description (which often accompanies exploration and discovery) and at the quantitative end are for validation. The fact that there is some level of shading for each category across all the roles, however, indicates that creative uses can be made in any of them, and sometimes their most creative application is in atypical roles.

SUMMARY

A variety of research approaches exist to be used by the researcher. For pedagogical purposes, these can be viewed on a continuum from qualitative to quantitative approaches, sample surveys falling about halfway between the two. Qualitative approaches use an inductive approach to design and collect verbal descriptions as their data; quantitative methods use a deductive approach to design and describe in numbers using measures and scales. Many research methods besides surveys, such as historical methods, evaluation methods, and longitudinal methods, creatively borrow from both approaches to achieve success—some more from one end, some more from the other. *The research question determines the most appropriate approach to be used.*

A Look Ahead

The mastery of certain basic methods provides researchers with skills for attacking a wide variety of problems. Hence, in this book we will provide considerably more detail on the basics of qualitative (Chapters 11–15) and quantitative methods (Chapters 17–21). Sample surveys, one method that combines the best of both quantitative and qualitative approaches (Chapter 16) is placed between them; it also includes useful basic skills such as sampling and questionnaire construction. In less detail we will examine two other examples of research categories, historical (Chapter 22), and evaluation and action research (Chapter 23), which use a variety of research methods and approaches.

So far we have proceeded as though everyone knows how findings make the trip from the researcher's report to the encyclopedia. However, few of us have thought about that trip. Although we might think we know what is involved, many of us will be surprised, perhaps even uncomfortably so. We tend to think of science as an almost mechanical process when it is really a human process; it works pretty well—although it is fallible. All science works this way; only the evidence is different in the physical and biological sciences. In the next chapter, because it is essential to understanding the criteria by which research is judged, we examine that trip and learn how findings become knowledge.

ADDITIONAL READING

Hoaglin, Light, McPeek, Mosteller, and Stoto
     (1982).

IMPORTANT TERMS

Creativity
Description
Dependent variable
Explanation

Exploration
Independent variable
Treatment
Validation

APPLICATION PROBLEMS

1. A group of researchers conducted a study to investigate the relationship between the age of viewers of an instructional film and the gender of the narrator. Subjects in the second and fifth grades were randomly assigned to one of two groups. One watched a film narrated by a woman, and the other group viewed the same film narrated by a man. The children's visual attention to the film was measured. The researchers also tested recall of the story ideas using a multiple-choice test. The results indicated that the gender of the narrator influenced the recall of the second graders but not that of the fifth graders. Also, fifth graders paid greater visual attention than the younger children. Identify the treatment and the independent and dependent variables.

2. A researcher compared low-achieving sixth graders who left their classroom one hour per day for remedial tutoring in reading to a comparable group that received only regular classroom instruction. She wanted to ascertain whether or not the special program made a difference. She found that the group that was tutored daily made significantly greater gains on a standardized test of reading skills than the other group. Identify the treatment and the independent and dependent variables.

3. Lewis Terman of Stanford University directed a classic investigation into the nature and development of gifted children. It was carried out over a 35-year period and consisted of a set of five published studies. In four of the studies, an initial group of approximately 1400 children from elementary to high school age were identified as "gifted." These children were then compared to a control group of 800 "non-selected" (randomly selected) students. A great deal of data was collected for these individuals, including IQ test scores, achievement test scores, interest questionnaires, reading records, a home information form filled out by the parents, an information form filled out by each individual's teachers, and medical data. These groups were

reassessed after periods of 6, 25, and 35 years. A separate study was conducted of the early years (childhood to early adulthood) of 301 men and women "of great historical eminence." A variety of materials was gathered, including primary sources such as letters, essays, poems, and diaries written by these people, and secondary sources such as biographies. From these data, psychologists estimated intelligence quotients. What research methods were used in this study? Where on the qualitative-quantitative continuum do they lie?

4. Two doctoral students at Syracuse University, one of whom was a librarian, were interested in the usefulness of the instruction provided as a part of a computerized reference work in the library of a local community college. (Reference works in such form are referred to as "databases.") They wished to know if the on-line instructions were sufficient to allow users to search the database satisfactorily or if users would require further help or instruction. They decided to collect data using several techniques. These included a questionnaire that would be filled out by users immediately after using the database, a rating of the printouts of their searches by an expert in on-line searching, semistructured interviews with staff librarians concerning their perceptions of student use of the database, and logs of student questions kept by the librarians during the same period. Do you consider their research study to be quantitative or qualitative approaches?

Compare your answers with those in the following section after you have written your answers and referred to the chapter text to correct any about which you had a question.

ANSWERS TO THE APPLICATION PROBLEMS

1. Two separate treatments were compared in this study: the film with narration by a woman and the film with narration by a man. The independent variables were viewer age (grade level) and gender of the narrator. There were two dependent variables: a measure of visual attention and a test of recall of story ideas. Both gender of the narrator and age were employed as presumed causes.

2. The treatment was the remedial tutoring received by the experimental group; the independent variable was prior achievement level

(low), and the dependent variable was each student's level of reading skills as measured by the standardized test.

3. Terman and his colleagues used a wide variety of methods to validate and to describe, although mostly they did the latter. No part of the study was truly an experiment. It took place entirely "in the field" (rather than in a laboratory or similar setup), and no treatment was applied. However, both the IQ and the achievement tests could be seen as validation of the category of giftedness (that is, quantitative research)

and certainly involved both measurement and statistics and structured data collection. Furthermore, the 800 nonselected individuals provided a group (a control) against which to compare the gifted group as in an experiment.

The interest questionnaires, reading records, information forms, and medical data, by contrast, were all forms of survey research. Most (like the interest questionnaire) would likely have provided numeric data, but there would have been narrative data to analyze as well. All were probably structured and hence are closer to the quantitative side of the continuum.

The study of the 301 eminent personalities was historical research. The case study method, a qualitative approach, was used, and the data were verbal. By assigning IQ scores based on these data, however, the investigators gave the method a quantitative twist. All in all, although the methods of Terman and colleagues spanned the continuum, their orientation was toward quantitative data.

4. The methods chosen for the study were used entirely in a descriptive manner and were to be used at the library (the natural situation). The questionnaire and the expert ratings were forms of survey research and produced numeric data. As such, they were a form of measurement and hence quantitative. The interviews and the logs were not fully structured and provided spontaneous verbal data. These latter methods were more qualitative. Thus the methods again span the continuum; it would be hard to classify this study because both quantitative and qualitative data make important contributions.

As these last two application problems illustrate, approaches to research studies need not be one or the other—quantitative or qualitative—but may be somewhere in between, perhaps a combination. The nature of the research problem usually determines the most appropriate investigative method, though researchers may adapt the problem to fit the method they are most comfortable and skilled in using.

From Findings to Knowledge

What needs to be understood is how, scientifically, we come to know what we know.

Gerard Piel, *The Social Process of Science*

I am tempted to say that we do not look for truth, but for knowledge. But I dislike this . . . for two reasons. First of all, we do look for truth, however we define it; it is what we *find* that is knowledge. And second, what we fail to find is not truth but certainty.

Jacob Bronowski, *The Identity of Man*

O V E R V I E W [1]

This chapter describes the process by which the findings of an investigation become knowledge. The process starts with a knowing decision by the investigator and continues through a process of examination by peers and editors to the building of a consensus around the generalization and the proper interpretation of the research data that support it. This process is contrasted with other sources of knowledge. The norms of science that function as guides and standards for the process are described.

Understanding the process by which findings become knowledge is important for a number of reasons. With that understanding you will realize:

- Why the characteristics of science are relevant to social and behavioral research merthods.
- Why publication is so critical to the development of science.
- How science differs from other methods of knowing.
- The importance of answering the audience's questions so a consensus forms around the researcher's interpretation of the data.

---

[1]This chapter is adapted from Krathwohl (1988), Chapter 11.

Further, it serves as the basis for the research criteria we will develop in later chapters.

CHAPTER CONTENTS

Introduction

The processes of science are taking place around us all the time; they are as natural as breathing. We rarely give them a passing thought except, possibly, when there is a dispute about what scientific facts are true. Even in this instance, such as the controversy over global warming, we typically focus on the issue rather than the processes. It is the processes, however, that determine what is good science and create the criteria by which a study will be judged.

Unless we cut the processes and criteria of science "out of their frame," so to speak, and assign names, conceptualize, and examine them, we are typically aware only of pieces of the picture—for example, such criteria as requiring valid instruments. We lack perspective on the whole process and the complete set of criteria. We need to understand how science works and how the criteria for what is good science flow from that understanding. Without these, we can't maximize the value of our research efforts. Indeed, without these, we may make serious mistakes.

Although there are occasional references to characteristics of social and behavioral science research or of natural science research, the chapter as a whole is intended to be descriptive of how findings become knowledge and the norms of science in all science fields.

An Illustration of the Journey from Findings to Knowledge

We tend to think of the researcher's job as a lonely one, one of pursuing a problem to solution, publishing the results, and then moving on to the next problem. In truth, science is really a social process, and each bit of knowledge involves many persons as it makes its way from being mere findings from data to becoming knowledge accepted by society.

We will use Kounin's research (1970) as our example of how research findings become knowledge. Kounin examined classroom practices to determine what teacher actions make a difference. If you've been in a classroom with an emotionally disturbed child, you know the havoc that such a child can produce; the learning process of the whole class can come to a standstill.

Kounin put boxes on tripods in classrooms, leaving them so the teacher and class became accustomed to them. Sometimes they contained a television camera to videotape classroom interaction, and sometimes they did not. Only Kounin knew. In this way, he gathered natural classroom reactions.

Kounin noticed that children diagnosed as emotionally disturbed acted up in certain teachers' classrooms but not in others'. Why? By videotaping teachers' classrooms where they often acted up as well as those where they did not, Kounin, Friesen, and Norton (1966) and later Kounin and Obradovic (1968) found several differences. Two of these differences they named *momentum* and *smoothers*. *Momentum* referred to keeping up the pace of instruction so that teaching was free from slowdowns—dwelling too long on a subject, nagging, giving overlaborious directions or comments. *Smoothers* referred to teachers who changed activities smoothly, as from art to mathematics. Their behavior was characterized by pausing, looking around, and sensing the group's readiness for change. In contrast, some teachers made changes whenever they felt the need, regardless of class readiness. Others did not follow through; they gave a transition direction and walked away to become immersed in something else, creating confusion. In examining classroom recitation sessions, Kounin found a significant relationship between deviancy and both slowdowns and nonsmoothing teacher behaviors.

How did this finding become knowledge? We can trace many steps in the publication records; others we must fill in.

1. First, there were the three researchers, Jacob Kounin and his assistants, Wallace Friesen and Evangeline Norton. Each had to make a personal judgment that the most appropriate interpretation of the evidence showed consistent differences between classrooms of equally emotionally disturbed children. Where momentum was maintained and transitions were made smoothly, there was less behavior deviancy. Let us call their personal judgments **knowing judgments.** These findings were beginning the journey down the road to becoming knowledge. Such judgments will be made by individuals all through the rest of the journey, judgments about whether they accept the interpretation of the evidence as the appropriate one.

2. It took a **consensus** of knowing judgments among Kounin, Friesen, and Norton for them to agree on the nature of their research report. Knowing is a personal judgment; that a finding is accepted as knowledge requires a consensus of such judgments. Furthermore, such a consensus must exist at each judgment point on the path from initial investigator to research consumer; these steps are examined in items 3-15 below.

3. The steps at the next stage vary, depending on the researcher's situation. If close colleagues work in the same or a closely related field, most researchers will share the report with them. If there are no close colleagues at their own in-

stitution, some send copies to professional friends at other institutions. At this or a later stage, some send copies to the **invisible college** in their field, a designation adopted by Garvey, Lin, and Nelson (1970) during their study of communication in psychology. It describes an informal (usually unorganized) cross-institution group of colleagues who have a common research interest. Their mutual admiration for what the others have done, their concern at others' unintentional errors, and their goal to become the first to present new findings in a research area drive a variety of informal means of communication.[2]

Because the publication process was (and still is) slow, each invisible college member formed a mailing list of colleagues who might be interested in his or her research or who may have been helpful in the past. Each routinely sent copies of his or her research reports to this group, keeping them more up-to-date than readers, who had to wait until it appeared in a journal. Persons who were cited in an important way in an article may also have been sent copies so that they could see how their research had been built on. Sharing data and interpretation in these ways provided feedback that could either confirm or modify notions about the proper interpretation of any set of data. The questions that invisible college members asked were likely to be among the most penetrating to be faced, since having worked in the same field, they could anticipate potential weaknesses.

Although there is no record, we can assume that Kounin and associates had an invisible college network and mailed them copies of the report. Note that we are talking about research done around 1964. Invisible colleges now are more likely to do their communication by e-mail. They may have a bulletin board or forum for the posting and discussion of the latest work. Professional association–supported bulletin boards or forums make the invisible colleges visible and accessible because usually anyone can join these forums.

4. Given positive responses, the authors probably decided to present their findings at an appropriate professional association meeting. They submitted an abstract of their report to the Program Committee of the American Educational Research Association (AERA) charged with selecting papers on classroom research for the annual convention. The abstract was sent to each member of the committee, who independently judged whether to schedule a presentation of the report. The committee members pooled their judgments and agreed to schedule the paper. Again, there was a consensus of knowing judgments that the proposed interpretation of the data seemed appropriate and contained potentially significant findings.

5. If, as we presume, the study was presented at the next AERA convention, a discussion period in which findings and procedures could be questioned followed the presentation. Informal discussions in the halls after the session

---

[2]This book owes much to Lee Cronbach's membership in an invisible college concerned with how knowledge develops. Professor Cronbach generously shared those files with me, putting me in contact with the mainstream and saving me hours of searching. As important as prepublication copies of articles was the correspondence. It indicated an openness about certain conceptions that could be only dimly discerned in publications, encouraging signs for work contrary to established dogma.

would raise further questions. Again, these were colleagues knowledgeable in the field, respectful but tough critics. Their questions cued the researchers to points in the report that were of concern to their audience. Because Kounin and his researchers believed they could satisfactorily answer these questions, they maintained their belief that their interpretation was appropriate and took steps in future reports to ensure that the questions were answered.

In addition, persons who did not attend AERA saw the title of the paper in the Convention Program and, if interested, wrote Kounin for a copy. Kounin did send copies. I know because I received one June 7, 1965, with Kounin's handwritten note "Unpublished as of 7 May, 1965." Although I didn't respond, others probably reacted to the paper in writing, raising questions, making suggestions, and calling his attention to relevant research of which he may not have been aware.

6. Kounin and his colleagues submitted the paper, revised on the basis of the questions raised in previous airings, to the *Journal of Educational Psychology*. The authors' names as well as any other identifying information were stripped from the manuscript by Ray Kuhlen, the editor. He sent it to one of the journal's consulting editors who knew the literature surrounding the study and to a couple of other researchers active in that same field who he selected as competent and interested. These experts made knowing judgments that the findings held up under scrutiny, were interpreted appropriately, and constituted significant additions to the field. They recommended that the article be published, probably with some minor modifications to clarify procedure and interpretation. Because both authors and reviewers were kept blind to each other's identity, the presentation had to stand on its own, unsupported by the reputation of the researchers or their institution. Similarly, because their identities were protected, reviewers were free to give their candid judgment.

Kuhlen considered the readers' comments and his own reaction to the article carefully. He had the authors make the few modifications needed and then scheduled it for publication. The consensus had continued to form.

7. The paper was published in 1966 under the title "Managing Emotionally Disturbed Children in Regular Classrooms" in volume 57 of the *Journal of Educational Psychology*. The editor thought the article sufficiently important to make it the opening article of the issue.

8. The previous seven steps were also involved in a **replication** of the earlier study by Kounin and another assistant. Replication involves doing the study again. This time, they used 50 schools instead of 30 and videotaped full days' classroom activities rather than half-days. The findings were replicated; terminology and coding of activities were further clarified. This study was published in volume 2 of the *Journal of Special Education* as "Managing Emotionally Disturbed Children in Regular Classrooms: A Replication and Extension," by Kounin and Obradovic (1968).

9. John Glavin and Herbert Quay were asked to write an article summarizing research on behavior disorders for the February 1969 issue of the *Review of Edu-*

cational Research. They read the Kounin studies and decided that those findings and their interpretations were sound enough that they should include them in their review. Their review was accepted and published.

10. The findings were now in a **secondary source,** removed from the initial evidence and dependent for acceptance on the reader's trust of the reviewers' judgments. By 1970, a dozen other authors had cited one or the other of the original articles in papers. The fact that the original findings had held up under replication was an important factor in their acceptance. Their confirmation by an investigator other than the original researcher, however, would have given even stronger confirmation. But there is in social science research neither the tradition nor the funding for replication that seems to exist in the natural science fields. Unfortunately, even Kounin's own replication of his earlier study is not a common practice.

11. In 1970, Kounin published a book that summarized the research to date: *Discipline and Group Management in Classrooms.* It began to take the place of the journal articles in citations by other researchers.

12. Robert Travers was charged with the responsibility of editing the second edition of the *Handbook of Research on Teaching* (1973). He asked Frank Hewett and Phillip Blake (1973), researchers who knew the literature, to write a chapter on teaching the emotionally disturbed. They included a section on classroom management and found the Glavin and Quay references to Kounin's work. They believed it of sufficient importance to read the original studies. They included a reference to the first study in their chapter, as did other chapter authors. In all, there were 20 references to this body of work. The new edition of the *Handbook* was published by Macmillan in 1973. The first edition had established it as an authoritative source; this second edition benefited from that reputation and rapidly became one, too.

13. Thomas Good and Jere Brophy (1977), leaders in the teaching research field, decided to write an educational psychology text. It was destined to become one of the most popular texts in the field. They had long known Kounin's work, since some of their own was based on it. They used the *Handbook* as a reference, and the many citations to Kounin's work strengthened their own impressions of its soundness and importance. They included his findings in their text, which was published as *Educational Psychology: A Realistic Approach.* Now thousands of students were exposed to the findings as knowledge.

14. Harold Mitzel was carefully chosen as editor for the massive task of preparing the fifth edition of the *Encyclopedia of Education Research.* On the advice of his board of editors, he asked Kevin Ryan to do an article on teacher characteristics. Ryan asked Debra Phillips to help, and they judged the Kounin work worthy of inclusion. The four-volume encyclopedia was published by the Free Press in 1982.

15. Subsequently, other writers of texts; encyclopedia articles; advice to teachers to appear in *The Instructor* and similar journals, and articles aimed at parents in popular periodicals, women's magazines, and *Reader's Digest* all treat the findings as accepted knowledge. A consensus of knowing judgments extends

all the way back to the first presentation of the study's results, which have now made the transition from findings to knowledge.

Compare this story with the stereotype of the lone scientist in a laboratory, antiseptically creating facts that are immediately accepted by a waiting public eager to be told the way the world really is. The true picture is one of a highly social process, developed, controlled, and maintained by people.

Important Characteristics of the Journey

The journey from the initial findings of a research study to the acceptance of those findings is a long one. (Note the elapse of 16 years—seven years from initial publication to inclusion in the *Handbook of Research on Teaching* and another nine years to the *Encyclopedia of Educational Research.*) The experts closest to the research and those with the greatest competency to judge it make the initial decisions as to whether findings merit a claim as new knowledge. Probably nobody is in a better position to make this judgment than those who have done research in the area and who therefore know the problems to look for—likely rival explanations, weaknesses in methodology, and so on. Their reflective skepticism is critical to the start of the journey in that they must determine whether the results were positive enough and the overall excellence of the study was great enough to merit reporting. The experts make a data-based judgment about the proper interpretation of the findings, which they then compare with the interpretation of these data by the original researchers.

This process of judgment assumes that a negative result would not be published, an assumption that is probably true. This is not entirely foolish; editors know that there are myriad ways of getting negative results but relatively few ways of getting positive ones. Therefore, they are likely to publish only negative studies that definitively close off certain otherwise attractive directions that would waste other researchers' resources.

In their journey from colleague experts to lay audience, the judgments pass to persons removed increasingly further from the knowledge and skills involved in the immediate focus of the research. Campbell (1988) has observed that the knowledge and skills of each individual regarding the phenomenon of concern overlap those of the previous person like the scales of a fish. Figure 3.1 illustrates this pattern using the **fish-scale analogy** to show the stages in process that we noted in the Kounin scenario.

We have traced only one path in the process, like the angled line in Figure 3.1. Unquestionably, other people were judging and using the Kounin results during the time frame we covered. They built on one another's work just as Kounin and colleagues did. These other researchers are portrayed in Figure 3.1 by all the other "fish scales" not intersected by the angled line. Although we often act like it is, no single research study is sufficient to result in knowledge. Knowledge requires an entire body of research—in our example, that of Kounin and the many who built on his work. The consensus spanning all these efforts results in the transition from research to knowledge.

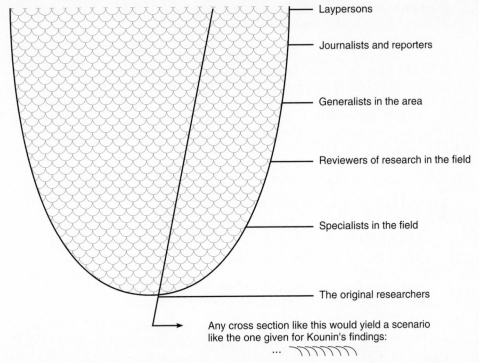

Laypersons

Journalists and reporters

Generalists in the area

Reviewers of research in the field

Specialists in the field

The original researchers

Any cross section like this would yield a scenario like the one given for Kounin's findings:

...

FIGURE 3.1 The fish-scale analogy of the transition of findings into knowledge.

Each individual making a knowledge claim, or encountering such a claim, must make a personal judgment to accept the claim as knowledge; that is, each must make a knowing judgment. The initial knowing judgments are based on the most appropriate interpretation of the actual data and are made by the people with the best basis for forming that judgment. As the claim is passed to persons further removed from those initial judgments, except as an occasional person goes to the source documents, the acceptance of the claim as knowledge is based on trust in the expertise of all below them in the fish-scale network. As knowing judgments agree, a consensus is formed and the claim is accepted as knowledge.

Sometimes a field moves so fast, or the communication patterns in a field are so slow, that it is difficult for a consensus to form around findings at the periphery of knowledge. Such a problem exists in medical and biological fields, where changes are rapid and researchers themselves may differ regarding what parts of the knowledge base are solid. The result is conflicting advice and critical comments about the research. Then experts lose credibility, and concern develops among practitioners and laypersons who would like to benefit from this knowledge. A technique of the National Institutes of Health (DeAngelis, 1988) is intended to speed up the process. Its "consensus conference" consists of a summarizing panel that evaluates the evidence and separates what they consider solid enough for practitioners to use from what is still experimental. In addition, journals such as the *New England Journal of Medicine* have made an effort to establish an "informal consensus view" in some fields. All these practices increase common recognition that science works by consensus.

Is knowledge the same as truth? If knowledge is determined by a consensus of critical judgments, is it possible that such judgments could be wrong? Truth lies elsewhere? Yes, of course. That gives us all an uncomfortable feeling we shall have to live with. Reread the quotation from Bronowski on this chapter's opening page; this is the point he makes. As close as we come to "truth" with our available methods is to be adequately critical of a finding and listen carefully to all the arguments and then see if a consensus can be formed that the conclusion is warranted. Phillips (1992) notes that the great philosopher John Dewey, reluctant to use the term "truth," decided to replace it "by 'warranted assertibility'" (p. 108), a considerably more descriptive term.

> ✦ *Each individual making a knowledge claim or encountering such a claim must make a knowing judgment regarding the appropriate interpretation of the evidence. As a consensus of such knowing judgments forms, findings become accepted as knowledge.*
> ✦ *The development of knowledge results from the creation of a consensus around the interpretation of data in successively widening circles of decreasingly specialized persons.*

Knowing Judgments in Everyday Life

Clearly, some results do not garner a consensus. Consider, for example, the controversy over whether there is a real crisis in the burning of fossil fuels. Findings in these areas are rapidly being accepted as knowledge by many people. However, some scientists are still uncertain whether these activities will result in a "greenhouse effect" and global warming or whether self-adjusting mechanisms are operating, making our concern unjustified. Until there is a consensus among the experts (acceptance as knowledge), it is unlikely that a crisis will be accepted widely enough that all nations will agree to appropriate action.

> ✦ *When experts disagree and cannot form a consensus, laypersons are leery about accepting research findings as knowledge.*

The picture is further complicated by the fact that there are different thresholds for acceptance as knowledge, depending on the seriousness of what is involved. Let us examine another way of considering this phenomenon.

Cronbach (1982) views the development of knowledge as one of **uncertainty reduction.** When our uncertainty about the proper interpretation of the data is high, we are unwilling to admit the research claim to the category "knowledge." When the evidence or the testimony of authorities sufficiently reduces our uncertainty below some threshold, we accept it as knowledge.

Conceiving that knowledge results from uncertainty reduction—or from its mirror image, the certainty with which we hold the knowledge—allows us to consider the matter of the certainty threshold for knowledge. This threshold varies with a matter's personal importance and relevance to our lives. For example, we may readily accept as true a claim that a certain individual has gone over Niagara Falls in a barrel because it means relatively little to us. However, a claim that a new chemical will facilitate weight loss without causing any bodily harm now or in the distant future may have a much higher threshold before the claim is accepted.

Furthermore, we make different knowing judgments in the various areas of our lives. We allow some sources of knowledge to push us over the threshold but reject others—we accept engineering specifications for the sizes of lumber for building a house, for instance, but we may reject advice to us as parents not to use physical punishment. The latter is an instance of behavioral science knowledge and points up the fact that despite the testimony of "experts" regarding the negative consequences of physical punishment, such "knowledge" is tested against our own experiences to see whether it "rings true."

Much of natural science's "knowledge" is so complex that we have no basis for knowing when not to trust the experts. Such complexity, however, is much less true of social and behavioral science knowledge, which deals with everyday life—a special problem for social science researchers. Further, behavioral science findings that run counter to what our intuition tells us is true are difficult to accept unless the explanation supporting them is strong.

Research findings in the social sciences face an additional challenge. Once stated, findings are judged "obviously true" and therefore not worth having been researched. Taking this point of view, some members of Congress have called the whole social science enterprise a search for the obvious. Wong (1995), however, showed that what often seems "obvious and true" may not be. Studying twelve "durable, replicable and potent" (p. 505) findings from research on teaching, she found that experienced teachers were no more accurate than nonteachers and regarded "as obvious the majority of both the actual and the opposite findings." All participants selected the actual research finding "in only 4 out of 12 items" (p. 509). Sample items: "Third graders learn more in reading groups when teachers ask a question first and then call a student's name" (opposite of finding) or "call a student's name first and then ask a question" (actual finding). "In Grades 1–9, students were found to get better scores on achievement tests in classes with more teacher control and less student freedom to select learning experiences" (actual finding) or "less teacher control and more student freedom to select learning experiences" (p. 511). Clearly the pervasive sense of what is obviously true is not always trustworthy. Research has an important role to play. Therefore, it is particularly important that social science researchers understand the process by which findings become knowledge so that they will design research that facilitates the process of consensus building.

> ◆ *Each new bit of evidence contributes to our evaluation of the certainty with which a finding or an assertion is accepted as knowledge.*
> ◆ *The threshold for when a finding or assertion crosses the border into the realm of knowledge varies, partly in accord with its personal importance to us.*
> ◆ *Social and behavioral science findings and assertions are tested against personal experience before being permitted to cross the threshold. This is not required of most natural science findings and assertions.*

You should sense that to build a consensus around the findings of a study it must satisfy a number of criteria that are widely accepted and understood by researchers. We will explore what those are more thoroughly in Chapters 7–9. But first let us compare the knowledge gained from science with that from other sources.

Different Sources of Knowledge

Science is only one source of knowledge. Knowledge comes from a variety of sources, and we are constantly making knowing judgments about whether a source can be trusted, whether the source is our eyes; our own past experience; some source of traditional wisdom like the Bible; or a person we respect as an authority because of training or status (for example, clergy), specialized expertise (nuclear engineer, petroleum geologist, philosopher), or professional license (physician, dentist, lawyer, teacher, clinical psychologist, social worker). It is worth examining the characteristics of other sources of knowledge to understand how science differs from them. Cohen and Nagel (1934) proposed a useful categorization—personal observation and experience, intuition, belief and tradition, authority, and science.

Personal Observation and Experience

Personal observation and experience is the source we trust the most. If you personally experience the maintenance of classroom order that results, as Kounin suggests, from making a smooth instead of an abrupt transition, you are likely to be convinced that this is solid knowledge. Indeed, personal observation and experience is a particularly important source of knowledge. It is the raw stuff of science, for the personal experience of scientists is the basis both for claims to knowledge discovery and for ideas and hunches that lead to new knowledge.

A characteristic of personal experience is the need for us all, infant and adult alike, to find an order, or pattern, to our existence. Where there are no patterns, we impose them. Judson (1980) notes, "Beat of the traffic, pulse of the phone, the long cycles of the angle of the sun in the sky. Patterns, rhythms, we live by patterns" (p. 28). One of the most important things that researchers do is to find order and pattern in nature. As Judson further notes, "Patterns set up expectations. . . . To perceive a pattern means that we have already formed an idea of what's next" (p. 28)—a hypothesis. Guessing "what's next"—predicting—is one of the most important outcomes of knowing. If we can predict, we have the chance to change the outcomes for the better—to improve ourselves, to help others solve their problems, to have a better society.

Experiencing how things move and change is the basic experience of childhood. A child is delighted by new discoveries; a scientist experiences the same pleasure with a discovery that leads to a knowledge claim. Re-creating that pleasurable sensation can be a powerful motivator—it is the fun of doing research!

Intuition

Intuition encompasses propositions so obviously true as to be self-evident; merely stating them is enough for their acceptance. Frequently, we infer such propositions from the world around us. It was accepted for centuries that the sun revolves around the earth because this appears to be self-evident. So, too, the earth was believed to be flat because that is how it appears. Accepting such propositions involves making a knowing judgment. Clearly, not all such propositions are true, however. It is threatening when any such proposition turns out to be false because then we have no basis for knowing whether others equally obvious may be equally untrue. How do we distinguish which ones to trust? Because there is no easy way, we tend not to doubt—not to open Pandora's box and let these evils fly out.

Belief and Tradition

As a source of knowledge, belief and tradition confirm all those things that "have always been true." The wisdom of the Bible, Koran, and Talmud and the advice of a culture passed from generation to generation are examples. Traditional knowledge, especially of the religious kind, tends to be set forth by authorities who help interpret it. Knowing relies on a personal judgment of whether to accept the tradition and the authority.

Authority

Authorities are, without question, the major source of our knowledge. Why? For one thing, we can personally experience only a small part of our world. For another, few propositions are self-evidently true. An **authority** is anyone we accept as being more knowledgeable than we are. Most professional persons earn their livings as authorities in some area. Although authorities are generally accepted as experts *only* in their area of expertise, this distinction is not always made. Heroes and persons of prominence often voice opinions on public policy matters in which they have no special expertise. For most persons, and most decisions, the knowing judgment becomes one of whether or not to accept a particular source as an authority.

All authorities are not alike. At one end of a continuum are the arbitrary or **dogmatic authorities,** who assert that something is true by reason of their position or ability to enforce its truth. In the middle are authorities who are believable by virtue of their position, experience, and training. At the other end are **reasoning authorities** who, though they have a believable case and might also rest on the laurels of position, nevertheless indicate the basis for their judgment and present the case for all to judge.

Dogmatic authority is found in some traditions and religions, especially when, if there was a rationale for a given truth, it has long since disappeared. For many years, the Soviet Union enforced Lysenkoism with dogmatic authority. This was the theory that a plant or animal could genetically pass on to its progeny environmentally acquired characteristics. Dogmatic authority generally regards challenges as threatening. If challenge is permitted in one instance, where will it stop? Of course, should such an authority be successfully challenged, the halo of authority vanishes.

In the middle of the continuum, we have the authority who, by reason of education, experience, and especially past success, is accepted. The past record is particularly important with respect to a current knowing judgment because it is one of the major bases for having been given the mantle of authority. Most licensed professionals, such as physicians, are in this category. Often they do not take the time to explain their decisions.

At the other end of the continuum is the reasoning authority. The characteristics of the reasoning authority are much like those of the scientist and help make science the source of much accepted knowledge. Unlike most authorities, however, every scientist's opinion is to be given as serious consideration as any other's. Thus when judging manuscripts, some editors routinely remove the authors' names so that reputation will not influence acceptance. Science does not always operate on this basis, however; we can surely think of many instances where the accepted opinions of senior scientists were wrong and impeded progress. That the sun revolves around the earth was perpetuated by scientific authorities long after contrary evidence challenged it.

A distinguishing characteristic of reasoning authorities is the logical force of their arguments. Consider Kounin's assertion that the teacher's smoothing behavior aids in controlling emotionally disturbed children. It is more easily accepted when we understand that the teacher's behavior continuously directs the child's attention to external stimuli and away from the internal turmoil that would result in acting up.

Another characteristic of reasoning authorities is integrity: openness about what is not known, willingness to reveal weaknesses in the case, and a balanced presentation of the positive and negative sides of the case. These make it less probable that something important and relevant is being hidden.

Challenges to the arguments of reasoning authority do not harm the authorities' expert status; in fact, such challenges are expected and welcomed. Only through challenge can the soundness of the case be tested. Furthermore, we can agree with such an authority in one instance where, in our judgment, the case holds up, yet we can disagree in another instance without rejecting the authority as a potential source of knowledge.

Of course, if a source is repeatedly found in error, there would seem to be some uncorrected problem in procedure or thinking. Unless the individual's integrity is challenged, however, as in faking data or being caught deliberately withholding knowledge that would affect its interpretation, any finding, no matter how unusual, is seriously considered by the reasoning authority. Typically the scientist is an example of a reasoning authority.

Science

The conception of knowledge as reducing uncertainty has the advantage of allowing many knowledge levels between the extremes of "rejected" and "accepted." Not everything that crosses the threshold into the knowledge category is held with the same certainty. We may reluctantly accept fluoridation of our water but buy bottled drinking water to be on the safe side. Sometimes we accept something as knowledge but retain some uncertainty.

That is the way of science, including, of course, the social and behavioral sciences. All scientific knowledge, even the most basic, is held with a tinge of uncertainty—just enough that it could be replaced should more valid knowledge come to light. Knowledge that is replicated and reconfirmed is held with considerable certainty—enough that we act on it as though it were unquestionably true.

Successful replication of research is considered essential in the natural sciences. **Replication** involves the repetition of a study, preferably by someone other than the original researcher and possibly somewhat differently. If the same results are obtained, especially by a different and improved study, they are considered confirmed or validated. *Replication, especially using enhanced methods in new situations, is the ultimate validation.*

Exact replication in the social and behavioral sciences is rare. In one common kind of replication, however, each successive researcher builds on the previous work. Should expectations fail to be confirmed, either the previous work was in some way invalid or the current researcher extended it incorrectly. If the researcher can find no fault in the extension study, a replication of the earlier work may be required.

As we have noted in the Kounin example, a finding must undergo the scrutiny of a host of **gatekeepers**—convention committees, editors, chapter authors, and so forth—to make the transition to knowledge. The researcher's interpretation of the evidence is repeatedly examined to make sure that it meets each gatekeeper's standards. This process of continual challenge, when combined with the tentativeness with which we hold all scientific knowledge, is relatively unique among the sources of knowledge. It allows knowledge to be changed as a natural part of the process without loss of the scientific community's status as an important source of knowledge.

Scientists understand the necessity of scrutiny, the tentativeness of knowledge, the importance of replication—the many steps to knowledge. However, the nature and length of the process is often not grasped by the public and by policymakers, who want concrete, correct answers and want them now! They frequently become impatient or do not recognize science as a social process in which a network of individuals assume responsible roles to make knowing judgments that coalesce into a consensus.

✦ *Knowledge comes to us from many sources: personal observation and experience, intuition, belief and tradition, authorities, and science. Of these, only science and the reasoning authority routinely seek and survive testing and challenge. The others all have trouble handling the challenges.*

✦ *In the natural process of science, knowledge is routinely challenged and replaced. Challenging findings previously considered knowledge affects science's status as an important knowledge source less than it does other sources.*

✦ *Replication, especially using improved research methods and new situations, is the ultimate validation of a proposition.*

The Norms of Knowledge Production

Science is a social system in which individuals assume important responsibilities in various roles:

- Researchers design studies, carry them out, and interpret the results with integrity.
- Journal, handbook, and encyclopedia editors; consulting editors; reviewers; and similarly trusted gatekeepers of knowledge dissemination ensure that studies selected for publication meet appropriate standards and that pertinent criticism of already published studies is disseminated so that an unwarranted consensus does not develop.
- Writers of reviews of research, textbooks, encyclopedia, and handbook entries carefully consider the results of studies and disseminate the deserving findings.

Each of these roles is governed by an informal but well-understood system of rules and norms. Although some are obvious, making them explicit describes the system and shows how it is maintained and its work is facilitated.

Merton (1968) described the following as the norms of science: universal standards for everyone's knowledge claims (he called this universalism), common ownership of information (his term for this was communism, a far cry from its usual meaning), integrity in gathering and interpreting data (he referred to this as disinterestedness), and organized skepticism of all knowledge claims. These, of course, apply to the natural as well as the social sciences. Let us examine each norm in more detail.

Universal Standards for Knowledge Claims

As a neophyte researcher, you would not want your research to be judged by harsher standards than those of a respected colleague in your field. As a member of a minority, you would expect your work to be judged by a standard identical to that applied to everyone else. As a researcher at newly established East Snowshoe State, you should not expect different standards from those had you been employed by venerable and distinguished Oxford University. The quality of the work itself, rather than its author, sponsoring institution, or financial supporter, should be the focus of a judgment based on **universal standards**—standards that are the same for all.

Each field establishes norms for what is acceptable research. Over time, these norms are raised as more is learned and the general level of methodological sophistication of the field rises. At any one point in time, however, the standards that gatekeepers apply should be the same for everyone.

Common Ownership of Information

That information is to be owned by all and shared freely—**common ownership of information**—is a norm subscribed to and maintained in academic and not-for-profit research settings. As we might expect, it is not always observed in the commercial sector since industrial research is often pursued for monetary advantage. Similarly, classified military research is beyond the reach of this norm. However, this is the norm for all the rest—the great bulk of science. Most major universities have rules forbidding sponsorship of research that cannot be freely published.

Thus publication is not only a right of the researcher, but also an obligation. Researchers who dabble in research simply to satisfy their own curiosity and then do not publicly share their findings not only remove themselves from the social system of science, but also are guilty of using for private amazement resources that are expected to be used for the public good. The "publish or perish" rule of many universities is simply an enforcement of this norm.

This norm also requires that the data of a study be shared on request, once the original researchers have used the data for their purposes. The efforts of others who might want to analyze the data differently, for instance, should be facilitated in every way possible. The reasonableness of the norm is self-evident: It enables others to make sure that no errors were made in processing the data and that the most suitable methods were used to extract their appropriate interpretation.

Integrity in Gathering and Interpreting Data

Merton named this integrity "disinterestedness." Gove[3] (1976) defines disinterested as "not influenced by regard to personal advantage." We all take for granted that researchers will gather and interpret data without regard to what they person-

---

[3]Gove, as editor of *Webster's International Dictionary,* is an example of an authority being accepted as a source of knowledge because of background, experience, and training.

ally believe they should show. This **disinterestedness** is one of the norms to which we are presumably most sensitive when it is violated. Thus advertisers use presumably disinterested laboratories to provide the basis for claims like "Powder-Milk Biscuits give 4 out of 10 shy persons the will to do what needs to be done!"[4] We rely on the integrity of researchers to be as critical of their own behavior as would outside observers.

The pressures for success cause a few individuals to violate this norm. Indeed, no doubt some of us did so when our physics or psychology laboratory course required replication of famous experiments with a certain precision. Not realizing that these assignments were intended mainly to teach laboratory technique, we felt it necessary to generate fictitious data to meet the precision criteria. With pressure for exact results rather than acceptable laboratory technique, such class exercises can teach behavior that could disastrously end a career if carried over to later research where unsuspecting colleagues expect integrity.

Broad's chapter in *The Dark Side of Science* (1983) details violations in both historical and recent times. These are instances where we know fraud did occur. How many uncaught cases there have been nobody knows. Fortunately the peer review process is in place in most settings where we seek to communicate a knowledge claim.[5] Both this process and studies that build on the findings of others are deterrents to fraud. The potential in active research areas for successful fraud seems small. Yet the possibility of any at all is unsettling, for the whole system is tarnished and loses credibility when just one member violates this norm.

Organized Skepticism

We have already described this norm in our detailing of the passage of Kounin's findings into knowledge. The editors, readers, and other gatekeepers embody organized skepticism at work. Merton called this aspect one of the most necessary, and you can see how it makes science unique as a source of knowledge. **Organized skepticism** means that it is the responsibility of the community of scientists to be skeptical of each new knowledge claim, to test it, to try to think of reasons the claim might be false, to think of alternative explanations as plausible as the one advanced. Challenging new knowledge is sought in all science instead of being avoided as in other knowledge sources.

Organized skepticism, however, cannot operate without the acceptance and observance of the other norms: The findings and the process by which data were obtained must be freely available—common ownership of information.

---

[4]Adapted from Garrison Keillor's radio broadcasts.
[5]The lack of peer review on the Internet and the problem of how to provide it has been a serious concern of those using this means of communication of research results. In response to this concern, some peer-reviewed electronic journals have been established.

Researchers must know that their work will be fairly and appropriately judged if they expose it to challenge—universal standards. We must assume integrity in gathering and interpreting the data if we are to accept the report at face value. Given these conditions, organized skepticism can do its job of keeping an inappropriate consensus from forming and preventing invalid knowledge claims from reaching people who might otherwise unwittingly try to use them. The esteem in which scientific knowledge is held is testimony to the conscientiousness with which scientists voluntarily play their proper roles and make the system work.

In addition to the Merton's norms, several principles that guide the development of science are worth noting. We have already considered one: Replication is the ultimate validation of a finding. Added to this is the importance of replicating studies with new samples of persons and situations, and different investigators, and research methods to assure the findings consistently reappear. Another is that when there are several equally reasonable explanations for a phenomenon, we chose the simplest that accounts for the facts—the principle of **parsimony.** The preference for theory-based research is another. **Theory-based studies** help tie together disparate findings into an integrated explanation. Findings without a theory base float off alone, can become one of too many to track, and are unlikely to be as useful as those that can be found through their relation to an applicable theory.

Each new version of how science works is tested against the historical record. It is clear from this record that science is by no means a perfect system. We have already indicated instances in which scientists should have been open to contrary evidence, were not, and dominated the thought of their day. There is no way of ensuring that science of a given day will tread the proper path. However, over time, progress is made, and wrongs are righted. It is this self-correcting characteristic of science that is reassuring.

If we observe all the norms, the process will uncover errors. However, any process is facilitated by an understanding of how and why it works; science is no exception. Much of the normative structure appears in one way or another in the codes of ethics of professional organizations so that we can pass these norms to new generations with an understanding of their vital roles. In fact, the perspective you gain from this text should enable you to play your role more effectively, whatever it may turn out to be.

The norms of science include at least those described by Merton:

◆ *The quality of research should be judged by universal standards regardless of the characteristics of the researcher—experience, race, sex, employment, and so forth.*

◆ *Scientific information is not proprietary but is owned by all in common and freely shared; publication is not only a right, but also an obligation of a researcher.*

◆ *The researcher displays disinterestedness—integrity in gathering and interpreting data without regard for personal advantage.*

◆ *It is the responsibility of the community of scientists to be skeptical of each new knowledge claim, to test it, to think of reasons the claim may be false, and to consider alternative explanations as being as plausible as the one advanced.*

✦ *Besides the norms, certain principles are observed: Studies should be replicated
with different methods, investigators, and new samples of persons and situations
to assure findings consistently reappear; the simplest—that is, most parsimo-
nious—explanation should be used; theory-based studies are preferred.*

Ethics

The previous discussion makes it clear that science is the result of a collaborative
social enterprise with rules the participants are expected to follow. If there are
rules, we might expect that the field of ethics would be an essential aspect of such
an enterprise, as indeed it is. As Grunder (1986) points out, "whether you wish to
become an ethicist . . . is not at issue. . . . You became one the minute you joined the
profession. The only. . . issue now is whether you are going to be a good ethicist or
a bad one. . . . You cannot use a human being [in a study]. . . without asking yourself, 'Ought I to be doing this, in this way, to this person, at this time?' The moment
the word 'ought' is muttered, you have entered the realm of ethics" (p. xi).

We shall discuss the necessity of obtaining the consent of those studied and
that of ethical standards at length in Chapter 10. (Because ethical concerns pervade many aspects of research, you will also find discussion of them scattered
throughout the book.) However, scientists are increasingly going beyond informed consent to a concern for the rights of those who help us gain knowledge.
We see this trend in the natural sciences as botanists, helped by indigenous people to discover the curative effects of an herb, are concerned they share in the rewards. So, too, some social scientists are concerned that informants and subjects
gain something from the research through being educated by it, helped to feel
empowered by it, or even, as in the case of at least one qualitative researcher,
sharing in the royalties accruing from publication. Action research, a topic considered in Chapter 23 is, in part, an outgrowth of this concern.

As with the scientists who helped invent the atomic bomb, however, the concerns go still further, to responsibility for whatever results from one's work. That
this requires a consideration of the choice of the research topic itself is made clear
by these two excerpts:

> Some years ago, I did research on attitudes toward cheating among college
> students. One could observe cheating, however, only by deceiving subjects. I
> could have used a technique such as returning already graded multiple-choice
> exams for (supposedly) self-grading and then counting answers that are changed
> by students during grading. Such techniques seemed to me to raise very serious
> questions about relations between people. . . . Was this my right as a scientist? I
> decided not to pursue the project in this direction.
>   I have conducted a number of participant-observation studies in which
> subjects were unaware that they were being observed. Each time I conduct such a

study, the ethical problem arises concerning the very act of disguised participant observation. My resolution of the ethical problem of invasion of privacy, disguising one's true role, and so on, essentially is based upon a rudimentary cost-benefit analysis. That is, I consider at length the value of the data sought, the possible effects of publication of the findings on the subjects, and the relative degree of privacy that actually is being violated. If I have serious misgivings about any of these factors, I will not conduct the research.[6]

Isolated researchers still pursue truth wherever it may lead regardless of the consequences. Science plays such a critical role in our society, however, that both scientists and nonscientists agree that the consequences of research need to be a consideration when it is undertaken. Even the consequences of testing, as we shall see in Chapter 18 on measurement, should be considered in determining the validity of a test. Although not all studies raise ethical dilemmas, it is the responsibility of the researcher to search for the ethical aspects of each problem and then to make a judgment as to whether to pursue it.

SUMMARY

In research, we continually make knowing judgments as to whether a knowledge claim is an appropriate interpretation of the evidence. As others agree with these judgments, a consensus forms, and findings become knowledge. A network of individuals extends from those closest to the research to the lay public, with decreasing levels of expertise in judging the evidence directly. The individuals at each level, as appropriate, either judge the evidence or determine whether to accept the judgment of others closer to the research in the network. Individuals are leery of accepting research findings on which experts cannot form a consensus.

We can also consider each new piece of evidence as increasing or decreasing our uncertainty about a knowledge claim. The threshold at which a finding or assertion becomes knowledge varies, partly in relation to its personal importance to us. Although it is not possible to test many natural science assertions, social and behavioral knowledge claims are typically checked against our own personal experience.

There are a variety of knowledge sources: personal observations and experience, intuition, belief and tradition, authority (dogmatic and reasoning), and science. Science and reasoning authority invite challenges to knowledge assertions to ensure their validity. In contrast, other sources have difficulty in handling challenge and typically avoid it, for once begun, there is no way of knowing where it will stop.

The development of knowledge reveals science as a social system of individuals in roles of important responsibility governed by well-understood rules and norms. Merton (1968) has suggested that as least four norms are essential: (1) that the same standards be used in judging knowledge claims for all individuals regardless of status, personal characteristics, institutional affiliations, or other considerations; (2) that information be understood as owned by all and freely shared; (3) that there be absolute integrity in gathering and interpreting data; and (4) that it is the responsibility of the community of scientists to be skeptical of all new claims, to test them,

---

[6]Both from American Psychological Association, Ad Hoc Committee on Ethical Standards in Psychological Research, *Ethical Principles in the Conduct of Research with Human Participants*, p. 20. Copyright © 1973 The American Psychological Association. Reprinted with permission.

to try to think of reasons why they may be false, and to seek alternative explanations as plausible as the ones advanced.

In addition to norms, certain principles direct the progress of science. Replication reduces the uncertainty surrounding any finding by showing it is not dependent on the circumstances, method, or investigator of the original study. Replication is the ultimate validation of any finding. Where multiple explanations are advanced for a phenomenon, use the simplest one—the principle of parsimony. Basing

studies in theory is critical to making science an integrated network tying together disparate findings. Merton's norms assume ethical scientific behavior.

A Look Ahead

It seems reasonable that a society with norms and standards may have found a format for reporting research that facilitates their application. We explore that format in the next chapter.

ADDITIONAL READING

Campbell (1988)
Cronbach (1982)

Merton (1968)

IMPORTANT TERMS

Authority
Common ownership of information
Consensus
Disinterestedness
Dogmatic authority
Fish-scale analogy
Gatekeepers
Invisible college
Knowing judgment

Organized skepticism
Parsimony
Reasoning authority
Replication
Secondary source
Theory-based
Uncertainty reduction
Universal standards

APPLICATION PROBLEMS

1. A Senate committee, concerned about safeguarding public funds spent on research grants, is questioning the methods of science used by the grant recipients. The committee is convinced that the process is rife with cronyism and that researchers are not adequately critical of one another's work. The senators wonder if public money is being wasted on findings of questionable quality. How would you reply?

2. You have been studying the use of color in illustrations in school readers, included to heighten children's comprehension of text. Having established that children prefer color pictures to either black-and-white illustrations or none at all, you had hypothesized that their inclusion would motivate students to pay more attention to the text and hence would increase comprehension. To your surprise, your results indicated that neither color

nor black-and-white illustrations had any significant positive effect. Indeed, there was some evidence that color actually impeded understanding. What should you do with these findings? Should you submit them for publication?

3. As editor of a prominent journal in the field of information studies, you receive a paper from a psychologist who has been studying the psychological barriers that students develop to the use of computer-based information systems. The particular study had focused on the on-line catalog system at the investigator's university. Should you consider publishing this study even though the researcher is not in your field?

4. You are a junior researcher in the department of reading and are being considered for tenure this year. A senior member of your department is well known for his advocacy of the phonics approach for teaching young children to read. He is adamantly opposed to a contending theory, the whole-language approach, which is the fad at other universities. You do a comparative study that produces significant findings that lend credence to the latter and undermines his position. What should you do with your findings?

5. Powers, Fowles, Farnum, and Ramsey (1994) were concerned about the inequality of computer access. Their study examining the hypothesis that essays written on word processors would be graded more favorably than handwritten ones appeared in a reputable peer-reviewed journal. Assigning students the same topics, they collected two sets of essays, one written on word processors and another, handwritten. Each was also converted to its opposite format and the papers were graded on a six-point scale by trained and experienced readers. Surprisingly, handwritten essays, when word-processed, dropped from an average 3.6 to 3.0; word-processed-changed-to-handwritten scores rose slightly from 3.3 to 3.4. Replicating the study, the authors trained the readers to overlook the effect of mode of presentation, checked for differences in scoring the modes, used both modes in training, and double-spaced word-processed essays to make them look longer. The direction of effect was the same: handwritten-to-word-processed dropped from 3.5 to 3.2; word-processed-to-handwritten increased from 3.5 to 3.7. It was noted that graders gave the benefit of the doubt to handwritten essays more often than to word-processed ones. Word-processed essays were longer (380 words versus 316) and length correlated with grades (.60). Poorer essays suffered more in word-processed format than in handwritten.

Now that you know about this study, you are given the option of word-processing your next examination. Would you take it? Why or why not? Would you consider this finding knowledge? Why or why not?

ANSWERS TO THE APPLICATION PROBLEMS

1. Respond to the committee by describing the journey of findings to knowledge, explaining the thoroughness and professionalism with which research findings are examined by members of the field even before they are published. Explain that research findings are normally submitted for judgment first to colleagues at one's own institution and then to members of the invisible college, an informal interinstitutional group of colleagues with a common interest in the particular topic. In this way, the people most likely to know the potential weaknesses of the study are given a chance to respond to the methodology used and to the interpretation given to the results. They make a "knowing judgment" of the study. Any findings that progress further in the journey would have already been subjected to substantial scrutiny.

Given positive responses to this point, findings would likely be submitted for presentation at an appropriate professional association meeting. Abstracts submitted to convention program committees normally have the names removed and are submitted "blind" to committee members. Each paper is again judged by members of the field who pool their knowing judgments. Therefore, before a paper is scheduled, a consensus has been reached that the interpretation of the data seems appropriate and that the findings are significant. At the presentation itself and informally during the convention, the findings would again be questioned.

Finally, if the researcher is satisfied that all questions have been answered appropriately, the findings would likely be submitted to a professional journal for publication. Similar to the process used by the convention program committee, the paper would be submitted to a blind review by both a consulting editor and other experts in the field. The findings are again subjected to knowing judgments. Only after these people are satisfied that the findings have been interpreted appropriately and are significant additions to the field is the paper published.

Although the findings may not yet be accepted by the field as knowledge, they have been subjected to a thorough and professional review process.

2. You should attempt to disseminate your information. Negative findings may function to close off otherwise attractive research directions that would waste other researchers' resources. By submitting your findings either for presentation at a professional meeting or for publication, you put them up for peer review and allow others in the field to judge their merit. In doing so, you are subscribing to the principle of Merton's communism, or common ownership of information. This principle implies that publication is the obligation of any researcher participating in the social system of science who uses resources intended for the public good.

3. The functioning social system of science extends beyond the perceived boundaries of a particular field. This researcher would presumably be following the same norms of knowledge production as members of your field. Merton's universalism (universal standards for knowledge claims) applies to this case. That is, you should judge the quality of the work according to what is considered acceptable research for the methods commonly used in your field. While you, as editor, must use your judgment to filter out obviously inappropriate submissions, findings from another field may provide the members of your field with enlightening and useful knowledge that might not otherwise reach them. Thus you must make an initial knowing judgment based on the nature of the study, not the identity of the investigator and, if appropriate, allow the findings to be judged on their merits by putting the study through your review process.

4. Although you are in a politically sensitive situation, you should submit your findings to the peer-review process and share your information with others in the field. As in the study on color illustrations in problem 2, Merton's communism applies: Ownership of the data is shared, and you have an obligation to disseminate your results. Perhaps your first step is to seek the feedback of the particular researcher concerning your interpretation of the findings. He will likely be one of your most severe critics and may help confirm or modify your analysis. You may also wish to provide copies of the study to other members of the department or friends at other institutions to garner their reactions. After seeking such informal feedback and making any appropriate modifications, you should submit your findings for presentation at a professional meeting or for publication. You should allow the community to judge the merits of the study.

5. Here we face the question of knowledge that has personal consequences, versus knowledge which does not. Taking the latter first, would these findings generally be considered knowledge? Since the findings appeared in a peer reviewed journal, we can trust that expert review assures these conclusions reasonably follow from the data. Given that the study is well done, is that enough to make them knowledge—especially when the findings are counterintuitive? We are more willing to accept findings as knowledge when the findings are replicated in additional studies. There is no evidence that these have been. Further, since we require counterintuitive findings to meet a higher standard before they are accepted as knowledge, it seems likely that these would be only very tentatively accepted until replicated. However, the explanation that handwritten material was given the benefit of the doubt does explain away some of the counter-intuitiveness of the findings. This often occurs when a problem is better understood; what appears initially as counterintuitive turns out not to be.

Should you use word processing for your examination? Here you must make a knowing judgment to guide your own behavior. Each of us might make the decision differently, depending on how much trust we put in the study. Some would be so bothered by the counterintuitive nature of the findings, they would still choose to use word processing. For myself, since the study appears to be a sound one, and, assuming I can compose as well in handwriting as with a word processor, answering in handwriting will not hurt and may increase the score, so it would be the safest course.

CHAPTER ADDENDUM

As far as it goes, this chapter's account of science would currently be widely accepted and provides a sufficient base for developing the model of internal and external validity and other criteria for judging research used in this book (see the graphic on the inside front cover). However, it skims the surface of a variety of philosophy of science issues being raised by persons who identify themselves as postmodernists, postpositivists, realists, and many others. There is not space, nor is this book the place, to go into this discussion. However, to give you a flavor, some dissenters argue because researchers have largely sought consensus among elitist, Eurocentric males to determine accepted knowledge, and this bias has marginalized less developed countries, female voices, and minority voices in that judgment. Furthermore, since all science is affected by the culture and context in which it is produced, objectivity is impossible. Some, like Bereiter (1994), seek to rescue science by suggesting that all that counts is that we can sense progress as, through open discussion, we achieve a consensus within the context in which we are working.

Intrigued? Read further: Bernstein, 1986; Carr and Kemmis, 1986; Friere, 1970, Habermas, 1984; and Phillips, 1987, 1992, 1994.

The Research Chain
of Reasoning

A chain is only as strong as its weakest link.

Old proverb

OVERVIEW

This chapter describes the way evidence is organized in the presentation of a knowledge claim. It thus builds on Chapters 2 and 3, which suggested that if many individuals are making knowing judgments about studies, they must have developed ways of facilitating the judging process. This is indeed true. An integrating framework or model for the presentation of knowledge claims is described here, and important implications for designing and critiquing research studies are shown to flow from it.[1]

CHAPTER CONTENTS

Introduction

Several federal reviewers are chatting about journal articles submitted as the final reports for projects they had funded:

> "I had a hard time with that last one. She started right off describing her data, and it was only later that I learned how and where she had gathered it. In the end, she

---

[1]This chapter, like the previous one, applies not only to social and behavioral science research, but also to research that sets forth a generalization in any science field.

had answered all my questions, but I guess I have a set of customary expectations about how a report of research should be written. I'm surprised this journal permitted such a deviation."

"Move over—I have the same expectation; there are a lot of us in that 'rut.' I must say, though, yours was an exception; the last one I reviewed was a dream—everything was there, and in good logical order."

"The report is the one thing for which we don't provide a standard federal form. I guess it is so the researchers are free to write their report in any way that makes sense to them. Sometimes I wish we did enforce a particular sequence or outline, especially for reports that are not in journal article form. It would make them easier and faster to read and critique."

"Whoa! Come on, now, you don't really believe we need another form, do you? There is more than enough bureaucratic regulation around here! Give them some freedom!"

"Okay, I'll grant you that we don't want to stifle creativity. But most journals create expectations in their readers and authors that certain parts of the research will be reported in a particular order. I think we should too. It makes such good logical sense to build one's case that way."

"Yes, and if there are headings, one knows just where to look for certain items."

"Sure, but even without headings, the organization of the write-up provides an orderly sequence so that readers can follow the argument and find what they need."

This conversation simply reinforces the fact that research is a social process; the researcher is communicating with an audience to present the study properly and to convey how carefully it was done. Similarly the reader or reviewer is trying to follow raising and answering questions as the report is read, judging whether it supports the knowledge claim that is being asserted, and making knowing judgments. It is not surprising, therefore, that a fairly standard form or sequence of presentation has evolved. The standard has been informal—that is, accepted by authors rather than being required by journals—though some journals rarely seem to depart from it so researchers conform in order to enhance chances of publication. It is exemplified by the Zimbardo article reprinted in Chapter 1. Although that particular journal saves space by eliminating headings used by many journals, the article is organized in typical sequence.

The Research Chain of Reasoning

Articles that present a research-based knowledge claim for a generalization are typically presented as logical arguments. The sequence of article parts corresponds to what we might think of as a prototypical or model **chain of reasoning** that applies to any research article. Even when the usual sequence is not followed, all the parts of the chain are required to supply adequate information to make a logical case. A representation of the chain of reasoning appears in Figure 4.1.

To make the research chain of reasoning more than an abstract conceptualization, let us see how it applies to the Zimbardo experiment.

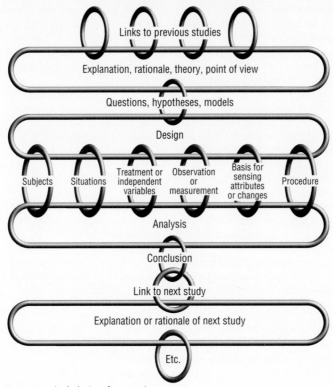

FIGURE 4.1 A prototypical chain of reasoning.

The Zimbardo Article as an Example of the Research Chain of Reasoning

Explanation, Rationale, Theory, or Point of View. Turn back to the Zimbardo article on page 6. How does it begin? The first three paragraphs describe the rationale underlying the relationship the study is intended to demonstrate. The article begins with a discussion of previous research, showing in the first paragraph that psychopathology, especially paranoia, has been clinically observed to accompany deafness. In the second paragraph, a mechanism is suggested as to why a relationship might develop. The third paragraph indicates how a psychopathological response could be reinforced and maintained. All paragraphs draw heavily on previous research and writing.

The **explanation, rationale, theory, or point of view** underlying a hypothesized relationship is usually laid out at the beginning of the article as is done here. It is important because it is the basis for understanding and interpreting the rest of the presentation. An explanation indicates how the relationship works. A rationale indicates the basis for thinking that it works this way. A theory indicates how this relationship fits into a larger scheme of things, how these variables relate to others. A point of view indicates how this researcher views this relationship and compares or contrasts this with the views of others. In building this section of the study, the researcher draws on previous relevant work, selectively citing it to indicate that the idea is not a "bolt from the blue" but is in fact solidly based on what has gone before. In Figure 4.1, previous work is represented by the combination of the small links at the top of the figure labeled *Links to previous studies*. The large link running through them all represents the explanation, rationale, theory, or point of view based on them.

Questions, Hypotheses, Models. Next comes the **questions, hypotheses, models** link. In the Zimbardo case, the hypothesis is at the end of the third paragraph: "In this analysis, paranoia. . . ." It is a hypothesis because we know enough to go beyond merely stating a question that tells us where to look. We know what we shall look for, the development of paranoia. We don't know how much paranoia or exactly how it is linked to a certain amount of deafness, so we can't make a precise prediction. That constitutes the next higher level of prior information, when we know even more about the phenomenon. When we can link all, or a great many, of the variables in the situation and make an even more precise prediction, we have a model. In Zimbardo's case, there is enough previous research to suggest that there is a relationship but not enough to make a precise prediction or build a model. Thus, depending on how much basis previous research gives us for anticipating what will happen, at this link in the chain of reasoning, with increasing prior information we have: a question, hypotheses that something will happen, that it will occur in a certain direction, that it will be of a certain size as well as in a particular direction, that it is also related to certain variables, that it is related in specific ways to certain variables—a model.

Adapting the Format to the Researcher's Purposes. The fourth paragraph is a summary of the rest of the article. It is evidence that the chain of reasoning format need not be followed slavishly and rigidly. Each author adapts the format to the requirements of the readers. In this case, this article appeared in a journal that is devoted primarily to biological and physical science reports. Non–social scientists might be interested enough to read a few paragraphs but are not likely to read the whole article. Thus, placing the summary early, right after the rationale and hypothesis, is savvy writing. It serves here as a motivator to read the rest of the article and provides an advance organizer for what will be found. For the hurried reader who is merely skimming the journal, this is a convenient stopping place that provides the essential information. This fourth paragraph is not part of the usual structure but illustrates an adaptation of the usual form to the needs of this particular audience.

Research Design. After stating the expected relationship, the article begins describing how the study was carried out. Implementing the study means translating the various facets of the presumed relationship into aspects that dramatize it, so to speak. A playwright, having described a plot as "Lillyann falls in love with Joe," must then write a script that translates that into a scene where individuals move to certain places at certain times, say certain things that convey love, and so on. Similarly, in this study, the researcher must translate such terms as *paranoia*, *deafness*, and *perceptual discontinuity*. But that is not all that has to be translated.

There are six aspects we should look for when we examine the translation of the hypothesis link into a study. Together these constitute the **research design** of the study. They are represented in Figure 4.1 by the six rings interlinked with *Design*. These rings correspond to the *five W's and an H* that all journalists learn to include in a story: who, when, where, what, why, and how. For research we want to know: (1) *Who* was involved in the study (the subjects ring in design)? (2) *Where* (the situation ring)? (3) *Why* did an effect occur (what was the cause—the treatment ring)? (4) *What* effect occurred (the observations or measures ring)? (5) *How* do we know an effect occurred (the basis for sensing attributes or changes ring)? (6) *When*, or in what sequence, did the various parts of the study take place (the procedure ring)?

This journalist's ditty, borrowed from Rudyard Kipling, is a useful mnemonic for the six facets of design:

> I kept six honest serving men
>
> They taught me all I knew:
>
> Their names were What and Why and When
>
> And How and Where and Who.

For research application, this can be translated as follows:

Who	Subjects. (*Who* are they?)
Where	Situation. (*Where* did it take place?)
Why (the cause)	Treatment. (This is *why* something would be expected to occur.)
What (the effect)	Observations or measures. (These tell *what* occurred.)
How	Basis for sensing characteristics and changes. (This tells us *how* we know an effect occurred.)
When	Procedure. (This tells *when* what subjects received what treatment, observations, or measures; where they received it; and when and where the effect is to occur.)

Paragraphs 5 through 9 of the Zimbardo article translate the hypothesis into the design and structure of the study, the middle links in Figure 4.1. Let us examine the choices Zimbardo and associates made in these six facets of the study. The whole of the fifth paragraph is devoted to the who—**subjects**. The where—**situation**—is implied rather than specified, and it is clearly a laboratory, presumably at the author's institution.

The cause or **treatment** (the why of the study) is described in the sixth paragraph, where part of the how by which the effect was sensed—the **basis for sensing attributes or changes**—is also described. In this instance, random assignment into three different treatment groups gives us a basis for sensing changes in the groups relative to one another that lets us sense the effect. It also, as we shall see, rules out alternative explanations. The Hoffmann-Riem study reprinted in Chapter 1, similar to most qualitative studies, instead of sensing change, sought common attributes across individuals, groups, or situations. In this instance, comparing the different interviews provided the basis for sensing the common attribute—a desire for normality across people who adopt children.

The **observations and measures** are described in the seventh and eighth paragraphs. Note that Zimbardo used multiple measures of paranoia so that even if we have questions about one, it is hard to argue that all three might be wrong.

The seventh paragraph also has extensive description of the **procedure,** as does the ninth paragraph. Thus we can see that all the important information regarding the design and structure of the study is presented in this midsection of the article. Here the concepts in the explanation that were pulled together into a hypothesis are translated into actions. These are the basis for gathering the data for analysis.

Data Analysis and Conclusion. The data of the study are presented in the tenth and eleventh paragraphs and the accompanying table. This is represented in Figure 4.1 in the link labeled *Analysis.* The data show that the hypothesized relationship is demonstrated across all the measures and observations. This claim in turn leads to the last link in the chain of reasoning for this particular study, the conclusion. This appears as the last paragraph of the article, paragraph 13. There the authors note that despite the artificiality of the laboratory procedure, the rationale is sound and the findings have a bearing on the problems of the elderly.

The Next Study. The last links shown in Figure 4.1 actually belong to the next study that builds on this one. That study is connected to this one by one of those *Links to previous studies* rings like those at the top of the figure. It would use the findings from this one to support some further explanation of this or a related phenomenon.

In summary, the chain of reasoning begins with links to the results of previous studies that are used to build forward to an explanation, rationale, or point of view. Depending on how much previous knowledge we find, we draw from it a question, hypothesis, or model. This in turn we translate into a design that consists of choices of subjects, situations, treatment (or independent variable), observations or measures, basis for sensing attributes or changes, and procedure. The design guides us in the collection of data, which permits us to demonstrate a relationship by means of data analysis. Future researchers may in turn pick up the demonstration of the relationship and conclusion in a new study.

Another Example: Use of the Chain of Reasoning in Study Design

A published study makes the choices in the chain of reasoning seem easy and obvious, like looking through binoculars focused on a particular phenomenon. But have you turned the binoculars around and looked through the other end? You will see far more—the phenomenon of interest is embedded in a whole distracting context. So it is in developing a study. Consider the example shown in Figure 4.2.

The literature suggests that there are naturally occurring zones of activity in the classroom that are normally occupied by high achievers. The rationale for the

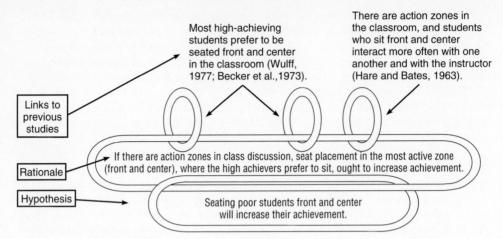

FIGURE 4.2 The first links in the chain of reasoning of a classroom seating placement study. (Adapted from Krathwohl, 1985)

study that grows out of this literature is that perhaps this phenomenon could be turned into a treatment for students who are achieving poorly if they are seated where high achievers normally sit.

Figure 4.3 shows, in the next links of the chain, a sampling of the alternatives that the researcher faces in translating this simple hypothesis into a design. Although merely touching on the possibilities, the figure gives an idea of the decisions involved in choosing a design, the basis for which we will be examining in

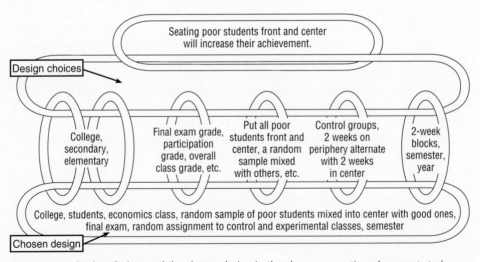

FIGURE 4.3 Design choices and the chosen design in the classroom seating placement study. (Adapted from Krathwohl, 1985)

future chapters. The chosen design in the figure suggests a set of reasonable alternatives that might have been combined into a study.

Four Useful Characteristics of the Chain Analogy

If the chain of reasoning were made of metal, it would have four physical properties that, by analogy, are helpful in understanding the use of the chain of reasoning in research (Krathwohl, 1985). Let us examine them.

A Chain Is Only as Strong as Its Weakest Link. Just as a metal chain breaks at the weakest link, so does an argument for a knowledge claim. As much as any part of the argument for a knowledge claim can be faulted, the whole chain is weakened, and readers are less likely to accept the claim. If the fault is serious, the chain fails and the claim is rejected. For example, if we were convinced that the paranoia of the elderly is different from that produced in the college men, then the *choice of subjects* link is weakened, and, depending on how serious we consider this problem, the whole argument either is weakened or fails to be convincing.

All Links in the Chain Should Be Equally Strong. A second characteristic of a metal chain, which is derived from the first, is that all links in the chain should be of about the same strength. This is typical of a metal chain; a set of strong links is not interrupted by a small, thin link. Yet this inconsistency sometimes happens in a study's chain of reasoning without our realizing it or its seriousness. It makes little sense that one link in the chain is thick enough to anchor a building in a hurricane and others are as thin as a decorative gold chain. Thus, there would have been little point in allocating considerable resources to the instrument link as Zimbardo did—he used three measures of paranoia—if he had developed the hypnotic technique only to the point where deafness was irregularly and unpredictably maintained. Better that he reassigned some resources from measures to improving the hypnotic technique. Resource allocation should ensure that all the links are equally strong.

In whose judgment should the links be of equal strength? Our audience makes the final judgment; we are building a chain intended to achieve a consensus about the interpretation of the findings. We must satisfy our own personal standards first, but the interpretation of the data being advanced will be accepted by others only if their standards are met as well. Anticipating what their thresholds are is a problem, but it is a problem we cannot avoid. Learning these standards is part of the socialization process that maintains science and results from the judgments made, among others, by panels awarding research grants, journal and convention program referees, and editors.

The real problem occurs when our personal priorities about what to strengthen differ from those we anticipate others will require and the resources are not sufficient to satisfy both. Because resources are always limited, **trade-offs** are usually required, and completely satisfying all parties may not be possible. Zimbardo obviously thought a laboratory study was preferable to a field study in a retirement home. He traded the positives of reality and generality and the negatives of trying to control the situation in a retirement home and its accompanying ethical problems for alternative sets: of positives—good control in the laboratory and fewer ethical problems, and negatives—artificiality and problems in generalizing the results. We try as best we can to find the choice that optimizes satisfaction for all.

Many trade-offs are hidden in the research process. This is the first we have encountered. There will be others, however, and you should look for them. Because researchers differ about trade-off solutions, we often have to consider more than one "right" way to do a study, an unanticipated characteristic of science. It makes many people uncomfortable; indeed, some argue that there is always only one best way to do a study—a position you may find difficult to support. But such arguments are also a part of the social process, one that seems to work itself out as efforts are made to replicate or build on studies and create consensus about a particular generalization.

Each Link in the Chain Is Determined by the Link Before It. The information must be logically linked together. Each link depends on the preceding one. The *explanation or rationale* is built on previous research. The *question, hypothesis, or model* grows out of that rationale or explanation. Because the extent of knowledge about the problem determines whether a question, hypothesis, or model is formulated, the second link is dependent on the first.

The next link, the *design* of the study, is a translation of the preceding link into the operations that constitute the study. What can be shown in the next link, *Analysis,* depends on the design choices. Analysis in turn leads to the *conclusion,* which is clearly dependent on how the analysis of the data turned out.

It is the way each step advances the argument for the knowledge claim that sets boundaries for the next; each step is shaped by the argument to that point. Thus, being aware of the desired breadth for the lower links, we need to build in sufficient breadth in the earlier ones. If Zimbardo wishes to generalize his conclusions to the elderly and sees the use of college students as narrowing the range of his conclusions, then he must make a different choice of subjects in the earlier links.

Where Links Share the Load, One of Them May Be Made Stronger to Compensate for Weakness in Another. This last characteristic of the chain is not quite as obvious as the previous ones. Although it rarely occurs with metal chains, it is important in research. Where several horizontal links across the chain's breadth connect the links above and below them, each of the horizontal links shares the load. Therefore, a weak link can remain if another of the horizontal links is made stronger. In the research chain of reasoning, this situation occurs at the design level. At that level, all six facets link the design as a whole to the demonstration of the relationship shown in the analysis link.

Zimbardo used this principle in his study; hypnosis is a weak treatment in the sense that it will not work with some individuals. For them, the posthypnotic suggestion might not have been effective. He strengthened the *subjects* link by choosing subjects who were especially susceptible to hypnosis, thereby making the treatment strong.

✦ *The chain analogy makes four important points about the chain of reasoning:*
1. *Because an argument is only as strong as its weakest link, the chain of argu-mentation must be viable despite its weakest part.*
2. *Links at all levels of the chain should be equally strong. At the design level, it is the combined strength of the six links that equals the strength at the other links. There is no point in lavishing care on one part of the argument if an-other part is weak.*
3. *The nature of each prior link in the chain constrains the nature of successive links.*
4. *Since all six links at the design level "help carry the load," weak links may be made up for if one or more of the other six links is strengthened.*

The Chain of Reasoning and Qualitative Studies

Does the chain of reasoning also apply to qualitative research studies using an in-ductive method to gather and analyze data—the Hoffmann-Riem study of Chapter 1, for instance? Yes, but only if the study presents one or more **generalizations.** That is, the study is setting forth findings that are expected to be true in samples of per-sons and situations beyond those studied. In such instances, the study may also be presented as a chain of reasoning. Although the study was carried out inductively, the findings can be presented deductively. Sometimes the details of procedure, de-sign, and analysis are put in a methodological appendix. Remember, one can adapt the presentation to one's audience. Frequently, the links of the chain are all present but not necessarily in the chain's order. The Hoffmann-Riem study is an example of the latter; this makes the chain more difficult to discern than in the Zimbardo article.

Hoffmann-Riem, instead of beginning by building on previous literature and advancing to a problem statement and hypothesis as did the Zimbardo study, uses paragraphs 1 through 8 to describe various aspects of method and design. In the course of these, the information describing the six parallel links in design are covered. For instance, paragraphs 1 through 4 deal with data collection methods, covering the procedure as well as the observation and measure links. As might be expected, the sample and situation links are described in the section labeled "Sampling," paragraph 5. The basis for sensing attributes or changes link is de-scribed in paragraph 7. As is true of nearly all qualitative research, there is no ma-nipulated treatment. Instead, in place of treatment, the link is filled by study of a naturally occurring process—the desire for a child, adoption, and normalization. So all the links of design are covered.

The other links in the chain are covered as well. Paragraph 6 deals with the analysis. Paragraph 9 is an early statement of her conclusion, which, of course, is also reflected in the section headed "Conclusion," paragraphs 25 to the end. More analysis and its results are described in paragraphs 9 through 24, which present the context and the process of adoption. The illustrative examples in these para-graphs provide a sense of reality to the data it would lack without them. Where appropriate, as in paragraphs 19 and 21, there are references to relevant previous literature. Clearly, the case has been built with all the parts of the chain, but without assembling them in the chain sequence. The chain describes the parts needed to make the case and they are all there.

The purpose of many qualitative studies, however, is mainly description; for example, a historical account of the development of Piaget's notion of conservation or a case study of a person, group, or culture. The intent may be to give you an insight into a corner of the world, or a community you are unlikely otherwise to encounter. Obviously, such studies need not follow the chain pattern.

SUMMARY

All studies setting forth a generalization are expected to supply certain information that allows readers to judge the study and make a knowing judgment whether to accept the interpretation of the evidence being advanced. Most, though not all, studies follow a standard sequence in presenting the findings of their research. If they do not follow the sequence, they nevertheless include the same information.

The case for a generalization is presented (or can be arranged) in a sequence that forms a chain of reasoning. A universal or prototypical model of such a chain of reasoning can be constructed that contains the essential elements. Such a model begins with an explanation, rationale, theory, or point of view that is linked to or grows out of prior research studies and writing. The generalization being advanced flows from this explanation, rationale, theory, or point of view.

The stronger the previous evidence, the more detailed in its development, the more comprehensive in its breadth, then the stronger the explanation, rationale, theory, or point of view, and in turn, the stronger the links that flow from it. With the strongest prior knowledge, we can pose a model that links many variables. With less prior knowledge, we may still be able to make a reasonably precise prediction of how large an effect will occur, as well as where and when it will happen. With still less, we may have a hypothesis that describes the direction things may take and how they are related. With the least prior knowledge, a question focuses our attention on certain aspects of the phenomenon of particular interest that presumably have potential for guiding further research.

The question, hypothesis, or model is translated into the design of the study. The result is the choices of who (subjects), where (situation), why (treatment), what (observations or measures), how (basis for sensing attributes or changes), and when (procedure). These choices determine how to gather data that demonstrate whatever relationship is being studied. These data are analyzed, and a conclusion is drawn to represent the most appropriate interpretation of the data.

The chain-of-reasoning model is analogous to a metal chain and has some of the same properties:

1. Because it is only as strong as its weakest link, the argument should be viable despite its weakest aspect.

2. All links should be of the same strength except when they share the load. Thus, resources of time, effort, and money should be allocated such that they strengthen the weaker links.

3. The nature of each prior link in the chain constrains the nature of successive links, so early links must be appropriate to the desired conclusion.

4. Where links share the load, as they do between *design* and *analysis,* one or more of those links may be made stronger to compensate for weakness in one or more of the others.

A Look Ahead

With the next section, we examine in some detail the top links of the chain of reasoning: finding a research problem in Chapter 5 and relating it to the body of literature from which we will build forward, Chapter 6.

We can infer from the chain of reasoning what evidence must be present in the report of a good study. But what criteria do we apply to that evidence? It should now be clear that audiences, in making the knowing judgments involved in forming a consensus, use criteria to assess links in the chain of reasoning. We will consider these criteria in Chapters 7 through 9 of Section 3.

ADDITIONAL READING

Krathwohl (1985)

IMPORTANT TERMS

Chain of reasoning
Explanation, rationale, theory, point of view
Generalization
Question, hypothesis, model
Research design and its six facets:

1. Subjects

2. Situation

3. Treatment (or independent variable)

4. Observations or measures

5. Basis for sensing attributes or changes

6. Procedure

APPLICATION PROBLEM

The following paragraphs summarize a 1987 study by Dr. David Jonassen of the University of Colorado in which he set out to verify "pattern notes" as a method to assess an individual's cognitive structure. Jonassen began his article with a brief discussion of instructional design theory. He noted that such theory had traditionally been based on experience with programmed learning and behavioral task analysis but was slowly giving way to cognitive theory. That theory assumes knowing is a process of individually constructing our cognitive structures, based on experience. Thus the purpose of instruction is to build the best of these structures in the learner. Instructional design theory provides techniques to determine the learner's cognitive structure and to organize content to fit it. The problem was to find a feasible procedure for mapping cognitive structure.

Jonassen proceeded to describe the available methods, dismissing most for reasons ranging from being limited to being too difficult. His solution was "pattern notes," a form of spatial word association task first developed as a technique for taking notes during a lecture. The student placed the topic of the lecture in the middle of the page and then added related concepts around it. Lines were drawn between concepts to indicate relationships. This simple technique, he noted, depicted the relationships between concepts associated with each other. *They should, he reasoned, represent cognitive structure.*

The purpose of the study was to verify this hypothesis. To do so, Jonassen proposed to compare a learner's pattern notes to a free word association task on the same topic. The free word association technique was, in his assessment, the most valid and reliable of the available methods for assessing the learner's cognitive structure. However, it requires the use of sophisticated statistical analysis. Relationships were measured by counting the number of common links between concepts— whether the lines from one concept to another in the pattern note corresponded to the response when one or the other concept was the stimulus in free word association.

Jonassen used both measures to assess the cognitive structures for Newtonian mechanics of 24 high school students. All were members of an advanced elective physics course and were presumed to be motivated and capable. The study was carried out on three separate days over a period of a week. The students were first administered the word association task. The order of concepts presented in each test was random for each student. The next week, they were taught how to construct pattern notes and finally were asked to construct one note for each of the concepts presented during the first test. Analysis of the data showed a significant relationship between the two measures, indicating that they could use pattern notes to assess cognitive structure as it was represented by free word association. In his concluding section, Jonassen then provided a number of suggestions for the use of pattern notes in instructional design.

1. Explain whether or not this summary of Jonassen's work follows the research chain of reasoning.

2. What do you consider the weak links to be in his argument?

3. For any weak links, indicate if Jonassen compensated by making other links stronger.

ANSWER TO THE APPLICATION PROBLEM

1. Jonassen did follow the chain of reasoning, but with a slight twist. He began with a rationale for the study and a statement of the problem rather than with conclusions from previous research studies. He described traditional instructional design theory first and then described how it was changing as a result of new theory, cognitive psychology. His rationale, though, was based on prior research. Once he had stated his problem—to find a feasible procedure for mapping cognitive structure—he explored the research, examining the available techniques. Only then did he offer a hypothesis— that pattern notes would provide a practical technique for mapping cognitive structure—and it, too, was based on previous research.

The next step was to translate his hypothesis into a research design. The *who,* 24 high school students in an advanced physics class; the *where,* in the high school classroom; and the *when,* over three separate school days, are clearly specified. To demonstrate *what* effect occurred, that pattern notes measure cognitive structure, Jonassen again returned to the literature to find a method to measure cognitive structure. He chose free word association, a technique that he thought was the most valid and reliable measure of cognitive structure available. A high relationship between the scores on the free word association task and on the pattern notes would demonstrate *how* he knew that the effect had occurred. Perhaps the most difficult task was to demonstrate *why* the effect happened—in this case, why pattern notes (and free word association) could be said to measure cognitive structure. This he did by means of a theoretical assumption—that the relationship between two concepts can be determined by their links in free association or in the notes. The why, then, was shown by counting the corresponding links between the concepts produced by the students in pattern notes and by free word association. Although not indicated in our summary, both the experimental and the analysis procedures were described in some detail. The relationship was demonstrated statistically, and the conclusion, that pattern notes were a valid measure of cognitive structure, was based on the analysis of the data. Jonassen concluded his report by relating the pattern note technique to instructional design theory and thus provided the link on which future studies could be built.

2. Possibly the weakest link is Jonassen's assertion that cognitive structure can be represented by the number of references of one concept to another. It is a means of inferring what cannot be observed directly. We must accept his argument that this is true in order to believe that cognitive structure was actually being measured.

We may also consider his choice of sample a weak link. First, it was quite small (24 students). However, a small sample under the right circumstances, to demonstrate an effect. (Know statistics? See power analysis, pp. 478–483.)

Second, the effect may have resulted from the characteristics of this one sample. The class was advanced, and the students were probably more capable than average, so maybe intelligence accounted for the relationship. Further, it was quite a uniform group; it did not have the variability of a group representative of that grade. This might not have been a weakness since it was necessary that each student have a well-developed cognitive structure in this subject to provide something to measure. The researcher's purpose was to demonstrate that pattern notes could be used to measure cognitive structure, not necessarily to show that the technique worked for all learners. The study would surely require replication with samples having different characteristics before we could accept the technique as widely useful.

Finally, we could advance an alternative explanation, that of the added motivation that results from the special attention of being part of an experiment (often called the Hawthorne effect). The experiment was carried out in the students' own classroom, however, which would probably dampen any such effect.

3. Not that you can tell from this summary. In the article, Jonassen (1987) strengthened the *observation and measurement* link for measuring cognitive structure by basing the technique solidly in theory and prior research. He indicated considerable theoretical and research support for it.

SECTION TWO

Foundational Research Skills

In this section we begin supplying the knowledge, insights, and skills to enhance your ability to handle various parts of the chain of reasoning, beginning with the top links of the chain. Foundational to any study is starting with a good problem. You'll also need to know about the marvelous array of reference works that helps you find it and then build on what about it has already been researched. If you are inductively developing your problem, prior work shows how others have understood it. With either approach, consulting the literature keeps you from reinventing the wheel. Thus, we commence exploring two foundational skills, problem finding and the literature search, skills that are important regardless of research approach.

- Chapter 5 discusses the criteria of a good problem and gives problem finding suggestions. Some persons seem particularly adept at selecting important overlooked problems. Clearly that is more than luck. We will explore a number of suggestions regarding the process of finding and conceptualizing a research problem that may strengthen your skill in this critical area.
- Chapter 6 explains the characteristics of a good literature search and the means for doing one. These topics are considered: relating your study to previous research and thought, the tremendous breadth of available resources, the different kinds of indexes, how to find where the cataloger put it, how the nature of your problem determines where to start, and how to organize the search.

Finding Research Problems

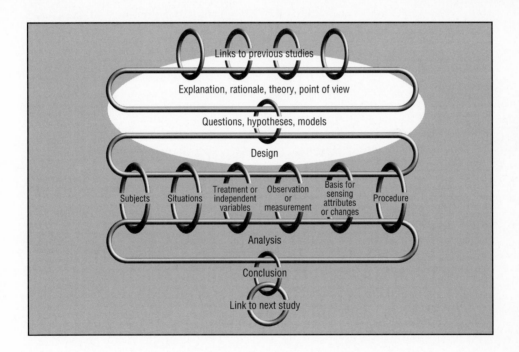

A question well-stated is half solved!

Anonymous

We need theories to live by. A theory is an intellectual armature which allows only certain facts in. . . . We will all die of word pollution if we allow our minds to become empirical dustbowls where every fact is as salient as any other. . . . what I must learn to do is to ask the right questions. And that, it seems to me, must come from having some working theories about what's important.

Warren Bennis as quoted in Wurman (1989)

OVERVIEW

Problem selection is critical because it sets the course for the study, yet it is also difficult for many of us. In this chapter, we explore the criteria of a good problem and problem development methods that biographies and literature suggest have been successful.

CHAPTER CONTENTS

The Problem of the Problem[1]

Not only is the choice of problem the most important decision each researcher makes it is also a real gamble! There is no certain way of telling at the outset whether the investment of time, energy, and resources will yield any return—with luck, a reputation can be made. Is it luck, however, that some persons are known as good researchers? No more so than that some people can make an honest living from the stock market, generally win at cards, or beat the odds at a racetrack. What research there is on problem finding suggests that some individuals are consistently better at it than others (Getzels, 1982). All of us know individuals who are particularly creative; I have known some from whom I got a good idea whenever I talked with them. But Osborn and others involved with industrial

---

[1]This is the title of an excellent chapter by Getzels (1982) on problem finding. He is one of the few people who have done research on problem finding and formulation.

training have data that suggest everyone's creativity can be increased (Osborn, 1959; Parnes, 1967).

Past studies have shown that relatively few researchers account for the bulk of useful work: 10 percent of scientists accounts for fully 50 percent of published research, and 10 percent of published research accounts for 40 percent of the citations in books and articles (Pletz, 1965; Price, 1963). There is little reason to believe the current situation differs. So often in reading research we find that it focuses on something in a familiar situation. We might have noticed it, but to our regret we did not act on it. Clearly, some individuals improve their odds for success by carrying thought into action. Modifying such behaviors as well as learning some of the behaviors that enhance problem-finding capacity will improve research capabilities.

How can we facilitate a creative process that by definition defies formulas or routine processes? We can describe the criteria of good problems so that when one appears, you will recognize it. We can note some problem types not amenable to research methods. Finally, we can describe behavior and activities characteristic of productive researchers and suggest some creativity enhancement techniques. You choose among these the ones you think may be personally effective. These topics outline this chapter.

Before we begin, let's re-emphasize the fact that, as we noted at the close of Chapter 3, we are ethicists whether we elected to be or not. As such we have an ethical responsibility to consider the consequences of whatever problem we choose.

Problem Finding and Research Method

Some persons find a problem, define it well, gather data, analyze them, and write them up, following each of these steps in sequence. Research is typically visualized this way, a stance usually associated with quantitative methods. It involves considerable investment in problem finding, problem redefinition, and the literature search (the latter, the topic of the next chapter). As we previously noted, other researchers immerse themselves in a situation of interest and let the research project emerge as they explore what is there, an inductive approach usually associated with qualitative research. In fact, however, we can adapt either approach to any method. With qualitative work, we can begin data collection as soon as we identify what might be called an "orienting question"—one that focuses and directs our attention. In the Hoffmann-Riem study of Chapter 1, the problem began as "how parents viewed adoption" and ended up as "how adoptive parents normalized their lives."

Novice researchers often concentrate on method before they are clear on what the problem is. To a certain extent, working on method can help formulate the problem if you don't go too far with method before you clarify the problem. *For most of us, however, research method follows problem choice.* Once we know what to study and how we want to do it, we adapt method of investigation and problem to one another until we personally feel comfortable. Often this is not a single method but a combination.

An Example. Mike, a part-time doctoral student, is also a school administrator whose School Board has been bargaining with his teachers. The teachers want the same pay as a nearby richer district. If he could show that to meet their demand would not cause budget defeat in the annual approval referendum, the Board could give the raise and everyone would be happier. If it would cause failure, that knowledge would give the Board a bargaining chip of value. This gets him interested in being able to predict the outcome of such budget referendums.

However, initially worried that the problem is too big for a dissertation, he begins talking about this problem to other students and his adviser. Someone suggests looking at the impact of taxpayer burden on such votes. While a smaller problem, he realizes that a given tax rate does not translate into an equal burden for rich and poor districts—it isn't the reality of the amount, it is the way it is perceived that counts. Worse yet, burden is only one of many handles on the problem. For some defeats, the main factor was how voters felt about the superintendent, for others it was the total tax burden, not just that of the schools. It becomes clear that he must first understand the major handles on the problem. What can he do?

Clearly one possibility is to look at the literature. But there is not a lot on predicting budget approvals. Further, his state law is relatively unique in requiring school district voters annually to approve the school budget, further narrowing interest in his problem. He turns to the closest literature, bond issue referendums. He begins to develop a list of variables involved in these studies. Can he translate these directly to his problem? Bond issues commit for 20-30 years, not just the next year. Though most variables seem applicable to both problems, he finds he must think carefully about each one.

He begins to list the variables but is bedeviled by questions. How complete is his list? Shall he look for others? Seek evidence about which are really crucial? Find which ones others believe to be critical? Try them out to see if they predict current referendums? Each option takes him down a different road.

Suppose that he wishes better to understand budget defeats, getting a complete roster of variables and their interrelationships. That might involve qualitative research, and interviews with individuals who can tell him stories about budget defeats and their perceptions about what caused them.

Suppose he thinks that he has a rather complete list, and would like to find which ones that experienced superintendents think are crucial in the cases they know about. Survey research of this group with a questionnaire might help him both add variables and point to the important ones.

If he believes he knows the crucial variables, he might use statistics to set up an equation to determine how accurately he can predict some actual school referendums. He would need to find or construct measures of the variables and learn something about quantitative correlational prediction techniques.

Alternatively, he might compare pairs of districts where his understanding of the problems suggests a particular variable is likely to cause defeat in both districts. Intervening in one of them, he can see if he can sufficiently ameliorate its effect—an experimental approach. If he can, then he has not only a method of predicting referenda but also a way of doing something about them. This, of course, is where he ultimately would like to be.

Of course, if he is wrong in having a good list, or in identifying the key variables, then neither of the latter studies is going to show positive results; they mainly tell him he was on the wrong track and may help discern why. But there are millions of variables that are not relevant to the problem and he must find the few that are. Finding these is fastest with a good understanding of the process; that is helped by either the qualitative, and/or the survey research.

Notice how research method follows from how well you understand your problem and what you want to get from it. *Don't freeze into method too early.* Good problem homesteading requires a nice balance between staying open with respect to focus and method until you understand your problem well enough to proceed further and making the necessary choices that allow you to make progress toward doing and finishing the research.

The names problem finding or homesteading suggest it is a one-time process—a problem, once defined, does not change. Nothing could be further from the truth. In qualitative methods, problem finding is usually expected to be a continuous process in which the possibility of redefinition continues even through data analysis. Although a less frequent expectation, redefinition also can occur with quantitative methods if something new and interesting shows up in data analysis. Indeed, the whole focus of the problem can shift, sometimes to a phenomenon quite different from the original one. With either approach, such redefinition often doesn't appear in the study's report, which is written as though the final choice were always the focus of investigation.[2] Yet when it occurs, reformulation is an important part of the research process. After all, only as complete data collection informs us sufficiently about the phenomenon do we understand the important questions to ask.

- ✦ Problem finding and the redefinition of the problem and its focus are continuing processes.
- ✦ In the typical case using quantitative methods, a clear conception of the problem emerges before data gathering, whereas in one using qualitative methods, it sometimes does not occur until the data analysis stage.
- ✦ Novice researchers often focus too tightly on method before they clarify the problem—not realizing they can use exploratory or validating approaches with either quantitative or qualitative methods.

Criteria of a Good Problem

A good problem is (1) of interest, (2) embedded in theory, (3) likely to have impact, (4) original in some aspect, and (5) feasible—within your conceptual, resource, ethical, and institutional limits. In addition, there are these adapted from Teplin's tongue-in-cheek suggestions (Youngstrom, 1990, p. 7) :

---

[2]The reader is more interested in the case you are presenting than in how you came upon it. Publication space is at too great a premium to include the whole story of the research.

- The Goldilocks test: Is the research question so broad it's untenable, so narrow it's dull—or is it just right?
- The five-year test: A five-year-old should be able to understand the purpose of the project.
- The persimmon test: Can you state the purpose of your study in 25 words or less?
- The blood test: People besides your blood relatives should want to read the research results.

Interest: A Necessary but Not Sufficient Condition

For most researchers, interest is the prime qualification, for it provides the motivation to work on the problem. As one doctoral student put it: "It's your baby, so it better be one you can love when you are up with it at night!" (Grant, 1986). Professor's files are full of projects that failed this test, and the many doctoral ABD (all but dissertation) candidates are further testimony to its importance. Clearly, it is one necessary condition; the other is feasibility. Besides these two, however, a problem should have as many of the following characteristics as possible: a basis in theory, some impact in its field, and some originality and creativity.

Basis in Theory

An isolated study typically has little impact. However, when a study contributes to explanations or significant ideas, when it modifies, contradicts, or extends them in some way, it multiplies its impact. As it affects the network of previous findings, it becomes embedded with those ideas and shares in their implications and effects. Problems that either build new rationale and theory or affect previous work are less likely to get lost. The power of Skinner to sway people to behaviorism lay not in his individual studies of learning, though these were important in building the base. Rather it lay in the rationale he built around these findings, a rationale that had important implications for explaining much of human activity. In fact, he even used the theory to suggest how language develops (Skinner, 1957).

What is meant by theory? Simply put, it means an explanation of behavior that makes good logical sense and either is consistent with the research and explanations that preceded it or convincingly negates or modifies them. Discussion of what constitutes good theory could fill the rest of this book. Although social scientists and educators don't have the kind of grand and precise theories that natural scientists have, theories help them find the significant variables, unify a variety of findings, assimilate them into a cohesive and interrelated body, and locate points where research is needed. Good problems are strengthened when they relate to theory.

When choosing or developing theory, be guided by what Yvonna Lincoln, in a speech at the American Educational Research Association convention, called the Coco Chanel principle: "Simple is always elegant, ultimately timeless and usually in fashion. Parsimony is prettier!" When choosing among explanations, choose the simplest that adequately covers the data.

Some Impact in Its Field

Beyond interest and feasibility, the criterion most researchers consider important is impact. Cronbach (1982) describes impact with the term *leverage*: "Leverage refers to the influence that reducing a particular uncertainty has on decisions . . . [it] is directly visible in the response of the community to the evidence" (p. 226). A social worker, concerned that the content of in-service training is determined by the supervisor instead of the workers, demonstrates this with a study. If she ignores the realities of administrators' responsibility and their role perceptions, however, she is likely to have little impact—leverage—in changing the situation. Predicting impact requires an accurate understanding of the dynamics of the situation and answers to such questions as: "Why hasn't it changed?" and "What would it take to change it?"

Originality and Creativity

A good problem reflects some of the originality and creativity of its author. As Morris Klein says: "I think that in research you want to satisfy your own ego. You want to know you did it before the other fellow" (Rosner and Abt, 1970, p. 99). Yet the hard fact of the matter is that we all stand on each other's shoulders. The competitive spirit provides a useful drive, but it gets in the way when it blinds us to our dependence on others. Graduate students often refuse problems they did not invent—perhaps one suggested by their major professor—in a kind of "second adolescence." They want to be independent and show they can do things on their own (Krathwohl, 1988). Researchers can make problems theirs by adding just enough of their own thinking to another's problem to get an "investment" in it. None of us starts from scratch; it is important to find that middle ground.

Feasibility

A good problem is feasible; that is (1) it lends itself to investigation with the instruments and techniques that are either available or can be invented; (2) it is within the capability of the investigator's available or acquirable experience and skills; and (3) it can be accomplished within whatever social, ethical, and resource limits must be observed. As a criterion, feasibility is obviously critical, yet in their zeal, novice investigators often believe that the only way to have impact is to choose a topic well beyond their capacity in terms of size, complexity, or required skills. This also is part of the "second adolescence" phenomenon—"I can do it, don't tell me I must cut it down, don't demean me that way!" Unless such advice is viewed from the perspective of the offerer seeking to help, it can be incorrectly perceived.

Social, Ethical, Institutional, and Resource Limitations. All studies must be done within limits, for example:

- The research time required may not be tolerated by a busy clinic.
- Having a control group without treatment may not be permitted by those who insist on receiving the experimental treatment as well.

- The potential for harm or unpleasantness in prying into people's value structures, political affiliations, or sex lives may not be warranted by the value of the information gained.
- The cost to investigate the number of subjects required to do a study well may be beyond the resources of the investigator.

Prime considerations are what an institution will allow, what a community deems appropriate, and what ethical constraints one's profession places on research (see Chapter 10). In addition, there are the limits on our own time, funds, and energy, which, though somewhat flexible, have boundaries that we must find and observe. Feasibility is important in regard to both not being overly intimidated by apparent limitations and acknowledging realities.

Ask yourself these questions about your problem:
✦ *Is it of sufficient interest that I will continue to be motivated through to its completion?*
✦ *Is it embedded in theory so that it is part of a network of propositions and explanations?*
✦ *Will it have some impact on the field?*
✦ *Has it an element of originality and creativity about it?*
✦ *Is it feasible in terms of my acquired or acquirable knowledge and skills, as well as being within my social, ethical, institutional, and resource limitations?*

A Researchable Question

Be sure your problem is researchable; not all are. The most common non researchable problems deal with what *ought* to be done—children *ought* to be able to read the classics by the sixth grade, clients *should* be permitted to find their own solutions in therapy. Notice the italicized value judgments: *ought* and *should*. Research cannot directly affirm or deny a value proposition. It can show what will happen if sixth graders try to read the classics or evaluate the success of a program in doing so. Others can use those consequences to make the "ought" decisions.

✦ *Research can help a decision maker determine the implications of something that is desirable or desired, but it can never determine what ought to be. That is a value judgment.*

Success-Enhancing Problem-Finding Behaviors

The following behaviors characteristic of productive researchers are drawn from the autobiographies of researchers, from observation, and from studies of problem finding and creativity.

Fill Your Mind with the Best Relevant Material. Filling your mind with the best relevant material from your area of interest is one of the most profitable ways to find a good problem. Have you had the experience of learning a new word that you thought was rare? Once you learned it, you were surprised at how often you heard it thereafter! It must have been there before. Research is no different; discovery favors the prepared mind. Fleming's discovery of penicillin was accidental, but his prior work prepared him to recognize the breakthrough when it appeared. He noticed that his bacterial cultures seemed not to grow where there was mold on the plate and wondered why this occurred. No doubt this had happened to other investigators. Fleming, however, being curious and having worked intensely with bacterial cultures, asked why. Acting on that query made a discovery worthy of a Nobel Prize.

Delve into what is already known about a phenomenon; immerse yourself in the literature and explore each of its important facets. If this search does not suggest the desired research problem, you will be sufficiently familiar with the area that when the unusual appears, you can recognize and act on it—like solving a jig-saw puzzle, where you have in mind the shape of a missing piece.

Keep a log of your ideas and review it from time to time to refresh the best of the log's possibilities in your mind. Old ideas may have new meaning in the light of something you have read since. New techniques, instruments, and models often suggest possibilities and extensions of past research. Other languages and cultures often hold possibilities that await discovery and development.

Read the Writings of the Seminal Minds in Your Field. Studies show that productive scientists read more deeply into the historical background of their problems. In addition, they read the original versions, not digests, of the best minds in the field. Often, those minds had already sensed something that was not well understood in their time. In other instances, they took a problem as far as they could, but you could now take it further. Reading such accounts against the background of what has happened more recently often gives a new perspective and meaning. For instance, Campbell and Stanley (1963), who made important contributions to understanding social science experimentation, start with a tribute to a 40-year-old book by McCall (1923). He described concepts they built on, setting them in a new and broader context.

You can sometimes stimulate ideas by reading the works of individuals with a creative turn of mind. They model the perceptiveness and fresh way of seeing that characterizes inventive researchers. For example, Milgram, Sabini and Silver (1992) is full of provocative questions of this kind. Ask faculty about comparable individuals with your interests.

Read Actively; Anticipate the Author. Active reading is one of the most important skills to develop. *Anticipate* where the material is going; *project* the argument that is being fashioned instead of passively following it. We process what we read more thoroughly if we underline or make marginal comments. This practice reduces reading speed and allows time to think ahead to where the argument is going. As we foresee what is coming, we will often find that the author zigs where our thoughts have zagged. Why the zig? Here is a question worth pondering. Our zag might have been a more profitable course to follow, but we should retrace our steps to be sure. Many new leads are discovered by active reading.

Reread Material. The mind can focus on only a few things at a time. Put aside those authors who seem to have the best grasp of your area and let them grow "cold." Then read them after they are again fresh to you, focusing on different things than when you read them the first time, looking for things you missed.

Actively Search for Inconsistencies in the Argument. Look for gaps where existing ideas do not adequately account for the phenomena. This step may call for revision of existing explanations or even for new ones. For example, Merton (1959) notes that regularities in cultural behavior are typically thought to result from prescriptions by cultural norms. However, he notes, "Men have higher suicide rates than women, for example, even when the cultural norms do not invite males to put an end to themselves" (p. xxiii). Apparently, regularities can result from something besides cultural norms, and the concept of cultural norms must be reworked to account for this anomaly; he has suggested an interesting topic.

Challenge Assumptions. When reading past research, examine the assumptions on which the arguments are based. Are they reasonable? Could you make less restrictive ones? What would be the result if you change the assumptions? Would such changes lead to different consequences? Consider the problem of the mentally handicapped. If you assume that they learn essentially as does everyone else but more slowly, given sufficient time and motivation they could achieve normally. The consequences of this view are to give the individuals more time, to isolate them in classes where the competition is less intense, and to motivate them to achieve.

A different assumption is that the conceptual structures into which the mentally handicapped fit what they learn are not the complex ones that others use. This assumption leads to the search for simplified conceptual structures they can learn—structures that will allow their learning to approximate that of more normal children. This is but one example of how different assumptions result in quite different consequences, in this instance for remediation, each of which could be tested for their validity. (See the application problems at the end of this chapter for other examples.) Try different assumptions to see where they lead.

Organize the Material You Have Read. In the Preface we noted that internal processing is important. Such processing results in "chunking" material into meaningful collections. The networking of these chunks makes connections that bring to mind new material. Furthermore, the "chunks" of experts are larger and more complex than those of novices. Some writers and artists seem to have learned this process intuitively since they often spend large amounts of time practicing and rehearsing their material before producing a masterpiece. Before he wrote a novel, Sinclair Lewis developed notebooks that described his characters and their complete setting—their personalities, what they wore, even maps of the community and floor plans of the buildings. Did he refer to the notebooks when writing? We don't know, but advance rehearsal chunked this material so effectively that he probably had little need; he could just let his characters interact and their characteristics and those of the situation they were in came almost automatically to mind. Similarly, before Andrew Wyeth painted his Helga pictures, he discarded on the floor sketch after sketch, which he even proceeded to walk on. They were chunks transferred to his mind for use in later drawings. Charles Darwin carefully indexed the books he read and organized the material into portfolios that he consulted at the beginning of each new project (Steiner, 1984).

Everyone uses chunks in their problem solving; however, the best writers and thinkers find that it takes work and time to build those chunks and their relational network. Maybe this is one of the differences between the greats and the not-so-greats: the willingness to do the work that is involved in building and relating the chunks that go into a masterwork.

Break Your Mind-set. We have all been exposed to problems that require us to think about them differently in order to solve them. Remember the game of passing the scissors? One person passes scissors to another saying, "I'm passing it to you crossed" or "I'm passing it to you uncrossed." Players unfamiliar with the game are puzzled; no matter how they position the scissors, they can do it correctly only by accident, if at all. They are concentrating on the scissors. Only when they realize that "crossed" or "uncrossed" refers to the position of the person's legs when the scissors are passed do they break the mind-set of concentrating on the scissors. Breaking the mind-set, viewing an area or a problem differently, is often the secret to an important piece of research. The next several tips are often useful mind-set–breaking tools.

Talk to Specialists in the Field. Experts who have worked in a field for a long time build their conceptions of it from their experiences. Researchers comparing the problem solving of experts and novices note little difference in strategies but find a significant difference in the repertory of experiences organized in long-term memory. Chase and Simon's (1973) study of chess players nicely illustrates this point. Grandmasters and masters were asked to reconstruct the positions of 22 chess pieces after viewing them for five seconds. When the positions were those from actual games, experts could place 81 percent of them without error, whereas novices could correctly position only 33 percent. When pieces were arranged at random, however, experts were no better than novices. Experts apparently identified patterns as games they had learned or experienced instead of memorizing the position of individual pieces. Note the specificity of their knowledge: Their capabilities would not apply to another subject matter. Since research on expert-novice differences suggests these long-term memory patterns are subject matter-specific, choose an expert in your field.

Assess experts' reactions carefully, however. Some persons discourage ideas that weren't original with them. Others, for whatever reason, fail to grasp your problem and react superficially. With these caveats in mind, you will find that experts can be extremely valuable and save you much time, especially by helping you avoid false and unproductive leads.

Look for New Ways to Tease the Problem Apart. Psychologist Daniel Kahneman suggests a trick for questions about behavior that he claims derives from

Lewinian psychology. Instead of asking, "Why does a person behave this way?" he asks, "Why doesn't he behave otherwise?" Instead of asking why a person is hostile in a particular setting, he asks, "Why isn't he more hostile?" "Why isn't he less hostile?" The kinds of answers made available by this reformulation are radically different from those derived from "Why is he hostile?" It may be much easier to remove the factors driving him to greater hostility and uncovered by the question "Why isn't he less hostile?" than to manipulate forces intended to suppress the hostile behavior. Sometimes it also helps consciously to switch the focus of attention from the end result to the process of getting there. Guns don't get used up in violent acts but bullets do. Maybe it would be easier and more effective to control ammunition than to control guns.

Another way of teasing the problem apart is to look for concepts that have not been effective in differentiating important aspects of a phenomenon. Merton (1959) notes that current concepts may have taken research as far as it will stretch. To go further we need new differentiations. For example, at one time self-concept was conceived as a single entity. Later, researchers came to realize that each of us has different self-concepts in different situations. Our self-concept of ability describes how capable we believe ourselves to be in solving academic problems, and this may be further differentiated into self-concepts of capability in different subject matters. The term *self-concept* has become highly differentiated, with several books delineating these different meanings (for example, Wylie, 1979).

Harness the Unconscious. There comes a point when we have read enough to have a flavor of the literature, but new approaches have not suggested themselves. Here it is well to recognize that our minds do not always do their best work when we are consciously pushing at a problem. William Safire gives the first rule of holes: "When you are in a hole, stop digging!" It is time for the unconscious mind to take over. Read Raudsepp's (1977) recitation of the testimony of the greats on this score:

> Dostoevsky found that he could dream up his immortal, moving stories and characters while doodling. Brahms found that ideas came effortlessly only when he approached a state of deep daydreaming. And César Frank is said to have walked around with a dreamlike gaze while composing, seemingly unaware of his surrounding. . . .
>
> John Dewey stated, "I do not think it can be denied that an element of reverie, of approach to a state of dream, enters in the creation of a work of art. . . . Indeed, it is safe to say that creative conceptions . . . come only to persons who are relaxed to the point of reverie."
>
> Thomas Alva Edison also knew the value of "half-waking states." Whenever confronted with what seemed an insurmountable hitch defying all efforts, he would stretch out on his workshop couch and let fantasies flood his mind (pp. 27–28).

Poincare (1913) concluded that the unconscious mind collates and sorts random possibilities among pertinent variables at a rate that defies the efforts of the conscious mind.

We must all find our own best means of commanding the muse, but the unconscious as an important resource is too rarely emphasized. Some people are helped by daydreaming, a reverie in which the mind floats over the problem, rejecting no possibilities. Some adopt a kind of half-awake, half-asleep posture. Still others get their best ideas at night and keep paper and pencil at hand to record ideas immediately, lest they be unable to retrieve their thoughts upon becoming fully awake.[3] Whatever your means, *use the unconscious; it is one of the most powerful tools of creativity available.* Then be prepared to record the results. Nothing is more frustrating than to have grasped a solution you are positive you'll remember, only to find it has slipped away.

Organize Material into Suggestive Patterns. There are many arbitrary ways of organizing material into suggestive patterns; one set of steps outlined by Zwicky (1969) was extended by Allen (1962). First, you put all the material onto small cards, spreading them out without order and reading them to transfer the material to your unconscious mind. Next, you work on something else for awhile. Then you organize the cards into groups and organize the groups into mega-groups, each with a title, continuing until you have seven or fewer mega-groups. Finally, you examine the interrelations of these groups and their components.

Having such a model to follow may have value in that all the possible options are touched. Elstein, Shulman, and Sprafka (1978, 1990) have shown that in medical problem solving, having a model, or heuristic, to follow increases effectiveness. Computer software is available that helps one organize material and suggests relationships.

"When you run onto something interesting, drop everything else and study it" (Skinner, 1959, p. 363). This quotation is one of a series of principles about research that the highly inventive researcher, B. F. Skinner, who founded a science of behavior, draws from studying his own research. Since often the most significant findings turn up when we are pursuing something else, it is advice worth following. He describes how, concentrating on a rat's learning, he treated the jamming of the food magazine as a defect causing him to discard data. Then he realized that the record he was getting showed the extinction of learning. He says, "I can easily recall the excitement." His tale makes fascinating reading as he illustrates this meandering "disorderly and accidental process" of science, so different from the stereotype of scientific method. Indeed, Skinner notes: "the. . . scientist is puzzled and often dismayed when he discovers how his behavior has been reconstructed in the formal analyses of scientific method. . . . it is a mistake to identify scientific practice with the formalized constructions of statistics and scientific method. These disciplines have their place. . . . They offer *a* method of science but not, as is so often implied, *the* method" (p. 260).[4] Don't be concerned if your trail

---

[3]The research of Robert Stickgold is suggesting that during REM (rapid eye movement) sleep, the brain is even better primed to make associations than during the day. Earlier, Carlyle Smith (1990) found that individuals who learned a complex logic task with a background noise of clicks, who were cued with those clicks during REM sleep, were better at solving those problems the next day than a control group.

[4]As indicated repeatedly in this text, the logical process described in the chain of reasoning, similar in many ways to what is often ascribed to scientific method, describes the way research is reported, *not* necessarily the way it is done!

of investigation zigs and zags. A direct approach is not the only way to do research, and many of the world's most significant discoveries were serendipitous findings.

Reduce the Censorship of Ideas. The process of brainstorming involves admitting possibilities for examination that would normally be rejected by typical problem-solving processes. Popularized by Osborn (1959), it consists of assembling a group of people to attack a problem with certain basic rules of interaction: Renounce criticism, avoid interrupting, listen, respect differing points of view, welcome freewheeling ideas, seek quantity but avoid repetition, inject humor, and try to combine and improve previous suggestions. At one time a fad, this technique is still useful. Although it can lead to time-consuming consideration of impossible suggestions, it may free individuals to consider desirable ones that would have otherwise been discarded. Thinking of analogies—even far-fetched ones such as "How is this phenomenon like an animal?"—have proven useful. Once the bulk of the ideas has emerged, select the best for further development and sometimes, in turn, as the focus of further brainstorming sessions.

Move Up the Causal Chain if Problem Focus Proves Elusive. Recall the story of the battle that was lost for want of a nail—for want of a nail the shoe was lost, for want of a shoe the horse was lost, for want of a horse, the rider was lost, and so forth. It demonstrates how everything is part of a causal chain. If you are interested in an area but have difficulty pinning down a problem in it, it sometimes helps to move to earlier links in the causal chain. For example, a researcher concerned with the in-service training of teachers wonders what to study. Move up the causal chain: Why do teachers seek training in the first place? For social contact with other teachers? Improved pay? Chances for leadership? These may be interesting possibilities.

Abelson (1995) found a formula in Tesser (1990) that takes a hypothesis a level deeper: State the hypothesis, then its opposite, and then find a way of reconciling the two. For example, "an outstanding performance by someone produces jealousy in those close to him. But the opposite can also be demonstrated, whereby an excellent performance arouses pride in close others, a 'basking in reflected glory' (Cialdini et al., 1976). The resolution of this contradiction is that what is at stake for the close other is the maintenance of self-esteem" (Abelson, 1995, p. 164).

Try Your Ideas in Simple Form Before Starting a Complex Investigation. When computers were still novelties, ideas that would have required writing expensive software were often tested for feasibility and to find difficulties by having humans play the role of computer in a paper simulation. Valenstein (1994) relates how Richard Jung missed discovering how the cortex of the brain received orientation information because he was warned against doing sloppy research. So he spent two years constructing a machine capable of presenting stimuli and recording the responses. Meanwhile, two other researchers, who received the Nobel Prize for their work, "made their discoveries by simply waving objects in front of cats" (p. 142).

Don't Close the Problem Definition Too Quickly. Getzels and Csikszentmihalyi (1976) found the most creative solutions to be those of artists who kept problems open longer. They suggest that solutions must be discovered by interaction with the elements that constitute it—mucking around in the problem. Superficial solutions are also likelier to be rejected if closure is delayed.

Formulate the Problem as a Written Statement. Setting down your thoughts is clarifying and organizing. As Merton (1959) puts it, try formulating questions that register your "dimly felt sense of ignorance" (p. xxvi). Writing enforces a discipline that helps articulate half-formed ideas. Something happens between the formation of an idea and its appearance on paper, a latency that somehow results in the clarification and untangling of our thinking. Writing helps bring unconscious processing to light as articulated synthesized statements—what we all are seeking! When we are reading widely, we cram the ideas into our memory, often without checking against what is already there; even contradictory material may exist side by side. Writing makes us confront these internal inconsistencies and assemble relationships.

Sometimes continued writing pays off. Listen to Albert Schweitzer in a translation of his autobiography:

> For months I lived in a continual state of mental agitation. Without the least success, I concentrated—even during my daily work at the hospital—on the real nature of affirmation of life and of ethics and on the question of what they have in common. . . . I saw the concept that I wanted to attain before me, but I could not . . . formulate it. While in this mental condition I had to undertake a long journey on the river. . . . Slowly we crept upstream. . . . Lost in thought I sat on the deck of the barge, struggling. . . . *I covered sheet after sheet with disconnected sentences merely to keep myself concentrated on the problem.* . . . Late on the third day,. . . there flashed upon my mind, unforeseen and unsought, the phrase, "reverence for life." The iron door yielded. The path in the thicket became visible. (Schweitzer, 1990, p. 155; italics added)

Particularly striking in this passage is the italicized sentence. It is so typical of good writers that even when they are blocked, they persist with provisional tries in order to formulate what they are seeking. Schweitzer "covered sheet after sheet with disconnected sentences" until he succeeded.

Slowing the writing process may help with difficult formulation. I can type when I know what I want to write, but I must write with a pen when I'm struggling. As a last resort, a fountain pen seems to work better than a ballpoint. Each method takes progressively longer to form the words on paper. I can hold longer internal discussions with myself about what comes next, do a memory search for the right concept or word, and still put it down without unduly interrupting my flow of thought. This flow is important. Poor writers are often so involved with grammar, spelling, or even word formation that they have difficulty remembering where their sentence is going.

Explain Your Ideas to Other People. Similar to writing is explaining our ideas to someone else, ideally an uninformed but intelligent observer. It is said that the best way to learn something is to teach it. Furthermore, an intelligent observer can often do better than we can for ourselves, especially if we are too close to it. Scheerer (1963), for example, assigned subjects randomly as observers and workers. The workers were to solve a problem that required use of a missing piece of string. A string that they could use was present but in the form of a hanger for a wall calendar. Only half the workers—but *all* of the observers—broke the mindset of the string as hanger and solved the problem. Talking with others may also restore a sense of excitement.

Try Your Ideas Out on the Internet. Increasingly, graduate students are asking for help with their problems on Internet forums and bulletin boards. We tend to think of colleagues as being those at our institution, but we must raise our horizons. Highly competent colleagues not only on our continent, but also around the world monitor these bulletin boards. Several emeritus professors, who apparently miss teaching, regularly respond to requests for help with sage advice on a listserv I regularly read. Most professional organizations have established such forums; contact them for information. Ask your professors for locations on the Internet you would find worth monitoring in regard to your problem area and then join the conversation.

Identify Your Most Productive Working Conditions. Become aware of the conditions that make you productive. For instance, you probably have an optimal level of motivation. At a higher level, you may be unable to stay focused long enough to perceive patterns. Administrators in particular are inclined to think that if a little motivation is good, more must be better. This is not necessarily so.

Where and when you work can be important. Find a place without too many distractions. Many productive writers set aside a regular time for writing, continuing with provisional tries whether they are blocked or not. Some rent a hotel room, having meals sent up until they finish.

Patterns of writing are particularly likely to be unique to each person. Outlining used to be considered a necessity by many English teachers. Neil Simon, the famous playwright, was advised to try it:

> "I . . . tried to make it go that way. It wouldn't! I did it 20 times! That is not the way to write a play. . . . because that is not the way life is. You don't know what the end is going to be so you don't twist and push it. It just carries you along, somehow, predetermined by your character." (Rosner and Abt, 1970, p. 363)

Clearly, outlining was not for him, and it may not be for others. There is, however, some pattern that is better for each of us, and we must find it.

Trim Away Your Entry to a Problem as Soon as It No Longer Fits. When the development of a human fetus is traced, there is always considerable surprise that it seems to go through all the developmental stages of a previous evolution—for example, developing useless gills that then atrophy and become something else. As a problem statement develops, its introductory statement tends to grow, retaining the problem's developmental history and repeating useless aspects that no longer contribute to the current problem. It is useful to us in that it retraces our thinking and gets us into the problem. But sometimes it is simply excess baggage. Other people can usually see this more easily than we can. It also is more apparent after the passage of time. The sooner we trim away this excess material, the stronger and more clearly we can develop the problem.

Some individuals find themselves rewriting the introduction to their problem every time they leave the work for a period of time. Not only is this likely to result in an introduction that needs to be trimmed, it tends to be unproductive labor. Write those sections you are ready to write rather than writing linearly from beginning to end; you are less likely to become blocked.

Rather than leaving the work at a point where a section is complete, stop at a point that cries out for completion and you know what you plan to do next. It will be easier to continue at that point.

Having trouble formulating your problem? Use the suggestions in the previous material as a checklist. Be sure you've tried those that are restated here to emphasize their importance.

Have you:
◆ *Filled your mind with the best relevant material?*
◆ *Read the writings of the seminal minds in the field, both past and present?*
◆ *Actively read material rather than simply following each author's lead?*
◆ *Reread the material after it has had a chance to grow "cold" to you?*
◆ *Studied the material sufficiently to "chunk" the material in your mind?*
◆ *Found ways of breaking your mind-set?*
◆ *Talked to experts in the field? Do they seem to organize or chunk the material in the field differently from the way you do? Whose organization seems more helpful to you?*
◆ *Read to fill your mind chock full of relevant material, puzzled over it a bit, and then let your unconscious take over as you work "off-center"—going to the movies or engaging in other forms of relaxation? Been ready to catch the answer when it came?*

SUMMARY

Choice of problem is the most important decision a researcher makes. Good problems are of enough interest to motivate you to carry them to completion, are typically embedded in theory, are likely to have some impact on the field, have an element of originality or creativity about them, and are feasible. Although feasibility in terms of personal skills often stretches further than you might initially think, the problem must be researchable within the ethical and institutional limits and the resources available. Research cannot affirm or deny a value judgment. It can only show the consequences of a given value

position or, through polling, find the support for or against it. This may be helpful to decision makers in determining policy.

Although some researchers are better at problem finding than others, you can learn the necessary skills. Discovery favors the prepared mind. Reading actively, reading widely, reading the seminal minds in the field, talking to specialists, challenging assumptions, looking for new ways to tease the problem apart and break conventional ways of looking at it—in short, filling the mind with the grist that allows the unconscious to sort matters and organize thoughts—all are highly conducive to finding new research ideas.

In addition, you can use techniques to enhance creativity, such as those that organize material into suggestive patterns and reduce the censorship of ideas (brainstorming). Formulate the problem as a written statement and/or explain it to someone else. Learn your most productive working conditions. When having trouble focusing, trace your problem back to earlier links in the causal chain. Don't close the problem definition too quickly.

A Look Ahead

Obviously, one of the most important sources of material to develop a "prepared mind" is the work of others. For this we need library skills, to which we turn in the next chapter.

ADDITIONAL READING

Getzels (1982), a helpful combination of speculation and data.

Leong and Pfaltzgraff (1996), a useful chapter on finding a research topic in a very useful book.

Meehl (1974), an argument for theory in social science research and some examples.

Merton (1959), still relevant advice from one of the greats in sociology.

APPLICATION PROBLEMS

1. Johnson (1978), drawing upon the theories of Carl Jung (1971), theorized that a person's psychological style is defined by how he or she makes decisions. He developed a two-dimensional decision-making scheme based on the way information is gathered (systematically or spontaneously) and on the way data are analyzed; that is, internally (the individual needs to think about it first) or externally (the individual needs to discuss it with someone). From this, Johnson surmised that individuals could be classified into four personality types: spontaneous external, spontaneous internal, systematic external, and systematic internal. If you were interested in researching psychological styles, how could you use Johnson's theory to develop a research problem?

2. Assume that you are a graduate student in educational psychology interested in "intelligence." You have read widely on the topic and know that over the years a number of theories have been advanced about its nature. These include such concepts as Thurstone's seven primary mental abilities; Spearman's *g*, or general intelligence factor; Guilford's structure of intellect model; and the idea of fluid versus crystallized intelligence championed by Cattell and Horn. To which of these should you look as the potential source of a research question?

3. A master's degree student in nursing is interested in the care of brain-injured patients. She has focused on a disorder called unilateral neglect, which leaves a patient unaware of one side of his or her body. The student wishes to investigate the degree to which such patients could carry out ordinary activities of daily living and what the implications of this would be for their nursing care. How might she proceed?

4. A doctoral student in the field of educational technology is working with an advisor who has gained international recognition for his instructional model for selecting and sequencing content. The student has identified a set of motivational strategies to add to the model and is considering their verification in an instructional setting as her dissertation topic. However, the student wonders if this topic is sufficiently original, since she did not develop the original model. What would be your advice to her?

APPLICATION EXERCISE

Beginning with this chapter, it is suggested that you choose a topic or problem that interests you and use it throughout the rest of the book to gain familiarity with the content of each chapter. Find a topic that you may be willing to stay with. Try some of the techniques described in this chapter to stimulate your creativity. Actively read some of the references found for your topic; the material in the next chapter will help you find references. See whether there is a member of the invisible college in your school or college or whether you can locate one at a nearby institution or on the Internet who will correspond with you. Get together with a small group and brainstorm. Have one person in the group play the role of observer to help you reflect on the process and make sure you follow the rules. Have this person summarize progress every 10 minutes or so or when there is a good breaking point and have her point out any breeches of the rules. Try the card sorting suggested on page 91. Read extensively and fill your mind with material; then concentrate on something else for a while and see what develops. Even if all this is effective, also try working at your project by yourself, filling a sheet of paper with ideas or whatever comes to mind to keep you engaged with the problem. Experimenting with these different approaches will help you learn what works best for you.

By applying the content of this and each succeeding chapter to your topic, you can easily end up

with a proposal for a study that has been subjected to analysis from the standpoint of the foundational skills and concepts of research and has been thought about in relation to various research methods. You will know which skills were applicable and useful for your project. You'll have compared the potential of the various research methods for it. What process could better strengthen your proposal for a research study than that?

Many students in the two-semester course in which this book was pioneered came out of it with proposals ready to go to their committee for final refinement. It gave them a big start on their doctoral program and helped save them from ABD status. By doing these application exercises and using the suggestions in the Appendix and/or *How to Prepare a Research Proposal* (Krathwohl, 1988), you can similarly benefit. See especially Chapters 16 and 17 of the latter which were designed specifically for doctoral students. Chapter 16 gives different perspectives on the meaning of the dissertation, and 17 reviews the steps involved in doing a dissertation.

ANSWERS TO THE APPLICATION PROBLEMS

1. Do you find these assumptions believable, or do you find yourself questioning them? One approach would be to challenge Johnson's assumptions. Examine their basis. Is there an alternate explanation that comes to mind? Are these personality types stable aspects of an individual's personality, or are they a function of the particular situation? If they are based on exhibited behavior, is there another way of explaining that behavior?

Conversely, you may find these assumptions appealing. Note that they have a basis in established theory. You would be well advised to review Jung's theory rather than relying on Johnson's interpretation. However, you may be able to come up with a way of extending, validating, or applying these conclusions. Coscarelli and Stonewater (1979), for instance, suggested that these personality types could be useful in a model of consultation to help determine the best way to work with a client.

2. All have potential. You could apply the criteria of a good problem here. First, which of the approaches interests you, makes most sense to you, perhaps gets you excited? Does any of them suggest a question to you immediately? Second, all of them are embedded in theory, but is one developing a

stronger network than the others? Does it seem to fit better into our developing knowledge base? Third, in terms of impact, which of them appears to be the most current? Exploring a problem based on a theory of prevailing interest in one's field is more likely to produce findings that have an impact than exploring one based on a theory that has been replaced or discarded. Fourth, which allows you to be creative? Do any of them lend themselves to analysis by a new technique, instrument, or model? This is one way to revive an older theory and still have impact.

3. She should begin, of course, by immersing herself in the literature of this topic. It would be worth her while to talk to anyone available to her who has experience or expertise with this disorder. Such experts may be able to answer questions about such matters as certainty of diagnosis, spontaneous recovery, and length of disorder. She should learn the best current explanation of the disorder and how well it is embedded in the network of theory that explains it and similar problems. Then she may turn to the problems of feasibility: Will patients with this disorder be available to her and, if so, in sufficient number to conduct a study? How would she evaluate how well they carry out the activities of daily living? Knowing that this is of concern in special education and with the mentally retarded, she might look for scales in those fields that could be applied here.

4. You should advise her to proceed with her question. If her adviser's model is indeed well recognized, she is in effect embedding her problem in current theory. She is more likely—particularly as a novice—to have an impact on her field in this way than to produce a more original but isolated study. Second, by adding her own touch to the model and providing an interesting and possibly useful extension to it, she has demonstrated originality.

CHAPTER ADDENDUM

Please reread the first two paragraphs of the Application Problem on page 73, which introduces Jonassen's pattern notes. Especially for those of you who are visual learners, this is a way of helping you organize and diagram what you learned. Figure 5.1 is an example of a pattern note for the preceding chapter that was made by Richard Kenny, the same person who wrote most of the application problems.

As you trace the lines and their titles, you will be reminded of the chapter contents and the interrelationships among its parts.

This was Kenney's way of organizing what he learned from the chapter. The intent of this appendix is to introduce you to the idea and to suggest that you experiment with it to see if you find it helpful and useful in future study. Use it in study-

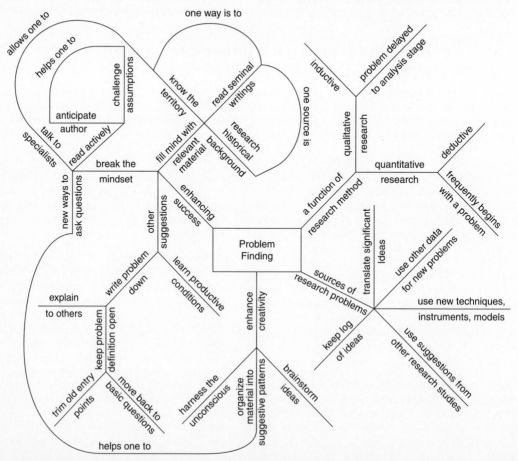

FIGURE 5.1 Pattern note based on Chapter 5, "Finding Research Problems."

ing the next chapters. Because this is a general example, it does not contain references to personal experience or prior learning as a pattern note should to tie what you are currently learning to your past personal and academic experiences. Adding such references to your pattern notes will make them more meaningful and the learning more permanent.

Because personal prior experiences differ, there clearly could be many ways to pattern-note this chapter; it depends on how you relate the material to what you already know. So, maps may differ significantly from person to person, though sections may be similar. Given differences in prior learning, one can argue there is no right way to pattern-note a chapter. Some persons have suggested that the more successful the teacher, the more closely a student's pattern note will resemble the instructor's.

The process of making the map is what is important: organizing your thoughts, relating parts of the chapter to other parts, and integrating new into your prior learning. The product, the pattern note itself, then serves as a short-hand for what one has learned and is useful in reviewing the material.

Finding Links to Past Research: The Literature Review

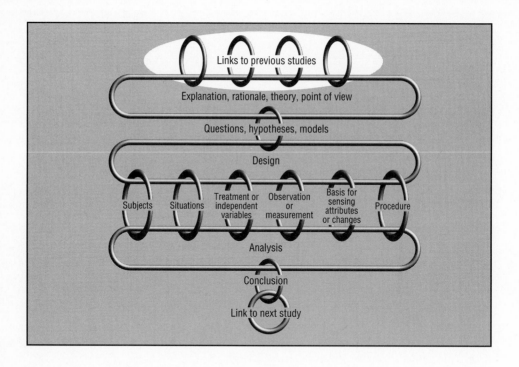

If no use is made of the labors of past ages, the world must remain always in the infancy of knowledge.

Cicero, *De Oratore II*

One of the diseases of this age is the multiplicity of books; they doth so overcharge the world that it is not able to digest the abundance of idle matter that is every day hatched and brought forth into the world.

Barnaby Rich, 1613 (As quoted in *De Solla Price, Little Science, Big Science*)

The longer we look back, the farther we can look forward.

Winston Churchill (As quoted in Coyne, 1995)

OVERVIEW

Problem formulation is facilitated by the literature review. Indeed, sometimes the problem is found there; more often, it is modified by what is found. Such reformulation is carried as far as is necessary, profitable, or allowed by time. The literature search forges the chain of reasoning links to past research and helps fashion the problem's rationale that contributes to building a credible explanation.

The variety of library aids is amazing. How to identify the key ones and to use different types of indexes will be the focus of this chapter.

CHAPTER CONTENTS

The Literature Search in Relation to Research Method

Except for individuals using an inductive approach, Hoffmann-Riem, for instance, the literature search is the phase in which they develop their research question and formulate the major direction of their study, an early step in the research process. They enter the literature search with an area of interest, an "orienting question," a hunch something worth pursuing—like a newspaper reporter's "sniff." These focus their attention, direct them to sources of information, and permit them to determine whether there is indeed something worth delving into.

These individuals leave their literature search with at least a more definitive notion about the area, its important variables, how they are interrelated, what the good questions are, and what research methods have been used. Sometimes a hypothesis emerges. Even better, if the literature base is solid enough, they may be able to make a prediction or create an explanatory model of the interrelations of variables. At a minimum, by exploring the literature, they move a long way down the road in the development of their research focus. At best, they can fully formulate the research problem.

Recognize, however, that research is a creative act. For every statement claiming that most people do it one way, there is another citing those who, for good reason, do it differently. For example, many researchers who use qualitative or inductive methods believe that to consult the literature too early will burden them with other people's perceptions. Their problems in this regard are discussed in Chapter 11. In the rest of this chapter, we will assume researchers are entering the literature search with only an orienting question and thus will discuss tools and skills that can help. However, this material will also serve those doing a literature search late in their study. First, we must be specific about what the literature search is trying to achieve.

Goals of the Literature Search

Often we are not prepared by our simple orienting question for the complexity of the problem shown by the literature. For example, when learning to swim, is it better to learn the Australian crawl as a whole or to master all the parts—arm strokes, breathing, flutter kick—and then put them together? The literature refers to this process as part-whole learning. It also shows there is more than one part-whole method. For instance, we can alternate practicing a new part and integrating it into the whole, or we can start with a part and then add successive parts until the whole is achieved. The problem has taken on a new complexity. Furthermore, the studies use these methods under different conditions of practice—massed in a single session or large, concentrated blocks or distributed over time. Distribution of practice is a concomitant variable that affects learning strategy; a second complexity has been added.

Thus, as a first function, the literature search shows which facets of the phenomenon are important; helps redefine the problem; suggests the nature of the relationship among the variables—in this case, patterns of practice as well as learning strategy; and, if investigating all the part-whole strategies seems too much, provides the basis for reducing the problem to feasible proportions.

A second function of the literature search is to show us the research frontier—how far previous research has come. Finding the frontier allows you to place your study in perspective to the work of others—shows how it fills a gap and advances what has already been done. You shouldn't assume that the newest work has advanced the field. Read in historical depth; the frontier may not have been advanced much by the latest efforts.

A third function, which will result from reading to the frontier, is to relate the problem to the network of theory, rationales, and previous explanations that already exists in the area. This is important because when research findings are isolated facts, they don't much advance our understanding of how things work. It is the latter knowledge that allows us to transfer findings to new situations and to improve the way we deal with the world. Explanations of how massed versus distributed practice affects learning will begin to suggest how the various swimming methods would be affected by this factor.

A fourth function is to find methods and designs to use as well as to avoid—you become aware of new refinements to methods. Furthermore, this literature includes instruments and measures that might be useful and it may also describe their validity; experimental instruments for hard-to-measure characteristics appear earliest in research studies. You can glean valuable ideas for data analysis from others' experiences. Studying distinctions in methods may suggest why study outcomes differ; the phenomenon may be more amenable to exploration with one method than with another.

We can look at the retrieval of knowledge on a cost-benefit basis; we are substituting relatively cheap literature search time for the expense of rediscovering it with new research. The more economically we can find how far previous investigators advanced, the more resources are available to "stand on their shoulders" and advance the field.

The literature search has several goals:
+ To assist in conceptualizing the problem, refining it, and, if necessary, reducing it to feasible size and scope.
+ To determine the major variables of importance in the phenomenon.
+ To understand the relationships among these variables.
+ To find the frontier of research on the problem—how far previous researchers could solidly reach.
+ To relate the problem to the network of theory, rationales, and explanations already existing in the field.
+ To get suggestions about how to do the study, what previous mistakes to avoid, and what new methods might be effective.
+ To substitute shorter, less expensive time doing the literature search for lengthier, more expensive research time rediscovering what is already known.
+ To put the conceptualized problem in the context of previous research, showing how the problem relates to it yet goes beyond it.

This long list of goals indicates how crucial the literature search is. Despite the massive increase in publications over the past several decades, new retrieval methods and index types have made access easier. This chapter introduces you to the tools that make retrievability possible.

The Variety of Information Sources Available

You will probably turn first to the information sources accessible in your personal or institutional library. This is fine, but recognize that the available resources now extend considerably beyond those. Figure 6.1 indicates sources to pursue.

Note that half the entries in Figure 6.1 refer to use of computers and most of these instances involve the Internet and World Wide Web. The role of the library is evolving especially with respect to the nature of their relation to the Internet and World Wide Web. Increasingly the front end of the library, what we now think of as the catalog, is becoming a virtual library. Some libraries are incorporating electronic versions of reference works into their on-line catalogs which have been accessed only on stand-alone computers through CD-ROM discs. In addition, some libraries are making their catalogs available on the Internet so that they can be searched with the same browser one uses to search the Internet. Additionally, as indicated in Figure 6.1 libraries are serving the role of information nodes, setting up home pages with hyperlinks to prescreened resources of the kinds that would be of special value to their clients. Look for one at your institution.

Sources of Information in a Literature Search

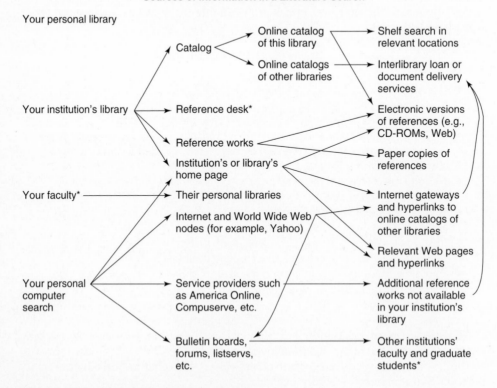

*Ask for additional suggestions from these sources

FIGURE 6.1 Information sources available in a literature search.

For the next few years, reference access will be uneven among institutions as some make access for their clients highly available through Internet means. Putting reference works on-line is clearly an expensive proposition requiring reallocation of old resources as well as new ones. No doubt library consortiums will bargain for packages of journals and reference works unique to their needs; a problem if your library is not one of them. Resource reallocation will be resisted; it is going to take time to shake out who pays for what. Be sure to keep abreast of the changes in access at your own and nearby institutions.

Note especially too in Figure 6.1 how faculty and libraries at other institutions besides your own are increasingly available by electronic means. For instance, your institution's library may already subscribe to the Research Library Groups' combined on-line catalog, which covers the holdings of a wide variety of research institutions, including the Library of Congress. Even without such subscriptions, sources on the World Wide Web provide gateways to the other libraries that have Web pages. Faculty at other institutions are available as sources of information and advice through the many forums, bulletin boards, and listservs.

Note also the document delivery services as a supplement to interlibrary loan. *The Genuine Article,*[1] is currently the largest collection of journal articles; University Microfilms International (UMI) can supply out-of-print books as well as dissertations. Journals and newspapers are also available but by volume rather than by article. For a fee, these services deliver by fax or paper (UMI in microform) an item that is unavailable locally.

The Breadth of References Available

The breadth of references available is unbelievable—books, journals, abstracts of journal articles, indexes, bibliographies, handbooks, and encyclopedias. For long-standing problems, books, encyclopedias, and handbooks are most helpful. In them, you can find summaries and reviews of work about which there has been a consensus—knowledge. Bibliographies in a field are listed in each library's on-line catalog under the subject heading "Bibliography of . . ." (fill in the appropriate subject heading).

Work that has not yet reached this level of acceptance is included in reviews of research. You can find such reviews in research review journals (for example, *Review of Educational Research*) or regularly issued review books (*Annual Review of Sociology*). A committee of relevant specialists usually puts together the annuals, allocating space to cover the topics of an area according to the importance and extent of recent work. Reviewers evaluate this material and place it in context in a way valuable to the novice.

Review journals and book, handbooks and encyclopedias are considered **secondary sources** because they give someone's opinion about what the research said, they do not reproduce the original research itself. Therefore, especially when you have doubts about the conclusions of a review or summary or wish addi-

---

[1]*The Genuine Article* is a service of the Institute for Scientific Information (phone (215) 386-0100, fax (215) 386-2911); reach University Microfilms International at: phone 1-800-521-0600.

tional detail, you should consult the **primary source** itself—the original article in which the findings appeared. Research reports are found in journals. Exceptions are reports of projects too large for a journal which become a monograph or book, or when researchers summarize their work in a book, as for instance in the Kounin example in Chapter 3. Journals are also where you will find the most recent work and can spot emerging problems.

The journal literature is accessible through a variety of indexes and abstracting services, with many specialized compilations available for nooks and crannies of subject matter (for example, *Language and Language Behavior Abstracts, Physical Education/Sports Index, College Student Personnel Abstracts*). To give you some idea of the wide variety of resources available, following is a list of selected references, including abstracting and indexing services. The list is not intended to be a comprehensive compilation.

General and Targeted Sources of Reference Works

Aby, S. H. (1987). *Sociology: A guide to reference and information sources.* Littleton, CO: Libraries Unlimited.

American Psychological Association (1992). *PsychINFO user manual.* Washington, DC: American Psychological Association.

Binger, J. L., and Jensen, L. M. (1980). *Lippincott's guide to nursing literature.* Philadelphia: J. B. Lippincott.

Conrad, J. H. (1982). *Reference sources in social work: An annotated bibliography.* Metuchen, NJ: Scarecrow Press.

Fletcher, J. (Ed.). (1984). *Information sources in economics* (2nd ed.). Stoneham, MS: Butterworths.

Freed, M. N., Hess, R. K., and Ryan, J. M. (1989). *The educators' desk reference.* New York: Macmillan.

Holler, F. L. (1986). *Information sources of political science* (4th ed.). Santa Barbara, CA: ABC-Clio.

Reed, J., and Baxter, P. M. (1992). *Library use: A handbook for psychology* (2nd ed.). Washington, DC: American Psychological Association.

Searing, S. E. (1981). *Women's studies: A recommended core bibliography, 1980–1985.* Littleton, CO: .Libraries Unlimited

Slavens, T. P. (1994) *Sources of information for historical research.* New York: Neal-Schuman.

Webb, W. H., Beals, B. R., and White, A. M. (1986). *Sources of information in the social sciences: A guide to the literature* (3rd ed.). Chicago: American Library Association.

Weeks, J. M. (1991) *Introduction to library research in anthropology.* Boulder, CO: Westview Press.

Weller, C. (1988) *Educator's Desk Reference for Special Education.* Boston: Allyn & Bacon.

Woodbury, M. (1982). *A guide to sources of educational information*. Washington, DC: Information Resources Press.

Woodbury, M. (1985). *Childhood Information Resources*. Washington, DC: Information Resources Press.

Annual Reviews

Annual reviews are published by Annual Reviews, Inc., in anthropology (for example, *Annual Review of Anthropology)*, psychology, and sociology as well as a number of other areas. The company also publishes reviews in some fields of medicine and in the biological and physical sciences.

Review of Research in Education is published annually by the American Educational Research Association.

Many professional associations publish yearbooks that serve the same purpose. For example, the National Society for the Study of Education publishes several yearbooks each year, each providing an examination of a particular topic.

Research Review Journals

American Sociological Review	*Reading Research Quarterly*
International Library Review	*Review of Educational Research*
International Nursing Review	*Social Work Review*
Psychological Review	*Sociological Review*

Abstracting and Indexing Services

Arts and Humanities Citation Index

Biological Abstracts

Business Periodicals Index

Business Index

Child Development Abstracts and Bibliographies

College Student Personnel Abstracts

Current Contents: Social and Behavioral Sciences

Current Index to Journals in Education (CIJE)

Dissertation Abstracts International (DAI)

Education Index

Educational Administration Abstracts

Government Reports Announcements and Index

Developmental Disabilities Abstracts

Exceptional Child Education Abstracts

Higher Education Abstracts

Index Medicus

Index to U.S. Government Periodicals

Language and Language Behavior Abstracts

Mental Retardation Abstracts

Monthly Catalog of U.S. Government Publications

Psychological Abstracts (PA)

Public Affairs Information Service (PAIS)

Resources In Education (RIE)

Science Citation Index (SCI)

Social Sciences Citation Index (SSCI)

Social Sciences Index

Sociological Abstracts

UNDOC: Current Index; United Nations Document Index

UNESCO List of Documents and Publications

Women's Studies Abstracts

Increasingly abstracting and indexing services are being compiled into computer searchable form. These compilations are referred to as **databases.** Databases may consist of past and current volumes of abstracts or indexes and of research or census data. The database form is sometimes given a different but related name from its base (and sometimes contains additional material). *Psychological Abstracts* as a database, for instance, is titled *PsychINFO. Sociological Abstracts* is called *Soclit.* New databases are continually being made available. Fortunately, the Gale *Directory of Online Databases* is updated annually (Nolan, 1983–). Lengenfelder (1988) is another listing and Gale Research Company (1983–) indexes surveys, polls, censuses, and forecasts.

Most abstracting and indexing services cover only journal articles, but there are exceptions. The citation indexes include references to books and book chapters where they have been cited in a journal article. PsychBOOKS which is a part of the PsychINFO database has included books and book chapters since 1987. One needs to check the reference's user instructions to determine what is and what is not covered.

A general source of information on reference works can be especially valuable not only in helping locate these indexes, but also in pointing out the variety of handbooks, bibliographies, review sources, and other access points. The most general of these, and the one used by general reference librarians, is *Guide to Reference Books* (Sheehy, 1986, and its update, Balay, 1992, often referred to as "Winchell" for its original author). It has sections on general reference works, the humanities, social sciences, history and area studies, and pure and applied sciences. In its subsection on bibliographies, among 14 entries, is "Bibliography Index," which is a bibliography of bibliographies arranged by subject. Its subsection on social science is organized in much the same way as are the social sciences departments, of a typical university and contains annotations on a wide variety of reference works. Another general reference is Hillard's *Where to Find What: A Handbook to Reference Service* (1991).

There are probably targeted reference works in your area of interest. The best current reference on where to look for material in any of the social sciences is White (1994). Devised to guide those seeking to do meta-analyses, which requires unusually thorough searches, it refers to both domestic and foreign sources. Webb, Beals, and White's *Sources of Information in the Social Sciences* (1986) is a general guide to the social sciences; the quality and the datedness of its chapters vary. Two especially excellent sources are Baxter's *Psychology: A Guide to Reference and Information Sources* (1993) and Reed and Baxter's *Library Use: A Handbook for Psychology* (1992). These are excellent for psychology and because they cover the widest boundaries of that field also cover parts of bordering social science fields. Reed and Baxter provides detailed information on how to access such commonly used reference works as *Psychological Abstracts, Sociological Abstracts,* and *Social Science Citation Index.* Freed, Hess, and Ryan's (1989) third chapter, which lists nearly 200 "Where do I go to find . . ." questions with answers, is a gem for education queries.

Computer Searches

With the increased availability of reference sources both on compact discs and on-line, **computer searches** have become an expected part of any serious literature search. It is tempting to say that nobody does hand searches anymore but since many specialized references and the early volumes of most abstracting and indexing services are not yet available in computer-readable form, that isn't true. The availability of fast desktop computers, however, has revolutionized searching for references. Further, the amount of additional information available on the Internet adds markedly to one's resources. Cooper (1985), in a study of the sources used by professional reviewers, found computer searches yielded the most references, and, short of using the references from previous reviews of the area, they yielded references with the greatest centrality and significance. Computer searches are especially appropriate in the following circumstances:

1. Where an aspect of an article is not prominent enough to include in the title or is not likely to warrant an index entry but would probably appear in the abstract. In a microsecond, the computer can read the text of the abstract as well as the title and all other words in the record, such as the identifiers. *Thus, every term in an abstract can be an indexing term.* For example, one can search for methodological details (stratified samples or statistical or research methods such as analysis of variance) or instruments or measures (*Stanford Achievement Tests, Minnesota Multiphasic Inventory*). Often looking at the indexing terms assigned to relevant entries suggests additional searches. Incidentally the capability to search abstracts depends upon the search software rather than the nature of the database.

2. Where the search words have a single stem like *psychology, psychiatry,* or *psychological,* each of which would require a separate hand search. A single computer search using a truncated term like *psych+* would allow the searcher to find all forms of the word.
3. Where you wish to find references best identified by a combination of two or more descriptors or index terms. Difficult for a human who must find the references common to two index entries, it is simple for a computer.
4. Where a search over a period of years must be pursued in individual printed volumes and the database cumulates across many years.
5. Where you wish a copy of abstracts and they can be easily printed from the computer.
6. Where you seek a particular title or the work of a specific author but do not have information on the journal or date of publication. (Note, however, most searches involving older references must still be done from the bound volumes until they are converted to database form.)
7. Where a topic is too new to have a descriptor but may be mentioned by a key phrase or term in a title or abstract.
8. Where a hand search might be constricted because of time or energy problems and a wide computer search using equal or, more likely, less time or energy would enlarge your horizons.

Whether or not available online, most university libraries have *PsychLIT* (*PsychINFO* in CD form), *Sociological Abstracts* (*Soclit*), ERIC (Educational Resources Information Centers), PAIS (Public Affairs Information Service), and other reference works on CD-ROM discs that can be computer-searched. It is also possible for individuals to access index and abstracting services from their own microcomputers at a reduced evening rate or to get a student rate. A variety of such services are available to individuals through vendors such as America-on-Line and CompuServe. Downloading the search in order to eliminate irrelevant entries with a word processor hastens getting the set you want.

One problem is finding the right-sized pool of relevant items. Sometimes the number of studies is overwhelming: Glass, McGaw, and Smith (1981) found over 2,000 studies evaluating psychotherapy. A broad search may yield too many references to screen; a precise specification may miss relevant items. Typically, you should search just beyond the immediate boundaries of the target area to include the relevant, but not too many irrelevant, ones. Finding that "just right" set of search terms is a matter partly of using preliminary searches to find the best set, partly of knowing the indexing terms of the database, and partly of learning how to combine search terms with *and, or,* and *adjacent* for the software you are using. Remember that *and,* which sounds as though it is the inclusive term, actually restricts your search to items containing both search terms, whereas *or* shows you items containing any one of the search terms and so is the more inclusive. With some software, you can also restrict your search with a modifier like *adj* to those where the search items are adjacent to one another (e.g., participant observation) rather than their appearing anywhere in the entry. Like *and,* this reduces irrelevant entries.

For example, suppose you were interested in the effects of inflation on education during recessions. To search for these keywords you would type them into the computer with instructions to search for them. The computer successively numbers its responses: 1) 3,605—inflation, 2) 605—recession, 3) 20,466—education, indicating how many entries contain one of the words. Since you are interested only in entries simultaneously containing all three, you ask for those with "1 and 2 and 3." The computer would give the answer: 4) 121. To reduce this number to those dealing with higher education, search for "higher"—5) 5,378. Then ask for "1 and 2 and (3 adj 5)," where the 3 *adj* 5 cuts the 121 to those where "higher" appears next to "education". Whereas *and* and *adj* are restrictive, *or* is inclusive. For entries dealing with either inflation or recession, you would ask for "1 or 2"; you would get their sum, 4,210 entries.

Usually listings are alphabetical by author. Unless the computer printout lists references together by year, you may not notice a change in the use of a descriptor over time. Significant breaks in the number per year may signal such changes (which you'd notice with a volume-by-volume hand search).

Be sure the database includes the earliest years you wish to search. Most databases begin with the year the publisher switched to computer typesetting using the electronic version created in that process. Therefore, as noted previously, earlier volumes are not available in database form and you must search the paper copies. However, some such as PsychINFO and the citation indexes have input earlier volumes. Indeed, PsychINFO is currently adding abstracts back to 1921 and has created abstracts for articles from volume one for eight of its major journals thereby giving a computer searchable record back to 1894.

The information accumulating on the Internet/World Wide Web is increasing daily and includes material relevant to social science research. Web searchers and Internet software change equally rapidly. Suffice it to say, use the best search tool available to you and trawl the Internet for material relevant to your search. Once a Web Crawler (the software you use to search the Internet) gets you close, clicking on successive appropriate hyperlinks (the highlighted words in text) will provide increasingly specific information.

Indexes and the Indexing Process

Library searches are one big game of hide-and-seek: the cataloger or indexer hid; you seek! Where did the cataloger place the material you want? Part of the difficulty stems from the imprecision with which we use words and the variety of terms for the same or similar phenomena. This imprecision requires you to find the terms researchers use to describe your problem (suggestions follow). Another part of the problem is that the searchers don't understand the ways in which indexes are put together and the different kinds that exist. The next sections describe the various indexes and their processes.

The On-Line Catalog

Assume you are a cataloger and that the Zimbardo article (see Chapter 1) is a book to which you must assign a Library of Congress catalog number before it can be shelved. Since a book copy can be in only one place, one number must describe it. Where would you put it? Under *paranoia? Elderly? Deafness? Hypnosis?* Probably under *paranoia,* since that is the main subject it concerns. You would turn to the Library of Congress *Subject Headings* volumes, look up *paranoia,* and assign to the book the call number that accompanies the paranoia entry, RC 520.

Have you ever been in a science museum's monochromatic light room? It is a room illuminated by only a single color from the spectrum instead of white light, which contains all the colors. Usually it is a yellow light, and all clothing that doesn't contain some yellow looks a nondescript black. People dressed in yellow can be described beautifully, but nobody else. This phenomenon is comparable to what the cataloger is trying to do, to get the right number (light color) so that the item is "described beautifully." To be so described, the illuminating light's color (the subject descriptor) must match the dominant hue (subject matter) of the item.

If you are a shelf browser like me, you'll appreciate a good cataloger who lets you find the books on a topic all in one place. You need only find the Zimbardo "book" to have access to other books on paranoia. This is tremendously valuable because you can browse books you didn't know existed and find books more recent than the one that brought you there. By looking around in that shelf area, you can find other relevant volumes. To test whether a given call number area is worth going to the shelves, do a call number search in the on-line catalog to skim the titles you would find there.

To find books in which paranoia is not the main topic, however, you'll need to discover where such books might be shelved. This is the purpose of subject indexing. Books may have only one place on the shelves, but they can have numerous entries in the subject catalog.

Traditional Subject Indexes

Instead of having only one color to shine on the item, the cataloger can use different colors to illuminate each important facet. The library catalog entry contains subject descriptors in addition to the subject classification of the call number. These are equivalent to multiple index entries. A library catalog will have at least two such entries, one for the author and one for the title, but there will usually be other descriptive entries as well. To return to the Zimbardo example, the other terms mentioned—*elderly, deafness,* and *hypnosis*—might all be subject descriptors.

There are two quite different kinds of subject indexes, however: traditional subject indexes and a product of the computer age, keyword indexes. Let us first examine traditional indexes.

Although the traditional subject index resembles a book index, there is one important difference. The book indexer uses terms unique to it and adjusts entries to the vocabulary of the author. Indexers of reference works such as *Psychological Abstracts* can't use a set of terms one year and another the next; you wouldn't be able to search across years. Of course, index terms do change with time, but slowly. When a topic like "computerized instruction" is new, you have to guess under what topic indexers will bury its references. Finally, convinced it is not a "flash in the pan," they will accord it a heading of its own. Although within a reference there is every attempt to maintain consistency in the way terms are used, there is little consistency from one service to another. Therefore, to some extent, you must learn each reference's indexing system.

Controlled Vocabulary Indexing. To return to the color analogy, if you use a tremendous variety of color names in an effort to describe an item precisely, you will use relatively rare terms like *mauve* and *puce*. Such names, like new technical jargon, make searches difficult for those not "in the know." All reference indexers maintain stability in indexing terms by having at least an in-house **controlled vocabulary.** Some indexers publish them, which means users have access to their headings. For book classification, the *Subject Headings, US. Library of Congress* (1986) is such a set. Psychological terms in the *Thesaurus of Psychological Index Terms* provide access to *Psychological Abstracts*. Education terms found in the *Thesaurus of ERIC Descriptors* are the list of ERIC's indexing terms for access to *Resources in Education* and *Current Index to Journals in Education*. Use *Medical Subject Headings (MeSH)* for access to *Index Medicus*. Consulting these thesauri or dictionaries is like getting an aerial view of a maze. It saves considerable time compared with a trial-and-error approach.

Use of the analogy "an aerial view of a maze" is intentional. Such schemes constitute a conceptual map of the field they cover. Typically, this is a hierarchical structure that starts with a set of main headings that divide the field and then subdivides these to take account of the specialties that develop within them. We might call this conceptually based indexing because it is based on a conceptualization of the fields of knowledge and how they are interrelated. (This is truer of academically oriented reference services—for example, *Psychological Abstracts*—than public library–oriented ones: for example, *Readers Guide to Periodical Literature, Education Index,* and *Social Science Index,* or the *Public Affairs Information Service.*)

Conceptual schemes tend to reflect the view of the field when they were developed. *Sociological Abstracts,* for instance, still uses its original organization, appending new fields to the end. The Library of Congress and the Dewey Decimal System, developed in the 1800s, also continue their original conceptualization, subdividing fields to create new ones. For instance, because psychology began as a branch of philosophy, it is juxtaposed with philosophy rather than being with other social sciences.

Because indexers feel constrained by controlled vocabularies, both *Psychological Abstracts* and *Sociological Abstracts* have appended descriptors to their abstracts that are not yet a part of their dictionaries. In the former, these appear only in the computer-searchable version known as *PsychINFO*. ERIC has done the same thing with what it calls *identifiers,* words that are not yet in its published scheme or are proper nouns. Such terms tend to be part of an in-house "authority list" of words that will be considered for inclusion in the next published edition.

Aids to Finding the Appropriate Index Headings. To find what terms are used in which reference work and to locate supplementary terms to search, use the

Cross-Reference Index (Atkins and Ostrow, 1989). This is a compilation of 42,000 subject headings used by eight major reference sources. Its tabular arrangement of headings permits you to find both the terms and the indexes in which they appear. It is particularly helpful in suggesting alternative headings. For example, it suggests that "Battered child" may be found under "Cruelty to children." In addition, dictionaries and thesauri include devices to assist you in finding the correct term; cross-reference lists are an example. The left-hand column in Figure 6.2 carries the entry "Day care services," taken from the ERIC thesaurus to show some of the **cross-references.** The right-hand column explains the entries.

   Such displays not only facilitate access to the index, but also help define the terms used in it. Most thesauri display the indexing terms used in different ways to enable selection of the most precise descriptors. Some, for example, use a *rotated display.* Rotated-descriptor displays list all controlled vocabulary terms in the middle of a column with modifiers on either side, like the display in Figure 6.3. Unless otherwise noted, all terms are part of the controlled vocabulary and may be searched.

Keyword Indexes

The key word index, a bottom-up approach, uses the author's orientation in contrast to conceptual subject indexing, a top-down approach oriented to the conceptual maps of the indexers and professionals. **Keyword indexing** takes the point of view that authors know best how terminology is being used. Under the oversight of editors who have comprehensive perspectives of their fields, authors title their articles using distinctions and new terms as appropriate. Because keyword indexes can be constructed from titles, they are a product of the computer age. At present, the only major references employing such a scheme are the citation indexes: *Science Citation Index, Arts and Humanities Citation Index,* and *Social Science Citation Index* (SSCI). **Permuterm indexing** of these citation indexes involves combining all the major terms of a journal title in word pairs and displaying them in

Day care services	The bold type indicates that this is an index term.
UF Day care centers	UF stands for "used for" and indicates that the index term "day care services" is used in place of "day care centers," which is not an indexing term.
NT Family day care	NT stands for "narrower term" and indicates that "family day care" is a more specific index term that could be looked up as well.
BT Human services	BT stands for "broader term" and indicates that "human services" is a less specific index term that could contain relevant material.

RT Attendant trainer
   Child care
   Child rearing
   Day camp programs
   Nursery school
   Preschool children
	RT stands for "related terms," and the list indicates index terms that are related to "day care services" and so also might contain relevant material.

FIGURE 6.2 Cross-references in a sample thesaurus of ERIC descriptors display.

American Indians
Nonreservation American Indians
American Literature
Spanish American Literature
American Studies
African American Studies

FIGURE 6.3 A sample rotated-descriptor display.

every possible combination (Figure 6.4). This treatment provides many access points for an article, sixteen on average. The analysis of word pairs is also likely to suggest other terms that the searcher can use to continue the search. The Permuterm index contains references only to journal articles. (References in the citation indexes themselves include anything an article cites, including books, reviews, and movies.)

The example in Figure 6.4 shows the term *aging*. We are first referred from an alternate spelling (ageing) to the spelling used in SSCI, *aging*, which alphabetically follows immediately. Alternative terms following the term *aging* should also be considered. They are designated with the initials *sa*, for "see also."

The first Permuterm entry is the pair *aging, accelerated,* where *aging* is the primary term and *accelerated* is the co-term; the title of an article by "A. Wilkinso" apparently contains those two words. (Computer-based records often lop off ends of words to fit allocated space; "Wilkinso" is probably Wilkinson.) The pair will also appear in the Permuterm index with *accelerated* as a primary term and *aging* as the co-term. Some terms, called stop words, are not used as primary-term entries; *ahead* is such a term in the example. Such terms appear only as co-terms because they are unlikely to be consulted. You wouldn't typically look up *ahead* in an index.

The arrowhead indicates that this is the first time that this article appears under the term *aging*. Note that "Wilkinso, A" also appears under *aging, society*. We now know three words in the title. If you were interested in all the articles under *aging*, you would skip the articles without arrowheads because these are repeats of earlier ones in the list.

Having found an entry of possible interest, you consult SSCI's source index to find its complete title and location. Although you can probably tell from the title whether the article is relevant, the source index also gives the references cited in the article as an additional check.

SSCI's Permuterm index is particularly useful in searching up-to-date terminology. For example, "tailored testing" is a relatively new kind of test in which the next item given to a testee is determined by how well he or she did on the previous one. *Tailored testing* may take years to appear in controlled vocabulary indexes like *Psychological Abstracts,* if indeed it ever does, because the examinations are also called *adaptive tests.* In fact, the latter is the heading *Psychological Abstracts* chose, apparently considering it the more standard terminology. However, should the article "Computerized Tailored Testing in England" be published, *tailored testing* will immediately appear in the Permuterm index. Furthermore, this title will be referenced six times under all the possible pairs of major terms: *computerized tailored, computerized testing, computerized England, tailored testing, tailored*

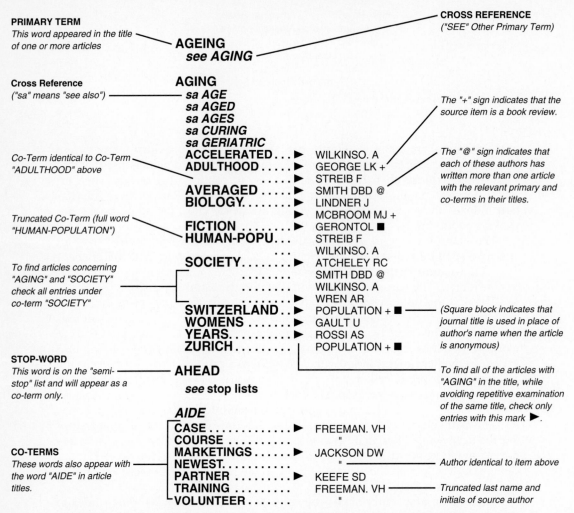

FIGURE 6.4 Guide to the Permuterm index for the *Social Science Citation Index (SSCI)*. (Copyright © Institute for Scientific Information. Used by permission. Permuterm is a registered trademark of the Institute for Scientific Information, Inc.)

England, and *testing England.* Pairs can be misleading because *tailored England* suggests clothing, but one or more pairs will capture the correct subject.

Citation Indexing

Citation indexing, a product of the computer age, is by far the best way to locate works that have built on and extended a previous research report because it identifies the published studies that cited that article. In addition, it finds articles in journals you might not normally check because each of the citation indexes covers an extremely wide range of journals numbering into the thousands. Whereas research reviews trace work backward, citation indexing allows us to trace it forward (and backward as well).

The *Social Sciences Citation Index,* the *Arts and Humanities Citation Index,* and the *Science Citation Index* together cover the relevant journal literature for most topics. They enter all of an article's references into a computer and sort them into an alphabetical index by each reference's author. Therefore, all the references that included a particular article in their reference lists are listed together in the citation index. If it will help you to know who cited an article, a book, a book review—anything that might appear in an article's list of references—citation indexing will tell you. Thus for the Zimbardo article discussed in Chapter 1, all the references in the section "References and notes" at the end of the article would be put in the computer (the note comments would be discarded).

Hoffmann-Riem separated notes from references at the end of her article; each item in her "References" section, from "Arbeitsgruppe Bielefelder Soziologen" to "Tyell, H.," would be entered. These would then be sorted by author, along with all the other references picked up from the over 2,000 journals covered by SSCI. Then all the articles that used the "Arbeitsgruppe" article would be listed in the citation index, Hoffmann-Riem's among them. This index will give a listing of all the authors, including Hoffmann-Riem, who used the material of the "Arbeitsgruppe" article in some way during the period the index covered. Maybe they fit it into their theory, used its findings, or copied its methods; you would have to consult the articles to know.

How is this index information useful? Suppose you want to know who is working on tailored testing and has built on Weiss and Davison's early discussion of the subject, *Test Theory and Method* (1981). You find in the SSCI citation index database all journal articles since 1981 in any given year which included that reference in their list. Suppose you find that in 1988 K. Johnson cited it in an article in *Educational and Psychological Measurement.* To make sure that the reference to Weiss and Davison is central to Johnson's article, you can use SSCI's source index to find the title of Johnson's article. If you are still in doubt, the source index gives Johnson's complete reference list. If you have learned the literature of the area, you will be able to tell something about the article from those citations. Citation indexing uniquely permits us to trace work forward in time, if you wish, to construct a tree of who followed up whose work and how the area grew.

More important, having found a good research article in your problem area, you can find out who has published work based on it and trace the development of that work to the currently published research frontier. Further, you can see the branches that stem from it, the alternative formulations and applications that differ from the original as you trace forward.

There are useful and interesting outgrowths of citation indexing. One is that you can identify the seminal articles in the field by noting which are most heavily cited. You can determine the premier journals from tables prepared by the publishers of SSCI. These tables indicate how often each journal is cited, in which publications a journal is most often cited, and how long a journal's articles are typically cited (an article's average "half-life"). By seeing which journals typically cite which others, you can identify a "family" of core journals.

The Relation of Starting Points to Problem Development

Table 6.1 suggests different starting points depending on where you are in the conceptualization of a problem. *Current Contents* in the bottom right cell is an unusual and important reference; it is a spin-off of the citation indexes and an excellent way to keep up with the most recent journal literature (subscribers may have a computer-searchable version delivered weekly by Internet. A web version is planned with hyperlinks). *Current Contents: Social and Behavioral Sciences,* for example, has sections for political science, sociology, psychology, education, special education, and so forth, each reproducing the table of contents of that field's major journals. You can quickly scan them to find what is going on. There is also a keyword index for each issue.[2] The *Index to Social Science and Humanities Proceedings* indexes convention papers and proceedings on a quarterly basis. ERIC is the best source of papers given at education conventions.

Why would you want to keep abreast of ongoing research? Isn't it enough to read the journal literature? It depends on how rapidly your field is moving. In a study of communication in the social sciences, Garvey, Lin, and Nelson (1970) found that the average research project took almost 2 1/2 years from start to publication, 3 if it was sent back by the editor for corrections. That is a significant lag, and since it is an average, approximately half of the articles take longer. Although an old study, journal backlogs are still long. Garvey and colleagues found that because of this lag, researchers tend to establish the so-called invisible colleges mentioned in Chapter 3. Finding persons who are part of the invisible college is a particularly good way of keeping abreast of what is happening. This is easier now that there are electronic journals, bulletin boards, and forums in so many areas. How do you find these? It seems almost any resource cited here will be out-of-date as soon it is written. One suggestion that may still be valid by the time you read this is to reach Yahoo! (http://Yahoo.com) or a similar node and use their search engine to find "directories of electronic journals, newsletters, and academic lists." One item that will turn up is the Association of Research Libraries' yearly publication of the *Directory of Electronic Journals and Newsletters,* which is available in hard copy and on-line. Kelley-Milburn and Milburn (1995) and Wallace (1997) list resources for psychologists on the Internet. Your faculty may know of invisible college computer sites that might be of interest to you. Posting a request for references on one of these targeted to your problem is a superb way to get expert help; the human mind is still the best retrieval system.

---

[2]Be sure to look at the frontmatter in each issue, which includes comments by the author of a heavily cited reference (a "citation classic"), a summary of current public comment regarding the social sciences, abstracts of new books, and an interesting column, usually by Eugene Garfield, founder of the company.

TABLE 6.1 *Entry Points in the Literature Search**

Entry Points	Purpose	Sources to Consult
A general problem area	To find the important sources of information in an area—encyclopedias, handbooks, reviews of research	General guides to reference books such as *Guide to Reference Books* (Sheehy, 1986; Balay, 1992) Reference guides specific to a field like Baxter (1993) or Reed and Baxter (1992) For computer searching, a guide such as *Gale Directory of Online Databases* (Nolan, 1983); Lengenfelder (1988) or Williams (1981–)
A specific problem area	To learn what research has been done, what terminology is being used, where the frontier is, what keywords to pursue in journal literature	A library's subject index or on-line catalog for relevant bibliographies, books, and other materials Compilations such as handbooks (*Handbook of Experimental Psychology, Handbook of Social Psychology*) and research reviews (*Annual Review of Anthropology, Annual Review of Psychology, Annual Review of Sociology; Review of Educational Research* [quarterly], *Review of Research in Education* [annual]), *Encyclopedia of Educational Research, Encyclopedia of Psychology* Thesauri (*Thesaurus of Psychological Index Terms*) and the *Cross-reference Index*
A specific problem	To find recent research, learn how terminology is changing, identify new fields related to the problem, explore current methodological approaches, determine the current frontier To identify the major aspects of a topic and the prolific writers in the area	Appropriate indexes and abstracting services, such as *Psychological Abstracts* and *Sociological Abstracts;* ERIC and its *Current Index to Journals in Education* (CIJE) and *Research in Education* (RIE); *Education Index; Dissertation Abstracts International;* Permuterm index of *Social Science Citation Index* (particularly good for current jargon, but requires that vernacular of the time be known for older references)
A research study basic to the problem	To find out what scholars followed up on this research and what they did with it To find the most cited authors in an area of work and the basic references to which other authors in the field refer To trace the historical development of an area by tracing back to who was cited first in an area, who cited this work, who in turn cited that work, and so on	Citation index of the *Social Science Citation Index; Science Citation Index; Arts and Humanities Citation Index*

*This is an important table that contains some material not in the text.

TABLE 6.1 *(continued)*

Entry Points	Purpose	Sources to Consult
Latest terminology for a problem or the names of persons who are doing extensive work in an area	To locate the most recent work in an area, including ongoing work	For latest published work, *Current Contents: Social and Behavioral Science* For ongoing research, the Internet, World Wide Web, or online services—to find web sites for lists of funded projects by government agencies Post requests for references and get into the discussions on relevant electronic bulletin boards and forums Do search on Internet/World Wide Web and follow hyperlinks to relevant material Look at electronic journals of which *Psycoloquy* and *Psyche* are refereed examples. Undoubtedly more will come Write directly to researchers who have been working in the area. Addresses are in convention programs and in membership directories of professional societies In lieu of convention attendance, search convention program for relevant material and write for copies. Some convention programs (e.g., Amer. Psych. Society) are on the Internet and are computer searchable

Organizing the Search

How organized should your search be? Most people begin by yanking at a corner of the problem, an aspect of it that interests them, like a loose thread on a sweater, tugging on it to unravel the garment. This technique often works; problems can usually be approached from a variety of directions. It is certainly difficult to organize a search for something you don't know much about. Thus, before organization, there is usually a period of broad exploration and, most important, of being flexible enough to recognize potentially profitable byways and side issues. Sometimes these turn out to be more important than what you set out to pursue.

Nevertheless, there comes a point in the process where you need to stop, get some perspective on what you have done, and carry out an organized search from that point on. It may come earlier than you anticipate—the only way to know is to take a few minutes every so often to reflect on what you

have done, to consider where you are going, and estimate further requirements to learn the dimensions and nature of the sought-for body of literature.
You will intuitively sense when this point of organization comes. You are comfortable with what you have learned, findings begin to repeat, and expectations of new surprises have dimmed. At that point, you should plan your future reference acquisition pattern, deciding what to cover heavily and what
more lightly.

To be sure you have found the boundaries of your topic, if you haven't done
so earlier, *do a computer search based on a careful consultation of relevant thesauri or
dictionaries.* Both activities, however, are *much more useful earlier* than as clean-up
activities.

Meta-Analyses

We have been considering literature searches in which the summary and analysis
of the literature is done purely in descriptive verbal terms. Increasingly, these are
accompanied or replaced by what have been termed meta-analyses, in which the
results of studies are summarized in quantitative terms. This process is described
in Chapter 21; the statistical techniques used are covered in the intervening chapters. Whether verbal or numerical, an integrative review of the literature around
unifying frameworks, theories, or explanations is what is to be sought. Let's consider some general suggestions.

General Suggestions

Aim for a coherent, integrated, critical examination of selected relevant literature. If possible, relate the problem to the network of theory and explanations already existing in the field. Show how this study fits with and "stands on the shoulders" of
previous work. Too often, authors aim at comprehensiveness instead of selecting
the best articles that bear on the topic. Too often, they merely cite previous work
instead of relating it to the problem with an explanation of its contribution. Some
authors accept the methods of others uncritically instead of being appropriately
critical or laudatory of aspects that deserve comment. They provide a loose collection of citations and miscellaneous facts that show coverage but little understanding. Avoid these errors. Keep these suggestions in mind:

1. Be selective in "following your nose"; do not check everything.
2. Read some primary sources, not just secondary ones, and do not depend on
   just one secondary source; read in depth to the cutting edge and backward in
   time. Include seminal sources, deep thinkers who really grasp the field.
3. Look for technical and design flaws to avoid and for innovations you may use.
4. Use a thesaurus or a search term dictionary, if one is available. It forces you to
   think through your search strategy and teaches the standardized terminology
   of the field. It adds to your search terms the descriptors used in highly relevant publications.

5. Record each entry immediately in whatever bibliographic style you plan to use; then you'll know you have all the required information.
6. When using a copy machine, be sure to label pages with the source when it is not in the heading or footer.
7. Especially if your topic is not covered well by the indexing terms, do a computer search of the journal literature. In fact, do one even if it is.
8. Check sources of current information to find others working on your problem. Use the Internet, the Citation Indexes' Permuterm index, *Current Contents,* the subject indexes of the programs of recent relevant professional association meetings.
9. Actively think about, argue with, praise, and otherwise react to your reading.
10. Discuss your search with the most informed expert in the field accessible to you. Despite the advances in computer searches, *the human mind is still the best retrieval device.*

SUMMARY

Figure 6.1 summarizes the variety of sources to consult in doing a literature search, and Table 6.1, in more detail, relates sources to the stage of development of your problem. Together with the general sugestions in the section above, these provide a summary of the chapter.

A Look Ahead

Your literature search has suggested how your variables are related, in most instances causally. Although we take causality for granted, nevertheless, it is worth examining to see on what basis one can reasonably infer it—the topic of the next chapter.

ADDITIONAL READING

Baxter (1993) and Reed and Baxter (1992) and Stockdale and Kenny (1996) for psychological topics and those at all related; Freed, Hess, and Ryan (1989) for education related topics; White (1994) for social sciences generally (excellent chapter).

IMPORTANT TERMS

Citation indexing
Computer searches
Controlled vocabulary
Cross-references
Database

Keyword indexing
Permuterm indexing
Primary sources
Secondary sources

APPLICATION PROBLEMS

1. You are beginning an examination of how instruction in learning strategies will affect the achievement of high school students in history. You are seeking an overview of research on learning strategies and key authors in this area. Where might you start both to better define the research questions and to answer these questions?

2. A colleague has referred you to articles by Wittrock and Jonassen for your topic of generative strategies in learning. How might you go about finding more on the topic and exploring the work of these researchers?

3. You are studying the use of the new whole-language approach in elementary basal readers. How might a computer search make this review of the literature easier to complete?

4. Designing instruction to accommodate different learning styles has gained attention in recent years. How might you sample recent research in the field to determine where the field of learning style–based instruction has come from and is going?

5. A project to teach adults the use of computers is being developed in the local school district. You are going to be studying how effective the chosen methods of instruction are with these learners. Why might you do a literature review first? Why not?

APPLICATION EXERCISE

Continuing the exercise begun in Chapter 5, take your chosen topic, and using Figure 6.1 and Table 6.1 choose the most relevant entry point. To gain familiarity with the reference works at "high" and "low" entry points, perhaps choose more than one point, pretending that you know more or less than you do. Consult the sources listed on pages 106-108.

Be sure to include the use of such references as a citation index, *Current Contents in the Social and Behavioral Sciences,* and at least one journal index or abstract source such as *Psychological Abstracts.* Do a computer search on a CD-ROM and on the Internet/World Wide Web. As you work, consult the general suggestions at the end of the chapter.

ANSWERS TO THE APPLICATION PROBLEMS

1. The education encyclopedias and handbooks might be the best places to start. You could determine what terminology is used for this topic, gain an overview of the field, and pick out keywords and authors. The information on keywords and authors might then be used to access the journal indexes. Descriptors or keywords (or both) may be used, depending on the index. If a CD-ROM or on-line search service is available, these might be used for a more comprehensive search once the terms have been determined. These indexes can provide an overview of current research, help locate review articles, identify authors who appear frequently, and show various aspects of a topic. Once key authors and works are found, the SSCI citation index could be used to determine who has cited these authors and thus possibly contributed to furthering the directions of this research.

2. To trace the works of the authors, you could search some of the major indexes by author to locate all their works. Then you might check the citation index of SSCI to determine who has cited their works on generative strategies. This could lead you to more recent work on the topic.

It would also be useful to locate review articles that deal with learning and specifically touch on generative strategies. This would help situate the topic on a conceptual map and lead you to other sources that might contain information on the topic or be related to it.

To find still more on this topic, you would probably first check the thesauri for cross-reference terms that are broader, narrower, related to, or used for "generative learning strategies." If "generative learning strategies" or its parts are not used in the major indexes with thesauri, keyword searching would be the next step. This is possible in SSCI or in ERIC or *PsychINFO* or on CD-ROM. When relevant articles appear, look at the descriptors or subject headings used to index those articles for further leads to search. References in the articles themselves are usually relevant to the topic and provide additional avenues to follow.

3. Computerized searching makes it easier to search for terms that are not descriptors or subject headings, such as *whole-language approach.* This is especially true for new terms or specific topics that might be subsumed in larger concepts. It also allows the search to combine more than one concept in a search. For example, the search in this case could look for articles that are about whole language, about basals, and about the elementary level all at the same time. This is a great time-saver.

Were the whole-language approach a recent idea in the literature, this computerized search would also help identify the appropriate indexing terms. It would point out the major authors in the field and reveal the research frontier on the topic.

4. Encyclopedias, handbooks, and the on-line catalog will give you a start in tracing the history of the field of learning style–based instruction. Bibliographies on the topic, located through the on-line catalog or through *Bibliographic Index,* would also be useful. Review articles on the topic can be found in ERIC and *PsychINFO.* This is especially easy when searching these indexes on-line or on CD-ROM.

You could use the large number of journal indexing and abstracting services to locate articles and then narrow the topic to something workable. *Dissertation Abstracts International* is good for locating dissertations, *Resources in Education* in ERIC for conference proceedings or speeches.

5. A literature review before the study begins would provide background on adult learners and methods of instruction in computer use. It could point out what methodologies work and what ones don't. It could help determine the variables, relationships, and confounding factors in other such studies. In addition it would show the state of research on the topic.

Others might argue that such a literature review done before the study might bias the observations through preconceived notions of what should happen. If the treatment and the sample are already set, it might predispose the researcher to expect certain results based on prior research.

SECTION THREE

Foundational Research Concepts

To build a firm foundation for studying research methods, in addition to the skills of the last section, you need to understand some basic concepts that underlie research. Comprehending these is important regardless of the research method employed. They provide the supporting structure and the criteria to be met for research to be accepted as contributing to knowledge.

- Chapter 7 discusses causation and the criteria used to show it. Cause and effect as concepts are more complex than we might think. A common logic, the chain of reasoning, forms the basis for the presentation of findings that support causation. This chapter describes the criteria that flow from the chain whereby a study can be judged to link variables in a relationship, the study's "linking power" (LP). Since this power is similar to what is commonly known as internal validity, it is designated internal validity (LP).
- Chapter 8 discusses generality. If variables are related causally, how generalizable is this relationship? Sampling is the basis for generalizing from one context to many. This chapter describes the principles of sampling and their application to various parts of the chain of reasoning. Sampling is shown to be pervasive throughout the chain. The set of criteria involved in judging the capacity of a study to support generalization determines a study's external validity (GP), where GP stands in parallel fashion for its "generalizing power."
- Chapter 9 examines additional criteria studies must meet and some constraints on them. Although these criteria are never completely satisfied, we try to optimize for each study: the extent to which we build credibility with the audience, the balance of internal and external validity, and the allocation of resources. All research is done in the context of limitations—limits on our resources, on what institutions will allow, and what is ethically permissible.

- Chapter 10 considers in more detail how we determine what is ethically permissible. It describes the safeguards that the federal government has erected to protect human subjects and the codes of conduct that professional societies have developed to guide researchers.

From the perspective of science as a social process (Chapter 3), it is apparent that the criteria and optimizing conditions logically follow from an analysis of the judgments that occur in developing a consensus around the chain of reasoning. The following chapters' description of that logic and those criteria combine into a model that will prove useful over and over again in conceptualizing, implementing, and evaluating research studies. For that reason, it is diagrammed on the inside front cover of this text for easy reference.

Causal Inference and Internal Validity

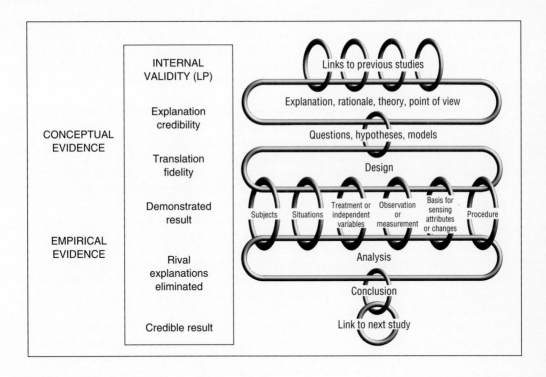

Rags make paper, paper makes money, money makes banks, banks make loans, loans make poverty, poverty makes rags.

Anonymous

For want of a nail the shoe was lost, for want of a shoe the horse was lost, for want of a horse the rider was lost . . . . For want of a nail, the battle was lost!

George Herbert (1593–1633)

OVERVIEW[1]

The review of literature discussed in Chapter 6 will often indicate what variables are related to the phenomena you are studying and how these variables caused the phenomena to come about. *Causation* is what is explained in a rationale, proposed in a hypothesis or model, and examined in the conclusions of the articles contributing to the literature review. The "basis for sensing attributes or changes" link (see p. 66) in the chain of reasoning of these articles provided the basis for inferring causation. The term *cause* is used loosely, however, and such usage hides at least three sets of complexities: (1) different understandings of what is meant by the term cause, (2) different perceptions of the nature of the world and their implications for the social sciences, and (3) the variety of complex as well as simple causal patterns to consider.

This chapter both sensitizes you to these different understandings and examines causal patterns other than the common ones. In particular, it examines the set of evidence we use to infer that a causal relationship exists. This set of evidence is defined as the *internal validity (LP)* of a study, where LP stands for linking power. Linking power is the power of a study to link the variables in a causal relationship. As we saw in Chapter 3, audiences make knowing judgments about the proper interpretation of data; hence, findings are presented as a logical chain of reasoning. This chapter describes the set of criteria audiences apply to the links of the chain of reasoning to make judgments of the validity of the inference of causality.

A second set of criteria concerns how widely the relationship applies—its generality. This generality is defined as the *external validity (GP)* of a study, where GP stands for generalizing power, the power of the study to show generality of the findings. It is the topic of Chapter 8.

Although discussed in the context of causality, internal validity (LP) and external validity (GP) apply more broadly than causal relationships; they work equally well with any cyclical, interactive and reversible relationships or processes in which either variable can be considered the cause or the effect. Thus, it is problematical to ask whether stress is a cause of failure or failure a cause of stress. Like the temperature and pressure of a gas, either can be considered cause or effect and the language of causality does not adequately describe the relation-

[1]I am most grateful to my colleague, Dr. Emily Robertson, for her helpful comments on the causation section in an earlier edition.

ship. In examining such relationships, however, we can usefully apply the concepts of internal validity (LP) and external validity (GP) and their five judgments to determine the existence, extent, and nature of the relationship and its generality.

CHAPTER CONTENTS

Association and Causation

The fact that things vary together and thus are apparently related doesn't mean that the relationship is necessarily a causal one. Many relationships are simply associations, possibly resulting from the fact that both are influenced by a third variable. Yet we often incorrectly impute causality where the evidence is sufficient only to establish association. Consider, for instance, this headline:

> Schoolwork Undermined By TV, California Survey Shows

Always read the small print under the headline, my teachers used to say, and of course, they were right. While the headline says television viewing caused poor schoolwork, the article itself interprets the evidence more cautiously:

> The more a student watches television, the worse he does in school. . . . No conclusions were drawn as to why television watching seems to go hand in hand with lower reading, writing and math test scores.
>
> *Report on Educational Research,* November 26, 1980

If not the headline writer, at least the author was careful to walk the fine line between association and causation; instead of ascribing causation, the author said they merely go "hand in hand." Indeed, that they vary together could be explained by the fact that poorer students prefer watching exciting TV to struggling with difficult and often unrewarding schoolwork. This is one example of the care we must use with the concept of causation.

Some people consider the conceptual difficulties of using the term *cause* so serious that they believe its use should be abandoned. For instance, Bertrand Russell wrote: "Causality. . . is a relic of a bygone age, surviving, like the monarchy, only because it is erroneously supposed to do no harm" (1953, p. 387). It is so pervasive in everyday speech and among academicians, however, that its abandonment seems unlikely. Köbben argues, "The notion of 'cause' is indispensable"; banning it "impoverishes our intellectual tool kit" (1973, p. 89). Causes have been called the "cement of the universe" (Mackie, 1974).

Philosophers have devoted years to analyzing the concept of cause and are still perplexed by it. We cannot do justice to that volume of literature here, but we can alert you to some of the common complications that may suggest some directions to explore.

Complications in the Concept of Cause

Causes Are Actually Parts of a Causal Chain

An important complication is that whenever we use the term *cause,* without realizing it, we are emphasizing a part of a causal history. Consider that a car stops with the gas gauge at empty. Did it stop because it ran out of gas? That seems to be the immediate cause. But perhaps the real cause was the driver's lack of attention to the gas gauge or the fact that the driver never learned regular habits of maintenance and the necessity of providing time for them. Perhaps, even more basically, because his parents always took care of the maintenance tasks, he never learned to be responsible for them. Each is a step back toward a more "fundamental" cause, and each is part of the causal chain.

The Cause Is the Most Appropriate Part of a Causal Chain

Use of the term cause *always means selecting the part of a causal chain that is the most appropriate for a particular inquiry.* Sometimes cause is defined as the last link that completes the **causal chain**—a football player flops into an antique chair; it comes apart, depositing him abruptly and painfully on the floor. He is perceived as the "cause" of the chair's demise. In reality, he is but the last link in a years-long causal chain as the glue changed to powder, the sockets dried out, the wood shrank, innumerable individuals of varying weights sat in it and loosened the joints, and so on.

We often attribute cause to the last link in the causal chain; it is the most immediate and obvious. There are many choices, however: the part that is most immediate in time; most important; most able to be remedied; or most fundamental, the part without which the event would not have occurred (the necessary part). As Lewis (1983) notes, one cause may be salient in a particular context, another in a different context. By selectively choosing from a causal history, he argues, we "explain" an action. That is, explaining an occurrence means giving some information about its causal history. Thus, we can describe the causal chain for a particular situation—as the chapter's opening quote traces the chain from the missing horseshoe nail to the lost battle. More usefully, we can describe a chain that generalizes across situations. That is what we do when we set forth a hypothesis or theory—for example, economic theory. "Lowering interest rates increases business activity" describes not just one causal situation, but a whole host of them. It is a proposition that has generality, and it is the kind that we seek in social science.

Solving problems is sometimes easier when we view them from the perspective of a causal chain. This approach can reveal where intervention will affect subsequent events. For example, the threat of acquired immunodeficiency syndrome (AIDS) may be combated at an early link in the chain through education for sexual abstinence. At a later link, we could promote the use of condoms or make sterile needles available free to drug users who might otherwise share them. At a still later link, we could seek a drug that will attack the virus. Of these, we might consider the earliest the least expensive, the most likely to succeed, and the most socially acceptable. Examination of the causal chain suggests where to break the cause-and-effect relationship.

Causal Relations Are Always Inferred, Never Proven

Assuming we continue to use the term *cause*, a continuing puzzle for philosophers has been to determine what conditions permit its use. David Hume (1902 [1748]) for instance, advanced the commonsense criteria: (1) Cause and effect occur close together in time, (2) the cause always appears before the effect, and (3) the cause is present whenever the effect is observed. We can think of exceptions to the first condition: the relation of smoking to cancer or emphysema. The effect of smoking is delayed rather then contiguous. As for the second condition, when a racquet hits the tennis ball, what precedes what? This criterion may be improved by changing it to "the effect did not begin before the cause began," but the change does not solve all the problems.

Some people have argued that we should find the **necessary and sufficient conditions** for a phenomenon. Sufficient conditions are all those conditions in the presence of which the effect will occur. But without trying all the possible causes, we would never know whether we had missed a sufficient condition— there may still be one we hadn't tried. *Causal relationships are always inferred, never proven.*

Causation is an inference for still another reason, a prime one: We never directly sense a causal connection. A billiard ball hits another and bounces away; we do not directly "see" the causal connection. The compression of the billiard ball material seems a reasonable explanation. Maybe oxygen atoms on the surface repel the balls. We must infer the most reasonable explanation from the circumstances; the attribution of causation is always an inference on our part.

Validated Causal Propositions Escape Disconfirmation

Popper (1959) points out that even though causal propositions and theories cannot be proven, they can be tested. Indeed, he argues that our major responsibility is to try to falsify such relationships by posing hypotheses about them and trying to prove them false—finding instances in which, although expected to do so, they do not hold. As he puts it, "man proposes, nature disposes"; "problem—> tentative theory—> error elimination—> new problem." This argument is similar to, and perhaps an extension of, Merton's *organized skepticism*, one of the essential norms of science. Suppose the evidence is consistent with an explanation, even where we have deliberately tried to find an instance in which it wouldn't work—as Popper would put it, "even when one has tried to falsify it." Then, as he notes, the explanation has "escaped **disconfirmation**." Theories and propositions are never proved; they merely escape disconfirmation. Of course, once they have escaped disconfirmation enough times, we consider them part of *knowledge*.

As noted in Chapter 3, Cronbach (1982) views this process of escaping disconfirmation as one of "reducing uncertainty." The uncertainty eventually is low enough that a research finding crosses the threshold for admittance into the realm of knowledge. Note that having escaped disconfirmation is consistent with the notion that we hold all scientific propositions as tentatively true and subject to disconfirmation—an important aspect of the uniquely self-correcting nature of science.

Social and Behavioral Science Variables Seem to Be Loosely Causally Related

Popper (1972) suggested ours may be a **clocklike world** with precise mechanical determinism like that which we find in the workings of an old clock with numerous gears. Turning a gear inevitably generates a response elsewhere. The physical sciences are often perceived this way. Contrast this with a **cloudlike world,** a reference to the normative behavior exhibited by a cloud of gnats in summer or a flock of birds flying south for the winter. A bird or a gnat strays only a certain distance from the center of the flock or swarm, returning when it becomes an outlier. Similarly organizations tolerate a wide range of normal behavior with occasional outliers. In such a world, predictions are probable rather than exact. With the loose coupling of events that the cloudlike model assumes, from time to time we would expect to find unusual results of both a positive and a negative nature. Clearly, it is much more difficult to find causal relations in a cloudlike world. That model, however, seems to fit all social and behavioral phenomena more closely than does the clocklike one—verbally skilled students are more likely to achieve academic success, it isn't a certainty.

Similarly, experts have argued that in contrast to the world of physical science, where the materials are inert and are acted on, the world of social science is one of complex interaction and so may never be predictable (Cronbach, 1975).

Some such individuals do not expect ever to find a science of rules and laws and propositions like those in the physical sciences. But, notes Phillips (1987), there are interactions in the physical sciences as well:

> Pressure and volume interact to affect the behavior of a gas—but temperature in turn is another interacting factor, and so is the initial mass of the gas and its purity. Furthermore, depending upon the precise chemical nature of the gas (another interacting factor), some surprising events may occur at specific temperatures and pressures—some gases will condense into liquids while others sublimate directly into solids.
>
> The difference between the social and physical domains is merely that the types of factors that interact are different, although, of course, the "merely" is not entirely without significance. . . . Humans are role-playing and rule-following creatures, while presumably gases neither consciously set out to follow Boyle's Law nor debate which role is appropriate for them. . . .
>
> Processes in the natural world in essence are arenas where a host of forces interact, and scientists cannot make accurate predictions because of the ensuing complexities. But this does not mean that theories are either unattainable, or useless when they are found. Popper uses the example of a storm shaking a tree and causing an apple to fall and bruise on the ground; Gage uses an autumn leaf wafting to the ground. In both cases, there are gravitational effects, air resistance, wind currents, biochemical actions in the plants that determined when the apple and leaf would fall, and so on. The situation in social science research undoubtedly is of similar complexity (pp. 55–56)[2]

A complex interactive world probably calls for equally complex patterns of causation and explanations of its phenomena.

- ✦ *Any explanation highlights some part of a causal chain.*
- ✦ *The term* cause *is often used to designate the last link that completes the chain, but there are many other possibilities: the most important, the most remediable, a necessary part, and so forth.*
- ✦ *Problem solving is often facilitated by considering not just the end point, but significant portions of the causal chain.*
- ✦ *Defined as the necessary and sufficient conditions for an effect to appear, causation is always an inference. Like all inferences, it can never be proved; there is always the possibility of a nonconforming case, as yet undiscovered.*
- ✦ *Each successful test in which propositions and hypotheses escape disconfirmation reduces uncertainty as findings move toward becoming accepted knowledge.*
- ✦ *In contrast to physical science phenomena, which seem to be tightly causally coupled, social and behavioral science phenomena appear to be loosely connected.*

---

[2]Reprinted with permission from D. C. Phillips, *Philosophy, Science, and Social Inquiry.* Copyright © 1987, Pergamon Press PLC.

Patterns of Cause and Effect Relationships

There are a variety of patterns of causation besides the simple *A causes B* that first springs to mind.[3] Knowing a range of such patterns makes it likelier that we can find a good match to data. When *A* and *B* occur together, it may well be that *A* causes *B*. This is the pattern we typically expect to find:

For example, we may think that spastic children's slurred speech and awkward movements (*A*) cause them to be dependent on other people (*B*). As Becker (1963) has argued, however, it is possible that the dependency (*B*) results because adults expect such individuals to be dependent on them. The child, getting desirable attention for obliging, displays dependent behavior. Becker turns around the causal direction that most of us would have inferred. He suggests:

A perhaps more realistic explanation might be that the child's awkwardness creates expectations and reactions in the adults, resulting in learned helplessness. That evokes even greater efforts by the adults, which reinforce the expressions of helplessness in the child, and so on. Here we are taking the perspective of a causal chain:

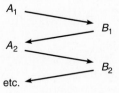

Although many of our studies deal with single-cause patterns, multiple-cause patterns are clearly more realistic. A single-cause analysis may be adequate to describe powerful variables such as intellectual ability, or conditions that totally dominate a situation such as overwhelming anger. But most variables act only in

---

[3]This section is a modification of Krathwohl (1985), pp. 214-221; the term *cause* is used loosely in this discussion.

concert with others, and their effects are noticeably modulated by this interaction. Such interrelationships can be illustrated by two more complex patterns:

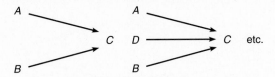

For example, visual acuity may be the result of the amount of available light and the strength of the person's uncorrected vision, an application of the left-hand pattern, *A* and *B* producing *C*:

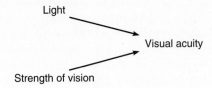

Or, like the right-hand pattern, *A*, *D*, and *B* producing *C*, it may be the result of those factors plus the size of the letters to be discriminated, as on an eye test chart:

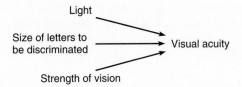

There are still other complications, as certain variables are more important in particular situations than others. Thus, when the light is very low, light may be the dominant factor in visual acuity despite the strength of the person's vision. Such dominance may reduce the relationship to a simple-cause pattern for that circumstance:

Light ⟶ Visual acuity

Some causation patterns involve what is called a moderating variable. For example, hostile individuals are often anxious. Why? Perhaps anxiety results from a concern that repression will only inconsistently hold hostility in check. In this instance the consistency of repression moderates (in the sense of affecting or controlling) the amount of anxiety:

Hostility ⟶ Repression ⟶ Anxiety

In still another pattern, two causal variables may be affected by a third. Inflation causes the Federal Reserve Board to raise interest rates as well as causes increases in car prices. Both of these factors depress car sales:

An interesting example of third-variable explanation is the explanation for the strange relation between the number of nesting storks and the birth rate. Storks like to roost in chimneys that have not been used by other storks, and neighborhoods with new homes are likely to have more newly married couples (Casti, 1992, as found in Miles and Huberman, 1994)! As you can see, *more complex patterns result in the inclusion of additional portions of the causal chain.*

In addition, effects may be delayed or cyclical; they may be all or none—nothing, then on reaching a threshold an all-at-once effect. No doubt you can think of others. Clearly, some understanding or reasonable anticipation of what is going on in the phenomena helps one delineate among these myriad of possibilities, hence the importance of theory. Without it, we would have all these possibilities to check out and hope that we are able to find the right one early.

With such a brief treatment of cause complexity, we have been limited to simple examples—causal chains can be infinitely complex. This realization reinforces the fact that we should consider a variety of possible causal patterns when we infer causation.

- ✦ *What we perceive as effects may often actually be causes or parts of a causal chain. Put another way, any effect is likely also to be a cause of some future event.*
- ✦ *Effects often have more than one cause, and this results in complex causal patterns. Such causal patterns may involve large portions of the causal chain.*

Internal and External Validity as Evidence of Causation

Now that we have examined some of the complications of defining cause, on what basis can we infer causation? We will answer this question on two levels: (1) by describing the evidence that permits the inference of causation and (2) by describing the situational patterns that facilitate drawing the inference of causation (the "basis for sensing attributes or changes" link in the chain of reasoning).

Research studies involving causation search for generalizations, and seek to build consensus around the evidence supporting them. What is a **generalization**?

Basically, it is a statement of a relationship between two or more variables that has generality; that is, it applies to persons, places, times, measures, and research procedures other than those involved in the original study. The two parts in the definition suggest that two separate concerns of any research are (1) whether a cause-and-effect relationship exists in the particular constellation of circumstances studied and (2) whether that relationship has any generality. A set of basic expectations applies to all research methods regarding the evidence and the judgments to be made of it.

The evidence that permits the inference of whether a cause and effect relationship exists is described by a concept called internal validity (LP) where the LP stands for "linking power"—the capacity provided by a research study for readers to link cause to effect. In similar fashion, the evidence permitting inference of generality is described by **external validity (GP)** where GP stands for "generalizing power"—the capacity provided by a research study for readers to generalize the casual relationship beyond the study's particular constellation of circumstances. Both internal and external validity are made up of conceptual evidence (evidence based on judgement and reasoning) and empirical evidence (evidence based on judgments of data), and both are derived from a set of five parallel judgments as you will see as we discuss them further.

Campbell and Stanley (1963) coined the terms **internal validity** and **external validity** to describe similar criteria for inferring causation. Their choice of the term *validity* was both appropriate and unfortunate. It was appropriate because the dictionary meaning of the term *validity* is "capable of being justified" or "effective, as in an argument" (Gove, 1976). This definition is quite consistent with the notion that the researcher is seeking to build a consensus about the proper interpretation of the data, a kind of argument.

It was unfortunate, however, because in the context of measurement, the term *validity* appropriately refers to the effectiveness of a test, measure, or evaluation. Whereas *internal validity* and *external validity* refer to basic characteristics of an entire study, *test validity* refers only to that part of the chain of reasoning involving measurement or observation. Students just becoming familiar with the technical language of research can find the multiple uses of *validity* confusing. Including a modifier such as *internal*, *external*, or *test* helps keep them distinct. To distinguish their use as summaries of a study's power to link variables in a relationship or to generalize that relationship, we modify them to *internal validity (LP)*—linking power—and *external validity (GP)*—generalizing power. Let us now turn to a closer examination of internal validity (LP), the evidence that permits an inference of causation. Then, in the remainder of the chapter, we will examine ways of designing the "basis for sensing attributes or changes" link of the chain of reasoning to facilitate drawing that inference.

- ◆ The term validity *can refer to different characteristics in different contexts.*
- ◆ Internal validity *refers to whether the evidence of a study supports the existence of a relationship between or among its variables.*
- ◆ External validity *refers to whether that relationship generalizes beyond the characteristics of the study in which it was found.*
- ◆ *External validity and internal validity are characteristics of an entire chain of reasoning supporting a generalization.*

◆ When used to indicate the power of a study to link variables in a relationship or to generalize that relationship, internal validity and external validity become in-ternal validity (LP) and external validity (GP).

◆ Test validity refers to whether a test measures what it was intended to measure.

◆ Test validity is a characteristic of the link in the chain of reasoning for measure-ment and observation.

Internal Validity (LP)

Internal validity (LP) is the power of a study to create a consensus that the appro-priate interpretation of the evidence is that the variables are linked in a relation-ship—to support an inference linking cause to effect. Zimbardo designed the study cited in Chapter 1 to have strong linking power, power to develop a con-sensus around his data interpretation that linked paranoia to a lack of awareness of developing deafness. Adding *(LP)* to *internal validity* distinguishes it from Campbell and Stanley's original definition of the term, which refers to relating only the operational definitions of the concepts used in the study rather than the concepts themselves. (The measure of a concept is referred to as its **operational definition** because the operations performed in measuring it define what the data represent. The answers to the problems on an intelligence test become what is meant by *intelligence*; the responses to a series of questions on government finan-cial assistance for destitute people become what is meant by "attitude toward welfare programs." The operationalizing of concepts is discussed further in Chapter 18.) In addition, Campbell and Stanley's definition included only empiri-cal evidence, not conceptual.

Many texts define internal validity as relating the concepts, although some fol-low the original definition. (For more information, see the appendix to this chap-ter). Because we are nearly always interested in linking the concepts, not just their operational definitions, internal validity (LP) seems the more useful definition and so is used in this text. Because it relates the concepts, it is composed of both con-ceptual and empirical evidence. What do we mean by conceptual evidence? Con-ceptual evidence for internal validity is what links the empirical evidence to the concepts. It is as important as the empirical evidence. It involves clarifying the constructs used to describe a relationship; embedding them in an explanation, theory, or rationale; and translating them into operational definitions. Judgments of how well these steps are done are typically the first appraisals made of a study and tend to color our view of the empirical evidence if they are not favorable. The conceptual evidence also helps us discriminate a chance result that has no expla-nation from one that makes sense because it has conceptual support.

Internal validity (LP) involves five judgments: explanation credibility, transla-tion fidelity, demonstrated result, rival explanations eliminated, and credible re-sult. The first two of these, *explanation credibility* (the reasonableness of the explana-tion or rationale for the relationship) and *translation fidelity* (the faithfulness to intended meaning with which concepts are translated into operational definitions), constitute the conceptual evidence linking the variables of a study. The next two, *demonstrated result* (the expected result did occur) and *rival explanations eliminated* (any explanation other than the original one was ruled out), constitute the empirical evidence linking the variables and are judgments of the data of the study. Finally, there is the judgment of whether there is a *credible result*. It considers the consistency of the findings with previous research and the strength of both the conceptual and the empirical evidence. Together the five judgments lead to an overall determination of the linking power, or internal validity (LP), of a study.[4]

> ✦ *A study with internal validity (LP) supports an inference linking the concepts of the study in a causal relationship, not just their operational definitions. It involves judgments of conceptual evidence, empirical evidence, and a credible result.*

Let us examine the five judgments that make up internal validity (LP) in some detail, starting with the two that constitute the conceptual evidence:

Initial Conceptual Evidence: (1) Explanation Credibility

Explanation credibility is a judgment of the credibility of the rationale of a study: the discussion and definition of the constructs involved in the study and the explanation of their interrelationships expressed as a question, hypothesis, prediction, or model.

What was the first thing that struck you about the Zimbardo study?[5] It probably was the rationale for proposing that paranoia might be related to the chain of events that begins when elderly persons do not realize their hearing is gradually disappearing. They no longer understand what is occurring in a previously comfortable social context. They become angry and confused and perceive the environment as hostile. This explanation is well presented, and it makes the study interesting and the results plausible. The hypothesis sets the stage for the rest of the study: "paranoia is sometimes an end product of an initially rational

---

[4]This chapter focuses on studies that explain or validate generalizable casual propositions. But do the criteria of internal validity (LP) and external validity (GP) have relevance for studies other than those setting forth such generalizations? For descriptive studies, for instance, like the famous *Streetcorner Society?* Through its description of the life of lower-class men, it is clear that the author expects the reader to see their behavior as quite reasonable given the circumstances in which they find themselves. Certainly this is very similar to an explanation. Further, the wide acceptance and acclaim the study has received derives from the credibility of the description (explanation credibility), the accurate translation of observations into the concepts used in the description (translation fidelity), the reasonableness of event following event rather than taking other paths (demonstrated result and alternative explanations eliminated), and it is not contradicted by other research (credible result)—all aspects of internal validity (LP).

Similarly, because the author hopes we will develop empathy for these men, and perhaps learn useful things for our own lives, there is a sense in which these descriptions are expected to generalize akin to external validity (GP).

So although application is not as straightforward as with studies yielding generalizations, clearly the criteria of internal validity (LP) and external validity (GP) have some relevance and applicability for descriptive studies as well.

[5]Please skim or reread the Zimbardo study, pages 6–9, to refresh your memory of it. We will be frequently referring to it both in this chapter and the next.

search to explain a perceptual discontinuity, in this case, being deaf without knowing it" (end of paragraph 3, page 7, of this text).

This first judgment of whether the study has explanation credibility is critical. If the explanation is plausible, we are willing to pursue the rest of the study to see whether the proposed relationship is borne out by the data. If it is not, we may only reluctantly pursue it. Einhorn and Hogarth (1986) note that if we do not perceive a reasonable causal link, we may still refuse to attribute causality despite the evidence.[6] Certainly, we will read it exceedingly critically because it will need to meet a high standard of evidence to be persuasive. Note that one of the strengths of the Zimbardo study was its explanation credibility; it is often the first item students discussing it note as a strength.

> ✦   Explanation credibility *is a judgment of the plausibility of a proposed relationship's explanation or rationale, built as it is on previous research and thought.*

More Conceptual Evidence: (2) Translation Fidelity

What is the next thing that attracts your attention as you read the Zimbardo article? After ending the explanation with the statement of the expected relationship, the hypothesis, the article begins an extensive description of how the study was carried out. This requires translating the various aspects of the hypothesized relationship into the choices that form the design of the study, the *5 W's and an H* of Chapter 4:

Who	Subjects	*Who* are they?
Where	Situation	*Where* did it take place?
Why (the cause)	Treatment	This is *why* something would have been expected to occur.
What (the effect)	Observation or measurement	These tell *what* occurred.
How	Basis for sensing attributes or changes	This tells us *how* we know an effect occurred.
When	Procedure	*When* subjects received what treatment, observations, or measures where they received it and when and where the effect was to occur.

---

[6]Einhorn and Hogarth (1986) explain that the inference of causation depends on the contextual field; the study's explanation, rationale, point of view, or theory describes this field. They note Mackie's statement (1965, 1974) that this field focuses us on the part of the causal chain involved in the phenomenon, distinguishing it as the "figure" from its background. (The causal chain also points to the background as an important field within which alternative explanations of the event should be sought.)

The hypothesis already translates *perceptual discontinuity* as "in this case, being deaf without knowing it." But such terms as *paranoia* and *deafness* have to be translated. They have to be operationalized—used in this study in ways faithful to their meaning in the hypothesis. This faithful translation is aptly termed **translation fidelity**. What does translation fidelity mean in the Zimbardo article? To see, we shall examine each of the six links of the design.

Subjects. Subjects are the *who*, the individuals chosen to be studied. For internal validity (LP) purposes, subjects can be anyone to whom the question, hypothesis, prediction, or model applies.

You probably decided that the use of college students in place of elderly in Zimbardo's study was a weakness of the study, that the translation fidelity was not good. The study's rationale leads us to believe that the subjects should be from among the elderly. Although the origin of the study was a problem of the elderly, the hypothesis is more general, stating that "paranoia results from a rational search to explain a perceptual discontinuity." It applies to *anyone* experiencing a perceptual discontinuity of *any* kind.[7]

The experimenters could not ethically test elderly subjects' hearing and then allow them to misinterpret their social world. A necessary condition in terms of choice of subjects for internal validity (LP) is that they be an example of subjects to whom the hypothesis would apply; college students are.

Situation. Situation is the *where*, the location of the study. For internal validity (LP) purposes—like subjects—any situation to which the question, hypothesis, prediction, or model would apply is appropriate.

As with subjects, you may have decided that the substitution of the laboratory situation for a social situation involving elderly persons was a weakness of the Zimbardo study. Consider, however, whether features of the normal social situation omitted in the laboratory are essential to the relationship expressed in the hypothesis. All that is important is that the situation be one where the phenomenon can be displayed—where there can be social interplay allowing individuals to discover that they can't understand the conversation. Thus, the laboratory was an appropriate situation. Furthermore, by bringing the study into the laboratory, the social situation could be controlled so that it was almost identical for each of the subjects. In examining the next three links of design we shall see the importance of this.

Treatment. Treatment is the *why*, the cause in the presumed relationship. In Zimbardo, the treatment is a sequence of three events: (1) the hypnosis of the

---

[7]For example, the proposition might apply to persons with Alzheimer's disease who cannot remember from moment to moment even that they have a memory problem. Often, someone will refer to something that occurred earlier that the affected individuals don't believe occurred. If they still trust their own senses more than they trust those of other people, they come to distrust others and view the world as hostile.

subjects; (2) three alternative posthypnotic suggestions; and (3) the social situation, which called the subjects' attention to the sensory anomaly and resulted in efforts to explain it. Each phase has to be operationally defined. The posthypnotic suggestions were operationally defined by tape recordings randomly assigned to the subjects. The social interaction leading to the discovery of the sensory anomaly was operationally defined as the role-playing of a "well-rehearsed standard conversation" by two confederates. Note the efforts to standardize all contact with the subjects, by using slides and rehearsed conversation, so that each experiences as nearly as possible the same situation and treatment. We will refer to this standardization later in discussing *rival explanations eliminated*.

Although we are told that the subjects were trained in self-hypnosis and heard "deep-relaxing" music, we are never told exactly how the hypnosis was accomplished. Zimbardo expects us to trust him that this was done well and properly. Because unrecognized partial deafness is essential to the study, and the experimenters couldn't intentionally make people really partially deaf, the use of hypnosis to create this condition temporarily is a clever solution, provided that we accept hypnosis as a tool capable of creating the condition.

Note that the treatment in this case was administered in a laboratory-type situation. But treatments are sometimes given under natural conditions, as in a study of the effects of intentionally varied housing designs (for example, the effect on security and privacy when residents can enter their apartments directly in contrast to when all must first pass through a single door to reach their apartments) or naturally occurring conditions (for example, studying the effect of these configurations in existing housing).

The complexities of representing a treatment are considered in Chapter 20. Here, suffice it to note that the treatment used in the study should faithfully represent at least one appropriate version of the treatment.

Observations and Measures. Observations and measures are the *what*, the measures of the effect showing that when the cause is present, the effect appears. The effect, paranoia, must be defined operationally. Zimbardo accomplished this by using both established and new tests as well as observations. The established measure was the Minnesota Multiphasic Personality Inventory (MMPI), a commonly used clinical tool. The new instrument, a clinically derived paranoia scale, had been used for an earlier study. Two unseen judges served as observers and rated the social interaction of all three groups for paranoid behavior. Note that three different types of measures of paranoia were used, possibly to assure the audience that paranoia really did occur. Readers can take their choice of whichever measure they trust most; all showed the effect. Surely, one of the three indicators should be acceptable as a measure of paranoia to those among whom Zimbardo hopes to form a consensus. Clearly included in translation fidelity is the judgment that the measures or observations meet the technical standards of good measures. These characteristics known as test validity and test reliability are discussed in Chapter 18.

There is another reason for using multiple measures, however: When all these measures indicate the same result, we are additionally sure of the outcome.

A surveyor establishes a particular location not with one measurement but by triangulation—that is, using two or more sightings from different angles.[8] Known as the **multiple-measure, multiple-method procedure**, such triangulation ensures that the result is not dependent on the peculiar characteristics of a single measure or of a measurement method. In the Zimbardo case, with multiple measures we find that each of three different, imperfect measures indicates the same outcome—triangulation support for the fact that the effect did occur. *Multiple method* in this instance refers to seeking agreement between two different ways of gathering data: the *self-reporting* involved in both the MMPI and the experimenters' own paranoia scale, and *observation* by the observers. Both should, and did, give us similar results.

In making a judgment regarding translation fidelity of measures or observations (or of the treatment, if it is subject to monitoring to assure proper treatment administration), we look for empirical evidence (data) on which we can base the judgment, and we also make a conceptual judgment about the fit of the measures to what is intended. If tests are used, we expect evidence of test validity and reliability; if observation scales are used, we require evidence of objectivity and, if two or more raters are used, interrater reliability (all are discussed in Chapter 18).

Basis for Sensing Attributes or Changes. The basis for sensing the particular effect of interest or the changes that resulted from treatment is the *how*. A useful way to show that a relationship exists is to demonstrate that the effect is present when the cause is also present and absent when the cause is absent. We could compare subjects with themselves under the two conditions or compare comparable groups. The Zimbardo study used the comparable groups condition, assigning subjects to three treatment groups at random so that they would be comparable. Two of the groups were alike in that both involved partial deafness, but they differed in knowledge of the deafness. The aware group would expect and understand the sensory deficit. The researchers used a third group with a different posthypnotic suggestion (itchy ear) to eliminate a rival explanation, posthypnotic suggestion with amnesia.

Discussions of the criteria for determining causality have involved some of the best philosophic minds over the centuries and are too extensive to recapitulate here. But you might note that the aforementioned design is only one of many suggestive of causation. For example, some other criteria are Hume's three: the cause, *A*, always precedes or is contemporaneous with effect, *B*; *A* is always present when *B* occurs; and a plausible mechanism links them. Additionally:

- With increases or decreases in *A*, *B* increases or decreases (possibly the opposite of changes in *A*).
- *B* never occurs before *A*.

---

[8]You will meet the concept of triangulation again several times in this book as a way of confirming the interpretation of evidence by viewing it through different "lenses" and from "different angles." In particular, it will importantly reappear in qualitative research and in measurement.

- A pattern of change in *A* is reflected in *B*.
- Everything present that is not *A* does not result in *B*, so the cause lies in *A*.
- A baseline of change in *B* is changed by the presence of *A*.

There are indeed additional conditions, but the point is that the basis for sensing attributes and changes link must include such criteria. They are embodied in the logic used in qualitative research in selecting data to link variables and in experimental designs used in quantitative research. Additionally, such criteria of causality are reflected in the other judgments included in internal validity (LP): the requirement of an explanation, that the explanation be correctly operationalized, that it be verified by the data, that it cannot reasonably be replaced by an alternative, and that it be consistent with previous research and appear to be replicable in a subsequent study.

Procedure. The *when*, the description of the study's steps, defines the operations involved in procedure. These include who received what treatment, when and how they received it, who was observed and measured, and where this was done. Note that besides ensuring comparable experiences for individuals among the three groups, the standardized procedure was designed such that the investigator, accomplices, and observers were not privy to the subjects' treatment assignment; these were given by tape recordings delivered through headphones. Judges were "blind" to what to expect from a subject.

The two links in the chain of reasoning, *basis for sensing attributes or changes* and *procedure,* are critical facets of design where causation is to be inferred. They provide important cues to causation: precedence of cause before effect, contiguity of cause with effect, indicators of change from some base state to a new one as the presumed result of one or more intervening causative agents, and—with a change in the state of the cause—a congruent pattern of change in the effect. When the effect is delayed rather than contiguous, a strong, plausible explanation is required for the delay.

The above review of the translation of each of the design links in the chain of reasoning into operational aspects of the Zimbardo study conveys the importance of this judgment to internal validity. It is critical and often the weak link of a research investigation. Indeed, if you review the list of strengths and weaknesses on pages 10 and 11, you will notice that many of them are concerned with translation fidelity. Without an accurate translation of the hypothesis, question, prediction, or model into the actual steps in a study, we do a different study from the intended one. If the gap in translation is serious, the evidence that is provided may be totally irrelevant. Translation fidelity is a second critical judgment in the sequence determining internal validity (LP).

◆ Translation fidelity *is the faithfulness of the design choices to the meaning of the question, hypothesis, prediction, or model as defined by the study's explanation or rationale. The design choices operationalize the concept in the explanation or rationale.*

Initial Empirical Evidence: (3) Demonstrated Result

What evidence contributes to a strongly **demonstrated result**? Data show these four attributes:

- Authenticity of the evidence.
- Precedence of cause.
- Presence of effect.
- Congruence of explanation and evidence.

Let us examine each of these attributes more closely.

Authenticity of Evidence. Although authenticity is important in any study, it is of particular concern in historical studies. It asks the question, "Is the evidence what it purports to be?" If we claim that the moldering notebook in our library is Napoleon's diary, we must have convincing evidence that it is. We assume that scores on a test were the result achieved by a certain individual. Can we be sure that someone else did not take the test in that person's stead or help that person with it? If the test was a take-home, this claim is not assured. Thus, **authenticity of evidence** is a legitimate concern we must be prepared to answer if we are to accept the evidence as authentic.

Precedence of Cause. The cause appears prior to or at the same time as the effect, never the reverse. If a person is nervous and smokes cigarettes, does the smoking cause the nervousness? Only if we have evidence that smoking started before or at the same time as the nervousness can we show **precedence of cause**. Precedence, obvious in laboratory experiments, is more difficult to establish definitively in natural situations. Often, because we didn't know until later what causal factor we should have been attending to, it may not be in our records.

Presence of Effect. With an experimental treatment, we are sure there was an intended cause, but was there an effect? We need no statistical test to know that penicillin is effective; however, most behavioral science effects are not so obvious. A small effect in the proper direction may be a chance deviation caused by sampling or other error. We use statistics to minimize the likelihood that a chance deviation is mistaken for **presence of an effect**. This assumes, however, that the correct statistics were used, were properly interpreted, and were sensitive enough to show a significant treatment result if one occurred. Cook and Campbell (1979) refer to these latter characteristics as *statistical conclusion validity*.

Congruence of Explanation and Evidence. Astronomy is not an experimental science, yet we consider it a strong one. Why? Its explanations prove to be good predictors; there is **congruence of explanation and evidence**. Einhorn and Hogarth (1986) note that we typically expect both contiguity of cause and effect and congruity of the effect to the cause. By congruity we mean, for instance, that a large cause would be expected to provide a large effect and a small cause a small one. When there are both contiguity and congruence, causation is often inferred with few conceptual links. When either contiguity or congruence is lacking, and especially when both are, a strong conceptual "bridge" is required for the inference to be made. When such explanations are provided and the effect appears as expected (for example, inferring causality of pregnancy from intercourse where both contiguity and congruence are lacking), this is potent evidence of causality.

Evidence for causality is most impressive when:

- *The effect follows a detailed prediction.* For example, one can accurately predict when the effect will appear, how it will do so, in what strength in relation to that of the effect, and so on. These are convincing aspects of astronomy; astronomers tell us where to look, when, and for what magnitude of heavenly body. Although there are few instances in the behavioral sciences where we can make such precise predictions, we can aspire to do so. The principle is sound.
- *The effect follows the pattern of a manipulated cause.* This cause-and-effect pattern is probably the most compelling evidence of all. The more complex the causal pattern, the stronger the evidence for causality. Would we not be convinced that a strong causal link exists between food coloring and emotionally disturbed behavior if we can show that the behavior appears when the coloring is in food eaten? Disappears when absent? Is greater when more coloring is added? Less frequent with less? That such behavior parallels even a random pattern of coloring devised by an independent observer? Such evidence can be produced by experimental time-series designs (discussed in Chapter 20).

The empirical support for inferring causation includes evidence of the following:
- *That the evidence was authentic—it was what it purported to be.*
- *That the cause preceded the effect—precedence of cause.*
- *That an effect did occur and, if statistics were used to sense it, that they were used correctly and were appropriately sensitive.*
- *That there was congruence between the explanation and the evidence of the effect. The evidence is weightier if there was a detailed and accurate prediction and/or an effect parallels a randomly varied cause.*

Let us examine the Zimbardo study with these four conditions in mind. Much of the responsibility for *authenticity of evidence* rests with the researcher. Typically the reader trusts the researcher. As noted in Chapter 10 and discussed further in Chapter 25, such trust is occasionally misplaced, but most researchers do not consider this a problem. There is certainly no reason to mistrust Zimbardo and his associates; he is an established researcher, and the article appeared in a respected journal with careful peer review and high standards.

Precedence of cause is easy to determine in an experiment such as Zimbardo's because the procedure used assures it. The next condition is that *an effect is found.*

In a quantitative study, we typically use statistics, as Zimbardo did. Without explaining the two columns on the right of Table 1 on page 9, the differences in the mean (average) scores of the groups in the first three columns of the table are apparent. Thus, for the moment, we can accept the researchers' interpretation of these statistics as showing that the paranoia of the treated group exceeded that of the other groups on all the measures.

Was the *effect congruent with the explanation or rationale* and its translation into a hypothesis, prediction, or model? Clearly in Zimbardo's case it was. All four conditions were met, and we have a demonstrated result.

> ✦ *A* demonstrated result *appears when the evidence is authentic, there was precedence (or concurrence) of cause, and an effect occurred as was expected in terms of the relationship described by the hypothesis, prediction, or model.*

More Empirical Evidence: (4) Rival Explanations Eliminated

Rival explanations eliminated is a judgment of whether there are equally plausible rival explanations that account for the data as well as the proposed explanation and whether these can be ruled out or rendered implausible.

Returning to Zimbardo, so far the study has met our criteria: The paranoia appeared when and where expected. Is there any other reasonable explanation for its appearance? Only when all reasonable rival or **alternative explanations** have been eliminated from consideration can we be comfortable at interpreting the data as demonstrating the expected relationship. There are nearly always a variety of possible alternative explanations, some close to the mark, some farfetched. It is the responsibility of the researcher to anticipate any rival explanations that the audience might consider reasonable and to design the study to render them implausible. A common way is to be sure that the alternative possible causative factors are present both when the treatment is present and when it is not. If the effect occurs only when the treatment is present, regardless of the presence or absence of the other factor, the alternative factor is not the cause. In the Zimbardo study, the researchers ruled out rival explanations in several ways.

There were two nontreatment groups: one of them partially deaf, the other with an itchy ear. The intent was to rule out posthypnotic suggestion as a cause of paranoia. If it had been the cause, the itchy ear group would have had as high an incidence of paranoia as the deafness groups. It didn't.

Random assignment of the subjects to the groups plus random assignment of the groups to treatment prevented the researcher from ensuring that the group most favorable to the hypothesis received the treatment. Furthermore, after the tapes for the treatment instructions were played in their headphones, the groups were exposed to exactly the same procedure. The posthypnotic suggestion and all succeeding directions were given by slides so that the two partially deaf groups would not be disadvantaged. The confederates conducted a "well-rehearsed standard conversation" for all the groups. This made unlikely the possibility that the social interaction situation for the groups might have varied and therefore might have been the cause of the difference in paranoia. Finally—and this is a critical feature—no one having contact with the subjects knew to which of the three groups a given subject belonged. In research terms, the judges were kept blind— they could not have favored the experimental group even if they had tried.

Clearly the researchers tried to anticipate many of the possible rival explanations and eliminated them in their design of the study. Note that the design of the study is the prime protection against these rivals. If we are to satisfy this criterion, rival explanations must be anticipated and the study so designed that they are eliminated.

> ✦ *For the projected explanation or rationale to be accepted, all reasonable rival or alternative explanations of the data must be eliminated.* Rival explanations eliminated *is the judgment of whether this has been accomplished.*

Final Judgment: (5) Credible Result

Credible result is the final judgment that sums the previous evidence, both conceptual and empirical. It also includes an examination of the external evidence to see whether this study is consistent with earlier studies. (This assumes, of course, that they don't all have the same flaws or, should that occur, that the researcher is capable of spotting them.) It results in a final judgment of how strongly we can infer that the study would create a consensus that the proper interpretation of the evidence links the variables in a relationship.

In the Zimbardo study, the four earlier judgments are all positive: the conceptual evidence of explanation credibility and translation fidelity and the empirical evidence of demonstrated result and rival explanations eliminated. The evidence is consistent with the literature, and there is no directly comparable study. We conclude that the study has strong internal validity (LP).

> ✦ Credible result is *a judgment that sums up the four earlier judgments and asks whether in terms of external prior evidence we can believe the result. It is a judgment of the extent to which the uncertainty regarding the existence of the relationship has been removed.*

Relationship of Internal Validity (LP) to the Chain of Reasoning

The five successive judgments of internal validity (LP) draw their evidence from the successive links of the chain of reasoning. Showing them in relation to the chain is instructive and provides an easy way to remember them (Fig. 7.1).

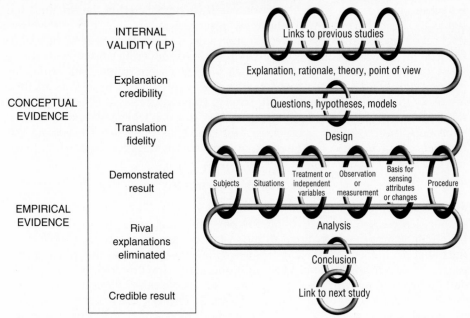

FIGURE 7.1 The judgments of internal validity (LP) superimposed on the chain of reasoning.

Each of the judgments in internal validity (LP) *can be placed alongside a certain part of the chain of reasoning where we find evidence used in making that judgment.*

Internal Validity (LP) and External Validity (GP) as Reduction in Uncertainty

Just as knowledge is better viewed as a reduction in uncertainty (instead of an all-or-none, true-or-false matter), so is internal validity (LP). In this instance, we are reducing our uncertainty that the relationship exists in the circumstances in which it was investigated. The better the study meets the criteria of internal validity, the greater the reduction in uncertainty.

In a similar vein, external validity (GP) is also a reduction in uncertainty—a reduction in the uncertainty that the relationship generalizes beyond the circumstances in which it was studied.

Patterns of the "Basis for Sensing Attributes or Changes" Link That Facilitate Inferences of Causation

An important link in the design section of the chain of reasoning is the "basis for sensing attributes or changes" link. This is the patterning of the situation (assuming we have some control of it) so that we can infer the relationship of the events—

we sense a change as a result of a treatment. If we do not control the situation, the link is the logic that we use to selectively observe events to infer a relationship—the basis for sensing the attribute(s) responsible. In 1843, John Stuart Mill elaborated on Sir Francis Bacon's recommendations for discovering causes in a series of what he called "canons," because he believed they were fundamental rules for proving causation. We now realize that they are not methods of proof; indeed, they are really impossible conditions. Although their conditions cannot be completely fulfilled, they describe the logic we use to infer causation when we believe we have sufficiently fulfilled their conditions. Mill called his patterns of reasoning the methods of agreement, of differences, of concomitant variation, and of residuals.

Method of Agreement

Mill (1868) formulated the method of **agreement** thus: "If two or more instances of the phenomenon under investigation have only one circumstance in common, the circumstance in which alone all the instances agree, is the cause (or effect) of the given phenomenon" (p. 428). It is extremely rare, of course, that phenomena, especially social phenomena, have only one aspect in common and everything else differs. Yet, by confining ourselves to reasonable possibilities, this is a commonly used logic for finding potential causes. To return to the Kounin example of Chapter 3, Kounin noted that smooth transitions by teachers was a common characteristic of classrooms where disturbed children were not acting out. Although not proof, it was suggestive of a causal relationship.

The method of agreement is often used with observation and descriptive case studies. It is the logic that underlies qualitative methods, the subject of Chapters 11–15, and is exemplified in the Hoffmann-Riem study of Chapter 1 (the common attribute across different adopting families was seeking normalization.)

The negative form of the method of agreement is also useful: Nothing can be the cause of a phenomenon that is not a common circumstance in all instances of the phenomenon. This method eliminates potential causes that were not present where the effect occurred. However, like the banning of carcinogens in food where presence is a matter of degree, it is sometimes difficult to define what we mean by "presence."

Method of Differences

The method of **differences** combines the method of agreement with its negative form and is the logic used in experiments. In practice, this calls for two groups as alike as possible, one of which, the experimental group, is exposed to the experimental variable, while the other, the control group, is not. If the effect shows only in the experimental group, we infer causation. Experimentation is probably the most strongly accepted evidence of causation.

The method of differences also requires an impossible condition—two identical situations. In reality, no two individuals are identical and no one is identical from moment to moment. Attaining sufficient functional equivalence for the logic to be effective is one of the most important aspects of experimental design. We shall give this logic much greater scrutiny in Chapter 20.

Method of Concomitant Variation

The method of **concomitant variation** is often used where it is not possible to manipulate situations experimentally. For example, it is used in correlational studies to determine how a measure of success such as future college grade point average can be predicted from the characteristics of students applying for admission.

This method determines whether cause and effect vary together in some regular way. Unfortunately, however, two things may vary together because of a common link in their casual chain instead of being directly causally related. A colleague of mine, Si Halperin, uses the illustration that, plotted over the elementary school grades, reading ability is related to weight. It is true that sixth-graders both weigh more and read better than first-graders, but would overfeeding first-graders improve their reading capacity? Of course not! Both vary with a third variable, the passage of time, so one must be wary of assuming causation with covariation.

The method of concomitant variation can be used to rule out potential causes since, usually, if something does not vary with an effect it cannot be the cause. Because level of poverty does not vary with artistic ability, it cannot be considered a cause (artists don't have to suffer to be good). Step function effects are an exception, however—effects that do not appear until some threshold (the "step") is reached. Combustion is an example. One doesn't get an increasingly visible flame as heat builds up; rather it bursts into flame as the ignition threshold is reached. One must be careful in making assumptions about the nature of the cause.

Method of Residuals

The method of **residuals**, more often used in natural science research, is rare in behavioral science research. This method asks us to account for as much of the situation as we can on the basis of prior work, and the cause is to be found in the residue not accounted for. This method is regularly used in trouble-shooting. A mechanic working on a stalled car pulls a wire from a spark plug to test for failure of the high-voltage electric system. If okay, the culprit is another system—carburetor, fuel pump, timing, and so on. The mechanic then checks these in order of their likelihood of failure.

Clearly the method of residuals works best in a well-explored system of limited scope. In comparison with the natural sciences, problems in the behavioral sciences tend to have fuzzy boundaries, broad scope, and less firm knowledge about constituent parts that would permit their elimination.

Possible Comparison Patterns of the "Basis for Sensing Attributes or Changes" Link

The logic of the "basis for sensing attributes or changes" link has only so many possibilities. We can compare an individual's present behavior with past or future behavior. Alternatively, this can be compared with that of other people in natural situations or ones designed for the study. It is therefore possible to lay these out in

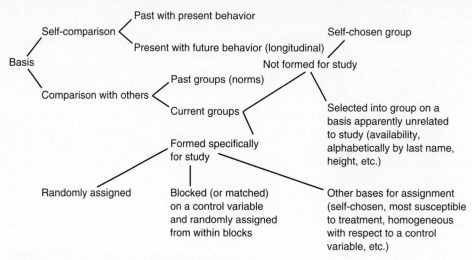

FIGURE 7.2 A decision tree of possible alternatives for the "basis for sensing attributes or changes" link in the chain of reasoning.

a decision tree like the one in Figure 7.2. The tree suggests alternatives to be considered in any study.

Can Causation Ever Be Inferred?

Mill's methods assume a single cause; they are not as successful in cases of multiple causation. This flaw is especially obvious with the method of residuals, as many car owners have discovered the hard way. Singularly a weak spark plug or a bad fuel mixture might not cause engine failure; together they may do so. A mechanic looking for a single cause might pass over each as adequate.

Mill's methods are often stronger when they are used in combination. The method of concomitant variation combined with the method of differences can show not only an effect, but also that it is related to strength of cause. For example, suppose we place food coloring in increasing concentration in a series of batches of processed food. We can show that presence of the food coloring only above a certain level causes hyperactivity in children (the method of differences), and by showing that the degree of hyperactivity corresponds to the level of concentration above the critical level (the method of concomitant variation), we have strong evidence of a causal relation.

Although Mill's methods describe the logic of single studies, we are increasingly going beyond them. Meta-analysis, a way of combining studies quantitatively that is described in Chapter 21, is proving to be a strong method of providing evidence for causal propositions. Replication of a study provides its ultimate validation—combining studies that are in some ways replications of one another provides strong evidence. Furthermore, depending on what evidence is available, a meta-analysis can plot the nature of the causal relation, show how it is affected by other variables, and determine where evidence is needed for more complete understanding.

Still another method of interest is causal modeling. If we can construct a model showing how variables are related in a situation, such causal modeling will describe whether these relationships are borne out by the data and show the fit of the model to the evidence. A model that fits well can be quite convincing.

The caveats of this chapter are well worth bearing in mind along with the possible complexities of inferring causation. It is evident, however, that we can and do construct strong evidence for causal relationships, and our methods of doing so are continuously improving.

- ✦ *The "basis for sensing attributes or changes" is a key link in the chain of reasoning for inferring causation.*
- ✦ *The logic described by Mill is used in our research methods and is embodied in the "basis for sensing attributes or changes" link. Mill proposed:*
  1. *The method of agreement (used in case studies and in historical studies).*
  2. *The method of difference (used in experimental studies).*
  3. *The method of concomitant variation (used in predictive studies and in studies examining data gathered after an event has occurred, after-the-fact natural experiments).*
  4. *The method of residuals.*
- ✦ *We approximate Mill's conditions as closely as possible, add such conditions as we can to strengthen the logic, and often combine the methods to support our inferences.*
- ✦ *New methods are improving our bases for inferring causation. For example, meta-analysis quantitatively combines the findings of studies and provides strong evidence for causation. We must be cautious, however, and bear in mind the complexities of causation.*

SUMMARY

This chapter has focused on some of the complexities in the concept of causation. For example, any statement of causation emphasizes a part of a causal chain that leads to the effect. Understanding this relationship helps to draw attention to the rest of the causal chain, which may be more amenable to study or control. Use of the term *causation* tends to imply that the world has a mechanical, clocklike nature, a view that some social scientists do not accept. Some prefer a cloudlike conception that yields predictions only in terms of probabilities or odds. Added to these complexities are the many possible causal patterns. If the simple *A causes B* does not fit the evidence, a variety of other patterns of causation should be considered.

Internal validity (LP) and external validity (GP) are two major criteria by which studies are judged. They are distinguished from internal validity and external validity as defined by Campbell and Stanley (1963) and Cook and Campbell (1979) in that they are more inclusive, encompassing conceptual as well as empirical evidence, and imply a relationship between the concepts involved, not just their operational definitions. Internal validity (LP) is the power of a study to create a consensus that the appropriate interpretation of the evidence is that the variables are linked in a relationship—that is, its linking power (LP). External validity (GP) is the power to create a consensus that the appropriate interpretation of the evidence is that the relationship has generality beyond the circumstances in which it was studied—that is, its generalizing power (GP).

Each of these validities consists of five parallel judgments. Internal validity (LP) consists of two kinds of conceptual evidence, explanation credibility and translation fidelity; two kinds of empirical

evidence, demonstrated result and alternative explanations eliminated; and a final summary judgment, credible result.

A Look Ahead

You are already aware that external validity (GP) consists of a set of judgments parallel to those of internal validity. Because in generalizing we are extrapolating from the sample of evidence on hand, we will consider external validity in the context of sampling. These are the subjects of Chapter 8.

ADDITIONAL READING

Many useful treatments of causation go beyond this discussion. Examples are Ellsworth (1977) in psychology, Köbben (1973) in anthropology, and Hage and Meeker (1988) in sociology. Chapter 1 of Cook and Campbell (1979) is a clear and readable summarization of the progression of the philosophical positions. Guba and Lincoln (1982b) similarly summarize them and argue for abandonment of causation

for "plausible explanations," a construct especially congruent with qualitative positions. See also the early sections of Messick (1989).

For treatments of internal validity, Brinberg and McGrath (1985); Campbell and Stanley (1963); Cook and Campbell (1979); Cronbach (1982); Krathwohl (1985); and Kruglanski and Kroy (1976);

IMPORTANT TERMS

Agreement (method of)
Authenticity of evidence
Causal chain
Concomitant variation (method of)
Congruence of explanation and evidence
Credible result
Demonstrated result
Differences (method of)
Disconfirmation
Explanation credibility
External validity
External validity (GP)

Generalization
Internal validity
Internal validity (LP)
Multiple measure, multiple method procedure
Necessary and sufficient conditions
Operational definition
Precedence of cause
Presence of an effect
Residuals (method of)
Rival explanations eliminated
Translation fidelity

APPLICATION PROBLEMS

1. Considering the definition of causation given in this chapter, how would you comment on the age-old question, "Which comes first, the chicken or the egg?"

2. Assume you are an elementary school teacher conducting an interview with the parents of a student who has consistently demonstrated low achievement. They claim that the "real" reason for

their child's performance is that he is "lazy." How would you answer them?

3. Weiner's attribution theory (1972, 1980a, 1980b) identifies several "causes" to which individuals "attribute" (use to explain) success or failure, including ability, effort, task difficulty, luck, mood, illness, and help from others. Each of these causes, Weiner asserts, shows the presence or absence of three properties: (1) stability (consistency of the attribution over time, as with luck versus ability), (2) controllability (degree to which the cause is under the person's control, such as mood versus illness), and (3) locus of control (whether the cause has an origin internal or external to the person, as in effort versus task difficulty). These are all factors in an individual's understanding of an outcome. Thus, future behavior is determined by a person's perception of these causes. Are these factors truly causes, or are some of them effects? How does this theory fit the definition of causation outlined in this chapter?

4. You are a researcher who is interested in the effect of cognitive styles on learning. It is your conviction that independent of ability, some individuals tend to be impulsive in their approach to learning activities, whereas others are more reflective. You set up an experimental study to determine whether these styles exist. What

conceptual evidence can you provide to show the validity of your idea?

5. You are a psychologist with a deep interest in the age-old practice of astrology. You suspect that there may be some validity to the belief that astrological sign determines aspects of personality. Consequently, you decide to try to show that people who are born under the sign of Taurus tend to be more stubborn than others. What conceptual evidence can you provide for the relationship?

6. Internal validity (LP) applies to qualitative studies as well as to studies like Zimbardo's; indeed, it is of concern wherever a generalization is developed. Use the Hoffmann-Riem study to illustrate the judgments to be made with respect to internal validity (LP) as the Zimbardo study was used in the text.

Compare your answers with those following the Application Exercise.

APPLICATION EXERCISE

Where does your selected problem fall in the causal chain? What part of the chain have you chosen? The most important part? The most recent? The most easily explored? What pattern of causation do you expect to find? Might others apply? After considering the various causation possibilities, have you changed your mind about what to expect?

Consider the internal validity of your problem. Do you have a strong explanation or rationale so that it has explanation credibility? Although the translation of the study into operational terms has yet to come, what problems, if any, do you sense

there might be with translation fidelity? Although demonstrated result will have to await the gathering of data, can you think of rival explanations that might be as plausible as your intended explanation? While you'll be more aware of common rival explanations to watch for after studying the research methods of Section Four, what do you anticipate now might be reasonable alternatives? Have you checked the other research evidence regarding your problem? Do you expect yours to be consistent with it? If not, are you attempting to refute prior work?

ANSWERS TO THE APPLICATION PROBLEMS

1. Needless to say, the question does not refer to any specific chicken or any particular egg but to chickens and eggs in general. It addresses the problem of precedence of the cause before the effect and is an example of what appears to be a simple causal pattern that has been, with tongue in cheek, turned around. Did there have to be a chicken egg from which the first chicken hatched? If so, where

did the egg come from? Which was the "cause" and which was the "effect"? Was the egg the cause, by hatching the first chicken (the effect), or was the first chicken the cause, laying the first chicken egg (the effect)? The saying is an example in popular terms of the fact that everything is part of a causal chain, and we use this saying in nonresearch problems to make the causal chain salient.

2. Your answer would naturally depend on the specific circumstances: the particular student, his instructional history, his environment, and so on. You would likely emphasize that patterns leading to low achievement are never simple and that there might be alternative explanations. In effect, there is a causal history to the student's behavior, and its pattern should be explored. Maybe the causes are multiple and affect each other in complex ways. What, for example, is the home situation? Have the parents encouraged or discouraged learning? What is the student's perceived or measured ability level? Has he in the past made an effort but not succeeded? Is he now achieving at his ability level? Is he learning-disabled? What is his medical condition? All are possible explanations for (or factors involved in) his behavior, some of which may be more important than others. It is likely that the cause is some constellation of these factors and not one simple answer (such as "The student is lazy").

3. The causes are probably best explained as all being part of a causal chain in a multiple-cause pattern. Some will be real and some perceived. Not all will be present in any one circumstance, but some group of them will act one on the other or in concert to affect an individual's understanding of a situation. Consequently, they will influence that person's choice of behavior in that situation or in similar ones in the future. Take an individual who normally does poorly on examinations and believes himself to be a poor student. He may prepare well for a test and be successful. Yet instead of identifying the cause of his success as his ability or his effort (or both), he may attribute it to conditions such as luck or the exam being "easy." He might then choose to depend on luck the next time rather than believing in his ability and therefore preparing for the exam. In each case, multiple factors or causes, both real and perceived, produce a behavior.

4. First, consider explanation credibility. Is your rationale plausible? In this case, it makes good sense intuitively that some people respond quickly to situations, while others prefer to take their time and ponder. It is especially apparent in examination situations. Is there existing research evidence that might help explain the idea? In fact, these categories *did* grow out of research into analytic versus global reasoning. Kagen and colleagues (1964) developed a

categorization test (the Conceptual Style Test) to compare the concepts. As a side product of their research, they found that children who adopted an analytic reasoning style took significantly longer to answer the test questions than those who gave relational answers. It led the researchers to wonder whether the tendency to delay responses was a stable characteristic of certain individuals. Their explanatory evidence, then, had its roots in prior research.

Second, consider translation fidelity. How well have you operationalized this explanation? What is your hypothesis here, and how have you designed your study? Kagen and associates (1964) operationalized the concept of *impulsiveness-reflectiveness* by stating it as a tendency to delay a response to a task. Because the hypothesis involved time, it was easily measurable. Furthermore, so was the individual's error rate. Kagen and associates developed another test, the Matching Figures Test, consisting of sets of similar pictures in which the task was to pick out the ones that match exactly. Time and error scores were kept. Individuals were classified as above or below average on each score. An impulsive person would be quick (below average on time) but would make many errors, whereas a reflective person would be slow (above average on time) with few errors. The researchers appear to have soundly operationalized their construct. That their studies were corroborated by other researchers gives evidence of this.

5. The evidence for this concept may not be as easy to provide as for impulsiveness-reflectiveness. Again, consider explanation credibility. To some people, the relationship between signs of the zodiac and personality is intuitively obvious; witness the popularity of astrology columns in many newspapers. To others, the idea of any relationship between personality and star patterns is inherently ridiculous. To the first group, the explanation is plausible, but to the second, it will be a hard sell! You will have to provide strong empirical evidence. Is there any research evidence to support the idea?

Think about translation fidelity. How would you operationalize this concept? Members of the sign of Taurus are indicated by birth date. But you will need a convincing measure of stubbornness. If you do find or develop such a test, you may be able to sense an effect—that is, demonstrate that a relationship exists. Even so, you will have a problem eliminating rival explanations. For example, how will you show that the relationship is caused by the zodiac and not the season of the year? Personality issues are extremely complex, and so are the influences on them.

6. To determine the internal validity (LP) of Hoffmann-Riem, we will have to consider the five judgments that contribute to it: explanation credibility, translation fidelity, demonstrated result, rival explanations eliminated, and credible result.

Explanation credibility: Is her explanation credible? Definitely, it makes good sense that adoptive parents would want to consider theirs to be just like children born to their parents. Hoffmann-Riem elaborates on this theme with quotations such as the one of the father who had "quickly come to believe that the priniciple of biological filiaton is almost irrelevant for an emotional relationship." The explanation she presents together with her description of the process by which normalization develops is entirely credible.

Translation fidelity: The term she uses, *normalization*, seems entirely appropriate to the process she is describing, and she includes sufficient quotations and description of the process so that one has a good grasp both of what the concept of normalization is and how it is operationalized in her data. This close correspondence of concept and operational definition is typical of qualitative studies in which the concept, in this instance normalization, has been developed inductively out of the data.

Demonstrated result: She provides evidence in her quotations that normalization occurs. There seems no reason to doubt these statements of the parents.

Rival explanations eliminated: She is silent on this point. We don't know whether she looked for any, and there are no clues as to what such rivals might be. As a reader, I had none to suggest.

Credible result: She does not give any indication that others have studied this problem, and unless this were one's specialty, one couldn't be expected to know whether these data are consistent with previous literature. Given what evidence we have, however, and assuming her study is not contradicted by other work (given the reasonableness of her findings, this seems not improbable), the study would appear to have strong internal validity (LP).

CHAPTER 8

Sampling, Representation, and External Validity

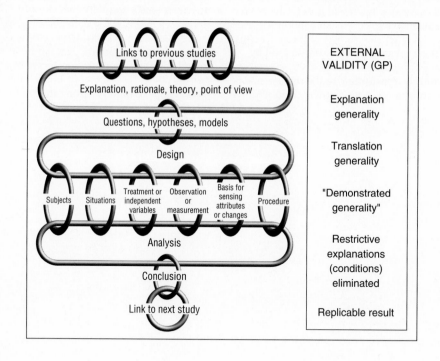

OVERVIEW

The evidence we use to infer how widely a relationship applies—its generality—is defined as the **external validity (GP)** of a study, where GP stands for the power of the study to show generality of the findings. This chapter describes the general principles of sampling; shows how they are used; and because sampling is basic to the inference of generality, examines the evidence used to infer it.

CHAPTER CONTENTS

Introduction

We intuitively use sampling principles in our everyday lives. Although without the formalities, we approximate various sampling methods, unconsciously applying the principles. From the slice we cut off, we judge whether the whole roast is done; from our neighbor's experience with a particular car, we judge whether that model provides reliable transportation—continually making the intuitive leap from a sample to the population or universe, making judgments on the basis of incomplete information. Our essential decisions are of this nature: whether to attend a college on the basis of a brief guided tour, which house or apartment to buy or rent on the basis of a short visit, which job to take after brief interviews. We continually gather information from specific instances and generalize to new ones on the basis of their belonging to a common population of instances. In doing so, we treat information as a representative sample. Thus, sampling is continually present in our lives. But the sampling just described tends to be haphazard, sometimes even biased, instead of methodical. Unfortunately, we often find out too late that the sample we chose was not representative—the neighbor's car was used over the road rather than on short trips, the apartment looks dreary at night compared with a daylight visit, the college's guided tour presented just the best side of college life. Systematically applying sampling principles has the advantage of giving assurance of representativeness.

Just as in daily life, sampling is everywhere in research. Some instances, such as those involved in polling and sample surveys, differ from those involved in historical studies and qualitative work, but the principles of sampling apply in all instances. Wherever our research points to a generalization, the questions are, "What does it tell us about other persons, places, times, and events in our world? What is its generality to persons, places, times, and events beyond the situation in which it was researched?"

The inference of **generality** is derived from the relationship between what is studied, the **sample**, and that piece of the world of which it is a component and of which it is therefore representative. The piece of the world to which we wish to generalize, in sampling, we refer to as the **population** or universe. Populations and universes are made up of units—usually in social science research the units are people or behaviors—and it is these we sample. Because we can interact only with small parts of our world at any given time, we are continually sampling it and, on the basis of what we can see or otherwise sense, making judgments about the rest, which we cannot sense directly.

✦ Sampling procedures *are ways of selecting a small number of units from a population to enable researchers to make reliable inferences about the nature of that population.*

Sampling is used in public opinion and consumer polling to make inferences about how citizens will vote on election day or how consumers will react to a new product or television program. Sampling is used in qualitative research in the selection of interviewees or persons to observe. Sampling is involved in all six facets of design choice. Its use to find subjects and situations is obvious. Its use in measurement and observation is less obvious but important (explored in Chapter 18). So sampling is universal to the methods and is an important tool.

Principles of Sampling

As a child, each of us may recall reaching into a cookie jar so high on a shelf we couldn't see into it. If we wanted to know the contents, we didn't necessarily take the top cookies but reached in, mixed them up, and then drew out a few cookies. We intuitively knew that we could judge from the handful we had withdrawn the freshness or staleness of the cookies we could not see or smell (*the inferential leap from sample to population*).

Further, we understood that the larger the sample of cookies we drew, the more certain we could be in our conclusion about the rest of the cookies. (*Certainty of the inference increases with sample size.*)

We also intuitively understood that if the first one was stale, as was the second, the third, and even the fourth, there was little or no variation in freshness. Thus, even with that small a sample, we inferred the jar contained stale cookies. (*Where there is little variation among the units of the population, a small sample will do.*

If the units are all identical, a sample of one tells the nature of the population.) If the first cookie were quite fresh, the second stale, the third in between, the fourth on the stale side, we would have a hard time judging the average freshness from a small sample. (*All things being equal, a larger sample is required to judge the nature of a highly variable population than one that is homogeneous.*)

Suppose we think the chocolate cookies are larger than the molasses ones in the jar but we aren't sure. How many cookies do we need to examine to find out? It depends. Let's say chocolate cookies vary one from another by as much as half an inch because of different baking conditions and so do molasses cookies. In our cookie jar, the typical chocolate cookie is two inches larger than the molasses, a difference easy to see even given the half-inch variability because of baking conditions. But there is another cookie jar over at a friend's house, and the difference between the chocolate and molasses cookies there is only half an inch. Remember, the normal variation in baking conditions also causes differences of half an inch. This could mask the difference between chocolate and molasses, especially in a small sample that might consist of a bunch of big ones or small ones by accident. In a large sample, differences in baking conditions average out over both the chocolate and molasses cookies such that the average difference in size of the two kinds will be apparent. (*A larger sample is required when a difference we are trying to sense—or estimate—is masked by the normal variation in the sample.*)

Let's stop for a moment and recapitulate what we intuitively know: We are interested in generalizing from a sample to some target we shall call a population or universe. In our example, the contents of the jar were the population about which we wished to infer freshness. As the cookie tale illustrates, sample and target need not be individuals. Although we generally think of populations as consisting of individuals, the terms *population* and *universe* can apply to anything; these words are broadly used in research. For example, we sample not only individuals, but also universes of situations, of instruments, of possible treatments or variables, of possible designs and procedures; each is a realm to be sampled. In the Zimbardo study, the college student sample represented the population of persons who might develop paranoia with an unrecognized sensory deficit. The laboratory interaction of subjects and confederates was representative of social situations. The measures of paranoia were a sample of possible instruments from the universe of measures of paranoia. Each choice stood for, or represented, a target population of persons or a universe of situations or instruments and was intended to allow us to generalize to it. Although there were good reasons for the particular choices made for the study, other choices presumably would have been acceptable. Said in another way, the choices made for that or any study are made from larger sets of alternatives. This same point is illustrated in the classroom seating placement study, p. 68. Other choices presumably could be made from those sets of individuals, situations, measures, and procedures and provide us with the same results. In other words, the study would replicate if it had generality.

 ◆ *Required sample size is related to four factors. A larger sample is necessary:*
   1. *The greater the certainty required of the inferential leap from sample to population. (We want to be absolutely sure the cookies are fresh.)*

2. *The more precise we desire to be about the exact nature of the target popula-tion. (We want to know accurately how fresh they are.)*
3. *The more the units in the sample vary from one another on the characteristic of interest—being heterogeneous rather than homogeneous. (Because if the small sample varies in freshness, it is hard to know just how fresh the cookies are on average.)*
4. *The smaller the effect to be sensed relative to the normal variation among the sampling units. (The variation in cookie size because of normal baking condi-tions is large in relation to the difference in size between two kinds of cookies.)*

Principles one and two above make good intuitive sense. We might do a quick pilot study with few cases, but we intuitively know that it will only approx-imate the results of a larger study. Our faith in the results of the former cannot be as great as it would be in the results of the latter. If we want to know the average height of men precisely, although we might be able to approximate it to the near-est inch with a sample of 20 or so, we can sense intuitively that a much larger sample is required to know it to the nearest hundredth of an inch.

The third principle also seems intuitively true. When the population varies considerably with respect to a characteristic, the cases in any sample typically vary widely on that characteristic as well. A small sample might contain only cases at one extreme of that characteristic (stale cookies). Because of the variabil-ity, we wouldn't know whether the whole population was stale or whether by chance that sample of cookies contained mainly stale cookies and those in the population were mainly fresh. Only with a larger sample is the chance factor minimized.

According to the fourth principle, the sample size is frequently increased to ensure that a study's positive result won't be missed. This is called increasing the sensitivity or power of a study. The waves left behind by a speeding boat are easy to follow long distances when the water has few waves but difficult to see even a short distance behind the boat in a storm. When the normal variability among units of a population is large and the effect we are looking for is small by compar-ison, normal variability may mask consistent differences.

Consider, again, our friend's chocolate and molasses cookies, remembering that in the population, on average, the chocolate cookies are half an inch larger. Remember too that variation in baking conditions can also create differences of half an inch. A small sample might, by chance, consist of a combination of under-sized (normally larger) chocolate cookies baked under unfavorable conditions and oversized (normally smaller) molasses cookies baked under favorable condi-tions. Inferring the relative sizes of the cookies in the population from this small sample, we might judge them equal—no difference in size. With a sample of 1000 cookies, however, favorable and unfavorable baking conditions would average out, and the average size of molasses cookies would be almost the same from sample to sample. So too would a larger sample stabilize the average size of the typically larger chocolate cookies. As a result, any sample of chocolate cookies would have a larger average size than any sample of molasses cookies. The differ-ence is no longer masked by the variations between samples when the samples are large and the averages therefore have little variation.

These principles govern sampling of all kinds. Indeed, it is through the use of these principles that different probability methods of sampling are devised. Hence, we shall refresh our memory of them as we study the various sampling methods.

Probability and Nonprobability Sampling

Sampling methods are typically divided into probability and nonprobability techniques. **Probability sampling** enables us to make inferences about characteristics of the population—for example, the size of its average value on some characteristic or the size of a measure of its variability with some estimate of the margin of error. You have seen announcements of polling results such as: "Johnson was favorably rated by 42 percent of the sample. The poll has a margin of error of plus or minus 3.5 points. This means that, with a confidence expressed by odds of 2 to 1, Johnson's favorable rating in the population is between 38.5 and 45.5." The margin of error and estimates of its size, given specified odds, are the result of reasoning with inferential statistics and probability based sampling. This topic is discussed further in Chapter 19.

All probability samples involve random sampling of units from the population at some stage in the sampling process.[1] If probability samples involve random sampling at some stage in the sampling process, it follows that **nonprobability sampling** does not. For example, the panels used in rating television programs' audience sizes are not random samples but meet the profile of typical families with television receivers. They may indeed be representative of such families, but they are not probability samples, because random sampling did not enter into their choice.

We noted that sampling pervaded all six links at the design level of the chain of reasoning. Where employed, random sampling is usually confined to the subjects link and occasionally the situation one. Nonprobability methods are typically used for the selection of measures, forms of treatments, designs, procedures, and other aspects of the study design. For example, in the choice of treatment involving the teaching of outlining in English composition, we would intentionally choose a particular teaching method. It would be selected to be representative of possible ways of teaching outlining rather than being chosen by randomly sampling. Furthermore, because one can add additional criteria such as ease of use and popularity, nonrandom sampling would be especially appropriate.

Probability Sampling Procedures

The list of units from which we draw the sample in any sampling procedure is called the **sampling frame.** For a survey of teacher morale in a school district, the sampling frame might be a list of all the teachers in the district. The population would be the teachers in the district, and from the data obtained on our sample we would infer the morale of the teachers in the district. A city directory, a faculty directory, a telephone

---

[1]It is from this process that statisticians can construct a probability model. That model allows the construction of statistics that give us probabilities, such as those in the Zimbardo study where there were statistics like (t=2.86, P<.01) and (z=5.00, P<.001) P refers to probability values that come from these inferential statistics, as do such statements as "significant at the 5 percent level."

book, and a club or church membership list are all examples of sampling frames. At some point in the sampling procedure, all probability samples must have a list of the units from which they intend to sample—the sampling frame. Some nonprobability sampling is done without listing the units, just taking what is available.

Problems of nonrepresentativeness can usually be traced to some inadequacy of the sampling frame. A famous case is the *Literary Digest* poll, which had had considerable success in predicting presidential elections using telephone books as a proxy for voter rolls. In 1931, their predicting Herbert Hoover as winner was wrong by a wide margin. Franklin D. Roosevelt's win was missed because their sampling frame excluded the many less well-to-do Democratic-voting families without telephones. (See Kish, 1965, for a discussion of frame problems.)

Simple Random Sampling

Simple **random sampling** is the basic method on which all other methods of probability sampling are built, and they all involve simple random sampling at some stage in the process. It can be defined as follows:

> Simple random sampling *requires that each unit of the population have an equal chance of being selected. A more precise definition is that all possible samples of a given size have an equal opportunity of being selected.*

The definition makes it clear that the choice of any unit is independent of the choice of any other. Recall that before we drew a cookie, we mixed the cookies. That was to ensure that every unit had an equal chance at each drawing. *Note that randomness is provided by the process by which we drew the sample.*

How do we obtain a random sample in research? The first task is to define the population and the sampling unit. The population is that group from which the sample is to be chosen and of which the sample is to be representative. Put another way, the population is the group to which we would expect the results of our study to generalize.

Although we may have a conceptual notion about what the target population should be, it is the translation of this conceptual notion into a sampling frame that makes the concept real and is the determiner of the generality. Suppose a university faculty member, concerned that students do not seem to be achieving as they once did, hypothesizes that they are elsewhere employed while trying to be students. She suggests surveying students regarding their employment while working for a doctoral degree. Sounds straightforward, doesn't it?

But what is the sampling frame? All students, both part-time and full-time? If only full-time students, what defines a full-time student? Those taking nine hours of credit? Aren't graduate assistants who take only six hours full-time students? In some cases, to exclude graduate assistants would exclude whole departments. But, since graduate assistants are not supposed to be employed outside the university, including them artificially lowers the averages for everyone. However we answer these questions, the definition of "full-time graduate student" determines the sampling frame and the population. The population definition clearly is a critical question in designing studies.

Disjunction between the sampling frame and the target population of generalization is the most common problem of simple random sampling. If we want to generalize to all college students, how representative of the target population is one university? The generality we can ascribe to the data of a study is always dependent on the study's operational definition of the population (that is, the sampling frame) and an inferential leap from it to the target population.

Sampling Unit. As might be expected from the chain of reasoning, the unit used in stating the problem is usually the unit used in the hypothesis, the sampling unit, the unit of analysis, and the unit used in stating the conclusion. In the morale survey of a school district cited earlier, the individual teachers in the district would be the sampling unit. But the choice of unit is less clear when we make comparisons between aggregated units. For instance, when we test a new curriculum in a school, we are not interested in how well, as individuals, Johnny did with the new and Rebecca with the old, but in how well Johnny's class did in comparison with Rebecca's. Is our sampling unit here students or classes? Ordinarily the rule to follow is that the **sampling unit** is the smallest unit receiving the treatment. In a typical curriculum study, this would be the class because all students experience the same treatment together rather than independently. Some studies examine both class and individual effects and require that attention be paid to sampling at both levels.

How to Choose Units. Typically, having numbered the units in the sampling frame, we use those numbers to choose the sample. This method can also involve using the page number, column number, and location in the column as a set of numbers to designate each person. In a 20-page, two-column, 25-names-per-column directory, this would be a randomly selected five-digit number. Presumably, as is done with many lotteries, we could enter the numbers on slips and then have someone who is blindfolded draw the required number of slips. Partly because of the labor and partly because of the difficulty of ensuring that the slips are really thoroughly mixed, we more often use a computer to generate random numbers. Alternatively one can, as we used to, use a table of random numbers. The RAND Corporation (1969) has produced a book containing a table of a million random digits.

As long as it provides an equal chance for any number to be chosen, any set of arbitrary rules is satisfactory. For example, using computer generated numbers, if the sampling frame consists of 423 units, choose for your sample each consecutive set of three numbers under 424, ignoring the numbers in between. To find where to start in the RAND book, with eyes closed, open anywhere and place your finger on the page. Use the set of digits under your finger to designate the page on which you begin drawing the sample. Use the pair of numbers immediately to the right to designate the row to start on that page (if there are only 20 rows, take the next pair under 21), and use the next two appropriate pairs to tell where to start in the row. Again, the units in your sample are designated by three successive numbers below 424 in any consistent direction from the starting place.

Representativeness and Bias. Why is so much emphasis placed on randomness? To avoid bias by ensuring that all relevant population characteristics have an equal chance of being represented in a sample. **Bias** occurs when a sample fails to represent the population (Jaeger, 1984). There are many possible causes. Without guidance from random numbers, interviewers sampling individuals in a shopping mall may choose more women or well-dressed people because of unconscious personal preferences. Such factors would clearly bias the sample.

A nice thing about a genuine random sample is that it will, on average, represent *all* characteristics of the population, especially with large samples. Thus we are protected even from characteristics that we were not aware could affect the study. What does that protection mean in practice? Let us suppose that we are interested in how well a new curriculum will fare with the average youngster in a school district. A random sample will, on the average, give us a group that has not only the same average intelligence level as the students in the district, but also the same motivation level and attitude toward whatever subject we are working with—all characteristics that might affect our study. In addition, it has the same average length of fingernails and shoe size—characteristics that probably will not affect our study—as well as exposure to and interest in TV programs—characteristics that might, although we couldn't anticipate such occurrences in advance.

Sample Size—How Big Is Big Enough? Notice that we have always hedged by saying "on average" and "with large samples." How big is big enough? The answer depends on the four principles of sampling we considered earlier: (1) How precise do we want to be, (2) how sure do we want to be of our answer, (3) how much variation is there in what we are studying, and (4) how small an effect do we want to sense in contrast to the normal variation in the sample units? Once we can answer these questions, as we shall see in Chapter 19, there are statistical formulas that tell us how large a sample is required. When using inferential statistics, *this is the only way we can determine needed sample size.* Conventional wisdom, such as "thirty cases are enough," won't do. While these principles apply as well to qualitative research, instead of planning ahead for a certain number of cases, these researchers more often continue gathering additional data until their analysis shows they are learning nothing new.

Are there other things we can do to ensure representativeness besides increase sample size? Indeed, we can use stratified sampling. Recall that a smaller sample will do the job of a larger one where the units are homogeneous. Stratified sampling uses that principle.

Stratified Sampling

Because researchers want to do what they can to ensure representativeness, **stratified sampling** is more common than simple random sampling. Suppose that when we eat some cookies, we notice—maybe because they help retain moisture—that the number of raisins in the cookie is an approximate guide to its freshness. Suppose further that the baker, afraid she might run out of raisins, started by using few but about the same number of raisins in each cookie. Later, realizing she had underestimated her stock, as the last ones approached, she grew more and more generous with each cookie sheet.

Several weeks later, we want to find the batch's freshness. The full range of freshness will be accurately represented, since each cookie sheet filled a jar, by sampling from each one of the jars. Although the number of raisins per cookie differs from jar to jar, each jar is homogeneous. Therefore, the batches' freshness can be represented by a smaller random sample of cookies from each jar than if each had the full range of variation.

This is the process of stratified random sampling: We classify the units in the sampling frame (the cookies) into strata (the jars) on the basis of a characteristic (first to last baked and therefore number of raisins) that, if not properly represented in the sample, might bias our inferences. This reduces the variability of that characteristic in each stratum. Randomly sampling from each stratum allows us to have representativeness yet reduce our sample size (or, using the same size, allows us to be more exact in our estimation of the population characteristic and surer of that estimate).

Proportional Stratified Sampling. The most common form of stratified sampling is **proportional stratified sampling.** Consider the determination of overall mathematics achievement in a junior high school. To ensure proper representation of each grade, we make each grade a stratum and randomly sample within each one, the proportion taken being determined by the size of desired sample in relation to the size of the school. For a sample of 40 from a school of 197 pupils, 20 percent of each stratum would be taken.

Stratification on More Than One Variable. We may stratify on more than one characteristic at a time, for instance, stratifying on gender in addition to grade to ensure proper representation of boys and girls. In a racially mixed neighborhood, we might additionally stratify African-American, Hispanic, Asian, and other minority children as shown in Figure 8.1. With a total of 197 students in the table, to obtain a sample of 50, we would randomly select one-quarter of the students in each cell.

Unless the stratifying variables are independent of each other, we gain little by using more than one characteristic. For example, because at one time most women were not given advanced education, gender and highest level of educa-

Minority:	African-American			Hispanic			Asian			Other		
Grade:	6	7	8	6	7	8	6	7	8	6	7	8
Boys	11	7	7	14	13	16	2	3	1	7	8	6
Girls	13	9	8	16	11	15	2	1	1	9	9	8

FIGURE 8.1 Three-way stratification on the basis of minority, grade, and gender for an achievement study of a junior high school. (The numbers in the boxes indicate the number of students in that cell from which a random sample of pupils would be drawn.)

tion were not independent and stratifying on gender achieved most of the advantage of also classifying on education. With increased education of women, this is no longer true, and the additional stratification is justified. It is rare, however, that more than a triple stratification is advantageous.

Intentional Oversampling. How does one handle situations like Figure 8.1, in which many cells are less than four? With small cell sizes, some groups might not even be present in a small sample. **Oversampling**, taking extra cases, perhaps everyone from those cells, permits us to study these groups separately and then combine them by appropriately weighting each cell. For example, a 25 percent sample of all Asians in Figure 8.1 would be only three students. With only one case in each cell, how would seventh-grade or eighth-grade girls or eighth-grade boys be included? All 10 Asians make up 5 percent of the school but would constitute 20 percent of the sample, an overrepresentation that would better characterize them. When the average achievement of the school is determined, however, they are weighted 10/197, or about 5 percent, their correct proportion in the school, for combination with data from the rest of the strata.

When to Stratify. You should stratify when a bias threat is serious (as, for instance, an unrepresentative religion sample would be in studying the abortion issue) or whenever you can do so easily. By randomly sampling within strata, you do no worse than simple random sampling, although you lose the extra time and energy involved. If stratifying turns out not to be needed, it still gains peace of mind—not an unimportant aspect. By the luck of the draw, ten pennies will come up all heads once in 1024 tosses, but if that one time is your sample it is little consolation that your sample is unusual. It is best to ensure representativeness through stratifying if you either have or can easily obtain accurate information that you need.

Advantages and Disadvantages of Simple Random and Stratified Sampling

Table 8.1 summarizes the advantages and disadvantages of simple random and stratified sampling. Note that where considerable information about a population is available, one must use stratified sampling to take advantage of it; simple random sampling doesn't. Where no information is available, however, random sampling obtains, on average, a representative sample of every characteristic of the sample.

Systematic Sampling

Systematic sampling is one of the most commonly used and simplest sampling patterns. Although not really simple random sampling, it can approximate it. To draw a sample of 50 from a sampling frame of 500 names, we would take every tenth name instead of bothering with random numbers. If the characteristic on which the sampling frame is ordered is related to the variable being studied, it will also have the effect of stratification. Suppose the sampling frame lists individ-

TABLE 8.1 *Advantages and Disadvantages of Random and Stratified Sampling*

	Description	Advantages	Disadvantages
Simple Random Sampling	Assign each population member a unique number; select members using random numbers	Requires minimum knowledge of population in advance Is free of possible classification errors Makes it easy to analyze data and compute statistics	Does not make use of knowledge of population that researcher may have Results in larger errors for same sample size than stratified sampling Requires identifying and in some studies traveling to units over whole population area
Proportional Stratified Sampling	Sort units of population into groups (strata) on basis of the characteristics to be properly represented in the sample, characteristics that might otherwise result in incorrect inferences Randomly select from each stratum cases equal in number to the ratio of that stratum's size to the population or sampling frame	Ensures sample is representative of whatever characteristic is used to classify units Depending on how closely the stratifying variable is related to the variable being studied, there will be greater homogeneity in each stratum so each can be represented with fewer cases. Compared with simple random sampling, fewer cases yield equal accuracy. If size is retained, we gain greater accuracy and more confidence in the estimates	Requires accurate information on proportion of population in each stratum, or else error is increased If information for classification is not available, may make it costly to obtain and prepare lists Risks improper classification of individuals in strata because of clerical error or poor measurement

uals according to their learning ability. A systematic sample of the top group would be just like a sample taken from a top stratum. The same is true for the middle and lowest groups, which would thus represent the sampling frame just as if we had done proportionate stratified sampling. Another advantage is that in an alphabetized list of names, this approach avoids repeat sampling from the same family.

When using systematic sampling, however, we should be sure there is no periodicity in the sampling frame that is related to what we are investigating. Let's suppose every tenth room in a list of dormitory rooms is a corner room, and, being preferred suites, these are assigned to student floor leaders. Then, depending on where we start in the sampling frame, we may have either all corner rooms or no corner rooms—neither a representative sample. Such a sample would make considerable difference in a study of the social life of students. Thus, when using

T A B L E 8.2 *Advantages and Disadvantages of Systematic Sampling*

Description	Advantages	Disadvantages
Using the sampling frame, select every nth item beginning at some random point and cycling through the list; the value of n is the ratio of the desired size of sample to size of the sampling frame	Makes sample simple to draw If population list is ordered with a variable related to what is being studied, has the effect of stratification on that variable	May result in nonrepresentative sample if n is related to a periodic ordering in the population listing If stratification effect is not taken into account, certain statistics yield biased estimates.

systematic sampling, we must beware of periodicity in the sampling frame. Table 8.2 summarizes the advantages and disadvantages of systematic sampling.

Cluster Sampling

We noted in Table 8.1 that if the selected units were scattered all over the city and we wished to contact them personally, random sampling would create a significant travel problem. Researchers use **cluster sampling** to solve this problem by dropping a grid over the city map to divide the city into geographic units, then randomly selecting units. We may use all the cases in a unit (which may be a city block or several blocks), or we may do multiple-stage sampling, successively performing different kinds of sampling. For example, after cluster sampling, we would stratify within each cluster on a relevant variable and randomly sample within each strata—cluster followed by stratified and then random sampling. Cluster sampling has the advantage not only of reducing travel, but also of requiring complete sampling frames only for the selected clusters. Because both travel and compilation of sampling frames can be costly, cluster sampling is widely used for studies involving interviewing.

You may ask, since people live in relatively homogeneous neighborhoods, how can a few units be representative of the whole city? Unless the selected units cover all neighborhood types, such lack of representation can be a problem. Indeed, the error in estimating population values is likely to be greater with cluster than with random or stratified sampling for the same size sample. To ensure that neighborhood types are appropriately sampled, researchers sometimes use a multistage process. They stratify clusters on a significant characteristic such as socioeconomic class and then take random samples of clusters from within strata.

Clusters need not be geographical areas. Depending on what we are studying and how we define the population, we may use classrooms, schools, or other institutions as clusters. The nature of any already existing unit, however, may result from factors that make it nonrepresentative for our study (for example, problem students are given to the new teacher, parents choose neighborhoods for its particular schools, occupations attract persons with certain skills and values). Users

TABLE 8.3 *Advantages and Disadvantages of Cluster Sampling*

Description	Advantages	Disadvantages
Use as sampling unit either squares in a grid placed over a map or any other arbitrary or natural grouping; take a random sample of units and then either all individuals or a random sample of individuals in each unit	Reduces travel if clusters are used for interviews Sampling frames need be constructed only for units used in sample Permits studies of individual clusters and comparison of clusters	May result in larger error in estimating population values than other probability sampling methods Requires each member of population be assigned uniquely to a cluster (thus, for example, if clusters are families, where should children born out of wedlock be assigned?); otherwise may omit or duplicate cases

of cluster sampling must be fully aware of its potential difficulties. Table 8.3 summarizes the advantages and disadvantages of cluster sampling.

Nonprobability Sampling

Nonprobability sampling methods are procedures that do *not* include random sampling at some stage in the process. Because of their convenience, they are common. Undoubtedly the most common is the grab or convenience sample, using whatever individuals are available: the researcher interviewing the first 100 persons encountered in a shopping mall, the graduate student's using students in an introductory course, the radio station inviting callers to phone in votes.

How representative are such subjects? Short of taking a probability sample, there is no way to know. Clearly the nature of situations, the constraints of time, and the characteristics of individuals predisposing them to act in certain ways all lead to a selective effect. For example, what kinds of individuals take the trouble to call the television station to praise it for a certain program? Or to complain? The kinds of persons entering a mall at certain times depend on whether it is in the morning, when homemakers, preschool children, and retirees are likely to predominate, or whether it is at a meal hour, when workers join in. Certain kinds of persons choose occupations that make them available to public access; others prefer to deal with things instead of people. These are all likely to be groups with characteristics that set them apart from random samples.

Because use of any nonprobability sampling procedure immediately raises questions regarding the representativeness of the sample, it is the responsibility of the investigator to provide the best possible answer. This usually involves comparing pertinent demographic characteristics of the sample to those of the community or population to which the researcher intends to generalize. To lessen such questions, nonprobability sampling methods often have some carefully considered base. Judgmental or purposive samples and quota samples are two such types.

✦ Nonprobability samples *are those that do* not *involve random sampling at some stage in the process.*

Judgmental and Purposive Sampling

Judgmental sampling uses the experience and wisdom of the researcher to select a sample representative of the population. In **judgmental sampling**, the researcher selects individuals presumed to be typical of segments of the population who as a group will provide a representative panorama of the population.

How good are judgmental samples in representing the population? In one sense, they are as good as the researcher's knowledge of the population. In another, the answer is a pragmatic one; if the researcher is able to extract consistently accurate new information from them, they are useful. Conditions often change, however, and if the researcher does not change the sample appropriately, inaccurate information can result. Such an inaccuracy caused the crash of the *Literary Digest* poll mentioned earlier. Only a genuine probability sample protects against such changes. The fact that researchers have continued to produce beneficial information from judgmental samples accounts for their continued use.

Purposive sampling is most often used in qualitative research to select individuals or behaviors that will better inform the researcher regarding the current focus of the investigation. But it is often used in quantitive research to find a site, for instance, with particular properties. For example, the General Accounting Office chose Maryland's enterprise zone program because it best matched proposed federal legislation.

Qualitative researchers might choose individuals to interview or observe who have information, perspective, contacts, or whatever the researchers need next. Such individuals may or may not be representative of the group to whom they wish to generalize. For example, after picking their initial sample and drawing some conclusions with that group, qualitative researchers often test the robustness of those conclusions by deliberately choosing individuals who will put their ideas to the test. Such sampling strengthens the logic of the method and, when done properly, is a stringent test of the findings.

Similarly, researchers may sample extreme or deviant cases either to see how far a generalization extends or to view the problem in an extreme light with the hope of finding some clue about more normal cases. Sometimes, anticipating audience questions, researchers sample cases that if not included might cast doubt on the conclusions of the study. Purposive sampling in qualitative research is discussed further in Chapter 12.

Quota Sampling

Quota sampling requires prior knowledge of the characteristics related as stratifying variables to whatever we are studying. A nonprobability form of stratification, it requires that we establish quotas for characteristics of individuals to ensure they are distributed in the sample as they are in the population. For example, knowing the community's gender ratio and the proportion of each racial group and religion, by establishing quotas for each of these variables we ensure that the sample has those characteristics. This assumes, of course, that providing accurate representation of these variables ensures sufficient representativeness with respect to whatever we are studying.

Fitting the sample to quotas often requires obtaining the respondent's profile at the interview's outset and proceeding only if he or she fits an open quota. Alternatively the interviewer can gather data regardless of fit and, provided that all quotas are sufficiently represented, simply adjust the results so as to represent each group's responses in a proportion appropriate for the population.

Despite the appealing logic of the method, the individuals in any quota are simply a convenience sample of that group. Unless properly supervised, interviewers will seek out busy areas to fill their quotas easily—shopping malls, entertainment areas, terminals and depots, and so forth. Depending on the problem, oversampling the kinds of individuals who collect in such places could result in a biased study. Even when properly instructed, interviewers are likely to avoid less desirable situations—upper floors where there is no elevator, dilapidated buildings, and so on. Clearly, nonrepresentative samples can occur many ways. Still, quota sampling is a favorite of pollsters who, with experience, have learned to avoid some of its problems.

Snowball Sampling

Snowball sampling (also called chain referral and referential sampling) is used to find members of a group not otherwise visibly identified. Suppose we wished to learn the influential members of the state legislature lobbying community. Although we could identify the members of the lobbying group, we would not know which were influential; indeed, such individuals might not be visibly identified with that group. Using snowball sampling, we start with a powerful state legislature member and ask the names of the most influential lobbyists and of others in a position to give an opinion. Interviewing the latter as well as other individuals we think would know, we continue until we come full circle, getting names of persons already identified. This method has been used to identify members of crime groups and others engaged in covert activities. (For additional reading, see Biernacki and Waldorf, 1981.)

- ✦ *Whenever nonprobability samples are used, the representativeness of the sample is a prime question in the reader's mind.*
- ✦ *Judgmental, purposive, and quota sampling all involve judgments by researchers of which characteristics of the target population they should seek in their sample. Judgmental and quota sampling are used by pollsters who select their samples, often on the basis of demographic data, to fit the appropriate profile of characteristics in order to be representative of the population. Qualitative researchers use purposive sampling to select individuals who can help them explore their problem, understand certain phenomena, test their hypotheses, and/or show generality.*
- ✦ *Snowball sampling is used to discover the members of a group of individuals not otherwise easily identified by starting with someone in the know and asking for referrals to other knowledgeable individuals.*

Sequential Sampling

Starting with an initial batch of cases, in **sequential sampling,** data from successive samples is cumulatively analyzed to determine if the needed statistical precision has been met. If not, sampling is continued until it is.[2] It is used in field samples where whatever is being studied is not continually changing, and the study itself has not caused an increased awareness of the topic, thereby biasing further data collection. Increasingly used in telephone polls, population values are cumulatively computed as interviewee responses are entered. Interviewing is stopped when the desired accuracy is reached, thus conserving resources.

Sequential sampling can be used with any of the probability or nonprobability sampling methods. It is of particular advantage when we know how precisely we wish to estimate the population characteristics but do not know the variability of the population. Qualitative researchers may be considered to do a kind of sequential sampling as they continue to observe or interview until they stop getting fresh insights or having new useful experiences.

✦ Sequential sampling *involves gathering additional data in successive waves until some criterion of adequacy is met. It can save resources but assumes that the subjects do not change during the sampling process.*

Generality, External Validity (GP), and Population Definition

The external validity (GP) of a study indicates the power of the study to support inferences of generality of the findings, where GP stands for generalizing power. Just as knowledge is better viewed as a reduction in uncertainty, so are internal validity (LP) and external validity (GP). Internal validity (LP) reduces our uncertainty that the relationship exists in the circumstances in which it was investigated, and external validity (GP) reduces our uncertainty that the relationship generalizes beyond the circumstances in which it was studied.

By now it must be clear that generality depends on what the study's sample can be presumed to represent—that is, its relation to the population to which the researcher intends to generalize. However, it is the judgment of the gatekeepers who form a consensus about the interpretation of findings that determines the useful generality—which is often less than that intended. But on what basis do gatekeepers make the judgment of generality? A series of five sequential judgments makes up external validity (GP). The judgments are parallel to those of which internal validity (LP) is composed; each is similar in name and content.

Again, we have both conceptual and empirical evidence and a wrap-up judgment, this time of generality. The conceptual evidence consists of two judgments:

---

[2]*Statistical precision* refers to estimating desired population statistics, such as the average income of the sample, with a predetermined accuracy, such as to the nearest $1000. The procedure for doing this involves developing a confidence interval, a concept discussed in Chapters 18 and 19.

The first is a judgment of the generality claimed, implied, or inferred from the explanation, or **explanation generality**; the second is the extent the generality claimed, implied, or inferred is operationalized in the choices made in the design of the study, or **translation generality**. The empirical evidence consists of the two judgments: "**demonstrated generality**" (the quotation marks are intentional and explained in the detailed discussion that follows) and **restrictive explanations (conditions) eliminated.** Finally, a judgment is made whether there is a **replicable result,**[3] and the evidence is summed up to gauge the strength of the study's external validity (GP). Figure 8.2 places these criteria with their parallels in internal validity (LP) on the chain of reasoning.

> ✦ *A study with* external validity (GP) *supports an inference that the relationship generalizes to persons, places, treatments, measures or observations, study designs, and procedures other than those used in this study. It involves judgments of conceptual evidence, empirical evidence, and a credible result.*

Partial Dependence of External Validity (GP) on Internal Validity (LP)

Some of the judgments of external validity (GP) depend on those of internal validity (LP). For example, if the explanation makes little sense and therefore lacks explanation credibility, explanation generality is generally irrelevant. Similarly, if the translation into the operations of the study is unsatisfactory (translation fi-

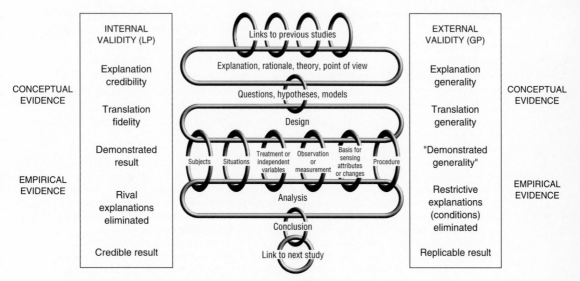

FIGURE 8.2 The judgments of external validity (GP) added to Figure 7.1.

_____

[3]This criterion was suggested by Cronbach (1982).

delity), it makes little sense to be concerned with translation generality. If there is no effect and no demonstrated result, there can be no "demonstrated generality." Some of the alternative explanations that were not eliminated may restrict the generality of the findings and may therefore be involved in the judgment of whether restrictive explanations were eliminated. Finally, of course, if we do not have a credible result, we can hardly expect it to replicate; thus, replicable result is affected. Let us return to the Zimbardo article to illustrate how we would make the five judgments of external validity (GP).

Initial Conceptual Evidence: Explanation Generality

Explanation generality makes a judgment regarding the generality stated or implied in the explanation or rationale of the study. The generality is not explicitly stated in the Zimbardo study, but by implication we can sense that the hypothesis is intended, at least, to apply to all elderly people. As we noted earlier, however, although the explanation is stated in terms of the elderly, the hypothesis is stated so broadly as to apply to anyone experiencing a "perceptual discontinuity" or "sensory anomaly." Certainly, this broader interpretation is necessary to make sense of data gathered on college students.

As in this case, the generality claimed by research studies often is not explicitly stated; it is implied or must be inferred. After all, explanations can be stated more simply and clearly if they are not cluttered with all the qualifications required to detail the boundaries within which they hold. Furthermore, many explanations start out without qualifications—as universals. Only as a body of research develops, are the explanations successively circumscribed as limiting conditions are found.

Regardless of whether clearly stated, implied, or inferred, explanation generality is a judgment of whether that generality is reasonable. Just as with explanation credibility in internal validity (LP), we judge the credibility of the explanation, so in explanation generality we judge the credibility of the claimed, implied, or inferred generality. If it seems reasonable, we proceed to translation generality to see whether that extent of generality was observed in the operational translation of the study. If we reject, doubt, or can find little basis for expecting generality, we are likely to be extremely critical of the study and will be convinced only by strong empirical evidence.[4]

---

[4]There are studies with little rationale that do present strong evidence. For example, some researchers—like the medical clinician who tries all kinds of plants as he or she looks for one with therapeutic properties—devise studies with only the loosest rationale for why they might uncover predictive relationships and then seek them. Such studies have created highly successful predictive instruments, such as the Strong-Campbell Interest Inventory and the Minnesota Multiphasic Personality Inventory (MMPI). Even though we can't conceptually explain why they do so, such instruments have proven to have wide "demonstrated generality" and have been shown to work in a broad range of situations. The Strong-Campbell, for instance, can usefully predict vocational success in a number of fields, and the MMPI is heavily used in clinical psychology as an aid in diagnosing mental illness in a wide variety of patients. Even for such uses the search to provide explanation credibility (LP) continues as clinicians seek explanations for why the instruments work.

✦ Explanation generality *is a judgment of the plausibility of the generality that is claimed, implied, or inferred for the relationship.*

More Conceptual Evidence: Translation Generality

The determination of generality is always an inference. It is a leap of faith to generalize from any given instance to others like it. That leap is clearly much safer if the instances in which it was demonstrated are representative of the target to which the leap is to be made. That is the importance of **translation generality.** Both translation fidelity and translation generality are concerned with accuracy of translation into operational terms. The former is concerned with the accuracy of translation of question, hypothesis, or model into choices at the design level; the latter, with whether the breadth of generality claimed, implied, or inferred is represented in those choices. Are the choices representative of the targets to which the researcher wishes the study to generalize—the individuals, situations, treatment versions, alternative instruments, alternative research procedures, times, and so on?

Usually the question, hypothesis, or model stemming from an explanation is only one instance rather than the breadth of expected generality that could have been explored. A test of the proposition "frustration leads to aggression," might study crowded elevators, but such a focus would not validate the extent of generality. That would require evidence from a variety of kinds of individuals, situations, and so on. Clearly, we should make design choices from within the population of situations to which we hope to generalize; however, in addition, these choices ought to be representative of them. Let us look at the six facets in which we make design choices.

Subjects and Situations. These two aspects of design are considered together because they are often linked in research studies. Kruglanski and Kroy (1976) make the point that when a particular group is the target of generalization, a representative sample is the only appropriate set of subjects. Consider studies of how well the Scholastic Aptitude Test predicts success at a particular college. A study of students from a particular high school would not be sufficient; a cross section of the variety of high schools represented in a typical freshman class would be needed. Cook and Campbell (1979) note that using a sample of convenience (usually college undergraduates in a required course) may save time and energy, but there is a trade-off. It is difficult to generalize to a larger universe of which the sample might be representative.

The same advice applies to situations. Bracht and Glass (1968) use the term *ecological validity* to describe whether the choice of situation is representative of the other situations to which generalization is intended.

By contrast, in instances in which a proposition is universally applicable, we can use anyone and any situation (convenience samples) except where subject or situational characteristics might be biased in support (or against) the proposition. Goldstein and Arms (1971), for example, hypothesized that watching aggressive athletic contests increases hostility and aggressiveness. They tested their hypothesis with spectators at a football contest. Suppose there were reasons to believe that their proposition might be more applicable to sports-minded individuals than to the population at large. Then, as designed, the study is a weaker demonstration of generality than, for example, one using a sample of shoppers at a mall.

In the Zimbardo study, the hypothesis seems intended to be universal—that is, intended to apply to all people who are unaware of their sensory deficit. Therefore, college students, a convenience sample, are as good as any other subjects unless something about them is particularly favorable (or unfavorable) to the hypothesis. Although the sample used was a subgroup of college students who were particularly susceptible to hypnosis, it is hard to see how this characteristic has any bearing on their developing paranoia in the instance in which they did.

Assuming one can find no reasonable alternative explanation, the fact that a proposition was supported by data from a convenience sample removes some uncertainty that the proposition has universal generality—applies to any one or any roughly comparable situation. As discussed on page 51 we may require more than a single demonstration, however, to remove sufficient uncertainty to act as though the proposition were true. But each such confirmation removes further uncertainty and moves it closer to acceptance as knowledge.

Treatment. In some instances, the treatment is carefully standardized. For example, in the Zimbardo study, directions were administered mechanically with slide projectors or electronically with tape recordings. Standardization was achieved in the social interaction by carefully training and rehearsing the confederates. Such standardization is typical when the goal is knowledge itself instead of its application in a typical field situation where such standardization is unrealistic. It is important for internal validity (LP) because it eliminates the alternative explanation that the differences in treatment application were in some way involved in producing the effect. Standardization that requires unusual situations or equipment may restrict the generality to similar situations or equipment.

When we are interested in the useful application of a treatment, there is likely to be variability in its application among the kinds of persons using it, the way it is applied, the equipment used, the circumstances preceding application, the application situation, and so on. For example, in studying various ways of increasing classroom learning, different teachers might apply the method in their own ways. Representativeness with respect to treatment involves including that variability in the definition of the treatment. One aspect of that definition of treatment is how the treatment will be mastered by the people who apply it. If it is to have useful generality, it should be mastered in the same manner as it is in normal practice. For example, if the new classroom procedure is to be mastered from a teacher's guide, learning from the guide alone is an essential aspect of the treatment. If, however, teachers would typically be given extra help and explanation, either by a supervisor or by in-service training classes, then either or both should be a part of treatment.

A second aspect of treatment definition is determining appropriate treatment variability for generality. Internal validity (LP) is concerned with maintaining treatment fidelity—that is, how much variation can be tolerated and still have the intended treatment. External validity (GP) is concerned with representation of the likely variability of application in practice. For example, Rowe (1974) noted that as the time that a teacher waits for student response increases, classroom discussion changes toward more considered responses, more student-to-student interchange, higher-level thinking, and so on. Treatment fidelity for internal validity (LP) would involve defining the range within which wait time should be increased (a teacher can only wait so long before discussion drags) and monitoring teachers to ensure it was maintained. Translation generality would involve ensuring there was a representative variety of wait times within this range appropriate to typical teachers.

Observations and Measures. How representative of all possible valid measures and instruments are the chosen measures or observation instruments? Could we substitute others for them without changing the results, or is there something unique about them? For example, is the measure affected by the way it is administered—paper and pencil, interview, observation? Might we get substantively different results if the information were gathered in a different way? In the Zimbardo study, the key factor to be measured was the development of paranoia. The researchers used three measures of paranoia providing data gathered two different ways—self-report and observation. Fortunately, all of them showed the effect. If they had not, the researchers would have been faced with the difficult problem of deciding and justifying which measure of paranoia had the greatest validity and seeking a reason for the disparate results.

Basis for Sensing Attributes or Changes Link and Procedure Link. These two final aspects of design also need to be representative of the kinds of designs and procedures that would allow generalization. For example, the Zimbardo study used a straightforward design comparing experimental and control groups. Except for the fact that the subjects were hypnotized, there was nothing about the way the treatment, measures, and observations were carried out that would prevent generalizing the results. The use of hypnosis, however, is a condition of the experiment that is in no way implied by the hypothesis and might limit generality. Suppose we considered hypnosis only a parlor trick or believed that easily hypnotized people are different from others. Then the results would be atypical of the universal population to which the study is intended to generalize. We look for such unusual aspects in the procedure link and basis for sensing attributes or changes link in determining translation generality.

Time. We seldom consider time as a factor in designing a study from which we wish to infer generality. Cronbach (1975), however, points out that some generalizations decay, especially as the culture changes. Child-rearing patterns effective in one decade may not generalize to a later one. This decay can be a serious problem for the behavioral sciences, which are often seen as progressing by assembling findings over time into larger generalities. Cronbach notes:

> The trouble . . . is that we cannot store up generalizations . . . for ultimate assembly into a network. It is as if we needed a gross of dry cells to power an engine and could only make one a month. The energy would leak out of the first cells before we have half a battery completed. So it is with the potency of our generalization (p. 123).

We are left with the uncomfortable feeling that our generalizations are becoming less valid even as we are discovering them—which may indeed be the case. Where a social or cultural aspect is undergoing rapid change (for example, the role of women in the past half-century), knowledge about it may not generalize to a future time. Thus, where possible, the circumstances of a study should anticipate those of the future time to which it is expected to generalize.

> ✦ Translation generality *is a judgment of the extent to which the generality claimed, implied, or inferred in the study is represented in the operational choices of its design.*

Initial Empirical Evidence: "Demonstrated Generality"

"Demonstrated generality" asks whether the generalization held up in the instances where it should have and did not where it should not have. In the Zimbardo study, paranoia was highest in the group that was partially deaf but did not know it and, on most measures, considerably higher than in the other groups. This finding is, of course, just what the explanation called for.

Why is *"demonstrated generality"* in quotation marks? To call attention to the logical impossibility of demonstrating generality in all the instances where it is intended to apply. No matter how exhaustively we research it, there is always the possibility it will not hold in one that has not yet been tested. Instead, we make an inferential leap from the sample to instances to which it should generalize. The quotation marks reinforce that it is an inference, not a certainty.

> ✦ *"Demonstrated generality" is a judgment of the extent to which the relationship appeared in all the instances of the study in which it would be expected to do so and did not where it shouldn't.*
> ✦ *There is always an inferential leap from the particular instances in which the relationship is demonstrated to those to which it is intended to generalize.*
> ✦ *"Demonstrated generality" is in quotation marks because generality can never completely be demonstrated. There is always some untested instance in which, presumably, it might not hold.*

More Empirical Evidence: Restrictive Explanations (Conditions) Eliminated

A study that fails to be representative of the targets to which it is to generalize has restricted generality unless those **restrictive explanations (conditions)** are **eliminated**.[5] For example, suppose that teachers were given extra assistance in interpreting the manual that describes how the treatment should be administered in a learning study. Then generality could reasonably be extended only to similar situ-

---

[5]Dr. Jason Millman pointed out to me that the rival explanations of internal validity (LP) became restrictive conditions in external validity (GP). To keep the names parallel, they are called *restrictive explanations (conditions)*. They are conditions that provide explanations for restricting the generality.

ations in which that kind of assistance was available. We couldn't be sure that the manual alone would be effective in conveying the essentials of the treatment from the data of that particular study.

Such restrictions are more common than might be anticipated. If the study were done with volunteers, their extra motivation might be necessary to make the treatment effective. If it were done in circumstances in which the subjects knew they were part of an experiment, the desire to please the researcher or to show up well might have been an important factor. A test given to determine pretreatment status might cue students as to what to attend to in treatment. The most appropriate generalization of data is to situations similar to those in which they were gathered.

Thus, this judgment looks backward to the way in which generality was translated into the study and looks forward to the intended generality of the conclusion. It places such restrictions on the latter as are necessary in view of the special conditions under which the data were gathered; or, if the study is still being designed, the researcher seeks to eliminate conditions that might be restrictive.

> ✦ Restrictive explanations (conditions) *that were part of the study but would not be part of the target of generalization must have been eliminated for the inferential leap to the target to be confidently made.*

Final Judgment: Replicable Result

The heart of external validity (GP) is replicability: Would the results be reproducible in the target instances to which we intend to generalize—the subjects, situations, treatment forms or formats, measures, study designs, procedures, and times? Do we have a **replicable result?** Of course, we can never be sure unless we actually do a study under each of those instances, and that is an impossibility. So the final judgment of external validity (GP) is a thought experiment about the reproducibility of the results under this variety of conditions. We can use comparable studies to facilitate this judgment, if such exist.

Would the Zimbardo study replicate with elderly rather than college student subjects, with subjects less susceptible to hypnosis, in a different laboratory, in a field situation rather than laboratory, with different measures of paranoia, or with observations of individuals suspected of growing deaf in a home for the elderly? These are the kind of questions this last judgment requires. If you can find no reason that the study would not replicate in those circumstances and the four prior judgments are positive, the external validity (GP) is strong.

Of course, this, the fifth decision of the sequence, is dependent on the previous four: (1) The explanation must specify or imply a reasonable generality, (2) this generality must be represented in (translated into) the choices for the study design, (3) the result must appear with the generality expected in those choices, and (4) the result must appear without restrictive explanations (conditions).

> ✦ *Replicable result is a summary judgment of the forgoing judgments and of the extent to which the results of this study could be replicated in the target to which it is being generalized.*

SUMMARY

Four basic principles underlie sampling: A larger sample is required (1) the greater the certainty required in the inferential leap from sample to population, (2) the more precisely we desire to estimate characteristics of the population, (3) the greater the variability of the population in those characteristics, and (4) the smaller the effect to be sensed relative to the normal variability of the population. All probability samples involve random sampling at some point in the process. Random samples require that each possible sample from a population be equally likely to be drawn. Probability samples allow us to estimate the population characteristics with specified accuracy and certainty. Random, stratified, systematic, and cluster sampling are all probability sampling methods. Often, they are combined in a multistage process. Their characteristics, advantages, and disadvantages are summarized in Tables 8.1 through 8.3.

Convenience and grab samples are nonprobability samples and are popular because of their ease of use. Judgmental or quota samples rely on the researcher's knowledge of population characteristics to sample appropriately. Nonprobability judgmental and quota samples are usually justified if it is shown they fit certain demographic characteristics of the target population. Quota sampling is in common use in surveys, especially telephone interviewing. Purposive sampling, often used in qualitative research, involves samples chosen to facilitate research on a problem, such as understanding particular cases, determining the breadth of variability, testing a hypothesis, checking generality, and so forth.

The generality that can be attributed to a study is a function of the quality of the sampling process. When well done, sampling makes the inferential leap from sample to population less tenuous. Not all studies depend on sampling for generality, only those that are intended to apply to a particular target population. Propositions that are assumed to be universal—that is, to apply to everyone—can be studied with convenience samples. Such samples are, of course, only one demonstration of the universality; we may want additional evidence. The fact that it worked on a sample with no special reason to expect it to, however, does make the case stronger.

The judgments involved in determining generality are those of external validity (GP), the power of a study to create a consensus that the relationship has generality beyond the circumstances in which it was studied—that is, generalizing power. Similar to internal validity (LP), external validity (GP) consists of two kinds of conceptual evidence, explanation generality and translation generality; two kinds of empirical evidence, "demonstrated generality" and restrictive explanations (conditions) eliminated; and a final summary judgment, replicable result.

A Look Ahead

It is already apparent that still other characteristics affect how we build a consensus and that other criteria apply to links in the chain of reasoning. In Chapter 9, we examine these other characteristics. In Chapters 18 and 19, we shall discuss how the basic principles of sampling are used in statistics and measurement.

ADDITIONAL READING

Jaeger (1984) and Kish (1965) are discussions of sampling. Bracht and Glass (1968), Campbell and Stanley (1963), and Cook and Campbell (1979) all are discussions of validity. Kruglanski and Kroy (1976) and Cronbach (1982) critique the Campbell and Stanley version of validities. Brinberg and McGrath (1985) propose a different set. Krathwohl (1985) is an earlier and fuller treatment.

IMPORTANT TERMS

Alternative explanations
Bias
Cluster sampling
"Demonstrated generality"
Explanation generality

Generality
Judgmental sampling
Nonprobability sampling
Oversampling
Population

Probability sampling
Proportional stratified sampling
Purposive sampling
Quota sampling
Random sampling
Replicable result
Restrictive explanations (conditions) eliminated
Rival explanations eliminated

Sample
Sampling frame
Sampling unit
Sequential sampling
Snowball (chain referral) sampling
Stratified sampling
Systematic sampling
Translation generality

APPLICATION PROBLEMS

1. A researcher wants a simple random sample of 150 students from the population of all sixth-grade pupils who attend private schools in Syracuse, New York. The total population is 900 pupils. What steps should the researcher use to get the sample?

2. Mary Wayne, doctoral student, wants to study the effect of postinstruction summaries on high school student achievement. She will use the Rochester school district, which consists of 3000 high school students (grades 10–12). She wants a sample of 300 cases by grade level (sophomores, juniors, and seniors), gender (male and female), and three different levels of reading ability (low, medium, and high). She wants to select a representative sample. (a) What type of sample should she select and why? (b) What steps should she take in selecting her sample?

3. A manager of a food company wants to test the effectiveness of a new product for marketing in California. He plans to administer a questionnaire and interview 75 persons individually. What sampling method should he use, and what criteria would influence his decision?

4. Dr. Hendrika Kuizenga of the Marley Nursing School was studying depression in first-year college students, its rate of incidence, and its relation to their level of perceived stress. She wanted a sample of 200 and obtained 133 randomly selected subjects proportionally stratified by level of parents' education and by race so as to represent the entering class. To do so required sending her graduate assistants into the dormitories to contact the students personally, a labor-intensive procedure that would deplete her funds. Therefore, she asked her assistants, while in the dormitories, to pick up an additional 67 cases of any first-year female students who would cooperate with them in filling out the instruments. To answer her questions, can she combine the convenience and random samples to get the desired sample size of 200? Why or why not?

5. The English faculty at Local University wanted to offer its introductory writing course, using distance-delivery methods, to adults who could not come to campus. In collaboration with the computer applications department, the English department produced a computer-based writing course that could be offered off campus without the need for an instructor. Field tests were conducted with first-year on-campus students, to whom the writing course was also normally offered. Those following the computer-based course showed significant improvements in writing scores as compared with those taking the equivalent course taught by an instructor. Proceeding from these results, the department decided to offer the course off campus in computer-based form. Was this the correct decision?

6. Criminologists conducted a five-year study of a boot camp–style correctional program for young offenders (age 20 or younger) at minimum-security institutions. Participation in the program was voluntary. "Graduates" of the program exhibited an extremely low incidence of recidivism (repeat offenses). The researchers were extremely enthusiastic about the results of their study and thought the program would work as well if required of any offender of any age throughout the United States. Was this enthusiasm warranted?

7. External validity (GP) applies to qualitative studies as well as to studies like Zimbardo's; indeed, it is of concern wherever a generalization is developed. Use the Hoffmann-Riem study to illustrate the judgments entering into external validity (GP) as the Zimbardo study was used in the text.

Compare your answers with those following the Application Exercise.

APPLICATION EXERCISE

Using the topic you have chosen to follow throughout the book, think about the generality you'd like your work to have. Then consider the kind of sample that would permit inference of that kind of generality. In addition, think about how you might apply each of the different kinds of sampling to your problem. Include both probability and nonprobability sampling processes. You may want to reconsider your original choice after examining some of the other sampling possibilities.

Consider external validity as well. What generality do you intend for your study? Are you examining a universal proposition, or is it bounded in some way in its applicability? What are those limits? Will the translation of your concepts plumb the boundaries of the generality you intend the study to have? Can your design choices be changed such that the generality is increased? What restrictive conditions do you see in your study as now planned that might limit generality? Would you expect your study to replicate with different design choices? If not, would better design choices allow it to replicate?

ANSWERS TO THE APPLICATION PROBLEMS

1. (a) Obtain a list of the names and addresses of all private elementary school principals in the city of Syracuse from the superintendent of schools. (b) Contact each principal by mail and request a roster of sixth-grade pupils enrolled in that school. (c) Assign a number to each name. (d) Use random numbers to draw the desired sample. If using a random number table, select a starting point randomly and then follow a row, column, or diagonal. (e) Since the population consists of 900 cases, read the numbers in sets of three. Skip any set of three on the random table that exceeds 900, since there are only 900 cases in the population. (f) Continue taking numbers until a sample of 150 pupils has been selected.

2. (a) A sample might be obtained through proportional stratified sampling, since Mary has to adjust her sample to more than one variable at a time (grade level, gender, reading ability). She should also take into consideration the proportions of variables in the target population. (b) The steps in the proportional stratified sampling are as follows: (1) Get the names, gender, and reading scores of the high school students from the superintendent of the Rochester school district. (2) Classify the students into sophomores, juniors, and seniors. This yields students in three cells. (3) Classify students as male or female within each grade level. The three cells are now divided into six. (4) Set scores that are the dividing points for low, medium, and high reading ability according to a reading ability test. Divide students in the six cells into high, medium, and low groups according to the reading test cut scores. This yields 18 cells. The cells will not have equal numbers because the classes may be of unequal size and boys more numerous than girls, and the scores determining low, middle, and high reading ability will not necessarily divide the whole group into equal thirds, let alone those in a cell. (5) Because there are 3000 students in the schools and we want a sample of 300, we can take 10 percent of each cell. We can use a table of random numbers to select a random sample from each of the 18 cells. Alternatively, because the list of names in each cell is probably unordered, taking every tenth name will likely give us a random sample (this is systematic sampling).

3. He should use cluster sampling. The state of California is so large that one researcher cannot cover every city, area, street, and block. Traveling and interviewing are expensive and time-consuming.

4. This problem nicely illustrates the difference between the inferences that can be derived from a random and a convenience sample. Where Dr. Kuizenga is concerned with the level of incidence of depression, she is concerned with a context-specific estimation, the incidence of depression in a specific population. The 67 convenience sample cases may or may not be representative of first-year college students at the institution; there is no way to know. They showed a 25 percent incidence, similar to other studies that used convenience samples. On average, however, the 133-case random sample will be representative, so incidence of depression should be estimated from it; it showed a 15 percent incidence. The difference in incidence rates, especially if it holds up with more research, may indicate biased sampling in prior studies.

The relationship of depression to perceived stress is not unique to first-year female students. The relationship of depression to stress, if it exists, is postulated as a universal, so there is no reason that she cannot combine the samples for purposes of examining the relationship of depression to a variety of stress variables. Because some of the stress variables may be related to culture, however, she may wish that she had oversampled certain combinations of parents' level of education and race.

5. No, the faculty should have repeated the study with a sample from the actual target audience. There is a problem here both with translation generality and with whether all restrictive explanations (conditions) have been eliminated. The field test was not conducted with the adult population to whom the course would be offered. The faculty members cannot be certain that the significant findings would be repeated with this group. Are the learning needs of adults and undergraduates the same? For example, the undergraduate students may be more experienced or more comfortable with computers.

In addition, the conditions of the study do not appear to be the same as those under which the course would be offered. Since the field test was conducted on campus, it seems likely that assistance from instructors, both with the subject matter and with use of the computers, was available to students taking the computer-based course. Any such assistance could be quite significant and could account for the findings. This is a restrictive condition with strong implications for "stand-alone" (without human intervention) computer-based instruction.

6. No, again there are problems with translation generality and with whether all explanations (conditions) have been eliminated. One translation generality problem is that these inmates had volunteered for the program and therefore probably already had a willing attitude. They may well have been in the process of "going straight" anyway, and this program only served to shorten their prison terms. Furthermore, there is a restrictive condition. The program may have taken them from an environment (prison) that could otherwise have negatively affected them and therefore contributed

to recidivism. If conducted in the prisons, it might not be as effective.

Further, these offenders were from a specific population (translation generality again). They were young offenders (20 years or under) who had committed less violent crimes. The investigators have no way of knowing if the technique would work with older, more "hardened" inmates or with the more violent. The study may hold promise, but it also needs replication.

7. We must examine the evidence contributing to the five judgments making up external validity (GP): explanation generality, translation generality, "demonstrated generality," restrictive explanations (conditions) eliminated, and replicable result.

Explanation generality: It is clear from this statement in her concluding section, "This research may be useful for adoptive parents, applicant couples, and agencies who deal with adoptive family life," that Hoffmann-Riem intends for this study to have wide generality. One might say that her generalization is intended to be universally applicable to adopting couples. Therefore, it must have strong external validity (GP).

Translation generality: Clearly, she can't sample from all the "adoptive parents, applicant couples and agencies" to whom she expects the results to be useful. What she can do is to select a typical sample to whom it should be applicable and show that the generalization does indeed hold there. She does this by choosing a discussion group of adoptive parents, a purposive and convenience sample. In her discussion of sampling, she notes that the members of such groups are "middle class, similar to most applicants for adoption." She also refers to a comparison she presented elsewhere which shows the similarity between the group she used and the characteristics of applicants for adoption over a year. Both of these pieces of evidence are intended to show that the sample she used is similiar to applicants for adoption generally. Readers must judge for themselves whether this evidence is strong enough for them to believe this group is typical of adopters.

"Demonstrated generality": As indicated in the discussion of explanation generality, one cannot really demonstrate generality. There may always be some untried instance in which the generalization doesn't hold, hence the quotation marks. However, does it hold with a group in which it would be expected to? Hoffmann-Riem indicates

that it does and provides quotations to back up the claim.

Restrictive explanations (conditions) eliminated: Because the data were gathered under the conditions to which the generalization would be expected to apply, there are no restrictive conditions.

Replicable result: Would one expect the same findings in studies of other groups of adopting couples? The main question one might have is whether individuals who attend these discussion groups are typical of adoptive parents. Hoffmann-Riem obviously thinks that they are. She indicates she has data indicating the parents in this group are similiar to adoption applicants over a previous year. Whether one judges the results would replicate is a thought experiment; I am inclined to think they would.

All five judgments are positive; the study has strong external validity (GP).

Research Criteria to Optimize and Constraints to Observe

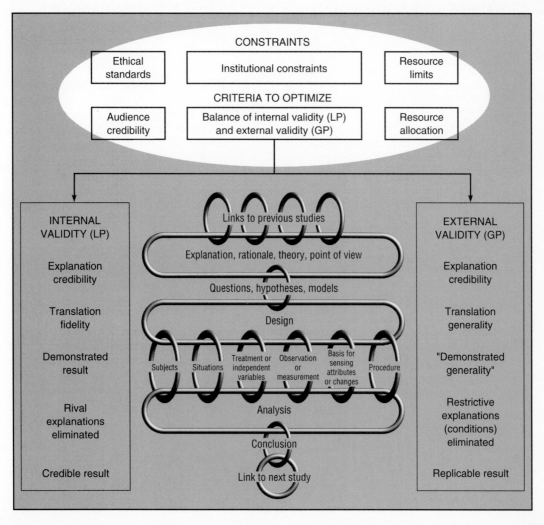

OVERVIEW

In addition to building a strong chain of reasoning and meeting the requirements of internal validity (LP) and external validity (GP), every study must optimize three aspects: (1) the building of audience credibility, (2) the relative weighting of internal validity (LP) with external validity (GP), and (3) resource *allocation*.[1] Furthermore, strengthening internal validity (LP) is usually bought at a cost to external validity (GP), and vice versa.[2] These three criteria are optimized because to some extent, they are part of a zero-sum game of resources; that is, resources spent on one part of the study cannot be spent on another. Furthermore, optimizing these aspects for one audience will not necessarily do so for another; researchers must keep their principal audience in mind.

In addition, these characteristics must be optimized within the limits imposed on every study: (1) what can be ethically done, (2) what an institution will permit to be done in the name of research when its primary goal is service to clients, and (3) resource *limits*. Although the available resources can sometimes be increased, they are always limited—usually too much so. This chapter demonstrates the relationship of these decisions to the chain of reasoning.

CHAPTER CONTENTS

Introduction

Internal validity (LP) and external validity (GP) may be the criteria by which most research studies are judged, but other important criteria affect study design and effectiveness. One is the credibility a reader attaches to a study—the *audience credibility* of a study. Researchers must elicit credence not only from gatekeepers to

---

[1]"Allocation" and "limits" are italicized to emphasize that, although both are concerned with resources, in discussing optimizing, it is resource *allocation* in the process of designing a study that is our focus, whereas in considering limits and constraints we are concerned with the *limit* on the resources that can be devoted to the study.

[2]This may seem to be contradicting Chapter's 8's discussion of the partial dependence of judgments involved in external validity (GP) on those of internal validity (LP), but it isn't. Those judgments are made of the way a study *was* designed. What is discussed in this chapter are decisions that *must be made in designing a study*. It is in designing a study that one must choose how to weight one relative to the other. For example, choosing to strengthen internal validity (LP) by doing the study in a laboratory reduces the generalizability of findings—external validity (GP).

publication or presentation, but also from the whole audience of relevant readers and reviewers after release to the public. Another is whether internal validity (LP) or external validity (GP) has the greater emphasis. The third, resource allocation, is a special concern of the researcher as the study is designed and implemented. The research report shows only the results of resource allocation, not the process that is at the heart of it. Differences in researchers' allocations of resources, especially personal time, energy, and attention, often explain how they arrive at different strategies for the same problem. Resource allocation is an important determiner of problem formulation and the design alternatives chosen at different stages in a study's development. Readers, however, are typically unaware of the alternatives that may have been considered. Finally, there are the constraints within which the researcher must work, constraints imposed by ethics, institutions, and resource limits.

Figure 9.1 adds all these aspects to the model we have been discussing and shows the complete framework of criteria and constraints.

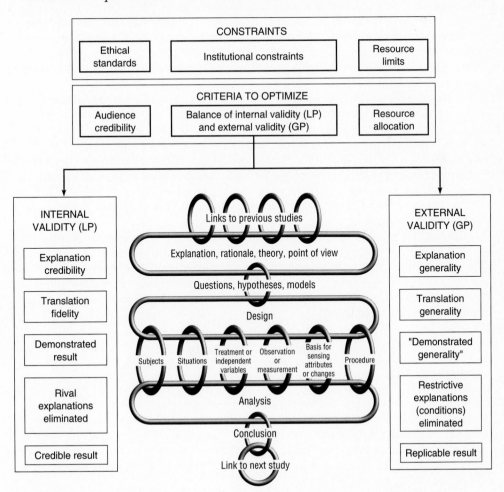

FIGURE 9.1 The complete framework of criteria, constraints, and chain of reasoning.

Criteria to Be Optimized

Why Optimization?

In Chapters 7 and 8, we discussed internal validity (LP) and external validity (GP) as though, if the proper choices were made, each could be raised to an entirely satisfactory level. Given a tractable problem, we could build a rationale that could be credible, get a satisfactory translation of the hypothesis with protection against both rival and restricting explanations, and so on. Attaining great strength in both simultaneously, however, is another matter because strengthening internal validity (LP) is usually bought at the expense of external validity (GP). Greater control gained by complex designs or taking the study into the laboratory typically results in decreased generality, external validity (GP). Furthermore, resources expended in pursuit of increased internal validity (LP) are lost so far as strengthening external validity (GP) is concerned, and vice versa. Because resources are always finite, and usually less than we would ideally like, we must find the proper balance of internal validity (LP) to external validity (GP) for our purposes.

Consider the problem of building audience credibility. Credibility with whom? Who are all the relevant audiences? Can we simultaneously build credibility with all of them? A difficult goal! We must choose one or a few and find the optimal choices for them.

Resource allocation is equally complex. We have already noted that the myriad of choices involved in building a design means that researchers may differ as to the ideal. In fact, within a given method, there may be alternative "best" choices leading to different resource allocations. What is the ideal design? Even if we construct what we consider to be a good design, others might construct a better one according to their view of appropriate resource allocations. All we can do is optimize the design for our purposes and intended audiences. With this introduction to the idea of optimization, we can understand it in greater depth as we look at each criterion.

Simon (1992) suggests that where problem solving is complex—as it certainly is in designing a research study—and since optimizing requires considering all the possibilities and that is impossible, we *satisfice* instead of *optimize*. We find a solution that at least partially meets (satisfices) our criteria. Probably this is a more accurate description of our attempts to optimize; although we set out to optimize, we end up satisficing.

Audience Credibility

Audience credibility is a judgment of the integrity of the researcher in carrying out the study, especially for the many aspects not described in the report. Creation of a consensus around the researcher's interpretation of the evidence requires the audience attribute credibility to the researcher. Cronbach (1982) ingeniously phrased the problem this way: "Validity depends . . . on the way a conclusion is stated and communicated. Validity is subjective rather than objective: the plausibility of the conclusion is what counts. And plausibility, to twist a cliché, lies in the ear of the beholder" (p. 108).

To build that consensus, the researcher must consider the expectations of the audience at each study stage: designing, implementing, and communicating the results. The audience may consist of gatekeepers (such as the committee members who select presentations for professional association programs, readers who review proposals for funding, and journal editors), fellow researchers, researchers in related areas, and practitioners interested in applying the results.

Ignoring concerns about audience credibility may prevent a good study from being adequately disseminated if the gatekeepers reject it. Even if they accept it, lack of concern for building credibility with the ultimate consumers of the research may delay or prevent consensus development. In basic research, if such a consensus is not formed immediately, it may form belatedly when the field is ready for it. In applied research, audiences who do not understand or accept the research will not apply it, and the purpose of the study will be negated.

Credibility is a function of both (1) substance—what steps the researcher has taken to ensure that the study is credible, and (2) presentation—how clear it is that the author is forthright about the weaknesses and/or problems of the study. For example, qualitative researchers, arguing that it may be impossible to prevent personal viewpoints from affecting their work, seek to be as self-aware of such influences as possible. They make that awareness part of their data and take it into account during interpretation. But taking such steps is only part of ensuring credibility. They must also inform the reader of the steps they took, and of the viewpoints and biases that might have affected their interpretations. Both taking actions that contribute to credibility in the research process and adequately communicating those steps in a way that conveys one's integrity are essential to building credibility with the audience.

Building Audience Credibility—Steps in the Research Process. We build audience credibility by conducting ourselves according to the highest code of professional conduct and then learning the particular expectations and concerns of our main audiences. A good place to learn the latter is at professional association conventions, where questions posed at the close of a presentation indicate audience concerns. In addition, here are a few suggestions:

- *Build on knowledge the audience has already accepted.* Remember the use of hypnosis in the Zimbardo study? For readers from the physical sciences, hypnosis is probably a stage trick, not based on solid accepted knowledge. Such readers would reject the study as soon as they encounter hypnosis in the report. Zimbardo and his associates assumed that the audience they wished to reach, behavioral scientists, would not find it objectionable and thus did not bother justifying its use.

    Policy studies are sometimes designed to show the generality of a finding, studies with strong external validity (GP). That goal is fine if you are less concerned with the mechanism itself than that it worked. Where you are trying to understand what is going on, as in basic research and many policy studies as well, you should make sure that the earlier work on which you are building had strong internal validity (LP) or that the lack of it has been taken into account.

- *Avoid the weaknesses of previous studies*. The audience likeliest to criticize your work knowledgeably consists of the real and self-perceived experts in your research area. If you are familiar with their past and current work, you will be able to convey how your study builds on past literature and avoids its errors. You may make some original mistakes, but repeating others' damages your professional credibility. If there isn't a better way, make that point explicitly to avoid inappropriate conclusions about your competence.

- *Use accepted techniques and measures*. Other things being equal, use accepted methods, measures, definitions, terminology, and knowledge. Accepted forms increase credibility—unless, of course, the contribution of the study lies in such areas as new methodology or measures. The audience's familiarity with conventional methods facilitates communication. It results in readers who feel more capable of judging the study and have more confidence in that judgment.

  Using standard methods permits the audience readily to find the hallmarks of excellence it has come to associate with particular approaches. In a questionnaire study, for instance, they will look for that special effort to obtain a sample of nonrespondents' replies. Showing that they were like those of respondents helps justify interpretation of respondent data.

  To reach lay or practitioner audiences, use common terminology with few technical terms. Using instruments that look valid may be particularly important.

- *Justify use of the nonstandard*. Whenever researchers depart from the accepted, they carry the burden of proof. Pioneering a new method, coining new terms, and developing a new instrument all require making it "self-evident" to the audience that these were appropriate. Usually, these new versions require comparison with the standard choices to demonstrate their advantages. Also, researchers should justify the use of a controversial technique or measure, particularly when the controversy has appeared in the literature.

  In some instances, we must first teach the hallmarks of excellence for the innovation and then show that these appear in the study in question. Instruction in methods and terminology may be especially necessary for an untutored or lay audience; otherwise, important aspects may seem unnecessary complexities.

  Sometimes an accepted instrument is not quite "on target" for a construct; a less well-known one measures it more precisely. We trade ready acceptance of the standard measure for a better measure, but we must exert the extra effort to educate the audience to its merits. Another of the many trade-off decisions in research, this is part of the optimizing process.

Audiences willing to grant that a study showed an effect in one setting, internal validity (LP), are often much less willing to grant its generality, particularly to their own situation. Credibility with each new audience may require repeating previous studies in circumstances relevant to them. Language laboratories, programmed instruction, and educational television have each had to be demonstrated anew in different contexts. For example, language laboratories had to be shown to work with each of the foreign languages and programmed instruction and educational television with each different subject matter. We have learned the importance of demonstrating effectiveness in each new field from the county agricultural extension agent. Through field trials, they learned they must demonstrate the effectiveness of a new seed corn in each county to convince farmers of the generality of its effectiveness. (Further discussed on pp. 641–643.)

> *Credibility with the audience is enhanced by several actions taken in the research process:*
> ✦ *By building on knowledge that the audience has already accepted.*
> ✦ *By demonstrating familiarity with the relevant literature.*
> ✦ *By avoiding the weaknesses of previous similar studies.*
> ✦ *By using accepted research techniques, measures, definitions, and terminology.*
> ✦ *By justifying the use of any nonstandard or controversial aspects and educating the audience to their superiority.*

Building Audience Credibility—The Presentation of Findings. *The essential audience with whom credibility must be built is you.* Maintaining your integrity as a scientist and a scholar is a first priority. Do you recall Merton's norm of disinterestedness (see p. 53–54)? This does not refer to a lack of motivation. It means not lack of interest, but that, insofar as they are able, researchers in general prevent their personal expectations, hopes, and aspirations from influencing how they gather, analyze, and interpret their data.

Usually the integrity conveyed when a study is presented is a reflection of your own. (True, it is possible for individuals to succeed in playing the role of a person of integrity when that is not the case, but few researchers appear to be accomplished liars.) Integrity may require paying attention to such things as building a chain of reasoning only as strong as the data permit and not using salesmanship or propaganda techniques to build an apparently stronger one. Scientists are chided for showmanship, and such work tends to be suspect. Once an audience discovers something it thinks it should have been told and wasn't, audience credibility disappears. That the audience may be wrong in its perception makes no difference. The line between a solid and appropriate presentation that takes full advantage of the strengths of the study without concealing its weaknesses and one that exploits its strengths and underplays its weaknesses may be a fine one. But it is a boundary that *must be found and observed.* Erring on the conservative side may delay proper recognition of a knowledge claim, but it is generally considered the lesser of the evils.

Is there a role that the researcher can adopt? The researcher's task is more akin to that of a judge writing a decision than to that of a lawyer trying to make a case. Having come to a decision, the judge prepares a document that, while recognizing the cons, presents the strongest possible argument for the pros, explaining how and why the conclusion was reached. Similarly the researcher, having made a knowing judgment about the proper interpretation of the data, prepares the case. He or she reports it in such a way that we can carefully examine the argument, and it does not depend for its appeal on the eloquence of the writer (Cronbach and Suppes, 1969). In preparing that decision, both judge and researcher must consider the expectations of the audience and what concerns its members are likely to have.

The foregoing should make clear that building credibility with the audience has nothing to do with hiding a study's weaknesses, misconstruing the data, or overgeneralizing. Protection of the progress of science is reason enough for such a stance. From a personal standpoint, such errors reflect on one's professional competence as well.

> *Credibility with the audience is important to acceptance of a study's findings. It involves presenting the findings in ways that:*
> ✦ *Provide the kinds of evidence expected by the audience.*
> ✦ *Answer the audience's questions and allay its concerns.*
> ✦ *Appropriately reflect the study's strengths and weaknesses.*
> ✦ *Convey the integrity of the researcher.*

Relative Weighting of Internal Validity (LP) and External Validity (GP)

Ideally, studies have enough internal validity (LP) to create a consensus that a relationship exists and enough external validity (GP) to show appropriate generality; preferably, both are optimized. Actions taken to strengthen internal validity (LP), however, tend to weaken external validity (GP); they tend to work against each other. Thus, for each study, the researchers must decide how to achieve the optimum **relative weighting of internal validity (LP) and external validity (GP)** to reach the goals of the study.

For example, to strengthen internal validity (LP), we tend to narrow the scope of the question studied. This permits us to observe easily the phenomenon under controlled conditions, possibly even laboratory conditions. This artificiality shrinks external validity (GP). Bronfenbrenner (1977) described the efforts to strengthen the internal validity (LP) of developmental psychology as resulting in "the science of strange behavior of children in strange situations with strange adults for the briefest possible time" (p. 513).

Internal validity (LP) is usually stressed in the early studies to ensure that a relationship does indeed exist. Once established, however, interest turns to how broadly it applies, and emphasis shifts from internal validity (LP) to external validity (GP).

Some policy studies determining whether a given program or policy works, however, place the initial emphasis on external validity (GP). Does it work across a variety of persons, places, and so forth? Take, for example, the Head Start studies of preschool programs for underprivileged children throughout the United States. They evaluated programs with every possible range of activity, cultural backgrounds, regions of the country, and school milieus. These initial studies showed no advantage to the program, so studies seeking the "effective ingredient" were delayed. More carefully designed later studies showed the expected gains both in Head Start (Royce, Lazar, and Darlington, 1983) and similar programs (Schweinhart and Weikart, 1985). They had strong external validity (GP)—change occurred widely. Typically, findings that a treatment worked in a variety of situations (that is, had generality) would be followed with tight internal validity studies to determine the cause.

Limited resources may restrict the size of the sample or the number of sites we can study; as a result, external validity (GP) must often be constrained. By contrast, in determining the presence of a relationship, we can use any one of the wide variety of design choices in which the relationship either is present or can be created. Thus, emphasizing internal validity (LP) typically results in a less expensive study.

The relative importance of internal validity (LP) and external validity (GP) varies with the disposition of persons. Some individuals are innovators, risk takers. We often refer to them as early adopters, persons on the "cutting edge." They eagerly take the findings of studies with internal validity (LP) and try them out before much external validity (GP) evidence is available. Others, more conservative, require stronger external validity (GP) studies before accepting a finding as likely to be useful to them—late adopters.

Similarly the nature of the decision influences which validity we emphasize. Suppose the decision requires a good bit of investment of resources (time, effort, money), with relatively small return. In that case, to be sure it will work in a new instance, we seek external validity (GP) evidence. This is one of the reasons expensive electronic equipment must be shown to work in each field of application before adoption. If little investment may yield big potential payoffs, trials in a variety of situations may not be as important, because individuals may make those efforts on their own.

Thus, the emphasis on internal validity (LP) or external validity (GP) can be affected by such factors as whether (1) it is a basic or applied study, (2) it requires a large investment, (3) the ratio of potential payoff to costs is large or small, and (4) the researchers are risk takers or conservatives. This may seem like a lot to bear in mind, but successful researchers manage to balance internal validity (LP) and external validity (GP) so as to meet their own and others' requirements.

♦ *Strengthening internal validity (LP) usually diminishes external validity (GP). Each study must find the proper balance of the two for its purposes. Basic research usually emphasizes internal validity (LP); certain applied research and policy studies may initially emphasize external validity (GP).*

Resource Allocation

When you read a study, you see only the final choices that were made in problem choice, formulation, design, analysis, and interpretation of findings. **Resource allocation** is concerned with decisions about investment of researcher (and staff) time, energy, and other resources—the actual choices rather than their alternatives. Resource allocation determines: How much time should be devoted to problem conceptualization? Study design? Data gathering? Analysis and interpretation? What will be required to procure research space, equipment, measuring instruments, and so on? Resource allocation also contributes to the determination of the relative emphasis of internal validity (LP) and external validity (GP).

We noted an earlier instance of resource allocation when, in discussing the chain analogy and "a chain is only as strong as its weakest link," we drew the conclusion that all the links should be of approximately the same strength (Chapter 4). That conclusion is a prime criterion of good resource allocation. It makes no sense to concentrate on only one link when another might allow the argument to come crashing down. Let us examine how resource allocation decisions affect the links.

Question Choice and Formulation. There is considerable testimonial evidence on the contribution of problem formulation to problem solution. Getzels (1982) quotes Einstein:

> The formulation of a problem is often more essential than its solution, which may be merely a matter of mathematical or experimental skill. To raise new questions, new possibilities, to regard old questions from a new angle, requires creative imagination and marks real advance in science. (Einstein and Infeld, 1938, p. 92).

Getzels notes that this idea is reinforced by Wertheimer (1945): "Often in great discoveries the most important thing is that a certain question is found. Envisaging, putting the productive question, is often a more important, . . . a greater achievement than the solution of a set of questions" (p. 123).

Although question choice and formulation are intertwined, the choice often precedes formulation. Given an "itch one wants to scratch," can we find a satisfactory formulation? Clearly, some questions lend themselves easily to investigation. Others, such as Zimbardo's problem in Chapter 1, are difficult—we couldn't let aged people grow gradually deaf and do nothing about it. Only by reformulating it to substitute temporary deafness through hypnosis on college students did Zimbardo make it tractable.

Once found, the answer is obvious, as in Zimbardo's case, but troublesome aspects often become apparent only during our search for a satisfactory formulation. For example, we would expect that the more we spend in educating students, the better the education should be. However, many problems appear in trying to unravel per-pupil expenditure figures—differences in salary schedules, determinants of salary increments, costs of space and maintenance, and so on.

Zimbardo doesn't state how long it took to come up with the reformulation. The general problem for researchers is to decide at what point to stop allocating resources to this process and proceed with the study. Frequently, researchers are not at all sure that they have stopped at the right place. It is possible that further work would have resulted in a more important problem or a better-formulated one—the reason why this criterion is optimized instead of being completely fulfilled. Researchers reformulate until some inner criterion of optimality is satisfied and then proceed, never knowing what might have been missed.

Other Links in the Chain of Reasoning. In a fashion similar to the analysis of the problem finding, the researcher must consider each link in the chain. How can we best design this study? What method or combination of methods should be used? What sample of subjects? What situations? What treatment or independent variable? The questions are legion; mostly, we allocate resources in accordance with the difficulty of finding a satisfactory choice. If an appropriate measure is not available, we must allocate resources for the construction of a new one. If the initial design does not rule out certain important alternative explanations, we develop a new design. Designs are often reformulated several times before a satisfactory one is found.

Concealed from the reader is the fact that the design choice may have been but one of a number that were explored. Alternatives, which may have been time consumingly explored, are not typically mentioned. Remember how long a trip seems the first time you make it? Retracing the route, without the wrong turns and byways, is so much shorter. Readers of a study see it in the latter way, not as it looked to the researcher the first time through. Thus, although you can judge the allocation of resources to the final design, it is difficult from the report to know the total allocation pattern.

✦ *Resource allocation is the hidden decision making that determines the relative strength of the various parts of a study. Although confined within resource limits, what is available may be allocated in many ways. The researcher's task is to optimize the allocation to fit the problem, goal, and audience.*

Limits and Constraints

Limits and constraints are our final set of considerations: (1) What can ethically be done? (2) What research will an institution allow? and (3) What are the resource limits?

Ethical Constraints

Because of its importance, we shall devote all of Chapter 10 to the question of ethics and discuss additional aspects as required throughout the book. It suffices to note here that professional societies have developed codes of ethics that can limit the kinds of problems open to study. Human subject protection committees (and similar committees for animals) are established by institutions doing research to see that **ethical standards** are observed by their researchers and determine whether the potential worth of knowledge gained justifies whatever discomfort or suffering may be incurred.

Institutional Constraints

Researchers who do studies in institutional settings find research a secondary consideration to whatever activity achieves the service goals for which the institution was established. Such **institutional constraints** limit what the institution will allow the researcher to do, especially if a study interferes with an institutional schedule or interrupts essential activities. Only a limited amount of time can be taken from classroom teaching or asked of a patient receiving therapy.

Limits are rarely fixed; exceptions must be negotiated by the researcher. Because most institutions try to maintain business as usual come what may, those institutions that allow their schedules to be disrupted by research are unusual. Such disruptions bear testimony to some combination of the negotiating skill of the investigator, the perceived value of the research, and/or the atypicality of an institution. The last, of course, weakens the generality of those findings in which nature of the institution is an important factor.

Access is especially difficult when controversial topics are probed or when a study could reflect unfavorably on the institution. Administrators often grant access for study of what they perceive as a desirable development only to find it reported unfavorably. Rist (1977), for example, observed the integration of African American children bused to previously all-white schools in Portland, Oregon—a program of which the administration was proud. He pointed out, however, that integration meant assimilation to the point that African American culture was devalued. The school administration was offended.

Similar incidents make administrators reluctant to approve researcher requests that appear more interested in revealing unfortunate conditions than in protecting the institution. Each additional highly critical report, as its controversy spreads, probably raises barriers to similar studies. A no-win situation sometimes develops, and the researcher must decide who shall be harmed instead of avoiding harm altogether. Taylor (1977), for example, found that institutional attendants drank beer to the point where it interfered with their duties to the patients. Yet he did not report this, rationalizing that the impact of the study on the institutionalization problem as a whole was more important than remedying this instance of impropriety.

Whether and how to "blow the whistle" on such social problems are also ethical dilemmas for the researcher. The researcher believes that society should know about such conditions. Yet such revelations may undermine support for the institution and deny what help is now given to people who need it. In addition, the professional careers of persons who cooperated may be damaged. Although some people might argue that if they created the conditions, they deserve to suffer the consequences, this reasoning in no way enhances the researcher's image. Researchers come to be perceived by the authorities as meddlers unsympathetic to administrative complexities and lacking real understanding of the problem. Such perceptions interfere with the study of social problems needing correction, and the institutions most needing study may become inaccessible.

The foregoing discussion has assumed the researcher is approaching the institution as an outsider seeking permission. Many take the position that research and especially evaluations (see Chapter 23) should be a collaborative affair between the researcher and the institutional personnel and/or administrators. In the case of action research, the research is often done by the institutional personnel who will be the research users, its prime audience (see also action research in Chapter 23). In these latter instances, the situation becomes one not of constraints externally imposed by an administrator but of researcher and institutional personnel mutually seeking to determine what institutional limits are appropriate.

> ✦ *Institutional constraints typically prevent researchers from engaging in activities that may interfere with their ongoing routine or may reflect unfavorably on the institution, its performance, or its personnel. Such constraints have serious implications for what social problems researchers can investigate.*
> ✦ *Where the research or evaluation studies are done collaboratively, or as in action research, the institutional limits are not externally imposed but internally determined by the researchers.*

Resource Limits

Resources are rarely sufficient for all we hope to do. We think of the main resources as our time and energy as investigators. Graduate students writing dissertations tend to think of these as relatively unlimited—they simply put in whatever it takes. Nevertheless, these resources are limited in a practical sense. Time expended on a study must be evaluated in terms of its alternative uses, what economists call its marginal utility or opportunity cost (for example, working to earn money instead of spending that time on more dissertation development). Hence, the real costs are rarely included in the researcher's decision making. Keeping a study in the perspective of alternative important activities and alternative research projects allows us to assign more reasonable limits to it.

Resource limits are often fixed by the available staff, equipment, instruments, and the like as well as by money—the size of a grant or budget. Given positive results, however, we can sometimes find new resources, and limits may not be as fixed as we tend to regard them. Nonetheless, expanding such limits takes time and energy and is usually far from certain. Thus, deciding to seek additional funds is itself part of the resource allocation process. Note also that seeking funding may subject you to the requirements of a sponsor. These can bring many changes to such areas as the focus of the study, the relative importance of various audiences, and the time schedule for completion—all factors that you must view in terms of the study's importance in the larger picture of your career, the needs of your discipline or profession, and your responsibility to society.

With some experience, you will discover that the same study can be built in a variety of sizes. This realization suggests that a resource limit may not be a bad thing because many alternative formulations of a study can be made to fit within it. However, different study goals—large and impressive studies for Congress and lay audiences, smaller studies done to very high standards for professional audiences—suggest that there are guidelines for resource size. Optimal size for a study is determined by such variables as the need for sufficient sensitivity to show the relationship, size for representativeness and generality, and impressiveness for uncertainty reduction. These also suggest that there may be a minimal level below which the study may not have the intended effect—a study too small to reduce the uncertainty of a nonprofessional audience or too small to sense an effect, even if it should occur (more on the latter point in Chapter 19).

Resource limits clearly determine the constraints within which resource allocation can take place. Because the latter is one of the essential tasks of a researcher, resource limits can be a determining factor of research quality.

✦ *Resource limits set the boundaries on resource allocation.*

✦ *There is considerable flexibility in the design of studies. Studies of a given problem can be built to different sizes to fit particular goals or designed in alternative ways to fit a resource limit.*

✦ *Resource limits imposed on a given problem often reflect its relative importance in the larger scheme of knowledge development.*

✦ *There is probably both an optimal and a minimal size for a study based on the expectations of the audience, the size required to sense the expected effect, and the generality intended.*

SUMMARY

Although it is apparent that internal validity (LP) and external validity (GP) are important characteristics of a research study, other characteristics also shape it. One, audience credibility, is a function of how well the design, implementation, and report of a study anticipates the concerns of its main audiences and alleviates them; provides evidence of the integrity of the researcher; and builds trust by using standard procedures, explaining the merits of nonstandard ones, and supplying an understanding of why the researcher made what may appear to be dubious or controversial design or procedure choices.

A second characteristic is the relative weighting of internal validity (LP) and external validity (GP) such that the evidence sufficiently supports the existence of the relationship and appropriately indicates its intended generality.

A third characteristic, resource allocation, is apparent in the complex process of allocating time, energy, and funds during the designing, implementing, and reporting of research. However, only the final product of the process appears in the research report. Ideally, it permits the intended balance of internal validity (LP) and external validity (GP) to be achieved and links in the chain of reasoning to be equally strengthened.

There are many ways in which each of the three criteria may be satisfied. Fulfilling one may be at the expense of another. Furthermore, there may be differences among researchers concerning the optimal level to be achieved on each criterion. Therefore, these criteria are optimized for each study rather than being fully satisfied.

This optimization must be achieved within: (1) the ethical limits prescribed by each discipline for the protection of both humans and animals; (2) the constraints of each institution that protect their operations in the face of research requirements; and (3) the limits on the investigator's personal time and energy as well as on the resources available from the institution, a research grant, or a contract.

A Look Ahead

This chapter noted the importance of understanding and abiding by the constraints imposed by ethical standards. Chapter 10 expands further on the nature of these constraints; how they have come about; and the role of the federal government, institutions, and professional associations in developing them and seeing that they are observed.

ADDITIONAL READING

Krathwohl (1985)

IMPORTANT TERMS

Audience credibility
Internal validity (LP) and external validity (GP),
    relative weighting of
Ethical standards

Institutional constraints
Resource allocation
Resource limits

APPLICATION PROBLEMS

1. Reread the summary of Jonassen's study of pattern notes (page 73). His purpose was to verify this technique as a simple, practical means of assessing a learner's cognitive structure. What has he done to build audience credibility?

2. You are a researcher who is interested in the acquisition of second languages. You want to test a newly developed technique for teaching correct pronunciation in French to high school students and to compare it with the program in current use. Both approaches are based on the use of listening tapes. You are considering whether or not to bring groups of students to the university's language laboratory, where you can randomly assign them to one or the other approach. You have the support of local school officials and can bring in several classes. Considering internal validity (LP) and external validity (GP), what would be the advantages and disadvantages of doing so?

3. Reread the description of the study on impulsiveness-reflectiveness by Kagen and asso-

ciates in the *answer* to problem 4 on page 156. Note that the concept was developed during research on analytic versus global reasoning. From the information available, what choices did these investigators appear to make in terms of resource allocation?

4. Psychologist Sarah Ellenova compared student-generated questions about a text passage with adjunct questions inserted by the author. She sought to carry out her study in several elementary schools in the local school system. She was granted permission to investigate only one group, the sixth grade class at the University Elementary School, a laboratory school run jointly by the university and the school board. It was, she was told, the only school properly set up to allow such research without unnecessarily disrupting school routines. How could these institutional constraints affect her study?

Compare your answers with those following the Application Exercise.

APPLICATION EXERCISE

What constraints do you think you might encounter with your problem? Do you anticipate ethical problems? If so, you may want to jump ahead to Chapter 10. Will institutions be reluctant to let you in to gather data? What might you do to lessen such problems? Entry is often a problem; we'll consider that further in Chapter 12. Do you anticipate insufficient resources of some kind? If you may need addi-

tional monetary resources, see section 4, "Finding Funding," in Krathwohl (1988), which examines sources of both public and private funding. What balance of internal validity (LP) and external validity (GP) do you anticipate? Is yours closer to basic research or applied research? Do you anticipate any particular problems with audience credibility at this point in your problem's development? You may want to think about this issue again after you have chosen a research method. As for resource allocation, as your plans for your study firm up, consider doing a work plan such as is described in Krathwohl (1988) beginning on page 73.

ANSWERS TO THE APPLICATION PROBLEMS

1. First, Jonassen built his study on knowledge that the audience had already accepted. He began his article with a discussion of existing instructional design theory and pointed out what he thought was missing. He next compared the various techniques available for assessing cognitive structure and, on the basis of that information, presented his rationale for choosing to use pattern notes instead. Part of this explanation showed why he believed the existing methods were not appropriate. Thus, he also attempted to avoid the weaknesses of previous similar studies.

Second, he used an existing, accepted technique, free word association, to validate pattern notes as an assessment method. It was, he noted, the most valid and reliable method available for assessing a learner's cognitive structure.

2. You want to demonstrate that the new approach is more effective than the current one—internal validity (LP)—but you would also like to show that this is true with other such groups and in other situations—external validity (GP). Conducting the study in the laboratory would allow you tight control of most variables and would probably help to strengthen internal validity (LP). Most important, you would be able to use such methods as the random assignment of students to either treatment and the standardization of your instructions to eliminate rival hypotheses. It is, however, an artificial situation (for these students) and not one in which the approach will normally be used. That in itself could account for a demonstrated effect.

Demonstrating the relationship through a study conducted in the schools—in the natural environment—would certainly improve external validity (GP). The new approach would be shown to be superior in the situation in which it would normally be used. Such a result would also be more difficult to obtain. Unless the schools also have language laboratories, it would be hard to standardize your treatments. Furthermore, random assignment of students to the two approaches could be unacceptable for ethical or administrative reasons. You would generally be less able to guarantee the equivalence of your samples, and it would be more difficult to eliminate rival explanations.

In this case, however, it is probably essential to know whether any advantage attributed to the proposed technique will hold up when it is used in the schools. So you may wish to emphasize external validity (GP) and conduct your study in the schools if at all possible.

3. Resource allocation reflects the hidden decisions that a researcher makes, such as what question to choose, how to formulate it, and where to invest time and energy. Perhaps the most obvious (and important) choice that Kagen and colleagues made was that of the question. They were originally studying these other concepts when they noticed the tendency of analytic individuals to take longer to respond to questions. It led them to wonder whether this was a stable trait and to want to investigate it.

Once they had chosen this question, its formulation was fairly easy: Measure the time taken to complete questions or problems and the error rate in doing so. They also had to invest considerable effort in the development and validation of a new measure, their Matching Figures Test, before they could actually test for the concepts in question .

4. They could strongly affect the generalizability of any results she might obtain. Although perhaps not totally a laboratory situation, such a school probably would not represent the other schools in the district. We would expect more (and more varied) visitors than in a typical school. It would likely be staffed with exceptionally enthusiastic and capable teachers who had agreed to work in a more public atmosphere and to be equipped with extra resources and paraphernalia for research, such as two-way mirrors.

All of this could contribute to an unusual atmosphere in the school, perhaps allowing for more highly motivated students than would be found in an average school. It is probable that the school would be the site of a variety of experimental programs. Further, if such a school were located in a residential district near the university, we might also find a higher proportion of children from professional families who might be expected to be, on the average, more capable than those in a more average school.

CHAPTER 10

Ethical Standards and Legal Constraints

> The scientific research enterprise is built on a foundation of trust. . . . To maintain that trust . . . more attention must be given to the mechanisms that sustain and transmit the values . . . associated with ethical scientific conduct. In the past, scientists learned [them] . . . by working with senior scientists. . . . That tradition . . . is no longer sufficient. . . .
>
> *Alberts and Shine (1994)*

OVERVIEW

Ethical standards, one of the three constraints on research discussed in Chapter 9, divides into two aspects: (1) the legal and institutional constraints designed to protect the people from whom data are gathered and (2) the responsibility of the individual researcher for proper conduct above and beyond legalities. The former, covered by U.S. federal regulations, ensures that the researcher's institution provides adequate safeguards for the protection of human subjects in all federally funded research. Most institutions require that these regulations be met for all such research, even unfunded studies, by both faculty and graduate students.

Because each widely publicized ethical problem not only tarnishes the perpetrator but also affects the work of other researchers, professional associations have established codes of conduct. Ethical violations that occur in the privacy of a professional office are almost impossible to police. Trust, integrity and voluntary compliance are the cornerstones that make standards work. This chapter discusses the ethical problems involved in research question selection, confidentiality and privacy, decisions in the field, data ownership, and relations with the institutional review board. Analyzing and reporting data with integrity are the topics of Chapter 25, which is concerned with whether and how well science works.

CHAPTER CONTENTS

Introduction

Although published professional standards in psychology were formulated as early as 1951 (American Psychological Association, 1951), extensive emphasis on the protection of human subjects arose primarily as a result of government intervention. Before that, many members of the professions were concerned by studies that, although they made important points, did so by deceiving the subjects. Milgram's (1963) study was one that provoked an early outcry. In his experiment, a first subject in a cubicle thought he was helping a second subject in an adjoining cubicle to learn. The first subject did so by applying electric shocks to the second subject at the request of the investigator. When asked to do so, the first subject moved the lever, presumably increasing the shocks into what was labeled as the "danger" level even after hearing a groan and then silence from the person receiving them. Individuals were informed during **debriefing** after the study that no shocks were given and that the other person was a confederate.

Milgram thought the study important, for it showed that ordinary persons could be made to do extraordinary things under certain circumstances. As Sieber and Stanley (1988) noted, blind obedience to authority is "more contextual and less characterological than most [people] have assumed" (p. 52). Milgram believed his evidence relevant to the questions involved in the Nuremberg trials of Nazi officials as war criminals when they claimed they were merely following orders. What a furor this interpretation created![1] People questioned whether the circumstances were comparable to those in Nazi Germany. It gave prominence to the issue of whether the value of the information gained was worth the discomfort of subjects requested to do such awful things.

A second issue involved the protection of subjects. They had neither asked to have such distasteful knowledge of themselves, nor did they realize they were go-

---

[1]Milgram (1974) notes, incidentally, that there were no objections to his study until the results were known. This raises the interesting question of how many of the criticisms resulted because the conclusions ran counter to what people wanted to believe.

ing to receive it. It could be very disturbing to realize that one was capable of such behavior. Whether deception of subjects that results in self-knowledge and stress is conscionable is at issue.

On what are such ethical judgments based? We noted early in the book that knowledge results from the development of a consensus around the appropriate interpretation of evidence. So, too, a consensus is required for actions to be judged ethical. In judging whether a study will meet standards, however, there are two differences from the judgments involved in findings becoming knowledge: Rarely is there evidence on which to base judgments—the consensus must be formed around what persons anticipate is likely to happen; and a value must be placed on the predicted consequences to determine whether gains outweigh costs. These conditions clearly make it much more difficult to form a consensus. People differ in their predictions of the likely consequences and of the seriousness of potential negative effects and in their estimate of the potential value of the knowledge we seek. Adding to the difficulty are absolutists for whom there is never any way gains in knowledge can offset harm to subjects; deception of subjects is always unacceptable.

How do we proceed? From whom can we gain a consensus that ensures meeting acceptable ethical standards? Two groups, the federal government and professional associations, have stepped into the breach. We shall first examine the federal apparatus for the protection of human subjects and then consider the principles established by professional associations to guide researchers.

Legal and Institutional Protection of Human Subjects

Two U.S. federal laws provide for regulation in ethical matters: the Family Educational Rights and Privacy Act[2] and the National Research Act 93–348 of 1974. The requirements of the latter are in *Code of Federal Regulations*, Title 45, Part 46, or 45CFR46, as it is usually referred to. It provides for what are known as **institutional review boards** (IRBs), which must approve projects forwarded for funding consideration. Technically the IRBs are responsible only for research funded by the US Department of Health and Human Services (HHS), but Grunder (1983) found that 96 percent of institutions have been applying the regulations to all research whether funded by HHS or not.

Institutional Review Boards

The membership of an IRB is specifically prescribed in the regulations:

- It must have at least five members.
- It may not consist of all men or all women.

---

[2]P.L. 93-380, Title V, Sec. 513 (b)(2)(i), 88 Stat. 574; 34 CFR Part 99. Regulations similiar to those for humans exist to protect animals used in research.

- It must include at least one nonscientist (examples given are lawyers, ethicists, clergypersons).
- It must include one person not affiliated with the institution or part of the immediate family of persons affiliated with it.
- Persons with a conflict of interest are to be excluded except to provide information.
- Persons with competency in special relevant areas may be invited to assist in the review but may not vote.
- If the board regularly reviews research involving a vulnerable category of subjects (such as the mentally retarded), the IRB must include one or more individuals "who are primarily concerned with the welfare of these subjects" (Sec. 46–107).

Approval is by majority vote. These boards not only have the responsibility of approving research plans, but also they may suspend or terminate approval of research that is not being conducted in accordance with the IRB's requirements or in which unexpected serious harm occurs. Adequate documentation of all IRB meetings and actions is required.

The criteria for IRB approval focus on the safety of subjects and include a lengthy discussion of informed consent:

- Risks to subjects are to be minimized; that is, the risks of harm must be "not greater, considering probability and magnitude, than those ordinarily encountered in daily life or during the performance of routine physical or psychological examinations or tests" (Sec. 46–103).
- "Risks are reasonable in relation to anticipated benefits, if any, to subjects, and the importance of the knowledge that may reasonably result" (Sec. 46–111). Note that this statement makes the IRB specifically responsible for evaluating the trade-off—for deciding how much risk this knowledge is worth.
- "Selection of subjects is equitable" (Sec. 46–111); that is, for example, that friends are not put at less risk or have greater potential benefits than strangers.
- Adequate provision is made for monitoring the safety of subjects, where appropriate.

As Grunder (1986) notes, the IRB is "a work of bureaucratic genius," a reasonably satisfactory solution to a complicated problem to which no solution will be lauded by everyone. It transfers the responsibility from the government to the institution but specifies what the institution must do to comply. Thus, there is no "Ethical FBI," as he puts it, to check out rumors; "no army of investigators lurking around thousands of laboratories" (p. 7). It solves the problem of where and among whom to obtain a consensus by specifying the board as the place where agreement must be found and by reducing "consensus" to a majority. It provides guidelines, leaving it to the board to interpret them and to decide when a rule is violated. The penalty for violation is the removal of eligibility for all future research moneys involving human subjects for the researcher *and the institution*—a severe penalty for a research institution.

The work of IRBs has become of such importance that they now have their own journal, *IRB: A Review of Human Subject Research*.[3] In it are discussions of such issues as IRBs being too responsive or too resistive to community pressure, too zealous in protecting subjects, and so on. Just as a body of law is developed by precedents, no doubt IRB judgments will be refined by experience and discussion.

    ✦ *Institutional review boards bear the responsibility for determining whether projects are ethically permissible and, if there are ethical questions, for deciding whether the potential knowledge that is gained is worth the potential risk that is involved.*

    ✦ *Although established under federal regulations for funded projects, IRBs are used for other research conducted at most institutions—regardless of funding sources.*

Informed Consent

A key part of work with human subjects is obtaining **informed consent**. It is especially important where:

- There is any possibility of risk.
- Minors are involved.
- Privacy may be invaded.
- Potentially distasteful self-knowledge may result from participation.

Similiar to other topics in the values arena, there is more to the issue of informed consent than meets the eye. Who can give informed consent? A jailed prisoner? A psychotic? A mentally retarded person? What constitutes sufficient information? How do we know when a person really understands and so can provide *informed* acquiescence? Certain safeguards have been put in place, and a number of aids have been developed. Grunder's text (1986) is such an aid, an excellent one providing a checklist on consent forms and procedures. Sample situations test the reader's mastery of the rules. Much of this chapter's material is patterned after Grunder. To begin, he notes that informed consent may be obtained on a short or long form.

Short and Long Consent Forms

The short form accompanies a verbal explanation and indicates the individual has been given information regarding the study, understands what he or she is committing to, and has received answers to all questions. Two copies must be signed and dated by the subject and a witness, a disinterested third party who was present during the presentation of the information. The verbal presentation

---

[3]Published by the Hastings Center, Institute of Society, Ethics and Life Sciences, 360 Broadway, Hasting-on-Hudson, NY 10706.

should give the information needed to make an informed decision. With short or long form, a reasonable opportunity must be given to the subjects to decide whether to participate. Those not signing should be dismissed courteously. Whether short or long form is used, the participant retains one of the two signed and dated copies.

The long form includes all the information that would be given verbally. It does not need to be witnessed, although Grunder notes that this is still a good idea. Under either short or long form, a witness can affirm that the assent was freely given, or the individual was allowed to leave with no sign of disfavor, and the individual was not coerced, or deceived into signing the form. When the long form is used, it is read aloud to the participant to reinforce its content and to be certain that it is read in its entirety. A brief verbal summary follows the reading. Although Grunder prefers the long form, Mann (1994), testing understanding with both long and short forms, concluded "the form should be as short and concise as possible" (p. 142). Furthermore, the long form apparently made some subjects believe that they had lost rights the form was designed to protect. She recommends reminding them, after they have signed it, that they have not.

Contents of the Consent Form

What must the consent form contain? These are its minimum requirements:

- Information as to who is doing the study; its nature; its purpose; procedures; hazards, risks, and inconveniences; benefits; if therapeutic, the alternative treatments that could be chosen; duration; and the identification of any experimental procedures.
- Availability of compensation and treatment if an injury should occur in cases of more than minimal risk.
- The extent, if any, to which confidentiality of records identifying the subject will be maintained.
- The name of the contact person to whom to address questions or report an injury.
- Notification that participation is voluntary and that refusal to participate or discontinue participation will be without penalty or loss of benefits to which the person is otherwise entitled.

In some instances, where appropriate, it should also reveal the following information:

- The fact that some risks are unforeseeable.
- The investigator's right to ask a subject to leave the study (usually the criteria for termination are given to show that this is not arbitrary).
- The promise that subjects will continue to be informed as information develops that may bear on participation.
- Additional costs to the subject resulting from participation.
- The consequences of withdrawal and the procedure for orderly termination of participation.
- The approximate number of subjects.

The consent form must be so written that its reading level makes it under-standable to the subjects. Readability formulas can be used to determine this, and Grunder (1986) includes those in his manual. Stanley, Sieber, and Melton (1987) note studies that have been made indicate that, in general, the risk disclosure re-quired by the consent process has had only a minimal influence on decision mak-ing with regard to medical procedures. This finding seems consistent with the few available psychological studies as well.

Altering or Waiving the Consent Process

The decision to alter or waive the consent process can be made only by an IRB. It can do so only if the research does not involve greater than *minimum risk*, the rights or welfare of the subjects will not be adversely affected, the research could not otherwise be done, and the subjects will be debriefed. Consent documenta-tion can be waived if the consent form links the individual to data that, if made public, could be harmful to the subject. For example, in a study of drug pushers, merely being identified as part of such a study might be considered the basis for subpoenaing the data to search for an illegal act. Humphreys (1975) makes fasci-nating reading on this latter problem. He studied an illegal act, homosexual be-havior in public places. He identified participants through their license plate numbers, tracked them down, and interviewed them. Realizing later that he could not protect his data from subpoena, he destroyed them. Only under special dispensation do social science researchers now have immunity under the law si-miliar to that of doctors and lawyers. This lack of a general immunity has been re-peatedly tested in the courts and is still the subject of litigation; its status may change. "Scientists engaged in research on mental health can obtain certificates of confidentiality from the Department of Health and Human Services which pro-vide immunity from subpoenas. The Department of Justice can provide grants of confidentiality to protect data gathered in research projects involving drugs" (Nelkin, 1984, p. 52).

Obtaining Consent When the Individual Is Incapable of Giving It

Can freely given informed consent be obtained from children, prisoners, and the mentally handicapped? Each is a special case. With children, informed consent must be obtained from *one* parent or legal guardian. In addition, assent—agree-ment to take part in the procedures—must also be sought from the child, and the IRB must determine if the child is capable of giving assent. The definition of a child is determined by state instead of federal statutes because the age of legal majority varies from state to state.

Prisoner consent must not involve procedures that would compare too fa-vorably with normal prison conditions so as to serve as enticement. Risks must be comparable to those of nonprisoner volunteers. The selection of subjects must be fair. Participation must have no effect on parole, and subjects must be so informed.

Procedures for working with the mentally handicapped and the elderly are not addressed by the regulations. Grunder (1986) strongly suggests using a professional who regularly works with the population in question and who has no ties to the project. This person can attest that consent procedures were followed; that consent or assent was obtained during a period when the subject was lucid; and that if assent is not within the realm of capability, the lack of objection may be enough if minimal risk is involved. In cases of more than minimal risk but benefit to the patient, approval from a court of appropriate jurisdiction should be sought. Grunder suggests reading Chapter 1 of the report of the National Commission for the Protection of Human Subjects of Biomedical and Behavioral Research as a guide.

✦ *Individuals used as subjects in a study, especially if there is any potential risk, if minors are involved, if privacy may be invaded, or if potentially distasteful self-knowledge may be gained, should give their voluntary signed consent. Problems arise when individuals are unable to do so because of such circumstances as incapacity, lack of freedom to make decisions, or status as a minor.*

Codes of Ethics from Professional Associations

Many professional associations have developed a set of ethical standards for their field. Typical of these is *Ethical Principles in the Conduct of Research with Human Participants* by the Committee on Protection of Human Participants in Research of the American Psychological Association (1982). The **code of ethics** consists of ten principles, each followed by "a discussion [that] relates the Principle to various problems, research settings, and populations of research participants" (p. 25). This excerpt includes the ten principles:[4]

> The decision to undertake research rests upon a considered judgment by the individual psychologist about how best to contribute to psychological science and human welfare. . . .
>   a) In planning a study, the investigator has the responsibility to make a careful evaluation of its ethical acceptability. To the extent the weighing of scientific and humane values suggests a compromise of any principle, the investigator incurs a correspondingly serious obligation to seek ethical advice and to observe stringent safeguards to protect the rights of human participants.
>   b) Considering whether a participant in a planned study will be a "subject at risk" or a "subject at minimal risk," according to recognized standards, is of primary ethical concern to the investigator.

---

[4]The committee's statement makes clear that the principles should be interpreted in terms of the context of the complete document, which is offered as a supplement to them.

c) The investigator always retains the responsibility for ensuring ethical practice in research. The investigator is also responsible for the ethical treatment of research participants by collaborators, assistants, students, and employees, all of whom, however, incur similar obligations.

d) Except in minimal-risk research, the investigator establishes a clear and fair agreement with research participants, prior to their participation, that clarifies the obligations and responsibilities of each. The investigator has the obligation to honor all promises and commitments included in that agreement. The investigator informs the participants of all aspects of the research that might reasonably be expected to influence willingness to participate and explains all other aspects of the research about which the participants inquire. Failure to make full disclosure prior to obtaining informed consent requires additional safeguards to protect the welfare and dignity of the research participants. Research with children or with participants who have impairments that would limit understanding and/or communication requires special safeguarding procedures.

e) Methodological requirements of a study may make use of concealment or deception necessary. Before conducting such a study, the investigator has a special responsibility to (1) determine whether the use of such techniques is justified by the study's prospective scientific, educational, or applied value; (2) determine whether alternative procedures are available that do not use concealment or deception; and (3) ensure that the participants are provided with sufficient explanation as soon as possible.

f) The investigator respects the individual's freedom to decline to participate in or withdraw from the research at any time. The obligation to protect this freedom requires careful thought and consideration when the investigator is in a position of authority or influence over the participant. Such positions of authority include, but are not limited to, situations in which research participation is required as a part of employment or in which the participant is a student, client, or employee of the investigator.

g) The investigator protects the participant from physical and mental discomfort, harm, and danger that may arise from research procedures. If risks of such consequences exist, the investigator informs the participant of that fact. Research procedures likely to cause serious or lasting harm to a participant are not used unless the failure to use these procedures might expose the individual to risk of greater harm or unless the research has great potential benefit and fully informed and voluntary consent is obtained from each participant. The participant should be informed of procedures for contacting the investigator within a reasonable time period following participation should stress, potential harm, or related questions or concerns arise.

h) After the data are collected, the investigator provides the participant with information about the nature of the study and attempts to remove any misconceptions that may have arisen. Where scientific or humane values justify delaying or withholding this information, the investigator incurs a special responsibility to monitor the research and ensure that there are no damaging consequences for the participant.

i) Where research procedures result in undesirable consequences for the individual participant, the investigator has the responsibility to detect and remove or correct the consequences, including long-term effects.

j) Information obtained about a research participant during the course of an investigation is confidential unless otherwise agreed upon in advance. When the possibility exists that others may obtain access to such information, this possibility, together with the plans for protecting confidentiality, is explained to the participant as part of the procedure for obtaining informed consent.[5]

In its annual directory, the American Psychological Association also publishes a set of ethical standards for psychologists, which cover not just research but all professional activities.[6] Most would apply to any social science.

In addition to ethical standards, associations have formulated standards for various fields of work, such as standardized testing (see Chapter 18) and evaluation (see Chapter 23). Although in no way intended to have legal standing, these carefully crafted statements are often cited as expert opinion in legal cases. They have therefore come to have a marked influence beyond what might otherwise be expected of pronouncements set forth for voluntary compliance.

    ✦ *Professional associations have developed codes of ethics and standards for the guidance of both the lay public and members of their professions. Although without legal standing, they are sometimes cited in legal cases.*

Collaboration with Research Subjects

There is increasing interest in making research collaborative. Because qualitative researchers think of those whom they study as informants, collaboration comes easily. Although such collaboration is less frequent among quantitative researchers, they also can often design their projects and identify and solve ethical problems by working with their subjects. Such a stance educates those involved in the ways of science. It gives them increased feelings of self-worth and motivates them to work with the researcher both to find the best solutions to the problems and to do well what is required of them as subjects. Although collaboration would too drastically change some studies, where it is practical, the researcher may be surprised by the quality of the collaborators' suggestions for improvement, some of which would probably not otherwise have been thought of. The topic of collaborative research is discussed as a part of evaluation and action research in Chapter 23.

---

[5]American Psychological Association, *Ethical Principles in the Conduct of Research with Human Participants.* Washington, DC: American Psychological Association, pp. 5–7. Copyright © 1982 by the American Psychological Association. Adapted with permission. APA cautions that the 1982 *Ethical Principles in the Conduct of Research with Human Participants* is no longer current, and is not enforceable by the APA Ethics Code of 1992, but may be of educative value to psychologists, courts and professional bodies.

    Although the APA insists on the permission wording above, the 1982 statement is their most recent version of this publication.

[6]To assist in the interpretation of the principles, a casebook has been developed citing actual instances considered by the American Psychological Association's Ethics Committee (American Psychological Association, 1987).

Common Ethical Concerns

Problem Choice

The ethical role often includes the choice of problem, as is made clear by the two excerpts on pages 56–57 from researchers who chose to forgo pursuit of a problem rather than take actions violating their sense of what is right. Clearly, not all studies raise such ethical dilemmas, but it is the responsibility of the researcher to search for the ethical aspects of each problem and to make a judgment as to whether to pursue it.

Deception. We can argue that some topics cannot be studied without **deception of subjects**, withholding true knowledge of the nature of the study. Studies of entrance procedures to college to determine the effect of racial and sexual identification, the effects of subliminal messages, the effects of certain drugs, and other topics may all require concealment of the true purpose of the study. The Zimbardo study of Chapter 1 is such an example. IRBs do approve such studies from time to time (for example, the Zimbardo study). Why do some persons categorically reject such procedures? Baumrind (1985), summarizing the arguments from different points of view, notes that such approvals fail to take into account long-range costs that are "unknown and therefore easy for investigators and review boards to dismiss" (p. 167). For example, deception may:

> offend participants or damage their self-esteem, give. . . research a bad name and work to the detriment of the research of others, lower the level of the participants' confidence in the quality of their relationships with others or provide them with a bad example on which they may model their behavior (American Psychological Association, 1973, pp. 11–12).

It is difficult to obtain evidence regarding the absence of harm to subjects that is acceptable to opponents of deception. For instance, Milgram (1974, 1977) argues that he adequately debriefed his subjects, and in a one-year follow-up, 80 percent said they were glad to have taken part and less than 1 percent of his subjects regretted it. Patten (1977), however, argues that the evidence comes from "destructively obedient" individuals; that is, we could hardly expect them to say otherwise. Furthermore, Baumrind (1985) notes that when queried about the study, such subjects need to deny they have allowed themselves "to be treated as objects, and . . . [therefore] most will say that they were glad to have been subjects" (p. 169). In the face of such arguments, it is difficult to gather evidence acceptable to people who oppose the practice.

Decreased trust of others is a cost to both the individual and society. Debriefed subjects have been found to be less inclined to trust experimenters to tell the truth (Fillenbaum, 1966). That same distrust rubs off on the rest of the profession. Baumrind (1985) also sees the practice as deteriorating the researcher's "ethical sensibilities and integrity." She argues that the continued use of such practices becomes self-defeating. As enough subjects are made suspicious, naiveté becomes a variable, and Page (1973) showed that naive subjects generally behave differently from suspicious ones.

There are clearly strong arguments against using deception, and IRBs no doubt carefully weigh any proposal for its rare use. Careful debriefing by a skilled professional certainly is one condition of its use. If it is employed, Sieber's (1983) recommendations are worth consulting, and Mills (1976), who attempted to educate his subjects, may provide a model.

✦ *Certain research topics cannot be pursued without deception. Some people believe that they should be excluded from the research agenda.*

Data Confidentiality and Personal Privacy

Confidentiality and privacy are often mistakenly assumed to relate to the same concern. **Confidentiality** refers to control of access to information; **privacy** refers to a person's interest in controlling boundaries between self and others (Sieber and Stanley, 1988). *Anonymity*, a related concept, refers to researchers' not knowing the identity of subjects or at least not being able to link data with specific subjects. In most research, ensuring confidentiality of data is just plain good practice.

As noted earlier, because researchers have no general immunity from subpoena like some professionals, *they must gather data in such a way that anonymity is ensured from the outset*.[7] The main use of identifiers such as name, address, and so forth is usually to link items of data such as test scores with other data from the same person. Data gathered with identifiers can be made anonymous by tearing off this information once it is no longer needed. Researchers can also use various means that do not violate confidentiality to link data or to gather responses to sensitive questions (see Chapter 16). Sometimes a neutral third party can receive the data, remove the identifiers, and pass the data on to the researcher. Keys for identification can be held by a neutral person in another country, where subpoenas cannot be served. As noted earlier, immunity from subpoena can be granted by the U.S. Department of Health and Human Services and the Department of Justice for certain kinds of projects. In short, there are enough ways of handling this situation that the problem more often stems from inadequate attention to solutions than from a lack of them.

Inadequate provision for confidentiality protection can cause problems. Consider the *Chronicle of Higher Education* report (Dispatch Case, 1986) that the government of Sweden ordered all clues to the identity of participants destroyed. It thus terminated and rendered useless past sociological information on 15,000 Stockholm residents who had been part of a longitudinal study since 1966. It quotes Jansson, who started the project, as writing: "It is grotesque that people under study can deprive me of material I have worked on for more than 20 years; fantastic that they think they own information on themselves" (p. 42). Critics called the comment "academic arrogance." We can criticize the researcher as not

---

[7]Nelkin (1984) reports that "between 1966 and 1976 at least 50 scholars were served subpoenas in 18 different cases, ordering them to reveal the identities of sources and subjects of research; another 30 scientists were threatened with subpoenas" (p. 51).

having adequately attended to confidentiality concerns. We should also note, however, that such concerns were not as great when the project started as they have become with the advent of computer databases.

Confidentiality of information from school records is within the jurisdiction of the U.S. Family Educational Rights and Privacy Act, also known as the **Buckley amendment**. This act requires that before information may be gathered from school records, a waiver must be obtained from the parent or guardian or, if over 18 years of age, the student. The waiver must indicate what records will be disclosed, the purpose of the disclosure, and the persons to whom disclosure will be made. The act exempts school personnel with a legitimate educational interest as well as organizations conducting studies for local or state agencies for the purpose of developing and validating tests, administering student aid programs, or improving instruction. Although this last category seems broad, the local institution is the final judge of what constitutes "improving instruction," and its approval must be obtained. Data so gathered must be reported so that individuals cannot be identified and destroyed when the study is completed.

Privacy of subjects is a problem when a person reveals more than intended to a skilled investigator. The subject may reveal this information more readily if he or she suspects that it is available anyway and that concealing or lying about it may create problems. Such information may then result in public policy such as mandatory AIDS testing, quarantine, or similar actions that might not have occurred had the information been withheld (Sieber and Stanley, 1988). IRBs are alert to this problem; however, ultimate responsibility for respecting privacy rests with the researcher.

> ✦ *Confidentiality of data must be maintained so that individuals or institutions cannot be identified in ways that may be harmful or invite undesirable comparisons.*
> ✦ *Invasion of privacy is a problem when subjects reveal more than they intended in the course of a study.*
> ✦ *Unless a special exemption is obtained from the US Department of Health and Human Services or the Department of Justice, social science investigators have no immunity from subpoena. Special steps must be taken from the outset of data collection to make sure that subjects are not at risk.*

Ethical Decisions in the Field

Perplexing ethical decisions are often encountered in the course of field research. They are specifically discussed in Chapters 12 and 13 regarding qualitative research, but they can occur with any method anywhere. Researchers in the field encountering such problems usually have to make their decisions on the spot without any opportunity to consult others or an IRB. Where illegal acts, incompetence, or serious mistakes are observed (such as an incompetent surgeon who makes a serious error), should the researcher report them? At the least, reporting them usually terminates the project. Therefore, some researchers believe that revealing the overall problem so it can be corrected is the better solution, as Bosk (1979) did with surgical errors.

A special problem is the administrator who wishes to control the flow of information from the study. Such a desire may seem unreasonable from a scientific point of view. Because unfavorable reports may cost the administrator's job, however, this is not an illogical request. The researcher may think that an administrator who has anything to hide ought to lose the job, but that belief only creates an attitude that may make it more difficult to gain entry. Once again, individuals' rights as human beings, society's needs for protection from incompetence or wrongdoing, and the scientist's freedom to explore and provide the free flow of information that is the lifeblood of science come into conflict. It is a conflict that each researcher must resolve. Many investigators prefer not to use a site rather than submit to censorship or to deceive to obtain the data.

✦ *Entry to field situations, especially where a negative report may reflect on the people giving such access, causes serious ethical dilemmas, especially when the public's right to know is also involved.*

Ownership of the Data

At least two ethical issues arise with respect to ownership of the data: availability to others for secondary analysis and apportionment of credit on publication. The rules are clear for each of these areas. With regard to the availability of the data, concern over possible fraud (see Chapter 25) makes it important for researchers to retain rather than discard it so that others could check their findings. Anonymity can be compromised, however, if individuals try to check on the way they were collected or to follow up on cases. Nelkin (1984) cites cases where federal granting agencies claimed *and were granted* access to data that researchers obtained under the promise of confidentiality. Ownership of data and maintenance of confidentiality should be agreed on at the time a grant is negotiated.

Who should get credit on publication? This is covered well in the American Psychological Association's ethical principles (1993). In deciding authorship of work on which a graduate student and a faculty member have collaborated—perhaps a dissertation initiated at the behest and with the guidance of a faculty member but carried out by the student—the American Psychological Association states:

> Psychologists take responsibility and credit, including authorship credit, only for work they have actually performed or to which they have contributed. . . . Principal authorship and other publication credits accurately reflect the relative scientific or professional contributions of the individuals involved, regardless of their relative status. Mere possession of an institutional position, such as Department Chair, does not justify authorship credit. Minor contributions to the research or to the writing for publications are appropriately acknowledged, such as in footnotes or in introductory statement. . . . A student is usually listed as principal author on any multiple-authored article that is substantially based on the student's dissertation or thesis (p. xxxix).

Other associations have similar statements.

◆ *The right of outsiders to obtain data for secondary analysis may pose a dilemma for the investigator who has promised confidentiality to subjects.*

◆ *Publication credit should be given in direct proportion to contribution to the project.*

Researcher's Responsibility to the Institutional Review Board

Although it is the IRB's responsibility to make the final decision, the board depends on the researcher to present the case. This responsibility can create a dilemma for the researchers, who must anticipate the negative consequences as well as the positive side of each new study. It is easy to see the IRB as the enemy to be thrust aside. But the attitude everyone must take is not much different from the impartial attitude that researchers assume, insofar as they can, in assessing data on which they have invested their time, their resources, and sometimes their reputations. As Koshland (1990) notes:

> Scientists are the servants of society, not its masters, and we should remain so. . . . It is our special responsibility to spell out the disadvantages as well as the advantages of a new discovery as far as we can. What is good for science is not necessarily good for the country. . . .
>
> As architects of change, we have occasionally oversold the product, implying that it will bring unmixed good, not acknowledging that a scientific advance is a Pandora's box with detriments or abuses as well as benefits. By confessing that we are not omniscient we may lose some awe and admiration, but we will gain in understanding and rapport.[8]

If an IRB turns down your proposal, try to understand their position. Simple adjustments in the research plan will often take care of the matter. In other instances, counterarguments can and should be expressed. Before a counteroffensive is launched, careful listening, genuine understanding, and a real attempt to view the situation from both sides are essential to keeping this decision process working as it should.

Researchers must also help IRBs understand the opportunistic nature of science. Quoting Koshland (1990) again:

> No one can assess at the inception of an invention all of its social implications. We could not predict that an understanding of radio waves would change the way we communicate, that understanding control of bacterial growth would lead to a population explosion, or that a simple equation, $E = mc^2$, would lead to a change in the nature of warfare. . . . [We must] explain the serendipitous nature of science, . . . display our own limitations with candor, . . . express our intentions and reservations in clear, nonspecialized terms, and . . . empathize and communicate with those whose lives . . . [may] be changed.

---

[8]From Daniel E. Koshland, Jr. "To See Ourselves as Others See Us," in *Science*, Vol. 247 (1/1/90), beginning on p. 9. Copyright 1990 by the AAAS. Reprinted with permission.

SUMMARY

Ethical principles to guide the work of the researcher have been established by the federal government and by professional associations. The government has entrusted the enforcement of these principles to IRBs, which must be established at institutions seeking federal funds for research involving humans. In most institutions, these boards must approve all such research, not just that federally supported. IRBs are responsible for holding subjects harmless, both physically and mentally. They also enforce specific rules regarding eliciting freely given informed consent from subjects and protecting the confidentiality of data and the privacy of subjects. Researchers must also observe federal specifications protecting the privacy of information obtained from school records.

In addition, through the publication of ethical standards, professional associations have sought voluntary compliance in research areas not covered by federal regulation as well as in such fields as testing, evaluation, and personnel selection.

Despite these standards, there is concern over possible fraud in science. Do scientists live up to the standards set for them? Can their work be trusted? These concerns raise questions as to whether the whole system works. Those questions are addressed in the final chapter of this book.

A Look Ahead

The concepts covered in this and the previous three chapters that make up this section will be referred to repeatedly in the next four sections of this book, which is devoted to discussing methods of research. Section Four begins the coverage of the continuum of methods with qualitative research. Chapter 11 discusses the characteristics of and different approaches to qualitative methods. Chapters 12–15 cover successive aspects of doing qualitative studies.

ADDITIONAL READING

Sieber (1992) contains sample consent and assent forms for children and parents. Good actual research illustrations are included. Sieber emphasizes a collaborative approach involving subjects.

Schuler (1982) examines ethical questions from a historical viewpoint. The codes of eight European nations are presented. Alternatives to laboratory experiments for sensitive problems are presented.

Koshland (1990) further discusses the issues mentioned in this chapter's quotations—the relation between science and society. Bersoff (1995) discusses ethical conflict in psychology and devotes Chapter 8 to problems in academia, research, and supervision. Use Schmidt and Meara'a (1996) checklist before presenting to an IRB.

IMPORTANT TERMS

Buckley amendment
Code of ethics
Confidentiality
Debriefing

Deception of subjects
Informed consent
Institutional review boards
Privacy

APPLICATION PROBLEMS

1. The rapid spread since the beginning of the 1980s of the virus that causes the acquired immunodeficiency syndrome (AIDS) has brought about considerable medical research on the topic and, with it, a series of controversies. One surrounds research into the effectiveness of drugs, such as AZT, meant to control the disease. Medical

researchers and government regulatory bodies such as the U.S. Food and Drug Administration restricted the distribution of such medications until they were clinically tested. Furthermore, during such tests, some groups of AIDS patients would receive the experimental drugs while others would not. Some of the latter might even receive a placebo to provide a control for the experiment. AIDS patients have objected strenuously. What is the ethical dilemma here?

2. The AIDS epidemic has led to another ethical problem. Two of the major groups identified as at risk are male homosexuals and intravenous drug abusers. Homosexuality is legal in many countries, including the United States and Canada; in others it is not. Regardless, many gays are subjected to discrimination. Drug abusers, most often, are breaking the law. Research to find ways to control and eventually cure the AIDS virus must necessarily involve these groups. What is the problem?

3. An educational sociologist was interested in determining if there was a relationship between teachers' socioeconomic backgrounds and their job performance. She decided to begin with an exploratory approach using several qualitative research techniques, including classroom observation, interviews, and document analysis. She met with a local school superintendent to negotiate entry to the schools and permission to interview teachers. The superintendent agreed to arrange for her to meet several school principals and, in the meantime, provided her with copies of various documents from the personnel files of teachers in the district. Is there an ethical problem here? If so, for whom?

4. A cognitive psychologist wanted to study the effect of modeling behavior on school-aged children's willingness to persist in a task. To do so, he chose a task, solving a wooden puzzle, and developed two videotapes to provide a model. The first showed a child of comparable age as the subject solving the puzzle easily (a positive model); the second featured a child having great difficulty, becoming frustrated, and not finishing the puzzle (a negative model). Each videotape was also accompanied by one of three audio messages explaining what to do in the task and stating whether or not the child would succeed. One

message was positive, one neutral, and one negative. Combining each audio message with each videotape provided six treatments. Having designed the experiment, the psychologist approached the local school authorities for permission to carry it out with local school children in grades 5 and 6. He received permission from the superintendent of schools and from the principal of the particular school. Need he have done more?

5. A team of social psychologists wished to investigate the cognitive processes underlying the concept of altruism. They decided to conduct a field experiment to study the phenomenon under "natural" conditions. This was carried out in an urban subway to determine whether assistance to an ill passenger would be affected by the severity of the problem (blood or no blood). A passenger (member of the experimental team) with a cane would collapse in a subway car. In some cases, blood would trickle from his mouth. The responses of the participants (regular, unsuspecting passengers) were observed and timed. If no regular passengers came to his aid within a specified time period, a helper, disguised, for example, as a clergyman, would assist the victim and help him off at the next station. What ethical issue was involved with this experiment?

6. Daniels (1983) used participant observation to study wealthy women involved in charity organizations. She gained acceptance into the group and, in particular, developed a close friendship with some of the women (her key informants), who were aware that she was engaged in research. This relationship involved such activities as frequent lunches together and the exchange of gifts. As the study wound down, the investigator found herself bored with the friendship and wishing to terminate it. In effect, it no longer served a research purpose. Is it ethical for a researcher to have developed such a friendship?

Compare your answers with those following the Application Exercise.

APPLICATION EXERCISE

Consider what problems of informed consent you might have with your proposed project. Will you be collecting data from individuals from whom informed consent can be obtained, or will you need to contact parents or guardians? Is there a problem in

terms of confidentiality? Will you be the only one seeing the data? Can you ensure that no one else has access to it? Is there any reason you can't destroy identifying information shortly after the data are collected? As a better alternative, can you collect data without identifying information and still get the subjects' cooperation?

Are you collecting data about which there might be a privacy question? If so, how will you handle it?

Does your institution require that both federally and nonfederally sponsored grants be approved by its institutional review board? If so, do you know the procedure? You might get one of the board's forms now and fill it out for your project. See what potential problems it brings to mind.

If you plan to do the project with others, have you tentatively decided how you will allocate credit and authorship?

ANSWERS TO THE APPLICATION PROBLEMS

1. The dilemma is the choice between the rights of the patients and the responsibilities of the regulatory agencies. The latter must ensure valid assessment of the drugs before their general use is allowed. Balancing this are the rights of terminally ill patients to any treatment that might offer them a chance of life. This may be a situation in which the cost to the subjects (probable death) outweighs the gain in knowledge about an effective treatment for a deadly disease, as is evidenced by the 1989 decision by the U.S. Food and Drug Administration to modify its policies and make certain of these drugs more readily available. The decision is not simple, however, even concerning the cost to the patient with AIDS. A drug that has not been thoroughly tested may well be discovered to have side effects that worsen the patient's condition rather than ameliorate it. There is a cost to society as well. Properly controlled tests of these drugs may be necessary to allow medical researchers to build knowledge about the disease and eventually find a control or a cure. Premature distribution of a particular drug may impede research into its effectiveness.

2. The problem is one of confidentiality. Researchers generally have no immunity from subpoena unless granted special immunity by government bodies such as the National Institutes of Health or the Department of Justice. For homosexuals and drug abusers, breaches of confidentiality could result in great social harm, including imprisonment and a criminal record, loss of employment, or loss of insurance. Furthermore, the disease of AIDS itself carries a stigma. Understandably, many members of at-risk populations would be reluctant to jeopardize their privacy to participate in research on this problem. To gain access to these important groups, researchers have to take extraordinary steps to ensure the privacy of their subjects.

3. There is a possible invasion of privacy here with legal implications that should concern both the investigator and the superintendent. It involves the issues of gaining access to and ownership of the data and obtaining consent. It appears that the superintendent released information from confidential files without the permission of the teachers involved. Since the consent of particular teachers was not sought or obtained, the question becomes one of ownership of the data. Were the data contained in the files the sole property of the school system, in which case the superintendent may have been within his rights, or was this a case of joint ownership? Without seeking the involvement and permission of the teachers, both the superintendent and the investigator could be leaving themselves open to possible litigation. Their best course of action would have been to obtain consent before the release of the information.

4. Yes, he should have obtained the consent of each child's parent or guardian and also of the children themselves. His institutional review board should have required him to determine if the children were willing to give assent. Furthermore, since his experiment seems likely to produce psychological discomfort in at least some of the subjects, in obtaining consent from the children, he would have the responsibility to make clear the nature of the task and to debrief the children afterward.

5. This controversial experiment was conducted as described by Piliavin and Piliavin (1972). It clearly involved deception and also likely invoked considerable anxiety on the part of subjects who were not given the opportunity to consent to the treatment. It was actually quickly terminated because of dramatic participant reactions and the possible danger to them as well as a result of harassment from subway police. The research was inspired by the highly publicized attack and murder of a young woman in plain daylight, observed by a number of people who did nothing to help. The research problem thus appeared to have significant social value (the gain). It was conducted surreptitiously to create a "natural" situation and allow "valid," interpretable results. The cost was to the subjects who had not consented, may have experienced negative effects, and certainly gained no direct benefit (other than perhaps the satisfaction of assisting a fellow citizen).

6. The question of ethics in the study by Daniels (1983) focuses on deception. There does not appear to be any serious breach of ethics. The respondents were informed that Daniels was conducting a research study and had consented to participate. The question the investigator was asking was whether or not she had deceived these women by appearing to have developed a friendship and then letting it lapse as the study wound down. Because friendships usually have a basis in some common interest and because the investigator was not otherwise involved in these charities, this may well have been the natural course of events.

INTRODUCTION TO SECTIONS FOUR THROUGH SEVEN

Portraying the world around us in words is as old as history. Almost as ancient are attempts to simplify and increase the precision of those descriptions by using numbers, counts, and various ways of summarizing them—tabulations, graphics and statistics. But where describing in words may lack precision, abstracting in numbers omits aspects only words can portray. Thus, the foundations of both quantitative and qualitative approaches to research lie deep in the past—and so, as well, do concerns about each approach. *But, the differentiation between qualitatively oriented research tools and techniques and quantitatively oriented ones can be exaggerated.* Whereas some researchers see them as opposites, in fact they are usually complementary. Indeed, where appropriate, the strongest studies will borrow the most appropriate aspects of all methods to present their case.

Therefore, to understand the research literature and to do the strongest research, you should become familiar with a wide range of tools and techniques. Concentrating on the methods most widely used, Chapters 11 through 23 cover the continuum you were introduced to in Chapter 2. On that continuum, tools and techniques with a qualitative orientation anchored one end and those with a quantitative orientation, the other. In parallel fashion, Section Four, comprising Chapters 11-15, describes tools and techniques with a qualitative orientation and Section Six, Chapters 17-21, those with a quantitative orientation. Similarly, the example in Chapter 2 of those fields located in the quantitative/qualitative middle of the continuum, survey research, is the subject of Section Five's Chapter 16. Two additional examples of the middle are described in Section Seven: Chapter 22, Historical Research and Chapter 23, Evaluation and Action Research.

The Continuum of Research Methods: Qualitative End

Qualitative research methods are particularly useful in understanding how individuals understand their world, in showing how individuals' perceptions and intentions in situations determine their behavior, in exploring phenomena to find explanations, and in providing concrete and detailed illustrations of phenomena. Three important changes have been taking place with respect to qualitative research:

1. For a variety of reasons—dissatisfaction with the pace of progress with quantitative methods, rethinking positivist philosophy, among others—qualitative methods and research have become the focus of extensive interest and debate. Whereas some quantitative researchers have considered their methods superior because of their presumed impartiality, and freedom from bias, the discussion of qualitative methods has made everyone more aware of how *all* methods are influenced by the researcher's perceptions and values. As a result, most quantitative researchers have become increasingly tolerant of other approaches, some even advocating increased use of qualitative methods.
2. Considerable thought has been devoted to methods of analysis of qualitative data and use of computers has opened new possibilities.
3. The importance of providing information on the data gathering and analysis methods used, ideally an audit trail, is increasingly realized. With such information other researchers can understand how conclusions were reached and presumably could reproduce the original findings; replication is the ultimate validation of findings in all fields of science.

Though some qualitative researchers desire to put "rigor" into qualitative methods, many covet the unhampered freedom to do whatever they think best. Whether because of these discussions, or in spite of them, these methods are increasingly taking a respected and useful place alongside other research methods, and the methodological advances make them appealing to a wider audience.

The five chapters in this section start with an overview, proceed to data gathering, and then to processing the data:

- Chapter 11 discusses when to use qualitative methods, describes their advantages, introduces a variety of approaches to them, considers how to find a qualitative problem, and describes the overall pattern of a qualitative study.
- Chapter 12 shows the different conditions under which participant observation—one of the main methods of qualitative data gathering—is carried on, and traces the various steps in fieldwork and observation—from gaining entry, through developing acceptance, to fieldnoting, memoing, and data checking. Problems are described and their solutions suggested.
- Chapter 13 summarizes much of what is known about the art of interviewing, one of the skills the field-worker needs for any face-to-face observation or data gathering. This chapter also lays the groundwork for sample surveys, a main method of data gathering, which is discussed further in Chapter 16.
- Chapter 14 describes how to code and analyze the voluminous data that are gathered in fieldwork, and how to begin the process of data reduction leading to drawing conclusions. Coding categorizes data into underlying concepts and dimensions and facilitates systematic retrieval. Interpretation is kept separate from description.
- Chapter 15 discusses the ultimate data reduction, the abstraction of the data and analysis into the development of the research report. The reports are usually written as a case study for descriptive research and as a chain of reasoning for studies presenting a generalization. Indicators of quality are discussed and shown to include the application of internal validity (LP) and external validity (GP) to qualitative work. Hallmarks for judging qualitative research reports are listed.

CHAPTER 11

Qualitative Research Methods

Reality is in the eye of the beholder

Miguel de Cervantes Saavedra, *Don Quixote*

If one wishes to understand the term *holy water,* one should not study the properties of the water, but rather the assumptions and beliefs of the people who use it.
That is, holy water derives its meaning from those who attribute a special
essence to it.

Thomas S. Sasz, *Ceremonial Chemistry* (1974)

OVERVIEW

This chapter provides the basic background you need as you begin studying
qualitative methods. It starts by suggesting when to use qualitative procedures.
Next, because qualitative procedures are employed by a variety of social scientists, each, like different brands of coffee, having their own distinctive flavor,
there is a brief description of some varieties. One, singled out for special attention, uses qualitative methods of data gathering and analysis but employs them
from a particular point of view, namely that reality is determined by the perception of the individual. This affects both the data gathered and the way it is
interpreted.

Unlike quantitive researchers who work on clearly identified problems
from the outset, qualitative workers often use an inductive approach to defining the problem to be studied. Some of the implications of this approach are
explored.

Qualitative researchers differ from one another not only in the traditions they
follow, but also in the ways and kinds of data gathered—for example, observation, interview, archival material, documents, photographs, artifacts. Some of the
many different ways of gathering data are discussed.

CHAPTER CONTENTS

Introduction

For two reasons, we begin the book's sections dealing with specific research processes with qualitative methods. First, qualitative methods build on the well-practiced verbal descriptive skills and the techniques for selecting and categorizing information that you have used in writing term papers and reports since the start of high school. Therefore, you come to them with both extensive experience and some skill.[1]

Second, familiarity with qualitative procedures is useful even if as researchers we choose to specialize in quantitative methodology. Use of them keeps us close to the persons in the situation and helps us to learn what lies behind quantitative numbers. Indeed, qualitative researchers typically view those they observe or interview as collaborators or teachers from whom they learn rather than as subjects to be held at arm's length and studied.[2]

Qualitative procedures are typically inductive in orientation during data gathering and analysis. Some qualitative researchers may object to the characterization of qualitative research as inductive on the grounds that it is too narrow. In their defense, we should note that we can use qualitative data to validate a proposition in a deductive study just as we can quantitative data. Because most qualitative studies are inductive, inductive logic seems useful as a distinctive characteristic in contrast to other methods of research. Qualitative studies that propose generalizations, like all such research reports, typically use a deductive format to present their findings.

---

[1]Don't assume, however, that qualitative methods are a breeze compared with quantitative ones. As you will see, both require skill, and qualitative methods are extremely labor intensive. It is hard to appreciate this fact thoroughly until you are confronted with the usual mountain of notes that you must organize, analyze, digest, and interpret.

[2]Are qualitative methods influencing quantitative? The 1994 edition of the American Psychological Association's Publication Manual (pp. 13–14) recommends the use of the term *participants* in place of *subjects* as in previous editions. "Participant implies a more active, voluntary role in research . . .: [replacing *subject*] involves . . . ideological change" (Madigan, Linton, and Johnson, 1996, p. 654).

Uses and Advantages of Qualitative Procedures

Qualitative procedures are ideal for complex phenomena about which there is little certain knowledge. Even if much is already known, however, qualitative researchers often purposely approach phenomena without consulting prior work so that they come to the problem afresh. For well-studied problems, this approach can be a waste of researchers', time unless through careful attention to some significant aspect that others had taken for granted, they find a way to make a contribution. (Regardless of method, researchers always risk wasting time; there is no sure payoff when venturing past present knowledge—research is an adventure!)

Qualitative methods are extremely useful for exploration—to find out how to understand a phenomenon. For example, Borman and O'Reilly (1987), studying children's social roles in kindergarten, discovered that boys' speech used to establish same-sex friendships was quite different from girls'. In asserting their status as friends, girls made no attempt to "conceal their 'goofs' and scribbles" whereas ". . . among boys, declarations of competence and extraordinary accomplishments in exploits such as running footraces . . . served the same purposes as the revelation of inadequacies . . ." (p. 63) by girls.

Qualitative methods have some distinct advantages. Consider Stake's (1995) description of the intent of qualitative research as "not necessarily to map and conquer the world but to sophisticate the beholding of it." By *sophisticate,* he means qualities that:

- Humanize problems and data.
- Make people, problems, and situations "come alive."
- Portray phenomena in context.
- Describe complex personal and interpersonal phenomena that would be impossible to portray with quantitative research's single dimensional scales.
- Provide a holistic view of a phenomenon.
- Help, in some instances, to "get inside" others to view the world as they perceive it (this is the anthropologist's *emic* perspective).[3]
- Help to attach emotions and feelings to phenomena—sometimes also faces and their accompanying personages, even their situation, context, and accompanying emotional and social climate and milieu.
- Help to find "handles" on problems without obvious starting places.

These qualities suggest that qualitative procedures may be useful when:

---

[3]In contrast to the anthropologist's *etic* perspective—that is, how it looks to the outside observer. As we will note later in the chapter, many qualitative researchers stress the internally perceived world's *emic* perspective, whereas quantitative researchers are seen as emphasizing the outside observer's *etic*. The latter seek to describe the world in an objective way. There is a reality "out there" that they are trying to describe. *Objective* refers to description that other observers of the same events agree is accurate. In comparison, qualitative researchers, describing thoughts and perceptions and supplying their interpretation of them in providing an *emic* perspective, may present different interpretations of the same phenomenon.

- Research is lacking in an area and must emphasize discovery rather than validation or confirmation. The focus and design of the study is not pre-planned; it develops as work proceeds, it emerges—it is an emergent study.
- The problem involves complex interactivity and feedback loops.
- The focus of study is on a process and its internal dynamics or its strengths and weaknesses more than on its product or effect; you want to understand the process of local causality in depth.
- Detailed, in-depth information is sought—for instance, on the implementation or quality of a program or process, description with many nuances and details.
- There is interest in the diversity among, idiosyncrasies of, and unique qualities of persons or processes (in contrast to comparing them on standard measures).
- The administration of standardized instruments (questionnaires, tests) would be obtrusive or impossible in contrast to observations and informal interviews.
- No valid standardized instrument is available, and it isn't worth the effort or it is too difficult to build one.
- The goals of a program or processes are sufficiently diffuse that goals are best discerned by the research rather than determined beforehand.
- Research progress in an area has plateaued; you are seeking a new perspective for a fresh start or to find something that was overlooked in previous work.
- You believe the perceptions of the participants differ from those of outside observers in such a way as to explain their behavior.
- A well-grounded explanation of a phenomenon is needed.
- A holistic picture of phenomena will restore perspective on the problem.
- Unexpected consequences or side effects may be important.
- Examples are needed to put "meat" on statistical "bones."
- You or your audience has a preference toward qualitative orientation (some points adapted from Patton, 1980, pp. 88–89).

As the next to last of these points suggests, the qualitative vignettes used to illuminate aspects of a research report portray a reality that is difficult to achieve with just the numbers and statistics of quantitative methods. Qualitative data's real-life translation of these figures makes it much easier for an audience to visualize and identify with what is being conveyed.

Qualitative methods require skillful interpretation of the data. In fact, although we don't generally make the connection, like historians, *qualitative researchers are judged by how insightfully they analyze their data, how well they present their interpretations, and how carefully and tightly they relate them to their information base.* Turn to page 574 and read the first two paragraphs on interpretive history, for these paragraphs apply equally well to qualitative research in general.

Stake (1995) sees quantitative work as primarily providing *explanations*—explaining how an effect is related to a cause. Although much qualitative work does this, Stake contrasts explanation with understanding. Qualitative research is especially helpful when it provides us with someone's perceptions of a situation that permits us to *understand* his or her behavior. For example, much has been made of how so-called culturally deprived children see the world as hopeless. But when, through qualitative research, a study reveals in detail the hopes, fears, dreams, and nightmares of a few cases, that general statement takes on new meaning. Stake and von Wright mean that the research provides, besides understanding, an emotional acceptance, an empathic feeling toward the individual as well. Qualitative research can do this especially well.

Hargreaves (1996, p. 110) contrasts academic knowledge with that of practicing professionals, such as clinicians, teachers, social workers, librarians, journalists, and so forth, as follows:

Academic Knowledge	*Practicing Professional's Knowledge*
generalized	context specific
propositional in form	metaphorical, narrative, story-based in form
rational	rational but also moral and emotional
public	interpersonal or private
written	oral
explicit	tacit
theoretical	practical

The characteristics of academic knowledge in the left-hand column are those of the scientific knowledge both quantitative and qualitative academic researchers in general seek. Note how much better, however, the characteristics of practicing professional's knowledge match the case study produced by qualitative methods. Such compatibility suggests that the qualitative case study may be particularly effective in communicating with practitioners.

Considerations in Choice of Research Method

A comparison of qualitative methods with quantitative methods is a bit like contrasting the use of essay questions with multiple-choice ones. Because there are always many ways of interpreting and answering essay questions, you collect the data and do the scoring and analysis later. In contrast, you decide on the correct answer and the alternatives of multiple-choice questions at the outset; thus, the scoring is a clerical rather than a judgmental task. Quantitative studies, like multiple-choice tests, are largely planned before data collection, and the pattern of analysis, like multiple-choice scoring, follows from prior work. Qualitative research, like an essay examination, typically involves much less structured collection of data and a large, time-consuming analysis stage where judgments are made. Each method involves precious research time, either in quantitative study planning and design or in qualitative data gathering and analysis—there is no getting around it.

Novice researchers often choose to do a qualitative study, for instance, for a dissertation, because it looks easier than learning all those statistics for a quantitative one. Or perhaps they have a math phobia and feel more comfortable with qualitative methods. But qualitative research requires skill as well. It takes a special ability to organize and reduce the incredible detail amassed in qualitative research to a significant generalization. Some researchers gather drawers of data and are unable to find a way to pull it together meaningfully. Further, qualitative procedures are time-consuming and require much hands-on attention from the researcher.

Choice of method has ceased to be a matter of *easier* and *harder*. Computer programs now do the computation and solve the equations of quantitative research. Furthermore, statistics can be learned conceptually at a verbal level without going through their algebraic derivations. Computer programs also facilitate qualitative data analysis. The truth is that appropriately disciplined procedures must be learned for the proper use of *any* research method. The crux is what approach is most appropriate for your problem; which best fits your personal problem-solving style; whether you prefer to, or are better at, working with people or things; your flexibility and tolerance for ambiguity; your ability to "pass" in fieldwork; and your commitment to accepting the discipline of whichever process you choose.

At one time, qualitative researchers were defensive of their method, and quantitative researchers were extremely critical of it. Unfortunately, there are still some quarters where this conflict has not abated. Because qualitative methods possess less resemblance to those of the natural sciences, some quantitative researchers view them as *unscientific* and, when used to infer causation, never as satisfactory as experimentation. Careful attention to allaying the concerns of the research audience, however, can help make qualitative evidence convincing.

In most academic circles, qualitative methods are assuming a respected place in the panorama of research methods. It is toward this goal that qualitative methodologists have striven as they have introduced more improved and disciplined procedures, procedures that are embedded in the rest of this section on qualitative methods. As these procedures are widely used and understood, the criticism that qualitative methods as a whole are unscientific will shift instead to the current position of quantitative methods in which each study is judged on its own merit. Thus, it behooves qualitative researchers, as it does researchers of any kind, to anticipate the concerns of their audience and allay them. The acceptance of their findings is a measure of how successfully they have allayed concerns.

In some instances, qualitative methods stand alone; in others, they are combined with other methods, often as a supplement to quantitative methods. All methods have strengths and weaknesses; the researcher's task is to learn when and where to capitalize on strengths and avoid weaknesses. This and the next four chapters present qualitative research as an approach to gathering and analyzing data that leads to the strongest conclusions its current methodology can provide.

✦ *Qualitative methods use familiar techniques for handling verbal material that make situations "come alive"; they keep the investigator close to the data and markedly facilitate understanding of the phenomenon being studied. They also can be usefully combined with all other research methods.*

The Variety of Approaches to Qualitative Methods

Adherents of qualitative research distinguish many variants. Figure 11.1 from Wolcott cleverly illustrates them as a family tree. There are many branches of the tree in Figure 11.1, some with abstruse names like human ethnology, micro-ethnography, ethnomethodology, and others more easily decipherable like com-

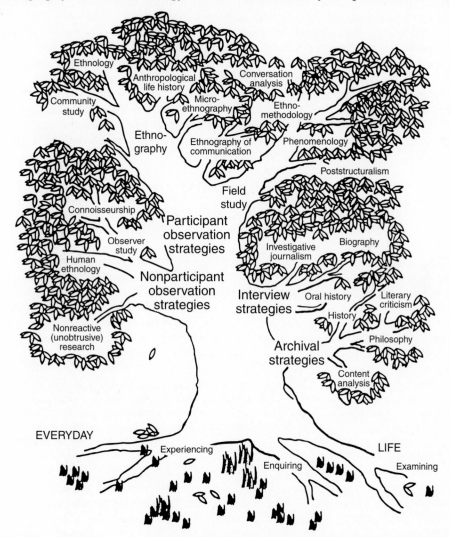

FIGURE 11.1 Different approaches to qualitative methods. (Graphic from "Posturing in Qualitative Inquiry" by Harry F. Wolcott in M. D. LeCompte, W. L. Milroy and J. Preissle [Eds.], *The Handbook of Qualitative Research in Education*, pp. 3–52. Copyright © 1992 by Academic Press and Harry F. Wolcott. Reprinted by permission of Academic Press and the author.)

munity study, investigative journalism, and content analysis. Some are labeled in terms of what is studied: culture, communities, conversation. Major parts of the trunk designate sources of data: observation, interviews, archives. All are rooted in experiencing, inquiring into, and examining everyday life. Wolcott's tree is an interesting and useful portrayal. Others however, might organize the field differently and/or include other of the field's terms such as naturalistic methods, case studies, responsive evaluation, or symbolic interaction. The point is there are a variety of uses of qualitative methods, they are applicable to diverse phenomena, and can be used by individuals with differing views of the world.

Examining, for example, how ethnography, ethology, ethnology, ethnomethodology, phenomenology, and connoisseurship differ from each other might be an interesting exercise but not an easy way of learning qualitative methods. To give a flavor of the variations, however, let us examine two of them. Social scientists with an anthropological orientation typically call their work ethnography. They emphasize the role of culture in influencing behavior, studying the meaning of shared patterns for behavior, and tracing how culture evolves. Physical aspects of the surroundings and the behavior of others are interpreted in terms of cultural standards.

> Researchers in this tradition say that an ethnography succeeds if it teaches readers how to behave appropriately in the cultural setting, whether it is among families in a black community (Stack, 1974), in the school principal's office (Wolcott, 1973), or in the kindergarten class (Florio, 1978). (Bogdan and Biklen, 1992, p. 38)

Some sociologists, although not denying the role of culture, tend to emphasize the interactions of persons with the meanings they attach to the persons and things that surround them—symbolic interaction. That is, people act according to the meaning of things and persons to them; their reality is socially constructed. From this viewpoint, it is necessary to see the world through the eyes of the actor to reach a full understanding of the purpose of that person's behavior. As Bogdan and Biklen (1992) note:

> People act not, however, according to what the school is supposed to be . . . but rather according to how they see it. For some students, high school is primarily a place to meet friends; . . . for most, it is a place to get grades and amass credits so they can graduate. . . . The way students define schools determine their actions, although the rules and the credit system may set certain limits and impose certain costs, and thus affect their behavior (p. 37).

We might add (as Bogdan and Biklen do) that the students' actions are also a result of how they see themselves: Seeing themselves as individuals who succeed or fail in such settings strongly influences their behavior as well.

Many of the traditions, the branches of Wolcott's tree in Figure 11.1, deal more with the *what*—a particular emphasis or orientation—than with the *how* of method. We can, and therefore will, concentrate on learning the important aspects of method—the "*how*"—without dealing with every "what." This downplay of differences, and the fact that so many researchers choose their method to fit their problem, may make you wonder if it is ever useful to identify your work with one of these traditions. Yes, to communicate well, you must know and be able to talk the language of the tradition that is your target audience. Further, with such identification comes advice based on the experience of knowledgeable colleagues. As Buchmann and Floden (1989) note, through association with such a community "the purposes, process and outcomes of one's work [will be critiqued] . . . by people who have some understanding of what one is about" (p. 247).

However, there is one of these differences in approach that we must discuss. It is illustrated in the second quotation from Bogdan and Biklen above. For these researchers, the term *qualitative* denotes not only a method of gathering and analyzing descriptions of phenomena, but also a point of view about reality. They argue it is important to study not only the objective reality that is the subject of the natural sciences, but also an individual's perceived reality because, to the individual, that *is* reality.

Clearly, not everyone using qualitative methods adopts this point of view. Further, both those who adopt this view and those who don't, use common data gathering and analysis tools and face common problems of entry and gaining acceptance. Therefore, we can examine separately:

1. Qualitative research as a point of view for understanding the perceived reality underlying individual and social behavior. This is the viewpoint taken by many who do ethnography, but it may be a part of other branches of Wolcott's family tree as well.
2. Qualitative methods as data gathering and analysis tools, their problems and solutions. This knowledge is of as much use to those adopting qualitative methods as a point of view as to those not so doing; they are important to understand even for those whose main research method will be quantitative.

Let us next explore qualitative as a point of view. Then, we pursue finding a research problem using an inductive rather than a deductive approach. Finally, we look at the different ways of gathering qualitative data, regardless of the point of view.

Qualitative Orientation as a Point of View

For some researchers, as Bogdan and Biklen (1992) note, doing qualitative research involves taking a particular point of view (also sometimes referred to as a phenomenological point of view or the **emic** view). They call this *thinking naturalistically* and argue that through our experiences, we construct a view of the world that determines how we act. These researchers try to understand how individuals perceive the meaning of the world around them and seek to view it through their eyes—how people understand their world and their surroundings. This strongly affects what data are gathered and how they are interpreted. Although some qualitative researchers argue that this point of view and qualitative method are inseparable, most do not. Those using a qualitative approach may or may not adopt this point of view.

Those taking this emic point of view argue that it is an individual's perceptions that count. It does not make any difference that you and I might not see an individual's supervisor as hostile. As quantitative researchers, evaluating her supervisory behavior on an observation scale, we might find little or no evidence of hostility. But, if subordinates see the supervisor's behavior as hostile, it will affect the way they react to that person's supervision. To understand that reaction, we must understand the world as the subordinates see it. This perspective explains many actions that are inexplicable from a strictly external point of view and therefore is an important one to recognize.

How can we contrast qualitative as a point of view with quantitative and qualitative method? An analogy, if not pushed too far, may be helpful. As noted in Chapter 7, Popper (1972) suggested that the world might be perceived as *clocklike* or *cloudlike*. A clocklike world, like the workings of an old spring-wound clock, would run with a mechanical determinism. The laws that govern behavior in such a world can be exact, and quantitative prediction is precise. This model may be appropriate for physics, but it is too mechanistic for most social scientists, especially for those who believe in self-determination—"I am the master of my fate, the captain of my soul."

Most social scientists prefer the more loosely coupled model of the world— the *cloudlike world*, like the normative behavior of a cloud of gnats. Qualitative predictions will more or less hold (since most gnats are in the center of the swarm), but there can be no precise prediction. Discovering rules and laws increases the likelihood of accurately predicting loosely coupled events. Most researchers with a quantitative orientation are trying to find those rules and laws to increase the accuracy of predictions about the behavior of the swarm—that is, normative statements. Other researchers, however, believe that when social science is sufficiently advanced, it will result in clocklike prediction. Note that we are describing the fundamental beliefs of researchers here, their orientation to what social science is all about, and what kind of a social science we can construct—not just the research approach they use.

Let us carry the analogy a step further. Those for whom qualitative is a point of view do not take the stance of the outside observer who is watching the clocklike gears or the cloudlike swarm. Rather, if we may treat the gnats as people, they try to perceive the situation like individual gnats, trying to understand how the swarm looks to them. How do they interpret the actions of other gnats? How do they understand the behavior of always returning to the swarm whenever they find themselves outliers? Then we are studying the meaning-making process, asking, "How do these individuals construct the meaning of their world?" This knowledge is a social construction of behavior, a joint product of the culture and the meanings assigned by the individual.[4] Thus, this viewpoint differs as to what it emphasizes as important to observe and how the researcher tries to understand it.

---

[4]So also, however, is quantitative interpretation. See the example of volume as the pitch of a sound on p. 423. What characteristics of a phenomenon are attended to and how they are measured are social constructions. Such measures are so much a part of our culture that we often consider them as natural, as though that were the only way to view them.

Another difference of this point of view is that knowledge is local in the sense that it applies to these gnats in this swarm. Gnats in other swarms may understand their situations differently. It is also context dependent; how gnats interpret what is appropriate to do under certain conditions of heat and humidity may not apply in other situations.

In addition, because there are differences in perception, different researchers may properly advance different interpretations of a situation without trying to reconcile the differences. As Glesne and Peshkin (1992) note, both Redfield and Lewis studied the Mexican village of Tepoztlan with different results. Redfield argued his hidden question was, "What do these people enjoy?" whereas Lewis's was, "What do these people suffer from?" As Redfield notes, "we must recognize that the personal interests and values of the investigator influence . . . the study" (Redfield, 1955, p. 136).

Researchers who adopt the qualitative point of view will not typically use tests or measures to learn how individuals construe their culture or perceive their world—at least not at first. Any such instrument would have been built with certain assumptions about what is important and what questions to ask. Therefore, many such researchers would argue that tests do more than record an individual's reactions. By the very assumption that something is there to be measured, Stake (1978), for instance, notes that the act of measurement transforms what is measured into a bearer of properties, into something in an array of characteristics. It objectifies it—there must be such a thing as intelligence if we can measure it with an intelligence test. As he states, "Measurement is not just holding a ruler to what we see, but seeing something to hold a ruler to." Thus, from a qualitative point of view, we might well never use a measure; however, if we did, we would certainly first plumb what a person's perceptions are. Only then might we be able to select a matching measure that could capture these perceptions as a way of gathering additional data.

The kind of social science that views such research findings as local and context bound and encourages multiple meanings of situations without encompassing the explanation of those meanings in a single generalization or reconciliation is quite different from that sought by most quantitative social scientists.[5] Social scientists in general may not embrace the natural sciences model, but most are not willing to move as far from it as those fully committed to this viewpoint believe is appropriate. Although anyone can use qualitative methods, not everyone who does so will adopt the qualitative point of view.

✦ *The* qualitative point of view *involves understanding how the world looks to the people being studied and how those people act on that information. Research findings are local and context bound. Multiple interpretations of situations may*

---

[5]How can there be multiple meanings of a situation? Phillips (1992) notes that societies construct their own meaning, an observation we make again in Chapter 18. The Eskimo believes there are 14 kinds of snow; we refer to only one. Are they right and we wrong? According to the philosopher Popper, each of us assumes a physical and a social world, and their nature at any given time reflects the level of our understanding of them.

be quite acceptable, depending on how various persons perceive it. This charac-
teristic is puzzling to people who seek single generalizable explanations of phe-
nomena, the typical goal of the natural sciences.

Finding a Problem

For the researcher with a clear idea of a research problem, the approaches of examining the literature and proceeding to develop a research design discussed in Chapters 5 and 6 are similar in both quantitative and qualitative methods. Many qualitative methodologists stress letting the foreshadowed problem develop inductively, immediately starting the gathering of data in the area of interest with considerable openness and looseness of design. They immerse themselves in the situations to see what emerges, it is an **emergent study**. The intent is that the researchers are instructed by the phenomenon as to what is important rather than imposing some framework on it that determines what is presumed important. Those using this emergent approach to problem finding need to find an area in which they'd like to work and then begin to immerse themselves in it in whatever way is available and appropriate—for example, observation, interviewing, reading records, examining artifacts.

As is clear from the above, some researchers using inductive methods believe that consulting the literature too early will burden you with other people's perceptions. They don't want you to miss what the naive eye might see; after all, you will come fresh into a situation only once. They want you to do the literature search after you have been exposed to the situation and have begun to form your own notions about what is important, how things are related to each other, the general context, and what explanations you can advance. Then, with a much sharpened notion of your study, you ask how others have understood it in the literature in contrast to your own understanding. With this approach, you begin the literature search with quite a different background from others just starting to define a problem.

As with other aspects of qualitative methods, however, researchers differ about how much preparation to do before data collection. For instance, Wax and Wax (1980) note that reading about the situation the researcher intends to enter "is a mark of respect to the hosts, as it demonstrates that one considers their affairs of sufficient importance to learn whatever one can about them before formal introduction. Preparation is also a mark of respect to the scholars who have studied the community in the past" (p. 6). For researchers who argue that this imposes a framework that may alter their view of the situation, Wax and Wax note: "True, when one enters the field, one may be hampered by inaccurate ideas gained from prior studies, [but] the researcher will always be entering with some freight of expectations. It is better that these be grounded in past scholarship" (p. 6). Given these differences of opinion, researchers must decide when to consult the literature for themselves in terms of their own style of working, their problem, and, especially, their ability to maintain openness to new perceptions.

Immersing yourself to see what emerges can lead to collecting data on everything, to initial diffuseness of effort, to breadth rather than depth of data, and, often, to bewilderment on the part of novices as to what details they should attend to and record and how to limit their study. The admonitions of openness and looseness of design are indeed appropriate for experienced researchers studying complex problems with reasonably adequate resources (it seems there never are enough; studies always consume whatever resources are available and then need more "for a solid completion" or to "round them out"). There are also examples in which novices handle these conditions successfully. In general, however, novices, especially when studying a structured phenomenon that has been the subject of prior work, may find that too open a design pursued too deeply will result in little new "pay dirt." Such individuals would do well either to cut their losses early if little appears or try a more focused and structured approach to a part of the area that has not been well explored.

Fetterman (1989) is right on target: The researcher "enters the field with an open mind, not an empty head." As Miles and Huberman (1994) point out, in most studies: "Something is known conceptually about the phenomenon, but not enough to house a theory. The researcher has an idea of the parts of the phenomenon that are not well understood and knows where to look for these things. And the researcher usually has some initial ideas about how to gather the information" (p. 17). These hunches begin to structure the approach to data gathering and make choices easier about where, from whom, and how to gather data.

Thus, most individuals know why they chose a particular phenomenon to study and what they hope to find, even when they use an open qualitative approach. They may not want to make it explicit for fear of appearing to slant the study to fit their predilections. But, qualitative researchers pride themselves on recognizing and making explicit potential sources of bias. They have more control over those that are made apparent.

On this basis, it makes sense to formulate the best possible statement of your problem as early as you can. This does not mean that it won't change with further data collection—certainly you must be open to that. But the formulation of the problem will help clarify your thoughts and feelings about the direction of your effort. You'll have an initial gut feeling that "No, that isn't quite right; it will do for now but I've got to. . . . " Or, "That doesn't capture what I'm looking for. May be I should. . . ." When the ellipses in those statements are filled in, they begin to chart directions for the study that can lead to boundaries and a clearer focus.

The very act of seeking a focus and verbalizing keeps you working at conceptualizing the problem—it is a facilitating process. Sari Biklen tells her students to keep trying to express the problem or purpose of the study in a single sentence. Others suggest trying out titles for the study. Gradually, you will be able to develop a problem statement and rationale for the study. It may even be possible to embed the study in some kind of an explanation or theory. Clearly the further you can go toward an explanation, the better. Whether that is best done near the outset or later depends on how open to change you can be from that point on.

Yin (1984) notes:

When Christopher Columbus went to Queen Isabella to ask for support for his "exploration" of the New World, he had to have some reasons for asking for three ships (why not one? why not five?), and he had some rationale for going westward (why not north? why not south?). He also had some criteria for recognizing the New World when he actually encountered it. In short, his exploration began with some rationale and direction, even if his initial assumptions might later have been proved wrong. This same degree of rationale and direction should underlie even an exploratory case study.

Ways of Generating Qualitative Data

Although observation and interviewing are the major qualitative data-gathering methods, diaries and other personal as well as official records and artifacts are frequently analyzed by qualitative researchers, especially historians. Similiar to quantitative data, qualitative data may be gathered from situations as diverse as the human imagination permits. To illustrate the many ways qualitative data may be gathered, suppose we are studying—as did Bogdan, Brown, and Foster (1982)—communication between hospital staff and parents in a neonatal ward where extremely premature infants hover between life and death. Once we have identified a problem of communication between staff and parents, we might begin observation of their interaction, asking to sit in as researcher-observer on their conferences. Since this may seem intrusive, we might simply take the role of a nurse or staff member but participate neutrally in such discussions as we try to fix in memory what went on. Alternatively, if it can be arranged, conferences might be held where staff and parents can be unobtrusively observed, perhaps through a two-way mirror. Such observations may be supplemented by informal interviews or, as we close in on particular data that we need, by structured ones. We might interview small groups of staff and parents about the problem of communicating the right amount of hope and pessimism to parents. The group setting gives them the chance to discuss and react to one another's ideas, possibly expressing thoughts and reactions we as researchers might not have anticipated.

We might also use projective techniques to gather data, showing pictures taken of parent-staff conferences in the ward and asking other parents and staff to describe what was going on. The pictures should be somewhat ambiguous to allow the respondents to bring their own typical and most salient interpretations to the scene. Using a more structured stimulus, we might put phrases on 3-by–5-inch cards describing what was going on in the ward, ask both parents and staff to sort the cards into piles, and then ask them to describe the piles and explain why they placed each card there. Like the pictures, this technique allows the respondents to project whatever organizing schemes are most salient in their minds, schemes that may or may not be readily apparent from their actions. We then compare the way parents sorted the cards with the staff's sorts.

We might use the stimulated recall method, which involves recording on videotape the actions we wish to learn about—in this instance, parent-staff conferences. We would then play the tape to each of the parents and staff individually. During this replay, we ask them to stop at points they think are significant, tell what they were thinking at that time, and indicate why those points were significant. In addition, we might stop the tape at points we think are significant and ask what was going through their minds at those points.

Note that these are all ways of eliciting how individuals perceive situations and what organizing frameworks come readily to their minds to make sense of them. We can record responses either on tape or in handwritten notes kept as close to verbatim as possible. If we have a categorizing and coding scheme, we can tally responses directly into it.

Thus, there are a variety of ways of generating qualitative data. Some come out of the sociological and anthropological traditions, in which interviewing and observation are central, some are closer to psychological ones, in which reactions to tests and specially designed stimuli are more central. Because Chapter 12 deals with fieldwork, we will examine observation as a means of gathering data more closely there.

✦ Qualitative data *may be gathered in as many ways as the researcher's creativity permits. Although the most widely used sources are observation and interviewing, analysis of records and documents is also common. In addition to observation and interviewing in the sociological tradition, methods of eliciting individual responses to specially designed stimuli, as do psychologists, may be useful.*

Overview of the Qualitative Process

Figure 11.2 presents an overview showing a process of doing qualitative research. Not everyone will do it just this way; as we will note later, some do not start the analysis until the data have been gathered. The figure describes a typical pattern, however, and it incorporates many of the suggestions for enhancing the quality of the study which are discussed in the following chapters. The stages of the study are listed down the left column and the data, report, and analysis streams of activity in the three parallel columns.

Note that in this pattern of work, gathering data and putting material aside for the final report and analysis of the data begin at the outset of the study and continue throughout it. The report stream provides initial guidance to data gathering and analysis in terms of whatever prior conception of the study exists, but as the focus of the study becomes increasingly clear they align with each other. The data and analysis streams become increasing interdependent as data determine the direction of analysis, which, in turn, determines what new data to gather, with both increasingly converging into the middle, the report stream, in the closing stages of the study.

This pattern has the advantage that you can note and correct deficiencies in data collection before leaving the field. Successive data collecting and analysis efforts can be kept maximally effective as you increasingly focus on the emerging problem. Further, collecting material for the study's report from the start keeps this goal as an ever-present priority; this is likely to improve the report's quality as you work at it throughout the study.

These cross-stream transfers of information occur throughout the process. The researcher transfers from the data gathering stream to the analysis stream in order to screen data which is at the study's focus from that which is at the periphery; from the analysis stream back to data gathering with information regarding

Stages of Study | **Streams of Qualitative Research Activity**

Stages of Study	Data Stream — Observations	Interviews videotapes	Documents: diaries, proceedings, meeting minutes, census statistics, etc.	Artifacts and Photos	Report Stream	Analysis Stream
Gathering data	Observe and develop fieldnotes	Transcribe interviews Code videos Reconstruct tapes as written notes		Develop descriptive verbal placeholders for each item	Set up title file Keep trying to summarize the study in a single sentence Set up file for initial chapter; put material in it during remainder of study	If pre-structured study do literature review. Set up quotation file Set up subjectivity file Contact summary reports on observations and interviews Search for relationships in data and write analytic memos on relationships to various potential frameworks and possible interpretations
	Review data and underline significant parts	Review data and underline significant parts	Review data and underline significant parts			
Summarizing and packaging it	Write memos re significant items	Write memos re significant items	Write memos re significant items	Write memos re significant items	Set up file for final chapters; put material in it during remainder of study	

Triangulation across persons, situations and/or methods as appropriate

Code and winnow for relevant data	←	Develop tentative codes
More triangulation as appropriate	←	Develop code list, revisions, and consolidation of codes
Recode and further winnow	←	
		If emergent study, do literature review. Determine and act on implications for coding. Set up quotation file

Stages of Study	Data Stream	Report Stream	Analysis Stream
Finding gaps in data	Selectively gather more data, memo, code, recode, and analyze		
Repackaging and selecting central data		Identify themes and related material	Do graphic, matrix, and network analyses and cross check tentative findings
		Reduce data to that related to selected themes and examples	
	Possibly gather additional data to eliminate alternative explanations		Search for alternative explanations
		Further reduce data to that related to the central theme	
Developing and testing propositions and constructing explanatory framework		Synthesize into an explanatory framework Organize data into a chain of reasoning or narrative report with methodological appendix	
Write report		Write report	

FIGURE 11.2 A representation of the stages in a study, illustrating the simultaneous pursuit of data gathering, report development, and data analysis; the continuous data reduction through the stages; and the merging of the streams of activities in the closing stages of the study (after Carney, 1990 and Miles & Huberman, 1994).

data needed; from the report stream to both data gathering and analysis streams regarding needed information; from data gathering and analysis streams to the report stream for summarization, narrative and/or chain of reasoning construction. To show all these and similar information transfers would create a mass of confusing arrows; they can generally be inferred from the activity descriptions.

The process is basically one of data reduction: Masses of data are gathered in the early stages, these are reduced to the relevant material in the middle stages, selective additions are made to round out the body of work in the middle and late stages, and the ultimate data reduction—the abstraction of the data into a descriptive final report—is the closing activity.

Study this figure and return to it as you read the material in the next chapters. It will keep the activities in perspective and help you see how each is fitting into the larger picture.

SUMMARY

Qualitative methods are especially useful for exploring a phenomenon, for understanding it, and for developing an understanding of it into a theory. These methods humanize situations and make them come alive. They are particularly useful in describing multidimensional, complex interpersonal interaction where the limited focus of quantitative measures would be inadequate. They more likely focus on process than product. They communicate well to practitioners.

Although qualitative methods build on one's verbal skills, they require skillful interpretation of data. Qualitative researchers are judged by how insightfully they interpret the data and present their findings and how well the interpretation fits their material. Qualitative research is extremely labor intensive. Appropriately disciplined procedures must be learned with any method, and qualitative research is no exception.

Qualitative procedures are increasingly respected, although its users have been somewhat defensive about them in the past because they differ significantly from the natural science methods. In part, the greater acceptance is due to the continued development of the method.

There are a variety of approaches to qualitative methods: ethnography, ethnomethodology, naturalistic methods, and so forth. One of these, derived from symbolic interactionism, we call here the qualitative point of view. It seeks to present the world as individuals perceive it. Whereas other persons might see a situation as conducive to growth, if an individual who is the subject of study sees it as stifling, it is their view and what impact it has on their

actions that is the focus of the qualitative point of view. Although some adherents see qualitative methods and the qualitative point of view as the same, many more individuals distinguish them and use qualitative methods without necessarily adopting the qualitative point of view.

Although observation and interview are two of the main methods of gathering qualitative data, such data can also be gathered from diaries, personal records, official documents, and artifacts.

A Look Ahead

Chapter 12 through 15 which follow discuss in sequence: 12) fieldwork and observation, 13) interviewing, 14) data analysis, and 15) drawing conclusions and reporting. It may seem, therefore, that these activities must follow one another sequentially. You may already have noted this is not the case from your study of Figure 11.2, where, for example, analysis and final report issues are worked at from the very beginning. While qualitative researchers adapt their method to fit their problem, issues such as gaining entry, securing acceptance, purposive sampling, data analysis, and ethics continue to be revisited throughout a study. It is difficult to do justice to this simultaneous processing of different aspects of the study in the linear presentation to which books are confined. So, while the text will remind you from time to time of the holistic nature of the process, it will help if you return to this figure as you read the material in the following chapters. That should allow you to put activities in perspective so you can see how each can fit into the larger picture at an appropriate time.

ADDITIONAL READING[6]

The following books have methodological discussions that illustrate the process of participant observation. Any will give a feel for the process; choose one in a topic of interest:

Medical situations: Becker (1961); Bosk (1979).
Academic situations: Becker, Geer, and Hughes (1968).
Special populations: Bluebond-Langer (1980); Humphreys (1975); Rubin (1976); Schneider, and Conrad (1985).
Social communities: Liebow (1967); Lynd and Lynd (1929), old, but appendix discusses use of mul-

tiple sources of data, including observation, documents, interviews, statistics, and questionnaires; Whyte (1993).

Other useful discussions of methods are: Bogdan and Biklen (1992); Denzin and Lincoln (1994); Glaser and Strauss (1967); Johnson (1975); Le Compte, Millroy, and Preissle (1992); Miles and Huberman (1994); Strauss (1987); Strauss and Corbin (1990); and Taylor and Bogdan (1984). See Lancy (1993) regarding different qualitative traditions.

IMPORTANT TERMS

Emergent study
Emic

Qualitative point of view

APPLICATION PROBLEMS

1. You are interested in determining what, if any, barriers exist to children's use of desktop computers in their schooling. You decide to conduct participant observation of children at a local elementary school where staff members are just beginning a computer education program for their students. A colleague who is committed to the quantitative tradition of research suggests you mix qualitative and quantitative methods. How would you respond to him? Your answer will depend on whether you believe that quantitative and qualitative methods can be usefully and successfully mixed, and whether you adopt qualitative research as a point of view.

2. Prof. James Oxford wants to validate the proposition that students in the 9th grade learn more with tight teacher control of learning experiences than

when they are allowed to select their own. He plans to use qualitative methods when a colleague warns him that these are inappropriate; he won't be able to validate the proposition. Prof. Oxford turns to you for advice; what would you tell him?

3. Dr. Penelope Wilgren is interested in gender differences in preschool play. She is planning to gather qualitative data in one intensive period from a pre-kindergarten day care center with all-day observation over the course of a week. She will then do an analysis of it. A colleague suggests that she would be better off analyzing it while she is gathering it. Any advice for her?
Compare your answers with those following the Application Exercise.

APPLICATION EXERCISE

How might you pursue your problem with qualitative methods? Is there some facet of it they might uniquely fit, might provide new insight into, or tell you whether your study is proceeding as expected?

Some of you may wish to explore a different problem better suited to qualitative methods for this and following four chapters which also deal with these methods.

[6]My thanks to Dr. Steven Taylor for many of these suggestions.

ANSWERS TO THE APPLICATION PROBLEMS

1. *Mixing Quantitative and Qualitative Methods:* Although some researchers who advocate the qualitative point of view likely might not accept the mixing of the two methods in the same study, most qualitative researchers see these techniques as complementary. From this viewpoint, qualitative methods provide an excellent exploratory device to allow researchers to develop a solid understanding of the circumstances in which they are interested. Qualitative methods can be extremely useful in identifying questions that will later be verified experimentally, which is your intent in this study.

The Qualitative Point of View: Some investigators are of the opinion that to carry out qualitative research, researchers *must* adopt this point of view. If you agree with this argument, you would explain that the qualitative point of view involves understanding how the circumstance looks to the people being studied and how that act on that information. From this standpoint, knowledge is a joint product of culture and the meanings assigned by the individual. Thus in your school study, you would expect a variety of behaviors, depending on the particular children involved. Your choice of participant observation as a research method will allow you to understand these behaviors from their point of view and to document them. The plausibility of your explanation would be induced from, or "emerge from," the data. The process is inductive rather than deductive. It is true that others looking at the data might come up with different interpretations. However, this methodology provides reasoned opinions based on the data.

2. I would have told him that, although it is more common to use qualitative methods to explore rather than to validate, they can be used in the latter role. However, Prof. Oxford needs to ask himself what is he expecting to accomplish and who is his audience. If he seeks to contribute to publications where quantitative learning studies on this subject are being published, then the sheer quantity of observations that would be expected to build a case that would gain a consensus among editors, reviewers and readers would likely be prohibitive. Such a case might be much better achieved by using achievement tests and gathering data from a large number of students in classrooms with differing levels of teacher control and student freedom.

Incidentally, this generalization that achievement tests scores would be higher with teacher than student control of learning experiences was one of the findings that Wong (1995) used in looking at the obviousness of social science findings. Achievement was higher with greater teacher control and less student freedom, but this finding was *not* obvious to teachers or non-teachers alike.

On the other hand, were Prof. Oxford interested in showing that "learning" rather than "achievement" was greater, he would probably be looking at a much wider range of outcomes than simply higher scores on achievement tests. Where students were allowed to choose their own learning experiences, one might expect changes in motivation to learn, interest in new fields, and so forth. Qualitative methods would easily permit the recording of a variety of such changes. Probably interpreting the statement as "learning" instead of "change in test score," is what many in Wong's study had in mind when they chose greater student freedom as the expected true finding.

As Wong's study showed, however, this finding is not obvious; it doesn't unmistakably "ring true," a usual test of such statements. Therefore, Prof. Oxford may also want to consider the intended audience and the evidence they are most likely to accept. If the intended audience were teachers and practitioners, they would probably find qualitative findings and their accompanying examples of great interest to them, and, especially if they could identify with the examples in terms of their own experience, they would more likely find that evidence convincing. This by no means is intended to convey that when communicating to practitioners, one must always use qualitative methods; generalities supported by quantitative evidence that "ring true" are also likely to be convincing. It is when the findings are less obvious that use of evidence that fits the pattern of communication of the audience is more likely to be effective.

3. Dr. Wilgren already has her focus of observation in mind; she is looking for differences in play patterns of boys and girls. So, her study is exploratory in the sense of looking for where these differences exist, but is targeted in knowing what activities are the focus of data collection. The latter makes more feasible gathering the data in a condensed period of time. In gathering all her data before analyzing it, she is assuming that she will have observed carefully those instances that display differences. However, were she to analyze her data as she collected it, as suggested in Figure 11.2, she would spot the types of instances where such differences typically occur. Then, using purposive sampling, she could concentrate further data gathering on obtaining many such examples as well as seeking the broadest instances of them to determine the limits of generality.

The flow of the process depicted in Figure 11.2 must always take into account, however, the reality of circumstances. If she does not have enough time and energy to do analysis during a concentrated period of observation why not spread observations out to allow interim time for analysis? As suggested in the discussion of sequential sampling in Chapter 8, this might be a good solution if the situation is relatively stable and one could return to the field to take up approximately where one left off. However, if it were the beginning of the school year and boys and girls are learning to play with one another, sensing this, Dr. Wilgren might decide to continuously observe so she will not miss this period of adaptation. This is an example of the on-the-spot decisions fieldworkers must make in adapting their pattern of work to specific situations.

Fieldwork and Observation

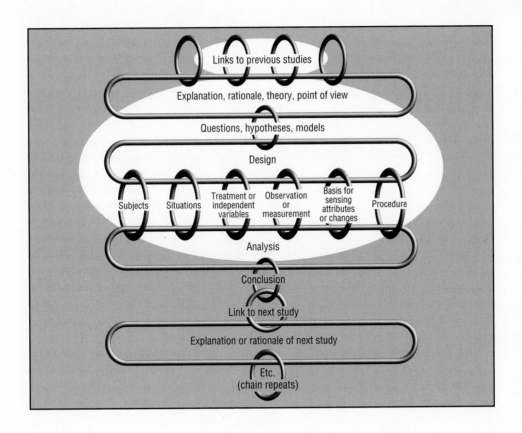

There is more to seeing than meets the eyeball.

Hanson, *Patterns of Discovery*

Unfortunately, events do not come with labels on them: "Look at me, I'm recurrent"; or "Ignore me, I won't happen again." Indeed, they do not even come labeled: "I am an event." Such labels must be imposed . . . by an observer. Until they have been, a scientist has nothing to work with.

George A. Miller, *Spontaneous Apprentices*

To be perceptive, we must . . . recognize the role . . . bias plays in everything we do. Point of view pervades information. Once we acknowledge that our perceptions are selective, we can allow the point of view to enrich our experience with information. When we know that Monet's eyesight . . . approached near-blindness as he got older, we can begin to understand his water lily paintings.

Wurman, *Information Anxiety*

OVERVIEW

Field-workers are faced with many tasks, beginning with gaining entry, finding a way to preserve the naturalness of the situation while gathering data and securing acceptance of their presence. On the basis of successive visits, they decide which persons, activities, situations, events, documents, pictures, and so forth, to sample and which informants to query. They continuously carry on analytic induction and constant comparison processes, checking their perceptions and hunches and building an explanation. Throughout, they must capture what is significant in descriptive fieldnotes and memos that form the basis for coding and analysis and for eliminating alternative explanations. They must check their data and emerging explanations for accuracy and for stability over time. They must decide how much fieldwork is enough. In addition, they are often faced with difficult ethical dilemmas that they must decide on the spot. When listed in the abstract, so many operations may seem overwhelming, yet, most field-workers find themselves capable of handling these tasks as needed and, with practice, becoming skilled with them.

Although titled "Fieldwork and Observation," most of the chapter content *applies to any kind of data gathering,* be it for instance, observation, interviewing, or gathering documents. But, you don't just do fieldwork; you do it in a context—you observe, interview, gather documents. Therefore, this chapter describes the tasks of fieldwork in the context of observation. Replace the word "field-worker" in the paragraph above with the word "observer" and you will understand the approach of this chapter. Therefore, the chapter has two tasks: 1) to discuss observation, how it is done, its possibilities and its problems, and 2) to describe the tasks of fieldwork both in general, and in particular using observation as a context.

The chapter begins with an introduction to the different ways of observing, some of their advantages and problems, and then proceeds to the tasks of fieldwork in the observation context: gaining entry, securing acceptance, and learning to observe (which, for example, because it also applies to fieldwork generally, might have been titled "learning to gather data"). Analytic induction and constant comparison are described, processes employed during data gathering to make sense of the data, and to develop constructs that help reduce the mass of detail to what is important. Notes written in the field, fieldnotes, capture whatever data one considers potentially useful. Memos capture one's reflections on the data and on the data-gathering process and start analysis. Both are discussed and examples given. Considerations regarding data quality begin with a discussion of data validity and triangulation; the topic is returned to in later chapters. The chapter closes with discussions of when one has learned enough to leave the field and the ever-present problem of ethics.

CHAPTER CONTENTS

Ways of Observing

Our perspective in observation is like a flashlight: It lights up only where it is directed. Indeed, observers are judged by whether they are sensitive enough to capture the critical aspects of what is occuring, how well they can make sense of these aspects, and how accurately the explanations they induce from them fit the data.

A central problem of observation is that individuals who are conscious of being under scrutiny are likely to behave differently from usual, often in the direction of what they perceive to be more socially approved or in accord with the observers' expectations. Such behavior is not always the case, as with resentful experimental school pupils tired of being observed. They may purposely act atypically to display their resentment. Indeed, sometimes it is hard to predict how individuals will react to observation; we just know that they usually do react.

Covert observation, in which the individual is not aware of being observed, is a way of solving the problem. A more common solution is to use participation by the observer to reduce obtrusiveness. With prolonged contact, it is usually assumed that reaction to an observer diminishes. We can construct a continuum of observation techniques from least to most obtrusive as shown in Fig. 12.1.

Covert participant observer	Concealed recording equipment or concealed observer	Visible recording equipment made unobtrusive	Participant observation, recording done out of sight of observed	Participant observation, recording done in sight of observed	Non-participant observer

FIGURE 12.1 Observation methods placed on a continuum of obtrusiveness (adapted from Bouchard, 1976).

Covert Participant Observation

Covert participant observation is the most difficult of all the observation roles. There is a constant tension between the mental vigilance needed to stay in character and the effort to relax so the role seems natural. The former is physically exhausting, yet the latter—too much naturalness—runs the risk that observers will "go native" and lose their professional identity. How exhausting is it? Sullivan, Queen, and Patrick's (1958) covert observer of basic military training lost 35 pounds, presumably from role tension. Weekend meetings with the research team helped maintain his professional perspective, as did visits with a chaplain who was privy to his real identity.

There are other difficulties as well. Reconstruction of events over a long time period between debriefings can be a problem. An alternative, a miniature recording device, produces voluminous records that are expensive and often difficult to transcribe (two persons talking at once, disturbing noise, voices too far from the microphone, and so forth). They also miss nonverbal cues. If a group is small and the behavior of the participants is neither routine nor prescribed, the observer's role may affect what the group does. To maintain a natural role in a small group, the covert observer may feel the necessity to initiate action, and this may result in group outcomes different from those if the observer were not present.

Covert participation also limits the kinds of inquiries that can be made to those consistent with the observer's role. Questions may be too personal, too prying, or too naive, although these questions might be asked by a researcher whose role is known and accepted (Ornstein and Phillips, 1978). The relationships that can be developed and maintained are also limited. A teacher would not be expected to spend much time with the superintendent or central office personnel. Certain records may be inaccessible as well.

Cultural background, age, sex, race, appearance, manner of speaking, physical build, family situation, and other relatively unchangeable characteristics may preclude not just covert but any kind of participant observation in certain groups. Age, for instance, precludes participation roles in any kind of youth situation by senior professors. The restrictions a role may place on the characteristics of an individual may well be impossible for many professionals to meet. Even under favorable circumstances, training may be necessary. The observer of military training referred to earlier was coached for nine months before assuming the part of a working-class enlisted man. Even then, he was nearly rejected by the recruiting sergeant "because by all appearances he was a juvenile delinquent" (Sullivan, Queen, and Patrick, 1958).

Of course, there is a problem if the ruse is discovered. Negotiated entry to institutions is already difficult enough for noncovert observers, especially when their findings may reflect negatively. It is not made easier by researchers who ask no permission and are discovered. Like research fraud, which is discussed further in Chapter 25, it reflects on the rest of us who did not transgress, and the reputation of the profession as a whole is tarnished.

On the positive side, however, participants gain access to data to which no one else could be privy. Behavior is uninhibited by the presence of an outsider. How else could a researcher record how a mental, penal, or other institution looks to an inmate; how the army feels to a recruit; or how certain religious, fraternal, and political groups view their world? Further, an informant can be a main-line actor rather than the marginal and often atypical person a researcher might otherwise have to rely on. Despite these advantages, it is rarely used because of the difficulties involved and the dilemma of whether to report observed illegal or unethical behavior (we discuss informants and the ethical dilemmas of observation later in the chapter).

Concealed Observer or Recording from a Hidden or Unobtrusive Viewpoint

Concealed observation from behind two-way mirrors or from some hidden or unobtrusive location is often feasible in institutional settings, especially if the researcher can locate where hidden observation is possible without suspicion. Experimental schools associated with universities frequently have such arrangements. As a matter of courtesy, teachers are usually informed when they are "on stage," and students are sophisticated enough to know the purpose of the mirrors as well. Requesting permission of the administration further reduces the possibility of covert recording without the subjects' being aware of it. Appropriately, few administrators will approve the latter. The value of the mirrors is that the observed become accustomed to observation because neither observer nor equipment is visible to remind them. Behavior usually returns to what appears to be normal. The video part of a record is likely to be clearer and more understandable than its sound track. The noise filter of the human ear and its ability to follow one conversation when several are occuring have yet to be duplicated by electronic equipment.

Unobtrusive placement of the equipment, the third position on Figure 12.1's continuum, is less expensive and probably as effective. Kounin (1970), for instance, placed boxes in classrooms that would conceal cameras; left in place, they came to be regarded as part of the furniture. Before a record was to be made, equipment was installed in the box when the room was empty. Of course, the location is fixed, and only with expensive equipment are tracking, closeups, and perspective views possible.

Unconcealed Participant Observation

Unconcealed **participant observation** is the role preferred by most observers. Although the fact of observation is obvious, that the researcher is acting as a participant at some level reduces the obtrusiveness. At the same time, it instructs the researcher as to what it is like to be in the situation. This role allows the researcher access to the important places and people while remaining "in character." With a high level of participation (the fourth position on the continuum), note taking may have to be done on the side, but at a lower level (the fifth position) it is often done overtly.

Nonparticipant Observation

The most obtrusive of the roles, **nonparticipant observation,** nevertheless provides the researcher freedom to concentrate entirely on observation and to become sensitive to the significance of what is occurring. Older participant observers often find that they must either adopt this role to continue in the situations they studied when they were younger or change the focus of their research to situations in which they can still successfully pass as participants. Just as it is difficult for an observer to play an unnatural role, so too is it difficult for the observed to maintain "on-stage" behavior over a long period of time. Thus, even with the nonparticipant role, over time there is usually considerable accommodation toward more natural behavior on the part of the observed.

Although some people might argue that without participation we are unable to appreciate fully the affective reactions of participants, there is little evidence that this is the case. Good observers train themselves to be as empathic as possible. They cultivate a combination of empathy and detachment—the former so that they can understand, the latter so that they can record and place in perspective what they are observing. Hughes (1971) has noted that a person who is of the culture, but feels not wholly a part of it, often makes a good observer.

Awareness of observation changes the behavior of the people being observed. Efforts to avoid this effect result in a continuum of observation methods:

✦ *Covert observation gains access to unique situations but is difficult to carry off and may involve complications if the ruse is discovered or illegal or unethical behavior is observed or participated in.*

✦ *Concealed observation is usually known to those being observed, who grow accustomed to it more rapidly in the absence of a constant visual reminder.*

✦ *Unconcealed participant observation makes the observer less obtrusive because he or she becomes a member of the group.*

✦ *Nonparticipant observation requires a longer period for accommodation by those being observed to return to natural behavior (if they ever entirely do), but it also allows the observer to concentrate on the observation process.*

Initial Steps

Gaining Entry

Field-workers seek a way of **gaining entry** that conveys they can be trusted. Often they seek the help of a friend or colleague who either is a part of the setting or is trusted by a member of it. Negotiating entry, particularly of institutions, is often complex. The experience of Bosk (1979), who studied surgeons' errors, is an example. He started with a surgeon he had met at a party who, as supervisor of residents, was a **gatekeeper**—one with authority to give permission for entry. Bosk's department also provided a letter of introduction. Although the surgeon expressed enthusiasm, he also feared his sponsorship would be a "kiss of death." (This is often the case when the sponsor is someone with an administrative position.) He felt that Bosk needed to talk to the residents directly and be seen as his own person. "I learned . . . there was no instant access for the field-worker." Being sent to the chief resident, Bosk was not sure whether he was being given assistance or the runaround. The chief resident also approved but needed to check with his supervisors. "Gaining my initial entrée was a multistage diplomatic problem," Bosk explained. "Each action was a test, and access was the result of continual testing and retesting. Entrée was not something negotiated once and then over and done with . . . but a continuous process" (p. 194).

Bosk is absolutely correct! Entrance and acceptance are continuous processes. Researchers are not only making an entrance with each new person and each situation, but they are also seeking acceptance to gain access to the data or situation they choose to study.

Bosk's experience is not uncommon, nor is his paranoia about possibly being given the runaround. Respondents may not like granting access when they fear being labeled "bad guys" who appear to be "against research and progress." They may refer the request to others in the hope that someone will find a legitimate objection that can be used to provide an excuse. Organizations that perceive themselves to be doing a good job and therefore might gain favorable publicity from a report are much more willing to grant access than organizations wary of criticism. Because of their poorer performance, however, the latter, less accessible ones, are more likely to be the subjects of study.

Sometimes it is possible to enter an area of an organization that feels secure and use the trust established there to gain entry to less accessible parts. This strategy can be a good one because, at time of entrance, researchers often do not know precisely all they will ultimately want to observe.

Often administrators ask for something in exchange for access. They want a report on some subordinates or an evaluation of "how we are doing." They may want some control over the project or the report, to see fieldnotes, to view the draft and make suggestions, to rule certain aspects of their operation "off limits," or perhaps even to approve the report's release. Such administrative approval requirements can create a very difficult situation because most such requests, if they do not violate academic freedom, abrogate the necessary confidentiality of informants. Clearly, the fewer restrictive conditions for entry, the better. Some researchers argue that access privileges can be renegotiated once the observer is at work and initial fear has been replaced by trust. Although observers can often renegotiate restrictive initial conditions, they should never promise things on the assumption that renegotiation is likely. It may be better to use another site.

Field-workers should always enter the field with an open mind. Nevertheless, presuppositions usually exist and can get in the way. For example, Barbera-Stein (1979, as found in Hammersley and Atkinson, 1995) wanted access to puppet-play sessions social workers used with children to explore their emotional development. Even after eight months of fieldwork, which should have established some trust, her access was still extremely limited. She presupposed interactional data in the home would be off limits also because clearly it was the subject of the puppet play. Therefore, she did not ask about access to those data. In reality, it turned out, the social workers did not have a problem with that request. Thus never take such presuppositions for granted; always check out all possibilities.

For many researchers, especially new ones, entering the field is an anxiety-producing experience. Ely (1991) quotes Hillary:

> A cold shudder hit. . . . the selfsame shyness which helped make me an attentive observer . . . could sabotage . . . my efforts to place myself. . . . What is this terror . . . all about? . . . among my fellow classmates, the sense of *angst* and inertia . . . is all too common. . . . I think this feeling comes from human self-doubts and fear of rejection. . . . So? So you could be refused! So what's so devastating about that? The trouble is that this rational line doesn't really reach what these fears may be all about (pp. 17–18).[1]

Experienced researchers suggest acknowledging such fears and then working through or around them. Writing memos about your feelings or keeping a log as the project continues are helpful in this regard. Hillary further states:

> The first and most important thing to do, I found, was to confront my feelings . . . via the log, where the naturalistic researchers record what they plan and feel about their experiences. . . . Here is a 'safe-place,' a haven where feelings, fears, doubts, suspicions, intuitions all have an honored place. [It] . . . gets them 'up front,' and gives them a reality and sense that they are perfectly legitimate and human (Ely, 1991, p. 18).

New students looking for a project are often tempted to study situations where they already have entry, situations that are familiar to them. There is a saying that the intent of qualitative researchers is "to make the strange familiar and the familiar strange," that is, they are looking at a familiar situation as though they were a stranger in it, trying to learn what is going on by emptying themselves of their presuppositions. In a familiar situation, this is difficult to do, not only because of previous experiences in it, but also because others may not accept your new role. For example, the principal who decides to observe in one of the rooms of her teachers may be trying to do so as a student seeking practice for a research course or a dissertation. But, to the teacher, she is still the school principal and she cannot escape that role—especially when principals are involved in teacher competency evaluations. The general advice is, at least initially, to choose a problem in a situation different from what you encounter every day. There will be less of a problem of "making the familiar strange," and, as you study it, you can concentrate on "making the strange familiar."

- ✦ Find a way of gaining entry that conveys "I can be trusted."
- ✦ It may be best to enter where those observed feel comfortable about being observed; then, having established trust, move to other initially less accessible areas.

---

[1]Excerpts in this chapter from *Doing Qualitative Research: Circles in Circles* by Margot Ely, Copyright © 1991 by Falmer Press. Reprinted by permission.

✦ *Writing in fieldnotes about discomfort in seeking entry or observing helps to objectify a view of these feelings; it places them "out there" where they can more easily be seen as expected and normal.*

✦ *Negotiated entry is a continuous process that must be repeated at each level in the organization.*

✦ *Gaining entry to institutions requires the approval of administrators who may impose conditions on the process or wish for something in exchange. This can be a serious problem.*

✦ *Choosing a situation because prior familiarity makes entry problems minimal may result in problems in making the "familiar strange," especially when the familiar includes the baggage of past experience.*

Securing Acceptance

To quote Bosk again, "Access—being allowed in the scene—is one thing, but approval and trust . . . is quite another. Just like access, cooperation . . . is earned again and again when the field-worker shows that he or she is trustworthy" (1979, p. 194). In part, the act of participating demonstrates approval of what was going on by offering help. In return, **acceptance** of the researcher is expected. Sometimes this means doing menial tasks, as when Bosk was asked to open bandage packages or retrieve charts. Sometimes the researcher is involved as a professional, as when Rist (1977) was asked to comment on classroom situations when he was observing the integration of black children bused out of inner-city schools.

Acceptance may be enhanced when the observer uses personal skills to assist the observed. For example, Liebow (1967), studying a street corner society, used his knowledge of criminal proceedings to assist one of the group who had been summoned to appear as a witness in a murder trial. Whyte (1993), in a much earlier and famous study of a similar society, employed his knowledge of the political process to organize a rally of 300 people that got hot water turned on in public showers.

The observer as participant is a difficult role. The observer must maintain close rapport with all from whom information is sought while maintaining sufficient psychological distance not to be identified with one adversarial group or another. Wax (1971) appropriately calls this "instrumental membership" and notes that host and researcher jointly construct a suitable role. Sometimes it helps for the observer simply to explain that a researcher is not supposed to take sides. Perhaps the observed will understand, even though they will believe that, as Ornstein and Phillips (1978) put it, "'deep down' he or she is on our 'side'."

Acceptance does not necessarily mean acting like the rest of the group. Whyte (1955) tried using some of the obscenities he heard all around him. Conversation stopped, and one of the members said, "Bill, you're not supposed to talk like that. That doesn't sound like you" (p. 304). The goal is to become a member of the group enough to be accepted but to remain an outsider sufficiently to retain perspective on the situation. The observer should not be constrained to do all the things the group normally expects of its members.

Acceptance in the sense of appropriate behavior—that is, suitable lack of eye contact, studied lack of interest in others, and careful management of physical contact—is important in public places even though access is open to the researcher and requires no permission as such (Hammersley and Atkinson, 1995). Loitering so as to observe may need to be explained (collecting for a charity, passing out advertising material) or otherwise carefully managed (leaving the site at random times).

✦ *Administrative approval of entry does not guarantee acceptance; indeed, it may delay it. Acceptance, like entry, is a continuous process and must be negotiated anew at each level and with each new informant.*

Learning to Observe

Ely (1991) quotes one of her students: "Well, thank heavens! I've finally come to an easy part in this. Participant observation is a snap," and continues, "Well, it isn't. . . . an attitude of curiosity and a heightened attention are required in order to attend to those very details that most of us filter out automatically in day-to-day life" (p. 42). Spradley (1980) delineates six "dos" that distinguish the participant observer from a participant:

1. Watch yourself as well as watching others.
2. Try to become explicitly aware of what others take for granted.
3. Look beyond the immediate focus of your activity—use a "wide-angle lens."
4. Try to experience the situation simultaneously both as an insider and outsider.
5. Be introspective as you watch.
6. Keep a record not only of what you see but also of how you experience the situation, and mark the latter in such a way that you can separate what you see occurring from how you experience it.

The last of these is important because later you may experience the same events quite differently and change your interpretation. You must then sort out the more appropriate interpretation or determine what caused the difference.

It is important to remember that no matter how unobtrusive you try to remain, your merely having entered the situation may have changed it. Ely (1991) notes an instance in which a teacher-friend who had invited the observer into his classroom became increasingly defensive and argumentative. Discussing this situation with other student researchers, one of them remarked: "That is because you have introduced the reflective mode into that room. No matter how unobtrusive and non-judgmental your presence it is *heightening his own awareness of what he is doing*" (emphasis added, p. 196). Few are entirely comfortable with their performances and when they become reflective they are likely to become defensive.

Most observers start at the same place, a first phase of trying to find what is significant in a situation. In that initial stage, the researcher is like a sponge, soaking up all that is around and listening intently. Interviewing is open-ended, and sometimes just observing is best. Starting with a broad focus can be very confusing to the newcomer—there is so much to attend to! One of Ely's (1991) students, Belén Matías, observing in a classroom put this very well: "There are so many things going on at the same time! My head is spinning. What should I write in my log? What should I leave out? And to top it all, . . . the minute I write . . . I'm disconnected from what's happening. . . . If I'm the instrument, I need to be sent to the repair shop" (p. 48).

Before you despair, just jot down as much as you can. Even things that don't seem significant at first, may later turn out to be important. Gradually, it will become apparent what is relevant, and what your focus will be. This is not to say that the whole process is automatic; you will have to think about what you have observed in the time between observations. Try to understand what is happening, and what is significant about it for your purposes. As you work at that, (and it *does* take work!) you will find yourself more interested in certain aspects than others and from those the focus will emerge. Here is an example, again from one of Ely's students, Marcia Kropf: "As I reread my log entries each week, it became increasingly clear that, because . . . of my own fascination with people, my topic had changed! I no longer noted, in explicit detail, the computer programming functions being explored and how students gained insight into how they worked. Instead, I was describing in great detail when students came to class, how they behaved when they entered the room, where they stood, what they said and to whom, and how they were greeted. . . . I did not develop insights into how students learn computer programming. . . . I did, however, learn a great deal about how students can be invited to participate in a class" (p. 55).

Observers tend to focus on the actions and interactions. However, things such as physical locations, what is present in the room, who is present and how they relate to one another, the sequence of actions, the inferred intent of their actions and their feelings about them are all things you should try to get into your observation notes. You can include a map of the situation; this serves both to help you find the best situation for observation and to locate individuals and objects in space for later reference.

Whyte (1993) notes that we must "learn when to question and when not to question as well as what questions to ask" (p. 303). For example, conversation stopped when Whyte remarked to a gambler, who was telling the group about his operations, "I suppose the cops were all paid off?" His friend Doc commented the next day that he should go easy on all the who, what, why, and when stuff or people would clam up. If he'd just hang around long enough, he would learn the answers without asking. Whyte declares: "I found this was true. As I sat and listened, I learned the answers to questions that I would not even have had the sense to ask" (p. 303). Apropos of the same point is this beautiful quotation from Huxley (1982, as found in Worthen and Sanders, 1987):

> The best way to find things out is not to ask questions at all. If you fire off a question, it is like firing off a gun—bang it goes, and everything takes flight and runs for shelter. But if you sit quite still and pretend not to be looking, all the little facts will come and peek round your feet, situations will venture forth from thickets and intentions will creep out and sun themselves on a stone: and if you are very patient, you will see and understand a great deal more than a man with a gun does.

Over the course of a study, researchers will consult a variety of documents (transcripts and minutes of meetings, court proceedings, diaries, letters, questionnaire responses, census statistics, photos and so forth). They also look for artifacts (pieces of art, choices of furniture, items on desks or tables, available equipment). In short, they will seek any evidence that will be helpful in extending and deepening their understanding.

Sadler (1981), in an article discussing the mind's cognitive limitations as they affect qualitative data gathering, notes that there is a long history of efforts to identify the sources of distortion that cause the mind to make errors of judgment and inference. He observes that after these have been the subject of considerable research, certain cognitive limitations have come to be recognized. He lists a number of research-supported "information processing limitations," of which two critical ones are listed below. Knowing these limitations is the first step toward disciplining their effect.

- *Data overload.* Research suggests that most individuals are able to keep only about seven things in their mind at one time. The mind can beat this limit by "chunking" things as we routinely do—we don't see four legs and a top; we see a table. When many aspects of a situation must be considered at once, however, observers may be fooling themselves in thinking that they are attending to more of the information than they really are. When others are also observing, comparing perceptions may help identify overload situations.
- *First impressions.* We commonly know that first impressions are important, but it has also been confirmed in research. Research on first impressions with regard to physical stimuli where individuals must estimate size indicates that they are affected by the first stimuli they receive. First impressions tend to be enduring, perhaps because new information constitutes a progressively smaller proportion of the information base: after a first piece, the second piece constitutes only half our knowledge base; the next similar addition increases the base only 33 percent, the next 25 percent, then 20 percent, and so on. Because information received later is a smaller part of the base, it becomes more difficult for a new piece to markedly affect the whole. If we are aware of this problem, later efforts to separate out and then verify early impressions become important.

As you may have already sensed, the role of the participant observer is a complex one. As Metz (1983) puts it, participant observers must be:

> constantly "on," defining themselves, guarding against misinterpretation, judging ambiguous situations, and forming an emergent agenda. Also they must be ingratiating themselves with others and appearing to interact spontaneously so that participants are not inhibited by their presence, while they, in fact, reserve their own feelings and use occasions and relationships others treat as ends in themselves, for their own instrumental purposes. They are always in the situation or relationship, but not of it. And even when their spontaneous emotions do arise and they develop feelings of affection and loyalty, they must hold these feelings at bay as sources of bias. (pp. 405–406)

All the while, participant observers must simultaneously be filing away for later recall the significant events, actions, statements, and other details that will make up the database for one's study. Juggling the multiple tasks of observing is difficult, but the fact that many researchers have successfully mastered this art and constructed fascinating and insightful studies should be encouraging to novices.

Because observation is so complex, the neophyte may easily be swamped by trying to monitor all aspects of an observer performance from the very beginning. As Winne (1995) indicates, for novices to monitor their own thoughts and behavior reduces the mental resources available to observe and select significant aspects from the situation they are observing. (Remember, most of us can handle only about seven things at a time.) As the student becomes more comfortable in the observing situation, attending and noting become routinized and resources are freed for self-monitoring—examining one's own behavior for the kinds of relational and bias problems mentioned in the preceding paragraphs. *The novice should probably build up a repertoire of observation behaviors gradually, aiming to add more of the complete set of desirable observer behaviors with each session.* It is not clear how transferable that repertoire and adjustment are from situation to situation or whether some adjustment is required in each new situation. Transferability probably varies with both the nature of the situation and the skills of the observer, but it appears that for many observers there may be a period of adjustment in each new situation.

- *Gradually build up a repertoire of observation skills.*
- *Observe and record what you are doing and thinking as you observe others.*
- *Try to keep everything in a larger perspective as an outsider would. At the same time, empathically try to sense how those in the situation are experiencing it.*
- *Learn when to question.*
- *Be aware of data overload.*
- *Double-check first impressions.*

Data Gathering

A substantial portion of each qualitative study is spent in data gathering: getting the study's target to emerge and focusing data gathering around the target. As you sift the data and are able to better identify your target, you focus your observations and inquiries, and you are able to select a purposive sample that includes individuals, documents, situations, events, processes, times, and other aspects that can further develop your understanding of it. Strauss (1987) and others use the term *theoretical sample* to indicate that the choice of the next subjects and situations is determined "on analytic grounds" for the purposes of developing and extending theory. Since this is covered by the term *purposive sampling* as it is understood in general usage as well as in Chapter 8, that term is used here with the understanding that sampling choices are made with the intent of developing understanding and an explanation.[2]

Analytic Induction and the Constant Comparison Method

Purposive sampling is particularly important in identifying cases needed in the analytic induction and the constant comparison processes. These processes are used to clarify the concepts and constructs developed to describe and explain the phenomena being studied. You might expect to find them described with the process of qualitative analysis, the topic of Chapter 14, instead of here. In the constant comparison method, however, data gathering and analysis are intertwined and both begin from the outset as the name implies. In contrast, complete analysis often waits until data gathering is finished with analytic induction. If feasible, however, the researcher may return to the field when already gathered data prove inadequate. Thus, data gathering and analysis are intertwined and we must begin discussing analysis here.

Both analytic induction and constant comparison are inductive processes used to develop and delineate the key constructs and concepts of a study. **Analytic induction** calls for finding commonalties in the data which lead first to a description and then to an explanation of that regularity. We also check the proposed explanation against already collected data to see how well it fits. Where it does not, as in adjusting an ill-fitting dress or suit, we move back and forth between checking and modifying until the proposed explanation accounts for the data. If we are stumped by cases that are not covered, we go back to these or similar cases for additional information that permits appropriate adjustment to accommodate them as well. In this manner, we gradually develop an understanding of the phenomenon and a theory, or explanation, of how the phenomena are grounded in our observations—that is, we have what Glaser and Strauss (1967) termed "**grounded theory**."

Analytic induction often begins as we leave the field as a result of having arrived at **saturation**—that is when new observations cease to add much to previous ones. We must be careful about declaring that saturation has been reached, however, for as Patton (1980) comments: "The moment you cease observing, pack your bags, and leave the field, you will get a remarkably clear insight about that one critical activity you should have observed . . . but didn't" (p. 195).

The **constant comparison method** involves the researcher in analysis to develop grounded theory from the very start of observation. Each item in the notes is coded in terms of the dimension or concept of which it is an indicator. New in-

---

[2]The implication in the discussion of purposive sampling above is that such sampling is of different persons or sites. The same principles of purposive sampling also extend to sampling the behavior of individuals over time. Thus we may observe particular individuals at set time intervals, or when certain behaviors occur; we may sample the behavior of a classroom every so many minutes or seconds recording verbal descriptions or tallying it, as Flanders's (1970) interaction analysis does.

dicators of each concept are sought until the same kind of instances are found repeatedly and the concept is said to be saturated. Concepts are linked with other
concepts in a theory, or explanation, of the phenomena. This explanation is constantly compared with new data from the field in which we try to find negative
instances, **borderline** instances, and key examples. It is a funnel-like process as
the range of new informants and situations is increasingly focused on the ones
that will add to and test previous formulations. Once core concepts and explanations are well developed ("densified") with detail and example, the funnel is reversed to broaden sample choice. The researcher then tries to find **negative cases**
that show the limits of the explanation and determines the generality of the theory. This step may lead to the choice of new sites to study and a comparison of
findings at the new sites with those of the old in a cross-site comparison.

Note the role of emerging explanation, or theory, in controlling the direction
of the study and therefore directing purposive sampling in the constant comparative method. Extreme cases may be selected to help illuminate aspects more difficult to discern in run-of-the-mill examples. Cases are chosen to "flesh out" description, densify theory conceptualization, and test and extend the formulations.
Cases especially suitable for these purposes are those with which your audience
can identify, that have aspects that suggest their generality (Patton, 1980).[3]

For example, Gouldner (1954) studied a factory and found that workers never
talked back to supervisors, did what they were told to do, adhered to a rigid
schedule, and left repairs to maintenance workers even though this practice meant
interrupting production. He considered these factors to be evidence of the construct "bureaucratization." (Note that whereas the quantitative researcher might
build a scale to be administered to workers to measure bureaucratization, Gouldner inferred it from the many indicators of the concept across the cases observed.)
Selecting a contrasting work site—a mine—he focused his attention on the same
indicators and found that workers stood up to their supervisors, made repairs
themselves, rotated jobs, and had no factory-like schedules. In fact, the track-lay-
ing gang, for example, was given only general instructions about where to work,
and the supervisor then asked them how long it might take. Gouldner considered
these behaviors to be indicators of a lack of "bureaucratization," concluding that
the red tape was greater in the factory than in the mine (Gouldner, 1954, in Ornstein and Phillips, 1978, p. 361). With both positive and negative examples helping
to define the construct, he then focused on "bureaucratization's" effects.

Figure 12.2 graphically portrays the constant-comparative process from its
start in the box at the upper left, following the solid lines to the box at the bottom
right. Researchers initially cycle through the activities in the upper left inner circle
as many times as necessary to formulate some kind of explanation or rationale for
the phenomena observed. With each cycle they are constantly comparing proposed hypotheses about what is significant and what is going on with the data

---

[3]Patton also notes that cases may be chosen because your audience would expect those cases to
be included. While these cases may or may not contribute to the constant comparison or analytic
induction process, they may be important to an acceptance of the study's findings by your chosen audience.

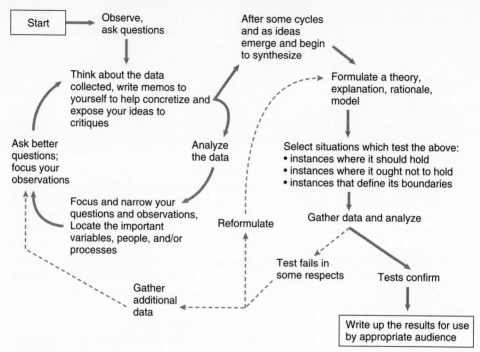

FIGURE 12.2 The process of developing and testing one's hypotheses and explanations in the constant comparison method. (Adapted from Gladwin, 1989.)

and successively modifying the former to fit. This cycle of formulation goes on in the field where observing, interviewing, and gathering artifacts and records provides the grist for the log of events. This feedback mechanism in turn leads researchers to consider what is happening and to write about it to themselves in memos—record their reactions to the situation, their hypotheses, suggestions for whom or what to observe or ask about next time, for what appears to be significant, and what is less so, and so forth. This material guides researchers to their next actions, which lead to further refinement until they feel either they are not learning anymore, or they have a firm enough idea about what is going on—its significance and explanation—to test it. Exiting the cycle, at the middle of the top of Figure 12.2, researchers then follow the steps leading, they hope, to confirmation and its write-up. Should confirmation fail, however, as the dashed lines show, beginning lower right of Figure 12.2, the process leads either to further data gathering to determine what was wrong, or to a reformulation with sufficient modification that they believe it ought now to fit the data. Then they test the reformulation and either confirm it or repeat the cycle of reformulation or additional data gathering until confirmation occurs.

The constant comparison process seems, in part, to have been built on sorrowful experiences at having left the field without sufficient data to complete the analytic induction process. In addition, however, whereas the analytic induction process adjusts a proposed explanation to account for accumulated data, the constant comparison method actively searches for cases that test the constructs in the explanation with negative and borderline cases to assure their clarification and completeness as well as their generality.

The two processes just described are examples of the efforts to increase the credibility of qualitative methods through descriptive procedures that improve and discipline the process without restricting it to a set formula. Glaser and Strauss (1967) described guidelines for analytic induction intended to develop "grounded theory" which had considerable impact. Such efforts have been joined by others, including Bogdan and Biklen (1982), Guba and Lincoln (1986), Levine (1985), Miles and Huberman (1994), Strauss (1987), and Strauss and Corbin (1990).

As an important aside, this process of defining a concept or **construct** was devised by philosophers and is called **conceptual analysis**. This process works by identifying key examples that characterize the heart of the concept being defined and then finding negative and borderline examples that delineate the concept's boundaries. Because it is a very useful way of distinguishing exactly what is meant by a concept and how a concept relates to its operationalization, conceptual analysis has been employed in a number of fields. We meet it here in the constant comparison method. We also find the same process used later in this chapter in the discussion of data validity. Long before the process was adopted as useful in other fields, Cronbach and Suppes (1955) calling it "construct validity" used it to show the validity of a test or other instrument. Therefore, it appears still again in Chapter 18 on measurement.

Conceptual analysis is highly useful whenever you want to clarify a concept or construct's meaning, develop a concept or construct, or show the relation between a concept or construct and its operational definition. For more on this method from a philosophical standpoint, see Green (1971), or Wilson (1971).

♦ *Most formulations begin as the observer—like a "sponge"—listens intently and observes open-endedly.*

♦ *With the constant comparison method, as the target emerges so do explanatory hunches that guide the further selection of cases and observations.*

♦ *Purposive sampling instead of random sampling is used to find cases that extend and densify understanding, to test an explanation, to find the limits of its generality, and to ensure the validity of information.*

♦ *Hunches are tested on new cases, modified as needed to fit, further tested, further detailed and related to other hunches, further modified and retested, and so on, until saturation is reached—the point at which further efforts add little or nothing.*

♦ *The intent of the constant comparison process is to develop an understanding and explanation grounded in and accounting for the observations —that is, grounded theory.*

♦ *Analytic induction also results in grounded theory. In contrast to the constant comparison process, which develops its theory during the observational process and guides purposive sampling throughout observation, analytic induction* focuses on theory development during the analytic process with already gathered data.

✦ Practitioners of qualitative research continue to provide discipline to their methods without restricting them to a formula.

Informants[4]

As noted earlier, qualitative researchers treat those being observed as individuals to learn from—an egalitarian perspective in contrast to using the term "subjects" as do those doing experiments. They see this view as more than a difference in designation; it involves an attitudinal change on the part of the researcher as well. As in any human contacts, our attitude has implications for how we interact with the people we observe and how we treat the data obtained from them.

Bouchard (1976) makes an additional distinction between respondents and informants. The former are random or systematic samples and may be considered replicable. **Informants** are selected for their sensitivity, knowledge, and insights into their situation, their willingness to talk about it, and their ability to help gain access to new situations. Bouchard warns that it is important to distinguish carefully between data from informants, especially those whose reasons for informing may influence what they say, and data from respondents.

Especially sensitive informants are persons who have less stake in the system (and so may be less defensive about it) and those who view it from a standpoint different from that of more central players. Examples are persons who come from another culture, social class, or community and who can contrast their impressions with their previous experience. As newcomers, they are especially likely to note things that others might take for granted. Individuals with a new role or status are similarly sensitive; they have left one role but are not yet comfortable in the other. All such people are likely to view their new situation in terms of their old role, a potential bias but one that can often be allowed for if we are aware of it.

Other informant types may similarly have hidden agendas: rebels or malcontents welcome the opportunity to "get things off their chest." These people and former insiders who have lost power are usually eager to share their views of current insiders, most likely in a negative manner. Some persons who are flattered by the attention are likely to say whatever they think the observer wants to hear in order to maintain that attention. Some persons are so much a part of the scene that they are too well entrenched to worry about repercussions from communicating with outsiders. They may be harder to tap, however, since they have the least to gain from doing so—unless they magnify their own roles in past actions, a problem to watch for.

Our original intent may be to represent a situation as viewed by its participants, but we often wind up with what Sieber (1973) calls an "**elite bias**," an over-

---

[4]Since typically, obtaining information from informants basically involves interviewing, much of the next chapter's advice applies here as well.

weighting of the elite of the system in the selection of informants and in the evaluation of statements. Sieber notes there are many reasons for "gravitating to the elite." Because the elite are the "gatekeepers" who grant access, the observer feels gratitude toward them and is careful to "keep on their good side." They are likely to be more articulate and give the impression of being better informed about the group. Sieber discovered his bias when he tried to predict the results of a survey he had given teachers. "It became obvious when observing these comparisons that I had unwittingly adopted the elites' version of reality. For example, I overestimated the extent to which teachers felt that the administration accepted criticism" (p. 1353).

The most desirable informant is the "natural" (Bouchard, 1976); he or she has a perspective on the situation and is able to communicate it. Whyte's (1993) "Doc" is the prototype of such individuals. Doc had a perspective not only on his situation but also on the role that Whyte should play in the community. He steered Whyte to situations and introduced him to persons helpful in the study. Every researcher should be so lucky! Some researchers have used informants as their eyes and ears in situations where they were unable to be present because they had to be elsewhere or would be too obvious or unwelcome—in essence, the informant becomes the participant observer. Dalton (1959, 1967) even had informants introduce certain topics into a situation so that reactions could be observed. His combination of experimental and qualitative methods illustrates that it is up to the ingenuity of the investigator to use methods in ways appropriate to the target situation.

The main caveat is that the observer must always be concerned with the questions: "Why are these persons willing to talk to me? What point of view are they using?" Only if you can answer these questions satisfactorily, can you determine the extent of bias that you must take into account as you use the information. To identify informant bias it helps if the interview takes place in front of others who can correct misstatements. Don't assume your informants will necessarily confront the misstatement at the time; provide later opportunities for them to do so privately. Perhaps even better, let the informants know that you are also gathering data from others. This practice not only helps you measure consistency but also is likely to make them more careful about their statements if they know there may be a check on their accuracy. Remember that you are talking not to a random sample of independent cases but to a social network. These individuals will be interacting with each other after you have left the scene and so must protect themselves. If the group learns who your other informants are, they may get together, compare notes, and possibly align their stories or otherwise misguide you.

+ *Informants help the observer to understand the views of the people being observed, introduce him or her to new individuals and situations, and may teach the observer how to behave unobtrusively.*
+ *Such cooperation may not be without its price. Therefore, observers must ask themselves, "Why is this person talking to me and being so helpful?"*
+ *Informants are often marginal persons who have less stake in the status quo or are not constrained by it. Because they may be atypical, their information must be appropriately discounted ("taken with a grain of salt").*

Accessing Cognitive and Affective Processes

Qualitative methods are particularly useful in studying cognitive and affective processes that cannot be directly observed but must be inferred from overt behavior. Indeed, inferring from careful observation is often the first method of studying such behavior. Sometimes such observation can be augmented by careful analysis of behavior in video recordings, especially nonverbal reactions. A second line of procedure involves retrospection. The interviewer reviews the situation and behavior with the respondent, asking her to describe what was going on in her mind. Such review can be enhanced by **stimulated recall** in which the interviewer and respondent view a videotape of the situation, with either of them stopping the tape at points where significant behavior might be taking place. Still another way of tapping such behavior is to have the respondents think out loud, reporting on their thoughts as the process takes place. Again, a review of the recording of this session, with the respondent in a stimulated recall mode, often enriches the data, and also helps find where the individual found the process slowed or changed by the necessity to think aloud.

Fieldnotes and Annotations

Fieldnotes and logs are the observer's records of what has been observed—descriptions of the individuals, the setting, and what happened, recapitulating the conversation and other interaction as completely as possible. Fieldnotes should begin as soon as the project gets underway. Notes on the initial contacts with gatekeepers, as you seek access, should all be part of the record. They may shed light on something that occurred later, but without these early notes you would have missed the connection. Rile's term *thick description* aptly captures the character of fieldnotes (in Geertz, 1977) .

Fieldnotes should especially try to capture the language used by the observees, as it shows how people define one another. Taylor (1977, pp. 117–138), for example, studied a mental institution and found that the attendants categorized patients in terms of their dominant mode of interaction with them: "troublemakers," "soilers," "vegetables," "runaways," "headbangers," and so on. Such terms suggested the attendants' attitudes, which could then be confirmed or modified by further observation.

Fieldnotes may require a different orientation than writing. Ely's (1991) student Donna Flynn wrote in her log:

> Thinking back to Nurse's Training, a great deal of emphasis was placed on clear, concise, to the point recording. . . . During our first field observation/informal interview my tendency would have been to log "E told me about her day as substitute teacher." Instead I had to learn to log: "E said: 'You'll never guess what I did yesterday. I subbed for a first grade class, and boy, was I wiped out at the end of the day. . . .'" All this was logged so that I could retain the flavor of her day and how she saw it and felt about it (p. 70).

Capturing as much verbatim speech as possible as well as all the details of the situation is especially important initially since, until the focus of the study becomes clear, you don't know what will turn out to be important.

You will also need to decide the basis for recording: videotaping, audiotaping, making notes while observing, catching up on noting later, or doing all the noting post-observation. If possible, make notes while in the field; you can then expand them after you leave the observation situation. As a participant observer, you may need to find excuses to visit your car, the washroom, or somewhere unobtrusive to quickly scribble placeholders to remind yourself later of events. My colleague Sari Biklen advises doing something subtle like turning a ring or watch to face inward as a later reminder of something important.

What about the use of video or audio recordings in place of notes? Certainly these capture conversation and give-and-take more faithfully than fieldnotes. They can be useful if you can't be present or wish to make an unobtrusive record with hidden equipment; if you were present, they can be helpful memory joggers. Most videorecording, however, is done from a fixed camera position without benefit of remote controls. Audio recording loses the nonverbal aspects, which can be crucial to understanding covert meanings. Neither recording process has the capability you have when personally present to listen selectively to one person's voice, filtering it out from a cacophony of background sound. Many researchers find that they must have the recordings transcribed, which is time-consuming and expensive. Extensive recording results in an overwhelming volume of detail, yet observers still have the job of making notes to extract the important information. Unless they can't be present, observers usually prefer to take notes in the actual situation. Furthermore, there is no guarantee that the important things will occur in the camera's view or can be inferred from the audio record.

On the other hand, you can do things with audio- and videotape that you cannot do with notes. For example, Erickson and Schultz (1982) subjected their audiotapes of counseling sessions to voice print analysis and analyzed the videotapes for nonverbal and kinesic patterns to determine points of emphasis and stress. Observers can view their videotapes with colleagues who may catch things that went unnoticed. Sometimes they provide a totally different perspective.

Write up your observations in detail as soon after the field trip as possible—certainly do so within 24 hours. "Forgetting begins as soon as the experience ends" (Ely, 1991, p. 79). Experienced observers suggest not talking about sessions with others before writing to avoid changing emphases as a result of the discussion. Although you can strengthen your memory by rehearsing what you have seen, such rehearsal will tend to be selective and likely lead to reflection on the events. This may change your first impressions. Such reflections are important to record—but separately from your initial impressions. Indeed, your ruminations on what went on may continue through the life of the project, and may change markedly over time both as events look different in perspective and as more context is available in which to understand them. Therefore, immediately record the notes as factually as possible, keeping separate any reactions or reflections on the data.

Keep a limit to the period of time you are observing. Ninety minutes is more than enough for most observers. Novices are typically concerned that they will not remember the conversations or be able to recreate them from their notes. Most are pleasantly surprised, however, to find out this is not a problem. Ely's (1991) student Laura Berns writes that she did not take extensive notes because she worried about missing significant activity. Then, when writing the log, she feared being unable to make sense of them. "Fortunately that fear turned out to be groundless . . . for those few notes were in fact sufficient to jog my memory, to bring back a wealth of detailed data—often more than I could conveniently manage. Later, comments of fellow students confirmed my experience" (p. 72). Contrary to expectation, Berns found following her notes easy: "There is no need to agonize over the best order, as you can whiz along, putting first what came first in time and continuing chronologically to the end. In addition, you don't have to be concerned about how many *t*'s in inputting because such polished details are unimportant in a text intended for your eyes only" (p. 74).

Novices are always amazed at how lengthy the notes become. Laura Berns again comments, "I routinely found that an hour of observation generated ten or more pages of log, an experience shared by many others in the course. . . . I found myself crossing the street to avoid conversations with [her observees] . . . because a pleasant five-minute chat meant adding five more pages" (p. 75).

If you are not planning to use one of the specialized computer programs for qualitative data analysis you will be analyzing and adding to your notes, so remember to provide wide margins, certainly on the left, and possibly on both sides. Double-space them to provide for interlinear notations. Because you will want to be able to refer to specific items in the notes, number the pages serially through the entire record and provide line numbers on each page. Most word processors can automatically do this for you. If you use page and line numbers as references, be sure to use software that allows addition of annotations without changing line numbers. Some researchers divide the paper vertically into thirds with a large middle column for fieldnotes, and narrower ones for analysis on the left, and for observer comments, reflections, and so forth, on the right. Numbering all pages, notes, memos, and comments sequentially will keep them in order so that the time sequence is clear. Making small paragraphs helps to keep like things together that you can more easily categorize when analyzing the notes.

For fast typists, the idea of making notes on a laptop computer is very appealing. There are advantages and disadvantages, purely aside from the obstrusiveness of the instrument and typing. Ragsdale (1992) notes that not only does typing the notes during the observation process shorten the writing process, but less data gets lost and the notes tend to be fuller. He adds, however, that there is a problem of confidentiality since the screen is visible to those sitting behind. Observers find persons trying unobtrusively to look over their shoulder. Turning down the brightness helps. Another problem with the use of the laptop is the inability to quickly sketch the setup of a room, or copy a graphic from a blackboard—it takes a lot more words to express the same thing. Some observers make hand-written graphics and later redo them in the computer.

There is also the problem of carrying the instrument around and finding a suitable place to type. Some field-workers set up their laptop in a convenient place and dash back and forth to make notes, but this is awkward and they miss the action while away from it. Although any word processor can be used, there are a number of special programs for qualitative research that facilitate analysis (discussed further in Chapter 14). Most of these programs can import text from any word processor.

Because all description selects aspects to emphasize, the notes preserve what the observer believed was important. This selectivity leads to a second aspect of the fieldnotes, the observers' reflections on the processes of selecting what was important to capture: their behavior in the situation (comfort, obtrusiveness, apparent impact on others, treatment by others); ideas or hypotheses explaining what was occurring; problems in observing, recording, or coding; suggestions for the next steps and from whence they were derived; and so on. It is customary to keep these remarks separate from the fieldnotes so that opinion is isolated from fact. Such comments are embedded in the fieldnotes so that they can be tied to the time and context but are labeled "O.C." for "observer comment" and indented, boxed, or written on new pages as personal **memos.**

Typically, fieldnotes consist of a chronological account. They may include relevant incidents from outside the formal observation process as well—comments elicited at a party, reflections on an interview from an informant encountered later, and so on. They may include diagrams of the situation showing the relative positions of the participants, furniture, and the like. They typically reflect on such things as a description of the room and the room furnishings, the physical characteristics and dress, and the mannerisms of the participants, so as to adequately convey the context. Conversation is quoted in so far as it can be gotten down, including gestures, accents, facial expressions, and so forth that give meaning to the speech. Observer actions should be recorded as well.

As you write your notes, mark comments so as to set them off from description. Comment on things you don't understand—your speculations on what is occurring, why you did what you did, your frame of mind and emotional state during the observing, and how you think they may be affecting your observing.

Figure 12.3 gives an example of fieldnotes (the inset remarks labeled "O.C." are observer comments). Only about one-fifth of the full set of fieldnotes is reproduced. An excellent example, the notes include an accidental contact at a party long after the observation which led to an insightful observer comment.

Note the wealth of detail (thick description!) in this fragment from the notes. Not knowing ahead of time what will be significant, the observer records what he was wearing as well as the attire of the important others being observed. Persons entering and leaving the school help establish the atmosphere, as do the notes about who was in the halls doing what and the observer's interaction with the students there. The use of a map of the classroom shows the relationships of students, teacher, teacher's aide, and observers. Further, note that every attempt was made to record the conversation verbatim. There is even a note that a quotation may not be exact because the observer was embarrassed about coming in late.

Note also the many observer comments marked "O.C." They include introspections by the observer about his feelings, explanations of the teacher's comments, evaluative observations (unsupervised halls), and questions to check up on later—material set off from the factual observations themselves yet important to understanding those observations.

Inexperienced observers tend to summarize what went on. Experienced ones, jot down detail, especially what they think may later be important and give the "feel" of the situation. Compare the two sets of notes (on page 272) on the same situation. Those on the right are by an experienced observer; those on the left are by an inexperienced observer:

March 24, 1980
Joe McCLoud
11:00 a.m. to 12:30 p.m
Westwood High
6th Set of Notes

The Fourth Period
Class in Marge's Room

I arrived at Westwood High at five minutes to eleven, the time Marge told me her fourth period started. I was dressed as usual: sport shirt, chino pants, and a Woolrich parka. The fourth period is the only time during the day when all the students who are in the "neurologically impaired/learning disability" program, better known as "Marge's program," come together. During the other periods, certain students in the program, two or three or four at most, come to her room for help with the work they are getting in other regular high school classes.

It was a warm fortyish, promise of a spring day. There was a police patrol wagon, the kind that has benches in the back that are used for large busts, parked in the back of the big parking lot that is in front of the school. No one was sitting in it and I never heard its reason for being there. In the circular drive in front of the school was parked a United States Army car. It had insignias on the side and was a khaki color. As I walked from my car, a balding fortyish man in an Army uniform came out of the building and went to the car and sat down. Four boys and a girl also walked out of the school. All were white. They had on old dungarees [jeans] and colored stenciled t-shirts with spring jackets over them. One of the boys, the tallest of the four, called out, "oink, oink, oink." This was done as he sighted the police vehicle in the back.

> O.C.: This was strange to me in that I didn't think that the kids were into "the police as pigs." Somehow I associated that with another time, the early 1970s. I'm going to have to come to grips with the assumptions I have about high school due to my own experience. Sometimes I feel like Westwood is entirely different from my high school and yet this police car incident reminded me of mine.

Classes were changing when I walked down the halls. As usual there was the boy with girl standing here and there by the lockers. There were three couples that I saw. There was the occasional shout. There were no teachers outside the doors.

> O.C.: The halls generally seem to be relatively unsupervised during class changes.

Two black girls I remember walking down the hall together. They were tall and thin and had their hair elaborately braided with beads all through them. I stopped by the office to tell Mr. Talbot's (the principal) secretary that I was in the building. She gave me a warm smile.

> O.C.: I feel quite comfortable in the school now. Somehow I feel like I belong. As I walk down the halls some teachers say hello. I have been going out of my way to say hello to kids that I pass. Twice I've been in a stare-down with kids passing in the hall. Saying, "How ya' doin'?" seems to disalarm them.

I walked into Marge's class and she was standing in the front of the room with more people than I had ever seen in the room save for her homeroom which is right after second period. She looked like she was talking to the class or was just about to start. She was dressed as she had been on my other visits—clean, neat, well-dressed but casual. Today she had on a striped blazer, a white blouse and dark slacks. She looked up at me, smiled and said: "Oh, I have a lot more people here now than the last time."

O.C.: This was in reference to my other visits during other periods where there are only a few students. She seems self-conscious about having such a small group of students to be responsible for. Perhaps she compares herself with the regular teachers who have classes of thirty or so.

There were two women in their late twenties sitting in the room. There was only one chair left. Marge said to me something like: "We have two visitors from the central office today. One is a vocational counselor and the other is a physical therapist," but I don't remember if those were the words. I felt embarrassed coming in late. I sat down in the only chair available next to one of the women from the central office. They had on skirts and carried their pocketbooks, much more dressed up than the teachers I've seen. They sat there and observed.

Below is the seating arrangement of the class today:

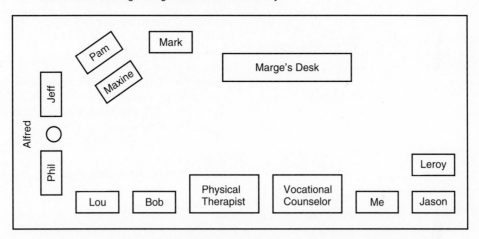

Alfred (Mr. Armstrong, the teacher's aide) walked around but when he stood in one place, it was over by Phil and Jeff. Marge walked about near her desk during her talk which started by saying to the class: "Now remember, tomorrow is a field trip to the Rollway Company. We all meet in the usual place, by the bus, in front of the main entrance at 8:30. Mrs. Sharp wanted me to tell you that the tour of Rollway is not specifically for you. It's not like the trip to G.M. They took you to places where you were likely to be able to get jobs. Here, it's just a general tour that everybody goes on. Many of the jobs that you will see are not for you. Some are just for people with engineering degrees. You'd better wear comfortable shoes because you may be walking for two or three hours." Maxine and Mark said: "Ooh," in protest to the walking.

She paused and said in a demanding voice: "OK, any questions? You are all going to be there. (Pause) I want you to take a blank card and write down some questions so you have things to ask at the plant." She began passing out cards and at this point Jason, who was sitting next to me made a tutting sound of disgust, and said: "We got to do this?" Marge said: "I know this is too easy for you, Jason." This was said in a sarcastic way but not like a strong put down.

O.C.: It was like sarcasm between two people who know each other well. Marge has known many of these kids for a few years. I have to explore the implications of that for her relations with them.

Her husband was seated next to her.	A man was seated next to her. (O.C. I presume her husband, but not sure.) He was dressed in faded but newish jeans and a black leather jacket and sat erect as though he had been in the military.
He turned to her and engaged her in conversation.	Turning to face her, he asked "What are we doing here? Can't we leave here now?" Somewhat slumped in her chair, she hardly seemed to notice he had addressed her.
I entered by the front door of the school and let the school secretary know I was here again.	Entering the front door of the school is like going to the gate at an airport; you pass through metal detectors and an armed policeman stands just down the hall. The school secretary sits near the entrance behind a sliding glass window. She opened it and greeted me cheerfully as though she was glad I had come back as I let her know I'd be in the school a couple of hours in Mrs. Seamon's room.

✦ *Fieldnotes are the observer's record of observations. They can be made while in the field if this can be done unobtrusively and without changing the behavior of those observed. Otherwise, they must be completed as soon as possible after leaving the field.*

✦ *Good fieldnotes include as much verbatim conversation as possible, as well as notes regarding context.*

✦ *Comments, inferences, and judgments are kept separate from observations—as observer comments or as memos.*

Memos

Miles and Huberman (1984) note that we become so fascinated with the flood of particulars that we "forget to *think*, to make deeper and more general sense of what is happening, to begin to explain it in a conceptually coherent way" (p. 69). Thinking is carrying on a conversation with oneself, and **memos** are records of those conversations. Strauss (1987) argues that memoing should take precedence over coding or data recording so that the ideas will not be lost. He suggests that if we do not have time to memo on the spot, to make at least a note to write the memo, and then set aside time for memoing as well as coding and analysis. In addition, if we write titles on memos, it makes them easier to code later and highlights their generality. Figure 12.4 is an example of a memo from a study of educational innovations in Miles and Huberman (1984). The researchers note that this memo pulls data from many sites and reformulates them around the issue of ca-

FIGURE 12.4 An integrating memo that shows the kinds of musings that lead to new hypotheses and guide future data collection. (Excerpt from *Qualitative Data Analysis,* 2nd Edition by M. B. Miles and A. M. Huberman. Copyright © 1994 by Sage Publications. Reprinted by permission of Sage Publications, Inc.)

Memo: Career patterns 2/22/80

In a general sense, people are riding the innovations in a state of transition; they are on their way *from* somewhere *to* somewhere *via* the project. . .

Where could people be going? They could be going

—*up*: from a classroom to a supervisory or administrative role or to a higher administration slot. Innovations are a lot faster then waiting for someone else to move on or going back for a *degree*. They get you visibility and good positioning. If it gets institutionalized, you get institutionalized with it in a new role. Also, they're less brutal than getting promotions by doing in the person above you and more convenient than having to move away to move up.

—*away*: from teaching by easing into a part-time or more flexible job. These projects tend to be marginal, loosely administered (although Tindale [one of the schools] is contrary), transition-easing. They also can allow for permutations, as in the up-and-away pattern Cary may be following at Plummet.

—*in*: the remedial programs are less choosy about formal credentials. They provide access to civil services like education to people with weird backgrounds. Aides can get positioned to become certified teachers; people from business or the arts can come into a marginal or experimental universe and ease gradually into a more formal role incumbency.

At "*my*" sites, the innovation services the purposes of two teachers moving into supervisory roles ("helping teachers"). One has now become Title I coordinator. The administrator at this site (Masepa) is now well positioned for promotion, since he has won (ECRI [the experimental program] has been mandated). At Banestown, the aide moves "in"; the head lab teacher does what the teacher at Masepa did with Title I: She gets the other half of her job in the same sector, thereby becoming "specialized" and ready to move "up" as *her* patron, the reading supervisor, moves "up" herself into a higher administrative post. The other lab teacher moves (back) "in" from non-teaching with a part-time post.

All this is very tentative, but it might focus us on this dimension, which is being independently flagged by 2–3 of us.

It is especially worth keeping track, as we dictate and code, of where these people have come from and where they are, or think they are, on their way to. I suggest we ask each informant:

—a little more directly, *why* he/she is doing this, in terms of roles and role changes.

—what he/she expects to be doing in 2–3 years.

—if he/she has a sense of being in a transitional period.

reer patterns. Because the writing of this memo occurred partway through the data collection, it affected subsequent collection and suggested specific means of doing so.

Memos are the basis for analysis and for further data gathering directions. Steinmetz (Ely, 1991) writes a memo (at a minimum) after every three sets of field-notes, finding that unless she does so, too much data accumulates and "we experience input overload and the uneasy realization that we are floundering because we haven't given ourselves the direction we need" (p. 80).

> ◆ *Memos are used to integrate thoughts, to record hunches and the gradual development of an explanation or theory and suggest future directions.*

Data Validity

We have already noted many of the things researchers in the field are required to do at the same time. Yet, another task—assuring the quality of the data—is equally crucial. We will further discuss the issue of data checking in the section on standards in Chapter 15, but some aspects of it are so integral to fieldwork that they are important to note here. Miles and Huberman (1994) describe 13 excellent data-checking aspects. One of these checks monitors representativeness. We assume what we are seeing is typical, but is it? For example, only a few board members took part in the discussion at the meeting you observed. Therefore, you check previous minutes to determine whether this is typical. Basically this is a purposive sampling problem. Taking larger samples and sampling aspects you know are important from the outset contribute to representativeness.

Unless you consciously attend to weighting sources of data, each tends to be regarded as good as the next. We know, however, that some sources are much more reliable than others. Data gathered in situations without the trappings of formality usually are more representative. So too are data gathered from those comfortable with us. Some individuals have a perspective on what is going on which others lack. Attending to these facts and consciously taking them into account is important in synthesizing findings.

Extreme cases, outliers, and surprise findings are all contrary to our expectations. They can be bothersome when they negate an explanation or rationale that otherwise would be solidly supported. We love data that support our ideas and hate data that do not. Our initial tendency may be to ignore such instances as aberrations of little importance. This would be a mistake; we need to find the cause of such deviation. Extreme instances may indeed highlight some aspect not very visible with run-of-the-mill cases. For example, students learn more rapidly if they form a circle and read aloud in order rather than having the teacher call on them individually at random. However, we occasionally find a reading circle where this is not true. Shall we ignore it and say that in general it works? Or should we try to find out why one instance didn't? With the latter we find that once a certain threshold in reading skill has been reached, the necessity to silently rehearse the section to be read aloud is no longer necessary; the generalization applies only with beginning readers. Outliers may have a simple explanation (for example, the individual was tired) that changes nothing, or one that causes us to modify our emerging ideas. With the former we buy peace of mind and an ability to explain such cases to our audience; with the latter, we modify the explanation in ways that add to its generality or show us its limits. Outliers, are used to modify rather than negate our ideas.

Triangulation

Bias is inevitable; as noted by historian Barbara Tuchman (1981, in Miles and Huberman, 1994) "[it] . . . is to be expected. . . . Even if an event is not controversial, it will have been seen and remembered from different angles of view by different observers. . . . As the lion in Aesop said to the Man, 'There are many statues of men slaying lions, but if only the lions were sculptors there might be a different set of statues'" (p. 19).

Triangulation consults different sources to determine the validity of data using purposive sampling. The concept of triangulation is borrowed from surveying. A property boundary can be established by simply measuring in the right direction from an established point, but it is more accurately found by using two established points as the baseline of a triangle to establish a third. The term has come to apply to any means that provides additional data to reinforce a finding where the new data are independent of the original set. Further, since data are subject to various errors, we can build on the strengths of one while minimizing the weaknesses of another. Guba and Lincoln (1986) compare it to a fisherman who uses multiple nets each with some rips and tears. When used together, the holes of one net are covered by intact sections of others. Denzin (1978) outlined three useful types of triangulation: (1) data triangulation, using multiple sources of data across time, space, and persons; (2) investigator triangulation, using multiple investigators; and (3) method triangulation, using multiple methods.

Data triangulation, the most common of the three, involves the use of two or more sources to establish factual accuracy. Thus, we confirm an informant's recall of a meeting by checking the secretary's minutes. Denzin (1978) argues for triangulating data across all three source types—time, space, and persons. His point is well taken. For example, a finding that a schoolboard's meeting procedures appear to discourage minority parents from presenting their concerns should be checked not only at more than one meeting but also with more than one set of parents and perhaps with regard to more than one issue. This is similar to sampling to establish the borderline of generality of a finding—external validity (GP).

Data triangulation can involve many different sources. For example, it may involve observing your informants in various situations that are relevant to your study. Answers to differently phrased questions involving the same concept should be consistent. Similarly, you can compare present observations with past records for invariability. You can check verbal responses against actual behavior, solitary behavior against that constrained by the presence of others. Nonverbal behavior is often a giveaway that contradicts verbal behavior—a teacher says she is concerned about the welfare of lower-class students but doesn't look at them while answering their questions or gives them less time to respond. You can compare volunteered responses with called-upon answers on the assumption that the latter may have an element of "polite agreement." Triangulation may be particularly important where you seek the covert meaning of a situation that differs from the expressed meaning.

Investigator triangulation refers to obtaining similar perceptions from different investigators of the same phenomenon. Thus, we might compare the reports of two observers of a teacher's lesson for similarities.

Method triangulation uses different methods to assess the same aspect of a phenomenon. The possibilities are legion and depend on the problem: minutes of meetings, interoffice memos, letters, excerpts from student records or portfolios, personnel records, test scores, performance appraisals, psychologist and teacher reports. Leinhardt (1989) used a variety of methods to compare novice and expert teachers: She observed, videotaped, transcribed the videotapes, interviewed each teacher before and after each lesson, and did stimulated recall interviews in which she asked teachers to comment on videotapes of their lessons.

Although triangulation is intended to provide support for a finding, as Mathison (1988) suggests, the result is often inconsistency or contradiction. As in the discussion of outliers above, the search for an explanation of the inconsistency frequently leads to new insights. In tracking teachers' activities with a new curriculum, Mathison noted that teachers reported including mathematical activities in unplanned times of the day, but a triangulation corroboration found only 14 instances in 200 classroom observations. The discrepancy turned up the fact that there was almost no unplanned time.

Taylor and Bogdan (1984) suggest that we discount the value of the information in terms not only of consistency over sources but also of such questions as these: Was it volunteered or solicited? Just asking a question may make salient a point usually ignored. Who was present? People often reveal things when authority figures are not present. Was it established through direct observation or hearsay? Finally, in regard to others' research, who paid for it?

Perhaps the best advice is this:

> Triangulation is not so much a tactic as a way of life. If you *self-consciously* set out to collect and double-check findings, using multiple sources and modes of evidence, the verification process will largely be built into the data-collection as you go. (Miles and Huberman, 1994, p. 267)

✦ *Triangulation is the process of using more than one source to confirm information: confirming data from different sources, confirming observations from different observers, and confirming information with different data collection methods.*

✦ *With the discovery of disconfirming information, seeking reasons for the contradiction frequently points to directions for extending or modifying explanations instead of discarding them.*

Integrating Multiple Perspectives

Triangulation uses multiple data sources to confirm a finding. Such sources, however, are equally critical to obtaining a complete picture. If we concentrate on confirmation to the exclusion of pursuing the meaning of data that are either inconsistent or contradictory, we may miss leads to new and important information. Each data source provides information from one perspective. By combining them we may complete a picture that would be incomplete without any one of them. The information from one source helps us to interpret the meaning in another. Patton (1980) provides an example from a wilderness education program. He had observed problems in communication between the technical staff who did the wilderness training and the program staff who conceptualized and had responsibility for the overall program. Through individual interviews he found that the program staff had all been university faculty, and the technical staff had been their students; the latter had taught the former wilderness skills, although the former had conceptualized the program. From correspondence prior to actual field activity, he learned the assumptions each had brought to the program. Documents often provide a behind-the-scenes view that would not be directly observable. "But," Patton notes, *"the documentation would not have made sense without the interviews, and the focus of the interviews came from the field observations. Taken together, these diverse sources . . . gave me a complete picture of staff relationships"* (p. 139, emphasis in original).

Leaving the Field

When do you have enough data to leave the field? That decision causes concern for beginners and sometimes experienced researchers as well. The usual advice is that you will intuitively know since you will find that the information is repeating itself—you are learning nothing new. True, you will find such a point. However, the anxious researcher, wanting not to miss anything, sometimes feels a compulsion to continue anyway. Ely (1991) tells of leaving for a tropical island on a sabbatical to analyze her data, spending several months doing so, but having a nagging feeling that she might not have done all she should. So she packed up, returned to the field, and gathered more interviews—only to find out that the new data confirmed her earlier work. Whether we are doing quantitative or qualitative work, research is the search for the unknown so the "real paydirt" may be just around the corner. Nobody can be assured this will not be the case, but we can allow ourselves to put more trust in our initial instinct.

Ethics

Because the observer faces more problems in the field with less support than most other researchers, it is important to discuss the issue of ethics here in addition to the previous discussion in Chapter 10. Observers must make on-the-spot decisions about ethical questions without the help of human subject protection committees or advisors. In some instances, they may witness illegal acts that should be reported. The problem is whether a researcher's own sense of justice should be substituted for whatever is the norm in the situation being observed. Bosk (1979), for instance, confronted the question of his responsibility to the patient and her relatives when he had witnessed a nursing or medical error. He decided that he would let the system handle these cases and that his disclosure of that system would be more effective than "tilting at windmills in one or two select cases" (p. 200). Unless lives are in danger, this is a fairly common ethical choice: to ignore the transgressions of individuals we are personally involved with in favor of making public those of the institution and its administration. The latter are perceived as the real culprit in need of reform. This is not to imply that this is an improper decision, but if made, the socially easier choice coincides with achieving the desired effect.

Maintaining confidences is especially difficult for the researcher who reveals witnessing illegal acts, since immunity from subpoena is not extended to scientists. Humphreys (1975), for instance, caused quite a stir when he reported that in order to study homosexual activity in public places, he had acted as lookout in public toilets and had learned the names of participating individuals by tracing their license plate numbers. When Humphreys learned that these data could be subpoenaed, he destroyed them. This problem is further discussed on page 375.

All observers encounter the problem of ambiguity in interpersonal relationships.

> Once the field researcher becomes involved in the daily life of the community . . . he develops personal friendships. . . . These friendships are usually quite important to everyone concerned, but they are tinged with doubt over authenticity. On both sides there is often doubt as to motives, and the limitations of the study versus the intimacy of friendship. At times this ambiguity can become quite disturbing. . . . There are no easy solutions . . . and this ambiguity . . . must be dealt with on a day to day basis as friendships develop. If the field worker is careful to keep confidences, . . . attempts to be as dependable as humanly possible, and eventually discusses this problem with people for whom it is a matter of concern, the ambiguity of personal and professional roles will be eased. . . . Field researchers often get so involved in observing and recording . . . that they forget to be human themselves. They forget to share their own feelings and personal histories. . . . On the other hand, this sharing makes it difficult to maintain objectivity and should for that reason be continually written about in field notes. (Fitzsimmons et al., 1973, p. A–15)

Along these same lines, P. Cusick (personal communication, July 28, 1980) writes:

> In every study I've done, I've . . . found people . . . with whom I could relate on a personal level . . . and [used them] to help with understanding how people really behave in the organization. All that is fine and according to the book. . . . The problem is that when one joins a small, normative unit he agrees to abide by an ethical agreement . . . and he has to internalize those ethical constraints. [The result is] when writing the study I was constrained by all the . . . internalized constraints that I took from those small affective groups. . . . I never felt it quite so strongly before, but prior studies had been of adolescents, not adults like myself. One doesn't tell tales on or even take a dispassionate view of his friends. . . . The argot of "informants" . . . etc. is one that denies affective relation. . . . All that research talk is just a little too glib and quick. It's a paradox of course; affective involvement is essential to the study's success, but involvement places a whole set of (from a researcher's perspective) irrational constraints on the process.

◆ *Ethical problems are inevitable in qualitative research, and many ethical decisions must be made on the spot without the support of committee discussion or ethicists.*

◆ *The betrayal of the bond of intimate friendship with informants, which occurs when the report is made public, is always a problem.*

◆ *Serious ethical problems arise when observations include acts that are either legally or morally reportable to authorities. To report them at the least interrupts, and more probably terminates, the study. The serious consequences of not doing so must also be faced but sometimes seem justified by the study's outcomes.*

◆ *Researchers and their data are not immune from subpoena. Therefore, data that might harmfully identify individuals should probably either not be collected or be quickly destroyed.*

Tips on Observation

1. Write up the notes as soon as possible. You will remember more than expected. Writing notes may require triple or quadruple the time spent observing; allow for it. Dictation is faster than writing but requires a certain amount of skill. Dictated notes will likely be more copious and more organized.
2. Talking about your observation before you record it may change the importance you attach to certain events. Indeed, it may change the way you remember them. Record, then discuss, then add separate notes regarding any changed impressions or new recollections (Bogdan and Biklen, 1992).
3. When something significant happens that you can't immediately record, change something inconspicuous until you have recorded it. Sari Biklen suggests moving a ring to the other hand or turning your wristwatch around to help you remember to record it.
4. Focus on the opening and closing of conversation; you can fill in the rest later. Include contextual factors.
5. Get down key words and phrases, outline what went on, and then go back and fill in. Develop a set of abbreviations appropriate to the study.
6. Draw a diagram not only to give the picture but also to trace your own movements.
7. Rehearse every 10–15 minutes what you have seen; this refreshes your memory. Play back scenes in your mind; try to visualize what your write-up of the scene will look like.
8. Keep track of your hunches; write them in the notes with *O.C.* before them to designate them as observer comments. Enclose them in parentheses to set them off from the narrative flow.
9. Separate inferences and interpretation from observations with observer comments and memos.
10. Ask, "Why is this person telling me this?" Be sensitive to others' and your own effect on the situation.
11. Ask not only why someone is doing something but also why the person is not doing something else!
12. Remember that actions and expressed attitudes may differ, as may verbal and nonverbal reactions. What someone does not say may be significant, too.
13. Don't be so intent on recording data that you forget to be human; share feelings and personal experiences. But also try to keep track of the effect of that sharing on the behavior being observed and your own feelings toward the situation.

14. Memoing is one of your most important field activities. Don't slight it—it is the beginning of analysis.
15. Zoom out occasionally to make sure you haven't lost sight of the larger picture (Lancy, 1993).

SUMMARY

The preceding tips on observation already summarize many points in the chapter. In addition, however, we discussed the problem of gaining entry, the initiation of the analysis process, the interaction with informants and covert processes, data validity concerns, and ethics.

Gaining entry for observation and acceptance by the observees are not one-time efforts but continual processes activated with each new situation and change of personnel. Furthermore, gaining entry is not the same as acceptance, which must be won from each group regardless of strong administrative approval and support of the research. Starting at the top of the administrative ladder is a convenient way to approach this task, but this may actually make entrance and acceptance more difficult at lower levels in the hierarchy.

Although data analysis is discussed in detail in Chapter 14, analysis and data gathering are intertwined, particularly when the constant comparison process is used. Coding data as it is gathered shows where concepts and constructs that inform explanation are developing and therefore suggest the nature of purposive sampling to flesh them out. Additional examples are sought until no more can be learned from them; negative and borderline examples then serve to delineate the boundaries and generality of the constructs.

Informants can help you view the situation from the inside, but you must always ask yourself, "Why is this person telling me this?" and appropriately discount it. Often you are interested in what persons are thinking as well as what actions they are taking. Therefore, thinking aloud and stimulated recall may be useful in probing the inaccessible.

Maintaining data validity is a state of mind for the appropriately cautious worker, who then uses triangulation for quality assurance. Triangulation judges the comparability of different sources of data, different observers, or different methods of data collection of the same events. Such multiple perspectives also may lead to new insights.

Field-workers must often make off-the-cuff ethical decisions in interaction with those observed. This is particularly true when they encounter professional errors, illegal acts, or improper decisions. In some instances, not reporting is itself an illegal act, but reporting may well end the study and require observers to accuse persons who placed their trust in them. Field-workers must decide whether to let the system take its normal corrective course or to "blow the whistle." Neither alternative is without problems.

A Look Ahead

The skills of interviewing, often called upon in observing, sometimes become the main data source for a study. Interviewing, therefore, is explored in the next chapter. Questionnaires, often employed in interviews, are discussed in Chapter 16, Sample Surveys.

ADDITIONAL READING

For useful general references see: Ely (1991); Miles and Huberman (1994); Hammersley and Atkinson (1995). Strauss (1987) illustrates different types of memos with 16 pages of memos from a project on the impact of medical technology on hospitals. He usefully comments on their intent and actual effect (pp. 111–127). Persons planning on doing participatory observation in a covert role may find Mitchell's (1994) exploration of the topic of interest. Those interested in life-histories, ethno- and autobiographies may find Casey (1995) of interest. See Edwards and Lampert (1993) about making a written record of a conversation or videotape which includes references to a variety of speakers, their intonation, loudness variations, nonverbal behavior, pauses, and other accompaniments to speech (and lack of it). Kidder (1981) has a useful discussion of negative case analysis. Wolcott (1995) is a chatty discussion of field work and reporting as an art.

IMPORTANT TERMS

Acceptance
Analytic induction
Concealed observation
Conceptual analysis
Constant comparison method
Covert participant observation
Elite Bias
Fieldnotes
Gaining entry

Gatekeeper
Grounded theory
Informants
Memos
Nonparticipant observation
Participant observation
Saturation
Stimulated recall
Triangulation

APPLICATION PROBLEMS

1. You wish to conduct a study at an inner-city high school located in a low socioeconomic district. You are aware that the community and the school have well-documented problems with juvenile crime and truancy. You want to engage in participant observation at the school in order to investigate how the youths who attend it view their schooling experience. How will you go about establishing your study? What problems might you encounter, and how will you overcome them?

2. Assume that you have gained entry to the school in problem 2 and have succeeded in conducting observations for several months. Many students have taken you into their confidence and have begun to accept you as one of them. You then observe that one of these students is selling cocaine to other students. What do you do?

3. You wish to study preschool children (aged 3 to 4 years) at a local nursery school. To understand how they interpret their experience, you decide to observe them over the period of the school year. On the continuum of obtrusiveness, which method would provide you with the most informative data?

4. Your study of children's use of computers has led you to some interesting conclusions. From your ob-

servations in two classes—one of third graders and one of sixth graders—it appears that elementary-aged children view computers as something alive or, at least, as an entity with psychological characteristics. This has caused you to reflect upon the question of animism. You wonder whether their apparent attitude is peculiar to these classes or this school or whether these conclusions are generalizable to other children of this age group. How will you go about extending the study using qualitative methods?

5. You live in Columbus, Ohio, a city with a large Greek immigrant population. As a researcher in the field of nursing, you are interested in the topic of folk health in immigrant populations. In particular, you wish to study the Greek folk-healing tradition, which practices *matiasma*, the beliefs surrounding the prevention, diagnosis, and treatment of the "evil eye." You wonder about the extent of this practice and how to take it into account as a nurse working with these people. Why might you incorporate both quantitative and qualitative research methodology into such a study?

Compare your answers with those following the Application Exercise.

APPLICATION EXERCISE

If you pursue your research project with qualitative methods, what problems of access do you expect, if any? How will you record what occurred? Are there persons who you think might serve as particularly useful informants? Where will you look for them? What memos will you write to yourself regarding your feelings about the project and your entry into

it? What problems do you anticipate in writing up your fieldnotes? Will you be able to do so right away? If not, how will you manage? What other sources of data might be available to provide triangulation of some of your findings? What ethical problems, if any, do you anticipate?

ANSWERS TO THE APPLICATION PROBLEMS

1. Your problem is the one faced by all investigators who wish to engage in participant observation. You have the dual task of gaining entry and securing acceptance.

Gaining Entry: You need to find a way to enter that conveys the message "I am to be trusted." Your first step will probably be to secure the approval of the school administration—possibly the superintendent—or begin the process of approval with a member of the school board. In one such study of students at a junior high school, the researcher, Everhart (1977), was able to legitimize his presence at the school through his role as evaluator for a government agency. Even so, the school administration resisted his entry for several weeks. The administrator with whom you are dealing may also impose conditions on your study or demand some sort of favor in return for the privilege. You must be careful that such conditions neither violate academic freedom nor abrogate the confidentiality of your informants. In Everhart's case, the school principal set the parameters for the study by limiting it to students (that is, excluding teachers) and by insisting that the researcher's role be one of observer and not "confidant." Everhart was restricted to specific classes and limited interviewing. Fortunately, he was able to renegotiate these conditions once on site for a couple of months.

Securing Acceptance: Once you are on site, you will have to gain the approval and trust of your field subjects—in this case, the students. Simultaneously, you must remain enough of an outsider to avoid the constraints of the behaviors the group expects of its members. Everhart slowly developed the role of friend to his respondents. He did so first, by developing an explanation of his presence (he was a writer there to do a story about what students did in junior high) that made sense to them and indicated that his presence was legitimate. He was then able to present himself as a friend both by spending a considerable amount of time with the students and by reducing his contact with the adults. In time, he became so well accepted by the students that he was able to become an ex officio member of certain groups in the school.

2. This is an example of an ethical dilemma to which the answer may not be as clear-cut as it first appears. It is a no-win situation that is frequently encountered in this kind of research. Reporting the people involved to the authorities may well identify you as a part of the authority structure and disrupt any special relationships that you have developed, thus terminating your study. Conversely, you may endanger yourself and your study by becoming party to a criminal act. A fairly common choice is to ignore such transgressions in favor of completing the study and letting the natural corrective forces of society come into play. You should understand, however, that unlike an attorney, you are not in a privileged position. You cannot protect the anonymity of your informants or subjects. Furthermore, once published, your information is public knowledge. Your notes can be subpoenaed by a court of law.

3. Depending on the equipment avaliable, you might consider two possibilities:

    a) *Covert Nonparticipant Observation*: If done from behind two-way mirrors it allows observation of "natural" actions. However, it limits action to special rooms and/or the range of equipment. It will provide behavioral and descriptive data but will not afford you the opportunity to gather explanations from the children's point of view.

    b) *Participant Observation*: Within this category is a continuum of possible researcher behaviors. At one end, you may make it clear that you are conducting research and make it obvious by means of low interaction with your subjects. At the other extreme, you may observe covertly. You could adopt an authority role within the situation, such as being a teacher (covert observation), or try to become a part of the situation (with minimal explanation—at least to the children). Some researchers conducting such studies have gone so far as pretending to be one of the children, playing with them as if they were a child. Perhaps the most common approach within this tradition, however, is to adopt the friendship role, maintaining your status as an adult but eschewing a position of authority. By adopting this role, you would be able to minimize your influence on the situation and to develop trusting relationships in which you are able to ask the children for their own explanations.

4. Your first step would be to conduct further observations in other classes in the same school and, if possible, at the same grade levels as those you have already studied. Develop your understanding and densify it with detail and example. Test your understanding with negative instances, borderline cases, and key examples. Extend your observations to other grade levels within the school. Once the concept becomes saturated (the same kinds of instances are being found repeatedly) within the school, reverse the funnel and broaden your sample choice to gather new data. First, include other similar schools (in terms of age level, socioeconomic status, exposure to computers, etc.). Then move to less similar schools until you are no longer able to discover new instances of your theory. Continue this process until you develop a solid understanding of the phenomenon—in this example, how children interpret their interactions with computers.

5. Such a study was carried out by Tripp-Reimer (1983) in Columbus with the intent of identifying the extent of such beliefs across the generations in order to help plan health care. She used the qualitative methods of semistructured interviews and participant observation in the Greek community in order to establish baseline data concerning the description of *matiasma* The descriptions she obtained allowed her to develop categories indicating levels of belief in *matiasma* and levels of knowledge of the practice.

Tripp-Reimer also used a questionnaire to quantify the distribution of these beliefs and practices within the population. It was devised to elicit demographic and social characteristics of the population, including sex, age, and generation.

CHAPTER 13

Interviewing

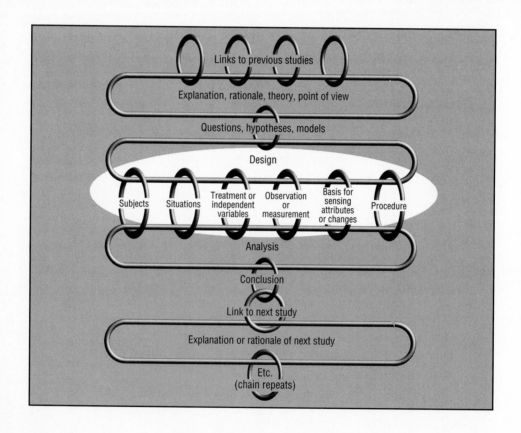

[Any response] is only in part a function of . . . the questions. It is also a function of the social interaction of the interview, of the interviewer's appearance, of the respondent's fear of similar strangers, such as bill collectors.

Donald T. Campbell, *Definitional versus Multiple Operationism*

OVERVIEW

Interviews are a prime qualitative data collecting tool and serve many useful purposes, including those of sample surveys. Although interviews may be spontaneous events, particularly during participant observation, once certain needed information is targeted, interviews typically become planned events, sometimes with structured questions to assure obtaining the desired information. But whether structured or not, spontaneous or planned, getting a response as close to natural conversation, unbiased by the fact that it is an interview, is critical. Rapport builders and the nondirective approach facilitate this. Equally critical is who to interview, a question usually answered by purposive sampling when using qualitative method (but more often probability sampling methods with sample surveys). Thought also needs to be given to the format of the interview—a number are available depending on one's purposes, and to the choice of interviewers—interviewer characteristics can affect the nature of responses.

Where responses are gathered as qualitative data, much of what is in this chapter applies equally well to sample survey method, the topic of Chapter 16. Similarly some of what is covered there, such as the formulation of questions, is usefully considered here. Were these chapters on a Web site, they would be full of hypertext links to tie them together.

CHAPTER CONTENTS

Introduction

Qualitative researchers often gather data by interview, some of which are spur-of-the-moment interchanges, whereas others are carefully planned and sometimes highly structured. Interviews and observations interact—observations provide new meanings to the interviews, and interviews suggest new things to look at or attach new meanings to the observations. Interviews are particularly useful in the following pursuits:

- Exploring, probing, and searching to determine what is especially significant about a person or situation. (For example: How would you describe your advisor-advisee situation?)
- Determining how individuals perceive their situation: its meaning to them, what is especially significant about it to them, what might be significant to others but is less so or unimportant to them, how it came to be what it is, how they think it will be changed in the future. (Tell me about your advisor, and how you came to choose her. How did your adversarial situation arise? How do you now perceive her? How do others perceive her? How do those perceptions affect your relationship to her?)
- Identifying the cause in cause and effect relationships. (What do you believe really lies behind this adversarial relation?)
- Finding explanations for discrepancies between observed and expected effects. (I'd expect you to be very disturbed about this situation but you don't seem to be. Why?)
- Finding explanations for deviations from common behaviors by individuals or subgroups. (Many students would be seeking another advisor. Tell me your thoughts about that possibility.)
- Providing clues to the processes and mechanisms called into play by the situation. (What factors do you think contributed to your situation? Milieu, background characteristics? What?)
- Making sure the respondent correctly understands what was asked. (I've described this situation as adversarial, how else might you describe it?)
- Following up incomplete or nonresponsive answers. (Tell me more about the latter. I'm not sure I understand you correctly. Are you saying that . . .?)
- Getting responses from individuals who might not respond to or might not understand a questionnaire.

These are some of the obvious reasons to interview; you'll undoubtedly think of others. Certainly, wherever there is a desire to tap an internal process, to gain knowledge of a person's perceptions, feelings, or emotions, or to study a complex individual or social behavior, some form of interviewing is most helpful. It is the major means of tapping thought processes.

We tend to think of interviewing as straightforward question-and-answer conversation between two individuals directed by the interviewer. But, interviews vary depending on whether the researcher is simply exploring, verifying a hypothesis, or determining the limits of its generality. However, there are a number of things to consider, of which the following are particularly important:

- Structuring the interviewer role: on-the-spot as opposed to predetermined questioning by the interviewer
- Structuring the respondent role: recording response verbatim in contrast to categorizing in predetermined response codes
- Focusing the interview: narrow and deep versus broad perspective; go-with-the-flow versus focused versus exploratory
- Sampling: nonprobability, convenience, or purposive in contrast to probability random, or stratified
- Explaining purposes: true purpose given respondent in contrast to giving a false purpose

- Using rapport builders, prompts, and nondirective responses
- Determining the number of interviewers and respondents: one on one, two on one, and so forth
- Determining the location of the interview: normal context as against special circumstances

Let us explore these in the following material.

Structuring Interviewer and Respondent Roles

One characteristic of interviews that can be varied to suit the interviewer's purposes is the extent to which the interviewer and respondent roles are structured, that is, determined beforehand. For instance, in order of increasing structure, the interviewer may be given: no structure (responsible for on-the-spot formulation of questions covering any content, in any order, and in whatever form seems appropriate), a little structure (areas to cover), more structure (specific information to obtain), or still more structure (an interview schedule to follow). Similarly, the respondent's answer may be recorded verbatim, may have his answer summarized, may have the answer coded into one of a preset number, or may be asked which of a set of responses best represents his answer to the question.

Table 13.1 combines these alternatives into a continuum ordered by the amount of structure—the predetermining of specific wording, order of presentation, and response recording process. Not all the possible combinations of these three factors appear in the table, but commonly used ones demonstrate successively increasing structure from left to right.

Strictly speaking, no interview is as unstructured as the title of the first column would imply. Even if it is simply exploratory, the researcher always enters with at least a focus of interest, sometimes a list of issues to be covered. In a free-

T A B L E 1 3 . 1 *Continuum of Interviews with Increasing Amounts of Structure*

Unstructured	Partially Structured	Semistructured	Structured	Totally Structured
Exploratory, only area of interest is chosen, interviewer "follows her nose" in formulating and ordering questions. Impromptu conversations that occur during observation are of this nature.	Area is chosen and questions are formulated but order is up to interviewer. Interviewer may add questions or modify them as deemed appropriate. Questions are open-ended, and responses are recorded nearly verbatim, possibly taped.	Questions and order of presentation are determined. Questions have open-ends; interviewer records the essence of each response.	Questions, and order are predetermined, and responses are coded by the interviewer as they are given.	Questions , order, and coding are predetermined, and the respondent is presented with alternatives for each question so that phrasing of responses is structured. Questions are self-coding in that each choice is preassigned a code.

flowing conversation, in which each rejoinder in turn follows the lead of the previous response, the interviewer gently bends the conversation so as to cover the variety of topics in which she perceives there may be paydirt.

With less structure, as shown in the first three columns of Table 13.1, interviewers can adapt the questions to the immediate situation so as to increase rapport. They can be highly responsive to individual differences and situational changes. But such interviewing is highly dependent on interviewer skills. Ely's student Ewa Iracka (1991, pp. 63, 64) says: "There were times when I used to . . . [think] Barbara Walters, the alleged interviewer of all time, . . . was overpaid. After all, she would merely sit comfortably in a lovely setting and glibly and effortlessly ask poignant questions which would elicit informative and sometimes sensational replies. Anyone can do that. After having indulged in this communication art form for the first time, [I realize] . . . perhaps I had judged Barbara Walters too harshly."[1]

Clearly, more structure is appropriate for a preplanned research problem than an emergent one—when the researcher has a hypothesis to test in contrast to probing for what is important. When the researcher has pretty well confirmed a hypothesis, and wishes to determine its generality, she seeks data from a variety of individuals and circumstances. Doing so with relatively unstructured interviewing is time-consuming, thereby reducing the number of interviews obtainable with available resources. This makes it difficult to get the same set of questions answered by a large enough group to feel confident that one can generalize across them. Further, if both questions and responses have been customized to individuals the data may take longer to analyze and the person-to-person variations make patterns harder to see. Considerable structure of both respondent and interviewer roles obviously facilitates larger-scale data gathering by reducing both interview and analysis time and is more appropriate for hypothesis validation than for exploration.

The ultimate structure is a standardized interview in which the questions are the same for all respondents, and clarifications, prompts, elaborations, and any needed additional information are built into the interview plan. In addition, interviewers are all trained to administer it the same way. Standardized interviews minimize interviewer effects and interviewee time. Also the instrument is available for those using results to judge its fairness for themselves. Of course, such structure restricts the pursuit of topics that were not anticipated, or new leads given by respondents. Because the researcher has the same data on all the persons sampled, he can confirm that patterns of responses exist, and can determine their generality and distribution in the sample. Such interviews must be tried out ahead of time to assure they obtain what is intended.

Obviously, the unstructured end of the continuum is closer to the qualitative approach tradition and the structured end to the quantitative approach. Sample surveys are between the extremes with interviews that range from open ended questions to the verbal administration of multiple-choice questions. Contrasting the extremes of the same continuum shown in Table 13.2—the relatively **unstructured interview** and the **structured interview**— highlights the differences in pur-

---

[1]Excerpts in this chapter from *Doing Qualitative Research: Circles in Circles* by Margot Ely, Copyright © 1991 by Falmer Press. Reprinted by permission.

TABLE 13.2 *Comparison of the Extremes in Interview Structure*

Relatively Unstructured Interview	Structured Interview
• Interview requires a researcher-interviewer who can direct it in directions that may be rewarding.	• Interviewer may be a clerk with good social skills who can comfortably follow a script while carefully making check-marks to record answers on well-designed forms.
• Nature of the sample may not be predetermined but may unfold as each interview suggests where leads may next appear. Unless interviewer is exploring the characteristics of some particular group, emphasis is not on generality but on covering the widest possible types of individuals that may suggest leads to better understanding.	• Nature of the sample will be carefully predetermined because the emphasis is on generality for some target population of which the sample is intended to be representative.
• Compilation of data is labor intensive and results in extensive records.	• Compilation of the data is easy and, if computer-assisted telephone interviewing (CATI) is used, results may be continuously compiled as the interview is conducted.
• Analysis of the data requires professional skill to catch "paydirt."	• With preplanning, most of the analysis can be carried out by a technician.
• Professional expertise required to catch unexpected findings. Often the most exciting part of the research, this aspect requires professional time regardless of how the data are collected.	• Same as relatively unstructured interview.
• Profitability of such interviews depends directly on the skill in interviewing, the "nose for paydirt," and the keen recognition of insights.	• Profitability of such interviews depends on skill in anticipating where "paydirt" lies during interview development and doing sufficient pretesting of interview to assure it elicits what was intended.

poses and the implications of structure. Interviews structured between the extremes typically also fall between them regarding the various characteristics listed earlier. An exception is the unstructured exploratory interview. With it, we may simply be exploring and not much interested in generality. With interviews of almost any other type, generality is important, and we are concerned with ensuring representativeness of the sample.

The contrasts make clear that the researcher must choose among many trade-offs. Among the most important trade-offs is the division of professional time: how much for gathering data in interviews, how much for the analysis of it, and what the balance between the two should be. Another is question type: whether to use open-end questions and devote professional time to compiling and analyzing the data, or to use professional time to set up closed-end questions that anticipate the meaningful responses. The latter method risks missing the unexpected, but it is much more economical with a large sample and is by far the most common practice, especially in sample surveys.

The Focused Interview

As noted in the discussion of structure, when we start an exploratory or emergent study, we search broad areas to find what is significant. As the study progresses and we form and test hypotheses, our questioning focuses on increasingly narrow areas, probing in some depth for detail. An interview format that encompasses both ends of the structure in a single interview, allowing exploration and targeted information gathering in the same sitting, is the focused interview (Merton, Fiske, and Kendall, 1956).

The **focused interview** begins with broad questions and with nondirective responses (discussed in the section after next), then moves to semistructured questions, and finally to structured ones. The last section tests the researcher's ideas about what was significant and its effects. For example, in the voting literature study the researcher might ask early in the interview: "What did you think of the cartoons?" But toward the end, the questions are quite structured: "Did the cartoon on the back page that showed neighbors poking fun at the protesting nonvoter make you want to prevent that from happening to you?" Early interview material provides focus for the structured parts so that the questions are continually evolving. Insights from early questions are validated by later ones.

Using Rapport Builders

No interview succeeds unless the interviewer builds a relationship with the respondent in which both are comfortable talking with one another. For example, Hoffman (1980, as found in Hammersley and Atkinson, 1995), seeking access to an elite group of members of boards of hospital directors, found access limited. He had difficulty getting appointments, time allotted was short, and interviews were frequently interrupted with "important" phone calls. Then he discovered he knew the family of one respondent and "the rest of the interview was dramatically different" (p. 46). He started to select interviewees on the basis of social ties and referrals. To demonstrate the "dramatic difference," he contrasts the responses to his "known" and "unknown" interviewer roles to the question: "How do you feel in general about how the board has been reorganized?"

Interviewer Unknown to Interviewee	Interviewer Known to Interviewee
"I think the basic idea of participation is good. We need better communication with the various groups. And I think they probably have a lot to offer."	"This whole business is unworkable. It's all very nice and well to have these people on the board, they might be able to tell us something here and there . . . but you're not going to run a hospital on that" (Hoffman, 1980, p. 48)

The contrast is startling. Compare the bland general comments where insufficient rapport has been established with the candid response where the interviewer is trusted. Although rapport here was enhanced by prior social contact, the ability to develop rapport at the same time one gets the information desired is one of the most important skills of an interviewer.

The initial experience of Ely's (1991) student Ewa Iracka is not uncommon: "My first interview can be compared to taking a puppy for a walk. In the attempt to make the respondent feel comfortable, I wound up being led everywhere except for where I had intended to go " (p. 64). Studying men who were primary caregivers of their children, Ely's (1991) student Steve Spitz, found it important to *adapt to the interviewee:* "During the next few interviews I was reminded of the never-ending variability among people. Not every participant was as open and articulate as Barry. Ira, for example, was much harder to get to know. . . . In the end it became a matter of . . . adapting the questions and probes to each participant's style. . . . My experience with Ira . . . heightened my sensitivity to each participant's unique style" (p. 68).

The rhythm of questioning, taking turns speaking so that the flow is natural and sustained, is important to develop. Various things can throw you off—a waiter drops a tray of dishes, or you are prepared for one person and find that another was substituted."Interviews suffered because I was busy trying to regain my equilibrium and switch gears . . . to ask appropriate questions for that [unexpected] person" (Ely's student Patricia Thornton, 1991, p. 63).

Avoid questions that can be answered with just a "yes" or "no"; they will stop the conversation—what else is there to say? To break this unproductive rhythm of interchanges, you might ask "Tell me how you felt in that situation" rather than "Were you happy in that situation?"

Some kind of rejoinder by the interviewer is important to stimulate full responses. Lansing, Withey, and Wolfe (1971) found that typically, only 28 percent of interviewers gave feedback for an adequate answer, and worse, almost as many, 24 percent, did so as well for an inadequate answer. Even more, 55 percent, did so for refusal to answer. The 55 percent may consist largely of probes, but if we consider any interviewer response as positive reinforcement, which their study shows it nearly always is, this pattern reinforces the wrong response tendencies. *Remembering to reinforce full and thorough responses is essential.*

The emphasis needs to be on the respondent. As Dick DeLuca, Ely's (1991) student, put it: "The best advice anyone can give is to LISTEN, LISTEN—AND LISTEN SOME MORE. . . . Take care to observe . . . body language—tone, gestures, posture, eye movements. For example, if a question evokes a startled look, . . . ask, 'From that look, I assume you didn't expect that question, could you tell me why?'" (pp. 66–67). Recall that Whyte (1955), when he asked an inappropriate question, was told to *be quiet and listen.* He did and found the answers to questions he didn't know enough to ask.

Particularly if you have an agenda for the interview, it is easy to slip out of the listening mode. This happened to Rosengarten (1981): "I played over the morning's tape. . . . I was astonished at how little of Ned's talk had reached my inner ear. The problem was, I had set out to question, not to listen. My mind was full of chatter and thoughts about my questions." (p. 124).

The solution reached by Rosengarten is worth noting: "Let the machine record and you listen. Afterwards, listen to the recording with an adversarial ear . . . [That is what I did.] I got into the pattern of listening deliberately to our tapes the evenings of the days we recorded. In these hours I planned questions, . . . listened for gaps in the stories, . . . for allusions to people or incidents I wanted to hear more about, . . . for extraordinary events . . . [to follow up], and for inconsistencies" (p. 124). *Using the time out of the interview situation to analyze and plan allowed him the best of both worlds, what he called "pure listening" and "deliberate listening."* He found that "You need to listen both ways. . . . Whenever I was stymied, I found . . . going back to pure listening had the effect of sharpening my sense of Ned." Thus he managed to put together Ned's autobiography "in a way that conformed to this sense—or essence—of him" (p. 124).

The interviewer telegraphs messages by body language, voice intonation, and other subtle clues. *If the interviewer signals discomfort, the tension often spreads to the respondent.* In a nonthreatening situation, the reverse may occur, secure respondent may put the interviewer at ease. But because setting the mood mostly depends on the interviewer, it is very important to learn the art of building rapport.

Respondents realize they are being interviewed when an interview is requested and its purpose given (Patton 1980). However, in the unstructured interview the respondent may not even realize he is being interviewed. Indeed, if questioned, the interviewer may give a false reason. This method is similar to covert participant observation and is subject to the same ethical and practical problems, especially that of misleading the interviewee.

The location of the interview can be important. *Often it is useful to interview in the respondents' home or office* since this allows them to relax in their own territory. But phone calls and other business may create complications. There also may be other distractions: for example, Skipper and McCaghy 1972 (from Hammersley and Atkinson, 1995) who interviewed a stripper in her dressing room: "It was clear to us that the nudity and perceived seductiveness of the stripper, and the general permissiveness of the setting had interfered with our role as researchers" (pp. 239–240). Thereafter, they conducted their interviews in a restaurant.

The Nondirective Approach

One technique that every interviewer should master is the **nondirective approach.** It requires the interviewer to rephrase and reflect to the respondent the central significance and *especially the underlying feelings* of what the respondent seems to be saying. For instance, in a study of voting literature, the initial question might be, "What do you think of the literature you received on voting?" Respondent: "I don't like people bringing literature to my home that implies I am not a good citizen if I didn't vote; I pay my taxes like anyone else." Interviewer: "I just want to be sure I'm getting this right; you were unhappy with the literature you received? It seemed too preachy?" When followed by the interviewer's look of anticipation, the respondent is encouraged to elaborate on the answer and, if necessary, correct the rephrasing. Note also, that the interviewer found the underlying feeling of unhappiness the significant emotion to reflect. In this style, the interviewer is attentive, and the restatement implicitly conveys the personal worth of the respondent. The restatement suggests acceptance of the respondent, whose answer was important enough to rephrase.

Nondirective interviewing doesn't mean that the interviewer cedes all direction of the conversation to the respondent. Whyte (1953, as found in Hammersley and Atkinson, 1995) gives an example of "steering" in the responses given to a union official handling grievances in a steel plant:

> Whyte: I'm trying to catch up on things that have happened since I was last here to study this case. . . . I think probably the best thing to start [with] would be if you could give your own impressions. . . . Do you think things are getting better or worse, or staying about the same?
>
> . . .
>
> Whyte: That's interesting. You mean that it isn't that you don't have problems, but you take them up and talk them over before you write them up, is that it?
>
> . . .
>
> Whyte: That's very interesting. I wonder if you could give me an example of a problem that came up recently, or not so recently, that would illustrate how you handled it sort of informally without writing it down.
>
> . . .
>
> Whyte: That's a good example. I wonder if you could give me a little more detail about the beginning of it. Did Mr. Grosscup first tell you about it? How did you first find out?
>
> . . .
>
> Whyte: I see. He first explained it to you and you went to the people on the job to tell them about it, but then you saw that they didn't understand it?

Notice, that, in contrast to reflecting the underlying feelings, which is what is normally practiced in the nondirective approach, the interviewer is responding to the overt content in the responses. He then questions to get more depth and detail. He uses the restating and reflecting of the nondirective approach, which maintains rapport. He keeps control of the direction of the discussion in the choice of what is restated until the last response—a method that, in restating the response, assures it was correctly understood.

Nondirective responses build rapport and are particularly valuable in getting respondents to talk about and elaborate on their answers. The response has an unfinished quality that calls for further elaboration, but it does convey the direction of what is significant to the respondent. If the restatement is incorrect or inadequate, the respondent can correct it: "I felt really mad!" An important effect of nondirective responses is that whereas, on average, structured questions result in more talk by the interviewer than the respondent, the nondirective approach reverses this ratio. Although the interviewer sets the stage for responses, the interviewee is the focus of attention.

In many instances the best response is minimal—a simple "Uh huh" or "Yes" said with a rising inflection that signifies "tell me more." "Yes, I see, I never thought of that, but . . ." Sometimes a wave of the hand, a questioning eyebrow, or a similar natural gesture implicitly says "and . . ." At other times more direct probes are needed: "Tell me about . . ." "Could you tell me more about that." "If I understand you correctly, . . ." Note how Whyte's responses start with approving comments: "That's interesting . . . ," "That's a good example . . . ," "I see." Sometimes materials are used for prompts. For example, Lancy and Zupsic (1991), studying parent-child interaction in learning to read, used a list of activities with which the parent was familiar as a basis for the interview, asking questions like "What do you think about item #8, 'Share family stories with your children'?" (p. 16).

Choosing Interviewees: Sampling Patterns

Selecting interviewees is, of course, determined by what information is sought. Purposive interviewing or theoretical sampling (Glaser and Strauss, 1967) is the most common pattern— that of selecting individuals who meet some information need or provide special access. The reprinted article in Chapter 1 by Hoffman-Riem provides an excellent example of the decisions involved in sampling. She wants a representative sample, and considers using the records of the adoption agency for perhaps a random or stratified sample. But note that under "sampling," (see p. 13) she rejects the idea because to do so would have connected her with the adoption agency and whatever experiences the parents might have had with its administration. Instead, she chooses a discussion group and compares its characteristics with those of a year's applicants to show typicality.

Access and openness in supplying the information may be important reasons for choosing interviewees. However, purposive sampling in which you choose individuals for certain purposes is a common and important tool. You choose individuals to fill in a missing piece of information, to check another person's statement, to validate a hypothesis or theory by including new cases to whom it ought also to apply, to find a theory's limits of generality by determining which cases are borderline and which are inapplicable,[2] to cover a kind or type of person not yet interviewed, and to find those who can extend in depth what is already known or take it into new areas.

There may be times, however, when you are simply trying to get a fix on the characteristics of a group as a whole. Then, either stratified sampling if you know certain characteristics that should be properly represented, or random selection may be best. In an observation situation, constructing a sampling plan ahead of time using a random number table avoids unconsciously being drawn toward better dressed or otherwise attractive individuals (for example, plan to interview the fifth person you meet, then the third, and so forth).

Multiple Interviewers and Respondents

Anyone who has done interviewing knows there are times when help would have been extremely welcome. For example, an interviewer who becomes exasperated may need to repair rapport and regain composure. It also helps an interviewer to have someone record responses while she concentrates on the interaction. **Tandem interviewing** is one answer. Kincaid and Bright (1957) used a male-female

---

[2]Conceptual analysis procedure again, see p. 263.

team to interview business elite. The team approach increased accuracy of questioning because help was available for rephrasing. Leading questions, which suggested the answer, were caught and ambiguous replies were identified and pressed to resolution. It is more difficult to "pull the wool over the eyes" of two people. Rapport was greater because the respondents had at least one interviewer's full attention at all times and one of the same gender to relate to. It also simplified recording and coding.

There can be multiple respondents as well as interviewers. Multiple respondents permit discrimination of unique responses from those that are mainstream by merely asking for agreement by a show of hands. Such groups determine meanings of a situation to various individuals, find the needed range of alternatives for closed-end questions, find what is significant about an issue or a political stand, determine how people feel about an issue or a product, or help get ideas for a questionnaire. They are used commercially to gauge the effect of television commercials, to find the desired characteristics of a projected product, to get reactions to new products, and so on.

The **focus group** is a specialized group interview that is usually used to learn how a group intended to be representative of a target population reacts to something presented to them—an idea, a product, a speech, an advertisement. It has become widely used in product development and advertising. It is also often used as an initial exploratory step in questionnaire development to learn what to ask and how best to ask it.

Such groups are typically small (7-10 persons) and relatively homogeneous in composition. Too much diversity causes some persons to withdraw. Circular seating facilitates spontaneous responses and interchange. Unless they are intended to obtain reactions to a specific item (for example a television commercial), focus interviews frequently start broadly and then target the questions to the area of interest. The broad inquiry provides the context in which to understand responses to more specific questions. Details and experiences of one individual may stimulate others. People have time to collect their thoughts before speaking, so the responses are often more considered than in an individual interview but may also be more carefully censored. At the same time, when one person speaks out on a sensitive issue, it releases the inhibitions of others who might not do so in a one-to-one situation. But, individuals with views contrary to those of the group may be less likely to share them than in individual interviews. Focus groups have been increasing in use because, for some problems, they can yield almost the same information as individual interviews, are less expensive, and more quickly gather information from a sample of people. The latest wrinkle is to assemble a focus group on-line and hold the discussion in a chat room on the Internet. Email directly to the moderator allows guidance of the discussion if the researcher does not fill that role. It appears that people's reactions may be more honest on-line than face-to-face.

Disadvantages include the difficulty of scheduling such a group and getting the right mix of people. Educational homogeneity seems to be an important feature. The moderator doesn't have the same control over the direction of the discussion the individual interviewer has. Remarks said in group context may have insider meanings difficult for an outsider to interpret (Krueger, 1994). There may be a selection effect as to who can or is willing to attend and to speak. Strong chairing may be required to prevent certain individuals from monopolizing the discussion or restructuring its focus on interesting but largely irrelevant material. (See Krueger, 1994, for more on focus groups.)

✦ *Unstructured interviews are useful for exploring issues. They must be conducted by skilled personnel and analyzed by professionals. The nature of the sample may be progressively determined as responses suggest new leads.*

✦ *Interviews can range from being highly structured to relatively unstructured.*

✦ *Highly structured interviews can be used with less skilled personnel, and are easier to analyze than less structured interviews. When they are used for measuring the responses of a population, the nature of the sample is generally carefully specified.*

✦ *Multiple interviewers may facilitate both the conducting of the interview and the recording of the responses.*

✦ *Focus interviews can combine exploration and structure, starting broadly and then narrowing.*

✦ *Focus groups, well suited to certain problems, gather data economically.*

Interviewer Characteristics Affecting Responses

The aim of the interview, like observation, where the invisible observer is the ideal, is to minimize the impact of the interviewer on what the respondent says. This may be difficult, especially when the interviewer is touched emotionally. For example, Ely's (1991) student Flora Keshishian, "found that I was too busy trying to imagine how he felt when called 'fat' to follow him, let alone tease a question out of that conversation. . . . In fact it was Sam who reminded me to take notes" (p. 60).

In an effort to build rapport, when the respondent describes an emotion-laden experience, interviewers are often moved to share their own similar past. While this does build rapport, care must be taken. Ewa Iracka, Ely's (1991) student who interviewed immigrants, had learned this: "Being a foreign born person myself, I wanted to tell them that I understood what they were feeling . . . . [But] expressing these thoughts . . . would have slanted the interview. . . . Detachment was and is a difficult state for me to maintain"(p. 60).

Numerous studies have investigated how interviewer characteristics such as race, status, sex, and religion affect the interview. It was originally thought that it was best to match the race of the interviewer to the respondent. However, a number of studies have shown significantly different responses under matching and mismatching conditions. For unknown reasons, as Ornstein and Phillips (1978) point out, some questions produce different results from white and African

American interviewers but others do not (p. 233). They note, for example, that Schuman and Converse (1971) used both African American and white interviewers to question African Americans two weeks after the assassination of Martin Luther King, Jr. Although they discovered differences, they also found no differences where some might be expected. For example, the race of the interviewer made no difference on questions such as whether the assassination would likely drive African Americans and whites further apart or whether interviewees had ever taken part in nonviolent civil rights protests.

Status and race are often confounded because whites are often perceived as high in status when interviewing low–socioeconomic status African Americans. Considering status alone, however, the results are still mixed. Some investigators have concluded that biasing effects are greatest both when the status of the interviewer and the respondent greatly diverge on one extreme or almost match on the other. Lack of rapport is a problem when levels of status are different, but when they are alike and rapport is high, it is possible that the interview "takes on the quality of a social visit . . . as both of the participants become overly concerned about maintaining the pleasant atmosphere." Good reporting suffers (Ornstein and Phillips, 1978, p. 234).

Religion may seem to be an invisible interviewer characteristic, but it has also been found to bias responses even when no apparent identification of the religion of the interviewer is given. Cosper (1972), for example, found that the consumption of alcoholic beverages related to the stereotype of drinking in the interviewer's religion. Protestant fundamentalists found few reports of heavy drinking, Catholics and liberal Protestants more. Hyman (1954), querying about Jewish influence in the business world, found more negative responses addressed to non-Jewish interviewers. These results seem to follow expectations with regard to the values espoused by the interviewer's religion. Perhaps an interviewer's values are conveyed more consistently than are differences in race or status, or more subtly so that they work subliminally and thus are harder for the interviewer to control.

Studies also show response differences with respect to same-sex and different-sex interviewers, but with the changes in attitudes toward women that have taken place, past data may not be a good guide to present research.

Most of these data on interviewer-respondent interactions come from survey research with hired interviewers. These findings are signals to the qualitative researcher doing his own interviewing, however, to be cognizant of the potential influence of sex, race, religion and other sources of bias in their work. They should be written about in memos, considered in interpreting the data, and conveyed to the audience so they may be taken into account in considering the findings.

All of these findings suggest that if we suspect there might be differences due to the match between interviewer and respondent characteristics, a pilot study of different matches and mismatches with the particular instrument and population in question may well be worth the effort.

◆ *Interviewer-respondent interaction effects appear to be quite subtle but can influence interview responses. Where they are suspected, pilot studies are appropriate to determine the nature and seriousness of such effects.*

Tips on Interviewing and Hallmarks of an Interview[3]

Heeding the following suggestions will improve your interview technique. Look for them as hallmarks in the interview procedures of other researchers.

1. Identify yourself and set the respondent at ease.
2. The respondent's reaction often mirrors that of the interviewer. The respondent will know if you are uncertain and uneasy. Your pleasant, positive, well-informed approach will be reflected in the interviewees readiness to respond.
3. If you want longer and detailed responses, reinforce those kinds of answers—say, "Yes," "Okay," or "I see," or nod. Using similar reinforcers for nonresponsive answers gives the wrong signal; save them for responsive answers.
4. To teach and motivate the respondent, use feedback expressions like these: "Thanks, this is the sort of information we're looking for in this research." "It's important to us to get this information." "These details are helpful." "It's useful to get your ideas (your opinion) on this." "I see; that's useful information." "Let me get that down." (Cannell, 1985b)
5. Master the **probe**: repeat the question; give an expectant pause (an expectant look or nod of the head); possibly repeat, summarize, or reflect the feeling tone of the reply. Say: "Anything else?" "How do you mean?" "Could you tell me more about it?" "I'm not sure I know what you mean by that (bewildered look)." "Could you tell me a little bit more?" However, don't overuse these, or the respondent will think you can't recognize a valid answer.
6. Where probing recall, use probes that give memory cues of items likely to be forgotten. For example, if probing hospitalization, say, "Well, people quite frequently forget; it is more difficult to remember just an overnight hospitalization, for instance. Was there any chance you had something like this?" (Cannel 1985a).
7. When overtly interviewing, sit in a comfortable spot where you can record the responses verbatim, using abbreviations to get them down. Record abbreviations, probes, and interviewer comment in parentheses. Write as the respondent talks.

SUMMARY

The preceding tips summarize important points to be aware of in interviewing. The interviewer's role and that of the respondent may be relatively unstructured or quite structured. The former is more likely to be used with the qualitative approach, the latter, the quantitative. Structuring refers to pre-planning the interviewer's role. In order of increasing amounts of structure, preplanning might in-

---

[3]Portions of this section are based on *Interviewer's Manual*, rev. ed. Ann Arbor, Mich.: Survey Research Center, Institute for Social Research, 1976.

clude: general areas to cover, specific topics to include, suggested questions to ask, specific questions to ask, or a specific set of questions to ask in a particular order. Similarly, the respondents role may be unstructured with open-end responses being sought, or quite structured in terms of choosing among options in response to questions. Exploratory interviews may follow whatever leads turn up. More often, however, interviews are structured because researchers are intent on covering certain topics or areas, answering certain questions, or getting specific information. Interviews often follow a combination of approaches, starting with broad exploratory questions and successively focusing on the target of interest closer to a session's end.

The skill of the interviewer is critical to getting good information. Rapport builders, which create a good feeling between interviewer and respondent, help build an atmosphere conducive to full and honest responses. The nondirective response, which reflects not only the content but also the feeling tone of the respondent's last response, is an important tool to learn. It encourages the respondent to answer more fully, conveys an attitude of respect and worth to the respondent, and assures that the interviewer is not misinterpreting the reply.

Purposive sampling is the dominant sampling mode in qualitative method. Cases for interview are chosen to densify examples of key concepts, to find the boundaries and general outline of applicable cases, and to determine how far the generalization will transfer.

The use of multiple interviewers and/or multiple respondents is frequently advantageous. For example, multiple interviewers permit one interviewer to pick up cues the other has missed, and allow the other to take over when one has lost composure. One can concentrate on questioning while the other focuses on making the record. Use of multiple respondents, or group interviews, allow the interviewer to quickly separate representative responses from those particular to certain individuals, and may encourage a shy respondent to talk when another adopts a frank manner. Focus groups, a particular kind of group interview, are widely used politically and commercially to fathom the reaction of relatively homogeneous groups of people to particular communications and products.

Although it is widely known that characteristics of interviewers can bias the responses, research has shown that it is difficult to predict in advance the exact direction and nature of bias. In some instances, it is counterintuitive. However, it is clear that bias effects may be more subtle than researchers might anticipate, making pilot studies mandatory where such bias is a possibility.

A Look Ahead

As noted in the previous chapter, analysis and data gathering are intertwined. We have begun describing some of the steps in the process. Because analysis is so critical to the success of the study, we need to examine it in more detail, a task we will undertake in the next chapter.

ADDITIONAL READING

For general discussions on interviewing: Whyte, W. F. (1984), Chapter 6; Ely (1991), pp. 57–69; Seidman, (1991); Fontana & Frey (1994); and Weiss (1994). Rosengarten (1981) discusses interviewing in the context of biography. For focus groups, see Morgan (1997a & 1997b), Krueger (1994) and Stewart & Shamdasani (1990). See also Chapter 16 of this book regarding the formulation of questions. Questionnaire development is similar to preplanning interviews.

IMPORTANT TERMS

Focus group
Focused interview
Nondirective approach
Probe

Structured interview
Tandem interviewing
Unstructured interview

APPLICATION PROBLEMS

1. David Apple is a researcher who is interested in establishing what barriers, if any, exist to children's use of personal computers at the elementary school level. He has received permission to carry out his study at selected elementary schools and has decided to supplement his participant observation by interviewing a sample of students from all grade levels (kindergarten to grade 6). What style of interview might he use?

2. Margy Darby is studying how the roles of secretaries have changed in her university as computerized word processing made faculty more responsible for their own correspondence. She knows she needs data on time spent on various kinds of activities, but she also wants to learn other ramifications. What kind of interview should she use?

3. Suggest a nondirective interviewer response that would build rapport, yet elicit further details to the following:

> I tried working as a salesperson in the funeral business and thought I was quite good at it. But no matter how hard I tried, I couldn't win the respect of the men. It was a boy's network and I just couldn't break into it. Finally I just couldn't take it any longer.

Would you change the response for a male rather than a female interviewer?

4. Comment on the interviewer's response in this interchange:

> Female informant: I know I owe him a considerable amount of money and that could affect our relationship of living together if I don't pay it back. Yet, I don't seem to be able to set aside enough to make payments.

> Male interviewer: You seem increasingly uncomfortable owing money, but not guilty enough to change the situation. How do you think it will get changed?

Compare your answers with those following the Application Exercise.

APPLICATION EXERCISE

How might interview data facilitate your understanding of the phenomena you plan to study? Who might you interview and for what purpose? How would you select that sample? How would you record the data? How much structure of interviewer roles would be most helpful? Of respondent roles? How much would you prepare for the interview? How would you do it? What kinds, if any, interviewer-respondent interactions would you anticipate might arise?

ANSWERS TO THE APPLICATION PROBLEMS

1. Children represent a special and often difficult group with which to conduct interviews. Further, the responses Apple might obtain from the youngest will likely be quite different from those of the older children. Given that and the fact that his purpose here is exploratory, he will want to use either an unstructured or a partially structured style. These approaches will allow him to ask open-end questions and to follow up any leads or unusual answers. Use of a nondirective technique would allow him to establish better rapport with the children and to encourage freer responses. Conducting group interviews, particularly with the younger children, might help overcome their natural shyness toward strangers.

2. A focused interview that begins with broad questions and then narrows to the specific "hard" data she needs regarding time allocations. The latter could even take the form of a questionnaire they might complete together.

3. A female interviewer: "You felt really shut out didn't you! Do you recall what made you first feel that way?" This suggested response, by stressing "really" shows sympathy for her situation. A male interviewer might change the lead to "Those guys really made you feel shut out didn't they!" "Those guys" is intended to distance himself from the males in that situation and thus to make him appear responsive to her feelings. The probe asking her about the beginning of the feelings takes her back to its start, thus providing a clear field to probe wherever it seems profitable between then and the present.

4. Presumably, because the final question is aimed at next steps, that is the direction the interviewer wants the interview to take. However, prior to that probe, his response far exceeds in feeling tone what the informant has admitted. The interviewer may be quite correct that she feels guilty but she has not said so. His response forces the issue out in the open and could well dispel what rapport exists. Even if it doesn't, it is more likely to become the focus of the following interchanges than taking steps to do something about the problem. The first part of his response is closer in style to non-directive and, phrased as a question, might be more appropriate: "You seem increasingly uncomfortable owing money but equally disturbed by your inability to begin paying it back?"

Qualitative Data Analysis

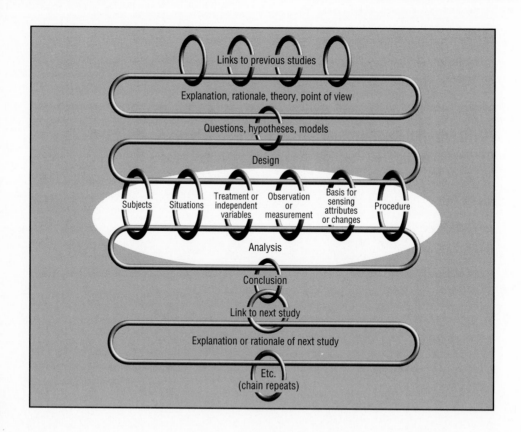

Art is the elimination of the unnecessary.

Pablo Picasso

You will need roughly two to five times as much time for processing and order-ing data as the time needed to collect it.

Patton, 1980, p. 295

OVERVIEW

Fieldwork, observation and interviewing often result in data from which impor-tant interpretations can be made. Qualitative data analysis is a process that facili-tates making those interpretations. Although, as described in Chapter 12, the analysis process is often integrated into fieldwork, because of its importance, it re-quires a more detailed examination than could be given there—hence this chap-ter. Most projects quickly gather more data than you can easily wrap your mind around; you must, therefore, find ways of reducing it so you can. Coding and analysis, processes of data reduction, do this by helping you highlight important aspects of the data, tag others as related but less important and relegate others to background. By thus reducing the conceptual load, you can focus attention on de-veloping an understanding and explanation of the important aspects.

First we will consider starting points for developing codes and coding. Then, a discussion of the process of drawing conclusions and their verification is begun in this chapter and continued in the following one. As explanations of the data de-velop, if they are to be accepted by your audience, any equally plausible alterna-tive explanations must be eliminated. Descriptions of some common alternatives that have plagued past research illustrate where vigilance is required. Finally, we discuss how using one of a variety of computer programs specifically designed for qualitative analysis can facilitate the process.

Qualitative analysis differs somewhat in a preplanned study, where one knows the problem focus from the outset, in contrast to an emergent one where one doesn't. The chapter is written from the standpoint of an emergent study, but the processes described are easily adapted to preplanned ones. Analysis for purely descriptive studies consists of deciding how to organize and selectively present the data.

CHAPTER CONTENTS

Introduction

Fieldwork tends to be an all-consuming activity with energy single-mindedly devoted to building a substantial database of notes. Fieldnotes pile up rapidly and become extensive as observation proceeds. Lila Sussman's fieldnotes for one day of observation at an elementary school amounted to 34 typewritten pages (Ornstein and Phillips, 1978, p. 327). Some studies run to many file drawers of notes. Clearly, **data reduction** is important.

You probably have never thought of art as the "elimination of the unnecessary" as suggested by Picasso, but this is what the sculpturer does in revealing the form hidden within the stone. It is also what the painter does in selecting which are the elements in a composition and arranging them creatively. The musician, as well, finds a melody and suitable embellishments among a host of possibilities. Doing good research is also part art, and—as Picasso's epigram suggests—part of the art of qualitative research is cutting away those notes and details that are not of consequence in order to concentrate on what is important—data reduction. Listen to experienced researcher Harry Wolcott (1990 as found in Stake, 1995): "The critical task in qualitative research is not to accumulate all the data you can, but to 'can' (i.e., get rid of) most of the data you accumulate. This requires constant winnowing" (p. 35).

Qualitative research is a successively selective (winnowing) process. At each stage, the researcher progressively selects and focuses. In an emergent type study, at the initial data-gathering stage, we attend to everything that might be important as well as to that which commands our attention. For beginners it is especially hard to focus, and that can be a problem. "In the early stages of a study, most of . . . [the data] looks promising. If you don't know what matters more, everything matters" (Miles and Huberman, 1994, p. 55). Nevertheless, we can't record everything. Sometimes, almost unconciously foci emerge and supplant attention to irrelevant detail. Other times, it is hard work and takes much rereading of the fieldnotes and reflection on their content to determine what is significant about the data being gathered. As we gradually sense more clearly what is important, interpretive memos suggest the meaning of significant events, elevating their importance and marking them for more attention than others. Through coding we can selectively attach meaningful tags to words, phrases, events, situations, and so forth, naming what is potentially important about them and distinguishing them as contributors to the study's findings. This successive selectivity guides on purposive sampling to find those individuals and situations needed to round out important study aspects. Finally, in setting forth generalizations that grow out of the data and stand above its detail and specificities—the ultimate stripping away of the unnecessary—we contribute to social science knowledge.

An equally important part of the analysis and interpretation process is assuring that all plausible rival explanations of the data have been eliminated. The search for such explanations has been facilitated by the identification of a number of common ones in past studies. Rival explanations were noted as early as the first chapter where it was explained that "mortality" concerned not death, but how people dropping out of studies might have affected results so as to constitute a rival explanation for the findings. Elimination of rival explanations is one of the five judgments involved in internal validity (LP). In this chapter, we discuss rival explanations that can be problems for qualitative studies. (We will meet these and others again in sample surveys, Chapter 16, and in experimentation, Chapter 20).

Because computer processing is becoming nearly as common for qualitative studies as it has been for quantitative ones, although what the computer does is quite different for each, we discuss how computers can aid analysis of qualitative data.

Early Steps in Analysis

We discussed steps that begin analysis in Chapter 12, the necessity of frequently summarizing and memoing. A **"contact summary report"** is a useful step beyond (Miles and Huberman, 1994). This one-page summary, completed after each major contact, reviews such questions as "What were the main issues or themes?" "What, in summary, was the information obtained (or still needed) on the target questions?" "What else was salient, interesting, illuminating, or important?" "What are the next or remaining questions for this contact?" A contact summary report not only summarizes a group of fieldnotes but also helps organize next steps. Again, analysis is concomitant with data gathering.

New qualitative researchers will want to try various suggestions to find those that work for them. Glesne and Peshkin (1992), for example, suggest keeping a number of files as data gathering and analysis progresses: subjectivity, title, thoughts for introductory and concluding chapters, and quotations from the literature. They describe these files as follows:

- The subjectivity file helps you keep track of your reactions during the study. In it you track feelings and reactions that may affect how you perceive situations and the actions you take in them—for example, avoiding talking to someone you find unappealing, spending too much time with those you are attracted to. The file should help you "get as fully as possible in touch with the embodied self who performs the acts of research" (ibid., p. 106). For example, the first observer comment (marked o.c. on page 270) would go in such a file.
- The title file holds the succession of ideas that encompass what you think the study is about. Given that you enter with only a general idea, "conjuring up titles as the data are being collected is a way of trying out different emphases, all of which are candidates for ultimately giving form to your data. . . . as your awareness of the promise of your study changes, so do your titles" (ibid., p. 29). One of Peshkin's students used banner software to print out her current working title so that "it guided her work whenever she lifted her head to reflect" (ibid., p. 131). The process of titling key memos will contribute to this file. For example, the title of the memo reproduced on page 273, "Career Patterns," might go in such a file, suggesting a study title like "Career Patterns of Teachers and Administrators."
- The file of ideas for the beginning and ending chapters, begun as data are being gathered, helps to ensure that the data needed for these chapters are not

missed. For the beginning chapter, this file includes the context, background, and conceptualization. For the final chapter, it is the detail required to flesh out the conclusions formed around the ideas in your title file. Starting early on these key chapters both focuses your mind on the larger picture and helps ensure that required material will be on hand. For example, as part of the description of context, the observer comments in the fieldnotes on page 270, which describe the unsupervised halls and the teachers saying hello, would be put in the "Beginning Chapter" file.

- The quotation file contains selected material from reading of literature on your problem that says something about your study in especially useful terms or has captured an attractive turn of phrase. "By resourceful use of quotations, you acknowledge that the world has not been born anew on your terrain" (Glesne and Peshkin, 1992, p. 129).

Coding as Indexing

Suppose someone had totally reordered the contents of a book, tearing out each index entry and stapling it to the fragment of a page or pages to which it referred. Never having seen the tome before, you are presented with this pile of papers ordered just as they appeared in the index and are asked to reconstruct the book! Impossible? Not really, if you are a qualitative researcher who has learned to construct a research report from such notes.

You would soon realize that only the logical interrelationships of the entries matter, not their alphabetical order. Thus you start by sorting the scraps dealing with the same topic into piles that made some logical or theoretical sense. You combine piles too similar to maintain the distinction between them. Then you move piles next to other piles that bear some relationship to them. Finally, you arrange the piles into an order such that there is a flow or logical or theoretical progression, with some piles acting as senior categories to junior piles related to them, perhaps hierarchically. In this way, you will be able to construct the book. If different people tried to reconstruct the book in this way, they might not all come up with exactly the same book. They may even come up with quite different books.

The better the "index," the easier this process will be. The topics with many entries are clearly central to at least certain parts of the book. The "see" and "see also" references tell something about the interrelations of topics. The topics with several levels of subentries suggest the hierarchical structure—which topics subsume which others—and therefore are central to the organization of the book. A good index does more than simply make the material accessible; it communicates the author's organization of it. The indexer has analyzed the author's text to determine importance and relations of topics and has inductively created an index that reflects that material. In addition, an indexer familiar with the field relates the author's material to the commonly accepted concepts and structures of the field where a reader might expect to find them.

You have sensed by now that this hypothetical problem was not an idle exercise, because it appropriately describes the process of qualitative research. Coding and indexing have much in common, but are obverse processes. Consider the problem of "indexing" (that is "coding") fieldnotes. Whereas a book has some structure, which the author imposed on the material to help readers understand it, fieldnotes are just running observations or interviews interspersed with comments. Their organization is chronological.

Like indexing, coding makes all these different kinds of notes accessible; however, it also helps us learn what is significant as we see aspects that repeat themselves—index items with many entries. As we examine these characteristics, relationships among them start to reveal themselves—the complex and "see" items in the index. These relationships may be organized into a theory to fit these particular data or may fit existing theory in the field so that some kind of organizational structure accounts for the characteristics and their interrelationships—the hierarchical complex entries of an index.

Thus, there are clearly helpful parallels to good indexing. Keep in mind that good coding, like good indexing, does more than granting access to the data: Coding provides lenses through which data can be viewed in a relational structure. Book indexers get most of this organization from the author; coders of fieldnotes must inductively develop the organization out of the items they themselves index (code).

There is an additional difference, however, between indexing and qualitative research. Our hypothetical researchers above all started with the same data, the index. Most likely, different qualitative researchers do not even start out with the same data. Thus they may end up with quite dissimilar books even though they are studying the same situations because they attend to different aspects of the same events, interviews, and so forth. But this difference is inherent in the inductive nature of the qualitative process. Indeed, it may be thought of as one of its strengths. As other individuals come up with new and creative ideas about how to gather, organize, and interpret the data, some are likely to be more useful or insightful than the initially obvious ones.

The Nature of Coding

Besides the summaries, memos, and contact summaries we discussed earlier, the most basic process of analysis is coding. **Coding** is interpreting; as my colleague Sari Biklen tells her classes, "it is making decisions about what things mean." What do you code and where do these codes come from? What you code depends on what you consider relevant and important. In coding, you assign a descriptive word or phrase to each unit of notes (not necessarily everything—some clearly will be irrelevant). Use the informant's language in the code title if you can, usually abbreviated for ease of use (numbers are shorter but removed from the concept involved and, if there are many, difficult to remember). Codes may be descriptive, merely labeling the salient aspect of the text. Consider this fragment from fieldnotes:

> Before class started, it was obvious that Johnson had decided to videotape the segment on statistics and place it in the Instructional Materials Center so students could review it at their convenience. But it was equally obvious that he had never

handled a video camera before and, even after class started, he was still fiddling with the equipment, apparently attempting to get it to work.

In a study concerned with instructional technology, the technology aspect is the subject of coding. In a study of the problems of new teachers the interest can be difficulty with the video camera. If you are merely concerned with which technology was being used, you might code this note fragment *vid* for videotape or *cl vid* for in-class videotape. If you are concerned with the skill with which technology was used because there was not sufficient training, you might code it *NT/c/vid*. Each of these codes emphasizes a different aspect. Your description of the salient aspect depends on the purpose of your study.

Initially you might be unsure of the focus of your study and ask yourself what code to assign. Don't worry, you can recode material and consolidate, or change or divide codes after you learn more thoroughly what is significant and what is not. This is particularly easy to do with one of the specialized computer programs for qualitative analysis which permit you to relabel material or combine codes with a few keystrokes.

Often descriptive coding is a first step to "see what is there." Make a list of the codes and examine it to see where there are apparent redundancies and categories that you can combine. The list will suggest categories that ought to be hierarchically related so that there are different levels of coding. But *read the fieldnotes or interviews themselves before making these changes*, since closer examination may reveal distinctions not conveyed by the code titles.

After this initial coding, or if this were a structured study to analyze the purposes of technology use, you might recode this same material at an interpretive level. You would then infer the intended use of the technology: *rev* (content review), *sk* (skill learning), *sk p* (skill practice), and so on. At a still deeper level of analysis, usually arrived at later, you might code patterns of activities, themes, causal links, and other more complex aspects that relate to the theory you are building. A repeated pattern might be the instructor who decides abruptly with no training or forethought to introduce technology into the instruction. You might, for example, assign a code (*imp instr*—impulsive instructor) for this action.

Steps in Coding

As we might expect, considering the varied styles people use to organize material for their own writing, there is no standard method of qualitative analysis. Some researchers do all their coding and analysis after they have collected their data. Most qualitative researchers, however, carry on all these processes concomitantly but with shifting emphases during the study as indicated by which phase is italicized and capitalized in the following: *OBSERVING*, coding, and interpretation are followed by *OBSERVING, CODING,* and interpretation; then observing, *CODING AND INTERPRETATION*; and, finally, observing, coding, *INTERPRETATION*.[1]

Although individuals may differ in the sequence of steps they take in qualitative analysis, the following list of such actions, each which can profitably be cov-

---

[1] I learned this way of expressing the process from my colleague Anne Shelley, a co-author of QUALOG one of the early mainframe computer qualitative analysis programs.

ered at some time in the process, provides some practical guidelines. The section following that offers starting points for developing codes that may be helpful to beginners.

1. The first time you sit down to read through your data is the only time you come to that particular set fresh. Underline significant parts and make marginal notes; otherwise you may lose initial impressions. Intervening experience changes perceptions. Early impressions may be wrong, or especially insightful; you will know better later. Be sure the data is all there. Are there gaping holes? Are there places where you intended to write something but neglected to do so?

2. Study and re-study the raw data to develop detailed, intimate knowledge of it. Reading and rereading the data seems to facilitate seeing patterns. It chunks the material in your mind so that you get past the details to the larger picture.
   - Look for repetitions and relationships and note these in the margin; they help devise codes.
   - Figure out what is important about these similarities.
   - Identify types of individuals or cases or situations that are important to what you are studying.
   - Qualitative method is particularly useful for examining systems and processes where there are interactive relations among variables. Rather than confining yourself to single dependent and independent variables you do better to reflect these complex relations in your coding and analyses.
   - "Unusual participant terms are always worth following up since they often mark theoretically important or interesting phenomena" (Hammersley and Atkinson, 1995, p. 211). Reflect participants' terms in your code abbreviations as much as possible to keep the "flavor" of the situation.

3. A process suggested for organizing the literature review (p. 90) applies equally well to qualitative data analysis! Fill your conscious mind and let your unconscious sort it out while you do other things. Even while you are away from the process of coding and sorting because you have read and reread the data, your mind will be processing and organizing. Be prepared to make a record when the ideas pop into your conscious mind so they won't get lost. Jotting down a note or two helps. The process of writing itself helps fix it in your mind, and the data helps you create the rest.

4. Make a list of tentative categories and code the raw data using this initial set.

5. Sort the raw data under the code titles either by putting scraps of paper in piles or folders,[2] or, if you are using computer software, by sorting it into files. You will find the latter easier to scan if you print them out.

---

[2]If you decide to use the scissors, folder and paste method, consider using colored paper, colored high-lighters, pinking vs. ordinary shears, and clipping corners or otherwise shaping cut-out segments to signal to yourself whatever you are likely to want to keep track of or separate out (variables; codes, data sources: observations, interviews, or cases, persons, sites; types of data: fieldnotes, memos; and so forth) (Radnofsky, 1995).

6. As you do steps 4 and 5, notice how well the material fits the code title; as appropriate, change the title for a better fit as you proceed. You may also find that distinctions you initially thought were important aren't; combine and retitle those codes. (Changing code titles is much easier with software than relabeling all the slips of paper; you won't as easily get locked into poor codes because of the labor of changing them.)

7. Review the results, looking for overlap and redundancy but especially for whether the codes reflect what you think is important about the data. Still further refine and revise the codes, especially titles, so that they fit.

8. My colleague, Anne Shelley—because a picture is worth a thousand words—argues for laying out the codes in a graphic. Graphics help us see the relation of one variable to another and facilitate developing explanations and theory. Further, they highlight code categories where the relationships are obscure—these may call for more data. Where you have major codes differentiated into more specific minor ones, lay out the relationships as you might a hierarchical genealogical chart of your relatives, with the more inclusive codes in the role of parents and the more specific codes as their children. Use dotted lines to show relationships across codes. Alternatively, if a hierarchical structure isn't a good fit, use pattern noting to show the relation of the codes (see p. 98). Again, some of the computer software facilitates this process by showing the material in a tree-like graphic, or a network of codes with the relation of one code to another shown on the lines relating them.

9. Select at least a couple of instances of verbatim narrative from the data for each of the codes. If you are seeking to view the situation as perceived by those in it, select material in the informant's own words. Write a definition of the code; delineate what falls under the code title. The definition shows its generality and also helps to define the boundaries of what is included. Constructing definitions is likely to help you see other relationships among the codes and the necessity for further refinement and revision of the structure.

10. If you have not previously done so, and before finalizing your coding and tentative explanation, do a literature search to determine what others have learned about your topic. The search may give support to the directions in which you were already going and strengthen the case you will present when you write it up. Conversely, it may cause you to rethink or modify your coding and hypothesizing, or possibly even require you to start over in a new direction. In some instances, it will suggest alternative explanations to the one you had found, thereby requiring additional field data that will test which explanation is best supported by the evidence.

11. Now or earlier, write statements describing what you believe you can best draw from the data: generalities, general perceptions or perspectives, typologies of individuals, actions, situations, central actions or events, processes, strategies, interactions, and so forth.

12. Select from the database at least a couple of the best or model examples of each of the generalities, typologies, and so forth.

13. If pursuing a generalization (for example, most teachers are intrigued into using technology by its promise as a labor saver; once they begin using it, however, they concentrate on the instructional improvement instead of the labor-saving aspects):

a. Look for data providing counterexamples of this generalization.

b. Determine if the generalization would lead to certain expectations and see if those expectations are supported by the data.

c. If they are not supported, determine if you can revise the generalization so as to fit both the new implications and the original data from which it was derived.

d. Repeat steps *b* and *c* to see if support can be found for the revised generalization.

e. Review the case that can be made for the generalization and assemble the data that bears on it, pro and con.

f. Proceed with a similar set of steps for any other generalizations you can infer from the data.

14. If seeking to construct descriptive typologies, assemble the best examples and describe the common features that characterize the group. (For example, there may be a group of teachers making considerable use of instructional technology who have these common characteristics: 1) were either the first or one of the earliest in the building to use instructional technology, 2) devised their own instructional technology materials, 3) are perceived as more oriented to things than to people. Presumably, these three characteristics identify a teacher type.) Then:

a. Look for persons who were not included in this initial set but who are as relevant as those you have chosen. (Are there other teachers who are equally intensive users of instructional technology?)

b. Determine if additions or modifications in the initial set of characteristics will permit inclusion of the new examples, making sure the set still fits the original group. (Do the new teacher examples have some of these characteristics but not others such as being early adopters and more oriented to things than people, but used commercially prepared materials? Depending on the purpose of the study, the type might be better defined by only two common characteristics if instructional material preparation were not relevant.)

c. If the statement cannot be modified to cover both new and original data, you have a different type in the new data. Determine if there are a set of distinctive features which characterize all or a part of the new group and add it to your set of typologies. (For example, there may be a group of intensive users who 1) were late adopters, 2) heavily used commercially prepared material, 3) were perceived as more oriented to people than to things. They might form a second type in the typology.)

d. Continue with this process until there are no more groups of sufficient size to be of interest with common characteristics. Then review the set of types to determine whether there is redundancy across types or whether similar types can be clustered into a typology of families. For example, these two might constitute a family of types dealing with early adoption; there may be other families concerned with other aspects of technology use.

Coding Starting Points

We noted earlier that, especially with focused and preplanned studies—for instance, the evaluation of a program against its stated goals—we can establish a set of tentative codes at the outset. For studies in which the problem is emergent, many qualitative researchers, including Strauss (1987), suggest reading the field-notes and inductively picking out the important aspects as provisional codes that can be revised later as necessary. Certainly, our initial ideas about what is significant will bear heavily on what we look for. How should you start? Some alternatives:

- Identify individuals or groups that contrast with one another on a behavior or dimension of interest. Observe or read accounts of those contrasted so as to become sensitized to what is different about them. If, individuals, look for others like those initially selected.
- Cut a copy of the parts of the fieldnotes dealing with them into segments, each containing an important aspect. Deciding what is a segment with an important aspect forces you to decide what aspects are important. Once the slips are laid out before you, you can scan them for similarities and differences and put similar ones together in piles. Sorting into piles forces you to decide what important aspects differentiate them. The size of the piles indicates the frequency with which each occurs so the prevalent ones become obvious. Although they may not be the key ones, they often are.

    If you have your data in a computer, it is very difficult to scan the material and get the larger picture when you are limited to a screenful at a time. With small amounts of data, or without specialized qualitative research software, go the paper route. Use a word processor to break the material into paragraphs, print it out, and proceed as above.
- To get started using computer analysis software, have it compile a listing of the most common words found in the data and their frequencies. While most will be no surprise, the ones that are may suggest overlooked aspects. Some software allows you to look for words in conjunction with others, permitting you to find the location of these patterns in the fieldnotes. You can infer such multiple word search patterns from the frequency listing.
- Search the data for common phrases as well as surprising, counterintuitive and unexpected material. Once you find the characteristics or aspects or wording that is significant, a computer is invaluable in very quickly finding other occurrences.
- Develop working hypotheses about repeating patterns, especially things that follow one another regularly. These will yield classifications and principles that permit you to sort the data and observe the consistency or inconsistency of that regularity. Test these patterns to see whether the proposed explanation works for enough of them to be a satisfactory explanation for a significant segment of the data. Then similarly analyze the rest of the data, testing with provisional trials until you are satisfied with the emerging explanations.

Strauss (1987) suggests, as a way of getting started, coding "conditions," "interaction among actors," "strategies and tactics," and "consequences" (pp. 28–29). To find conditions, look for words like *because, since, as,* and *on account of* (easy with the "find" command on the computer). To find consequences, look for *as a result of, because of,* and similar expressions. Look for phrases or terms that appear repeatedly, and then ask questions about those items and their significance to get at the kinds of codes to use. Categories will evolve as research proceeds, although you will most likely have to recode fieldnotes along the way. This approach results in well-grounded codes, tightly knit into the theory being developed. (See especially Strauss and Corbin, 1990.)

Next, Strauss (1987) suggests moving to dimensions (abstractions, concepts, constructs, generalizations) as quickly as possible, each of which will suggest comparative cases to be examined for these dimensions. For examples, see Strauss (1987) and Turner (1981).

By way of providing more structure, especially for beginners, Miles and Huberman (1994, p. 61) suggest using Lofland's (1971) generic scheme to code:

- Acts: action in a situation that is temporarily brief, consuming only a few seconds, minutes, or hours.
- Activities: action in a setting of longer duration—days, weeks, months—constituting significant elements of people's involvement.
- Meanings: the verbal productions of participants that define and direct action.
- Participation: people's holistic involvement in, or adaptation to, a situation or setting under study.
- Relationships: interrelationships among several persons considered simultaneously.
- Settings: the entire setting under study conceived as the unit of analysis.

Bogdan and Biklen (1992, pp. 167–172) provide a different scheme:

- Setting/context codes: general description of the setting that allows you to place the study into a larger context—for example, descriptions of elementary schools.
- Definition of the situation codes: how subjects understand, define, or perceive their setting or relevant study topics—for example, feminist perspectives.
- Perspectives held by subjects: ways of thinking shared by subjects toward the setting or some aspect of it; try to capture shared understandings—for example, "be honest but not cruel," a common recognition of what is best in informing parents in a medical setting.
- Subjects' ways of thinking about people and objects: understandings of each other, of outsiders, and objects that make up their world—for example, teachers differentiate students as "immature" or "ready for school."
- Process codes: sequences of events, transitions from one status to another, changes over time—for example, turning points, benchmarks, stages, phases, and careers.
- Activity codes: regularly occurring kinds of behavior—for example, the showing of films, morning exercises, and so on.
- Event codes: particular happenings that occur infrequently or once—for example, a strike, or a pageant.
- Strategy codes: ways people accomplish things, tactics, methods, techniques, ploys—for example, how students get out of hall duty.
- Relationship and social structure codes: cliques, friendships, romances, coalitions, enemies, and other regular behavior not defined on the organizational chart.
- Methods: problems, joys, dilemmas of the research process; usually consists of observer comments.

Drawing and Verifying Conclusions

A process of coding and inference is briefly but clearly described in the Hoff-mann-Riem study of Chapter 1. Reread the section "Data Interpretation" on page 14. Note how the author wrote up each couple's story, sectioning them into standard broad areas: motivation, adoption process, and relation development (a coarse coding to be further refined). Then she proceeds with analytic induction across the cases to find commonalities. Next, using certain common aspects within each of her broad initial three categories, she seeks their boundaries by determining case variety. Finally she constructs "polar"—that is, opposite—types to see how cases differed from one another and fills in between the extremes with other cases. Her process in perspective: establishing rough coding, seeking commonalities, developing finer coding, relating codes to dimensions representing major findings, and selecting cases to illustrate and give meaning to the ends and middle of each dimension. This is a common sequence. But, how to find interrelationships and generalizations seems to vary with the individual.

Bosk (1979) kept a running analysis separate from his fieldnotes. Gans (1962) abstracted generalizations from his field diary onto more than 200 cards, which he sorted and classified. He then digested these into notes listing the major generalizations. He reread the diary and wrote the report. Strauss (1987) suggests finding families of categories and core categories that represent the higher-level abstractions making up the theoretical network. Note that these all involve writing down ideas. Putting ideas on paper, as we noted earlier, does more than provide a record; it helps to organize our thoughts.

Miles and Huberman (1984) find that matrices and diagrams that display the interrelationships among variables, persons, and situations are of considerable help in organizing the data, finding relationships, and eliminating alternative hypotheses. In qualitative analysis, a **matrix** is a table displaying information that describes the relation between two or more variables. Table 14.1 is excerpted from an example of a matrix summarizing the results of a school improvement program across sites. Sites were arranged from top to bottom as having high (Masepa), medium (Carson), or low impact (Burton). Program objectives, the direct positive and negative results, and the indirect effects and side effects for each site are indicated in successive columns across the page. Each effect is marked to indicate the sources of data: U for user (teacher), A for administrator, C for counselor, P for parent, E for evaluator, and S for student. Underlined letters indicate a mention by at least two persons. An *x* indicates the presence of a dissenting or conflicting opinion.

By using such a symbol system and by the juxtaposition of data to be compared, this matrix facilitates the interpretation of a tremendous amount and variety of information. For example, by comparing rows, you can see that at a high impact school, Masepa, many effects were observed, both direct and indirect, whereas at a low impact one, Burton, there were few effects and only direct ones. Some important effects were observed by both the teacher users, and confirmed by an administrator or counselor (those labeled U, A, C). Few observations are labeled "x" so dissenting opinions were rare, although one appears next to what would otherwise be a very important result at Masepa: "Low achievers, more

TABLE 14.1 *Matrix Summarizing the Effects of a School Improvement Program across Different Schools*

Sites	Objectives	Direct Effects		Indirect and Side Effects	
		Positive	Negative	Positive	Negative
Masepa (externally developed innovation)	Improvement in full range of language arts skills More on-task behavior Improved discipline	Improved skills: vocabulary U, A, P; spelling U, A; phonetics Ux; punctuation U; reading comprehension Ux, E; reading decoding U; grammar U; written expression U Low achievers more productive Ux	Retention levels not good U Too little diversity U Student fatigue U	Concentration, study skills U, A Fewer discipline problems U, A More attentive to errors U Better academic self-concept U More enjoyment, enthusiasm U, A	Some lagging, failing mastery tests U Boredom U
Carson (locally developed innovation)	Increased achievement Clearer career interests Friendliness Improved self-concept as a learner More internal locus of control	Career knowledge U, A, C		Achievement composite (use of resources) E Better classroom attitude U Attitude to school E, U Self-concept as a learner (high school) E Friendliness E Self-understanding U	Little effect on achievement U
Burton (externally developed innovation)	Knowledge & practical skills re political/ government/ legal processes (voter education, state government, individual rights)	Concept learning by being in different roles U Experienced active learning approach A	No effects discernible U		

Source: Adapted from M. B. Miles and A. M. Huberman, *Qualitative Data Analysis*, 2nd ed., p. 191. Copyright © 1994 Sage Publications Inc.

productive." Thus, from this matrix, in addition to comparing the impact of the program at different schools, you can assess evidence in terms of the source of the data and whether it was confirmed by more than one source or contradicted by a dissenting opinion.

In addition, such matrices as that of Table 14.1 enable us to see other things. Do administrators always show up only on the positive comment side? Apparently. Are locally developed innovations more successful? Not according to these data. They make clear where we have data and where they are missing. Like Mendeleyev's periodic table of the chemical elements, they permit prediction and search for missing entries, sometimes with useful and surprising results.

Miles and Huberman (1994) is a superb source of suggestions for such graphic displays, matrices, and network designs. Their book contains many examples and excellent advice on their construction and use. Matrices such as that of Table 14.1, show the interaction of two or more variables. Graphic displays and networks show events in time sequence or relationships.

Not everyone thinks visually and, to some researchers, such devices suggest too structured an approach to method. Indeed, Miles and Huberman advise that at the outset the researcher roughly sketch matrices from the research questions and key variables, and then get colleagues and others to help examine the assumptions and to suggest alternatives. Provided the researcher can stay open to the unexpected, such an approach works well with structured and focused research questions; where research uses an emergent approach, such displays may be more appropriate later in the analysis process.

Matrices and memos are useful for another reason: they provide an **"audit trail"** that others can follow to reconstruct how an analysis developed, to check how well coding terms are grounded in the data, and to determine the logical validity of conclusions. Researchers argue leaving a clear audit trail helps critics to track the steps of qualitative method and is likely to provide for greater methodological rigor. Without in any way restricting the options available to the researcher, an audit trail allows others to check the reasoning and makes the process explicit. Studying trails of past research can provide a perspective on the qualitative analysis process that would help novice researchers decide how best to proceed with their studies.

✦ *Observation and interviewing often result in amounts of data that are well beyond human memory capacity to retain and integrate as a whole. Coding and analysis are the data reduction processes that make the database manageable.*

✦ *Coding, an inductive reasoning process, involves extracting similarities in behavior or perceptions from the data and abstracting the important concepts and dimensions for easier access and retrieval.*

✦ *Codes are the concepts used in the explanation, and the coded data are the definitions of the concepts. In turn, codes are knit into an explanation, or theory, hence the term* grounded theory, *since it is "grounded" in—that is, built from— the coded data.*

✦ *Coding and memoing go hand in hand; memos capture the inferences underlying the codes.*

✦ *Various generic coding systems can assist novices.*

✦ *Graphics and matrices provide a perspective on data that facilitates spotting trends and relationships, missing data, and data that does not follow the pattern.*

✦ *Providing an "audit trail" is important not only for others but also for ourselves en route to provide perspective on the process.*

Threats to the Validity of Interpretation: Rival Explanations

Regardless of research method, qualitative, quantitative, or other, now that you have a particular explanation for a relationship in data, or a theory that explains it, you want your work to be accepted by others. For that to occur, you must determine that no rival explanation accounts for the data as well as the one being advanced. Campbell and Stanley (1963) coined the phrase "threats to validity" for such especially plausible rival explanations. In some cases, the researcher may not be aware of alternatives; in others, she may be aware but did not, or could not, protect against them. All research is besieged by such alternatives: general ones we can name in advance and that are common to most research, specific ones that plague certain research methods, and unique ones resulting from the configuration of a particular study. Even one uneliminated alternative that is apparent to the audience, however, may be sufficient to destroy a consensus that the proposed explanation is the valid one. Thus, these are serious matters.

Of the common rivals that were given names and definitions by Campbell and Stanley (1963) and Cook and Campbell (1979), some have applicability to qualitative methods.[3] Although their names are, in one sense, descriptive—mortality, instrument decay, selection—they sometimes bring the wrong picture to mind. **Mortality** refers not to the death of subjects but to the loss of individuals from a group, thereby making it no longer representative. For example, an instructor asks his students to complete a questionnaire on his teaching, which is to be left in his mailbox. The responses are quite positive, but only a small proportion of students return the forms. An alternative explanation is that those who thought poorly of his teaching did not reply, afraid recognition of their handwriting might influence their grade—the mortality factor.

Does mortality apply to qualitative research? It often does, and worst of all, it sometimes occurs unnoticed. One may be concentrating on the persons active in a group without perceiving persons have left it who might have had an effect had they remained. For example, in trying to understand the impact on children's play patterns of new playground equipment, one concentrates on how children take turns, their ease in adapting to the equipment, and similar aspects. One might not notice that some former playground users, afraid of the new equipment, have avoided the playground altogether and gone elsewhere. In this instance, the mortality in the group strongly suggest that had they stayed, one might have an equally or more plausible, yet quite different, picture of adaptability to the new equipment.

Instrument decay refers to the inconsistency in measurement or observation that results from a change in a measuring instrument or observation procedure

<hr>

[3]You will find the discussion of "threats to validity" placed in the discussion of experimental methods in most research texts. Because it is important that the applicability of alternative explanations and threats to validity be recognized as relevant to any, not just quantitative work, we shall begin describing them here and note them elsewhere as they are relevant. For good measure, we will cover the set of them again when we discuss experimentation in Chapter 20.

over the course of the study. For instance, it refers to rules made up in the course of using an observation checklist for which, on encountering a situation not provided for by rules for checklist use, the researcher makes up an arbitrary addition on the spot. Forgetting the decision, he may make up a different rule for the next instance. Others in the study also using the instrument may make up their own rules. Inconsistency in using the instrument may be a reasonable alternative explanation for a finding.

In qualitative research, the observer is the instrument. We have to wonder how, over the period of the study, the observer changes in the perception of the observed, and how that affects the observations. For example, the data may suggest that a remedial treatment became more effective over time. In actuality, sympathetic to the struggle the participants were making to succeed, the observer loosened the definition of what constituted a positive change over the course of observation. Although observers often write about this in memos, it is still a problem. Wax (1971), having studied Japanese Americans interned during World War II, found that it "made it impossible that I ever again approach or talk to them in the way that I had . . . three or four months before" (p. 31). Clearly, the observer must be alert to such changes and take them into account.

The most serious change of this type is **"going native,"** that is, losing perspective on the group being observed and becoming entirely one of them. Lang and Lang (1960) report that, during a study of a Billy Graham crusade in 1957, an observer left her observation task and "somewhere in the course of the sermon she decided to step forward. . . .The next thing she knew was that she had risen and was hurrying to the main floor to declare herself [a believer]" (p. 424).

A variation of instrument decay is the tendency to overlook or ignore the negative aspects of a group the researcher has come to identify with. Thus Ornstein and Phillips (1978) criticize Liebow's (1967) "compelling description of street corner men" because he "presents no description of their involvement in crime or drugs or violence; he describes few instances of cruelty or times when they actually were impulsive or improvident, as we all are sometimes" (p. 350).

Sadler's (1981) analysis of the mind's cognitive limitations we considered two chapters earlier suggests some things to watch for in the process of analysis.[4] Knowing these limitations is the first step toward disciplining their effect.

- **Positive and negative instances.** Evidence that supports tentative hypotheses is much more likely to be noticed than evidence that negates them. Research shows that people tended to ignore information that conflicted with already held hypotheses; "even intelligent individuals adhered to their own hypotheses with remarkable tenacity when they could produce confirming evidence for them" (p. 28).
- **Correlation and co-occurrences.** Co-occurrences are often seen as evidence of correlation when they may be chance occurrences. Ability to construct a reasonable explanation helps delineate chance occurrences from correlated ones.
- **Novelty of information.** Two equally credible sets of data about a particular phenomenon might differ, one being more extreme than the other. For exam-

---

[4]Sadler (1981) cites research studies that support each of these points.

ple, one observer watching a teacher discipline a student describes it in routine terms; the other reports it quite graphically as an aberration in the
teacher's behavior. How shall we characterize her behavior? As long as the
report is believable, the novelty of the aberration makes it stand out and we
tend to discount the less extreme data. Positive and negative information do
not typically cancel each other out; the more extreme tends to win. This is
more likely to occur where there is a paucity of information than when, with
more information, the less novel behavior is shown to be closer to typical.

- **Base-rate proportion.** The base rate is the natural frequency with which a behavior occurs (for example, aggressive acts in daily life) independent of some
intervention such as an experimental treatment (for example, solving a frustrating puzzle), or of some cause one is studying such as a particular influence or
context (for example, aggression among spectators at a boxing match). Judging
base rates from small samples is very difficult; the occurrence of a particular behavior in a small sample may be large, but its actual base rate over all behavior
may be small. Insensitivity to the real base rate and a tendency to clinically form
impressions from small amounts of observational data seem to be common
problems in intuitive data processing. These may account for the novelty problem just noted. Further, as statisticians know but often themselves underestimate, there is much greater variability among small than among large samples,
a factor rarely taken into account. Instead of realizing that the actual sample
size may be very small, individuals tend to base their judgment on the sample's
perceived representativeness or the proportion of the population it constitutes.

- **Uneven reliability of information.** People tend to treat data from an unreliable source almost the same way as they do data from reliable sources. In one
study, subjects arrived at a conclusion, and then each source was shown to be
less credible than originally thought. As each source was discredited, the revisions of the original hypothesis became smaller. Even when all sources had
been discredited, a residual of commitment to the hypothesis still remained.

- **Revision of ideas.** New information tends to be either overweighted or un-
derweighted. With a single-stage inference, there is considerable evidence of
underadjustment, as noted in the preceding example. However, there is likely
to be overadjustment with second-stage inferences. For example, clinical psychologists, once having formed a prediction of the future success of students
in training, are then given new evidence from their second most favorite clinical instrument. They seem for some reason to overadjust to accommodate it.
Apparently, they carry over only the most salient of data to the second-stage
inference. Similarly, qualitative researchers, who feel they must accommodate to new data, may overadjust.

- **Confidence in judgment.** As noted, "once an assessment is made, people
have been shown to have an almost unshakable confidence in the correctness
of their decisions, even in the face of considerable, relevant, contrary evidence" (Sadler, 1981, p. 30). Training to remain open to new evidence is very
important for the qualitative researcher.

The last item, as well as others on the list, suggests that, since the researcher is
the data collection instrument, temperamental characteristics probably contribute

to good qualitative research. Impulsiveness, for example, might cause individuals to jump to generalizations too early. A tendency toward holistic approaches in contrast to "missing the forest for the trees" seems a necessity to induction. Flexibility, openness, and willingness to entertain the "new" are important, though not to the point that the new automatically displaces the old. This last point, the ability to appropriately integrate new information into the whole, may be one of the most critical since the order of events is beyond the researcher's control and initial events form the base on which the rest is built.

This section has dealt with some problems common to research in general and others mainly applicable to qualitative research. Of course, some alternative explanations arise out of the particular configuration of the study, the sample, the methodology, and so forth. For example, a study of secretarial responsibilities in universities may conclude that increasing faculty computer literacy has resulted in a major change in secretarial responsibilities, with faculty largely doing their own correspondence and manuscripts. Such a study, confined largely to state-supported institutions, might be subject to the alternative explanation that faculty-secretarial ratios have always been higher in public universities than privately supported ones. Faculty in private universities have always been responsible for their correspondence and manuscripts so that secretarial responsibilities would have changed little. Tightened finances in state institutions may have been a major cause, in addition to the fact that as faculty used their computers the secretarial budget could be reduced with less outcry and pain than would otherwise have been the case—a rival explanation unique to this study.

Clearly, there are many sources of problems. Qualitative or quantitative researchers who wish to build audience credibility in order to secure a consensus about their findings should attend to these concerns and allay them in their research report.

- ✦ *The elimination of alternative explanations is a concern of all methods, including qualitative methods.*
- ✦ *Certain common alternative explanations, or "threats to validity" as they have been called, are applicable to qualitative methods. Examples are mortality and instrument decay.*
- ✦ *Besides the common alternative explanations, others, often unique to the individual study, are the responsibility of the researcher to ferret out.*
- ✦ *A variety of information processing limitations affect the researcher. These can constitute special problems for qualitative researchers since they are the data recording instrument.*
- ✦ *The anticipation of alternatives that will be of concern to the audience is essential if a consensus is to be formed around the proposed interpretation of the data.*

Use of Computers in Analysis

Increasingly, qualitative researchers are expected to use computer programs to ease their labor, just as quantitative researchers have for years used them to avoid routine computation. As Behrens and Smith (1996) note, however, using such programs " does not render one's assertions more valid than using the time-hon-ored method of cutting up fieldnotes and putting sections in file folders. All qual-itative analysis is a cognitive process, and all such programs can do is facilitate clerical and indexing tasks so the researcher has more time for thinking about the data." (p. 984). Increased ease of handling vast and cumbersome qualitative data files is a significant advance that makes recoding and refinement of analyses feasi-ble and therefore leads to more complete analyses. However, some have resisted their use. In part this is because they want to stay close to their data whereas cer-tain computer features may make the process seem mechanical. Indeed, Weitz-man and Miles (1995) suggest some program designers have omitted characteris-tics other programs incorporate so the user will attend to certain tasks requiring contact with the data.

It has been argued that the learning time required to use a computer com-bined with the likelihood that you will attempt more complex analysis with a computer program than you would otherwise, makes the scissors and paste ap-proach preferable. Computer users, however, argue that programs have succes-sively become easier to use, learning is not as difficult and prolonged as imag-ined, and the increased ability to analyze the data leads to better studies.

Most computer literate individuals undertaking a project of any size will ben-efit from using one of the qualitative research software programs. Find the likely required investment in learning for yourself by searching the World Wide Web for the names of qualitative software of interest and see if they have demonstra-tion programs. Such demonstrations are currently available for several including two of the more complete and user friendly programs—ATLAS/ti for DOS and Windows (Muhr, 1993), and QSR NUD•IST for most operating systems (Qualita-tive Solutions and Research Pty. Ltd., 1997).

Unless one works from handwritten notes, the big task is typing the material into a word processor—a labor intensive process. Although scanners can shortcut this step for already existing documents, they currently do not provide a com-pletely accurate copy. Treatment with a spelling program catches many of the problems but they require proofreading. Word processing capabilities markedly facilitate entering and editing fieldnotes, memos, and interim and final reports. Computers make writing and rewriting so much easier.

Advantages of Specialized Software Programs. Coding by hand usually in-volves placing codes in the margin of the typescript; highlighting, underlining, cutting out the segments to which they apply; and making duplicate copies where segments overlap or have more than one code. The mechanical problem of getting together all the material dealing with a single code or related codes usually in-volves cutting up copies of the typescript and putting the slips into folders or by placing them on cards that can be sorted into piles.[5] Qualitative analysis pro-

---

[5]This process assumes the researchers are looking for generalizations and patterns. If instead they are interested in life histories or other narrative accounts, they may wish, instead of "tradi-tional approaches to qualitative analysis . . .[that] fracture [respondents'] texts . . . by taking bits and pieces, snippets of a response edited out of context . . . [to organize material around] the se-quential and structural features that characterize narrative accounts" (Riessman, 1993, p. 2, as found in Casey, 1995).

grams not only assist with these tasks but also do still more. You can use a word processor program for simple coding, for instance, placing codes in the text with symbols around them—#support#—and even do multiple level coding—lower-case for first level and upper case for second. Such codes can be found with a search command, and the text selected and copied to a new file. Provided one has paragraphed the text by homogeneous segments, this may be adequate for small, simple projects. Good qualitative software will go considerably further, however:

- Content can be easily analyzed. The computer can quickly compile a list of the most frequently used words which can be scanned for suggestions of coding categories. It can also locate and count certain words or phrases.
- Codes of key words or "tags" are easily assigned to sections of the text, whether paragraphed or not, to permit later retrieval.
- All the material for a code can be brought to one place, printed out for scrutiny, recoded, moved, and otherwise manipulated. Because it is difficult to skim material on a computer's screen, repeated printing, reading, skimming, and recoding may be required.
- Codes and code titles can be easily changed when codes are combined, divided for finer coding, or otherwise revised.
- Codes can be linked to form larger categories, clusters, and networks. The most complete programs even have the capacity to permit construction of graphics depicting the code structure.
- Some programs connect to software that facilitates making video clips part of the viewable and analyzable base. Photographs and other artifacts may be included in that base as well as with place-holders.
- Some programs encourage quantitative analysis of qualitative data since it is so easy to tabulate and export data to quantitative analysis programs.

Clearly computers save time and drudgery over old cut-and-paste methods. Computers make writing and rewriting so much easier. Easy recoding is a revelation to those who formerly considered keeping a barely adequate or poor code because of the labor required to change.

Software Features to Consider. Some programs require you to decide on how to chunk your data at the time of input and you are then limited to coding those chunks. What Weitzman and Miles (1995) call free-form coding allows you to select any portion of a text after input for coding, even to select overlapping sections to receive different codes. While most projects will benefit from such flexibility, for emergent studies, where the foci may change with the analysis, ability to free-form code can be very important.

Some programs allow multiple level codes so that one can combine codes hierarchically (for example, "encouragement" and "tutoring" as forms of "support") and display them in graphical forms. Some do this as a hierarchical tree such as one would construct to show the generations of a family. Like pattern noting (see p. 98), others can handle non-hierarchically related data with different arrows or lines to distinguish different relationships (for example: "together form," "are examples of," "results in," "follows," "belongs to"). These software, ATLAS/ti and QSR NUD•IST for example, facilitate the understanding of relationships in the data and thence the development of theory which may extend one's findings beyond the cases studied. Glesne and Peshkin (1992) note that use of graphical displays force organization and planning and encourage systematic work, all of which help provide an audit trail. But they also suggest that the ease of analysis may lead researchers to too readily adopt what the software puts before them, in essence letting the computer make the decision rather than adequately thinking it through themselves.

Most individuals who dismissed computers as merely high-priced page-turners have changed their minds as they became familiar with the Internet's ability to jump from place to relevant place through hypertext links. While many programs facilitate linking by telling you what is linked to something else so you can search and find the related material, some programs link them as does hypertext. These allow you to immediately pull up and view the linked text. Some, as you select text for coding, will search for and show similar material and, if desired, link it for coding. Clearly, such "page-turning" can be a real advantage in most analyses.

Many of the program authors or publishers have formed list-servs or have sites for description, demonstrations, updates, help and discussion on the Internet. Their availability may be another factor in program choice. Among the more complete and user-friendly personal computer programs, according to Weitzman and Miles (1995) analysis, are: QSR NUD•IST for Macintosh, DOS, Windows, and UNIX; Atlas/ti (Muhr, 1993), and Kwalitan (Peters and Wester, 1990) for DOS machines; HyperQual2 (Padilla, 1993) for the Macintosh. They analyze, and describe with sample screens, 24 programs in terms of their capabilities. Because at present (and probably for some time to come) each program has strengths and weaknesses, they suggest that choice of the most appropriate software program depends on the expected nature of the study.

✦ *The mechanical aspects of handling data can be substantial. This task is increasingly being taken over by specialized computer programs. While computer processing eases data management, its greatest contribution is to facilitate development of better coding structures. Ease of recording means the researcher is likely to work longer at getting a good fit. Further, some programs, through providing graphical portrayals of the code structure, give a perspective that facilitates theory building. Some programs can incorporate video clips as data and export and import tables and data for quantitative analysis.*

Fitting the Analysis Process to the Study

The process of analysis should be adapted to the nature of the study. The earlier descriptions of the qualitative process assume the researcher is engaged in an emergent study begun without a pre-structured goal. However, not all qualitative studies are of this nature. Some studies seek only to describe, leaving any generalization or extrapolation to their readers. Many case studies of unusual niches of society are of that type—for example, Whyte's (1955) and Liebow's (1967) famous studies of street corner societies. Presumably their intent is to make readers aware of such situations and to feel empathy for the persons involved. Although such studies may require selection and organization of the notes for presentation, complex coding is usually unnecessary. Arranging the material in time sequence or a simple sorting into topics for discussion may provide enough organization for writing the report.

In contrast to emergent studies, from the topic of a preplanned one, one can infer the codes and their interrelationships one would expect to find. This is true as well for studies that start with a clear focus even though the design may develop as work proceeds—for instance, an evaluation of a program of job training for the homeless. Miles and Huberman (1994) is an excellent description of this more structured process. In contrast to this chapter's "clean slate" approach, they suggest beginning with a provisional "start list" of codes devised prior to fieldwork. The list comes "from the conceptual framework, list of research questions, hypotheses, problem areas, and/or key variables that the researcher brings to the study" (p. 58). These initial codes are revised and supplemented for a better fit as data is gathered. Although some qualitative researchers would argue the start list might bias data collection, it may be favored by beginners with a need for some initial structure. In any event, good qualitative researchers will look for things outside the start list codes; those are sometimes the most important results of a study. (Goal-free evaluation, page 596 discusses this topic a bit further.)

Tips on Analysis

1. Underline or highlight notes for future ease of scanning and sorting.
2. Look for themes. Frequently, people's language gives clues. Look for repeating events, routines, and concepts.
3. Develop typologies and classification schemes of how people categorize other people and things.
4. Have professionals in your field unfamiliar with what you are studying read the notes and point out what they see as themes, commonalities, and points of significance.
5. Consult the literature of others who have studied the same phenomena and see what themes and explanations their work suggests. Include relevant fiction; removed from the constraints of scientific precision, such authors' intuitive insights may be suggestive of useful ideas.
6. Give priority to memoing over everything else. Sort your memos from time to time, and link them conceptually.
7. Begin early to set the goal of your study by trying various one-sentence titles, and by establishing files for the introductory and the final chapters of the report. Also set up a sensitivity file to remind you of the reactions, attitudes, and other concerns that might bias your interpretations.
8. There is a fine balance between sticking to a particular line of thinking and abandoning it to the lure of a seemingly more promising one. You don't want to get stuck in unproductive tracks, yet you need to follow them far enough to sense their potential. Strauss (1987) advises that you trust yourself, "your subliminal thought processes as well as your memory, [and the process of sorting

to bring back your older ideas] when the time is ripe. They all integrate better that way" (p. 211).

9. Remember, there is no one right way to handle your data; there are lots of "roads to Rome." Pick one that makes sense to you and is comfortable.

10. Once you have determined your core coding categories, those central to the support of your explanation, relate other categories to them. Examine what is left to see whether the core needs modifying or whether there is something significant that has been missed. After this process, discard categories that are totally or relatively unrelated.

11. Test each section for completeness, and whether it hangs together. This process can result in the need to recode old data or gather new. Beginning early reduces the extent of such work. Strauss (1987, p. 213) notes that writing the report is an excellent integrating mechanism and suggests beginning it even before integration is complete.

SUMMARY

The tips on analysis provide a summary of many important points in the chapter, but we might note several additional ones. Fieldwork accumulates data requiring processing to extract whatever it contains of value to the researcher. Coding and analysis are data reduction processes whereby the amount of data is winnowed out to those directly relevant to the study's focus. Their generalizable characteristics are then abstracted to form the study's report. Coding is the process of tagging the significant parts of the data with names indicating their importance to the study and their relation to its central focus. Coding is the obverse of a book's index; the index is prepared from the book's narrative whereas coding develops an index from which the researcher must inductively construct the report's narrative. Aids have been developed to help the novice researcher get coding started. Specialized computer software programs markedly facilitate analysis and, in so doing, contribute to more tightly defined, more directly relevant codes. Qualitative research, like any research, must eliminate explanations alternative to the one proposed in the study. Some common rival explanations, such as mortality and instrument decay, can cause problems for qualitative studies. In addition, since the researcher is the instrument, certain information-processing limitations need to be kept in mind.

A Look Ahead

In the next chapter, we will discuss the final step in the qualitative study, developing the report. In addition, we will examine some of the quality indicators of such research and how to ensure that our research meets these standards.

ADDITIONAL READING

See Miles and Huberman (1994) on matrices, graphics, causal analyses, and networks. See Strauss and Corbin (1990) on coding and analysis. Tesch's (1990) reviews of computer programs are dated but she describes 26 types of qualitative analysis. She describes four directions for qualitative research: (1) studying the characteristics of language, (2) discovering regularities of action, (3) determining meaning through understanding of text or action, and (4) discovering patterns through reflection.

For analysis processes closer to quantitative method, see the qualitative comparative analysis of Ragin (1987 and 1993), a halfway house between quantitative and qualitative. He uses the presence or absence of target items and Boolean algebra to build a case for causation. Griffin and Ragin (1994) introduce a special issue of *Sociological Methods and Research* devoted to further discussion of this and other "in-between" methods.

IMPORTANT TERMS

Audit trail

Coding

Contact summary report

Data reduction

Going Native

Instrument decay

Matrix

Mortality

APPLICATION PROBLEMS

1. How might you code this segment from a study of the onset of Alzheimer's disease? Would you code it differently if the study were of caregivers' reactions to the disease? If so, what?

> *Interviewer:* Tell me when you first noticed your wife's memory problems.
>
> *Dave:* She was a very bright lady who had a much better memory than mine. Then suddenly, as we left on a long trip, for which she had exhausted herself in preparation, her memory was gone! I just couldn't believe it. She seemed not to be able to remember what had happened yesterday. I was shocked! But then after we arrived at our destination, her disability disappeared as suddenly as it had come. So I didn't really think about it again until years later when she began to have trouble handling numbers.

2. Genvieve Le Conte is studying the effect of the availability of day care on families. Will day care allow the mother to become a wage earner or will she use the time for less economically helpful purposes? She starts interviewing every mother with an odd-number address in a low-income housing unit where a free day care program has been established and plans to reinterview them every month. About this time, a new and better housing unit opens across town. Some of her informants move to these new units. Since the new unit does not yet have day care, Genvieve decides to continue her study with the cases at the unit where day care is already established. Comment on this decision.

3. Frank Annanias has gathered data in a number of school libraries regarding its usage by the students. He has interviewed students in their classrooms and in the library itself. He has also recorded data about the make-up of the library, the way shelves are arranged, the training of the librarian, and many other factors. He is interested in the factors that

make for increased library usage. How would you suggest that he analyze these data.

4. Wharton (1996) interviewed 30 women from 17 real estate firms "to identify the factors that lead women to choose and keep this occupation" (p. 217). Following are excerpts from her interviews. If you were doing this study, how would you code these? Code each quotation in turn, adjusting your codes as you move through the set.

a. The flexible hours: thinking that I'd be able to play tennis and do some other things that I wanted to do during the day. In teaching I got really tired of being stuck in a classroom from 8:00 in the morning until 3:30.

b. I can schedule my home time and my time away from home. . . . Like in the summer, every Wednesday we [her family] go out on the boat. And I've had my weekend that I take off. I allow more time. I go to all the kids' games. I find that I can control my time better now: Once I learned that I had to say I had another appointment or commitment, then I could block off time.

c. Without a college education, I found myself limited in what I could do that would have income potential, let alone flexibility. Real estate did not require college, gave me unlimited potential depending on how hard I elected to work, allowed me to be my own boss while I could juggle my schedule around my family and basically take control of myself.

d. At that point in time, I thought the nicest thing about real estate would be that if I didn't like somebody, I just wouldn't have to work for them! I wouldn't have to worry about it!

e. Every transaction is a little bit different. I think the part that I like best is, that it is a dream and to see that face when that dream comes true, you know, when they get into the house. I just like real estate basically because I have that personality where I like helping people. I like to make money too [laughs], but I like helping people and it gives me gratification when you get into that house.

Compare your answers with those following the Application Exercise.

APPLICATION EXERCISE

Considering the questions you hope to investigate, the data that you plan to gather, and its likely key terms and important foci, can you begin to set up a possible set of codes that might help you get started on your data analysis? What problems of analysis do you expect at this point? Does one of the coding suggestions in this chapter seem to fit your problem better than another? Are there likely relationships that lend themselves to your developing tentative blank matrices that you will fill in later? Can you devise graphics depicting sequences or interrelationships of events that you anticipate encountering?

ANSWERS TO THE APPLICATION PROBLEMS

1. What is coded depends on what you consider significant for your study. Researchers coding this passage with different studies in mind would code it quite differently. Studies of the development of the symptoms of Alzheimer's might give it one or more of several codes such as "short-term memory loss recovered," or "short-term memory loss from stress," or "numeric aphasia," or "slow symptom appearance." All of these are potentially important characteristics mentioned in this segment of the interview, and might be relevant to the analysis. Note: The actual codes would be some abbreviation of the code titles that were easy for the researcher to remember—for example, for the above codes: *strec, ststress, numaph,* or *slosymp.*

Were the researcher studying caregivers' responses, the codings might be "denial of seriousness of symptom"; "I was shocked" (using the informants' words for a code title); or "slowness in observing onset." It is quite possible that the first and third of these might be merged if other examples showed little distinction between them. They might then be more appropriately titled to fit the whole body of excerpts.

2. This is an example of what is called mortality, individuals leaving the initial sample whose absence could well account for, or at least affect, the study's outcome. It is quite possible that the more ambitious ones who might be expected to take advantage of the day care center to find employment are the same ones who would be most likely to try to improve their lot by applying for new and better housing. Thus, those leaving the sample might be a selective group. Mortality could therefore be a rival explanation to a failure of the day care center to have an effect.

3. This problem is ideally suited to a matrix display. Frank should list the names of the schools, in order from most usage to least, down the left side of the page, one school to a row. Next he should draw as many columns as he has information items about the libraries, including those items on which he may have data for some but not all the schools. He should label the columns across the top with the items of information they are to contain and then proceed to fill in each row with the information he has on the school designated by that row.

Finally, he should scan down each column and look for consistent, gradual change. Some columns will be a jumble with no consistency, but those which change in a consistent direction from top to bottom are the factors associated with increased usage. Where there is only partial data in the column, he will want to go back to the schools with the missing data and fill it in and see if it completes the pattern. Once the data is complete for all the schools, he should add some new schools, especially ones for which the data might be expected to not support the generalizations developed from the initial set. He should then fill in the matrix for them on the same items as showed trends in the initial set and see if the generalizations hold, need to be modified, or are invalidated.

4. As in so many of these application questions, there is no single correct answer. Your answer may pick up some insight missed in the answers presented here which are intended more to show the process and illustrate rules than to present "right" answers.

a. It is desirable to use the language of the informants for codes where possible; such language usually captures the feeling tone more accurately. Therefore, in this instance, the first code might be *flexible hours.* Multiple codes capture other ideas in a statement and this one has at least a couple of ideas. Something reflecting freedom would capture the idea in the last sentence, perhaps *autonomy.* That code term captures the idea but is far removed from the informants' language! Maybe a later interview segment will provide a better name.

b. Here we have the idea of autonomy again, but this statement suggests there are different aspects to autonomy that may need to be separated out. Statement *a* suggests "freedom from confinement." Statement *b* adds "freedom to enjoy family," and "control of time." Perhaps autonomy is a good concept after all since it captures the different meanings, but it should be viewed as a major code with subcodes under it.

c. Here the job characteristics suggest two new codes: "low education requirement" and "earning potential." Apparently we can divide job characteristics into three groups, those set: (1) by the job requirements, like the education requirements, (2) jointly by the salesperson and the real estate organization, like earning potential; and (3) set by the salesperson, like their freedom to enjoy family. These might be considered superordinate categories for which you might write a memo to yourself describing this idea, then set it aside to see whether it is still helpful as coding proceeds.

In addition, this statement adds a new subcategory to autonomy: "own boss." Another subcategory, "autonomy—control of time," is a repeat of an earlier theme.

d. Still another new aspect of autonomy: "control over those worked with." This seems to apply to bosses, colleagues, and clients.

e. Even more new attractive facets of the job: "every transaction is different" and "gratification of helping people." The theme of earning potential repeats.

Note how in the above, we devise new codes, preferably in the informants' language, as new aspects are encountered. However, we try to relate them to what has gone before, and to see whether a deeper concept, in this instance autonomy, captures the essence of many of them. We then revise our coding scheme to reflect this, and go back and recode previously coded sections. Computer software makes recoding easier—a major advantage. Note, too, the attempt to find all the themes in each statement, and to multiply code the statement. Then, with computer software (or by sorting if they are on separate cards), gather all the statements with a common code to determine whether the name still fits or something better can be found. As you develop an encompassing explanation of what attracts and holds women as real estate sales persons, you will also further interrelate codes into a structure, often hierarchical with major codes and subcodes. You can see the beginnings of the hierarchical structure in the "autonomy" code above.

Incidentally, do you think these women really talked in nice, neat sentences as portrayed by Wharton (1996) in these quotations? Probably not, it seems likely Wharton cleaned them up while retaining the feel of the original statement. This common practice avoids embarrassing your informants when they see themselves in print.

CHAPTER 15

Conclusions, Reporting, and Quality Considerations in Qualitative Research

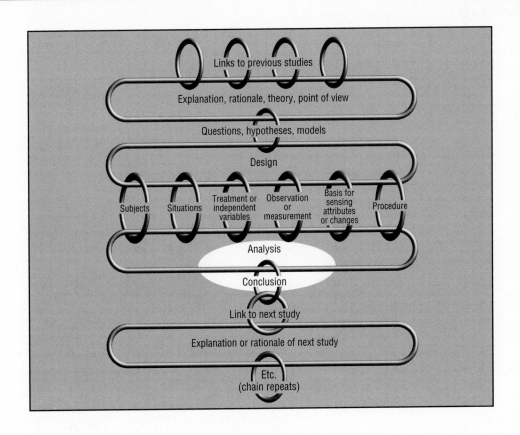

Links to previous studies

Explanation, rationale, theory, point of view

Questions, hypotheses, models

Design

Subjects | Situations | Treatment or independent variables | Observation or measurement | Basis for sensing attributes or changes | Procedure

Analysis

Conclusion

Link to next study

Explanation or rationale of next study

Etc.
(chain repeats)

329

Of all the roles, the role of interpreter, and gatherer of interpretation is central.

Stake, 1995, p. 99

How do I know what I think until I see it in writing?

Miles and Huberman, 1994, p. 299

OVERVIEW

Regardless of the research method used in the study, there is certain basic information readers need to understand the study, to determine whether to trust the evidence presented, to judge whether the evidence supports the findings, and to learn how the findings bear on whatever it is the study is addressing. Readers have certain additional expectations whenever the qualitative research approach is used. Therefore we can indicate what a report of a qualitative study should include. But what format and style of writing should be used? Just as in the analytic phase where qualitative researchers can follow many different paths, so qualitative reports can follow a variety of forms, especially if the study is mainly descriptive such as Whyte's *Street Corner Society*. If the study's finding is a generalization, however, it is usually presented deductively as a chain of reasoning, just as quantitative findings would be. Although some parts may not be in the usual order, all should be there.

What characteristics of the qualitative research report indicate its quality? Internal validity (LP) and external validity (GP) apply to qualitative as well as quantitative studies. We will discuss how they apply as well as other details of the hallmarks of qualitative research.

CHAPTER CONTENTS

Introduction

The line distinguishing analysis from the preparation of the report of findings is a thin one. As Glesne and Peshkin's (1992) student Gordon comments: "Another interesting discovery is that the writing process actually is an important part of the analysis. A lot of my insights . . . came through . . . writing. . . . Next time I will begin writing sooner" (p. 149). Up to this point, we have been writing analytic memos and other material, much of which will find itself, in one form or another, in the report. But writing the report raises questions like: "Am I sure of that?" "How consistently did this event actually follow that one?" "Maybe I'd better look at the data again!" Yet there comes a time, when, rather than working for our own amazement, our emphasis must shift to assembling the material for presentation to others.

Report Format and Organization

Whether a qualitative or quantitative study, the researcher must convince the reader that the evidence warrants the conclusion reached. When they present a case for a generality, qualitative researchers use a deductive format like the chain of reasoning as much as they would for quantitative research. In place of numbers and statistics at the "demonstrated result" link, they intermingle their interpretation with vignettes, quotations, and other examples to illustrate the points they are developing. The qualitative study of Hoffmann-Riem cited in Chapter 1 exemplifies such a study. Note that she starts by laying the groundwork for her method, and discusses her research questions (p. 13). These two steps lead to her description of sample and methods of data collection (pp. 13–14). Her analysis of what she found includes a number of interview quotations illustrating the points she is making about normalization (pp. 16 and 17). Her final section deals with her generalizations, tying together the material in the previous analytic section (p. 17). Thus, she has developed a chain of reasoning with some variation: question statement, followed by a section on research design, a large section on analysis and data presentation, and conclusions. Hoffmann-Riem lacks the literature review and the search for alternative explanations that are typical of quantitative studies, but she grounds the analysis and conclusions in well-chosen interview excerpts. Hers is not a great variation from the chain-of-reasoning format. Some qualitative studies adhere even more closely to the chain of reasoning, however, and include the links that she omitted.

Although many qualitative reports follow this pattern, especially for studies heavy on generalization rather than description, there really is no standard reporting format. The 1974 observation by Lofland that "qualitative researchers lack a public, shared and codified conception of how what they do is done and how what they report should be reformulated" (p. 101) is still true twenty years later. Whereas there are clear expectations that quantitative research will be reported as a chain of reasoning, qualitative research is variously reported. For instance, the researcher may prefer that the report reflect the inductive nature of the qualitative process such that the data's description gives rise to the generalization at the end rather than being anticipated in the problem statement. "A write-up can be organized any way that contributes to the reader's understanding of the case" (Stake, 1995, p. 122).

The standard report format of quantitative research has the advantage that the reader knows where to expect certain parts of the study and so may move directly to a part of special interest. Readers of qualitative studies, however, must encounter the study as presented since, not knowing where to expect what, it is difficult to intelligently skip around. And qualitative researchers do show considerable creativity in organizing and presenting their material. "The challenge is to combine theoretical elegance and credibility appropriately, . . . to combine propositional thinking of most conventional studies and more figurative thinking [of qualitative research]" (Miles and Huberman, 1994, p. 299).

Often qualitative research is written as a **case study.** Case studies have their origins in the medical and legal profession where, vividly and precisely conveying the characteristics of a single individual, situation, or problem, they are used to illuminate a generic problem. Case studies are bounded by a particular individual, situation, program, institution, time period, or set of events. Within those boundaries, whatever is the focus of attention is described within the perspective of the context surrounding it. Case studies are ideal for illustrating the complexity of causation. The case study is sometimes a step in a larger study where cases are combined in support of an overall explanation or theory that arises out of cross-site analysis.

In many instances, the time-bound nature of the material results in a time-line type of narration that organizes the presentation of a qualitative study. We can, however, make an informed choice if we consider different organization arrangements and their analytic implications. In addition to those discussed above, Hammersley and Atkinson (1983) suggest five for consideration:

- Natural history—tells the story of the investigation, how understanding unfolded, the history of progressive discovery.
- Chronology—focuses on the evolution over time, the development and unfolding of a character, or the situation.
- Narrowing or expanding of the focus—starts small and gradually increases in generality, like Russian doll sets with increasingly larger dolls enclosing one another, or follows the reverse—starting large and successively narrowing the focus.
- Separation of narration and analysis—provides a section for the narration and follows it with analysis. Note, however, that the narrative implicitly, by what it includes and what it excludes, is itself analytic,
- Thematic organization—(a) presents the culture or social structure in terms of sociological components such as kinship and marriage, political institutions, economic institutions, and so on; or (b) presents the insider's view in terms of how those studied organize and view themselves.

Similarly to generating a thematic organization, as mentioned in the last point, the researcher can develop an organization in the explanation and description. For this method, see Strauss (1987) who argues for clearly specifying all the theoretical elements and their connections and then adding such illustrative material as is needed to convey reality, enhance comprehension, and build trust.

Content to Include

While the reporting format may differ from study to study, there is certain information the reader needs to know in order to judge the study and determine whether to trust its findings. Generally we look for a number of elemental building blocks. Sometimes these are integrated into the body of the study report as they are in the Hoffmann-Riem study of Chapter 1. This is especially true of studies presenting a generalization. Other times, especially when it is a descriptive case study and such details would get in the way of the narration, they are put in a methodological appendix, as they are in Whyte's (1955) classic *Street Corner Society*. The report should include:

1. The topic, or what the study is about—the area of investigation, questions, hypotheses, theories or models around which the study is framed.
2. The circumstances—who did what, when, where, and how; how key concepts emerged; if problems in the field and in data collection occurred; and whether problems of bias or tendencies to "go native" interfered with the study.
3. The development of a rationale, explanation, or theory.
4. An indication of how this study stands on the shoulders of others and goes beyond any previous work in the area.
5. A complete meshing of facts and theory, in which choice of facts must demonstrate intelligence and internal consistency and honesty must shine through the description to show how well facts support theory.
6. A talented selection of vignettes, stories, and quotations that illustrate and interpenetrate the rationale, explanation, or theory, making the extent of the match clear. Good stories interweave chance and regularity in keeping with the theme that this is a unique conjoining of forces. Both chance and regular elements must be made clear.
7. Possible alternative explanations and, where possible, evidence for their elimination.
8. A reference concerning the intended audience with respect to both content and method. If the report is not addressed to a particular audience, reasons must be given.
9. A documentation of the researcher's background and how it affects data collection, analysis, and interpretation. (More often thought of as negative and potentially biasing, such disclosure can be quite positive, as when an individual has special knowledge and experience in an area).

Where and how each of these items is covered is the province of the writer, but all should be included.

Writers differ in how much of the interpretation they do for the reader. Stake (1995), noted for presenting large amounts of data for the readers to self-analyze, suggests seven sections:

1. Open the report with a selected vignette—"I want my readers immediately to start developing a vicarious experience, to get the feel of the place, time."
2. Describe the issues "that will help them understand the case" as well as who the researcher is and how the study developed.
3. Present a body of data "not unlike that they would make themselves if they had been there."
4. Develop a few key issues, "not for the purpose of generalizing . . . but for understanding the complexity."

5. Probe the issues with considerable experiential data and indications of how points were confirmed and attempts made to disconfirm them.
6. Summarize understandings about the case and how the generalizations have "changed conceptually or in level of confidence."
7. Use a closing vignette—"I like to close on an experiential note, reminding the reader this is just one person's encounter with a complex case." (Stake, 1995, p. 123)

"For a while we worry about having enough to say; before we know it, we have too much. . . . It is an effective author who tells what is needed and leaves the rest to the reader" (Stake, 1995, p. 121). Stake's own work exemplifies his recipe except that he tends to underweight the even-numbered points and to overweight the odd-numbered ones, especially number 3; he presents large chunks of data. The outline, however, is a good one when presentation and interpretation are balanced.

> ✦ *Many qualitative investigations are written up as case studies, which are ideal for describing complex causal systems "in living color."*
> ✦ *Inclusion of many illustrations from the data is a characteristic of these reports; it makes them highly readable. Empathy permits readers to "try on" the explanation to test its validity and estimate its generality.*

Style

Whereas academic writing is generally formal and uses the third person, qualitative research is often informal, and frequently uses the first person. For instance, Hoffmann-Riem's section describing her study is full of "I examined . . ." "I sought . . ." "I first showed . . ." and so on. Hammersley and Atkinson (1983) note that the use of "I" may be appropriate where these are personal choices, personal interpretations, or the result of personal characteristics or biases.

We face a number of perplexing problems in preparing materials to communicate with others. For example, what can we do about the grammatically flawed material we would like to quote from the data? Should the quotes be used just as they are? How many of us talk in complete sentences, especially when under stress or in a hurry? These problems may well convey the reality of the person or situation but be embarrassing to informants. By now, they seem more like friends than persons "out there to be studied." It is a matter of judgment, but many researchers prefer to clean up the quotes as much as possible while still making them sound as recorded. Incomplete sentences can include a description of a non-verbal gesture to show that it was finished.

How many examples are enough? The inclusion of "real" illustrative material is a strength of the qualitative path, which consists of "the concrete particulars of events," as Erickson (1986, p. 150) puts it. The narrative "persuades the reader that things were in the setting as the author claims . . . because the sense of immediate presence captures the reader's attention (ibid.). Strauss (1987), however, warns not to overload because the material is "colorful and interesting—at least to the author"; "data should function . . . in the service of . . . theory" (p. 220). It is a judgment call, but there is a strong tendency to include too many examples because they are particularly well phrased, clever, or "right on target." They become decorations instead of serving to connect evidence with claims.

Unfortunately, the authenticity so well achieved by such material can also cause loss of privacy and embarrassment to informants if "real illustrative material" leads to their identification. Unless there is reason to identify them, they should be protected not only by pseudonyms but also by the deletion of material that would uniquely identify them or their situation. Usually you can do this easily without losing the feel of reality. As extra protection, it sometimes is useful to have your colleagues try to identify locations and individuals and, if they are successful, query them for the clues they used to see whether such clues would be known to your audience.

Can you mix numbers and words? Why not? Some qualitative researchers believe that numbers have no place in their work. But the problem faced by the researcher is how best to convey the sense of the data. If that is best done with words alone, so be it. But if you are trying to convey relative sizes, frequencies, averages, and similar concepts, then numbers and appropriate statistics are as appropriate for qualitative research as for quantitative. They may play a minor part in the overall description, but there is no reason not to use them where they can be helpful.

Another dilemma is how to convey trustworthiness and be taken seriously yet write in such a way that one's audiences feel what one is describing "at the gut level." One of the appeals of qualitative methods is that they get behind the intellectual side of problems to the affective, to the emotional. Qualitative researchers often deal with problems they want the audience not just to "understand" but to "feel," to have empathy and concern. Rothman (1986) expresses the problem exceptionally well. She studied women who had undergone amniocentesis to learn whether they carried defective fetuses and whether to consider abortion. Worth reading in the original, here are some excerpts:

> The heart of the book is the women who got the bad news. I used their experience of grief and anguish for what it tells about motherhood, about pregnancy, and about a society that develops this kind of technology—and expects gratitude for it. . . . the challenge was to write it in such a way that *others* . . . would feel the emotion. . . . Yet I know that when we do that . . . we open ourselves to charges of being not scientific, of being journalistic, . . . sensational journalism. . . . It is a real bind. If I stick to the neat hypotheses . . . I don't get to . . . the core of the experience women face when they use amniocentesis. But when I share the horror at the core I risk being dismissed as not only not scholarly . . . but just plain hysterical, overemotional.
>
> When I wrote the chapter on their grief, I let it go . . . wrote like a person possessed. *I* cried—*you* cry. . . . At every level, from their most intimate relationships to the medical institutions, these women suffered. I wanted the whole society to know it, to know what we are doing (pp. 52–53).

Such research deeply involves the researcher in the data-gathering process, but then she must distance herself from it long enough to get it into perspective to write it up, change gears, reverse the process. The researcher "who fails to achieve distance will easily fall into the trap of recounting 'what happened' without imposing a coherent thematic or analytic framework" (Hammersley and Atkinson, 1983, p. 213). Having "made the strange familiar," she must now stand back to "make the familiar strange." Yet, to have the intended affective impact, she must keep that emotional edge. The title of Rothman's article says it well "Reflection: On Hard Work." No question, it was—and is.

✦ *Qualitative reports can be organized any way that contributes to the reader's understanding.*

✦ *They are often written in an informal style using first-person references.*

✦ *Quotations are often "cleaned up" enough to avoid embarrassing the informant but still retain a sense of authenticity.*

✦ *Informants are protected from identification by using pseudonyms and removing or changing identifying context.*

✦ *Inclusion of examples and direct quotations contribute to the success of qualitative methods, but can be overdone.*

✦ *Numbers and words can be mixed, numbers should be used wherever they can be helpful.*

✦ *In some studies, writers must balance the tone of their writing to achieve the emotional impact they seek without destroying the trust usually attributed to a scientific study.*

Quality Considerations in Qualitative Research

We have already discussed triangulation across persons, situations, and methods as we checked on data quality. Certainly, this is one kind of check we might expect careful researchers to use as they deem appropriate. In addition, we have considered the necessity of memoing regarding the potential for bias, and how we can be affected by what we are hearing or observing. Appropriate summarization of these, together with comments on parts of the observer's background and prior experiences that might affect him or her as the instrument of data collection, should also appear in any carefully crafted qualitative report.

Considering the wide variability in qualitative methods, however, can there be standards against which to judge quality? Some researchers suggest that, since one interpretation is as good as another, standards are impossible. "They hold the position that analysis is their . . . [unique] creation which can only be internally confirmed by them, and if they do a good job of communicating their reasoning, perhaps their results can be understood and even supported by others" (Ely, 1991, p. 164). Others take the stand that "there is a reasonable view of 'what happened' . . . and . . . we who render accounts of it can do so well or poorly." (Miles and Huberman, 1994, p. 277).

Qualitative inquiry, like all research, has real-world consequences. Therefore qualitative researchers cannot escape quality judgments whether or not they subscribe to standards. They can, however, suggest reasonable bases for making such judgments. Many have sought to fill this gap, adapting and supplementing criteria common to quantitative research to fit qualitative method and data (see, for example, Miles and Huberman, 1984 and 1994; Goetz and LeCompte, 1984; and Guba and Lincoln, 1989). In a 1995 speech to the American Educational Research Association, Yvonna Lincoln set forth Guba's and her parallel terms describing quantitative and qualitative research:

scientific rigor	trustworthiness
internal validity	credibility
external validity	transferability
reliability	dependability
objectivity	confirmability

Qualitative researchers are much more comfortable with the terms on the right than with those on the left. Ely (1991) and others argue that "while issues about reliability and validity apply equally to both quantitative and qualitative work, they are conceived of and arrived at in different ways. . . . For many of us, the use of different terms for 'validity and reliability' is a . . . liberating act" (p. 94). Reliability, validity, and objectivity are terms used in the quantitative approach which we will examine more closely in Chapter 18 in the section on quantitative method. As the Ely quotation indicates, however, they are not lacking but viewed differently in the qualitative approach.

Given that for studies concerned with a generalization, the criteria established in Chapters 7 through 9, which include internal validity (LP) and external validity (GP), are equally applicable to qualitative as well as quantitative approaches, let us examine the terms on the left in the above listing and see how they apply to qualitative research and the terms on the right. The last two on the list, reliability and objectivity, will be included in the discussion of internal validity.

Scientific Rigor and Trustworthiness

Guba (1982) set "scientific rigor" parallel with "trustworthiness," a good translation since, in building credibility with the audience **trustworthiness,** is essential for *any researcher!* Lofland (1995), in describing the seven characteristics of what he called analytic ethnography (ethnography dealing with generalizable propositions), usefully describes this as "exercising and exhibiting methodological concern and caution" (p. 50). It is amazing how much detail is omitted in the ordinary research report, quantitative or qualitative. Anyone trying to replicate a study will immediately become aware that there are gaping holes where the reader must trust that the researcher made reasonable decisions in carrying out the study. The audience credibility of qualitative work tends to be very high. The dense data that make the rationale and explanations come alive are much more effective than mere numbers in conveying the characteristics of situations and people and their interrelationships in detail. Some persons supporting the quantitative tradition may raise questions about the quality of data, sources of bias, and problems of causal inference, but their number is far fewer than it used to be as the qualitative approach is increasingly respected.

The section on research methods in most quantitative studies helps build this trust. However, such detail has not been and still is not a routine part of qualitative studies. Further, the emphasis in many of the most widely read descriptive qualitative studies seems to have been on fascinating storytelling. Methodological details would be considerably less fascinating; indeed, they might get in the way. Increasingly, however, there are calls for the inclusion of methods sections.

Lofland (1995) speaks of Sanjek's (1990) three "canons of ethnographic validity. . . . [1] . . . providing a chronological, intellectual and personal account of how the analysis evolved. . . . [2] with whom researchers interacted, in what sequence, and how. . . . [describing] the path connecting the ethnographer and informants . . . (p. 40), [3] the procedures of assembling and processing data and . . . practices of presenting data in the report" (p. 49).

Miles and Huberman (1994) argue that each study should compile an audit trail, such that another researcher can follow the path of the researcher through the data to determine whether the conclusions are reasonable. This is markedly facilitated by good documentation of actions—a methodological diary that records changes in design, steps in analysis, and so forth. They suggest that not only does such a record ease production of the methods section of the report, but both the act of recording and the presence of a record provide a perspective on past actions that will likely strengthen the study.

Predictably, the inclusion of such information will increasingly become a part of qualitative studies, whether in the main body, or as a methodological appendix. It shows the concern of the researcher with establishing the reader's trust and with meeting the expectations for rigor in a study contributing to scientific knowledge.

✦ *Including evidence of the researcher's attention to expected methodological concerns associated with rigorous work facilitates building credibility with the audience.*

Internal Validity (LP) in Qualitative Research

Internal validity (LP), you will recall, is composed of five judgments: explanation credibility, translation fidelity, demonstrated result, rival explanations eliminated, and credible result. Let us examine how each of these translates into the qualitative scene.

Explanation Credibility. Since "explanation credibility" is one of the main components of internal validity (LP), it is indeed reasonable that Guba & Lincoln independently settled on *credibility* as a term parallel to internal validity. Miles and Huberman (1994) added the term *plausibility*. Its meaning is the same for all research methods—namely, that whatever generalization is being advanced is plausible, or credible. Thus, there is no need for special interpretation for qualitative research.

Translation Fidelity. As a judgment of the research report, translation fidelity is the same for qualitative and for quantitative research; it is a judgment of whether the meanings of the terms used in presenting the proposed explanation, rationale, hypothesis, theory, and so forth, are congruent with the behaviors and other aspects of the study intended to represent them. It is the translation of these terms into the steps of the study in quantitative research which become the real concept definitions for that study. The researcher makes choices of persons and situations, of characteristics of the treatment, of measures or observations, of the basis for showing some effect, and of procedure that are congruent with the concepts involved in the study. The judgment of translation fidelity is a determination of whether the subjects and situation, the measures that were found or constructed, the available and feasible treatment, and so forth, were indeed congruent with the problem described at the outset.

In the case of qualitative research, however, the congruence of the terms used in the explanation, rationale, hypothesis, and theory, with the behaviors and aspects defining them in the data result from an inductive process. The judgment of congruence is whether the concepts and constructs used in the explanation or theory are a good match to the excerpts of data selected as supporting evidence. In some instances, the audiences may believe, for example, that the researcher has read too much into those excerpts or, perhaps, that more appropriate or accurate terms for the concepts and constructs should have been used. Although for both qualitative and quantitative research it is a matter of judging congruence, the congruity is created by deduction in quantitative method and by induction in qualitative.

For quantitative research, probably one of the biggest quality problems of translation fidelity is that of finding a test that measures what it is supposed to measure—a special problem for measures of cognitive processes and personality. It is avoided by qualitative methods in which the researcher relates the construct terms for cognitive processes or personality aspects directly to appropriately chosen excerpts describing those behaviors and the context in which they appear. For instance, Hoffmann-Riem relates the construct of "normalization" to excerpts like "It is your *own* child and that's it."

Translation fidelity also includes the matter of data quality, a concern easily apparent with quantitative measures that are expected to give consistent results. Such inconsistency problems are present in qualitative research as well. There are many kinds: for example, inconsistency from observation to observation—the behavior identified with a particular construct is not stable; inconsistency from one observer of the same phenomena to another—low interrater reliability; inconsistency between records of the same situation such as when the secretary's minutes differ from observation fieldnotes of those meetings. Lofland (1995), a major contributor to qualitative methodology, wraps together these problems using the terms *true content* and *factual trueness* for qualitative data. *Factual trueness* refers to "correctly representing the empirical facts of a situation or setting" and analytic trueness to "constructing analyses that accurately amalgamate the welter of empirical details into one or another kind of proposition" (p. 47).

"Factual trueness" includes bias, authenticity and such inconsistency as objectivity and stability. We have already addressed the problem of bias in discussions of memoing and analysis, where we noted that qualitative researchers do not pretend to be neutral, but seek to understand the directions of bias and take

them into account. Part of the judgment that audiences must make about translation fidelity is how successful researchers have been and how much audiences
must discount the findings where that success was questionable.

One check on the authenticity of a researcher's analyses is whether those in
the situation agree that the researcher has accurately portrayed them. Having the
report read by gatekeepers and the subjects of the study, a process referred to as
member checking, provides a useful review of both the data and their interpretations. Whyte (1993), for instance, went over the various parts of the report in detail with his informant, "Doc": "His criticisms were invaluable in my revision" (p.
341). This practice has its dangers, of course. Grant (1979), in a study of compe-
tency-based education, found the case study of one university so objectionable to
its administrators that he had to delete it from the final draft. Even when informants recognize the accuracy of the description, they may reject this view of
themselves and claim that it is inaccurate. Overall, most researchers have benefited from this process. Yin (1984) notes that one evaluator found the reviews by
five school districts of their case studies "so insightful and helpful, the investigators not only modified their original material but also printed the responses as
part of their book" (p. 138). This check is probably especially important if the
study is concerned more with how the informants perceive the situation than
with how the observer sees it.

A second check is that for **objectivity**—defined as consistency between the
way other observers would view the evidence and how the researcher did. The
consistency of two or more observers in describing the same phenomenon is also
referred to as **interrater reliability**. These concepts may be problematical for
some qualitative researchers. If they take the stand that their interpretations are
unique, then there is no reason to consider objectivity important and they can ignore it so long as their audiences accept the work. Many researchers who take this
stand provide no evidence in the study bearing on this topic; but for those who
agree that a situation may be poorly portrayed, comparing fieldnotes with a second observer may be helpful. It may highlight biases affecting one or the other
which can be dealt with in memos and further analyses. Sometimes it is helpful to
have the notes reviewed by one or more informants.

Lofland's analytic trueness also involves consistency in the sense of objectivity. We have to ask would others, using our coding schemes, classify the data the
same way as did the researcher and would they draw the same conclusions? **Peer
checking**—having others code samples of data and draw conclusions from it, and
comparing their work with that of the researcher—provides evidence of interrater
reliability of coding as well as of analysis.

Consistency in the sense of stability has two implications, whether the researcher has viewed the evidence consistently over time, and whether there is sufficient stability in the observed phenomena to render the data representative. With respect to the former, repeated close contact over time changes our perceptions of and
relations with those being observed. Whether researchers can remain consistent in
their fieldnoting and in use of terms to describe situations, or whether they change
terms and therefore meanings to describe the same kinds of situations over time, we
have to rely on them to report. With multiple observers or videotape records that
can be watched repeatedly, the extent of this problem can be determined.

Consistency of the phenomena observed over time, so that one has a representative sample of it, is a matter of prolonged engagement and deep familiarity with the phenomena being studied. Indeed, Lofland (1995) includes "deep familiarity" as one of his seven criteria identifying what he calls "analytic ethnography." Some experienced qualitative researchers are unhappy with the short periods of fieldwork in many current qualitative studies; the observation period does not seem sufficiently long for representativeness. But it is also true that natural change occurring over time can be a problem for a prolonged field study.

Clearly, we must consider a number of aspects of translation fidelity in judging qualitative studies.

Demonstrated Result. Qualitative studies provide evidence of a demonstrated result through the congruence of their data with their emergent grounded theories. The conformity of explanation with data is strengthened as relevant data intermingles with the theory presentation. On page 145, we noted four attributes contributing to a strongly demonstrated result: authenticity of the evidence, precedence of cause, presence of effect, and congruence of explanation and evidence. How do these relate to qualitative research?

- Authenticity of the evidence: If we trust the researcher, certainly the evidence is what she claims it to be. Member checking, noted above, adds to this trust. In addition, the detail in qualitative research reporting making it reminiscent of our own experiences helps make its authenticity apparent; it has a ring of reality that quantitative research often lacks.
- Precedence of cause: Unless the cause is under the researcher's control, precedence may be difficult to establish. Indeed, when the researcher delays analysis until after he has left the field, he may not always have attended to precedence of cause. This may be particularly true of relationships that become more important during analysis than they were perceived to be during observation. If he has gathered enough data, however, there may be enough instances in which he can infer precedence that he can satisfy this condition.
- Presence of effect and congruence with the explanation: The last two conditions of demonstrated result are part of the evidence gathered in the development of grounded theory. Theory is linked strongly to convincing instances where the relationship held. Since the researcher may fit the explanation to the particular circumstances in which she first noticed it, evidence of additional instances in which the relationship can be shown to hold is important. If the researcher notes the relationship after leaving the field, she may or may not have captured additional instances resulting either in a return to the field, or in the presentation of a weaker case than she might otherwise have obtained.

Rival Explanations Eliminated. We have already discussed the problem of eliminating rival explanations in Chapter 14 (and will do so further in Chapter 20). Since we have no control over what occurs in the field, elimination may be difficult and may depend on our "discounting" certain instances—postulating what would have occurred had not some contaminating alternative influence been at work.

Credible Result. The strength of the judgments of explanation credibility, translation fidelity, demonstrated result, and the elimination of rival explanations together with the congruence of the study to prior research all substantially contribute to the credibility of the result and the strength of internal validity (LP). As the above discussion indicates, there is no reason why qualitative studies cannot have strong internal validity.

- ✦ Internal validity and its five judgments apply to qualitative research concerned with linking evidence with a generalization.
- ✦ Explanation credibility *requires that the generalization being advanced is plausible and credible.*
- ✦ Translation fidelity *requires that the terms used for constructs or concepts match well the data excerpts intended to illustrate them. Problems can arise from inconsistency of the behavior identified with a construct over time, from inconsistency in the way an observer takes fieldnotes, from inconsistency in the records of two observers or recorders of the same phenomena, from inconsistency in the coding process by an individual coder over time, or the way different persons apply the codes (determined by peer checking). Member checking is a way of authenticating the data.*
- ✦ Demonstrated result *requires these judgments:*
  —*that the data is what it claims to be. Since the researcher is usually the data gathering "instrument," this is only a problem if he has not established our trust (but trust is enhanced by member checking).*
  —*that cause precedes effect. This can be a problem unless precedence is directly observed or there are enough instances where an inference of precedence is reasonable.*
  —*that there was an effect which is congruent with the explanation advanced for it. Data gathered in support of grounded theory provide evidence for this, particularly as it is bolstered by examples beyond those in which the theory was first developed.*
- ✦ Eliminating rival explanations *may be difficult if evidence to eliminate them is not gathered while still in the field.*
- ✦ Credible result *is attained when the above judgments are positive and the findings are consistent with previous related work.*

External Validity (GP) in Qualitative Research

Because of the small, and purposive instead of representative samples, evidence of external validity (GP) is often problematic with qualitative research. Indeed, many studies make no claim to it, and some discussion of standards or criteria do not even mention it.[1] With the exception of studies that do cross-site sampling, the local nature of the data and the limited, purposive sampling of most studies will provide little empirical evidence for it.

However, the rich and detailed illustrations of qualitative research allow readers to "try the examples on for size" to see whether they fit their experience and thus facilitate transfer to new situations. Some studies attain considerable transfer like, for example, Margaret Mead's (1928) *Coming of Age in Samoa,* one of the first widely read qualitative studies. In her Samoan data, she found insights with implications for raising children in America, which, although later challenged, had substantial impact at the time. Although not all researchers are explicit about the implications for generality, nearly all researchers hope their work will provide useful insights for other situations. If you did application exercise 7 of Chapter 8 (p. 184), you realize this goal is certainly true for Hoffmann-Riem. Generality always involves an inferential leap—a leap of faith. Although that leap is often not supported by empirical qualitative evidence, it is clear that many useful conceptualizations have been found in qualitative research. Often they have later been validated with quantitative or additional qualitative studies.

Increasingly, qualitative researchers are using multiple sites and multiple case studies to increase the generality of their findings. **Multi-site studies,** particularly where the additional sites are used to confirm and validate generalizations derived from a prior site, may develop considerable external validity (GP)—particularly if the additional sites are chosen randomly from an appropriate sampling frame. But, as Miles and Huberman (1984) point out, "If each site produces 200–300 pages of field notes and ancillary material, we are rapidly awash in waves of data" (p. 151). These data must be managed well or they will be poorly analyzed. Extending the methods of single-site analysis to those of cross-site analysis, Miles and Huberman note the necessity of standardizing the codes, reporting formats, and organizing data displays for each site. They then suggest a number of tools for managing and comparing the data across sites using matrix-type displays such as Table 14.1, where the data desired make up the vertical divisions and each row is a site (see also Ragin, 1987).

◆ *External validity (GP) involves a conceptual leap from the evidence of one study to similar situations. Although this leap occurs in all research, the limited and selective nature of qualitative evidence makes it more speculative.*

◆ *External validity is enhanced by multiple site and multiple case studies employing standardization of data gathering and analysis. Especially where sites are chosen by probability sampling methods, such studies can have strong external validity (GP), but are rare because qualitative research is so labor intensive.*

◆ *Although the empirical evidence is typically lacking, most qualitative researchers hope their findings will have generality. The examples through which the expla-*

---

[1]Miles and Huberman (1994), Stake (1995), and Lincoln and Guba (1985) are exceptions, the last using the term *transferability* to which the first added *fittingness.*

nation is usually presented facilitate readers' successful test of it against their own experience to show its generality.

Social Consequences—An Additional Criterion?

Researchers increasingly reflect about the **social consequences** of their research, the impact of their research on those studied or others who are affected in some way by the results. This concern seems to have become an especially important issue among qualitative researchers. Perhaps it results in part from the bond between researcher and informants that develops over the course of a study. Researchers often comment on how significantly their view of those they studied has changed, how they have become friends. Lincoln (1995) describes how some researchers helped their needy informants long after the study ended. At least one has shared royalties with them. Along with the increased interest in qualitative research has come increased concern with its impact on those researched, the researcher, and those audiences reached. Miles and Huberman (1994) use the terms *utilization/application/action orientation* to convey this. They note that Kvale (1989) calls it *pragmatic validity*—a good term in some respects, but one that does not capture the ethical concern for those researched and how the research affects them. Lincoln (1995) lists a whole series of such aspects: "Does it speak for those who do not have access to the corridors of knowledge or the venues of academic disciplines?" (p. 12). Does it empower them? Are they educated by it? "Have we 'come clean' about the advantages which accrue to us as knowledge 'producers'" (p. 17). She argues that "This dissolution of the hard boundaries between rigor and ethics . . . signals the new research is a relational research—a research grounded in the recognition and valuing of 'connectedness' between researcher and researched, and between knowledge elites and the societies and communities in which they live and labor" (p. 19). Many researchers are still content to do the research, publish it, and let it go at that. Undoubtedly there is much research for which this is quite appropriate. The question of social consequences, however, adds another criterion and highlights considerations that have not been taken into account by many researchers.

Hallmarks of Qualitative Research

A section on hallmarks is included for each of the research methods described in this book. A hallmark was the mark a guild used in the Middle Ages to signal a work of quality. These listings similarly indicate quality characteristics. Since the listing here is the first, it includes considerations that are universal to research, regardless of method; these are marked with an asterisk. [Some have been adapted from Stake (1995) or Miles and Huberman (1994).]

*1.   The author has special competence in the research method used as evidenced by previous work in the area, or by the details given about method in the body of the report's methodological appendix. Methodological detail is especially important, if the author lacks a prior reputation for competence.

*2. Unless it is strictly a descriptive report, the study includes a conceptual structure, explanation, rationale, or theory.

*3. The research questions are clear and the features of the design are congruent with them.

*4. Data were collected across the full range of situations, settings, persons, times, and artifacts, as would be anticipated by appropriate interpretation of the research questions and by whatever generality is claimed for them.

*5. If multiple field-workers and/or sites were involved, consistency was observed across researchers and sites in both data gathering and analysis.

*6. There is no reason to believe that the researcher has special biases that would distort his view of the phenomena; or, if he has such biases, he has described them so that they can be taken into account in judging the findings.

*7. The study was not sponsored in such a way as to create expectations regarding its outcomes.

*8. Observations appear to have been made in such a way that the behavior observed was not changed by the process of observation. If it was, allowances were made or the changes were documented.

*9. From the excerpts given in the report, recording of observations appears to reflect accurately what was observed.

10. The research examines the phenomena in context rather than concentrating on a part to the exclusion of aspects that might give a different perspective.

11. Observations and interpretations appear to have been triangulated and otherwise checked for deviation from standards of consistency in the sense of objectivity and stability appropriate to the point of view on qualitative research of the researcher. The role and point of view of the researcher are apparent. Negative evidence for findings was sought.

12. Where appropriate, observations seem to reflect how those that were studied understand or view the phenomena.

*13. The time required to complete the study was long enough to provide deep familiarity with the phenomena and provide a representative sample. It was not so long, however, that the phenomenon under investigation might have changed in such a way as to raise questions about the generality of the results.

*14. A thorough search for rival explanations has been made and they have either been eliminated or the remaining ones are discussed.

15. Checks were made of the consistency of coding across time and across data samples; similarly, checks were made to ensure that others can use the coding framework consistently with the way the researcher did and will arrive at the same conclusions. When shown to the informants (member checking), either the analyses are confirmed, the rejection can be reasonably explained, or their comments are incorporated into the report.

*16. The findings are internally consistent with the data that are presented—conclusions are neither over- nor underinterpreted and areas of uncertainty are identified. Findings are congruent with, connected to, or confirmatory of prior theory.

17. The report appropriately illustrates the complexity of the phenomenon with rich detail. It includes enough appropriate quotations and examples so that

the match between generalizations and observations can be judged. Abstractions are tied down with illustrations. Data summaries are displayed where appropriate. The study appropriately takes into account the influences of personalities, politics, and time on the phenomenon.

*18.   The generality of the findings is tested in other appropriate circumstances. The characteristics of the sample of persons, settings, processes, and so forth, are sufficiently fully described to permit adequate comparisons with other samples, and their limiting aspects are discussed.

*19.   Ethical concerns raised by the research have been allayed.

*20.   Enough methodological detail is presented that there is an adequate audit trail; another researcher can replicate the study by making reasonable inferences about procedures where there are gaps in the account.

SUMMARY

Descriptive qualitative studies are frequently written as case studies of an individual, group of persons, situation, event, or phenomenon. These, in particular, can be written in any format that adequately presents the case. Studies advancing a generalization, however, usually follow the chain-of-reasoning pattern; if not in exact order, at least all the pieces are present. A key to a good qualitative report is combining the explanation with sufficient (but not too many) informant quotations to give the feel of the individuals, the climate of the situation, and the atmosphere of events. Qualitative reports create pictures in the minds of the readers that are fleshed out with feelings as well as factual details—not only the "concrete particulars of events" but also the immediate presence of the individuals that are involved. This ability is one of the unique advantages of the qualitative method. The writing can be appropriately informal to achieve factual trueness to the original situation. Although words will carry the main message, there is every reason to combine them with numbers, charts, and graphs where these convey the meaning more appropriately. Although the format is not specified, we can clearly indicate what the report should include as indicated by the listing on pages 333.

Indicators of the quality of qualitative research deserving emphasis include not only such data-checking aspects as triangulation across persons, situations, or methods, but also appropriate self-disclosure of the background of data gatherers as well as reactions to persons and events during the study that might bias data choice and interpretation. In addition, both internal validity (LP) and external validity (GP) apply to qualitative as well as quantitative studies concerned with presenting a generalization.

A Look Ahead

With the next chapter, we move to a middle position on the quantitative-qualitative continuum to examine survey research methods. Surveys can emphasize qualitative or quantitative approaches. They very frequently use questionnaires, which therefore are a focus of the chapter. Learning how to ask questions is equally important to interviewing, however. Thus, as we might expect of a halfway point on the continuum, much of what we will cover in the chapter has relevance for qualitative research.

IMPORTANT TERMS

Case study
Interrater reliability
Member checking
Multi-site studies

Objectivity
Peer checking
Social consequences
Trustworthiness

ADDITIONAL READING

All of the many general works cited at the end of Additional Reading for Chapter 11 have something to say on writing the report. In addition, some researchers like Firestone (1993), for example, have examined the kinds of generality possible with qualitative research. Wolcott (1995)—chatty and helpful.

APPLICATION PROBLEMS

1. In her study, Margaret Johnson concluded from her interviews that in contrast with men, women talked about the difficulty of handling both their work on the job and that at home as though it were her responsibility to handle both. Using the first person throughout, she wrote the research report as a narrative, describing how she came to interview these particular people, the nature of the interviews, and so forth. The report concluded with the generalization that women have not yet internalized men's conception of the workplace. Comment on the nature of her report.

2. Describe how well you think the Hoffmann-Riem study in Chapter 1 meets the quality standards of this chapter.

APPLICATION EXERCISE

In writing up your proposed study, what format seems to be most appropriate? A sequential narration of what occurred? A chain of reasoning? Another format? What data quality problems do you anticipate and what can you do about them?

ANSWERS TO THE APPLICATION PROBLEMS

1. In one sense, she can write the report anyway she wants to, because there is no standard format. In another sense, if she wishes to make acceptance of the conclusion of her study the focus of her writing, she would do well to write it as a chain of reasoning and reserve the use of the first person for those instances where she is expressing her opinion.

2. Christa Hoffmann-Riem's presentation of the research is very workman-like and inspires confidence in her findings; trustworthiness as well as credibility with the audience are not problems. She provides sufficient description of the way she did the study that the reader can follow the general outline and another researcher could probably replicate it. But that assumes such a researcher has the interviewing skills of Hoffmann-Riem who, without a set of preinterview-developed questions, appears to have been able to draw the information she wanted from the parents.

The internal validity (LP) and external validity (GP) of the study were already analyzed in, respectively, application problem 6 of Chapter 7 (p. 157) and application problem 7 of Chapter 8 (p. 184). If you did not yet work on those problems, do them

now. Next read the answers to the problems and then the next paragraphs.

Two of the additional characteristics we would expect to find in a solid qualitative study are evidence of data checking and of self-disclosure. With regard to checking the data for validity, we have no indication of any kind of triangulation—person, situation, or method. There is no evidence that she used other than interviews as data; for instance, she did not observe the parents and children in their homes. She is the sole data gatherer. Although this is not atypical, having another person observe or interview can provide a basis for determining whether there may be a bias affecting the inductive reasoning.

Do we need triangulation in this instance? Is there any reason to doubt the validity of the parent interviews? Should we be concerned that what is actually happening is different from what parents say it is? Would parents have anything to gain by such statements? Respondents generally try to be cooperative and give the interviewer what is being sought; they want the interviewers to think well of them and want to please them. Did Hoffmann-Riem cue the parents to the answers she sought? Probably not, if we believe her interview procedure which starts broadly. If all the normalization statements came at the end when she was narrowing in on what interested her, this might be true, but we are given the impression they just tumbled out in the interview.

If we sensed that her findings were counterintuitive, we might press such concerns further. Where findings confirm what seems to make good sense, however, it seems petty to raise such considerations. This is part of what makes up explanation credibility—and her explanation is highly credible. It would seem much less petty to raise such concerns were her findings counterintuitive.

One can certainly question whether "raising the bar" and pressing such concerns is appropriate. Sometimes, it is precisely because someone questioned what nobody else did that a new significant finding comes about. Since far fewer counterintuitive findings turn out to be true than intuitively

true ones, this can be a very expensive way to spend your energy. You need either to be sharp enough or lucky enough to question the right findings.

With respect to self-disclosure, we would look for some background to indicate possible biases. Since she is the main data-collecting instrument, were there any personal reactions during the study that might have affected her interpretation of events? She gives no such indication. Further, she does not comment on why this particular problem intrigued her, so we don't know if there are any prior dispositions that might have influenced her. Some comments on this point would have allayed such concerns. Summarily, the report does not offer any clues that suggest that bias is a problem, or that others might have used an alternative strategy for the interviews or analyzed or interpreted the data differently. Again this kind of question might be pursued further if the findings did not make such good sense.

The Continuum of Research Methods: Qualitative–Quantitative Middle

This section could have been the largest of the book, describing the variety of ways researchers select from the continuum of methods those aspects that best fit and then adapt them for their particular study. Instead, survey research has been chosen as representative of such selection and adaptation because, located midway on the continuum, it uses aspects of qualitative and quantitative methods as appropriate. Furthermore, it adds to our inventory of useful research skills the extensive knowledge of questionnaire development and use. Sample surveys draw upon the sampling techniques of Chapter 8, the interview expertise discussed in Chapter 13, and the question formats of measurement in Chapter 18.

CHAPTER 16

Survey Research and Questionnaires

> The validity of survey data depends on persuading a scientifically selected group of people to provide accurate and detailed information about themselves, their opinions and expectations, their sense of well-being, their activities, their family finances and educational background—all to a complete stranger.
>
> Charles F. Cannell, *1985, Overview: Response Bias and Interview Variability in Surveys*

OVERVIEW

Survey researchers gather data from a carefully selected sample of a population, all of whom are considered informants, and extrapolate their responses to the population. Surveys may be either qualitative, as when interviews or open-ended questionnaires are used, or quantitative, as when closed-end or multiple-choice questions or both are used. For the same resources, we can collect considerably more information about a target population from a representative sample than we could afford to collect from the entire population, as in a census. This trade-off is faced by researchers in adjusting sample size, and in choosing between depth vs. breadth of data gathering to stay within available resources.

We will explore survey research by examining topics common to interviews and questionnaires: the purposes of surveys and the selection of the sample. Then, building on the discussion of interviews in Chapter 13, we explore the kind of structured interviewing used in surveys and some of the advantages of computer-assisted telephone interviewing (CATI). Next, we visit the formulation of questions with special reference to the questionnaire—but with applicability to the interview as well. We then seek solutions to the problems raised by nonrespondents, response sets, and sensitive topics. Finally, we will compare with respect to a number of characteristics, four methods of data collection: individual interview, group interview, telephone interview, and mailed questionnaire.

CHAPTER CONTENTS

Introduction

The practical effect of surveys on your daily life is amazing: They influence what television programs you watch and therefore what is scheduled, what foods show up on the grocer's shelves and how they will be packaged, what main and side effects a drug or ameliorative practice has had and whether its therapeutic value exceeds costs, and even which potential jurors lawyers should accept or reject. Surveys guide politics: what election campaign strategy your representative will use and how she will counter her opponent's tactics. Preelection polls help voters identify front runners, and potential financial supporters rush to jump on those candidates' bandwagons. While highly sophisticated interviewing and/or instrumentation is often involved, basically surveys involve getting reactions to questions or other stimuli from a representative sample of a target group, to which the researcher expects to generalize. The researcher is usually interested in the commonality of their responses, how and how much their responses differ—their variability, how closely some responses are related to others—and how responses vary with certain demographic variables or with measures of social, political, or psychological variables. The response record may be in the form of an interviewer's account of an interview, self-report answers by the respondent to multiple choice or open-end questions, an audio or videotape recording of an interview, an immediate coding as the response is given on a interviewer form (called an interview schedule) or some combination of these.

Survey Purposes and Planning

Survey researchers are typically more target oriented than most qualitative method researchers, who often enter a situation with only a hunch about what is significant. Surveys range, however, from only slightly more targeted (you interview a school social worker to learn her responsibilities) to highly targeted (you ask how often during each day she meets with parents). The angle of the questions, wide or narrow, depends on what the researcher wants to explore: general values implied by how time is typically spent on a case, or a focused hypothesis (female social workers are more responsive to parental requests than are male social workers). **Sample surveys** may determine the incidence of a characteristic in a target group (the extent of child abuse) and its distribution (frequency among racial groups or socioeconomic classes), including its relationship to other variables (parents abused as children).

Because surveys are targeted, they usually require more preplanning than emergent qualitative studies. Such planning is especially important for questionnaire studies which, in addition to the researcher's own time, involve out-of-pocket expenses for duplication and distribution. Plans must include the sample, the instrument, the method of gathering data, and preliminary plans for analysis.

Sampling

A distinguishing characteristic of survey research is the care used in selecting the sample of respondents. Cluster and quota sampling, discussed in Chapter 8, are an outgrowth of survey methodology.

Sampling Plans. As noted in Chapter 8, the first step in choosing a sample is determining precisely who is included in the population of interest. In trying to predict a town council election, it would seem evident that the population is all persons eligible to vote. Not so! It is those who actually will vote! Persons who have never voted in these elections, who can't get to the polls, or who are too disaffected to vote in this election will not help the researcher to predict the outcome. Precise definition of the population is critical to the sample choice.

The stereotype of a sample survey is that it typically picks a random sample of the population. The sample is actually taken from the sampling frame, which is an enumeration of the population or the part of it that we are sampling. (Where the frame is incomplete—for example, the telephone directory omits individuals too poor to have a phone—this will be reflected in the sample.) Random sampling is often used with questionnaires, although systematic sampling (say, taking every tenth name) is more common when a sample of a mailing list is taken. Because stratified sampling costs little more if the information on the stratifying variable is available, random samples are often stratified. Stratified sampling requires accurate foreknowledge of the correct classification of each sampling unit so that units can be accurately assigned to a stratum.

Quota sampling is common in commercial surveys. Savings in cost and time accrue when the initial questions serve to classify respondents into quotas so that members of full quotas can be passed over for those in unfilled ones. Cluster sampling markedly reduces travel for face-to-face interviewing and is usually part of a multistage sampling plan (see p. 170).

Sampling to Observe Changes Over Time. Because results can be available while the question is still of interest and because they are less expensive, most studies that examine change over time are **cross-sectional studies.** These, for instance, compare older respondents with younger ones in a cross-section sample of the target population. Inferences from such samples are subject to important alternative interpretations, however. Older individuals are a product of the events and context they have experienced. Therefore, differences between age groups are often better traced to the age group's developmental history—for example, a flu epidemic or economic depression. Equally important, selection may change the composition of the older group—for example, college satisfaction is overestimated by comparing seniors with freshmen; it omits the pre-senior dissatisfied dropouts. Thus we must view conclusions from cross-sectional studies with caution.

Longitudinal studies, which take samples over time, solve some of these problems but, depending on the particular sampling process, may incur others. Several kinds of longitudinal patterns—trend, cohort, and panel—are graphically depicted in Figure 16.1.

A **trend study** follows the changes in a particular population. If we are interested in following the change in attitude toward involving college students in making educational policy, we might sample students at three-year intervals. Not only will we be taking new samples, but the population itself will be changing over this time. Therefore observed changes may also be due to sampling variability in taking a new sample or to persons leaving or entering the population.

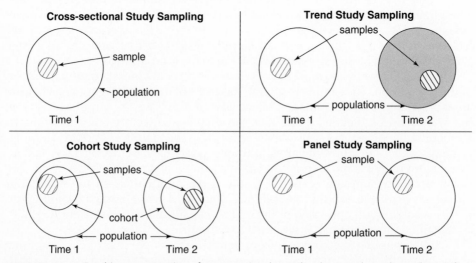

FIGURE 16.1 Graphic representation of cross-sectional, trend, cohort, and panel sampling. Differences in shading from time 1 to time 2 indicate a new sample, or changed population.

A **cohort study** keeps the population constant but takes new samples from it. The cohort serves as the sampling frame but is usually a preformed sample of a population, as is shown by the white circle in Figure 16.1. For example, the cohort might be the graduating class of 2001, which we follow as they go through college, taking new samples of that class to determine their attitude toward being involved in policy making. A rival explanation of observed changes is mortality (see p. 317), the selective drop-out of cohort members.

A **panel sample** is a cohort study in which the sample is retained throughout the study and is queried two or more times. It gives a stable basis for comparison provided the panel stays relatively intact during the study. If the likelihood of member loss is great, we would make the panel larger than needed at the outset to compensate. Alternatively, we can try to find satisfactory replacements. Because "movers" and "stayers" tend to differ on certain characteristics, if these are related to what we are studying, exact replacement may prove difficult. Again mortality may provide a rival explanation for observed changes. Because of the problem of retaining an intact group over time, panel studies tend to be of short duration.

The retesting or reobservation that occurs with panels, however, can have effects of its own. Having experienced the instrument or interview once, individuals have time to consider their answers for the next data collection. This rival explanation for observed changes is known as "testing." We meet it again in experimentation, p. 512. Further, knowing that they are panel members may create expectations. For example, Terman's study of talent identified a panel of child geniuses. The identification itself probably created expectations that may have been self-fulfilling and changed the nature of the results (Terman et al., 1926; Cox, 1926; Burks, Jensen, and Terman, 1930; Terman and Oden, 1947, 1959).

A panel study enables us to see the changes taking place in individuals over time. Further, since the same individuals are remeasured, it is sensitive to smaller changes than comparably sized random samples would be. Further, panel studies have the advantage of noting specifically who is changing. We can then track back to the events, the characteristics of the individuals, and the situations that might have contributed to the change. Thus, there are advantages and disadvantages to each kind of study. Table 16.1 on page 356 summarizes some of these.

Sample Size. The most common sampling question is, "How big a sample must I have?" The precise answer to this question is given on pages 481–483. Summarily, additional cases increase accuracy considerably for small samples, but much bigger increases in sample size are required for proportionally comparable increases in accuracy in large samples. A useful rule is that halving the error requires a quadrupling of cases. For instance, suppose there is a question to which the population responds 50 percent "yes" and 50 percent "no." If 100 cases will give a 10 percent error, an additional 300 cases (total 400) cuts it to a 5 percent error. But an additional 1,200 cases (1,600 total) are required to cut it in half again! Keep in

TABLE 16.1 *Advantages and Disadvantages of Survey Designs for Studying Changes Over Time*

	Description	Advantages	Disadvantages
Cross-sectional design	Data collected at one point in time from groups different in age and/or experience	Considerable savings in time and money	Researchers cannot be certain that results are the same as those obtained from longitudinal data
Longitudinal trend study	Samples taken twice or more over time from the population that is allowed to change in the interim	No need to keep track of a group over time; no problem with dropouts	Changes may be caused by differences in persons sampled rather than changes in population, and/or by persons entering and leaving the population
Longitudinal cohort study	Population is kept constant with new samples taken twice or more over time	Changes in group can be traced; events affecting group are known and can be linked to changes	Changes may result from dropouts rather than changes in population; researchers must keep track of all in cohort
Longitudinal panel study	Selected group of individuals measured two or more times; sample kept constant throughout study	More sensitive to changes than random samples of same size; since reasons for dropouts are known, changes in group can be adjusted for; changes can be traced to individuals and therefore possibly to their causes	Panel is difficult to keep intact over long periods of time; researchers must keep track of all in panel; dropouts may be hard to replace; repeated testing or observation may create self-fulfilling expectations and/or change the nature of measured or observed behavior

mind that unless the population is small and the sample is a substantial part of it (10 percent or more), the *population size is not an important variable.*[1]

[1]For example, suppose you have a small freight train of coal (the population) only five cars long. Since small chunks burn faster than large ones, you need to know the average chunk size in order to determine how long that load will satisfy the requirements of a particular power plant. You can estimate the average chunk size from a sample taken from each of the cars, or, if we assume the cars are all the same, from a sample of just a couple of cars. But that sampling process would be exactly the same if the train (the population) were 50 cars, 1,000 cars, or a train as long as from the earth to the moon. The estimate from a couple of cars would be just as valid and just as accurate for the larger populations as it was for the five car train. *The size of the population does not matter.* You might argue that with a longer train, you would want a more accurate estimate; fine, *then* increase your sample size *to increase accuracy.* You increase the sample size to increase the accuracy of the estimate for the population, *not* because the population is any larger.

Sampling, in place of a census, of course, is based on certain assumptions: All the cars must be just as they came from the mine's coal crusher—the variability of chunk size must be uniform throughout (that is, the unit sampled is the same throughout), and the chunks (sampling units) must be "well mixed," the variability is uniform across the cars.

Of course, because in reality people tend to congregate with others like themselves, many human samples are "lumpy" and if the variables on which they congregate relate to what we are studying may affect our results. However, if we know the variables around which these "lumps" occur, we can get data on the "lumping" (stratifying) variables. Then we can use stratification to ensure that the "lumps" are represented appropriately. *The size of the population still doesn't matter.*

Survey Plan Guide

Following is a typical sample survey plan. The sequence of steps can be used as a guide to doing such a study.

1. Determine the purpose of the survey; try to state it in about 25 words. Check it with colleagues and your survey sponsor, if any. For some problem areas it is worth checking with typical informants from the target population for potential hidden problems.

2. Develop a sampling plan appropriate for the survey's purpose. Determine its feasibility and the availability of required information (for example, names for sampling frame, completeness of stratifying information for all individuals, cost of acquiring, and so forth).

3. Form a representative group from the target population. Describe the purpose of the survey and get their help in formulating relevant questions. Try out questions of your own and get the group's reactions; move from broad to more specific questions. Refine questions with them until there is only one interpretation—the one you intend. (See discussion of focus groups, p. 295)

4. Develop your instrument, interview, or questionnaire. Get feedback from colleagues and your survey sponsor, if any. Do a pilot-test with a small sample of the target group using a feedback technique to determine if they interpreted questions as intended, had appropriate knowledge, and, as far as possible, answered honestly. Develop a preliminary coding scheme and analysis plan and make sure that they are congruent with each other and with your goal. Reformulate the instrument and repilot as necessary. For quantitative studies, determine the needed sample size from the pilot data.

5. When using questionnaires, prenotify, then mail first class with stamped return envelopes (preferable to return postage–guaranteed envelopes). Mail reminder postcards one week later so they will arrive while questionnaires are still on the respondents' desks. For interviews, prenotify and then phone to confirm appointment. Follow up nonrespondents with second mailings, postcards, and callbacks as appropriate. Do callbacks in the early evenings or on Saturday mornings to reach weekday workers.

6. Record time of questionnaire receipt. Analyze responses in order of receipt to determine if there is a pattern; since late mailers may be like nonrespondents, this may indicate direction of nonresponse bias. Contact questionnaire nonrespondents by phone to ask the most important questions.

7. Consider interviews with key informants in the target group to determine reactions that should be taken into account in interpretation.

8. Compile, analyze, and interpret responses with computer software tools.

✦ *Surveys, except for those using entirely spontaneous interviews, require advance planning to determine how data will be collected, to pilot the questions for the interview or questionnaire, and to determine the sample.*

✦ *Studies tracking changes over time may use cross-sectional, trend, cohort, or panel sampling.*

✦ Cross-sectional studies estimate such things as the effect of growth, experience, or the passage of time by comparing younger with older persons at a given point in time in a cross-section of the population. They are the least expensive and quickest to do because the researcher does not have to wait to collect the data.

✦ Trend studies collect data from different samples of a population over time; the population is allowed to change as it naturally would.

✦ Cohort studies collect data from different samples of an identified group of individuals over time; that is, the sampling frame is kept constant.

✦ Panel studies collect data from the same selected sample of individuals over time.

Interviews

Survey researchers can rarely afford the open-ended, unstructured interviewing described in the first column of Table 13.1 on page 287. To reduce expensive interviewing time, phenomena are accessed rapidly and directly with the partially to totally structured formats described in the other four columns. Table 13.2, comparing structured with unstructured interviews, shows the reduced professional time required by the former.

There is extensive literature on the techniques of interviewing, some of which borrows from counseling and clinical techniques. Organizations that commercially engage in surveys have their own manuals for training their interviewers. (Survey Research Center, 1976, explains well how it conducts its surveys.) Various approaches to interviewing have been proposed, each with its own advantages.

The material in Chapter 13 is directly relevant to surveys: the uses of interviews, the different styles of interview (the nondirective approach is especially important for interviewers to master), and some of the factors affecting interviews. Interviews are particularly useful in tracing causes, especially when these lie in the personal meanings of a common experience—what was significant to the respondent (Merton, Fiske, and Kendall, 1956). For example, if literature was used to stimulate voting in an experiment, an interviewer might find what aspects of the literature were significant factors, whether these factors were effective, with what groups they appeared to be effective, and what underlying mechanisms were driving voting behavior.

Tips on Face-to-Face Interviewing[2]

These tips on survey interviewing supplement the tips on general interviewing (pp. 298):

1. Don't ask, "May I come in?" Simply assume that the interview will take place: "I would like to come in and talk with you about . . ."

2. Answer questions about the survey as if the person were interested and friendly. Comment in a nonspecific way: "We are interested in how people feel about . . ." which does not bias the interview.

---

[2]Portions of this discussion are based on *Interviewer's Manual,* rev. ed. Ann Arbor, MI: Survey Research Center, Institute for Social Research, 1976.

3. Have copies of clippings that show the value of past studies as an example of the worth of the interview.
4. Collect the data uniformly. Ask questions exactly as they are worded. If there is an interview form, follow the specified order. Read slowly and repeat questions that are misunderstood.
5. Record the responses verbatim, using abbreviations to get them down. Record probes and interviewer comments in parentheses. Write on the form as the respondent talks. Figure 16.2 (p. 360) shows a sample interview form.

Computer-Assisted Telephone Interviewing

Unique to surveys is **computer-assisted telephone interviewing (CATI),** which automates as many aspects as possible. Once area codes and local telephone number prefixes of the sample have been selected, random-digit dialing generates and dials the last four digits. The computer keeps track of whether the number responds. If it does not, the computer files it for callback at another time of day and, by analyzing the accumulated information, determines the most appropriate time to reach individuals in that community. Although random-digit dialing reaches even unlisted numbers, unless a system to target residences (see, for example, Waksberg, 1978) is used, it also reaches many businesses. Once a potential respondent is reached, the interviewer's script is displayed on the computer screen, and the interviewer is led through the interview by the computer.

Interviews usually begin with questions to determine whether the respondent is part of the target sample or to ask for the person in the household who qualifies. The interviewer enters responses into the computer, which determines whether to break off the interview because the demographics do not fit quotas needed to fill the sampling plan or whether to continue. To personalize the interview, the computer can insert the respondent's name or other demographic information into appropriate points in the script. It can recall previous answers and point out inconsistencies so that the interviewer can probe for reasons. The computer can tell the interviewer he has made a clerical error in case the coding does not fit any of the acceptable codes for a given item. An important time and error saver is the computer's capacity to branch the interview to relevant questions, skipping whole blocks judged inappropriate on the basis of previous responses. Light pens or touch screens can eliminate the need for keyboard skills to enter data. Close control of the interviewing process (and useful research) is possible because all the interviewers are typically in the same location and the supervisor can easily monitor and correct errors. Lavrakas (1995) argues that these quality control measures recommend CATI "as the preferred [survey] . . . mode" (p. 5) if the required data can be so gathered.

Telephone interviews tend to elicit shorter responses than face-to-face encounters, but total length does not seem to be shorter. With shorter responses and no transportation time between interviews, the number of interviews per worker-hour is much higher than with face-to-face interviews. Of course, nonverbal cues that add meaning are lost, and maintaining rapport may require additional interviewer responsiveness. In exchange, the impersonal aspect also permits a kind of anonymity that allows sensitive issues to be handled with less embarrassment.

(CARD C2, ORANGE) Some people are primarily concerned with doing everything possible to protect the legal rights of those accused of committing crimes. Others feel that it is more important to stop criminal activity even at the risk of reducing the rights of the accused.

(RQ-What #on scale shows how feel?)

Throw them all in jail!

Protect Rights of Accused						Stop Crime Regardless of Rights of Accused
1	2	3	4	5	6	7

(INTERVIEWER RECORD NUMBER)

C2a. Where would you place yourself on this scale, or haven't you thought much about this?　　　a. ___4___

    ┌─────────────────────────┐
    │ 0. HAVEN'T THOUGHT MUCH │   ┌──────────┐   *I don't know any*
    └─────────────────────────┘   │ 8. DK   │   *policemen (what*
         TURN TO P. 10, C3   └──────────┘   *think? most*
                                                     policemen)
C2b. Where would you place most policemen?　　　b. 6 or ⑦ ←
                                                     (which closest)
    ┌──────────┐
    │ 8. DK   │
    └──────────┘

C2c. Where would you place most people who have gone to college? *My generation or now? (most people)*　　　c. ___2___

    ┌──────────┐
    │ 8. DK   │
    └──────────┘

C2d. Where would you place most people who have not gone to college?　　　d. ___—___

                              (R didn't
    ┌──────────┐   *want to be*
    │ 8.✗DK   │   *grouped)*
    └──────────┘

C2e. Where would you place most people about your age?　　　e. ___4___

    ┌──────────┐   *About where*
    │ 8. DK   │   *I am*
    └──────────┘

C2f. Where would you place most people your parents' age?　　　f. ___6___

    ┌──────────┐   *They're all*
    │ 8. DK   │   *squares (where place*
    └──────────┘   *on scale?)*

(I had to keep reminding R about the scale.)

FIGURE 16.2 A completed page from an interview form. (Survey Research Center, *The Interviewer's Manual*, Revised Edition, Copyright © 1976 by the Institute for Social Research, The University of Michigan, Ann Arbor, MI. Reprinted with permission.)

Completely automated surveys have also been developed with precoded lead-ins and questions. Respondents answer by pressing telephone buttons: "Press 1, 2, 3, 4, and up to 5 to indicate how strongly you agree with this statement." The computer responds to such responses as if an interviewer had keyed them in, but the respondent has actually done so. This method does away with the trained interviewer, one of the most costly parts of the process. However, it introduces other selective factors such as who is willing to respond to prerecorded queries.

As software becomes more sophisticated and equipment costs decrease, automated telephone surveys may become ever more prevalent. How much resistance will they encounter on the part of potential interviewees? Some experts argue that if the topic is of interest, individuals still enjoy the opportunity to express their opinions. This puts a premium on sample selection procedures.

In sum, computer-assisted telephone interviewing has many of the advantages of face-to-face interviewing; it is the method of choice when results must be obtained in a short time. Software into which questions can be inserted are available for desktop computers, is relatively inexpensive, and is increasingly flexible.

Notebook computers make computer-assisted personal interviewing (CAPI) feasible, so that responses can be entered into a computer instead of handwritten on a form. These completed face-to-face interviews can be downloaded into the main data bank by modem, providing quick data return and allowing interviewers to remain in the field. CAPI requires a skilled touch typist who can maintain eye contact with the respondent while recording answers. Unlike CATI, nonverbal responses may be noted. Further, many of the advantages of CATI such as branching, and catching inconsistent responses are possibilities.

♦ *Computer-assisted telephone interviewing has many of the advantages of face-to-face interviews, can obtain results quickly, eliminates travel, tends to elicit shorter responses, can have the advantage of anonymity for sensitive issues, can use the computer to generate the sample, can warn of respondents in already filled quotas, can make automatic callbacks, can use less skilled personnel if the computer leads the interviewer through the questions, and can automatically check the consistency of answers. Its main disadvantage is that it cannot pick up nonverbal cues. There may also be a selective factor as to who responds to face-to-face but not to telephone interviews, and vice versa.*

Questionnaires

A questionnaire gathers large amounts of data from many respondents very inexpensively. If the topic is of interest to the respondents and there are few questions, you might use open-ended queries, just as in an interview. You will get less depth and richness of information, however, because people will say more than they will write, and the latency involved in writing means that respondents may censor their replies. But mail questionnaires may get past the screening of doormen and secretaries who keep interviewers at bay. Also, you can ensure the confidentiality of responses if the questionnaire is returned anonymously.

Questionnaires may be designed to get at intangible constructs, with all the problems these entail. Just as with other measures, regardless of what is intended, the questionnaire or interview becomes the construct's operational definition. The validity of the questions seems apparent but, as we shall see, the interpretation of questions is not always as straightforward as it appears.

Important considerations in questionnaire construction are what to ask, how to ask it, how to order the questions, how to format the questionnaire, and how to improve it. These topics form the basis of the following discussion, much of which, especially as it relates to question development, applies equally well to interviewing.

What to Ask

Although some questionnaires are probes to explore, more are targeted to obtain specific information or to relate certain variables:

- questions of knowledge or fact (demographics, descriptions of past behavior under particular circumstances, participation in past events, or awareness of products or events)
- prediction of behavior (voting in future elections, possible need for training, anticipated occupation)
- expressions of opinion, interest, or valuing, problems to react to, or statements to agree or disagree with (how much aid to give the homeless, all homeless people are mentally disturbed: strongly agree, agree, undecided, disagree, or strongly disagree)
- demonstrations of capability (problems to solve)

An early step in planning a questionnaire is to lay out a "blueprint" to guide question construction. Called a **table of specifications,** such a table is shown in Figure 16.3 for a study of the impact of various election events on the voter; subjects of the query are listed down the left; queries are listed across the top. The cells where intended queries meet desired content specify items for the questionnaire—the numbers in the cells (for example, one item—first row, first column—elicits the respondents initial reaction to [the first positive] television advertisement of the candidate). From the mass of queries in the top row of this example, it is clear this 15-item questionnaire will emphasize the impact of television on voting. We will encounter such tables again in Chapter 18 in the service of test construction.

Some researchers work backward—from what the report should contain to the needed questions. This method minimizes the "get-that-now-in-case-I-can't-later" tendency, which can result in overly long questionnaires and items that never get analyzed. You should yield to the impulse to add questions that allow explanations of responses, but add them only where it is important.

Study of impact of various election events on voting behavior	Initial reaction	Considered reaction	Expected effect on vote	Actual effect on vote
Television advertisement for candidate				
First positive ad	1	1		1
Second positive ad		1		1
Negative ad		1	1	1
Newspaper ad for candidate				1
Newspaper endorsement of candidate	1			1
Candidate's performance during televised debates			1	1
Literature delivered to home	1			1

FIGURE 16.3 Table of specifications to guide question construction for a study of the impact of various election events on voting behavior.

How to Ask It

Careful wording is essential to portray accurately what is to be asked, to avoid biasing or leading questions, and to ensure that the response is to the full question without confusion over which part was answered or what else caused the response.

The variety of question types is limited only by your imagination. In addition to open-end questions, common types include short answer, checklists, rankings, response on a verbal scale ("very difficult, somewhat difficult, not difficult"; "very poor, poor, good, very good"), response on a graphical scale ("Check on the bar to show how clearly this instruction is written: very clearly ____ | ____ | ____ | ____ | ____ not clearly at all), weighing alternatives ("Indicate the relative importance of these statements by distributing 10 points among them") and a variety of other multiple-choice forms ("Use the following scale to judge the expressions of opinion: strongly agree, agree, undecided, disagree, strongly disagree). Measurement books with sample test items may suggest forms (see references, page 446). Payne (1951, in some respects outdated but still one of the best books on the subject), Converse and Presser (1986), Sudman and Bradburn (1982), and Foddy (1993, a successor to Payne), among others, give excellent advice and suggest item formats. Past surveys are often helpful in suggesting the wording of questions. Gale Research Company (1983–) lists databases of past surveys from 1983 on.

Projective Techniques. Private attitudes that control our behavior are often different from those publicly expressed. Therefore, direct measurement through scales asking the extent of agreement with certain stated positions may fail. Hence indirect measures are often used (see Webb et al., 1981). **Projective techniques** are one form of indirect measure. Three commonly used projective approaches are association, fantasy and ambiguous stimuli, and categorizing (Oppenheim, 1966).

In word association measures, we ask for the first thing that comes into the respondent's mind in response to a stimulus. The stimulus may be a word, a picture, or a graphic. This technique tends to work better in an interview because the respondent does not have time to think and censor responses. Even with a questionnaire, however, if there is a large number of items, responses tend to become less guarded and more revealing of underlying attitudes.

Respondents can be asked to construct a story suggested by fantasy and ambiguous stimulus measures ("Tell me a story about an African American person") or a response to a stimulus (a picture of an African American child and a Caucasian child playing—"What are they saying to each other?"). Such responses are revealing of the person's "building blocks" of experience and attitudes. Using ambiguous stimuli such as cloud or inkblot pictures ("Tell me what you see in these pictures") requires the respondent to assign meaning and reveal personal outlook.

Categorizing and labeling reveal how individuals see the world and thus their attitudes. Asking them to cluster photographs of faces "in whatever way you think they belong together" and then "Please explain the groupings" may tell how respondents categorize people and what characteristics of individuals are dominant in their minds. These reveal underlying thinking and suggest the attitude structure.

Ordering the Questions

The **order of the questions** is important. The opening of the questionnaire sets the tone for the respondents regarding both motivation and purpose. Grabbing their attention and "pulling them in" is good practice, and titles often help. Erdos (1970) suggests questionnaire titles that appeal to the ego ("A Survey of Industry Leaders"), emphasize the topic and its relevance ("Taking Inventory of Your Personal Health"), underline its importance ("A Nationwide Survey of . . ."), or emphasize the respondent-researcher tie ("For Alumni Only—A Confidential Survey").

The first few items are important in setting the tone, reducing defensiveness, and allaying anxiety. Begin by asking easy-to-answer questions that personally involve the respondent: "What do you like about the location of your home?" Questions that arouse the interest or curiosity of the respondent are a good beginning, even if you don't tabulate them later. Early questions also set the frame of reference for later ones. The **funnel-sequenced questionnaire** parallels the focus interview in design; it starts broadly and then narrows to the topic of specific interest. As with the focus interview, the intent is to prevent the early responses from biasing later ones. Broad questions obtain the respondent's general frame of reference. When asking about a new topic about which an informed opinion is desired, invert the funnel and cover the aspects of the question in detail. Then, at the end, you ask "Now, taking all these things into consideration . . ."

Other tips on ordering questions:

- Cluster similar questions to minimize the respondent's "mental set" changes.
- Order logically for flow and movement across topic coverage—such orderings as specific to general, past to present, or familiar to unfamiliar.
- Leave demographic questions to the end unless you are trying to determine whether the respondent should be questioned at all. It is well to explain why the demographics are important: "To determine how people of different backgrounds respond to this questionnaire, we'd like a few facts about you."
- Leave sensitive questions to the end; usually, respondents feel they have invested enough time in the questionnaire to answer them rather than discard the whole effort.
- Save respondent time and reading with "Skip to question X" where intervening questions are irrelevant. Arrows leading to the next pertinent question or other clever devices can help ensure that directions are followed.
- Check the effect of question order with a preliminary trial by using different orderings that seem to have merit. Often ordering affects the nature, length, and spontaneity of responses.

Tips on Questionnaire Format

Returns are highest on mail questionnaires that are short, easy to respond to, attractive, and of personal interest:

- Keep the length within an uncrowded two to four pages; feature plenty of white space. Avoid a slick advertising look—otherwise recipients may confuse it with junk mail. A personal rather than commercial look makes it clear that the person's response is important to you.
- Make the first page especially appealing and easy to read.
- Don't number consecutively if there are many questions. Number within sections and use sectioning with interesting headings ("About You and Your Department") to provide a feeling of progress. Break lists every five lines or so.
- Put write-in lines or boxes for responses in a uniform place, usually at the right, so that the question is visible as subjects respond (unless you are dealing with a left-handed sample).
- Use an easy to read typeface and be sure the printing is of high quality. Print both sides, so that the questionnaire appears shorter. Use good but lightweight paper.
- Arrange the questions on the page so that the respondent easily understands the flow through the questionnaire; this not only saves respondent time but also gives a feeling of progress.
- Use software that markedly simplifies questionnaire production by providing templates whose answers can easily be scanned into computers to produce reports with spreadsheets, graphs, and charts.

Tips on Question Construction and Hallmarks of Questionnaires

1. Use phrasing and language that will be understood and will appeal to all segments of the intended population. *Keep your questions short, grammatically simple (avoiding qualifying phrases or clauses), specific, and concrete!* This is sometimes difficult because education and experience may vary widely, so that what is simple enough and clear for one person may seem condescending to another. Be sure to pretest with varied groups. Be careful of colloquial terms and jargon (*winnow* may be known to farmers but not city dwellers). Slang becomes outdated quickly and may vary in interpretation from place to place.

2. Be sure respondents interpret the question as intended; pretesting is essential for this. ("What kind of headache remedy do you use?" may refer to the brand, type of medicine, or therapy—pills, liquids, or lying down in a dark room for an hour.)

3. Keep both the questionnaire and individual items short and simple. Short, simple questions are better than long, complex ones for maintaining interest and imparting a feeling of movement. They are also more likely to be understood.

4. Avoid double-barreled questions. **Double-barreled questions** pose two issues at once, obscuring the one being responded to. ("Have Russia's improved housing and industrialization raised the standard of living?" What if the respondent believes that housing has but industrialization hasn't?)

5. Avoid the equally subtle one-and-a-half-barreled question, where the second issue is introduced into the alternatives, for example:

    The United States is now negotiating a strategic arms agreement with the Soviet Union in what is known as SALT II. Which one of the following statements is closest to your opinion on these negotiations? (1) I strongly support SALT II. (2) SALT II is somewhat disappointing, but on balance. I have to support it. (3) I would like to see more protection for the United States before I would be ready to support SALT II. (4) I strongly oppose the SALT II arms agreement with the Soviets. (5) I don't know enough about SALT II to have an opinion yet. (Sudman and Bradburn, 1982, p. 136)

    The third response introduced adequacy of defense as a new issue and swayed responses negatively, whereas other surveys reported stronger support for the treaty.

6. Avoid biasing the response by the question. This is an obvious point, but often both sides of the issue are not included in the lead. Payne (1951) notes that when questioned on whether companies could arrange things to avoid layoffs, 63 percent of respondents said they could and 22 percent said they could not. But adding the other side of the question—"or do you think layoffs are unavoidable?"—dropped the 63 percent to 43 percent and almost doubled the 22 percent to 43 percent. Choice of words may also result in bias. Anglos react differently to "wetbacks" and "Mexican Americans." Asking about "big busi-

ness" gets a response different from that for just "business." Every modifier can make a difference!

7. Be aware of the importance of the **framing of questions.** Slovic, Fischhoff, and Lichtenstein (1982) found mandatory seat belts favored by only 54 percent of respondents when the likelihood of being injured was expressed as once in 100,000 trips. However, when the question was phrased in terms of a lifetime of driving which changes this to a chance of one person in three, fully 78 percent favored it. Tversky and Kahneman (1981) give a number of examples showing how "seemingly inconsequential changes in the formulation of choice problems caused significant shifts of preference" (p. 457). They reinforce the importance of trying out all formulations on small groups ahead of time to be sure they communicate as intended.

8. Allow respondents to protect their egos while responding. Otherwise, they may make up answers to avoid embarrassment. For example, lead with a question undercutting the expectation of a response. Instead of starting with, "What books does your child read?" first inquire, "Are you able to keep track of your child's reading?" Rephrase questions such as "Did you graduate from college?" to "What is the highest grade in school you completed?"

9. Assuage the guilt of responding negatively by first asking for the positive: "What do you like about General Bullmoose?" "What do you dislike about him?"

10. Use an impersonal lead, because it often gets responses when direct questions cannot: "Do persons like yourself generally believe . . . ?" "Are you like them?"

11. Avoid negative questions, if possible: "We should not admit tiny nations to the United Nations." Respondents may miss the *not*. If the affective tone would be lost by positive phrasing, emphasize the *not* with underlining or italics.

12. With multiple-choice questions, be sure that the list of alternatives is complete or an "other than the above" alternative is provided. Trying out the questions in an open-ended form with a sample of the target group helps determine the range of likely responses and whether a "none of the above" or "other, please specify" is necessary. Supplying the respondent with an incomplete list reflects negatively on questionnaire preparation, which, in turn, may be reflected in the care taken with responses.

13. Make sure the context in which a question is asked is appropriate. In a questionnaire about the reasons for buying a new car, a series of questions about conservation of energy preceded the main issue. Not surprisingly, "fuel economy" turned out to be the most frequent response. For a more accurate answer, the question regarding purchase of a car should have been asked before the questions on conservation of energy.

Comparison with results from an earlier poll is often helpful in determining whether new results are trustworthy. Such analyses help spot context and wording effects not otherwise noticeable. Because such effects are so pervasive and important, for very important issues, some pollsters suggest being very wary of a question from one poll. Data archives (Gale Research Company, 1983–) sometimes can be helpful. In addition, such repositories contain a wealth of question ideas that may be useful as you develop your own instrument. Further, reused questions can show changes in attitude, opinion, and practices.

The Letter of Transmittal and Its Hallmarks[3]

Motivating the respondent is central to getting a reply with good data. The **letter of transmittal,** which, together with a return envelope, accompanies the questionnaire, is a major means of motivation. Respondents will answer many, many items and even open-end questions if they are inspired to do so. Erdos (1970) provides an excellent list of characteristics of the letter of transmittal and provides an example of such a letter in Figure 16.4. The numbers on the figure identify the corresponding characteristic in the list below.

1. Personalize the communication.
2. Ask a favor.
3. Indicate the importance of the research project and its purpose.
4. Indicate the importance of the recipient.
5. Stress the importance of replies in general.
6. Note the importance of replies even from readers who consider themselves not qualified to respond.
7. Indicate how the recipient may benefit from the research.
8. Note that completing the questionnaire will take only a short time.
9. Point out that the questionnaire can be answered easily.
10. Include a stamped return envelope.
11. Describe how the recipient was selected.
12. Indicate that answers are anonymous and confidential.
13. Offer a report of the results.
14. Include a note of urgency in the request for response.
15. Express the sender's appreciation for the response.
16. Indicate the sender's importance to the respondent. Special populations respond to appeals from their own organizations.
17. Make the letter look professional.
18. If an incentive is included, describe it and indicate its purpose.
19. Avoid anything in the letter that might bias responses.
20. Keep the letter brief.

Note the number of items above concerned with motivating the respondent through conveying the importance of the project, the respondent, and the reply—they make up almost half the list! Be sure that comments about the importance of the respondent sound sincere; obvious flattery may backfire. Limited sample size emphasizes the importance of replies ("You are one of few individuals who have moved into this area in the last 12 months; therefore . . ."). Ask for replies even from those not qualified, to keep track of them. ("Send your return even if you are not a homeowner; otherwise, we'll never know.")

---

[3]Adapted from Erdos (1983), p. 102.

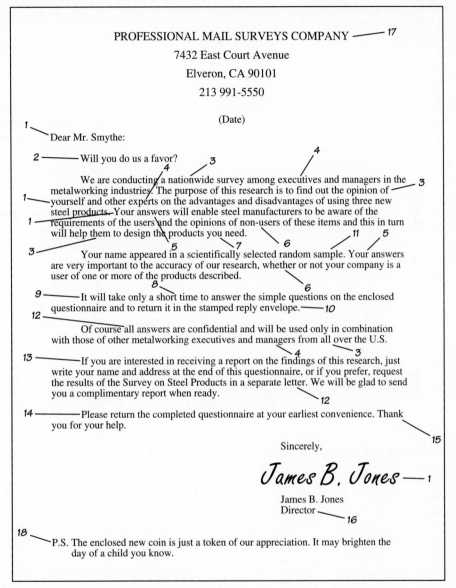

FIGURE 16.4 Sample letter of transmittal. The numbers identify the parts of the letter that correspond to the numbered characteristics listed in the text. (Excerpt from P. L. Erdos, *Professional Mail Surveys,* p. 103, Copyright © 1983 by Paul L. Erdos. Reprinted by permission of Krieger Publishing Co.)

Computer-personalized letters are so common these days that they may have lost some of their original appeal, but probably not all of it. If the topic is sensitive and confidentiality is important, it is probably better to make the letter impersonal and routine. If you are offering a report, be sure to supply a separate request form. A stamped envelope produces a higher response rate than a business reply envelope.

E-mail Questionnaires

We conventionally think of questionnaires as being mailed, but if there is a new two-way communication medium, survey researchers will try it—hence E-mail questionnaires. Too new for much empirical research, we can, however, note some characteristics. The restriction of samples to those with Email addresses is a limitation for most problems but a boon for topics related to computing. Obtaining e-mail addresses would seem to be a problem, but if so-called junk mailers can get them, so can researchers. The extra labor of scrolling to assure consistency with earlier responses may make for more spontaneous answers. But, similarly, the restriction to a screenful at a time may limit what can be asked and how it can be queried. E-mail's inclusion of the sender's address limits anonymity of response from organizations using some variant of the person's name in the address—not a problem, however, where an on-line services's clients construct their own login name. E-mail's novelty will only initially improve return rates. The sender's name, subject and size of message, which are all that typically appear on an "in" box, will be critically important in getting the message opened rather than immediately discarded.

Coding of Interview and Questionnaire Responses

Coding and analysis of exploratory interview data are done just like the analysis of qualitative data described in Chapter 14. Again, because surveys are so often targeted to obtain particular information, you can determine the items to code and how to code them before you gather your data. If it is an interview, interviewers can quickly learn the codes and can code the responses as they are given. Listing the response codes on the form adds to the clutter and clerks quickly become familiar with the codes. Keeping responses on the same edge of the paper speeds tabulation. Consider machine-readable response forms if the equipment is available to you. It saves keying the responses into a computer, with its attendant errors. Be sure to review the forms, however, both to ascertain that the clerk or machine will read them correctly and that the respondent has followed directions. Here are some tips:

1. From the outset make all the distinctions in coding that may help in analysis later. Retrospectively, you can always merge codes, but when, for instance, you give all the "Other, please specify" responses the same code, you cannot distinguish them without recoding.
2. Make codes exhaustive of the response range but mutually exclusive so that a given response will always carry the same code.
3. Be consistent (for instance, use 1 for yes and 0 for no consistently).

4. If missing data may be a significant factor, distinguish the different causes: doesn't know, skipped question, refused to respond, indecipherable, inappropriate response, and so on.
5. If you are allowing multiple responses, you can often usefully assign codes to the most common patterns.
6. Check consistency of coding across coders and over time. Determine the desired coding of certain sheets and slip them into the batch at random intervals to provide a coding audit.
7. Provide each coder with a coding manual, and keep all manuals up-to-date as resolutions of coding problems are agreed upon.

Analysis of Interview and Questionnaire Data

Most survey data are tabulated, compiled and analyzed with statistical computer programs these days. New software makes available statistics, many of which were simply impractical to process before the advent of computers. In some instances, these complex statistics are based on assumptions important to their interpretation which may or may not fit the data. Most of the statistics commonly used are covered in the next section of this textbook. Additionally, the next chapter describes measures of central tendency (mean or average, median, mode), measures of dispersion (for example, the standard deviation which indicates how widely people differ in their responses), and correlations (which indicate the strength of a relationship). Inferential statistics, indicators of statistical significance, are described in Chapter 19.

In general, use the simplest applicable analysis. It will require fewer assumptions and be understood by a wider audience. Simple percentages or averages very often suffice. If you wish to relate variables (for instance, to determine the influence of education on voting behavior), construct **cross-tabulation** or **cross-break** tables like that of Table 16.2. This table lays out the data from two questions: "What is your political party?" and "What is your highest level of education?" The raw data are given under the heading "Number of Cases." Turn-

TABLE 16.2 *Cross-tabulation of Political Party Registration and Level of Education*

Level of Education	Number of Cases N = 423		Percentage of Cases		Percentage by Education Level Within Party	
	Democrats	Republicans	Democrats	Republicans	Democrats	Republicans
Elementary	68	21	16	5	27	12
High School	123	80	29	19	49	46
College	42	47	10	11	17	27
Beyond College	17	25	4	6	7	15
Total	250	173	59	41	100	100

ing these first two columns into percentages of the whole group as in the middle two columns, shows that they split roughly 60–40 with more Democrats than Republicans. About half (29 + 19 percent) have a high school education. From these data it seems that the Democrats have a lower level of education than the Republicans, but this point is made much clearer if we compare the percentages by education level within party as in the last two columns. This makes it apparent that the Democrats' education level is lower than the Republicans', with about twice as many Democrats having only an elementary education, and about half as many having a college education or beyond. For many purposes, such simple percentage analysis is enough. However, we could translate these data into a correlation to show the strength of the relationship between party affiliation and education as shown on pages 414 and 416 of the next chapter.

♦ *Coding must be done carefully to maintain data validity.*
♦ *Quality control can be provided by training coders, using code books that are kept up-to-date as questions are resolved, and sampling coded questionnaires for coding accuracy and consistency.*
♦ *Development and analysis of cross-tabulated tables provide information on the variation of responses with various demographic and other independent variables that can throw considerable light on the respondents' underlying characteristics, value structures and thinking processes.*

Improving Questions, Questionnaires, and Letters of Transmittal

All interview schedules, questionnaires, and letters of transmittal must always be subjected to **pilot testing** *before being used!* Use test respondents who closely resemble those you intend to query. Then review with a sufficient sample of the pilot group, question by question, what they reacted to, what they meant by their answer, and why they answered as they did. (How big a sample do you need to take? As with qualitative research, pilot test until you are saturated!) This process will confirm that you have conveyed what you intended by each question and that you can interpret responses as replies to what you were asking. It will also help ensure that respondents understood the letter of transmittal and will give some indication of its motivating qualities. The time and effort you spend in pilot testing will be more than repaid by the elimination of confusing wording, ambiguous questions for which the results would be uninterpretable, and frustration among both respondents and interviewers

Interrupting an interview to ask about particular responses disrupts the flow, yet memory is selective, and underreporting of what actually occurred increases as time elapses. Further, querying about responses after a long session may not be fruitful. Audio- or videotape the session for later **stimulated recall**. Stimulated recall involves playing the tape for the respondent, and stopping it where you wish to query responses. For example, Bloom (1954) studied the thought processes of students in a discussion class. He replayed an audiotape, stopping it at important points and querying students about what had gone on in their minds. Kagan, Krathwohl, and Miller (1963) and Kagan, Krathwohl, and Farquhar (1965) used a similar process to study therapy and instruction with stimulated recall by videotape. Their students or clients held the control, stopping the tape at points they thought significant or as requested by the researchers. Given the stimulation of video- or audiotape replays, respondents are able to report both events and inner feelings with an apparent authenticity that suggests they were reliving those moments. The quality and depth of the questionnaire or interview pilot study data may be markedly enhanced by the use of stimulated recall.

An alternative to stimulated recall is to have individuals think aloud as they move through the questionnaire and letter of transmittal. This practice may slow reading, but most individuals can process the letter and questionnaire at close to normal speed while giving their reactions. Or you may supplement these data by using stimulated recall on a think-aloud recording. Such data will also allow you to judge whether the material elicits the responses expected. This can be important in motivating adequate responses.

Where the questionnaire is intended to measure a construct, the procedures of item analysis used with tests, discussed on pages 440–441, are also applicable as well as are estimates of test reliability and validity also discussed in Chapter 18. Discovery of nonfunctional items may allow shortening the questionnaire.

The Nonrespondent

Nonrespondents can cause a serious problem for questionnaire interpretation, another example of the problem of mortality mentioned on page 317. Note that there are two potential sources of mortality: loss of members of a cohort or panel sample and lack of response from current members. Refusals are rarer with personal interviews and to some extent with telephone surveys, but answering machines used as "electronic peepholes" to screen calls are a selective factor. Whether this bias occurs depends, as always, on whether nonrespondents' answers differ from respondents'. Professional survey organizations leave a message on answering machines designed to interest respondents sufficiently to return the call on a toll-free number. The effect on response rate of caller ID, which identifies the calling number, is as yet unknown.

What is a good return, and when should we be concerned about nonresponse? The answer lies in (a) the representativeness of the target population of the people reached and (b) the difference in answers between respondents and nonrespondents. If those reached are representative, and nonrespondents answer like respondents, a low response rate is acceptable.

The problem is that respondents are essentially volunteers and therefore likely to conform to Rosenthal and Rosnow's (1975) list of volunteer characteristics—see page 518. Are these characteristics relevant? Only if they relate to what you are studying. A questionnaire study of welfare mothers would yield highly spurious results if only the better-educated and more intelligent of them volunteered to reply. In contrast, a questionnaire on the prevalence of cancer in the family, which seems to strike persons irrespective of these volunteer characteristics, might be relatively unaffected.

The best defense against the nonrespondent problem is motivating respondents in the first place. Not all obvious ploys work: Dillman, Gallegos, and Frey (1978), using the person's name to increase rapport in telephone surveys, found that it had little impact. However, both they and Traugott, Groves, and Lepkowski (1987) found that an advance letter had a significant effect. Beside an effective letter of transmittal, the presence of an incentive such as a coin or trinket may improve returns, but it probably does little to enhance quality of response. The best motivator is the internal one of wanting to do it for its own sake rather than the external one of being bribed.

The "foot-in-the-door" technique —obtaining prior commitment from a potential respondent—is effective (Hansen and Robinson, 1980; Snyder and Cunningham, 1975). For example, a postcard is to be returned indicating a willingness to complete the questionnaire. Telephone interviews are helped by solicitation of willingness to respond to a callback at a convenient time (Groves and Magilavy, 1981).

Follow-ups do increase returns, with each successive one being less effective. A well-written postcard on first follow-up may do as much as a more expensive complete second mailing, but the latter are also often effective. Experiments with certified and overnight mail have shown increased returns but at considerable expense. Try to allow sufficient slack for follow-ups in the time schedule; the bulk of questionnaires are returned about two weeks after receipt, but may dribble in for months. You should also set a cut-off date.

Typically, we assume that questionnaire nonrespondents are merely very late respondents. Tabulating receipts by three- to five-day periods, or comparing those received before and after each follow-up, reveals progressive response pattern changes. Extrapolating such patterns suggests the most extreme nonrespondents' responses so we can judge how seriously they diverge.

As mentioned earlier, when questionnaire follow-ups prove ineffective, you can phone for answers to essential questions. Remember, because these respondents are clearly identified and their responses are verbal and spontaneous, they may differ from questionnaire replies—especially for sensitive topics.

✦ *Questionnaires can provide structured responses. They must be carefully developed, pilot-tested, and revised (sometimes repeating the latter steps) to obtain valid data.*

✦ *Proper framing and ordering of questions are important for obtaining valid data.*

✦ *Poor response rate is the single biggest problem for mailed questionnaires. This is of concern when the answers of nonrespondents might have differed from those of respondents in ways related to whatever is being studied.*

✦ *The letter of transmittal can be important in setting the frame for responding and in obtaining a high response rate; therefore, it warrants careful development and pilot testing.*

✦ *There are a number of ways of increasing response rate for mailed questionnaires. Research shows that prior commitment works, as may some kind of re-*

> *ward, but the best motivation is intrinsic interest by the respondent in having their response count toward the results.*
> ✦ *Follow-ups do increase returns, but each wave brings decreasing results, and responses may trend toward those of nonrespondents if respondents' and nonrespondents' answers differ.*

Inquiry into Sensitive Topics

Getting honest responses to questions regarding sensitive topics is a special problem. Wentland (1993), synthesizing studies of response accuracy, as might be expected, found it negatively correlated with the sensitivity of the topic as well as the social desirability factor. Questionnaires were less affected by these factors than interviews. However, respondents must believe their responses will be kept anonymous—there should be no secret code. It is here that the sins of shady researchers haunt the innocent. Researchers caught secretly coding presumably anonymous questionnaires reflect on all researchers. *Always* honor anonymity promises. Pay the extra postage for comprehensive follow-up mailings.

Various forms of the randomized response technique originated by Warner (1965) are useful in providing the respondent with greater security (Himmelfarb and Edgell, 1980; Schuman and Kalton, 1985). Instead of being confronted with a single sensitive question, the respondent is confronted with two or more questions, one or more of which is not at all sensitive. A random device determines which the respondent is to answer. Assuming that the respondent understands the process, it removes most of the embarrassment surrounding the questioning. For instance: "Please flip a coin, but do not show it to me. If the coin came up heads, *when I ask you to*, please answer this question 'Have you ever used marijuana, cocaine, or heroin or some form thereof?' If the coin came up tails, please answer this one 'Is your birthday in December?' Now tell me your answer, please."

With a random coin flip, half the sample will answer each question. Since birthdays are spread about equally across the year, about one-twelfth or 8.33 percent, will answer "yes" to the second question and 91.67 percent will answer "no." Since they constitute half the cases, subtracting half the 8.33 percent, or 4.17 percent, from the *yes*es and, similarly, 91.67/2, or 45.83 percent, from the *no*s will yield the percentages of *yes*es and *no*s for the other half of the group. Doubling the other half's percentages will yield an estimate of the percentages had all persons been asked the sensitive question, yet no one will know who answered which question.

Miller (1984) suggests dividing a sample randomly in half, each getting a different list. One list contains only innocuous behaviors; the other includes the sensitive behavior as well. Subjects are asked to report only the number of activities engaged in on the list. The difference between the two lists provides an estimate of the frequency of the sensitive behavior. This method is simpler; there is nothing to be explained to the respondent, and it may appear less intrusive.

Neither of these two techniques allows the sensitive responses to be linked to other items, for example, demographics. If the respondent needs more than the researcher's guarantee of anonymity, you might try putting such information in a separately mailed questionnaire linked by the CDRGP (for "<u>c</u>ontext-<u>d</u>etermined, <u>r</u>ule-generated <u>p</u>seudonym") technique. It also usefully links data gathered anonymously across different instruments or the same one over a period of time. Everyone follows a common rule to generate pseudonyms for identification (Carifio and Biron, 1982). Using information well known to the respondent but not to the researcher eliminates error in pseudonym recall since the same rule is used for all instrument administration in a given study. For example, respondents might be asked successively "the first letter of your birth month," "the first letter of your street's name" "the first letter of your mother's first name," "the first letter of your father's first name," and so on. For school research, you can base the questions on information that, by law, schools cannot disclose without the consent of those involved.

Response Sets

Interview and questionnaire responses can be affected by **response sets,** stances predisposing individuals to respond in certain ways (for example, toward social desirability, acquiescing, "nay-saying"). Particularly with attitude, personality, and interest scales, respondents may give false answers slanted toward their sense of what is desirable, possibly to gain social approval from the interviewer, to preserve their self-images, or to avoid feelings of discomfort (Phillips, 1971). For instance, when they were asked whether they had contributed to the Community Chest, a check of responses against records revealed that 44 percent of respondents gave false answers (Cahalan, 1968–69). View admissions of socially undesirable tendencies with suspicion until you try different wording that elicits these tendencies differentially to find how much, which groups of individuals, and which wordings are affected.

Yea-sayers give more positive responses to agree-disagree, true-false, and yes-no response modes. In an effort to combat this acquiescence set and obtain more valid responses, you can make the desired response negative. However, though less common than acquiescence set, some individuals are nay-sayers and tend to respond negatively to the above kinds of questions. Reversing the questions reduces the validity of the nay-sayers' scores, though there are considerably fewer of them. Alternatively, you can include both negative and positive wordings in the same questionnaire and eliminate the responses of people who contradict themselves. Note, however, that dropping these individuals reduces sample size and therefore may affect generality—yea- and nay-sayers probably respond differently from others in a variety of areas. The best way of avoiding the problem of response sets is using item formats that do not incur them.

◆ *Methods exist for maintaining respondent anonymity while querying sensitive topics and for anonymously linking data from several instruments.*

◆ *Researchers need to be alert to response sets, particularly the tendency to acquiesce to socially desirable responses; these can create data validity problems.*

Additional Hallmarks of Survey Research

We have already noted hallmarks of interviews, questionnaires, and letters of transmittal. Here are additional hallmarks:

1. The intent of the survey is defined clearly.
2. The target population definition is consistent with the study's intent, and inferences to the target are made consistent with the quality of the sampling process.
3. The sampling technique is clearly specified, the likelihood of systematic bias is described and, if possible, negated by demographic data from the sample. If possible and appropriate, the sample is stratified on key variables and probability samples are used.
4. Questions, questionnaires, and letters of transmittal are pilot-tested to determine whether they elicit the intended response. As appropriate, "think aloud" or stimulated recall procedures are used to make sure that the respondent's interpretation corresponds to the intended one. Revisions are also pilot-tested, as needed, to ensure that corrections worked.
5. Interviewers are selected on appropriate bases—usually being matched to interviewees' background (there are instances in which matching does not work as intended and pilot tests are required). Data gatherers are adequately trained so that their technique does not constitute an unintended contaminating variable.
6. If sensitive data are gathered, assurances of anonymity and procedures for guaranteeing it are implemented. Data are so reported that individuals or institutions cannot be identified without their consent.
7. Appropriate data-gathering methods are employed: structured, partially structured, or unstructured interviews in person or over the telephone, questionnaires administered in person or by mail, or similar methods.
8. Procedures, including follow-up of nonrespondents, indicate that a representative sample was reached. Regular checks ensure that respondents represent nonrespondents as well. Comparison of late with early respondents or a similar practice gives clues about possible nonrespondent bias.
9. Sample size is adequate to ensure sufficient statistical sensitivity (see pp. 481–483).

A Summary Comparison of Four Survey Data-Collecting Modes

Table 16.3 summarizes much that appears in the chapter in an unconventional way. It examines the relative advantages and disadvantages of four ways of gathering data with respect to a variety of considerations that arise in sample surveys. It distinguishes individual from group interviews and provides some additional information to that in the chapter.

TABLE 16.3 *Comparison of Data Collection Methods on Critical Characteristics*

	Individual Interview	Group Interview	Computer-Assisted Telephone Interview	Mailed Questionnaire
Sample	Restricted geographically and numerically by cost Field interviewer determines those chosen Possible bias toward those most accessible and pleasant if sampling plan is not carefully followed With good interviewer, nature of sample can be better controlled than with other methods Highest response rate	Group is geographically restricted and number of groups is restrained by cost Selectivity among invitees who actually attend may reduce representativeness Not all ages, sexes, etc., available at same time Right mix of people necessary for good response	No geographic restrictions Geographically dispersed sample can be contacted quickly Sequential sampling is easily implemented Can control sample representativeness by screening respondents for match to unfilled quotas Reaches unlisted numbers with random-digit dialing but, alas, also businesses Although poorest may be phoneless, it reaches about 95% of households Has advantage in urban areas over face-to-face interviews where doors are closed to strangers	No geographic restrictions May get past secretaries, which interviewers can't always Some segments will not respond (e.g., illiterates, disorganized people)
	Good sampling frame unavailable for some target populations (e.g., working mothers)			Low cost allows mass mailings to find targets without sampling frame
	Actual representativeness of sample depends on persons reached			
Length	Very long interviews of a day or more have been held successfully	Hard to keep a group together for long periods	Generally shorter than face-to-face interviews	Obtains shorter responses to open-end questions than interviews
	Respondent motivation determines length limits			
Nonresponse	Few people refuse; but callbacks are expensive	Selectivity in those who respond to invitations	Few people refuse but more than in individual interviews Callbacks are inexpensive	Typically selective Low response rate can be somewhat reduced by follow-ups, by activating respondent motivation, and by incentives

	Individual Interview	Group Interview	Computer-Assisted Telephone Interview	Mailed Questionnaire
Interviewer Bias or Coding Errors	Reduced through good training and regular supervisor checks for standardization, bias, or cheating		Supervision especially easy; computer identifies interviewers with atypical rates (e.g., refusals)	Scanner and computer highly consistent; training and supervision required for hand-coding same as interviews
			Computer shows inconsistencies in respondents' answers which can be probed for cause or correction	
Anonymity	Respondent is known, but interviewer can reassure most persons	Some anonymity in group responses as when interviewer asks "All those who agree, say 'yes' "	Impersonality of telephone better for sensitive issues	Can provide genuine anonymity when respondent trusts researcher's assurances
Sensitive Issues	Characteristics of both interviewer and respondent(s), as well as ability to observe race, socioeconomic status, dress, and other nonverbal clues, may affect both interviewers' questioning and respondents' answers	Respondents who open up, encourage others to do so	Impersonality of phone encourages responses that would be limited to the socially desirable or be inhibited in face-to-face interviews	Anonymity encourages fuller responses than face-to-face interviews
	Random response methods and artificial pseudonyms provide anonymity			
Visuals	Can be used	Can be used	No	Can be used
Speed	Slow	Relatively fast	Fastest; 10 interviewers @ 4 hrs. per day = 400 to 500 20-question interviews in 3 days (Lavrakas, 1993)	Slowest, if high return rate required
Probing?	Yes; can clarify questions, ensure understanding, determine underlying rationale for responses	Yes; further, generality of responses can be elicited by asking how many in group agree or would answer similarly	Yes, but somewhat limited if rapport is to be maintained. Can easily change interview schedule to pursue leads	No; omissions are common but difficult to interpret. Probing by follow-up contact destroys anonymity

TABLE 16.3 *(continued)*

	Individual Interview	Group Interview	Computer-Assisted Telephone Interview	Mailed Questionnaire
Spontaneous Reactions, Unguardedness?	Yes, spontaneous but more likely to get socially desirable responses Can control that others are not suggesting responses	Yes, gets both initial, spontaneous, and later, considered responses Fear of contradiction by others minimizes information distortion	Yes; lowest search time for answer yields most spontaneous but also shortest responses; may increase "don't know" responses	No, person can mull over and change answer Respondent checking of previous answers can inflate consistency
Adaptation of Language to Level of Respondent?	Yes	Yes	Yes, if interviewer catches on soon enough	No, must be preset as much as possible to accommodate sample
Inclusion of Persons Who Work?	Only with increased cost of evening and weekend interviews			Yes
Cost	Most expensive and time consuming	With large groups, can be the least costly of interviews on per-person basis; some researchers believe data is as good or better than individual interviews	Substitutes much lower phone costs for expensive travel; but adds equipment overhead costs	Large samples contacted at very little cost; but extensive follow-ups of non-respondents add expense
Pluses and Minuses Not Covered Elsewhere	Context for question interpretation is limited to respondent's memory of immediately preceding material; this makes order of questions and of responses within a question important Provides flexibility to follow significant leads			Less order dependence since all questions are available No control over who actually formulates questionnaire responses
	Can establish rapport and control over interview environment	Can establish rapport and control over interview environment but could have trouble with some in group which could affect others	Limited length; tiresome after 20–30 minutes Most important advantage: control over data quality from sampling through interview supervision to data entry (Lavrakas, 1995)	

Source: Adapted from *Research Methods in Economics and Business* by R. Ferber and P. J. Verdoorn, 1962, New York: Macmillan.

SUMMARY

In addition to the useful summary provided by Table 16.3, Jaeger (1984) has developed questions that apply equally to interview and questionnaire data. Reminding yourself of the considerations involved in answering each of the following questions will help fix the major points of this chapter in your mind. Starting with the sample and queries to be made, they track through to the interpretation:

- Was the sample representative of the target population?
- Was it large enough?
- Did the respondents understand the questions?
- Did the respondents interpret the questions as intended? Were they willing to respond?
- Did they have the knowledge or information needed to respond?

- Would responses change with equally appropriate rephrasing? With question order changes?
- Were respondents honest in their responses?
- Were responses recorded accurately?
- Were responses transcribed and aggregated accurately?
- Were responses interpreted accurately?

A Look Ahead

In the next chapter we explore the quantitative end of the continuum beginning with descriptive statistics. Such statistics are applicable to surveys in which the data lend themselves to quantitative summary or to the description of relationships.

ADDITIONAL READING

Surveys in general: Cannell (1985a, 1985b), Foddy (1993), Sudman and Bradburn (1982), Schwartz and Sudman (1996) and Survey Research Center (1976). Computer-assisted telephone interviewing (CATI): Chen (1996), Frey (1989), Groves (1990), and Lavrakas (1993). For a good self-instructional work-

book for both telephone and personal interviews: Guenzel, Berckmans and Cannell (1983). Focus groups: Morgan (1997a & 1997b), Krueger (1994) and Stewart and Shamdasani (1990). Sensitive topics: Lee (1993).

IMPORTANT TERMS

Cohort studies
Computer-assisted telephone interviewing (CATI)
Cross-break
Cross-sectional studies
Cross-tabulations
Double-barreled questions
Focus group
Framing of questions
Funnel-sequenced questionnaire
Letter of transmittal
Longitudinal studies

Nonrespondent
Order of questions
Panel sample
Pilot testing
Projective techniques
Response sets
Sample survey
Stimulated recall
Table of specifications
Trend studies

APPLICATION PROBLEMS

1. Christopher Easter, Dean of Student Services at Upstate University, wishes to determine how well his unit's services are contributing to the academic life of the university. It was his perception that there was a lack of awareness among faculty of the unit's contributions. He decided to conduct a survey to determine what information faculty had about the unit's program, how this information was received

and utilized, and at what level the faculty was currently involved. How might he carry out this survey?

2. Ruth Anne Blanchard, dean of a privately run community college located in a city of 500,000, wished to gather information to help plan the courses the college would offer over the next five years. In order to develop projections, she decided to survey a sample of the city's residents to determine their perceived needs. How should she proceed?

3. Kristin Phillips, a member of a large national professional association, wished to know whether fellow members shared her view on the need for a local chapter and the activities and services it might offer. She mailed all other members a questionnaire soliciting their opinions. Assuming that she had constructed an appealing, well-designed instrument and an accompanying letter of transmittal, what further problems should she be alert to, and what should she do about them?

4. David Apple is a researcher interested in investigating what barriers, if any, exist to children's use of personal computers at the elementary school level.

He has received permission to carry out his study at selected elementary schools and has decided to supplement his participant observation by interviewing a sample of students from all grade levels (kindergarten to grade 6). What style of interview might he use?

5. Kathy Mentor, the family life and sex education teacher at a large urban school, offers a program on human sexuality beginning at grade 7 and continuing until the end of grade 12. She wishes to determine whether the approach she uses and the information she imparts, are having an effect on the sexual behavior of the students. How might she do so using a questionnaire?

Compare your answers with those following the Application Exercise.

APPLICATION EXERCISE

Consider how you might explore your problem with a sample survey. Does it have aspects that might differ over time and be of interest? If so, what kind of design might you use to study them? Cross-sectional? Longitudinal? Which longitudinal design? Would interviewing gather useful data? What interview approach would you take? Nondirective? Structured? Funnel? Could you use a questionnaire approach? Who would be in your sample, and how would you choose these people? How would you learn what questions to ask? What kinds of questions might you use? Why? How might you pretest your questionnaire and, if a mail questionnaire, the letter of transmittal? What motivational appeal would you use?

ANSWERS TO THE APPLICATION PROBLEMS

1. Dean Easter can use either a mailed questionnaire or some form of interview, depending on whether or not he wished to reach all the faculty or a sample thereof. The choice may depend, in part, on the urgency of getting the information. The questionnaire represents a method of reaching a majority of faculty easily but unless the faculty view it as a priority, they may be slow in returning them. With support of the academic administration, however, a higher return rate might be expected. In light of a possible unwillingness to be critical of a colleague's operation, the anonymity of the questionnaire might provide more open and honest responses. On the other hand, the structured questions might restrict the answers given, possibly allowing important information to be missed. Dean Easter could also consider two forms of interview: individual or telephone. Both offer the flexibility of probing answers and ensuring that questions are answered clearly. Individual interviews offer the opportunity to establish rapport but are time consuming and would therefore likely restrict the survey to a small sample of the faculty. In this instance, since the calls are local and inexpensive, telephone interviews might permit more thorough coverage while retaining most of the advantages of both the individual interviews and the questionnaire.

2. Dean Blanchard is faced with two problems: finding the perceived educational needs and determining the size of the clientele for each educational program designed to answer a need. These problems call for different survey techniques. An exploratory technique, such as some kind of in depth open-end interviewing with a small sample to find the unfilled perceived needs, is required for the initial phase. A focus group might work well too. Once the perceived needs have been determined, a sample questionnaire or telephone survey of potential clients would permit estimation of demand.

The Continuum of Research Methods: Quantitative End

This section exploring quantitative methods begins with the tools of the method—descriptive statistics, measurement, and inferential statistics—and then describes the experimental method and meta-analyses that use these tools.

- Chapter 17 deals with the numerical description of data, how to describe phenomena in numbers. This chapter shows how to display data and summarize them into statistics descriptive of central tendency, variation, and relationship.
- Chapter 18 explores measurement, testing, and observation. Some things can be counted (number of words produced in a minute) or measured (time between each response). To be described by numbers, concepts and constructs must have their definitions translated into the observable behaviors that constitute a measurement scheme such as a test or observation schedule. This chapter examines the criteria of good measurement and the means for determining how well the criteria have been met.
- Chapter 19 builds on the descriptive statistics of Chapter 17 to describe the logic of inferential statistics which shows whether it is likely a real effect exists. It also describes the elimination of the rival explanation of sampling error. The most commonly used inferential statistics—*t*test, chi-square, and analysis of variance—are discussed.
- Chapter 20 describes how experimental design can eliminate a host of common rival explanations that plague studies. From simple to more complex designs, the logic of controlling to eliminate rival explanations is explored and rules for constructing new designs are discussed.
- Chapter 21 describes meta-analysis both (1) as a method of combining quantitative findings across studies to determine the average size of an effect or relationship, and (2) as a method of research in its own right to tease out likely causative factors embedded in those studies. Meta-analysis was expected to replace verbal literature summaries, but the two can be complementary, and, increasingly, reviews incorporate the best aspects of both.

CHAPTER 17

The Numeric Description of Data: Descriptive Statistics

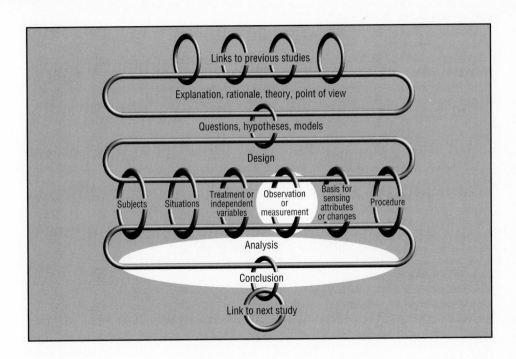

For in relation to economics, to politics and to all the arts, no single branch of educational science possesses so great an influence as the study of numbers.

Plato

OVERVIEW

Describing behavior with numbers or measures, as did the Zimbardo study of Chapter 1, initially produces too many numbers for us to comprehend as raw data. Only as we summarize them in some way can we draw conclusions from them. Descriptive statistics such as Zimbardo's do this very well. We can also summarize numbers as a chart or graph. This chapter first briefly shows how to portray a set of data in different graphic forms and then concentrates on common descriptive statistics such as mean, median, mode, measures of variation, simple correlation, and some more complex forms of correlation. Descriptive statistics facilitate analyzing and summarizing data and thus are important to the lower links of the chain of reasoning.

Correctly interpreting data is essential to its use. This requires using the proper statistic—for example, shall we use the mean, median, or mode, two of these, or all three? But taking data at face value is not always warranted. More often than not, we need to explore what underlies them.

CHAPTER CONTENTS

Introduction

The process of describing something requires that we abstract its important parts: in painting a scene, we sketch in the important features. Similarly, in describing phenomena in words, we almost automatically select what is important to us. Doing so is second nature; indeed, so much so that Travers (1961) used it as a predictor of teaching ability. To find what was important to teachers, he asked them to draw a classroom. Did they include pupils? Where did they put the teacher? The more successful teachers not only included pupils, but also drew the teacher in the classroom working with children, rather than behind a desk.

Because we are continuously surrounded by numbers, we often point out the significant aspects of our world with numbers: the gross national product, the population of a community, the temperature of the oven, or the Scholastic Aptitude Test (SAT) score of a college freshman. Nouns name these objects or characteristics: product, population, heat, verbal learning ability. We select each of these names from a range of possible nouns to fit the phenomena we wish to convey. To further convey them, when describing in words, we use adjectives to modify those nouns: *enormous* gross national product, *small* town population, *hot* oven, *bright* college freshman. When describing numerically, we use numbers instead of adjectives.

We must decide what it is we wish to convey: a measure of some particular ability, an economic or geographic fact, or, in the case of statistics, some characteristic of a set of data. Thus, numbers take the place of adjectives to describe nouns: $4 billion gross national product, a population of 267 persons, a 12-inch table lamp, a freshman with an SAT verbal score of 800. We speak of a batting average of .325, or an average income of $20,000. As used in the social sciences, numbers specify some condition in a category (such as how many) or a point on some scale.

Numbers in the social sciences modify their nouns by giving us a count of units (267 persons), by indicating a rank (the twelfth-smallest town in the state), or by placing the characteristics on some scale (12 inches, SAT score of 800, a mean of 500). They refer to only a single dimension, or characteristic, at a time, just as an adjective does—32 inches tall, a mean of $20,000. Numbers have the considerable advantage that we can differentiate far more precisely with numbers than we can with words. For example, students with SAT scores of 800 and 750 are both very bright, but their scores differentiate them. Even using a less-than-perfect measuring instrument, with a scale running over a large range, we can differentiate many more levels of learning ability than we have adjectives to describe them.

All the advanced fields of science that can predict and control use numbers to describe phenomena. In fact, using numbers has come to be such a hallmark of science that some people look askance at fields that do not use them. It is true that the use of numbers has proven effective and efficient in describing phenomena. Some experts, however, believe that because certain characteristics have not yet been measured adequately words still do a better job. At the current level of development of the social sciences, there is room for both points of view—and both have merit.

♦ *As used in the social and behavioral sciences, numbers specify a condition in a category or on some scale. Most fields of science that have made advances in prediction or control have used numbers to describe their phenomena.*

We have noted three operations for numbers: naming and counting, ranking, and placing on a scale. These correspond to different levels of measurement, each containing more information than the previous and requiring a greater degree of precision.[1] Thus, if we discriminate no more finely than to put people into categories (Caucasian, African American, Hispanic, Asian, Native American), all we can do is to name the categories and to count their contents. Such use is designated as the **nominal level of measurement**. The names apply to persons or things with common characteristics that we place into the same category. The UPC bar code on merchandise that is read at the cash register by a laser scanner is a nominal use of numbers; it names the product. We can also use numbers to modify that name by telling how many of a thing there are, that is, by counting them.

If we can differentiate among the individuals within a group, we can move to the next higher level of measurement: ranking, or the **ordinal level of measurement**. We can rank several teachers in terms of their apparent skill but perhaps would not want to say that the differences in skill between the first and second and between second and third are equal. So we are not placing them on an equal-unit scale, but we do know that one is more skillful than another—ordinal measurement. The Mohs hardness scale is an example of a very useful scale. It is formed by determining which mineral will scratch the other when the two are rubbed together; diamonds, scratching everything else, rate the hardest. We have no way of expressing diamond's hardness other than this ranking.

Finally, at the next two levels of measurement, we place numbers on scales: one with an arbitrary zero point like the Fahrenheit temperature scale—an **interval scale**—and one with a real zero point like the scale of inches —a **ratio scale**. The advantage of the latter is that we can say that a distance of 12 inches is twice as long as one of 6 inches. Conversely, we cannot say that a day on which the temperature reaches 80 degrees is twice as warm as one on which it reaches 40 degrees. Similarly, a student with an SAT verbal score of 400 does not have half the verbal learning ability of the student with the top score of 800. Most psychological and educational measures are of the arbitrary-zero type. These are called interval scales because the units from one score point to the next (400 to 401, 401 to 402) are presumed equal, but the zero point is arbitrary.

Just where ordinal scales cease to be useful and interval scale statistics become permissible has been much discussed.[2] A response scale such as "never," "sometimes," "frequently," and "always" is clearly ordinal. We often assign the values 1, 2, 3, 4 to these responses and compute averages; that is, we treat them as though the attribute were being measured on an interval scale. We have no evidence that the distance from "never" to "sometimes" equals that from "some-

---

[1]This discussion of nominal, ordinal, interval, and ratio measures perpetuates a legacy of S. S. Stevens (1946, 1951), which, some statisticians argue, is best left forgotten. Certainly, Stevens scale types are incomplete, as Duncan (1984) observantly notes. Further, this textbook includes counting (which Stevens ignored) in the nominal category. It deserves a place, for when combined with good theory, counting can be as important as measurement and is certainly less controversial than measurement. Discussion of these measurement levels is needed because the *interpretation* of statistics is determined by the level of data from which they were computed. We can calculate arithmetic averages on ordinal data, but a comparison of such averages is meaningless unless we assume that the data come from scales or measures whose units we can assume are approximately equal.

[2]For an excellent discussion, see Knapp (1990).

times" to "frequently." Since, however, the data yield useful generalizations when interpreted that way, we assume the underlying concept to be acceptable. Because it works, we use it.

Where the zero point is not arbitrary, we call the scale a ratio scale because we can legitimately interpret ratios such as twice as much or half as much. Time and most physical measures have this property. It makes sense that one can do something in half the time or that one person is half as tall as another. What does a zero SAT score mean? There is no such thing.

Some statistics are designed to deal with categorical data or nominal measurement, some with ranked data, and most with interval or ratio scale measurement where it is assumed we have a scale that measures in equal units.

◆ *Four uses of numbers are:*
  1. *Nominal: numbers name the members of a category or indicate the number in the category.*
  2. *Ordinal: successive numbers order data in terms of some common characteristic (size, hardness, ability, etc.). No assumption is made that the differences between the numbers are equal.*
  3. *Interval: successive numbers on a scale mark off equal units, but the scale's zero point is arbitrarily chosen.*
  4. *Ratio: not only do numbers mark off equal units, but the zero indicates an absence of whatever the scale measures.*

Representations of Groups of Numbers (Data Sets)

How would we describe each of these data sets (the list of data describing one or more characteristics of a group): The gross national product of a variety of countries? The populations of the communities of a state? The heights of a shipment of table lamps? The SATs of a freshman class? A common way is to use descriptive statistics, summarizing one feature of the data on a characteristic at a time—the average, the spread, the bias toward high or low, and so forth.

We tend to rush to use statistics or graphs, forgetting that clever use of words can also bring life to a disembodied set of numbers. Consider this from Wurman (1989, p. 176):

Statistics about the distribution of income may not mean much, but imagine if people's height reflected their income. An hour-long parade of 30 million British income-earners would start with several minutes of people with no height at all (people who, although working, are losing money), to more than a half-hour's worth of very short people (mostly women, pensioners and teenagers). Only after forty minutes would people of average height appear, followed by a few people who would be ridiculously tall, towering 20 miles over the heads of the people who started the parade.

This dramatic quotation also lends itself to a pictorial representation, the use of a graph or chart. Graphs and charts can depict all of this at once holistically and in easily understood pictorial form, letting us instantly grasp what is significant about it. Although the rest of this chapter is devoted to descriptive statistics, it just takes more pages of text to explain them. Before using statistics, first consider whether they are the best means of communicating what you wish to convey. Graphical representation has been underused, perhaps because of the extra preparation and printing costs. Today, however, they are so easily generated by a variety of computer programs that their use should be increasing. And, as the verbal illustration nicely shows, creativity and imagination help enormously.

Some common graphical representations are shown in Figure 17.1, which presents nine different ways of graphically portraying exactly the same data, the scores of 18 persons on a test of aggression (hence, the boxing figures in chart G). Each data point is individually represented in chart A; in total, the points depict a **frequency distribution**. Frequency distributions are strongly recommended to show how scores are arranged. In one picture, a frequency distribution conveys multiple layers of information: the spread of scores, the location of the middle scores, whether the scores cluster around one or more points, and whether the distribution is symmetrical, among other things. As Cohen (1990) puts it, without them you won't know that "there are no cases between scores of 72 and 90, or that this score of 24 is somewhere in left field, or that there is a pileup of scores of 9. These . . . become immediately evident with simple graphic representation" (p. 1305).

The variety of charts and graphs in Figure 17.1 only scratches the surface; their forms are as numerous as human ingenuity. For example, quality of life can be portrayed by superimposing faces on the states of a U.S. map. The features of the face each represent a quality-of-life characteristic (for example, eyebrows = crime; mouth = education, etc.) and can be given a positive or negative look to reflect that aspect. A high crime rate has arched eyebrows; lots of educational opportunity has a smiling mouth, little a frowning one; and so on. We can convey an overall impression of a state yet allow specification of a characteristic.

Some charts and graphs, including the histogram (C), the bar chart (F), and the figure chart (G), permit reconstruction of the data more easily than others. The **stem-and-leaf diagram** (D), invented by Tukey (1977; see also Emerson and Hoaglin, 1983), is easy to construct by hand for small data sets. It shows the values of the numbers in the "leaves" at the same time as it portrays the shape of the score distribution. In this diagram, the tens digit appears to the left of the "trunk," the unit digits to the right. Therefore, the top number is 11, with a 1 in the tens column and a 1 in the units column. Elevens and 12s would be tallied in this row or "branch," 13s and 14s in the next, 15s and 16s in the next, and so on. Thus, in the second branch there are two 13s and four 14s, represented by the two 3s and four 4s, respectively. The tens digit is not repeated until it is changed, as it is for the

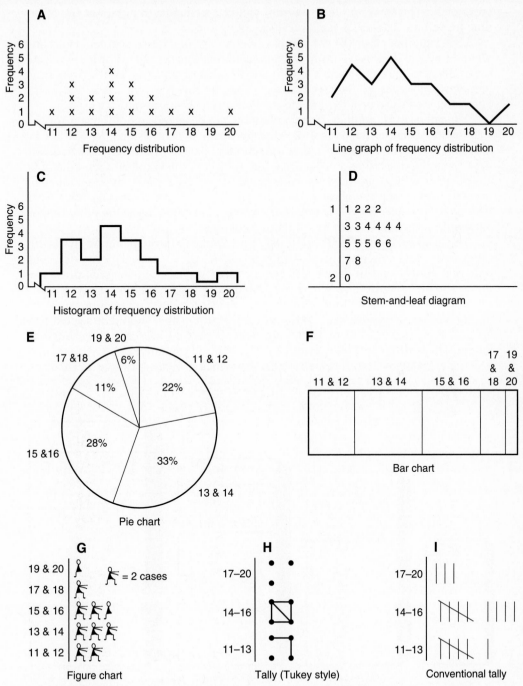

FIGURE 17.1 Different ways of portraying exactly the same data for the scores of 18 persons on a test of aggression.

score of 20. The stem-and-leaf diagram yields a frequency diagram at the same time that all the data are present for inspection.

Using the pie chart (E) we can easily compare one circle segment with another. However, unless we insert percentage figures, as here, it is harder to reconstruct the data since it is harder to estimate the area of circle segments. Area comparisons are easier in the bar chart (F), but percentages are an added help. Percentages can also be added to the columns of the histogram (C).

The tallies in H, another Tukey invention, are designed to minimize errors in a conventional tally such as chart I. Sometimes, due to carelessness, we add the final cross mark when there are either too few (three) or too many (already five) tallies. Arranging the tallies in a square is less subject to this error provided the dots are made heavily. The first four tallies are dots for the corners, the next four are the lines connecting the corners, and the final two, are the diagonals, for a total tally of 10. The tally for the scores 14–16 in chart H is nine cases; the other diagonal would constitute a tenth case if there were one.

The icons in figure chart G accurately portray the data. Such picture charts are often misleading, however, because the artist scales the characteristic of interest in only one dimension but draws it in two or three. A three-dimensional presentation is shown in Figure 17.2, where the gasoline pumps are actually scaled according to price only in one dimension, height. As Tufte (1983) points out, to avoid giving the wrong impression, it is the *area* of the pumps that should be scaled. The actual increase in price from 1973 to 1979 is 195 percent, which is the change in height. The width is also slightly scaled up, so the accompanying increase in area is actually 200 percent. But drawn in three-dimensions instead of two, or made as

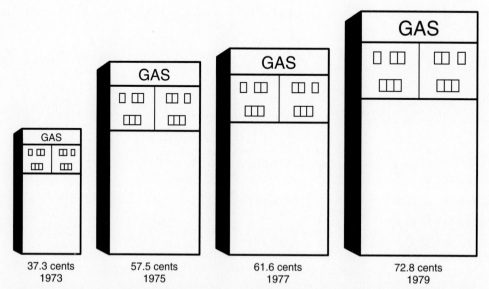

FIGURE 17.2 Misrepresentation in a picture chart of the average price of a gallon of gasoline for odd-numbered years, 1973–1979 (after a graph in *Time,* April 9, 1979, p. 57).

THE
NORMAL
LAW OF ERROR
STANDS OUT IN THE
RECORDS OF HUMANS
AS ONE OF THE BROADEST
GENERALIZATIONS OF NATURAL
PHILOSOPHY ◆ IT SERVES AS THE
GUIDING INSTRUMENT IN RESEARCHES
IN THE PHYSICAL AND SOCIAL SCIENCES AND
IN MEDICINE AGRICULTURE AND ENGINEERING ◆
IT IS AN INDISPENSABLE TOOL FOR THE ANALYSIS AND THE
INTERPRETATION OF THE BASIC DATA OBTAINED BY OBSERVATION AND EXPERIMENT.

FIGURE 17.3 Print formed into the shape to be conveyed, in this instance, the normal probability distribution, or normal curve (Tufte, 1983, p. 143).

clay models, when we compare the suggested volume, the apparent increase in price is 586 percent![3]

We typically choose a graphic form that facilitates the intended interpretation of the data. Charts E and F in Figure 17.1, for instance, facilitate comparisons among segments—for example, how big a portion of the federal budget is spent servicing the national debt or how small a portion of a nonprofit organization's expenses goes toward raising funds. Other forms emphasize outlines, flatness, peakedness, pileups at either end, where the bulk of cases lie, and so on.

Figure 17.3 shows an adapted version of a whimsical portrayal devised by the statistician W. J. Louden. It shows the bell-shaped form of a very common frequency distribution, the normal curve. His is an ingenious combination of chart and typography.

Graphics have much to recommend them, especially when, as is usual, they display all the data. Always examine the frequency distributions for your data. Though you can infer certain characteristics from descriptive statistics, the frequency distribution will corroborate the accuracy of your inferences as well as your computations. You can spot computational errors if a statistic looks unreasonable compared to the graphic representation. You can also see other interesting characteristics of the data, such as flatness or peakedness, number of peaks, lack of balance around the middle or in one direction, and so on.

Proper formulation of charts and graphs is essential to avoid misconceptions Tufte (1983) very crisply describes the goal: "Graphical excellence is that which gives the viewer the greatest number of ideas in the shortest time with the least ink in the smallest space" (p. 51). To achieve this, he suggests:

- Keep the representation of numbers, as physically measured on the surface of the graphic itself, directly proportional to the numerical quantities represented.

---

[3]Tufte (1983) is recommended reading for anyone interested in presenting data graphically and artistically. The book not only gives good advice but also is full of interesting examples.

- Use clear, detailed, and thorough labeling to defeat graphical distortion and ambiguity. Write out explanations of the data on the graphic itself. Label important events in the data.
- Don't let the number of information-carrying (variables) dimensions depicted exceed the number of dimensions in the data. (p. 77)

✦ *Charts and graphs have the advantage of showing the data while highlighting certain aspects of them. Unlike a descriptive statistic, such as an average, they can show more than one aspect at a time. Some, such as the frequency distribution, histogram, and stem-and-leaf diagram, show all the individual data points while displaying their distribution shape.*

✦ *Before (or at the same time as) you consider using descriptive statistics, determine whether the goal of your communication can be as well or better conveyed by a graphic. If it can, remember to heed Tufte's maxim to "convey the greatest number of ideas in the shortest time with the least ink in the smallest space."*

Descriptive Statistics

A descriptive statistic enables us to summarize some single attribute of a set of numbers. Adjectives that describe tallness, width, and other dimensions help us to visualize an object. Thus, each descriptive statistic describes a different aspect of a set of data and helps us gain an understanding of it. The most commonly used descriptive statistics are those describing the "central tendency" of data. They tell us something about the middle point around which most elements of a data set are found. Three descriptive statistics, the mode, the median, and the mean, are commonly used.

Measures of Central Tendency

The **mode** is simply the score, measure, or category that occurs the most often. Categorical (nominal-level measurement) data have a mode; it is the category with the most persons or things in it. In census data displaying the number of Caucasians, African Americans, Asian Americans, and other groups, the modal category is the largest. In the case of the frequency distribution of Figure 17.1, chart A, 14 is the mode, the score with the highest frequency.

The **median** is the point below which half the scores lie. In a sample with an odd number of observations, it is the middle observation, or score: In the sequence 10, 14, 15, 17, 20, the median is 15. With an even number, it is the score halfway between the two middle ones: In the sequence 10, 14, 16, 17, the median is 15. If the middle score lies within a set of equal numbers, such as the 14s in the sequence 13, 13, 14, 14, 14, 14, 15, 16, 16, finding the median is more complicated. In the distributions in Figure 17.1, chart A, the median score is 14.25. Why is there a fractional quantity? Because, if more than one case has the median score, we must divide the score appropriately.[4] A score of 14 technically includes scores from 13.5 to 14.4999+, and three of the 14s are below the middle score. Therefore 0.75 is added to 13.5, making the median 14.25. No median can be formed for nominal data because they have no order, but we can find one for ordinal or higher-level data.

By far the most commonly used indicator of central tendency is the **mean,** or arithmetic average. This is simply the sum of the observations divided by the number of observations. It assumes that the data are at least at the interval level of measurement. If the scores are displayed as a frequency distribution (Figure 17.1, charts A–D), it is the point on the baseline around which the distribution would balance if it were cut out of cardboard and put on a knife edge. The mean of the frequency distribution in Figure 17.1 is 14.5.

Like a seesaw on a child's playground, cases that are on the extremes have a major effect on the mean. Picture two children in balance on the seesaw but sitting in toward the center. Now move one child to the far end of the board. Because the fulcrum has to be moved toward the distant child to restore the balance, an extreme score pulls the mean significantly toward it.

Imbalance in a frequency distribution is referred to as **skewness**; if the distribution is asymmetrical, with a long tail on one side, the mean is pulled toward that side. A long tail toward the larger values is called a positive skew; one toward the smaller, a negative skew. A skewed distribution can be detected by the order of mean, median, and mode. When the mean is largest, the median next, and the mode smallest, as in frequency distribution B of Figure 17.4, the skew is positive (a long tail toward the right); when the size order of these measures is the opposite, the skew is negative (C). When they are all very close, the distribution is likely to be symmetrical (A).[5]

A negatively skewed distribution may result when we have a test with a "ceiling" effect; the test is too easy for high achieving students, nearly all of whom get very high scores, yet it discriminates well (provides a spread of scores) among low achieving ones. Similarly, a test that is too difficult for low achieving students

---

[4]Finding the median is a little more complicated than counting to find the middle case if we have more than one score in the interval, as in this instance, or if we have grouped data. Charts E, F, and G of Figure 17.1 display grouped data; they combine the frequencies for more than one score. Charts H and I combine them three or four at a time—in these instances, each of two or more successive score intervals. Where the score range is large, it is common to group data in intervals of 5 or 10. To find the median where there are multiple cases in the score interval within which the median lies, follow these steps—the bracketed material following each step applies it to the data of Figure 17.1, chart A: (a) Find the middle case, $N \div 2$ [$18 \div 2 = 9$]. (b) Find the interval within which the middle case lies [14]. (c) Determine how many cases are needed out of the interval to add up to $N \div 2$ cases [3, counting from the bottom]. (d) Divide the number needed by the number in the interval [$3 \div 4 = 0.75$]. (e) Multiply this fraction by the size of the interval [in this case, the interval is 1, since each score is tallied and scores are not grouped]. (f) Add the answer to the lower limit of the interval [the interval 14 runs from 13.5 to 14.4999+. A 10-point interval of 10 to 19 runs from 9.5 to 19.4999+. In this case, the lower limit of 14 is 13.5, so we add the 0.75 to it to obtain 14.25, the median].

[5]Note that we say "likely" to be symmetrical but not "certain." Large clumps of scores close to the mean on one side can be offset by small clusters on the other side distanced further from the mean. This distribution will be asymmetrical even though the mean, median, and mode are all lined up in the middle.

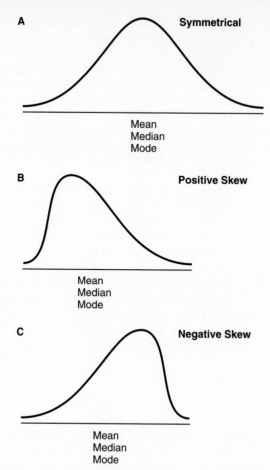

FIGURE 17.4 Symmetrical and skewed distributions and their effect on measures of central tendency.

will bunch up the very low scores and therefore have a "floor" effect, but it will spread out the high achieving students. A floor effect could have created the "cliff" at the left end of B in Figure 17.4, just as a ceiling effect could have created the right end of C.

With a skewed distribution, we are more likely to use the median or the mode rather than the mean to represent the data's central tendency. For example, the distribution of pay in large corporations is usually skewed with the mean moved higher by the salaries of top executives. The pay of a typical employee is better represented by the median or mode.

Not all distributions are bell-shaped.[6] Those that deal with social conformity,

[6]True, but many are, and even Plato noticed this. In *Phaedo*, Plato remarks to Socrates, "There are not many very good or very bad people, but the great majority are something between the two. . . . Have you never realized that extreme instances are few and rare, while intermediate ones are many and plentiful?" (Duncan, 1984).

for instance, are likely to be J-shaped. In Figure 17.5, graph A shows such a distribution for the number of parking tickets acquired by individuals in a year. Most had none, one, or two, and the drop-off is severe from there. Some curves have more than one peak and are multimodal. An example is the bimodal graph B in Figure 17.5, which is a frequency distribution of SAT scores for a high school with a combined rural and a suburban attendance area. The score distribution of the suburban feeder elementary school is represented by the higher peak, that for the rural feeder school by the lower one. When the students are merged in the high school, the combined distribution still shows these two peaks.

+ *Three statistics describe the central tendency of a data set:*
  1. *The mode is the most numerous category, measure, or score.*
  2. *The median is the point below which half of the scores, or measures, lie.*
  3. *The mean is the arithmetic average, the sum of the scores divided by their number, the balance point of the score distribution.*
+ *In a symmetrical frequency distribution, the mean, median, and mode are nearly equal.*
+ *In a negatively skewed distribution (tail to left), the mean is smallest, the median is in between, and the mode is largest.*
+ *Conversely, in a positively skewed distribution (tail to the right), the mean is largest, and the mode smallest.*
+ *Negative skewness can result from a "ceiling" effect (measure is too easy for high-scoring students).*
+ *Positive skewness can result from a "floor" effect (measure is too hard for low-scoring students).*

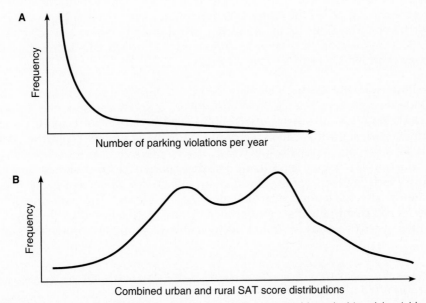

FIGURE 17.5 Frequency distributions for a social conformity variable and a bimodal variable.

We began this chapter with a discussion of four different levels of measurement: nominal, ordinal, interval, and ratio. Each level contains more information about the phenomena being described than did the previous. Nominal measures group people, ordinal measures rank them, interval measures use scales with an arbitrary zero point to show distance between ranks, and ratio measures use scales with a true zero.

Statistics require a certain level of information in order to be correctly interpreted; therefore, we can use only certain statistics on the lower levels of measurement. For example, since we cannot order nominal measures, they have no median and, of course, no mean. Since we can tell which category contains the largest number, we can determine the modal category. Where we have ordinal measures, we can determine the middle case; thus we can find a median. If there are ties in rank, there is a modal rank; without ties, all ranks have one case, so there is no peak. Finally, with interval and ratio measures, we can find all three— mean, median, and mode.

In using a statistic designed for lower-level data on higher-level data, we discard the additional information of the higher scale. Thus, the mode alone includes no information from cases other than those in the modal category. The median finds the middle case, but the clustering or spread of cases on both sides of it does not affect it; such information affects only the mean. As we have discussed earlier, this differential sensitivity can be helpful, for example, in detecting the presence and direction of skewness.

Measures of Dispersion and Variability

Range. The second most common characteristic of a distribution summarized by a descriptive statistic is its dispersion: how far apart the highest and lowest observations are and how scores are bunched around the center. The former, the simplest measure, is called the **range.** It is the distance from the highest to the lowest observations. The range for the frequency distribution in Figure 17.1 (A) is $20 - 11 = 9$. Because the range is totally dependent on the two extreme scores, it is likely to vary considerably from sample to sample.

Semi-Interquartile Range. One way to take account of the middle scores but to include the notion of how far they are spread, is to choose specified points toward the middle of the distribution and to see how far they are apart. The most common such statistic is called the **semi-interquartile range.** A **quartile,** like the median, designates a point below which a given proportion of the scores falls; for quartiles this is one-quarter of them. The first quartile, or Q_1, designates the point below which 25 percent of the observations fall; Q_2, the 50 percent point (thus the median is also the second quartile); and Q_3, 75 percent.[7] The semi-interquartile range is half (semi-) the distance between Q_1 and Q_3 (the interquartile range). We find the quartiles just as we found the median, except that we divide the number

---

[7]In Figure 17.7 (page 404), on the percentiles scale, the 25th percentile is Q_1, the 50th percentile is Q_2 (median), and the 75th percentile is Q_3.

of cases by 4 instead of 2. In Figure 17.1 (A), because there are 18 cases, the first quartile is halfway between the fourth and fifth cases, 12 and 13, or 12.5. The third quartile is in an interval with two cases. Thus, we use a procedure similar to finding the median, except that for the third quartile we encounter the point below which three-fourths of the cases fall.[8] It turns out to be 15.75. The semi-interquartile range is half the distance between Q_1 and Q_3, (15.75 − 12.5 = 3.25; 3.25 ÷ 2 = 1.625).

Since we are trying to find the distance between points, merely ranking them will not do; we must assume interval or ratio scale measures. We use the semi-interquartile range primarily when we report only descriptive statistics for a study. Unlike the standard deviation, it has no use in inferential statistics. Because the latter statistics are common, the standard deviation is the most frequently used measure of dispersion.

Standard Deviation and Variance. Standard deviation and variance measure how the observations are spread around the mean. The standard deviation is the positive square root of the **variance**. To obtain the **standard deviation** (SD), we find the distance of each observation from the mean, square that distance, find the average of those squares, and take its positive square root. Engineers call this the "root mean square deviation," which states the computational operations in reverse order. The variance is the square of the standard deviation (SD^2).

The formula for the standard deviation of a set of scores is

$$SD = \sqrt{\frac{\Sigma(X - M)^2}{N}}$$

where Σ indicates summation, X stands for each score, M for the mean, and N for the total number of scores. Translating the formula into a sequence of operations: the mean is subtracted from each score; these differences are squared and then summed; the sum is divided by the number of scores. The quotient of this fraction is the variance. The positive square root of that quotient is the standard deviation. When a set of scores is a sample from some population and it is the population that is of interest rather than the sample, we use $N - 1$ rather than N in the denominator in order to estimate the population standard deviation. This correction is necessary in order to adjust for a bias in estimation, which is of greater concern with small samples (the effect of subtracting 1 from a large N is negligible).

The standard deviation indicates how broadly the scores in a distribution are spread one from another, the deviation of each score from the mean contributing its bit. Hence, a class that is very heterogeneous in ability has a large standard de-

---

[8]Counting from the bottom, we need three-quarters of the 18 cases, which is 13.5 cases. This point falls in the interval 16, in which there are two cases. Because there are 13 cases through the score of 15, we need only half a case from the two that are there, or .5 ÷ 2, which is .25. We add this to the lower boundary of the interval, which is 15.5, to find Q_3, which is 15.75.

viation on its ability measure, whereas a class grouped by ability to contain high or low students, but not both, has a much smaller one.

The standard deviation is affected by extreme values even more strongly than the mean (on which it is based). The distance of a score from the mean is squared, and the squares of numbers rise much faster than the numbers themselves. For example, let's consider scores of 5, 6, 7, and 8, which are but one unit apart. Their squares (25, 36, 49, 64), however, are 11, 13, and 15 units apart, respectively, and the distance between numbers continues to increase as the numbers get larger. Thus, the more extreme the case, the more leverage it will have.

Figure 17.6 shows the two measures of dispersion on a normal frequency distribution. The **normal frequency distribution** is one of several ideal models of data. It corresponds closely enough to the score distributions of many behavioral measures to be useful. Note that the semi-interquartile range, by definition, includes the middle half of the cases. The standard deviation usually includes about the middle two-thirds of the cases. Therefore, the middle band including ±1SD on each side of the mean is broader than the semi-interquartile range. The range is not shown, because the highest score for a normal distribution is infinity, and the lowest is minus infinity.

Three measures of dispersion:
1. The range is the distance from the lowest to the highest score.

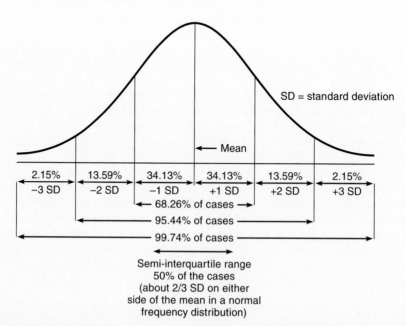

FIGURE 17.6 Two measures of dispersion shown for a normal frequency distribution (normal curve).

2. *The semi-interquartile range is half the distance from the point below which a quarter of the observations lie (Q_1, first quartile) to the point below which three-fourths of them lie (Q_3, third quartile).*
3. *The standard deviation is the root mean square of the deviations from the mean. The square of the standard deviation is the variance. The standard deviation is the dispersion measure most used; it is strongly affected by cases far from the mean.*

Standard and Derived Scores

Standard deviations provide a useful gauge as the unit permits development of a constant scale across measures. Thus, we can compare scores to show relative standing on very different tests. A raw score typically conveys little information. There is no meaningful zero point; some tests are easy, others difficult; some are extremely long and some very short. However, describing a score in standard deviation units, especially if the score distribution is roughly a symmetrical bell-shaped curve, tells us whether that score is high, low, or in the middle of the score distribution.

Standard scores (or z-scores) are simply the raw (original) score translated into its distance from the mean in standard deviation units. For example, in a distribution with a mean of 100 and a standard deviation of 25, a raw score of 75—a score that is one standard deviation below the mean—will have a standard score of –1.00. Standard scores, as such, are not much used because negative numbers for scores below the mean are troublesome to handle and carry a negative connotation. Instead, a close relative, **derived scores** (also called **scaled scores**) are commonly used. With the addition of a constant like 50, 100, or 500 to all scores so that the mean becomes 50, 100, or 500 instead of zero, derived scores translate standard scores to a scale where all scores are positive.

Figure 17.7 shows a variety of score scales that set some arbitrary serviceable number as the mean and similarly set the standard deviation conveniently (usually to 10 or 100) and then translate the scores to that scale.

We met the bell-shaped curve earlier as the normal curve in Louden's clever chart-graph (Figure 17.3) and in Figures 17.4 and 17.6. Numerous test score distributions resemble it, as do many physiological functions such as height and reaction time. Examine Figure 17.6, which is an approximation of a normal curve. The curve is really a frequency distribution just like chart B in Figure 17.1. In chart B, a line joins the tops of the columns representing the number of observations at each score value. Similarly, the normal curve joins the tops of an infinite number of columns running from the highest to the lowest score. When we mark off successive standard deviation distances on the baseline, starting at the mean, we will find that one standard deviation falls just at the point where the curve changes from convex to concave.

One of the advantages of the normal curve is that we know what proportion of the cases fall between any two scores. The percentages between successive standard deviation demarcations in Figure 17.6 indicate what proportion of the scores falls into each area. Adding the figures for the two areas adjacent to the mean gives 68.26 percent; thus, slightly more than two-thirds of the cases lie between ±1 standard deviation. When we extend the range to ±2 standard deviations, we cover 95 percent of the observations (the middle four areas add to 95.44

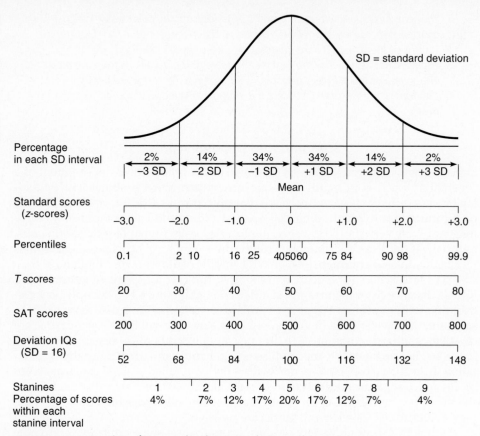

FIGURE 17.7 A variety of score scales shown in relation to the normal curve.

percent), or to ±3 standard deviations, which includes all but 3 cases in 1,000 (99.74 percent).

Many intelligence test results are reported in deviation IQ scores with a mean set at 100 and the standard deviation at 16 (for example, the Stanford-Binet; the Wechsler tests use 15). From our knowledge of the normal distribution, we can then interpret an intelligence test score of 148 as very high, for it is three standard deviations from the mean. Since only 3 cases in 1,000 exceed ±3 standard deviations, and that includes the observations in both tails, only 1 or 2 such scores in 1,000 might be expected in the upper tail alone. Similarly, a score of 84 is one standard deviation below the mean. With half of the cases above the mean and about 34 percent between the mean and one standard deviation below it, we know that 34 + 50 = 84 percent of the cases are above the score of 84 and only 16 percent below it. Whether such inferences are accurate depends on how closely the shape of the sample's frequency distribution approximates that of a normal curve.

The percentage below a given score is called the **percentile** score. Figure 17.7 shows where some percentile values fall in terms of standard deviations. Knowing the proportion of cases at points along the normal distribution, we can easily translate raw, standard, and derived scores into percentiles. Many tests have tables showing the translation.

To ensure the accuracy of inferences made on the basis of a normal curve's proportions, some tests use normalized *T* scores, usually with a mean of 50 and a standard deviation of 10.[9] The raw score scale is stretched and shrunk to make the proportion of cases fit those of a normal distribution.

Some tests use **stanine scores**. The name is a contraction of "standard nine." Each stanine is half a standard deviation wide; the middle score of 5 straddles the mean. Because so few cases normally fall into the end categories, they are open-ended, extending to the highest and the lowest scores possible on the test. Like normalized *T* scores, stanines are normalized; thus, the percentages in each stanine correspond to those of the normal curve. Stanines cut the score scale into nine categories of equal raw score size. If we consider the lack of precision of most tests, this cruder categorization of scores may be more appropriate. Two- and three-digit derived scores invite spurious interpretations. In a scale with a possible range of 600 points, like the SAT, the comparison of small score differences, such as a score of 704 with one of 720, reflects only one more correct question. This trivial real difference is made to seem important by the 16-point derived score difference.

Using half-deviation steps to define each stanine, however, results in different percentages in each stanine score (4, 7, 12, 17, 20, 17, 12, 7, 4, respectively). It is easier to remember that a fifth of the cases (20 percent) fall in the middle category and that the categories to each side are successively smaller by 3, 5, 5, 3 percentage points (see the bottom line of Figure 17.7).

Standard scores are used most often to compare scores on different tests, relative standing of a student on a verbal ability test, for instance, with achievement on an English test. We would expect comparable standard scores on each if students are living up to their potential.

✦ *Using the standard deviation as the unit of measure and the mean as a base point, standard scores replace the raw score mean with zero and adjust the raw score standard deviation to 1.*

✦ *With this new scale, or "ruler," we can translate any score to show where it will fall on a standard or derived score scale—we can then compare relative standings of scores across tests for individuals.*

✦ *A variety of derived or scaled scores are available to translate raw scores into scales with easy-to-use means and standard deviations that facilitate usage and interpretation.*

✦ *Such scores typically use the frequency distribution of the normal curve as a basis for interpretation.*

✦ *Percentile scores indicate the percentage of scores falling below a given raw score.*

---

[9]Check the test manual, the name is used for *T* scores that have not been normalized.

Measures of Relationships

So far we have dealt with the description of a single variable, but more often we deal with at least two variables and wish to describe the extent of the relationship between them. Suppose we have grade point averages (GPAs) for a group of students both in high school and in their college freshman year. Thus, we have a pair of GPAs, one high school and one college, for each individual. We can then plot each pair as a point on a graph, as in Figure 17.8, where each *x* represents a pair. We can see that, in general, individuals who did well in high school also did well in college, because the two variables vary together—they co-vary or are correlated. Such a plot is called by several names: **scatterplot**, scatter diagram, scattergram. The oval line surrounding the points is added to show the area within which the pairs of scores fall. Not a part of the computation of a correlation, the oval line will be used in other figures to represent the scatter diagram.

Pearson Product-Moment Correlation. The **Pearson product-moment correlation**, more commonly referred to just as "the correlation," is represented by the symbol *r*, and indicates the extent of relationship by a number between +1.00 and −1.00; thus it is usually reported as a two-digit decimal, for example, .85. The correlation is computed from pairs of scores for each individual in the sample; each individual has a pair of scores, one on each of the two variables on which the correlation is being computed. A correlation of +1.00 indicates a perfect relationship such that if we know that the individual has the highest score on one variable, we also know she has the highest score on the other. Similarly, with a perfect positive

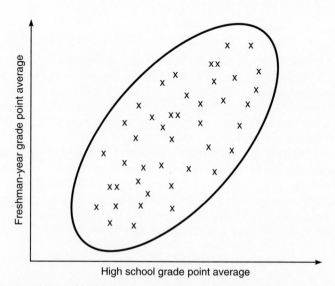

FIGURE 17.8 Correlation of high school and college grade point averages.

correlation, all the other pairs of scores are similarly predictable; they track each other exactly. With a negative correlation, they track one another inversely; with a correlation of −1.00, the highest score on one variable is paired with the lowest score on the other. A correlation of *less* than one, either positive or negative, indicates that each member of a pair of scores tracks the other *less* than perfectly so that the highest score on one variable in a positive correlation might be accompanied by a medium high score on the other variable. The lower the correlation, the more poorly one tracks the other, until, with a zero correlation, there is no regular relationship between the two scores. Knowing only one of the pair, we cannot predict what the other is likely to be.

Just as we learn to interpret the standard deviation, so we also learn the meanings of different sizes of correlation. Coat or sweater size bears a close-to-perfect positive relationship to the distance around a man's chest. High school academic achievement bears a zero relationship to shoe size or social security number, a negative but less than perfect relationship to the amount of conflict in the family or hours of television watching, and a positive but less than perfect relationship to the level of education of one's parents or to achievements in elementary school.

Anyone using correlations is well advised to create a scatterplot of the observations. Figure 17.9 shows scatterplots for correlations of various sizes. Correlations are often portrayed by encircling the majority of the points with an oval. As the oval narrows, it becomes a straight line for a perfect correlation, as in scatterplots C (*r* = +1.00) and D (*r* = −1.00). When the correlation decreases, the oval gets fatter until, at the zero point, it becomes a circle, as in plot E (*r* = .00). Plots A (*r* = about .80 to .90) and C are positive correlations. Plots B (*r* = −.20 to −.30) and D are

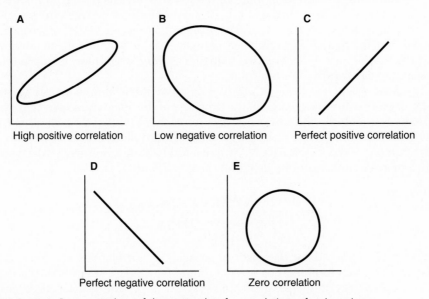

FIGURE 17.9 Representations of the scatterplots for correlations of various sizes.

negative. An exact size is not given for each scatterplot in Figure 17.9 because the correlation depends on the distribution of the scores as well as the shape of the envelope. Thus these are approximations.

The extent of relationship is indicated more accurately by the square of the correlation coefficient than by the coefficient itself. Thus, the amount of relationship displayed by a correlation of .40 is more accurately represented by .16, which is considerably lower. Further, an increase of .05 in correlation from .90 to .95 when these are squared is a change from .81 to .90, a change of .09. This is the same as the difference between a correlation of .10 and one of .32 [$(.10)^2 = .01$ to $(.32)^2 = .10$], which is a difference of .22 in terms of the coefficients. Because the connection between the amount of relationship and the size of the correlation coefficient is not constant from .00 to 1.00, a large change is needed at the low end of the correlation scale to achieve the same amount of increase in relationship as a small change attains at the top end of the scale.

The square of the correlation indicates the proportion of the variance that is accounted for by the relationship. For example, with a correlation of 1.00, 100 percent of the variance of the variables is common or accounted for by the relationship. With a correlation of .80, the proportion of variance that is common is .64, or 64 percent.

We noted earlier the importance of examining the scatterplot of a correlation. This is underscored by data from Anscombe's quartet (Anscombe, 1973, as given in Tufte, 1983, pp. 13–14). These are four sets of data of 11 cases, each of which produces exactly the same correlation of .82; they all even have the same means for both variables. However, the sets produce the four scatterplots shown in Figure 17.10. Note how different they are from one another. A is a typical correlation scatterplot; B is a curvilinear plot; C is an almost perfect positive correlation except for one point ($X=12$, $Y=13$). In D, all the y scores but one ($X=12$, $Y=19$) are the same. Were we to try to infer the nature of the relationship between the variables from just the number .82, the size of the correlation alone, we would make a grave mistake. Yes, the figures were adjusted to make a point, but they make it—examining the scatterplots as well as the statistics is very important! Computerized software can easily provide scatterplots.

The formula for the Pearson product-moment correlation is simple in standard score form; it is the average of the products of the standard scores (z-scores). Therefore, we multiply the pair of z-scores for each individual by each other (one from the x variable and one from the y variable), sum those products, and divide by the number of scores ($\Sigma z_x z_y$) ÷ N. Since we rarely have scores in standard score form, a more common formula using raw scores (X and Y) is:

$$r_{xy} = \frac{N\Sigma XY - (\Sigma X)(\Sigma Y)}{\sqrt{(N\Sigma X^2 - (\Sigma X)^2)(N\Sigma Y^2 - (\Sigma Y)^2)}}$$

Although designed for use with interval data, correlations are often computed on categorial (nominal) or ordinal on demographic data to show relationships with variables of interest in sample surveys. For example, let's consider the relation between political party registration and level of education previously shown in Table 16.2 on page 371. Although percentages depict the relationship, if

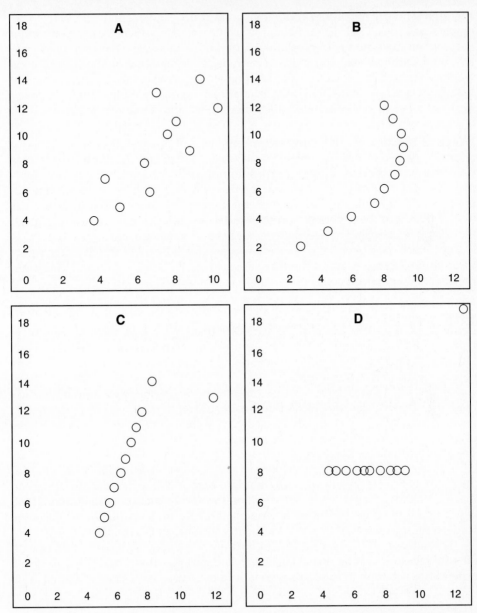

FIGURE 17.10 Scatterplots of four very different sets of scores for 11 subjects. Each set has the same mean for both variables, and the scatterplots for all four sets yield correlations of .82 (after Anscombe, 1973, as found in Tufte, 1983).

we wish to summarize the relationship with a correlational statistic, we assign arbitrary numbers to the categories and compute a Pearson product-moment correlation. For instance, we can assign 0 to the Democratic column and 1 to the Republican column (a nominal variable); similarly, 0 to elementary-level education,

1 to high school, 2 to college, and 3 to beyond college (an ordinal variable).[10] This process provides a pair of numbers for each case from which we can compute a Pearson product-moment correlation. Computed this way, the correlation between educational level and political party is .23. Depending on the assumptions we are willing to make, we can also use one of the correlations designed to handle data from special situations. These correlations are described in Table 17.1 (page 415) and other correlations are applied there to the above survey data also.

Effect of Outliers on the Correlation. The size of a correlation is particularly strongly affected by one or more extreme scores. Called *outliers*, these are observations that lie outside the ellipse that would normally encompass them. An example is the observation ($X=12$, $Y=13$) at the far right in scatterplot C of Figure 17.10. It is considerably off the line formed by the others, and notably lowers what would otherwise be a perfect correlation. In opposite fashion, in scatterplot D, there is no relationship between the *y*-axis scores (which are all 8s), and the *x*-axis scores (which vary over the score range) except for the outlier far up in the right-hand corner, which changes the correlation to .82.[11] As these examples indicate, the effect of outliers on correlations can make interpretation difficult.

Effect of Range on the Correlation. Because the correlation is sensitive to extreme cases, the score range of the variables making up a correlation should be typical of the relationship of interest. An atypical **restriction of range** leads to an underestimate of the size of the typical relationship, just as an atypical extension of range leads to an overestimate.

Figure 17.11 shows how, because of restriction of range, we might underestimate the effectiveness of selection into college. The data in the entire figure are what we would like to have—an unselected sample—to evaluate the effectiveness of using the high school grade point average (GPA) to estimate success in college. The typical situation, however, is that a test, or variable, is used to select those to be admitted and then only those already selected cases are available to estimate the success of selection—the cases to the right of the AB line. It is readily apparent that a correlation based on those cases alone would be markedly lower than that based on all the data. The former would markedly underestimate the selection value of high school GPA, yet it is frequently the only data available.

Thorndike (1947, as found in Guilford and Fruchter, 1978) describes one of the rare selection evaluations using unselected groups—they are costly, requiring expenditures to train individuals who would otherwise have been excluded. The

---

[10]If there are three or more categories, the variable must be ordered in some way—for instance, by the amount of education in this example. If we include independents among the political affiliations, for example, we can assign independents a value of 2 and Republicans a value of 3 if it is reasonable to assume that independents can be ordinally ranked on a scale from liberal Democrats to conservative Republicans.

[11]Without the outlier there is no variability; without variability there can be no correlation. Without variability the standard deviation in the denominator of the equation is zero. Recall from your study of algebra that dividing by zero makes no sense; thus there is no meaningful correlation coefficient.

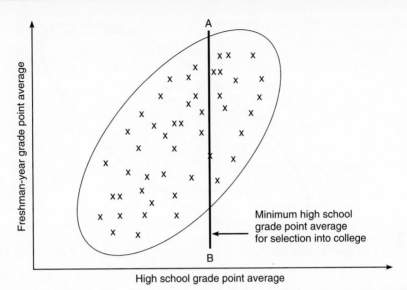

FIGURE 17.11 Selection of students for college on the basis of their high school grade point averages.

task was to evaluate the effectiveness of tests in predicting success in training pilots during World War II. The correlation between scores on a test of complex coordination and training success was .40 for the 1,036 unselected cadets but only −.03 in the top 13 percent that would have been selected. Restriction in range to that top group, which is all that might typically have been available, would have caused the test to appear useless.

In parallel fashion, if the range is extended to cover cases not typically included, the correlation will be an overestimate. Suppose you are considering using a reading test as a measure of how well a student is likely to achieve. Figure 17.12 shows the relationship of a reading test to overall achievement for each of grades 3 through 6. Note that the correlation *within any one* of these grades is not very high. The ellipse is very fat, almost the circle that you obtain for a very low or zero correlation. But the children do learn as they progress from grade to grade, which stretches the overall range of scores. When combined into a single scatterplot, the total range of scores increases markedly. Although the correlation was moderate to low in each of the grades taken individually, it is high (the heavily outlined ellipse) over the three grades. If you wish to use the reading test to examine children's likely progress in their own grade, the more modest correlation is the one you should heed.

Effect of Nonlinearity on the Correlation. From the fact that a perfect correlation is a straight line, you might guess that the Pearson product-moment correlation assumes that the relationship we are examining is a **linear relationship** (also called a straight-line relationship). As one variable changes, the other also changes in a proportionate amount. Relationships are not always linear, however. For example, a student with very little anxiety about a test may not exert himself

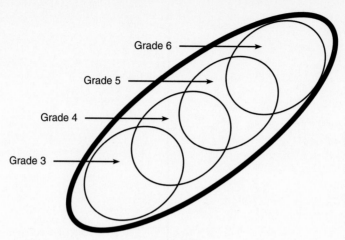

FIGURE 17.12 Effect of extended range on correlation.

and will receive a low score. But too much anxiety may lead to nervousness and also a low score. Only when moderately anxious will he attain his maximum score. Correlations of many ability scores with age are often nonlinear with growth spurts and plateaus.

Figure 17.13 shows a scatterplot for a class, some members of which have too much anxiety about the test, some too little, and some just enough to be well motivated. Such relationships yield an inverted U-shaped, or curvilinear, scatterplot. Such a relationship would be markedly underestimated by the Pearson product-moment correlation. However, we can use the correlation ratio (represented by the Greek letter *eta,* η) to estimate **nonlinear relationships** described in Table 17.1 later in the chapter.

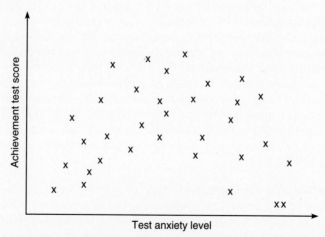

FIGURE 17.13 Curvilinear relationship between level of test anxiety and an achievement test score.

+ *The Pearson product-moment correlation shows the extent of a linear relationship between two variables on a scale from −1.00 to +1.00. It is usually reported as a two-digit decimal, for example, .76.*
+ *A correlation is computed from pairs of scores, a pair from each individual in the sample. For a correlation between variables A and B, the pair consists of an individual's scores on A and on B.*
+ *A correlation of .00 indicates no linear relationship.*
+ *A positive correlation shows that the members of the pair vary together; when one is high the other is also.*
+ *A negative correlation indicates that the variables vary inversely; low scores on one variable are associated with high scores on the other.*
+ *The extent of relationship is portrayed more accurately by the square of the coefficient than by the coefficient itself.*
+ *Size of the correlation is affected by outliers, nonlinearity, and inappropriate range (restriction in range or too broad a range to estimate the relationship in typical situations).*

Correlation and Causation. The fact that a relationship exists as shown by a correlation does *not* allow us to infer that the relationship is causal. Often the relationship is the result of a third variable or a combination of other variables. The statistician Helen Walker was fond of noting that comparing footprints in the sand of older women next to footprints of younger women might lead to the conclusion that women tended increasingly to walk with their toes pointing outward as they grew older. Actually, there is no causal relationship here, much rather it was considered a sign of femininity to walk with toes pointed out when these older women were young. Because the link often occurs earlier in the causal chain, we must be careful in inferring causation from a correlation.

Regardless of whether a relationship is causal, a correlation allows prediction; thus such relationships are extremely useful. An extensive body of literature describes predictors of various kinds: to enhance learning conditions, to increase the effectiveness of teaching, to predict the stock market, to forecast college success. The higher the correlation, the more accurate the prediction. Unless the correlation is perfect, however, the predicted value is always less extreme—that is, closer to its mean—than the value from which it was predicted. This relation of the predicted value to the size of the correlation is commonly described as follows: Predicted scores regress toward their mean—the smaller the correlation, the greater the regression toward the mean. Regression toward the mean reaches the mean itself with a zero correlation. With a zero correlation, the best prediction we can make from any score (such as high school GPA) is the mean of the other variable (mean college GPA).

The prediction of one variable from another is discussed in statistics books under the topic of **regression**. Regression, however, is too complicated a topic to cover here; see Guilford and Fruchter, (1978) or Hays (1981).

Other Correlations for Special Conditions. A variety of correlation statistics have been devised for special situations. Some of these have the same properties as the Pearson product-moment correlation coefficient; many of them do not.

Table 17.1 lists a number of these, indicating where you can read more about them, the assumptions they make about the data (special situations they fit), their special characteristics, and their limitations.

Earlier in the chapter, we computed a Pearson product-moment correlation on the sample survey data of Table 16.2 (p. 371) and found that it produced a correlation of .23. Alternatively, we can use appropriate choices from the special correlation methods described above. If we assume that Democrats and Republicans lie on a liberal–conservative continuum that has been arbitrarily divided and that level of education is an interval scale, we can use a biserial correlation. It produces a somewhat higher correlation of .29. If, on the other hand, we assume that political affiliation is a dichotomous variable, not an arbitrarily split continuous variable, we can use a point-biserial correlation that produces the same result as the Pearson product-moment correlation, .23.

Another possibility shown in Table 17.2, is to reduce the data to a two-by-two cross-break. Table 17.2 (p. 416)shows this process applied to the data of Table 16.2; it combines the top two rows into one and, similarly, the bottom two rows. This discards some of the information regarding education and assumes, for our purposes, that high school and elementary level are pretty much the same as are college level and beyond. We can use the tetrachoric coefficient to estimate the relationship of two arbitrarily categorized variables such as these, which is .32. Depending on the assumptions made, we use different statistics to compute the size of the relationship, and somewhat different estimates will result.

Treatment of Outliers

We have already noted that outliers strongly affect certain statistics such as means, standard deviations, and correlations. Should you, then, discard them? Or do they tell us something special about the topic? You must judge each situation on its own. You can interview persons with extreme scores to seek an explanation. An outlier may be the result of illness, trauma, or English as a second language and you might appropriately discard it. Be careful, however. An art test outlier's score, for example, that is due to color blindness raises questions about what is really being measured. Whether you decide to keep outliers or discard them, tell what you know and explain your action in the report. Calculate statistics both with and without the outliers so that readers can see their effect and judge for themselves.

Appropriate Interpretation of Statistics

Basic to proper interpretation is understanding what the data really represent. In part this requires: examining the data to determine that statistics were properly applied, examining the sample for representativeness, and examining what underlies the data from the standpoint of those from whom it was collected. If we expect to attain a consensus around the interpretation of data, we must anticipate problems our audience may have in these three areas. This general research strategy is especially important with statistics. We have already examined the

TABLE 17.1 *Correlations for Special Situations*

Correlation	Assumptions	Attributes	Limitations
Spearman's rank correlation (Guilford and Fruchter, 1978, p. 294)	Two ranked variables (e.g., rank in class achievement and rank in social activities), equal intervals between ranks, linearity	A product-moment correlation for ranks; is easy to compute for small data sets	Is often slightly smaller than the Pearson when raw scores are changed into ranked data
Biserial correlation (Guilford and Fruchter, 1978, p. 304)	A linear relationship between an interval or ratio scale variable and one that has been arbitrarily dichotomized (e.g., liberal-conservative); the latter would be considered normally distributed if measured continuously	Estimates the product-moment correlation for this special situation	Cases between dichotomized parts must not be missing; oddly shaped distributions may yield $r > 1.00$; always larger than point biserial
Point biserial (Guilford and Fruchter, 1978, p. 308)	A genuinely dichotomous variable (male-female, living-dying; not a continuous variable arbitrarily split), an interval or ratio scale variable; linearity	Cannot be interpreted on the product-moment scale but is an index of the relationship	Never quite reaches 1.00 but is at its maximum when split in the dichotomous variable is 50:50
Tetrachoric correlation (Guilford and Fruchter, 1978, p. 311)	Two normally distributed, arbitrarily dichotomized variables (achievers-nonachievers vs. tall-short), linearity	Approximates Pearson if assumptions are observed; shortcuts are typically used to estimate it	Should not be used with extreme splits (e.g., 90–10); when one cell is empty, it equals 1.00 even if other cells indicate the relationship is considerably less
Contingency coefficient (Hays, 1973, p. 743)	Two categorical variables (male-female, living-dead)	Goes between zero and 1.00 with no direction to relationship; equals Pearson when number of categories increases indefinitely	Has a maximum value of less than 1.00 for small number of categories (e.g., .87 for 4×4, .97 for 15×15); Cramer's *phi* prime overcomes this
Intraclass correlation (Guilford and Fruchter, 1978, p. 270)	Two or more sets of interval or ratio data sets	Is excellent for use in judging similarity of raters of a common situation or the reliability of repeated measures of individuals; can show members of a category or class are more alike than are nonmembers (e.g., twins vs. siblings)	Theoretically, minimum is −1.00 but actually is dependent on number of cases in a class; is sensitive to differences in mean and variances of groups being related; as these differences increase, intraclass correlation decreases
Correlation Ratio, eta (η). Used for nonlinear relationships; estimates fit of data to column or row means (Guilford and Fruchter, 1978, pp. 296–304)	Two interval or ratio scale variables, one treated as nominal for each eta	Two etas, one estimating fit of data to column means, other to the row means; goes between zero and 1.00 with no direction to relationship	Size dependent in part on number of columns or rows

TABLE 17.2 *Data of Table 16.2 Reduced to a Fourfold Table*

Level of Education	Number of Cases N = 423		Percentage of Cases	
	Democrats	Republicans	Democrats	Republicans
High school or less	191	101	45	24
Some college or beyond	59	72	14	17

matter of appropriate use of statistics in this chapter—for instance, in the discussion of outliers and nonlinearity. The old saying, "Figures don't lie, but liars figure!" clearly indicates that misuse of statistics is an important problem. Huff (1954) remains an excellent survey of statistics misuse. Let us examine the other two areas.

Representativeness of Sample. We are rarely interested in the sample itself, but rather in what it tells us about some larger group or population of which it is representative. If our sample comes from a laboratory school, our readers will suspect that, compared to typical public schools, students are well above average in ability and the ability range is smaller. If our research is to apply beyond the laboratory school, we should indicate the effect that range curtailment had on the data, what might be expected under more typical conditions, and how all these atypicalities affect the interpretation and generality of the results.

Understanding What Underlies Data. We are always tempted to take data at face value, but qualitative researchers in particular, remind us that data are always the result of a social construction and may not mean what we think they do. As Bogdan and Biklen (1992) point out, the very act of gathering data often changes it. When Congress mandated that 10 percent of a remedial program should consist of handicapped children, the programs magically produced the required number of such children. Were there really that many previously unrecognized handicapped children? Was the local definition of *handicapped* changed? "Statistical data on minority, or handicapped children . . . the number of athletic injuries, acts of violence, or incidence of drug use in schools does more than numerically portray phenomena; it changes how we experience them" (Bogdan and Biklen, p. 149). Depending on the reward or penalty for reporting them, data collection itself may increase or decrease the visibility of violence, injuries, or drug use; result in recruiting of minority groups; strengthen countermeasures toward undesirable behavior, and so forth. Changes in rates must be particularly scrutinized for such influences as well as the effects of newly visible efforts to collect the data, changes in definitions, new ways of data gathering such as a more sensitive test, and inconsistency in data collection procedure. Counts can be strongly influenced where the funding level depends on a quantitative indicator. Remember, accuracy depends on the data producer and "some commonly heard terms among data collectors include *fudge factor, numbers game, massaging the data, and padding*" (ibid., p. 151). Understanding what underlies the data is critical to its proper interpretation.

Exploring with Statistics

We usually don't think of statistics as useful in an exploratory mode because their use in the research literature is almost always to confirm or disconfirm some hypothesis, structure, or model. However, statistics have long been used to check data for unexpected relationships though that activity is not usually mentioned in the research reports. Scatterplots are universally used in this way. Researchers love the exhilaration of finding in them something unexpected that sometimes results in restructuring the whole direction of a study.

Having once experienced that "high," experienced researchers use descriptive statistics for the titillating exploration of data. They love looking for the next curiosity that could be just around the corner. Novice researchers should try exploration with simple statistics; it is a major joy of research. If you are interested in reading more about exploratory statistics, read Tukey (1977) or Leinhardt and Leinhardt (1980).

Exploration has been discouraged by the dictum that it is cheating to look at the data to see what they show, next develop a hypothesis, and, finally, proclaim to all that the data confirm it. When you know the hypothesis will be confirmed from the start—that is not research. Most statistics books warn against exploration as "data dredging " or "bottom fishing." As the derogatory names imply, such practices are deemed undesirable since chance relationships that are not generalizable may be interpreted as real.

Even if you rationalize after the fact, however, "Ah, now I see why," results that make reasonable sense may be worth confirmation research and further exploration. If you can, show that the explanation holds in a new sample; if it is confirmed, it probably is not happenstance. If you don't have time, leave testing for later or for someone else to follow up. *With clear indications that the results were found during exploration and explained after the fact,* you may include exploratory results in your report separately from the original hypotheses. Considering the time and effort invested in data collection, it is only sensible to seek all it can tell you. Wherever feasible, researchers ought to probe for additional findings that appear to make sense and then follow them up with further research for confirmation.

SUMMARY

The problem of describing a set of data is parallel to that of describing a situation in words. In both we select the features that are important to convey, name them, and then modify them to portray the situation more accurately. Graphs and charts convey more than one feature of a data set and therefore can communicate the sense of the data very effectively, but are underused. Statistics convey single features such as central tendency, dispersion or variation, and relationship. With descriptive statistics, we select the feature that is important (such as central tendency) and then modify it with numbers that convey more exactly the location or amount of that feature.

The statistics that convey central tendency are the mean, median, and mode; those that convey variation are the range, semi-interquartile range, and standard deviation. The mean and standard deviation are the most commonly used descriptive statistics and form the basis for standard scores. They can be used to translate raw scores into a variety of convenient score scales that are, in combination with the normal frequency distribution, more easily interpreted. Translating raw scores into a common derived score scale facilitates comparison of an individual's results on different tests

The Pearson product-moment correlation is most often used to convey the strength of relationships. Relationships are portrayed by means of a scatterplot, the shape of which indicates the general size and nature of the relationship. The correlation assumes that the relationship is best described or approximated by a straight line. The correlation ratio, *eta* (η), is used when the relationship is nonlinear. Regression permits the prediction of one variable from the other; the accuracy of prediction increases as the correlation increases. A variety of special correlation statistics have been developed for special situations.

A Look Ahead

As we will use many of this chapter's statistics in determining quality of measurement, we will meet them again in the next chapter on measurement, testing, and observation. Chapter 19 on statistical inference, inferring the size of a population value from a sample's statistics, also will build on this chapter's statistics.

ADDITIONAL READING

In addition to Tufte (1983), recommended earlier, see Henry (1997) for examples and discussion of graphical presentations. Guilford and Fruchter (1978) is a conventional but understandable statistics text; Jaeger (1990) is unconventional and an easy read. For exploratory data analysis, Tukey (1977) is the classic presentation; also see Leinhardt and Leinhardt (1980).

IMPORTANT TERMS

Derived scores
Frequency distribution
Interval scale
Linear relationship
Mean
Median
Mode
Nominal level of measurement
Nonlinear relationship
Normal frequency distribution
Ordinal level of measurement
Pearson product-moment correlation
Percentile
Quartile

Range
Ratio scale
Regression
Restriction of range
Scaled score
Scatterplot
Semi-interquartile range
Skewness
Standard deviation
Standard score
Stanine score
Stem-and-leaf diagram
Variance

APPLICATION PROBLEMS

1. A Department of Guidance and Counseling faculty member wished to determine how the graduates of its master's program rated the effectiveness of instruction they had received. She asked graduate students to rate each course on a scale of 1 to 5 (in which 1 = superior and 5 = inferior). She then calculated the mean rating for each course. The department course in statistics was given a mean rating of 1.56; the courses in psychological foundations and sociological foundations had mean ratings of 3.05 and 3.21, respectively. Suppose she had concluded, on the basis of the mean ratings, that the master's graduates considered the instruction in the latter two courses twice as effective as that in statistics. Would she be correct in her assumption?

2. The following is a frequency distribution of house sales at a large real estate firm in Gotham City for the second-quarter of the year:

Price Range	Houses Sold
$225,000–$249,999	3
$200,000–$224,999	5
$175,000–$199,999	10
$150,000–$174,999	25

$125,000–$149,999	35
$100,000–$124,999	55
$75,000–$99,999	40
$50,000–$74,999	5
Total	178

a) Calculate the median price of houses sold that year.

b) If total sales were $23 million, what was the mean house price?

c) Which is the better representation of central tendency of this distribution, the median or the mean?

3. A newly hired chemistry professor at Beltline University is put in charge of the first-year undergraduate chemistry course, which has an enrollment of over 200 students. He decides to teach the class in sections. He will assess students by a midterm and a final examination, each worth 50 percent of their grade. He wants a way of making it possible for students to compare their standing on successive examinations even though the difficulty of the examinations varies. What do you advise him to do? How should he go about it?

4. Drawing on Bandura's (1978) self-efficacy theory of motivation, Salomon (1981) suggested that the relationship between attitude toward media and learning can be conceptualized as an inverted U. He proposed that students invest effort on the basis of two factors: the perceived difficulty of the task and the students' assessment of their skills in relation to the task requirements. Thus students who perceive a medium such as television as easy will invest little effort in television instruction. The more difficult students perceive the medium to be, the more their effort increases until they begin to consider it too difficult. At that point, effort begins to decrease. Dr. Gladys Southwind conducted an experiment to test this relationship, examining subjects' ratings of the difficulty of various media and their effort on a task using the medium. A Pearson product-moment correlation coefficient determined that the strength of the relationship was only .35. Dr. Southwind concluded that there was not a strong relationship. Do you agree or disagree with her? Why?

Compare your answers with those following the Application Exercise.

APPLICATION EXERCISE

Consider the data that you are likely to collect for the study you plan. How can you best summarize them? Graphically? What kinds of symbols or graphs will best convey what you want understood? Will statistics like means and standard deviations be helpful? How else can they be presented? Will correlations display the strength of relationships among your variables?

Some students lay out "dummy tables" so that they can anticipate what data analysis they plan to do and can then fill in the tables when they get the data. Although this method avoids surprises, it can also lead them to believe they can anticipate all they are going to find. However, half the fun of research is playing with the data to explore what is there. Don't limit yourself—plan to explore as well.

ANSWERS TO THE APPLICATION PROBLEMS

1. No! Scales such as this have no real zero point; therefore, they are not ratio scales. We don't even know for sure that the units of measurement are equal to one another for an interval scale. The scales are at least ordinal, and we treat the data as though they were interval because we have found that we can make useful interpretations this way that correspond to real-world phenomena when we test them out. Although it is convenient and useful to calculate mean ratings by way of comparison between groups, it is not correct to interpret them in terms of ratios.

2. (a) To get the middle case, divide the number of cases by 2; $178 \div 2 = 89$, which is in the third category ($100,000–$124,999). Counting from the bottom, 44 more cases are needed from that category, which contains 55 cases. So $44 \div 55 = 0.8$, and $0.8 \times $24,999$ (the size of the category) = $19,999. To find the median house price, add $19,999 to the lower boundary, which is $100,000. Thus the median price is $19,999 + $100,000 = $119,999. (b) Mean sales price = $23,000,000 \div 178 = $129,213. The median would be a better representation than the mean because the frequency distribution is positively skewed; that is, the majority of house prices are in the lower part of the distribution. The mean is more sensitive to extremes and in this case is high because it is influenced by the expensive houses sold.

3. Advise him to change the raw scores to a derived score with some easy-to-remember mean and standard deviation, such as a mean of 50 and a standard deviation of 10. To do this, he would subtract the test's mean from each raw score on that test, divide it by the raw score standard deviation, multiply that standard score by 10, and add 50. Then all the tests would have a mean of 50 and a standard deviation of 10 regardless of how easy or hard they happened to be.

4. From the description of Salomon's theory, Dr. Southwind probably should have expected a curvilinear relationship: little effort for easy media, increased effort as a medium was perceived as more difficult, and effort falling off again as the medium was seen as very difficult. Nonlinear relationships are underestimated by the Pearson product-moment correlation. Statistics like the correlation ratio (η), would provide a more accurate estimate of the relationship. A scatterplot would be very useful in showing whether the relationship really is U-shaped.

CHAPTER 18

Measurement, Testing, and Observation

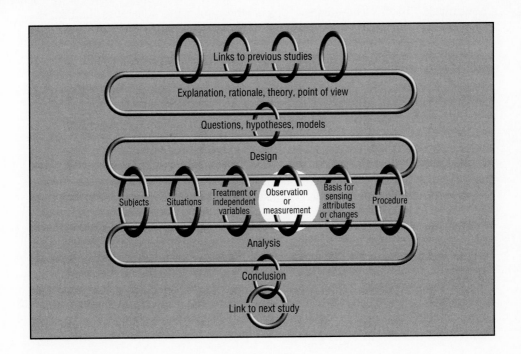

It is the faith of all science that an unlimited number of phenomena can be comprehended in terms of a limited number of concepts [constructs]. . . . The constructs are . . . man-made inventions . . . not a part of nature. It is only a way of comprehending nature.

Louis L. Thurstone, *Vectors of the Mind*

There is no descriptive language that does not consist of general words, that is, of concepts. The gift of humanity is precisely that, unlike animals, we form concepts. . . .

Jacob Bronowski, *The Identity of Man*

OVERVIEW

In Chapter 17, we noted that numbers are adjectives indicating "how many" or "how much." In this chapter, we look at the nouns the adjectives modify, the items or observations that are counted or measured. The problems of measurement are few when the scale can be physically sensed—length (how far an individual moved) or time (latency or duration of response), for example. The measurement of concepts and constructs that cannot be directly sensed is more problematic.

How do we know, if we cannot sense them, that we are measuring those constructs? What evidence can we find that an instrument is, in measurement terminology, valid? There is considerable evidence, but we must learn which evidence to use and when to use it. Consistency is also a problem. Scores may vary from one measurement to another or from one measurement form to a parallel one; the testee may be less motivated or more tired. Evidence of consistency of measurement, of reliability as it is called, is also important. This chapter examines the characteristics of good measurement.

Constructing good measures is time-consuming and costly. What aids exist for finding already developed measures? (There are many!) What are the strengths and weaknesses of various data-gathering methods? We will also explore these questions in this chapter. Whenever the word "test" is used throughout the chapter, the material applies equally well to any kind of measure, for instance rating scales, structured observation instruments and so forth.

CHAPTER CONTENTS

Introduction

Measures record, or "freeze in time," a sample of behavior—for example, the ability to visualize the rotation of figures in space—for later evaluation. Observation scales provide a means for recording perceptions of a sample of behavior (who talks, who listens), judgments of persons' behavior (actively discussing), internal state (happy), and characterizations of the environment (everyone is free to contribute). When properly summarized and interpreted, these evaluations, judgments, and perceptions convey information about variables of interest (spatial ability, classroom climate). They provide a symbolic representation of the behavior or its perception and allow inferences about the state of constructs affecting it.

We tend to think of units and measures, especially physical ones, as obvious or "givens." Indeed, some dimensions of phenomena stand out, whereas others, such as "good character," are more difficult to discern even when we are clear about them conceptually—and often we are not. It is worth noting, however, that dimensions and measures, even of physical characteristics, are social constructions. As Duncan (1984) observes, what we now think of as the result of multiplying width by length (area),

> was measured by cultivators in southeast [*sic*] Asia by the number of baskets of rice seed required to sow a field. . . . The Chinese even defined a standard vessel for measuring grain and wine in terms of the musical pitch produced when it was struck, so that a pitch pipe, its length measured by millet grains, was . . . [the] measure of capacity. (p. 15)

Thus, cultures choose aspects from phenomena, name dimensions, and select ways to describe them—in our culture, usually in units and numbers. Measurement is also part of a theme begun in the early chapters, which shows knowledge as the result of a social process.

✦ *Measures select from our world concepts of interest to us and operationalize them in ways determined by our culture.*

✦ *Measures record information for later use and provide a representation of one or more dimensions. Measures of constructs symbolize their state.*

Measurement—A Sampling Process

Measures and observation scales represent phenomena by sampling:

- The content of a course to find how well a student has learned on the assumption that the questions represent the material in the course (content or domain sampling)
- A student's behavior with respect to that content on the assumption that the sample represents that student's typical behavior with that content (behavior sampling)
- A candidate's ability to solve typical problems involved in a position he or she is seeking on the assumption that today's demonstrated ability is representative of the tomorrows' on the job (time sampling)
- The interaction of a group, coding at specified intervals the nature of the focus of the group and the interaction, the assumption being that this record of the group's behavior is representative of a complete record such as a videotape (time and behavior sampling)
- A pool of questions regarding ways of handling various interpersonal situations on the assumption that certain answers represent the construct of an individual's assertiveness (domain sampling)

All sampling principles apply to measurement:

- Other things being equal, for the same precision, a larger sample is required (a longer measure or period of observation) the more heterogeneous the target area or skill being sampled—for example, the complexities of American history in comparison with the relative homogeneity of multiplying single-digit numbers.
- Similarly, a larger sample is required the more precise we wish our measurement—confidence that an individual's true score is within 2 rather than 5 points of his observed score as expressed by odds of 1 to 20.

Stratified sampling and sequential sampling are also used in measurement.

✦ *Measuring is taking a sample of behavior at a sample time (which is a sample of possible times) on a sample of items taken from a domain that is a sample of a larger universe. The principles of sampling apply to measurement; some measures use stratified or sequential sampling methods.*

Advantages of Measurement and Observation Records

Measures extend our senses, gathering more data than we can otherwise comfortably digest and summarizing them in a single number or a profile of numbers. They allow us to differentiate individuals, groups, or classes as having more or less of whatever we are measuring. An alternative is to observe or interview individuals to obtain certain desired information, judge it, and then verbally summarize it in ways that differentiate hundreds of individuals. This comparison makes apparent the efficiency of tests like the Scholastic Aptitude Test (SAT), which, with all its faults, still gathers a great deal of information, in a single day's time, simultaneously, from tens of thousands of potential college students, and puts it into usable form.

Measurement often corrects faulty impressions. We may believe that dissatisfaction is widespread but be shown by a survey instrument that the problem is confined to a very vocal few. Or, when a student does poorly in high school but attains high scores on the SAT, we learn that the individual is not stupid, as we might infer from the grades, but is perhaps bored or otherwise not academically motivated.

Observation scales are used to make records of targeted persons (for instance, the group leader), to describe kinds of interaction (praise or reinforcing statements), and to indicate who interacts with whom and how. An example is Flanders's (1970) interaction analysis in which an observer classifies student and teacher talk in a set of categories. It is only a partial record, colored by the viewpoints of the scale and observer, but since categorizing and coding occur simultaneously with observation, the record is less voluminous than a video recording and is immediately ready for analysis and interpretation. Use of observation scales with video recordings allow more detailed analysis—like the instant replay used in telecasting professional sports—than is possible when observations are done in the field. Knowledge growth seems to follow the ability to record, analyze, and measure the phenomena of a field.

Many observation scales require observers to record the frequency of certain behaviors, rate certain dimensions or record their observations in similarly structured ways. Simon and Boyer (1974) is a collection of such observation scales for the classroom. Although not always mentioned in the remainder of this chapter, nearly everything in the chapter is applicable to such instruments; just consider a rating on a dimension, or the frequencies of a particular action as a test item.

+ *Measures allow us to differentiate individuals more precisely and accurately than we can with words.*
+ *Measures permit us to collect enormous amounts of information efficiently and quickly.*
+ *Observation scales abstract from behavior the characteristics of interest. We can use them either in the field or with film, audio, or video records of field experiences.*
+ *Some evidence shows that a field of research develops rapidly as the precision of its measures increases.*

Measures as Operational Definitions

We refer to the measure of a construct as its **operational definition** because the operations performed in measuring the construct determine what our data really represent. The ability to answer the problems on an intelligence test become what we mean by "intelligence"; responses to questions about how we feel about financial assistance for destitute people become what we mean by "attitude toward welfare programs."

The operational definition of a construct may specify:

1. Operations that bring the construct about.
2. Situations and circumstances that may evoke the construct.
3. Descriptions of behaviors that occur when the construct is present and so may be used as indicators of it.

We often use the first form of definition to bring about conditions we are interested in studying. For instance, to examine the effect of the constructs "hunger" and "thirst" on ability to concentrate, we use deprivation of food and water as the operations to bring them about.

The second form describes most of our measures; test items are situations developed to evoke a behavior, and the testing situation is the circumstance in which those situations are presented. For example, we set a problem in a test situation intended to elicit the correct behavior: "Predict the increase in temperature of hydrogen gas when the pressure on a 20°C 10-gram sample is doubled from 15 ppi." If the student knows Boyle's law, this problem should evoke a correct response.

The third form is reflected in observation rating scales: for example, tally the number of times each individual was an asserter or victim where assertiveness is defined as interrupting another person, or not giving another a chance to talk. (Other specific behaviors could be listed, perhaps as a checklist with space for tallies of occurrences.)

All three forms are useful ways of defining constructs.

✦ *The operations followed in measuring a construct are its operational definition. Operational definitions may specify the operations that bring it about, the situation that evokes it, or the behaviors that, being regular concomitants of it, can be used as indicators of it.*

Evidence of Construct Validity

Construct validity provides evidence which forms the basis for intended score interpretation (Messick, 1995). To show the **construct validity** of intended score interpretations is to provide an evaluative summary of the evidence for them. While the definition of construct validity has been broadened so that it applies to any score, it is of special concern wherever we are measuring a construct. A construct is a characteristic which is presumed to exist but which cannot be directly measured—for instance, intelligence, anxiety, or self-esteem. Its presence and strength or amount is inferred from the sample of behavior gathered by a measure designed to assess it. Construct validity is the unifying framework for all evidence regarding **validity.**[1] Basically the evidence sought is that the measure behaves as would be expected if it were a valid measure. This evidence usually combines theoretical and empirical sources; theoretical in the sense that our knowledge of the construct allows us to predict what to expect under certain conditions, empirical in that we gather data to confirm the prediction. Certain kinds of data are useful in assembling the evaluative summary of evidence:

- To assure that the score represents mastery of the content in a particular domain such as achievement in a particular subject matter, or mastery of certain job aspects, we seek *evidence based on content.*
- To assure that the test is assessing not only the proper content but also that intended mental processes, skills, and abilities are being displayed in responding to the measure, we seek *evidence based on response processes.*
- To assure that the structure of the measure conforms to our understanding of the nature of the construct we seek *evidence based on the measure's internal structure.* For example, if the construct (for example, anxiety) has two dimensions (current conceptions of anxiety suggest it has state and trait dimensions), then an analysis of a measure of the construct should display that structure (a context dependent dimension—state, and a person dependent one—trait).
- To further assure the measure is tapping the proper construct in relation to other possibilities we seek evidence *based on relations to other variables.* That is, we seek convergent and discriminant evidence—convergent evidence that other measures of the construct with which we would expect the measure in question to relate, do indeed correlate with it as expected, and discriminant evidence "indicating a distinctness from measures of other constructs" (Messick, 1995, p. 746) such that low, zero or negative correlations with them are found.
- To assure that the positive value of using the measure outweighs any possible harm, we seek evidence of the consequences of measurement.

We will examine these different kinds of evidence in detail below, but first note that there is a kind of validity evidence not recognized in the test standards. Where measurement results involve important decisions that must be accepted by lay personnel, we may ask whether the measure appears valid to these unsophisticated users. For example, for a long time, studies have shown that a multiple-choice test of English usage correlates with ability to write almost as much as does a very carefully scored written composition (Breland, 1987). Nevertheless, the College

---

[1]Conceptions of test validity have gradually changed over the years as experts in measurement have revised standards for measurement use (American Educational Research Association et al., 1985). These conceptions have become the accepted ways of viewing validity. The revision expected to be issued shortly closely follows Messick (1995) in which construct validity encompasses what, in previous editions of the test standards, were other co-equal validities, criterion-related validity, for instance. This chapter's presentation is based on Messick so as to be congruent with the forthcoming standards. Notice that rather than being a property of the test, since a test can be used different ways, validity applies to the intended score interpretations.

Entrance Examination Board still uses actual composition samples instead of the multiple-choice test which would be less expensive, less time-consuming, and faster and easier to score. Why? An important reason is that the appearance of validity, the **face validity**, of the multiple-choice test is so poor that many of the test's clients refuse to accept that it is almost as valid as an actual writing sample. Face validity can be important if there is considerable discrepancy between what the measure appears to measure and what it is claimed to. This problem is often faced where a cut-off score affects the futures of individuals or where policy decisions are involved.

Evidence Based on Content

Since we know the content of the subject matter that the measure is intended to sample we can analyze the measure to show that it does, indeed, representatively sample it. Evidence of **content validity** (also called curricular validity) is important for tests that are used to measure academic achievement, or competency. Examples are minimal competency examinations required for high school graduation or for obtaining a teaching certificate. The term "content," usually thought of as a curriculum area, is used broadly to include, for example, assembling a rifle or using a specific software program on a computer. In some instances, a job analysis provides specifications of the skills and content with which a measure can be compared just as a curriculum does for a course in school. Measures provide evidence of content validity if they adequately represent the content of the curriculum, task, job analysis or construct. Validity is a judgment supported by both empirical evidence and theoretical rationales; content-related evidence provides rationales.

Evidence of content validity is a representation problem and therefore involves sampling. We show how well the various parts of the measure represent the content by comparing it with a table of specifications. We met such a table before in Figure 16.3 (p. 363), a "blueprint," or table of specifications, for a questionnaire. Similarly we can construct a test from such a blueprint or prepare such a blueprint from a curriculum guide. By comparing the test with the table we can show congruence—evidence of appropriate sampling of the domain.

Table 18.1 shows such a table for an examination dealing with the main topics of this chapter: validity, reliability, and objectivity.[2] The table is constructed from behavioral objectives or goals of instruction. Such objectives state the combinations of behavior and content that the individuals are expected to be able to show upon completion of instruction.

The whole table represents the domain to be sampled by stratified sampling of two variables: the content arrayed down the left side of the table, and the behaviors across the top. Each cell is considered a subdomain, with a potential pool of items of varying levels of difficulty to be sampled. Because some behaviors and certain content may be more important than others, we weight the columns and rows to indicate the proportion of the whole test that should come from each.

---

[2]If programs rather than individuals are being evaluated, each student might be given a different sample of only a few items from the table so that testing time for an individual is minimized but coverage of the whole table is maximized. This process, called matrix sampling, is used by the National Assessment of Educational Progress.

TABLE 18.1 *Specifications for a Test of Test Validity, Reliability, and Objectivity*

Subject Matter	Skills					Row Weight in %
	Has Knowledge of Major Terms and Concepts	Can Use Terms Correctly and Intelligently	Can Apply the Concepts to a Situation	Can Construct a Table of Specifications	Can Evaluate the Usage of Concepts in a Study	
Validity	9	9	18	10	18	64
Construct	(4)	(4)	(8)		(8)	
Predictive	(2)	(2)	(4)		(4)	
Content	(2)	(2)	(4)	(10)		
Face	(1)	(1)	(2)		(2)	
Reliability	5	5	10		10	30
Internal consistency	(2)	(2)	(4)		(4)	
Stability	(1)	(1)	(2)		(2)	
Equivalence	(1)	(1)	(2)		(2)	
Stability and equivalence	(1)	(1)	(2)		(2)	
Objectivity	1	1	2		2	6
Column weight in %	15	15	30	10	30	100

These are shown as percentages at the bottom of the column and at the far-right of the row. Each cell entry not in parenthesis is the product of the percentages for the row and column defining that cell, and this number shows the percentage of the whole test that is to come from the cell. Where the domain's main emphasis is on particular cells, it may make more sense to assign weights to cell entries directly rather than to use row and column weightings. The numbers in parentheses show how many items are devoted to a subtopic; since this is a 100-item test, percentages and numbers of items are identical. By comparing the test's actual sampling of items with those shown as ideal by the table of specifications, we provide evidence of content validity.

Evidence Based on Response Processes

In addition to assuring that the expected content is appropriately sampled by the measure, we must also be concerned that the expected response processes are being sampled as well and that the persons actually use these processes in responding to the instrument. For example, a student taking a multiple choice arithmetic test may be solving the problem not by doing the arithmetic as intended, but by eliminating the most unreasonable answers and guessing among the rest. Having the students talk aloud about their thought processes as they take the test often provides evidence of the actual response process which can then be compared with those expected. Response times and/or eye movement records may provide evidence as well. So might stimulated recall (see p. 372). Similarly keeping a record of the development of writing skill by comparing successive drafts would provide evidence of process.

Evidence Based on Internal Structure

The internal structure of the construct is often known or hypothesized from the nature of the construct. For instance, many argue that intelligence is a multi-dimensional construct with many, at least partially independent, aspects. Evidence of the structure of an instrument is often obtained by **factor analysis.** Factor analysis is a statistical procedure that, by examining interrelationships among items or tests, help to identify the dimensions underlying a measure and hence what it is measuring. Suppose we correlate the scores of each item in a test with the scores of every other item in that test across a sample of individuals. A factor analysis identifies clusters of items measuring the same things (factors). One infers from the common characteristics of those items the nature of the constructs each measures. One can then show the relationship of each item to each factor, as well as the number of factors making up the test. Factors that correspond to what the test was intended to measure provide evidence of construct validity. The items of a homogeneous test will all strongly relate to one factor.

Evidence Based on Relations with Other Variables

By factor analyzing a battery of test scores that include both new measures we are validating and tests already accepted as valid, we can also gain evidence of the validity of the new tests. For example, we might anticipate that verbal fluency and flexibility will be two of the factors underlying a new measure of verbal creativity. A factor analysis of the intercorrelations of a battery of test scores that includes already accepted measures of verbal fluency and flexibility will show how the new test relates to these factors—further evidence of construct validity.

We make predictions about how we expect the properties of the construct to manifest themselves under particular conditions, or with certain kinds of people, and then we provide evidence that they do. For example, given a new measure of creativity, we can develop a set of propositions about how individuals who are creative will behave in certain artistic situations. We might expect that creative people will be flexible, but not that all flexible people are creative. Therefore, flexibility is a contingent (necessary but not sufficient) condition for artistic creativity. Thus, there might be people with both high and low creativity in their art who are flexible, but no inflexible people will be highly creative. We can inspect a scatterplot of the creativity measure against a flexibility measure to see whether it is triangular—people with high flexibility scores and both high and low creativity scores but no persons with high creativity scores combined with low flexibility scores. This would provide evidence of construct validity.

Similarly, we can correlate daydreaming with creativity. Again, however, we expect a low correlation in that daydreaming might facilitate creativity but is a contributing condition, not a necessary condition for it. A low positive correlation under these circumstances would be further evidence of construct validity.

Convergent and Discriminant Evidence. If we examine the network of measures of which our measure is a part and find that other measures correlate with it as we would expect, we have evidence of construct validity: Already accepted measures of the construct correlate highly with it and measures expected to be only weakly related to it, show only low correlations, or if inversely related, have negative correlations—convergent evidence. Those distinct from it and not related have close to zero correlations—discriminant evidence. Suppose we have a new measure of children's reading ability; we expect it to show a high correlation with widely accepted reading tests like the reading part of the *Iowa Test of Basic Skills*. We might expect a moderate to small correlation between arithmetic achievement and reading achievement and a low or zero one with a test of spatial visualization. Measures of opposite characteristics (sad vs. happy) should correlate negatively. Showing expected relations to other measures provides evidence of construct validity.

Does this procedure sound familiar? It should! Recall in describing the constant comparative method and delineating a coding category (construct) in our study of qualitative method we were to find (a) key instances of it, (b) borderline instances, and (c) instances that were beyond the border (see p. 263). We noted that this was a general procedure called conceptual analysis. We use that same logic here to examine whether the measure we are validating appropriately correlates highly (key instances), correlates weakly (borderline instances) and does not correlate at all—or negatively with inverse measures (those beyond the border).

Recall also the concept of triangulation wherein we used data from different sources (across persons, situations, and methods) to ensure that our data were not overtly influenced by one point of view. So too with construct validity, we are seeking data from different methods of validating measures: relating it to other measures, showing that the measure relates to how the construct would display itself, and showing that the measure samples its domain or context appropriately. The logic we apply to both quantitative and qualitative methods is basically the same, but we adapt it to the specific kind of data.

A combination of convergent and discriminant evidence with multiple methods of measuring (for example, free response, multiple choice, observation) provides very persuasive construct validity evidence—method triangulation we met on p. 275. It is known as **multi-trait, multi-method** evidence. For example, to assure his audience that the construct paranoia was being measured, the Zimbardo et al. study of Chapter 1 provided three measures in two modalities: a clinically derived paranoia scale (self-report), the Minnesota Multiphasic Personality Inventory (self-report) and judges (observation). They would be expected to show congruent results, and did.

Evidence Based on Test-Criterion Relationship. Evidence showing the measure might usefully predict certain criteria, called **criterion-related validity,** also contributes evidence of construct validity. A **criterion** is some measure generally accepted as valid. We show that a measure can predict a criterion measure: grade point average, number or dollar value of sales, number of patents when using the measure to select individuals for graduate school, a sales job, or a research program. We usually divide criterion-related validity into concurrent and predictive validity. These terms describe when the criterion measure was obtained. If obtained at the same time as the predicting measure, it is evidence of **concurrent validity;** if obtained later, it is **predictive validity.** Let's consider the salesperson example. Suppose we give a test that should predict good salespeople and then correlate test scores with each salesperson's sales that month. This is concurrent validity. Had we given the test when the salespeople were first hired and examined the test's relationship with a month's sales six months later, it would be predictive validity. But, since salespeople who were unsuccessful during their first six months quit or were fired, the test must discriminate not between all the unsuccessful and the successful salespeople but among the successful ones who survived, a much more difficult job. (This restriction in range results in a lowered correlation similar to that in Figure 17.11, p. 411).

What is the relationship of concurrent validity to predictive validity? We have two counteracting forces: (1) the restriction in range lowers concurrent validity but not predictive validity; (2) the instability of the trait over time lowers predictive validity, but not concurrent validity since criterion and test data are gathered at the same time. Restriction in range is usually the stronger factor, so concurrent is usually considered a lower-boundary estimate of predictive validity.

Evidence Based on the Consequences of Measuring

The consequences of measuring are not always only those that were intended. Some unintended consequences may have negative impact that outweighs the positive results. For instance, when an individual makes a poor showing on a measure, it may become a self-fulfilling prophecy—individuals then fail because their scores made them believe they couldn't do the work when perhaps they could. Is this occurence sufficiently rare and the selective and diagnostic value of measures sufficiently great that their use is justified? This difficult judgment is an example of consequential validity evidence; it recognizes that measuring has important consequences that must be taken into consideration wherever measures are used.[3]

The Specificity of Validity

We have seen that various kinds of evidence are used to establish that a particular use of a measure is valid. Further, evidence of validity is always gathered in a particular context, and one of our concerns must be the generality of that context. A measure that is useful for selecting individuals for entrance to East Snowshoe State College may not be selective enough for a prestige institution. We ask whether specificity in a situation makes it unique and limits the generality of the

[3]There is no debate that the consequences of testing are important and should be considered, but some believe they should not be included in the definition of validity. This is another of the increasing instances in the social sciences where exploration of the interlocking of values and science makes still more apparent the socially constructed nature of science.

results from it. Is there specificity in a job or task that similarly limits generality? Because important decisions are often based on tests and because validity evidence can vary widely from instance to instance, courts have held that validity is specific rather than general.[4] Further, texts and the 1974 version of standards for psychological tests (AERA et al., 1974) have specified that validity coefficients are specific to the situations in which they were obtained.

This point of view has been contested, however, by those examining the evidence. As Messick (1989) and Hunter and Schmidt (1990) show, a good case can be built for validity generalization if we can establish the relationship of the instance of proposed use to the accumulated evidence. Further, we must also look at the social consequences, where important trade-offs are sometimes hidden. These can be positive as well as negative and can change with time. The National Teacher Examination (NTE) was originally hailed as valid when African American teachers could use a high enough score to attain the same pay scale as Caucasians in certain states. Later, when pay was no longer differentiated by race, many viewed the NTE as invalidly discriminating against the minorities it had originally helped.

Table 18.2 summarizes information regarding the kinds of evidence of validity, purpose, questions posed, and methods of obtaining evidence.

TABLE 18.2 *A Validity Summary: Construct Validity and the Evidence That Contributes to It*

Kinds of Evidence of Validity	Purpose	Questions Posed	How Obtained
Construct validity (the unifying framework for all evidence of validity)	To show that the measure is a valid measure of a construct	Does the measure behave as would be expected of a valid measure of the construct?	Determine how the measure would behave if valid and demonstrate that it does so
Content related evidence	To show how well the measure covers the domain of a subject it is designed to measure	Does the measure sample the content and behaviors of its domain with adequate coverage and proper emphasis?	Determine the match between the measure's items and the table of specifications that describes the relative emphasis (number of items or percent of the test) to be given to each intersection of the content covered, and behaviors to be displayed
Response processes related evidence	To show the response processes elicited by the measure are those one would expect if it were a valid measure	Are the response processes used by those being measured the processes one intended the measure to elicit?	Ask a person being measured to talk aloud about what is going on in his mind as he responds. Use stimulated recall to facilitate remembering

---

[4]*Griggs v. Duke Power Co.*, 401 U.S. 424 (1971).

TABLE 18.2 *(continued)*

Kinds of Evidence of Validity	Purpose	Questions Posed	How Obtained
Internal structure based evidence	To show the internal structure of the measure is as one would expect if it were a valid measure	What is the internal structure and how does it relate to what would be expected?	Factor analyze the measure and infer the nature of the dimensions (factors) underlying the test from the nature of the items or tests contributing to the factor
Evidence based on relations to other variables Convergent and discriminant evidence	To show the test has strong positive correlations with other measures of the construct and smaller positive ones with those related to the construct (convergent evidence); has low or zero correlations with measures of variables not related and negative correlations with those inversely related (discriminant evidence)	Does the measure relate to other measures as would be expected if it were a valid measure of the construct?	Correlate the test scores with other established tests of the construct, with tests of other constructs related to the construct, and with constructs independent of, or inversely related to, the construct in question
Criterion-related evidence: Concurrent validity	To show a relationship with a criterion or to estimate predictive validity	Does the measure correlate strongly with the criterion or predict success and failure of survivors?	Correlate scores obtained from measure taken at the same time as the criterion. When both criterion and measure's data are gathered at the end of a training or induction period, because data is missing from subjects who had failed prior to that point, usually underestimates predictive validity
Predictive validity	To demonstrate how the measure will work when used to predict success and failure	Does the measure predict future success and failure?	Correlate scores obtained at, or prior to, entrance to a program or job with a criterion measure of success obtained later—for example, at end of probation period
Evidence based on consequences of measurement	To determine whether the advantages of measurement outweigh the disadvantages	Do the negative consequences of measurement, transcend positive ones?	Assess the consequences of measuring both positive and negative, including unintended ones
Face validity (not formally a part of construct validity)	To show that the measure appears to be valid; especially important for a measure used for public policy purposes with lay persons untutored in measurement	Does the measure appear to be a valid measure?	Examine the measure

Reliability of Measures

Reliability refers to the consistency of an instrument in measuring whatever it measures. We seek validity first, however, because if there is evidence of adequate validity for our intended purpose, we don't need to worry about reliability. In providing evidence of adequate validity, we will have also shown the measure is consistent—has reliability.

Think of a measure's reliability as comparable to firing a gun at a target where the bull's eye represents a person's construct to be measured and each shot represents an attempt to measure it—a score. Validity involves repeatedly hitting the heart of the target, as in the middle target of Figure 18.1, which shows a measure with both validity and reliability. When the measure is reliable, it tightly clusters the shots wherever it is aimed, as in the middle and right-hand targets. The right-hand target represents a reliable but invalid measure; the shots are clustered but are measuring something else and do not hit the bull's eye. An unreliable measure, as in the left-hand target, spreads shots (scores) all over; it will not accurately measure the attribute in any given instance. We might, however, get an estimate of the attribute by averaging the shots—in essence, lots of measurings—or a very long measure. Indeed, lengthening the measure is one strategy we use to increase reliability.

Without evidence of validity, an instrument may be consistent in measuring the wrong thing. Thus, reliability is a necessary condition for validity, but it is not a sufficient condition, not a guarantee that the measure is valid.

Operationally, reliability is the consistency with which persons evidencing the same amount of whatever is being measured are assigned the same score. Because various factors may prevent this consistency, there are different measures of reliability:

- The measure may consist of items from different unrelated domains (for example, spatial visualization and creativity) so that a score may represent excellence in only one (for example, spatial visualization) or the other (creativity) or middling levels in both. As a result, we would not know how to interpret the score—the measure lacks **internal consistency reliability**.

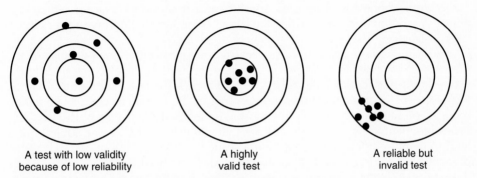

| A test with low validity because of low reliability | A highly valid test | A reliable but invalid test |

FIGURE 18.1 Reliability and validity portrayed as an analogy to firing consistent and inconsistent guns at a target.

- Different samples of items assign a different score to the same level of compe-tence or ability. Form A of a measure yields scores different from those of form B—the scores from the different forms lack **equivalence reliability**.
- The individuals' responses vary over time either because their perceptions of items change or because the level of the construct changes. Today the world looks rosy and I responded accordingly; yesterday I felt depressed by the rain and darkness and it affected my answers—the scores lack **stability reliability**.

We will examine each of these in detail.

✦ *Reliability refers to the consistency of results produced by a measure.*
✦ *Reliability is a necessary but not sufficient condition for high validity. A measure that is valid for a given purpose is reliable, but a reliable measure may or may not be valid.*
✦ *As with validity, we seek evidence of reliability to fit the kind of consistency desired.*

Internal Consistency Reliability

Internal consistency refers to the consistency with which all the items are mea-suring the same thing. We expect a reliable measure to be affected only by the construct of interest; all the test items should measure that construct and nothing else. Individuals at the same level of the construct ought to respond the same way to similar items. Such a test will have high reliability, and we say it is homoge-neous. Homogeneity will be lowered by items that receive different responses de-pending on how they are perceived (like the double barreled question on Russia, p. 366 which might tap attitude toward housing or industrialization), or by items measuring different unrelated or only partially related skills (in a mathematics test, algebra items require recall of formulas, geometry ones visualization in space). The responses can be affected by a pattern of random errors, as when test-ing conditions are poor and students are distracted while responding. Because low reliability often results from some combination of these factors, responses to certain parts of the test may be less closely related to those in another part. When scores are affected by such factors, we have difficulty knowing how to interpret them. What does the score represent? Skill in the construct we intended to mea-sure? More of one construct than another, and if so, which one for which stu-dents? A random error? Some blend of these? Score interpretability requires inter-nal consistency reliability.

For achievement tests and other learned responses, the homogeneity of the measure is not solely a function of the measure itself but is also affected by the way what it measures was experienced or learned. Homogeneity indices can be high for tests of students shown how events of the twentieth century had their roots in the nineteenth but low for those who learned the events of the two cen-turies independently and so do not see them as interrelated. Some subject areas tend to be more homogeneous in that a student who succeeds in one part of the domain also tends to succeed in another. Mathematics is such a subject, since those who do better at puzzling out one geometric proof or solving one equation can usually do other, similar problems. The more differently individuals experience the material, the more they will diverge in terms of what is easy and what is hard, and the lower the internal consistency or homogeneity.

Measuring Internal Consistency Reliability. There are several ways of estimating the internal consistency of a measure. One is to split the measure into two halves, randomly assigning the items to halves and examining the consistency of the scores between them. A perfectly reliable measure will have identical scores on each half; divergence will indicate less than perfect reliability. A correlation coefficient (see p. 406) expresses this internal consistency reliability. Considering the fact that half the test is a smaller sample of behavior than the whole, and therefore less consistently representative, the half-test correlation will underrepresent the reliability. Fortunately, there is a way of estimating whole-test reliability: the Spearman-Brown prophecy formula (see this chapter's appendix). Such reliabilities are sometimes referred to as Spearman-Brown reliabilities.

Where similar items are grouped (a math section, a social studies section, etc.), we assign odd-numbered items to one half and even-numbered to the other—parallel split-half reliability. Because this method stratifies the halves so that each correctly represents the groups, these reliabilities will be higher than random splits.

Because there are many possible random splits, each slightly different, we need an estimate of the average reliability for all random ones. **Kuder-Richardson reliability** formula 21 (KR21) for tests scored right and wrong, and Cronbach's **alpha coefficient** (or Hoyt's analysis of variance reliability) for any kind of scoring, provide estimates. Because KR21 requires only the mean, the variance, and the number of items, it is widely used. It assumes, however, that all items are equally difficult, a condition that is almost never the case. It, therefore, yields a slightly lower estimate of reliability than the parallel split-halves procedure, or KR20, a formula with fewer assumptions than KR21. KR21 is considered a lower boundary to KR20 estimates. Time limits so short that many testees do not finish result in artificially inflated reliability estimates of internal consistency. Because end items not attempted are scored as wrong, an artificially consistent score pattern is created that results in inappropriate estimates for such tests.

Another way of looking at internal consistency reliability assumes that each test randomly samples all possible items that measure its domain. Each individual will have a score on this universe of items—a universe score. Correlating observed scores with universe scores shows how representative this measure is of the universe. Although we have no universe scores, perhaps you can intuitively sense the parallel to estimating the average random split reliability. Thus, another interpretation for Cronbach's alpha and the Kuder-Richardson formulas is that they estimate how well the measure represents the universe or domain of which they are a sample.

Equivalence Reliability

Equivalence reliability is parallel split-half reliability with whole tests—that is, different forms of a test. Experiencing the first testing may cause scores to increase with the second. **Counterbalancing** is a general technique for eliminating the serial effect of order for tests, treatments, and so on. We divide the sample into as many equal groups as there are possible orderings. With two test forms, we divide the group in half, one receiving form A first and the other form B. With three forms we divide into six: ABC, ACB, BAC, BCA, CAB, and CBA.

Stability Reliability

Stability reliability asks, "How consistent are the scores over time?" It is the correlation of two score sets-test—retest of the same individuals—obtained at different times. How much elapsed time? For the period over which you wish to estimate stability. If you are comparing achievement test scores at the semester's beginning with those at the end, ideally, you can use testings a semester apart. However, since over such a long period some learning is likely, in practice, such periods are shorter. In principle, the period should approximate the target interval. The trade-off between using the proper interval and avoiding irrelevant influences is a matter of judgment.

What if we plan to use one form of a test at the opening of a semester and the other at the end? Then we need a combination of **stability and equivalence reliability**—we correlate scores from different test forms we have administered with a suitable intervening period. The two sources of inconsistency typically yield a reliability lower than either alone.

Table 18.3 summarizes information regarding the kinds of reliability, the question posed, the kind of consistency, its purpose, and how it is obtained.

Although we are very much concerned with reliability where we must interpret measurements for individuals, given reasonable sample sizes we are less concerned when we compare group means. For a discussion of this point, and an excellent discussion of reliability in general, see Feldt and Brennan (1989).

Norm-Referenced Tests and Criterion-Referenced Tests

Norm-referenced tests show where an individual's score stands with reference to the range of scores achieved by the norm group. For instance, an achievement test's grade norms indicate how far a student is working above or below others in the same grade. **Criterion-referenced tests** determine whether an individual has achieved a given criterion level with respect to particular content or skills and abilities. The criterion is a level accepted as satisfactory by a teacher, a standard-setting group, or research determining a mastery level needed for advanced work. A person may have to pass a criterion-referenced test before being allowed to proceed to further work or for licensing or certification. High school graduation tests sampling the content and skills individuals should have mastered are an example. In an experimental context, a criterion-referenced test that nearly all testees pass might not show differences between treatment groups unless it differentiates between levels of passing.

The measures of reliability discussed in this section require the spread of scores found on normed tests. Since criterion-referenced tests are built so that most students obtain a nearly perfect or passing score, conventional reliability estimates are not appropriate. Alternative measures have been devised by Berk (1986), and Subkoviak (1988).

TABLE 18.3 *Summary of the Different Kinds of Reliability*

Kinds of Reliability	Purpose	Questions Posed	Estimates Consistency of Responses over:	Method of Estimation
Internal consistency	To determine the homogeneity of the measure and the interpretability of scores	Are all items measuring the same thing—a single construct or dimension? Is the score interpretable?	Items of varying difficulty and content— e.g., low scorers get easy items and miss hard ones	Use random-split halves (split the measures into random halves, correlate the scores from each half, and correct the correlation with the Spearman-Brown formula for half-test length); the Kuder-Richardson formula for items scored "right" and "wrong"; or Cronbach's alpha for measures with other score schemes
Equivalence	To determine whether the forms can be used interchangeably	Are different forms of the measure equivalent?	Different forms of a measure	Correlate the scores of form A with those of form B given at the same time; half the sample get form A first, the other half, form B
Stability	To determine the stability of the construct over time	Is the behavior stable over time?	Different testing times—interval should approximate that of intended use	Correlate the scores at one testing with those of a later testing
Stability and equivalence	To determine the stability of the construct over time and comparability over measure forms	Will one form of the measure produce the same results as another form used at a later time?	Different forms of a measure given at different times	Correlate the scores from one testing with one form of an instrument with those on an alternate form at a later testing

* ✦ *Norm-referenced tests spread the scores along a scale so that the researcher can determine how well individuals did relative to a norm group.*
* ✦ *Criterion-referenced measures determine whether a certain content has been mastered.*

Generalizability Theory

Cronbach developed generalizability theory by adapting the approach he originally employed in developing coefficient alpha, which measured only lack of item homogeneity and extending it to estimate a variety of sources of unreliability (Cronbach et al., 1972; Shavelson, Webb, and Rowley, 1989). Generalizability theory allows us to examine the contribution of, for instance, whether the reliability of a measure is best increased by making it longer, by using more raters to evaluate each response, by improving the conditions under which measurement was made or by some combination of them.

Generalizability theory considers a score to be a sample from a universe of possible scores and reliability to be the accuracy with which it estimates the universe value of these scores (the "true" score). It requires a partitioning of the variability of scores (analysis of variance, see p. 490) to determine, as does Cronbach's alpha coefficient, the variability due to the items (item homogeneity). Beyond that, it also determines the contribution of such attributes as different samples of persons being measured, different samples of items making up the measure (such as different forms), different conditions of measurement, and lack of consistency in scoring from rater to rater. From such an analysis, we can estimate the expected variance of the scores in the universe and the expected variance of the scores in the sample; their ratio yields a generalizability coefficient. This figure indicates how well the measure embodies the variability of the universe it is intended to represent.

Generalizability theory has many useful aspects, especially for indicating the sources of unreliability in order to construct a cost-efficient measurement design. Researchers are increasingly using it. However, Jones and Appelbaum (1990) suggest that "given the complex assumption base, both conceptual and mathematical, and the basic difficulties in the definition of a domain [universe in generalizability terms], a cautious approach to the use of generalizability theory still appears warranted" (p. 31).

♦ *Generalizability theory extends the internal-consistency approach from merely estimating the impact of a lack of item homogeneity to assessing the variability of additional operationally definable sources of inconsistency. It is particularly useful as a diagnostic procedure to determine how best to improve measurement by showing the contribution of various sources to reliability of measurement and to error.*

Improvement of Validity and/or Reliability Through Item Analysis

We can use **item analysis** to increase validity, reliability, or both. Let's first examine whether some items are too easy or too hard for most examinees. The percentage passing an item is its **item difficulty index.** Unless the measure has very high internal consistency, items with too high or too low a difficulty index—too easy or too hard for most students—contribute less to validity and reliability than do items in the middle range. We can either rewrite items to adjust their difficulty or substitute new ones.

Next let's consider item discrimination, the contribution of the item to predictive validity. Suppose that on a test predicting sales ability, we ask the question "Do you like to show off at parties?" We can correlate a valid criterion measure, such as average total value of sales per month, with responses to this question (1 for yes and 0 for no). The correlation, the **item discrimination index,** shows whether salespersons with high criterion scores (sales per month) answered the question differently from those with low sales. If they did, the item was a good predictor of success, and perhaps we might add similar questions. While we might expect a "yes" answer to predict sales success, direction of correlation, positive or negative, is not of interest since a "no" answer predictive of success is also useful (see "empirical keying" in the next section). But if successful and unsuccessful salespeople answer the same way, we can drop this question from the test, repair it, or substitute a functioning item.

If we have no valid criterion to check validity, we can at least improve internal consistency reliability using the test score as the criterion. The item discrimination index shows how well each item predicts (contributes to) the total score. Items measuring something different from most other items will have a low correlation with the total score. Eliminating them usually increases reliability, even as it shortens the test. Patterning new items after the remaining ones augments reliability.

Item response theory (IRT) not only examines the contribution of the correct response through correlational statistics but also plots the relationship of each possible response in a multiple-choice item to the criterion. This is a rapidly developing area of psychometric theory (Hambleton, 1989).

Empirical Keying

We also use item analysis in **empirical keying** to determine how to score a test. The item analysis shows which responses correlate with a criterion we wish to predict. Items showing a significant relationship with the criterion are assembled into a key. Positively correlated items are scored as "right" answers. Responses that are negatively correlated are either subtracted from "right" answers, tallied as a separate score with its own interpretation, or the testee is given credit for avoiding that response by scoring the other responses to the item "right."

For example, the U.S. Army wished to select the best of its officers for retention during World War II's demobilization. While units were still intact, they obtained a criterion measure on a large sample of officers—peer ratings by fellow officers. These officers were also administered a "biographical inventory blank" which contained a large number of questions about background and attitudes. Items discriminating the best from poorest officers were keyed as the best officers answered them. So scored, the test successfully predicted the criterion. The key showed that the best came from small towns, were from large families, and were the firstborn.

Could the Army have anticipated this? Probably not. Can we rationalize these keyings after the fact? Yes, but there are also counterarguments. Because of their weak face validity, such findings are usually subjected to repeated studies (called cross-validation). Empirical keyings require large numbers of representative cases to get keys that are stable from sample to sample. But these tests often succeed where others have failed, as is shown by two of the most widely used measures, the Strong-Campbell Interest Inventory and the Minnesota Multiphasic Personality Inventory (the latter was used in the Zimbardo study in Chapter 1).

♦ *In item analysis we use item difficulty indexes to identify too easy or too difficult items, and item discrimination indexes to find items that correlate poorly with the criterion. Modifying or replacing these items improves the test's validity or reliability.*

♦ *To improve validity, we correlate the items with the criterion we want to predict. To improve internal consistency reliability, we correlate items with the total test score.*

♦ *By empirical keying with item analysis, we can determine which responses to include in the key because the response correlates with a criterion. Some of the keyings may be counterintuitive.*

Objectivity of Measures

Objectivity refers to the similarity of two or more independent judgments of the same phenomena—as for example, when two or more judges score a given performance or when they make a record of, or categorize, their observations of the same behavior. Multiple-choice tests are called objective measures because the correct answer is decided before the test is given. Any two clerks can then assign test answers to the "right" or "wrong" category with 100 percent consistency, barring clerical errors. There is no judgmental inconsistency. With essay tests, we defer judgment of responses until the test is given. Since the questions may be answered quite differently by various students, the task of judging the answers is much more difficult. Similarly, two raters are less likely to agree unless they carefully work out in advance their scoring basis for at least the most common answers.

A judgment of the correct response must be made in either case. If done beforehand, as in a multiple-choice format, consistency of judgment of responses is ensured. But the responses a testee can make are limited. This need not be the barrier it is generally considered to be, however. There are many more forms of multiple-choice items than are typically used (Gerberich, 1956; Gulliksen, 1986; Bloom, 1956). These extend the range of skills and abilities that can be tapped by such tests. Even so, it is still not easy to measure creativity, the ability to assemble thoughts and other complex intellectual skills. Alternatively, instead of using multiple-choice format, we can leave the response open and obtain constructed responses involving these skills. Then we must work hard to ensure that the scoring of those responses occurs with consistency—that is, objectivity.

Interest in objective measurement of a student's knowledge structure, a major determiner of problem solving and retention, has increased with the development of cognitive science. It is instructive to see the progress that has been made in this area with computer programs that allow students to develop graphics that describe their structure (cognitive maps[5])or to arrange "knowledge trees" that are derivatives of it (see Lane, 1991). These methods and others (see Frederiksen et al., 1990, and especially Marshall, 1990), not only extend the range of measurement possibilities but also better integrate instruction and assessment of learning.

Observation scales of social interaction vary greatly in the objectivity of the inferences to be made. High-inference scales require the observer to rate dimensions or statements such as, "Group members reinforce each other's actions ___ always, ___ most of the time, ___ about half of the time, ___ occasionally, ___ almost never." Such scales require training to ensure that observers have a common framework for deciding what is "most of the time" or "occasionally."

In contrast, low inference and, therefore, more objective scales specify the target behaviors sufficiently so that they need only be seen to be recognized. For example, Flanders's (1970) interaction analysis for school classrooms consists of ten easily learned, clearly specified categories. The observer categorizes the behavior in the classroom every 5 seconds, recording a sequence of category numbers. This record permits analysis of questions such as, "What happens when a child finishes talking?" Does the teacher try to clarify the child's ideas or ignore them and go off on a tangent? Many such rating scales for instruction exist. Simon and Boyer (1974) is a compilation of them.

Low-inference scales have the advantage of objectivity, but because of their highly targeted nature they may miss the larger picture. This can be captured by high-inference measures, which provide a summary judgment on a range of group characteristics. Which is better? The researcher is facing a trade-off.

Objectivity is also a problem for projective measures, for example, the Rorschach Test, the Thematic Apperception Test (TAT), and the House-Tree-Person Test, which are closer to qualitative than to quantitative measures. Rorschach testees report what they see in black or multicolored inkblots which look much like symmetrical clouds. Testees read meaning into the TAT's illustrations depicting people in ambiguous situations by constructing a story about each one. Skill and training are required to interpret these free responses. Bellak (1993), Exner (1986), and Aronow, Reznikoff, and Moreland (1994) make the scoring of these tests more objective, but many believe that, although something may be gained in objectivity and in comparability of one person's test with another, much clinical evidence is missed by structured scoring formats.

As must be apparent by now, one of the differences between quantitative and qualitative research is the importance given validity, reliability and objectivity and the way they are conceptualized. This is a good place in the discussion for you to compare this chapter's presentation of these concepts with their explanation in qualitative research; pp. 337–341.

♦ *A measure has objectivity when different individuals judging the evidence arrive at the same score or rating. Multiple-choice tests are considered objective because two persons can score them identically except for clerical errors. Essay tests*

---

[5]See the appendix to Chapter 5, pp. 98–99, for an example. Comparison with the instructor's map reveals the effectiveness of instruction and with whom it succeeded.

and projective tests require great effort to achieve objectivity. Measures calling for low inference tend to have objectivity; those requiring high inference, less of it.

Measurement Trade-Offs

Earlier in this chapter we noted a trade-off between structured and unstructured items. Structuring a measure for objectivity, as in using multiple-choice items, makes it difficult to construct examinations for hard-to-measure complex skills and with broad questions. But the examination can be graded by a clerk. These conditions are reversed if responses are free from restraint as in essay questions. Thus, we can put in the professional time beforehand in constructing the measure, or afterward in grading it. There is a trade-off.

The most common trade-off in measurement, however, is the breadth-versus-depth problem, that of measuring broadly but shallowly versus measuring narrowly but deeply. If we measure broadly, we get little information about weaknesses and strengths since only a few items, possibly just one, will sample a subarea—too small a sample for reliable diagnostic scoring. Alternatively, reducing the scope of the measure, we sample each subarea with many items and get good information on strengths and weaknesses. This trade-off is ever present: For example, should we measure reading ability as part of a broad achievement battery or with a diagnostic reading examination?

Another trade-off is between the use of an established test (for example, a widely used general reading test) that only partially covers what we wish to measure (students' knowledge of phonics) and a not yet accepted test (our experimental test of phonics mastery) that is more on-target (phonics, one on many influences on the general reading test score, is the focus of our experimental test.) Our problem of attaining credibility with our audience, is compounded by limited publication space. Do we: divert testing time and resources to multiple measures, like Chapter 1's Zimbardo et al. study—both the established MMPI and their own paranoia scale? Choose the established test which needs no validation, and removes a hurdle to consensus building, but may also produce less dramatic results? Provide evidence of the new test's validity, publication space taken from other aspects of the study? Each choice is a trade-off.

Still another trade-off is that between obvious evidence gathering and unobtrusive measurement. The former may suppress the target behavior we wish to study whereas the latter may only obliquely, and possibly inaccurately, get at what we want. Unobtrusive methods include, for example, library records to measure reading behavior (which fail to include magazine and newspaper reading) and one-way mirrors for observation (which require a good sound system to be effective) See Webb et al., (1981) for a more complete discussion.

Advances in Measurement

Computers have made it possible to shorten conventional tests using **tailored tests**, also called adaptive tests. These start everyone in the middle, and then branch to easier or harder items, depending on whether the preceding item was answered incorrectly or correctly. Such tests make maximum use of testing time, because the items are so chosen as to place the individual on the scale accurately with a minimum number of items. They require high internal consistency reliability to achieve the same accuracy of classification in less testing time. In structure, these tests are analogous to the sequential sampling plans described in Chapter 8. The idea is not new, and with special printing can be done for groups but was mainly employed where tests were given individually, such as the Stanford-Binet Intelligence Test and the Wechsler Intelligence Scale for Children. A set of guidelines for computer-adaptive tests have been developed (American Council on Education, 1995).

Computers have also made item response theory (IRT) and the Rasch models practical; these are methods of equating items on a scale that is presumably invariant with respect to population. A given test item may be easy for a college population but very difficult for elementary school pupils. Item response theory places the item on a single scale of difficulty regardless of whether the data come from college or kindergarten students, but it requires a large number of cases for stable results across samples.[6]

♦ *Adaptive, or tailored testing uses fewer test items and thereby reduces testing time when it is applied to measures tapping homogeneous domains. Computer software analyzes the testee's record on items previously passed and failed to determine the most appropriate next item in order to extract maximum information.*

Locating Existing Measures

Because construction of new measures is such an expensive and lengthy process, retrieval systems have been developed to help find already developed tests. Traditionally, these have been print resources, but, like so many retrieval areas, use of the computer to interactively access these resources is becoming the preferred path. Currently, you can use a computer to access the ERIC/AE site at: http://www.cua.edu/www/eric_ae

Since ERIC Clearinghouses are rebid periodically and the locator could move from this address, an alternative is to look for ERIC with a search engine. You are seeking access to the ERIC/ETS Test Collection Test File of more than 9500 entries, *The Mental Measurement Yearbooks* and Pro-Ed's *Test Critiques*. The yearbooks, begun in 1938 by Oscar Buros and now produced by the Buros Institute at the University of Nebraska at Lincoln, are noncumulative and currently appear about every other year, with supplements between issues. Each provides reviews of the standardized tests published since the last issue. The Institute's *Tests in Print* is a comprehensive bibliography of commercial tests (English only), as is a similar publication *Tests*, by Pro-Ed of Austin, Texas. *Test Critiques*, is also an an-

---

[6]For additional reading on test theory, see Weiss and Davison (1981) and Linn (1989).

nual publication of Pro-Ed. Only references to the measures and reviews are on-line, the actual measures and reviews must be accessed in print form.

In addition, here are a some useful sources of information in print:

Backer, T. E. (1977). *A directory of information on tests.* ERIC TM Report 62–1977. Princeton, NJ: ERIC Clearinghouse on Tests, Measurement and Evaluation, Educational Testing Service.

Chun, K. T., Cobb, S., and French, J. R. P. (1975). *Measures for psychological assessment: A guide to 3000 original sources and their applications.* Ann Arbor, MI: Institute for Social Research, University of Michigan.

ETS Test Collection Catalog, Volumes: 1, Achievement tests (1992); 2, Vocational tests (1988); 3, Tests for special populations (1989); 4, Cognitive, aptitude and intelligence tests (1990); 5, Attitude measures (1991); 6, Affective measures and personality tests (1992). Phoenix, AZ: Oryx Press.

Fabiano, E. (1989). *Index to tests used in educational dissertations.* Phoenix, AZ: Oryx Press. Covers 1938 to 1980.

Fabiano, E., and O'Brien, N. (1987). *Testing information sources for educators.* TME Report 94. Princeton, NJ: ERIC Center on Tests and Measurements, Educational Testing Service. Brings Backer, mentioned earlier, up to 1987, but is not as comprehensive.

Krug, S. E. (published biannually). *Psychware Sourcebook.* Austin, TX: Pro-Ed, Inc. A directory of computer-based assessment tools: tests, scoring, and interpretation systems.

Goldman, B. A., and Mitchell, D. F. (1974–1995). *Directory of unpublished experimental mental measures.* Vols. 1–6. Washington, DC: American Psychological Association.

Rubin, R. B., Palmgreen, P., and Sypher, H. E. (1994). *Communication research measures: A sourcebook.* New York: Guilford Press. Covers four communication contexts: interpersonal, mass, organizational, and instructional.

Sweetland, R. C., and Keyser, D. J. (Eds.) (1991). *Tests: A comprehensive reference for assessments in psychology, education and business,* 3rd ed. Kansas City, MO: Test Corporation of America.

With so many sources of information, in most instances, researchers can devote energies to adapting and improving measures rather than starting anew.

SUMMARY

Measurement, an important characteristic of any field, increases the distinctions that we can make among phenomena and improves our ability to describe them. Measurement is basically a sampling problem: We are sampling an individual's behavior at a single time or a series of times with respect to a sample of content or of situations.

Validity is the most important characteristic of measuring, and construct validity provides evi-

dence which forms the basis for intended score interpretation. To show construct validity is to provide an evaluative summary of the evidence for intended score interpretation. Therefore, construct validity is inclusive of other kinds of validity evidence. Basically, we show construct validity by predicting how a measure should behave were it valid and then gather evidence from appropriate sources to show that it does so. We gather content validity evidence to show that a measure is a representative sample of the content domain it was intended to measure. We gather evidence from response processes to show that the individuals are using the intended mental processes, skills and abilities in responding to the measure. We gather evidence of the measure's internal structure to assure that it conforms to our understanding of the nature of the construct. To assure it is a measure of the intended construct we examine its relations to other variables. For example, we show the measure correlates strongly with other measures of the construct and less strongly with associated constructs (convergent validity evidence) and does not correlate with unrelated constructs (discriminant validity evidence). We show that the test predicts a criterion measure of success—either when the criterion measure is gathered long enough after testing to determine how well the individual succeeded on a job or in school (predictive validity evidence), or when both test and success or other criterion measures are gathered at the same time (concurrent validity evidence). We gather evidence to assure the positive value of measuring outweighs it consequences, even unintended ones. Face validity—the test appears intuitively valid—is an important factor for tests used in important decision making since they must undergo scrutiny by lay persons, but it is not usually considered part of construct validity.

Reliability is a necessary but not sufficient condition for validity. Reliability indicates consistency, whether the measure's sample of behavior is sufficiently representative so that there is consistency across different samples at the item level (internal consistency reliability), at the test level (equivalence reliability), and over test samples obtained at different times (stability reliability). Some test uses require both stability and equivalence reliability.

Norm-referenced measures show where an individual's score stands relative to some norm group—for example, whether at, above, or below their school grade level. Criterion-referenced measures show whether an individual can achieve at a required level—for example, a high school proficiency test. Since such mastery measures result in a large proportion of high or perfect scores, reliability measures for criterion-referenced measures are different from norm-referenced ones.

Item analysis is a development process for improving the validity and/or reliability of a test. To improve validity, responses to each item are correlated with a criterion that is an acceptably valid measure. To improve the internal consistency reliability, the total score is used as the criterion. Items that do not correlate with the criterion are either discarded to shorten the measure or changed to improve the correlation.

The Spearman-Brown formula, the correction for attenuation, and the standard error of measurement are covered in this chapter's appendix. There it is noted that we can estimate the effect on reliability of changing the length of any test by any amount with the Spearman-Brown formula. With the correction for attenuation, the correlation between two tests that are less than perfectly reliable can be estimated as if they were perfectly reliable. The standard error of measurement is useful for indicating how far the true score may possibly lie from an observed score, given the unreliability of the test.

A Look Ahead

In this and the previous chapter on descriptive statistics, we have accumulated two of the three quantitative tools employed in experimentation. The next chapter adds the third, inferential statistics.

ADDITIONAL READING

Measurement texts: Anastasi & Urbina (1997), Cronbach (1990), Hopkins, Stanley and Hopkins (1990) and Mehrens and Lehman (1991). Linn (1989) is essentially a handbook on measurement. See Haladyna (1994) re test item development, Gable and Keilty (1994) re affective measurement, Zwick (1997) re innovative computer tests, and Table 24.1 (p. 624) re a data gathering methods summary.

IMPORTANT TERMS

Alpha reliability coefficient
Concurrent validity
Construct validity
Content validity

Counterbalancing
Criterion
Criterion-referenced tests
Criterion-related validity

Empirical keying
Equivalence reliability
Face validity
Factor analysis
Internal consistency reliability
Item analysis
Item difficulty index
Item discrimination index
Kuder-Richardson reliability
Norm-referenced tests
Objectivity
Operational definition
Predictive validity

Reliability
Sealed scores
Stability reliability
Stability and Equivalence Reliability
Standard scores
Tailored (adaptive) tests
Validity

Terms in Chapter Appendix
Confidence interval
Correction for attenuation
Spearman-Brown formula
Standard error of measurement

APPLICATION PROBLEMS

1. Refer to the description of Jonassen's study in the Application Problems for Chapter 4 (page 73). The purpose of the study was to "validate" the use of pattern notes as a measure of cognitive structure. With what type of validity was Jonassen concerned and why?

2. The dean of Watertown University was concerned about the number of freshmen who were failing and dropping out. She decided to try a prestigious testing firm's new University Entrance Competency Test (UECT) and carefully examined the data indicating the test's validity. (a) What kind of validity evidence should she look for? (b) How might she improve the test's validity?

3. Dr. Keith devised a typology that assigns an individual to one of four personality styles: spontaneous external, spontaneous internal, systematic external, and systematic internal. Coscarelli and Stonewater (1979) proposed that consultants use this model to help understand client decision-making behavior and thus to allow themselves to respond to the client in a supportive manner. In what sort of validity would these researchers be interested if they were to develop a scale to measure these constructs?

4. Elizabeth Cleghorn developed a computer-based course for teaching introductory calculus that should result in increased achievement. To verify this hypothesis, she compared a randomly selected group of 30 first-year college students with a "control" group who are taught by the "regular" (lecture) method. Each group was given a calculus achievement test at the beginning of the semester and a parallel form at the end. With what kinds of validity and reliability would this investigator have been concerned?

5. Recall the investigator who thought that there might be a relationship between a teacher's effectiveness and the teacher's enthusiasm. She had to measure both effectiveness and enthusiasm. To measure the latter, she decided to use two techniques: ratings by independent observers and a diary kept by the subjects. The observers were trained and filled out a 5-point rating scale for a series of indicators of enthusiasm such as facial expression, body movements, and varied vocal delivery. The diary was open-ended. Assess the strengths and weaknesses of each measure.

Compare your answers with those following the Application Exercise.

APPLICATION EXERCISE

Can you find measures for the study you are thinking about? If you are dealing with variables that are standard, look up possible measures in Buros' *Mental Measurement Yearbook*, or search the ERIC/AE site on the Internet. Given the kind of study you plan, what kinds of validity and reliability will you look for? Do the tests that are candidates for your study appear to have useful levels of validity for your purposes? What about reliability? As you can tell from the foregoing material, creating your own measures is likely to be difficult and time-consuming—a study in and of itself. Try to find measures in experimental form that you can build on if nothing seems to fit exactly.

ANSWERS TO THE APPLICATION PROBLEMS

1. Jonassen's study sought evidence that the technique of pattern notes measured cognitive structure—the latter, a construct not directly measurable. To demonstrate construct validity, Jonassen provided convergent evidence showing it related to the free word association technique, a cognitive structure measure already accepted as valid.

2. (a) She would have been interested in criterion-related validity evidence and, specifically, in predictive validity evidence, a predictor of a student's first-year grade point average. Presumably she is into the academic year when she notices freshmen dropping out because of failing grades. She could ask the remaining freshmen to take the UECT and correlate its scores with the end-of-year grade point average. This would be concurrent validity evidence, which would underestimate predictive validity because students who have already dropped out are not included in the testing. To obtain predictive validity evidence, the UECT should be given to next year's freshmen at the beginning of the academic year and be correlated with their GPA at the end of the year or at time of dropping out.

(b) To improve predictive validity, she might item-analyze the test to determine which items did not predict failing dropouts, replacing them with new items similar to those that did predict them. To do this, she would compare the way dropouts answered each item with the way those who did not drop out answered it. Items that showed a large difference would be predictive of dropping out.

3. They would first be interested in knowing whether the scale truly did measure the existence of the four personality styles theorized by Keith's model. For this, they might gather convergent evidence of construct validity. For example, they might ask individuals to nominate people who know them well. The latter persons would then be asked to rate the individuals on each of the four personality types, and these ratings would be correlated with the test scores. High correlations would be evidence of construct validity.

Second, after developing a scale that would indicate to which of these four types a client belonged, consultants would administer the scale to the client prior to working with them. Client's scale classifications would then be compared with the consultants' judgments of their decision-making

styles after the consultants had worked with them long enough to determine it. Since the judgment data was gathered later than the scale data, a comparison of them would provide predictive validity evidence.

4. She should check the content validity of the test against the course. The table of specifications for the examination should match the content and skills taught in the course in both coverage and emphasis. In terms of reliability, she would be concerned with a combination of stability and equivalence reliability. Since she will be measuring the effect of semester-long instruction, she will be comparing the results from two tests given several months apart. She would want to know that without instruction, the control group students' scores would stay approximately the same over that period of time. She will also be comparing the students on two parallel forms of the test and would be concerned that the two forms consistently measure the same concepts—that is, that they are truly equivalent.

5. The data collected by the observers were a direct measure of the teachers' behavior and perhaps the most objective measure available to the investigator. Since a checklist was used, analysis of the data would have been straightforward. However, the presence of the observers likely had an effect on both the teachers and the students. Moreover, the observers were restricted to predetermined indicators of enthusiasm, which may or may not have been valid measures. Thus, enthusiastic behavior not reflected by the checklist may have been overlooked. These observations would have been time-consuming, and possibly costly, if the investigator had to pay the observers.

The diaries were a form of data produced by the subjects themselves. Their flexible form could have provided comprehensive insight into a particular teacher's behavior, particularly into private thoughts and feelings. They were inexpensive. The major weakness of this form of measure is that it depends on self-perception and may not accurately reflect how others (in this case, the students) would have perceived the teacher's level of enthusiasm. In addition, filling out a diary requires recall of past events, albeit recent ones, which may have been modified by the teacher's memory. Finally, the diary data would have been time-consuming, and possibly difficult to analyze and summarize.

Chapter Appendix

If you are as concerned with doing research as with being able to read it intelligently, you do well to familiarize yourself with the formulas for certain of the topics in this chapter. Further, not only are topics such as the standard error of measurement (SEM) critical for score interpretation, but understanding them also gives you a running start on inferential statistics, the topic of Chapter 19. The SEM is probably the most important of the three topics covered in this appendix.

The Standard Error of Measurement

The opposite of reliability or consistency of measurement is inconsistency—variability. When you hear the word *variability*, think "standard deviation" or "variance." Score variability is shown by the **standard error of measurement**.

Consider the score as composed of two parts: a true score—the score if the measure were perfectly accurate—and an error component—the influence of all the factors that might cause inconsistency in measurement.[7] For any individual, the true score will not vary with remeasures (unless the underlying construct does—so assume stability). The error component will vary at random—sometimes positive, sometimes negative, usually small, rarely large, the bell-shaped normal probability curve of Chapter 17. The standard deviation of this error distribution, called the standard error of measurement, is as big as the standard deviation of the scores themselves with no reliability but approaches zero as reliability improves. A commonly used formula for the standard error of measurement is $\text{SEM} = \text{SD} \sqrt{1-r}$, where SD is the standard deviation of the measure and r is the reliability.[8]

We often report scores as an interval rather than a single score. Erected around the person's score using the standard error of measurement, it is called a **confidence interval** (a topic developed further in Chapter 19). Its size depends on how confident we wish to be that the interval includes the true score. Our confidence is expressed as odds, as in a wager. Let's suppose we had a test with a reliability of .91 and a standard deviation of 10. The SEM is 3. (The square root of 1.00 – .91 is .30, which, when multiplied by the standard deviation of 10 gives a standard error of measurement of 3.) Figure 18.2 (opposite page) shows the score distribution for persons with a true score of 63. With perfect reliability, scores will all pile up at exactly 63. Since we have error with a standard deviation of 3 (the SEM), the scores scatter around 63 as shown. Given a close to normal probability distribution, two-thirds of the observed scores will lie between ±1 SEM, or 60 and 66, 95 percent between 57 and 69, and 99.9 percent between 54 and 72.

Let's suppose we wish to locate Rebecca's true score with a certainty expressed by odds of 2 to 1. Graph A in Figure 18.3 (page 452) shows an interval from 56 to 62, one SEM on each side of her observed score of 59. This is the confidence interval within which the true score lies with odds of 2 to 1. Setting those odds assumes our willingness to be wrong the one time out of three when Rebecca's true score lies outside the confidence interval.

Put another way, the confidence interval in graph A locates the set of true score distributions to which her score of 59 can belong: 56, 57, 58, 59, 60, 61, and 62. We don't know

---

[7]This is a traditional test theory formulation; more modern test theory involves the latent variables underlying a test. The traditional formulation is simpler and serves our purposes here.

[8]For other formulas, see Lord (1968); for a description of item response theory see Weiss and Davison (1981). Both their formulas produce slightly different standard errors of measurement for different score ranges and larger ones for extreme scores.

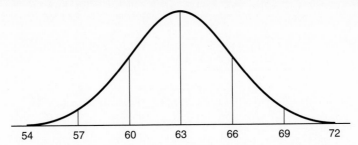

FIGURE 18.2 Distribution of observed scores for persons with a true score of 63.

which it is but graph B shows that, since 59 falls within their central ±1 SEM bands, it can be any. With confidence expressed by odds of 2 to 1, therefore, her true score is between 56 and 62. We do not know whether we are right or wrong, just the odds; that is 2 to 1, we will be wrong a third of the time.

We would have been wrong if Rebecca's true score were 63. But at odds of 19 to 1, a band four SEM wide, from 53 to 65, as shown in graph C, our confidence interval includes her true score in its 12-unit span. Precision of location is traded off for certainty; we must decide the optimum balance.

Knowing the SEM is important for scores that categorize an individual. Let's suppose scores of 60 or below fail the nurses' licensing examination; we can say with a confidence expressed by the odds of 1 in 6 that Mary Jane, with a score of 57, has a passing score! Why 1 in six 6? With a standard error of measurement of 3, at odds of 2 in 3, Mary Jane's score lies in the area labeled B in Figure 18.4 (page 453, top). Therefore, at odds of 1 in 3, it lies in the remaining areas, A and C, with equal probability of being in either. However, we are interested only in the odds of its being in C, the area above the passing score; therefore, the odds are half the 1 in 3, or 1 in 6.

Because candidates who fail a certification examination can legitimately use this argument, actual cut scores are often placed one or more SEM *below* the desired cut score. Some who should fail will pass, but, considering the personal devastation caused by an error, this may be the lesser evil. However, in licensing nuclear engineers or airline pilots with the safety of large numbers at stake, we may switch errors. Setting the cut score *above* the minimum level of competency increases the chances that those certified have a passing true score. Some will fail who deserve to pass, but consider the consequences of an error at a nuclear power plant or 35,000 feet in the air. Adjusting cut scores involves trade-offs for the "greatest" good.

- ✦ *The standard error of measurement permits us to establish a confidence interval within which we can say, with a confidence expressed by specified odds, that a person's true score will lie.*
- ✦ *The size of the confidence interval reflects the amount and kind of unreliability used in the determination of reliability—stability, equivalence, and so on.*
- ✦ *Requiring greater certainty increases the size of the confidence interval, thereby reducing precision in locating the true score.*
- ✦ *The standard error of measurement is often used in establishing a cut score for licensing and certifying examinations. The direction in which potential error is allowed depends on whether the individual's or society's protection is the prime consideration—a trade-off.*

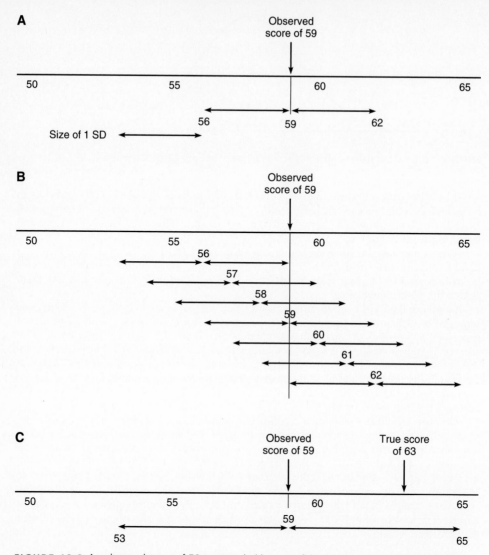

FIGURE 18.3 An observed score of 59 surrounded by a confidence interval one SEM wide (A), the central one-SEM-wide bands of true scores that overlap that confidence level (B), and a two-SEM wide band around an observed one of 59(C).

Estimating Reliability for Measures of Different Length

In discussing the split-half reliability, we noted that the **Spearman Brown Formula** adjusts the reliability for a measure of full rather than half length to avoid an underestimate. We can use the following formula to estimate reliability for any amount of change in the length of the measure (halving it, tripling it, and so on):

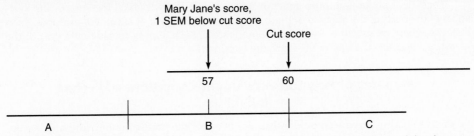

FIGURE 18.4 A score one SEM below a cut score on a certification examination and the chances of being failed in error.

$$\frac{Kr}{1+\left(K-1\right)r}$$

where K is the ratio of items in the new measue to those in the original form (for example, it would be 2 to double the length) and r is the reliability of the original form.[9]

Internal Consistency Reliability Formulas

The earlier discussion of the Kuder-Richardson formulas indicated that one of them, KR21, assumes that all items are equally difficult. This formula is simple to compute and therefore widely used. Its formula is

$$r = \frac{k}{k-1}\left(1 - \frac{M\left(k-M\right)}{k\left(SD\right)^{2}}\right)$$

where k is the number of items on the measure (and the maximum possible score), M is the average score on the test, and SD is the standard deviation of the measure.

KR20 uses the percentage passing each item and therefore is a more accurate estimate. Its formula is:

$$r = \frac{k}{k-1}\left(1 - \frac{\Sigma pq}{\left(SD\right)^{2}}\right)$$

where p is the proportion of students passing an item and q is the proportion of students not passing it. The Σ indicates that these pq values are summed over all the items on the measure.

---

[9]Generalizability theory provides a more accurate estimate where, for instance, multiple judges of constructed responses are involved (see Brennan, 1992).

Coefficient alpha is a more generalized form of KR21 in which the sum of the variances of the parts of the measure replaces Σpq in the numerator of KR21. For example, in an instance where items are scored on a 10-point scale, each item is considered a part of the measure, and the variances of the items are summed.

Estimates of Relationships Under Conditions of Perfect Reliability

Predictive validity is reduced by unreliability of either the predicting measure or the criterion. The **correction for attenuation** is a handy way to estimate the improvement in correlation if both criterion and measure were perfectly reliable. Its formula is

$$\frac{r_{xy}}{\sqrt{r_{xx}r_{yy}}}$$

where r_{xy} is the correlation to be corrected and r_{xx} and r_{yy} are the reliabilities of the measures involved in that correlation (see Guilford and Fruchter, 1978).

Used to correct any correlation between two imperfectly measured variables, the formula determines the size of the relationship between them with perfectly reliable measurement. We need to know the relationship between constructs devoid of measurement error when we build theory. We can also use it to tell whether improving a measure's reliability is worthwhile. For instance, what would the size of the relationship be if the salesman selection test and the sales manager ratings were perfectly reliable? The sources of inconsistency should reflect the sources of error we wish to eliminate. Because we want to predict over time, we use stability reliability. For example, if our stability reliability is .80 and our criterion reliability, based on correlating two judgments over time, is .60, the original total sales predictability of .40 becomes .84, a marked change.

Like any statistic, the correction depends on the accuracy of the underlying data. The usual underestimates from KR21 can result in nonsense correlations of over 1.00; overestimates from a speeded test's parallel split half (students didn't have time to finish the test) can give underestimates.

✦ *The correction for attenuation estimates the size of a correlation if both the measures involved were perfectly reliable. It is useful as predictive validity evidence showing that a measure is "on target" and merely needs to have its reliability improved. Its estimate of the size of the relationship between constructs without measurement error is useful in theory building.*

The Nature and Logic of Inferential Statistics

Mathematics does not develop the scientist's powers but puts its powers at his disposal; [with] its creation, something of the genius of the mathematician . . . is made available to every schoolboy.

Abraham Kaplan, *The Conduct of Inquiry*

Like many things, statistics, though opaque in bulk, is transparent in thin slices.

Anonymous

OVERVIEW

Inferential statistics became important to social science research because so many research effects are small. For most social science journals, inferential statistics serve a gatekeeping function, distinguishing "publishable" from chance results. (Natural scientists think it strange that social science researchers concentrate on whether there was an effect instead, as they have, on measuring how big the effect is. Interestingly, just as the social sciences are moving toward estimating effect sizes, the natural sciences increasingly use inferential statistics.) Chapter 17 explained how we use numbers for description—descriptive statistics. This chapter shows how inferential statistics build on them to provide confirming or disconfirming evidence for a hypothesis—a validating role.

However, just as descriptive statistics can be used in an exploratory role to check out hunches, so too can inferential statistics. Often they guide us to new insights or provide leads to next research. Both roles are important. Because exploration is rarely included in research reports, however, it doesn't get much visibility.

Inferential statistics are so named because they permit us to infer the characteristics of a population from a representative sample. They do two jobs. First, applied to data from a sample, we can estimate the size of a characteristic of interest, such as the mean of a population, by constructing an interval that tells the range within which the value lies with a certainty that we can determine (for instance, odds of 95 to 5). Second, we can determine whether an effect other than that of sampling and chance error exists in a study, with a certainty expressed by odds we set. We do this by determining whether the interval described above includes zero which would be the size if there were no effect. If it does not, with a certainty expressed by odds we set, we can rule out sampling and chance variability as causative factors. However, whether the effect is due to the cause we intended, depends on ruling out all other plausible explanations—a matter of study design instead of inferential statistics. Thus, inferential statistics contribute to two of the five key judgments of internal validity (LP): (1) If we can show there was an expected effect, there was a "demonstrated result," the third judgment contributing to internal validity (LP). (2) If we can show there was little likelihood that the effect resulted from sampling and chance error—usually a prime rival explanation—its elimination contributes to the judgment "rival explanations eliminated," the fourth appraisal in determining internal validity (LP).

This chapter concentrates on the logic of the processes of estimation and hypothesis testing. Because the logic is the same regardless of the inferential statistic used (for example, t test, analysis of variance, chi-square), once we understand the logic, it is easier for us to understand how a given statistic works and when and how it is appropriate for us to use it. In the course of exploring this logic, the chapter explains the concepts of power (sensitivity), Type I and Type II error, and the difference between statistical and practical significance. Explanations of the t test, chi-square, and analysis of variance demonstrate the logic of inference in use.

CHAPTER CONTENTS

Prologue

Inferential statistics seem to be made up of complex operations foreign to any of us but the initiated. Nevertheless they are omnipresent. Although we do not think in statistical terms, we are continually making inferences in our daily lives. Indeed, a large chunk of the workforce earns its living because it is good at making inferences! Further, our logic structure resembles inferential statistics in important ways. Consider this example.

When you drive someone else's automobile or a rental car, one of the first things you do is learn the normal noise and vibration the car makes, especially older models with lots of rattles and squeaks. Having learned what is typical, you can detect subtle but atypical noises such as a dragging brake pad or a wheel bearing starting to break up.[1] You then take the car to a garage.

Garage service managers make a good living determining what is atypical and why. How do they learn this? Probably from listening to lots of cars. A few normal cars are very quiet, a few are very noisy even though they are OK, but most are just slightly noisy—that bell-shaped curve we keep encountering (for example, pp. 395 and 402). Service managers know what is typical. The manager takes your car for a test ride—but only a five-minute ride because other customers are waiting. It is a small sample to use for a decision, but it is a typical one; we usually have less information to make decisions than we wish. From this small sample, a five-minute test drive, the manager must judge the kind and range of noise that currently characterizes this car. He practices estimation, inferring the population value from a sample—the car's typical noise over a long normal drive.

The next inference is whether the noise belongs to a population of noises made by "healthy" cars or to a population made by cars with defective wheel bearings. Defective wheel bearings are a serious problem. If ignored, they become more expensive to repair and, on a highway, can even get hot enough to seize up, freeze the wheel, and cause an accident. Is the sound atypical enough that something may be wrong? The manager can tell for sure only by pulling off the wheel. This will deprive the owner of the use of the car and cost something for the labor. Figure 19.1 on page 458 illustrates the dilemma.

These are the risks we run in making inferences. We can determine what is to be judged atypical at whatever level we wish. That will determine our **Type I,** or **alpha error**—saying the bearing is failing when it is OK. If it is cheap to pull a wheel, we might not mind making such errors because it will avoid a possible accident and a **Type II,** or **beta error**—saying the car was OK when the bearing was failing. But if the level of what is judged atypical is set too conservatively, thereby increasing Type I error so that many noises are said to be atypical when they are really typical, we will anger many unhappy customers who will have paid to pull the wheel when nothing was wrong.

Thus, we can decrease Type II (beta) errors, all other things being equal, by increasing Type I (alpha) errors, being conservative in saying there is a problem when there may not be. Alternatively, we can increase the accuracy of our diagnostic judgments by taking a bigger sample on which to base the judgment—a

---

[1]A flat tire is easy to sense—the effect is so great that we can recognize it immediately without knowing the normal background noise. In the same way, we don't need inferential statistics to determine that penicillin is effective because the before-and-after contrast is so great. When the effect is small, however, inferential statistics become important.

	Car is OK; noise is typical.	Car is not OK; noise is atypical; bearing is starting to break up, could cause accident if not corrected!
Manager says car is OK; noise is typical.	Manager is correct; customer has no further problems and has increased trust in manager's judgment.	Type II error in judgment (beta error). Customer has accident on road and says, "I *beta* never go there for service again!"
Manager says car is not OK; leave it for check and repair.	Type I error in judgment (alpha error). Customer says, "If you're wrong, do I *alpha* pay da bill?"	Manager is correct; repair is made; potential accident is averted; customer builds trust in manager's judgment.

FIGURE 19.1 Type I and Type II errors of inference described as automobile service manager's choices. Puns are intended to facilitate recall.

longer test drive—or otherwise increase sensitivity to the atypical—use a stethoscope or an electronic amplifier to increase the loudness for sound location.

The problem faced by the mechanic is also faced by the surgeon deciding whether surgery is warranted (every human being is built a little differently), the physician prescribing a drug (each of us metabolizes chemicals at different rates), the teacher diagnosing a student's reading ability, the librarian trying to decide how open the shelves can be without unacceptable rates of book loss, the social worker trying to decide how much aid can be given a family without its coming to depend on it, the economist trying to determine the interest rate that will stimulate the economy yet not cause inflation.

Thus the consequences of Type II (beta) errors may be more far-reaching than our wheel bearing example. For example, they may be judging a drug ineffective when it is efficacious and so missing the use of a valuable drug. Each situation has its own set of consequences and its own possibilities for increasing the sensitivity of the study to make a better diagnosis.

The logic of inference is obviously not foreign to any of us so neither will its use in statistical inference be.

Introduction

A typical poll result is reported as follows:

> Seventy percent of those queried said "yes" when asked whether they thought next year would be better for them financially than this one has been. Twelve hundred people were questioned, and the margin of error is three percentage points.

The phrase "the margin of error" comes from inferential statistics. The intent of the poll is to estimate what the response to the question would be in the population the sample represents. The response of the sample is used to estimate population values. Without any other information, and given a 70 percent "yes" response in this instance, our best guess is that the percentage of the U.S. population is the same as, or close to, the percentage that so responded in the sample. But how close? That is the margin of error. It indicates that an interval of three percentage points on either side of the observed value of 70, or the range 67 to 73, contains the population value with a confidence expressed by odds of 2 to 1.[2] The odds of 2 to 1, like odds in horse racing or betting, express our confidence that the statement is true ("I'll give you two dollars for your one that my horse, Beccaboo, will win!"). Although such polls are rarely explained in this way, it describes estimation in inferential statistics. And it is these techniques of estimation that we use in hypothesis testing.

These statistics are inferential because they permit us to infer the characteristics of a population from those of a representative sample. However similar the characteristics of the sample are to those of the population, they are probably not identical to them. Thus, having set acceptable odds for possibly being wrong, we can describe on the basis of a sample the range or interval within which statistics descriptive of characteristics of the total population will fall.

Inferential statistics, because they estimate the population value from the sample, can tell us whether a difference between means, for example, is likely to result from chance error or is a "real" difference.[3] They do this by asking whether, if we examine the typical range of chance differences between the means of samples taken from the same population, it includes or excludes the observed difference: Is the difference typical or atypical? If it is in the range of typical values, it is likely due to chance. If it is atypical, however, something probably influenced it besides chance and it is a "real" difference.

Briefly put, inferential statistics will help us in terms of estimation in several ways:

- Given a mean, standard deviation, or other common descriptive statistic from a random sample, we can describe an interval within which, at a chosen level of confidence, will lie the population value of that statistic. For example, with a certainty expressed by odds of 2 to 1, we can find the interval within which falls the percentage of people in the population responding "yes" to the poll's question.
- We can also find such an interval for a correlation, a mean, and a standard deviation—indeed, a variety of descriptive statistics.

---

[2]The media often say, "the chances are 2 to 1 that the real vote proportion is between 67 and 73 percent." The chances (odds) actually reflect our *confidence* in where the population value lies with respect to this observed value—a subtle distinction but one to keep in mind.

[3]Quotation marks are used around "real" because, although the difference between means is very likely the result of something in addition to chance, it may or may not be the result of whatever the study hypothesized was the cause. We accept that explanation only after we have eliminated every other reasonable alternative argument. Moses (1986) suggests that if chance is rejected as the sole cause, the hypothesized cause should be accepted with the qualification "maybe so" (p. 123).

- How sure do we want to be that the interval contains the population value? We can set the odds at whatever we wish; odds typically used are 2 to 1, 19 to 1 (or 95 to 5), or 99 to 1. The size of the band increases (our estimate is less precise) as we insist on being surer (for example, from odds of 2 to 1 to 19 to 1).

Similarly, here is what inferential statistics will do for us in terms of hypothesis testing:

- By hypothesis testing we learn, for example, at specified odds, whether a difference between a mean from a treated group and one from an untreated group (the effect of treatment) is likely due to sampling and chance error or is a "real" effect. We can do this for a variety of common statistics.
- Such testing can show the likelihood of one common alternative explanation of data—that we should consider chance factors as an alternative cause of the effect.
- It allows us to determine how sure we wish to be (for example, odds of 2 to 1) that we are not in error in calling a result a real effect when it really is a chance difference.
- It allows us to design a study with sufficient sensitivity to identify an effect of a given size as not due to chance at specified odds. Usually this will involve determining appropriate sample size, but sensitivity can be changed by other adjustments in the study's design.

Estimation

Estimation's Application Beyond Measurement

We encountered **estimation** when we discussed the standard error of measurement in the appendix to Chapter 18. We used that standard error to estimate the range within which, at given odds, the true score lay. Although that same logic applies to the estimation of population values, there is a change in terminology. Instead of true scores we estimate characteristics of a population. Numbers descriptive of a population are called **parameters.** When they are descriptive of a sample, we call them sample statistics or just statistics.[4] This is why estimation is concerned with parameters.

What are the similarities between the estimation of a true score in measurement and the estimation of a population mean in statistical inference? In both contexts, we can think of the value we wish to estimate as a mean of means. The population mean can be considered as the mean of a distribution of means computed from samples, or, said another way, the mean of the average values from repeated random samples of the same size taken from a population. The distribution of average values from samples is called the **sampling distribution of the mean.** Similarly, in the measurement context, the true score is the mean of the distribution of

---

[4]To help you remember, note the alliteration: *sample statistics* and *population parameters*.

scores for an individual resulting from repeated testing. Each score is a sample of the subject's behavior. Scores can also be considered means as one can sense when they are expressed in percentage terms.[5]

Carrying the parallelism further, the standard deviation of the sampling distribution of the mean is called the **standard error of the mean.** It indicates the variability of the mean due to sampling and chance error. In the measurement context, the standard deviation of the distribution of scores for an individual is called the standard error of measurement and indicates the variability of the observed scores due to sampling variability and the other chance characteristics we lump together as measurement error—inattention, lack of motivation, and so forth. The standard error of the mean includes measurement error as "chance" in the phrase "sampling and chance error." With these shifts in terminology, we can now apply what we learned in measurement to the context of general estimation.

With the standard error of measurement, we constructed a confidence interval within which we could say, at a specified level of confidence, the true score lay. Let's refer to Figure 18.3 on page 452. In part A, a confidence interval ±1 standard error wide was constructed around the observed score of 59. Recall that the middle portion of the normal curve between ±1 standard deviation includes about two-thirds of the frequency distribution (68.26 percent, to be exact); ±1.96 SD, 95 percent of it; ±2.58 SD, 99 percent; and ±3 SD, 99.9 percent. The sampling distribution for the mean is also a normal probability distribution.[6] Therefore, the same percentages apply. Thus, for any observed mean of a random sample from a population, since standard errors are really standard deviations, we can say with 68 percent confidence that the population mean lies between ±1 standard error (SE) of the parameter value, with 95 percent confidence that it lies within ±1.96 SE, and so on. Those figures represent our confidence that the population's mean score will be in those zones.

The intervals described in the foregoing discussion are called **confidence intervals,** and they represent the range of values that includes the population value with a given confidence expressed by a percentage (for example, a 95 percent confidence interval) or odds (19 to 1). The ends of such intervals are the **confidence limits** (for example, the 95 percent confidence limit).

The **confidence level** is the probability (for instance, 68 percent) that we will be right in saying that the confidence interval contains the population value—in this case, 68 percent of such intervals constructed on random samples from the population will contain the population value. The downside of this, however, is that 32 percent (100 minus 68) of them will not.

---

[5]Say a subject gets 30 items correct on a test with 60 items (50%). A percentage score of 50 is a mean score—the sum of scores for each correct item (one point each) divided by the number of items.
[6]Statisticians know this is true as a result of the central limit theorem, which states that as the sample size increases, the frequency distribution of sample means from a common population will increasingly resemble the normal curve, whether or not the population itself is distributed normally.

◆ *Numbers descriptive of populations are called parameters; those descriptive of a sample are sample statistics or just statistics.*

◆ *If we calculate a descriptive statistic (for example, a mean) on repeated random samples from a population, the frequency distribution of the resulting values is called the sampling distribution of that statistic (for example, the sampling distribution of the mean). The standard deviation of that distribution, a parameter, is called its standard error (for example, the standard error of the mean).*

◆ *We can use the standard error to describe a confidence interval within which the parameter lies with a specified confidence—the confidence level. The ends of the confidence interval are the confidence limits.*

An Example

As dormitory director, you are switching from an all-meals-in-the-dormitory policy to meals in any campus restaurant. You need to know how many meals on the average to budget in the dormitory. You interview 100 randomly selected students to ask how many meals per week they will take in the dormitory and find an average of 14.6 with a standard deviation of 2.4. How useful is that information? Not very, unless you can relate it in some way to the meal-taking habits of the rest of the dormitory population; it is a sample statistic, whereas it is a population value you want. Without further information, you would have to say that the mean of the sample, 14.6, is your best estimate of the population mean. This is called **point estimation.**

Each random sample is different, however, and this one might have more classes close to or far from the dormitories. In that case, its meal taking might not be exactly average. In any event, you can't be sure its mean is the same as the population mean, even though most random sample means will be closer to the population mean than not. The range depends on the variability from student to student. If it is large, samples may differ widely.

If the variability of samples and their means reflects that of the population, there ought to be a way to estimate the variability of the sampling distribution of means from the sample's variability. Statisticians have found a way: Divide the standard deviation of the sample by the square root of the sample size minus one.[7] In the dormitory meals example, this means you divide 2.4 by the square root of the sample size of 100 less one, which is 9.95, yielding a standard error of 0.24.

If the standard error of the mean is 0.24 and our sample mean is 14.6, the population mean of meals taken in the dorm per person per week, at odds of 2 to 1, lies between 14.36 and 14.84. If we wish to be more certain and construct a 95 percent confidence interval, the confidence limits become 14.12 and 15.08. When multiplied by the thousands of students in the dormitories, this difference between the upper and lower confidence limits of almost a full meal per week is quite a gap.

---

[7]In a statistics text, the "minus 1" is explained as the loss of one degree of freedom. For more on degrees of freedom, see page 489.

Were you this dormitory director, you should go out and get additional data to refine the estimates. A larger sample will reduce the size of the standard error.[8] If the students have gone home for the summer and these are all the data you can get, which confidence level do you use? That depends on many factors, such as how much of a problem an error in estimation causes, how quickly it can be corrected, and how tolerant your supervisors are of error. All you can do is make a choice of confidence level based on all the factors involved in the decision, including how sure you or your supervisors wish to be.

Confidence Levels. In the examples, we could have used any level of confidence we wished. But we repeatedly use confidence levels of 68, 95, 99, and 99.9 percent. Why? Somebody made a judgment a long time ago as to what was appropriate, and it has become a matter of convention. Pollsters tend to use ±1 SE, or 68 percent confidence, which they translate for the layperson as 2-to-1 odds. Most social and behavioral science publications use 95 percent and 99 percent levels.

The purpose for which the data are to be used is the most important factor in determining the confidence level. When we seek new information and will be able to remedy an error when we replicate a study, the odds of being wrong, on average only 5 times in 100, seem quite acceptable. However, we will never know in any given instance whether that study is one of the 95 or the 5. If a great deal is at stake, as in a life-or-death matter, or decision involving considerable expense, then we may wish to be wrong only once in 10,000 or 100,000 instances. Then we would extend the size of the confidence interval accordingly. We will return to this topic later.

Where do we find levels other than those already noted? Tables that statisticians provide show what proportion of the cases lies in the tails of a probability distribution. Table 19.1 (page 464) presents selected entries from a table of the normal probability distribution to give an idea of what it looks like and how the percentages change as we go further from the center of the distribution. Most of the statistics social scientists commonly use are distributed as one of five theoretical sampling distributions (the normal, binomial, t, F, and chi-square distributions). Tables such as Table 19.1 for all the distributions are available in most statistics texts, but they typically show values for more and smaller intervals than appear here.

✦ *The confidence level expresses our certainty that the population mean (parameter) falls within the confidence interval. Conventionally used levels are 68, 95, and 99 percent. Although these choices have become standard, we can set any level appropriate to the data's use.*

---

[8]Recall that one way of reducing the size of the standard error of measurement is to increase the reliability of the test—taking a larger sample of behavior by increasing the length of the test. Similarly, increasing the size of the sample reduces the standard error of the mean by reducing the variability of the sampling distribution. Imagine a sample of 5 women and another of 10,000 women. Count the money in their purses. The average value for samples of 10,000 will possibly vary only at less than the penny level; samples of 5 might vary at the dollar level.

TABLE 19.1 *Selected Entries from the Normal Probability Distributions*

Distance from the Mean of the Distribution	Percent of the Sampling Distribution in Both Tails	Percent of the Sampling Distribution in One Tail
0.00	100.0	50.0
0.44	66.0	33.0
0.50	62.0	31.0
1.00	32.0	16.0
1.65	10.0	5.0
1.96	5.0	2.5
2.00	4.6	2.3
2.58	1.0	0.5
3.00	0.3	0.1

◆ *We must set the confidence level in relation to the kind of decision that flows from the data.*

◆ *A multiple of the estimated standard error (for example, ±1.65 SE), determined by the confidence level we have chosen, marks off the boundaries of the confidence interval (the confidence limits) around the sample value.*

The Logic of Confidence Intervals

The logic of confidence intervals is just like the logic for finding the true score in measurement. In Figure 19.2, three means are shown, chosen simply for purposes of illustration from the infinite number in a sampling distribution: a likely one, L_1; a borderline one, B_1; and an atypical one, A_1. When we extend a ±1 SE confidence interval around the likely mean, L_1, the band includes the population mean, the thick line running down from the middle of the distribution. The borderline value, B_1, is almost as extreme as we can get, and include the population mean in its ±1 SE confidence interval. If we had constructed ±1 SE confidence intervals around the means of all possible random samples, the middle 68 percent of those intervals would contain the population mean. These are represented by the likely (L_1) and borderline (B_1) examples. The atypical example (A_1) represents the intervals that would not.

When we extend such a confidence interval around the atypical value, A_1, *it does not include the population's mean*. With a ±1 SE confidence interval, about a third of the means of random samples will be atypical and not include the population value. Thus, we will be wrong one-third of the time in saying that the population mean is contained within that interval.

How often we are likely to be wrong is under our control. It depends on the confidence level we set. Frequently, we use a wider interval to lower the error rate, for example a ±1.96 SE, or 95 percent confidence interval. As we do this, the confidence interval broadens and we locate the population's mean less precisely. Other things being held constant, we can trade off precision of location for certainty.

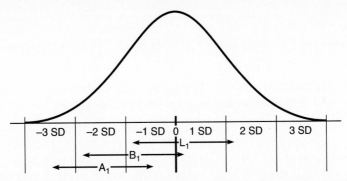

FIGURE 19.2 The ± standard error confidence intervals for likely (L), borderline (B), and atypical (A) values in a distribution of means of random samples from a common population.

♦ *A confidence interval is a region around a sample statistic (such as a mean) that contains the population value (for example, population mean) with a certain confidence that we can express in odds or as a percentage.*

♦ *We determine the width of the confidence interval by how confident we wish to be that it contains the parameter. The wider we make it, the surer we can be that it contains the parameter. Since a broader interval locates the parameter less precisely, however, we trade off precision for certainty.*

♦ *A confidence expressed by odds of 2 to 1 accompanies a 68 percent confidence interval, which is ±1 standard errors (SE) wide; odds of 19 to 1 accompany a 95 percent confidence interval, which is ±1.96 SE wide; and odds of 99 to 1 accompany a 99 percent confidence interval, which is ±2.58 SE wide.*

The Logic of Hypothesis Testing

We can extend the logic of estimation to **hypothesis testing.** In estimation, we are seeking a *range* of values that probably contains the population value. Therefore, we focus on the values *inside* the confidence interval. In hypothesis testing, by contrast, we are looking at differences. These might be differences between the mean of a sample and some population value. Therefore, our question is whether our sample differs from the population value ("Are our students like a normal hearing group?"). Our usual expectations are that they are not (they are partially deaf or have extrasensitive hearing), that they lie outside the "normal," the "typical," the "expected," the "likely." Our focus, then, is on the *atypical* values, those values that fall *outside* the confidence interval.

As another example, we often have two means (for example, like Chapter 1's Zimbardo et al. study, one mean from a sample of subjects that have been hypnotized and told they would be hard of hearing and not realize it, and one from a similarly treated group who were told they would realize they had a hearing deficit). We examine the difference between them in relation to a sampling distribution of differences between means. Our question is whether the difference is *atypical,* larger than would be expected as a result of sampling variation and random error built into a study. The logic involved in "Is this difference between means typical?" is simply a twist in the focus of the same logic we used in: "Does this value belong to this population?" which translates into "Is this mean atypical?"

Determination of the Atypicality of a Mean or "Does This Mean Belong to This Population?"

The logic of hypothesis testing builds on estimation by adding some steps. Suppose we are concerned that adolescents who are repeatedly exposed to loud music from headphones, cars, dances, and concerts are ruining their hearing. We test a randomly selected sample of 26 teenagers attending a recent concert who say they regularly listen to loud music. We find that on the Syracuse Hearing Tests, their mean score is only 69, whereas normally hearing samples have a mean of 80. We are about to go public with our results when one of our colleagues says that she is not at all sure that these students are hearing-deficient. This sample could be no different from the normal hearing population except for random sampling variation and the error built into the study, such as the error of measurement of the Syracuse Hearing Tests.

Our question is whether we can reasonably account for the difference between the sample mean of 69 and the mean of a normally hearing population of 80 by sampling and chance variation. Inferential statistics permit us to determine whether this explanation is reasonable or unreasonable. Figure 19.3 is helpful in illustrating the logic.

The upper left bell-shaped curve of Figure 19.3 is the frequency distribution of hearing scores for a population of adolescents who are regularly exposed to loud music, from which we have taken our sample of 26, shown on the right. The mean of this population is unknown as is indicated by the question mark. We are trying to establish whether the mean, whatever it is, differs from that of a normally hearing group. This problem is illustrated in step 1 of the figure. From what population was our sample taken? Is its mean from a population with a mean on the hearing test of 80—that is, a mean such as we might typically expect to obtain with a sample of this size from a normally hearing population? We define "typically expect" as the range within which most (for example, 95 percent) means of random samples will fall. Or is it atypical and therefore more likely from a population with a mean different from 80? Notice that it is the population value about which we make inferences.

Step 2 in the figure translates the hypotheses of our problem into proper logical form for this statistical test. This step involves establishing two hypotheses: the **null hypothesis** (A) and an alternate hypothesis (B). The null hypothesis (H_0) is that when we take into account the sampling and random error of the study, the sample value is typical for a sample of this size from a normally hearing population. Put another way, it is suggesting that in reality there is no (null) difference between the mean of the sampling distribution from which this sample came and that of a normally hearing population. Put still another way, the strategy is to nullify, or reject, this hypothesis (Cohen, 1990). The alternative hypothesis (H_1), which we must consider if the first hypothesis proves false, is that the sample

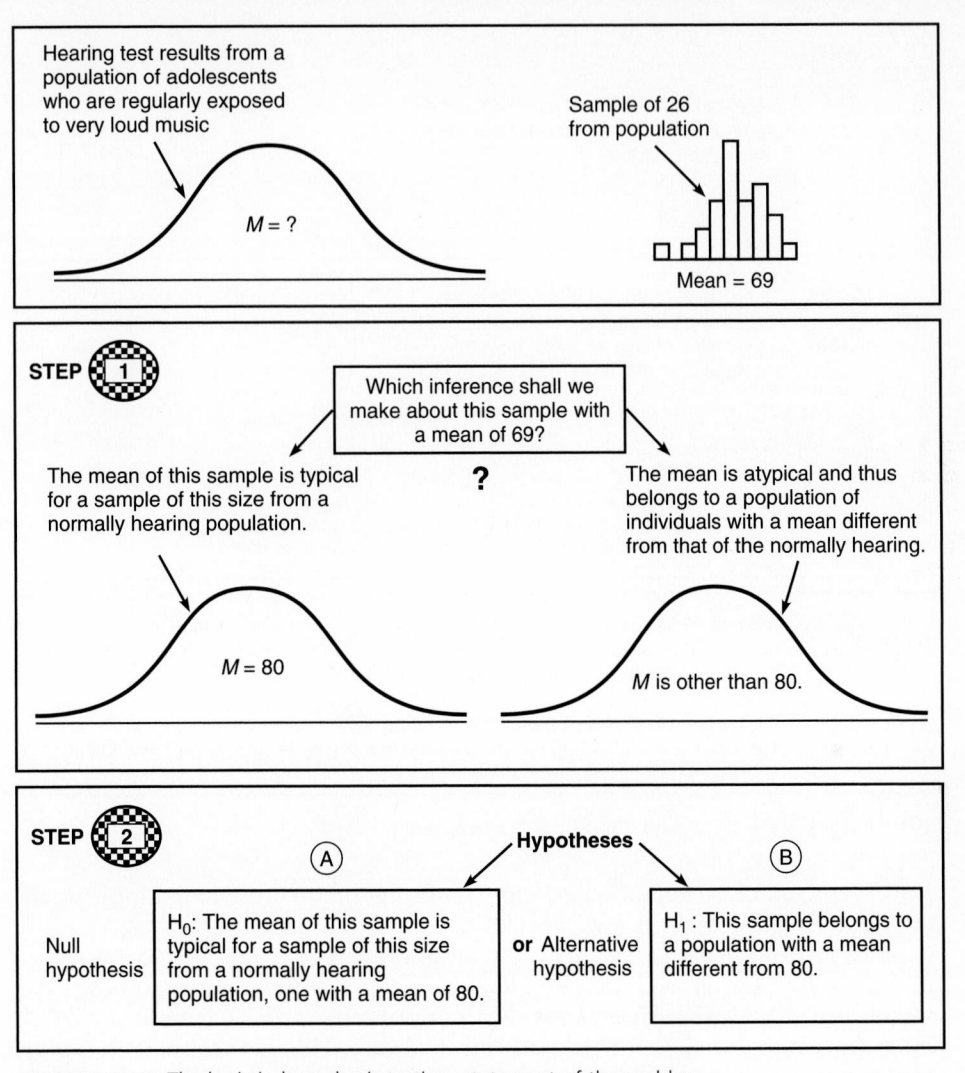

Hearing test results from a
population of adolescents
who are regularly exposed
to very loud music

$M = ?$

Sample of 26
from population

Mean = 69

STEP 1

Which inference shall we
make about this sample with
a mean of 69?

The mean of this sample is typical
for a sample of this size from a
normally hearing population.

?

The mean is atypical and thus
belongs to a population of
individuals with a mean different
from that of the normally hearing.

$M = 80$

M is other than 80.

STEP 2

(A)

Hypotheses

(B)

Null
hypothesis

H_0: The mean of this sample is
typical for a sample of this size
from a normally hearing
population, one with a mean of 80.

or Alternative
hypothesis

H_1: This sample belongs to
a population with a mean
different from 80.

FIGURE 19.3 The logic in hypothesis testing: statement of the problem.

came from a population with a mean different from 80. The question then becomes whether or not we can reject the null hypothesis.

In Figure 19.4, we find a way to choose between the two inferences. Step 3
shows the calculation of the standard error of the mean which for this example is
6.2. In step 4, we have extended a ±2 standard deviation confidence interval
around the mean of 80, just as we did in discussing estimation earlier. In this instance, the confidence interval is the region within which we will find samples
that differ only by sampling and chance error from the true mean of 80. Thus, it is
the region within which we will accept the null hypothesis (there is no real differ-

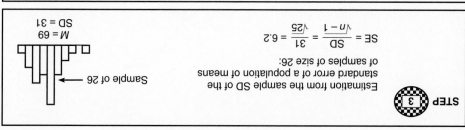

STEP 3

Estimation from the sample SD of the standard error of a population of means of samples of size 26:

$$SE = \frac{SD}{\sqrt{n-1}} = \frac{31}{\sqrt{25}} = 6.2$$

Sample of 26 → [histogram]
$M = 69$
$SD = 31$

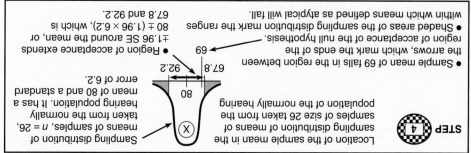

STEP 4

Location of the sample mean in the sampling distribution of means of samples of size 26 taken from the population of the normally hearing

Sampling distribution of means of samples, $n = 26$, taken from the normally hearing population. It has a mean of 80 and a standard error of 6.2.

[curve labeled X, with 80, 67.8, 92.2, 69]

- Sample mean of 69 falls in the region between the arrows, which mark the ends of the region of acceptance of the null hypothesis. Shaded areas of the sampling distribution mark the ranges within which means defined as atypical will fall.
- Region of acceptance extends ±1.96 SE around the mean, or 80 ± (1.96 × 6.2), which is 67.8 and 92.2.

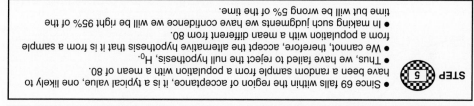

STEP 5

- Since 69 falls within the region of acceptance, it is a typical value, one likely to have been a random sample from a population with a mean of 80.
- Thus, we have failed to reject the null hypothesis, H_0.
- We cannot, therefore, accept the alternative hypothesis that it is from a sample from a population with a mean different from 80.
- In making such judgments we will have confidence we will be right 95% of the time but will be wrong 5% of the time.

FIGURE 19.4 The logic of hypothesis testing: the solution.

ence)—a region of acceptance. As before, we construct its size to an appropriate confidence level.

In hypothesis testing, however, we concentrate on whether the value is atypical, falls within the shaded tails—regions of rejection of the null hypothesis. We are concerned with **significance levels,** the complement (for example, 1 − .95 = .05) of the confidence level. This is the error we are willing to tolerate in saying that the value is atypical when it really is not; that is, when the null hypothesis is true. It is usually indicated by p = .05 ("p" for probability) or by the lower-case Greek letter alpha (α), α = .05. We say, "The **alpha level** is .05" or "The significance level is .05." In statistical tables, this is often indicated with asterisks, a single asterisk for the .05 level and two asterisks for the .01 level. In our examples, we have used the 5 percent significance level.

We are trying to determine whether 69 falls inside the range of values within which we will typically expect to find the population mean. If it does, there is no reason to say that the sample mean of 69 comes from a population with a mean different from 80. Although it is numerically different from 80, it differs by an amount that we can easily account for by sampling and measurement error. Therefore, in step 4, the thick arrowed line under distribution X is the region of acceptance of the null hypothesis if we assume the null hypothesis to be true. It

shows the range of values around the mean of 80 within which we will find the population value in 95 percent of samples of size 26. This interval extends across the center of the distribution from 67.8 to 92.2, enclosing all but the most extreme 2.5 percent of the means in either tail, the shaded parts at opposite ends of the distribution. It includes our sample mean of 69. As sample means falling inside the interval are typical, we accept the null hypothesis as true. Means falling inside the shaded areas are considered atypical, and not from a normally hearing population with a mean of 80. The shaded areas are regions for rejection of the null hypothesis as false.

Since the mean of 69 does not fall within the shaded regions—it falls inside the region of acceptance and so is typical—the data support H_0. Accepting the null hypothesis, however, does not mean we assume that the mean is really 80.[9] Rather, this indicates that within the sensitivity of this study we simply cannot re*ject* the null hypothesis. If we cannot reject the null hypothesis, we cannot accept the alternative hypothesis, H_1, which is usually what we wish to do. It is a matter of **statistical significance;** the difference between this mean and the mean of 80 is not statistically significant. This means it can be accounted for as well by random sampling variation and chance error as by the loss of hearing we expected. Of course, in saying this, we are assuming that this study is sensitive enough to show as statistically significant a difference in hearing that is a practical hearing deficit.[10] Thus, we would have been in error had we concluded earlier that this group was hearing-impaired simply because its mean hearing level was lower than that of the normal group.

♦ *A difference between an observed and an expected value which falls within a re-*
 gion of acceptance is considered to be typical; the difference can be accounted
 for by sampling and chance error.

♦ *A difference that falls outside that region is considered to be atypical, more ex-*
 treme than would be accounted for by sampling and chance error. It is consid-
 ered a statistically significant difference.

One-Tailed and Two-Tailed Tests of Statistical Significance

Notice that in our example we defined atypical values as being in both extremes of the distribution. Our alternative to the null hypothesis in step 2 was that the sample belonged to a population with a mean not equal to ($\neq$) 80. We were saying that a mean that was atypical in either direction was of interest. But defining the upper tail as atypical is tantamount to saying that our expectations include the

---

[9] If it is not 80, what is it? Using the technique of estimation covered earlier in this chapter, we can construct a confidence interval around the sample mean (with whatever confidence level we desire) to show the range within which the true mean is expected to be.

[10] We will consider statistical and practical significance, as well as studies designed to accept the null hypothesis, later in this chapter.

possibility that the hearing of this group might be more acute than normal as a result of being exposed to loud sounds (that is, the mean of the sample is statistically higher than that of the normally hearing group). This hypothesis seems highly unlikely. If there is any effect, we are expecting hearing to be diminished. Therefore, we should confine our search for atypical values to the lower extreme.[11] The alternative to the null hypothesis then becomes that the mean from which our sample came is less than (< 80).

We made what is called a **two-tailed test** for statistical significance where the alternative is nondirectional (≠ 80). This is appropriate when we do not know what to expect, for example, whether hearing might be made more sensitive or di-minished. Such might be the case if the causative factor were extensive training in pitch discrimination of very loud sounds. The training might increase sensitivity to pitch differences, but the loudness might diminish hearing entirely. We would not know whether one took precedence or whether they canceled each other out. In our example, however, where loudness is suggested as causing deafness, we know in which tail to look, the lower one (the alternative < 80). Thus, a **one-tailed test** is more appropriate.

Figure 19.5 indicates in bold type the changes that we must make in Figure 19.3 to accommodate a one-tailed test of the hypothesis. Notice that the definition of the population with nonnormal hearing has changed to be not merely different from normal but lower than normal (< 80). This has also changed the alternate hy-pothesis, B, which we will accept if we will reject the null hypothesis from "differ-ent from 80" to "less than 80."

In parallel fashion, Figure 19.6 shows in boldface the changes that we must make in Figure 19.4 to accommodate a directional hypothesis and its accompany-ing one-tailed test. Note that the shaded area is all in the lower tail of distribu-tion X in step 4 of Figure 19.6 rather than split between the two tails as in Figure 19.4. When split between both tails, half the 5 percent was in the lower tail, and a mean had to exceed −1.96 SE to be defined as atypical. We need only go out as far as −1.65 SE, however, to include 5 percent of the cases in one tail. (Where does the 1.65 come from? See Table 19.1.) Since 80 − (1.65 x 6.2) = 69.8 with a one-tailed test, 69 is just a bit smaller than the limit and would be atypical. With a two-tailed test, it was not. Thus, with a one-tailed test, we *reject* the null hypoth-esis that the sample belongs to the population with a mean of 80 and *accept* the alternative hypothesis that it belongs to one with a mean lower than 80. Com-pared with the normally hearing population, this group, on the average, hears less well.

With the one-tailed test, we have increased the sensitivity of the study. That is, the sample mean did not have to be so extreme to be judged statistically signif-icant. If the logic of the study permits us to make a sound directional prediction so that differences in only one direction are of interest, using a one-tailed test is one of the easiest ways of increasing sensitivity. It requires no changes in design, nor does it incur the cost of gathering additional data or increasing the size of the sample (the latter is the most common way of increasing sensitivity). As we shall

---

[11] In the Appendix to Chapter 18, this reasoning was demonstrated in the case of Mary Jane (p. 451). There, however, we were looking at the upper extreme rather than the lower.

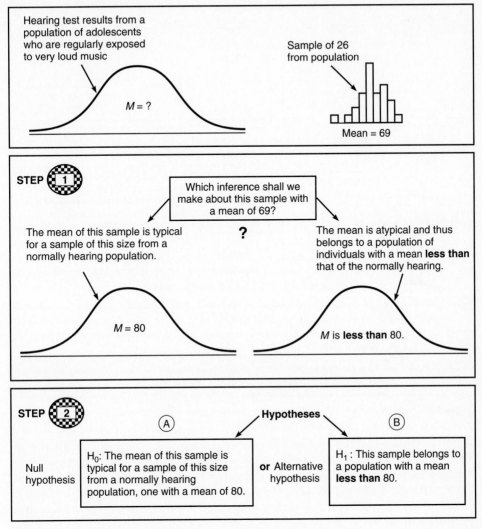

FIGURE 19.5 A one-tailed test. Changes to Figure 19.3 appear in boldface.

shortly see, there are other ways of increasing the sensitivity (sensitivity is also called the precision, or power, of a statistical test and is discussed later in this chapter).

Directional hypotheses and therefore one-tailed tests are appropriate whenever we are studying a treatment with an expected effect, and we can ignore a finding of the opposite effect (for example, a presumed sleeping pill causes agitation rather than sleep) and consider it as not resulting in new information (it can cause some agitation, but we thought it would be overcome by sleep). In improving reading scores, keeping students from dropping out, or reducing an individual's anxiety, we are interested in positive treatment effects. We do not expect

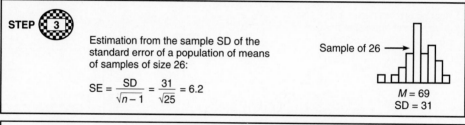

STEP 3

Estimation from the sample SD of the standard error of a population of means of samples of size 26:

$$SE = \frac{SD}{\sqrt{n-1}} = \frac{31}{\sqrt{25}} = 6.2$$

Sample of 26 →

M = 69
SD = 31

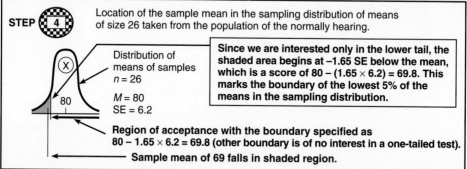

STEP 4

Location of the sample mean in the sampling distribution of means of size 26 taken from the population of the normally hearing.

Distribution of means of samples
n = 26

M = 80
SE = 6.2

80

Since we are interested only in the lower tail, the shaded area begins at –1.65 SE below the mean, which is a score of 80 – (1.65 × 6.2) = 69.8. This marks the boundary of the lowest 5% of the means in the sampling distribution.

Region of acceptance with the boundary specified as 80 – 1.65 × 6.2 = 69.8 (other boundary is of no interest in a one-tailed test).
— **Sample mean of 69 falls in shaded region.**

STEP 5

- Since 69 falls **outside** the region of acceptance, it is an **atypical** value, one **unlikely** to have been a random sample from a population with a mean of 80.
- Thus, we **reject** the null hypothesis.
- We accept the alternative hypothesis that it is from a sample from a population with a mean **lower than** 80. In doing this we have a confidence that we will be right 95% of the time but will be wrong 5% of the time.

FIGURE 19.6 A one-tailed test. Changes to Figure 19.4 appear in boldface.

negative effects or, if they occur, we presume them to be the result of chance or some factor other than the treatment. Of course, should we find the opposite of the expected, we will have the basis for another study to see why it happened and whether it is an artifact of the way the study was done. If we can replicate it and it is a real effect, then clearly our understanding of what is going on is in error and we must remedy it.

    ✦ *One-tailed tests of statistical significance increase the sensitivity of a statistical test. We can use them whenever we have a directional hypothesis, one that tells us in which direction to look for results that will be statistically significant. In that context, we would consider a result in the opposite direction an aberration rather than a reliable result.*

    Returning to our example, since 69 is statistically significant, we have a "demonstrated effect," the third judgment in internal validity (LP). There is a cause at work. What cause? We would like to say that it is exposure to loud music. If (1) we assume the previous three judgments in internal validity (LP) are positive, (2) if we can find no other reasonable alternative explanation [we have eliminated rival explanations, the fourth judgment of internal validity (LP)], and (3) if there is no reason for us to assume that we do not have a credible result (the fifth judgment), then the study has internal validity (LP), and we would say that the loss in hearing is due to the teenagers' being exposed to loud sounds.

✦ **Summary of the Logic**

In abstract form, the logic of inference to determine whether an observed value be-longs to a particular population is as follows:

1. *We translate the study's hypothesis into two statistical hypotheses: the one we test, the null hypothesis (H_0); and the alternative (H_1), which we wish to accept if H_0 is rejected:*
   - H_0: The observed value is typical of means for a sample of this size from the sampling distribution of means created by random sampling and chance error.
   - H_1: The observed value is atypical, not one that belongs to the population sampling distribution created by random sampling and chance error. It belongs to a population with a mean that differs from the mean of the chance distribution (or, for one-tailed tests, a population with a mean that is higher—or lower—than the mean of the chance distribution).
2. *We set a significance level that expresses the risk we are willing to run of being wrong in this particular instance. Whether the observed value is atypical depends on whether it falls outside the region of acceptance of the null hypothesis constructed around the expected value.*
   - If it does not fall outside, we have failed to reject H_0 and cannot accept H_1.
   - If it does fall outside, we reject H_0 and accept H_1 with a "maybe so."

Determination of the Atypicality of a Difference Between Two Means

Suppose we find in our survey research that one candidate was chosen by 45 percent of men and 40 percent of women. Is there a real difference in her appeal, or is this just a chance difference? Or suppose we believe that studying from the general to the specific is more conducive to learning than studying from the specific to the general. For instance, learning the logic of inferential statistics before studying specific statistical tests should result in superior achievement to studying specific statistical tests first. A pool of 40 volunteer students is randomly assigned: 20 undergo the general-to-specific treatment and 20 the specific-to-general. A posttest of inferential statistics is given to both groups. The general-to-specific group's mean on the test was 46.5, and that of the specific-to-general was 38.0.

Do these means come from populations with the same mean so that the difference results from sampling variation and chance error? Or are they from populations with different means and the treatments presumably made a difference? These are among the most common questions asked of inferential statistics. A group received some experimental treatment, such as the general-to-specific treatment, and a control group received either a neutral treatment or, as in this case, a less favorable alternative treatment. We want to know whether the difference between them is statistically significant—that is, reliably different from zero.

Here we appear to have two means whereas before we had only one, and an expected value. How do we proceed now? We reduce the problem to the same formulation. Instead of dealing with the two means, we deal with the *difference* between them and test it against the sampling distribution of *differences between means*, finding an interval for that sampling distribution that differentiates the typical from the atypical. We follow the same logic as before with a different application.

Let's assume that these two means are from sampling distributions with the same mean and same standard error. We have one observed difference between two random samples from these distributions. Presumably, we could take many more samples, find their means and, subtracting the first from the second, construct a distribution composed of *differences between means*. On the average, the two means would be about equal; only occasionally would a large positive or negative difference occur. Therefore, the mean of this distribution would be zero, and it would have the shape of a normal distribution as the number of differences grew larger. Obviously, we don't go through this process in practice, but this is conceptually what we mean when we talk about the sampling distribution of the differences between means.

The variability in differences between means will be a function of the variability in each of the sampling distributions from which the means came. Therefore, we use the standard errors of both distributions in estimating the standard error of the sampling distribution of the differences between means. The logic is similar to that we used before, but here we want to know whether the difference between the two groups belongs to a sampling distribution of differences between means with a mean of zero or to one with a mean greater than zero. Figure 19.7 shows the logic in the same kind of diagram as we used for previous examples. The top box states our study question, and step 1 translates the problem into an examination of the difference between means.

The standard error of the differences between means is the square root of the sum of the squared standard errors of the two individual distributions:

$$\sqrt{SE_1{}^2 + SE_2{}^2} \quad \text{or} \quad \sqrt{\left(\frac{SD_1}{\sqrt{n_1-1}}\right)^2 + \left(\frac{SD_2}{\sqrt{n_2-1}}\right)^2}$$

This formula holds for independent means. If the means come from samples where individuals are matched or paired, the product $2r_{12}(SE_1)(SE_2)$ is subtracted from the amount under the square root sign (r_{12} is the correlation between the scores for the paired subjects).

We build a region of acceptance around the expected value with a width determined by the error we are willing to tolerate. We use a one-tailed test, since our hypothesis is directional; we expect the general-to-specific treatment, M_1, to be superior. Therefore, all the atypical values will be in the right tail, since we expect the difference, $M_1 - M_2$, to be positive. We then determine

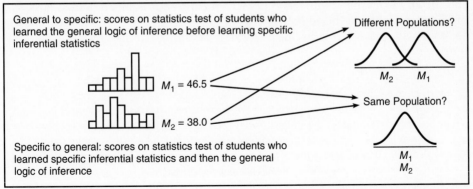

General to specific: scores on statistics test of students who learned the general logic of inference before learning specific inferential statistics

$M_1 = 46.5$

$M_2 = 38.0$

Different Populations?

M_2 M_1

Same Population?

M_1
M_2

Specific to general: scores on statistics test of students who learned specific inferential statistics and then the general logic of inference

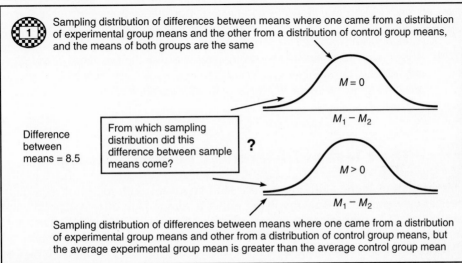

1 Sampling distribution of differences between means where one came from a distribution of experimental group means and the other from a distribution of control group means, and the means of both groups are the same

$M = 0$

$M_1 - M_2$

Difference between means = 8.5

From which sampling distribution did this difference between sample means come?

?

$M > 0$

$M_1 - M_2$

Sampling distribution of differences between means where one came from a distribution of experimental group means and other from a distribution of control group means, but the average experimental group mean is greater than the average control group mean

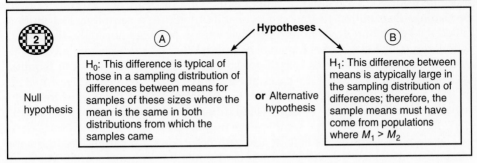

2

Hypotheses

Ⓐ

Ⓑ

Null hypothesis

H_0: This difference is typical of those in a sampling distribution of differences between means for samples of these sizes where the mean is the same in both distributions from which the samples came

or Alternative hypothesis

H_1: This difference between means is atypically large in the sampling distribution of differences; therefore, the sample means must have come from populations where $M_1 > M_2$

FIGURE 19.7 The logic of inference applied to a difference between two sample means with a one-tailed test of significance.

whether the difference falls within the region of acceptance or the atypical area, the region of rejection. If it falls within the area where values are typical, we cannot reject the null hypothesis and thus cannot accept the alternative. There is no statistically significant difference between studying from the general to the specific and from the specific to general. If the difference falls outside the region of acceptance, inside the region of rejection, we reject the null and say "maybe so" to the alternative, that in this instance it pays to learn the general logic of inference first.

+ *Hypothesis testing of a difference between two observed values involves a null hypothesis: The difference between the two means is typical of differences in a sampling distribution of differences between means from samples of these sizes, where the mean is the same in both populations from which the samples came. A simpler way of saying this is that the mean of the sampling distribution of differences is zero. We wish to nullify the null hypothesis.*
+ *The nondirectional alternative hypothesis is that the difference between means belongs to a population of differences with a mean other than zero. With a directional hypothesis, the alternative states whether the difference is greater or less than zero.*
+ *Working with the difference between means rather than the two means individually allows us to reduce the problem to the logic we used previously for whether a value was typical or atypical of those in the distribution.*

The *t* Test of Differences Between Means

Most studies examine a difference between two means with the *t* test, especially in relatively simple designs involving either a comparison of two experimental treatments or a comparison of a control with an experimental group. The *t* test and analysis of variance are probably the two most commonly used inferential statistics in the behavioral sciences. The *t* test uses the same logic that we have just examined but adds a couple of refinements. First, instead of using the normal probability distribution to find our probability, we use a sampling distribution called the *t* distribution. Although this distribution becomes normally distributed with large samples, it differs for small samples. Whereas the 5 percent level of the normal distribution requires 1.96 SE for statistical significance, the *t* test requires the higher value of 2.5 SE for 6 cases but the only slightly higher value of 1.98 SE at 100 cases. To use the table, we look up a number called degrees of freedom, usually abbreviated *df*. For most *t* tests of differences between means, this is simply 2 less than the sum of the sample sizes ($n_1 + n_2 - 2$).

Second, the formula we usually use assumes a common variance for the populations from which the samples came and pools the samples' variability for a better estimate of the population value. The formula also gives greater weight to samples of larger size:

$$SE_{M_1 - M_2} \sqrt{\frac{(n_1 - 1)SD_1^{\,2} + (n_2 - 1)SD_2^{\,2}}{n_1 + n_2 - 2} \cdot \frac{n_1 + n_2}{n_1 n_2}}$$

Then

$$t = \frac{M_1 - M_2}{SE_{M_1 - M_2}}$$

The *t* test also assumes that the groups are independent samples of a population. This is not the case where individuals are matched and then assigned to groups. As we noted before, where matching occurs, we should use a special formula. If we do not, we may make a Type II error and attribute a possible real difference to sampling and chance error (see May, Masson, and Hunter, 1990, pp. 272–276; or Moses, 1986, pp. 189–192).

A rank test comparable to the *t* test and useful for small samples is the Mann-Whitney *U* test. It involves combining both sets of scores into a single distribution and then assigning ranks to the scores in order, giving the rank of 1 to the lowest, 2 to the next, and so on. We next sort out the ranks belonging to each group and sum them. If the experimental treatment is effective, the sum of its ranks should be higher than that of the control group's. Using the simple formula

$$U = n_L n_S + \frac{n_L \left(n_L + 1 \right)}{2} - T_L$$

we consult the table of the *U* distribution to determine whether the product of the formula is significant. In the formula, n_L is the size of the sample with the larger sum of ranks, and n_S that of the smaller, and T_L is the larger sum of ranks (see Shavelson, 1996; Hays, 1973, 1981; or Siegel and Castellan, 1988). We can use the Mann-Whitney in place of the *t* test where we suspect the populations deviate significantly from normal or the variances are unequal. However, if the variances are nearly equal we can use the *t* test and fairly large departures from normality can be tolerated (Hays, 1981).

An Example

Culler and Holahan (1980) used the *t* test to examine the differences in study-related behaviors between two groups of college freshmen, one with low test anxiety (*n* = 31) as measured by Sarason, Pederson, and Nyman's Test Anxiety Scale, and the other with high test anxiety (*n* = 65). It is one of a large number of studies examining this problem among students. Test anxiety is "thought to produce task-irrelevant responses (concern for passing, thoughts of leaving, etc.) in the testing situation that interfere with the task-relevant responses necessary for good test performance" (p. 16). An alternative explanation is that the well-documented poorer grade performance of those with high test anxiety is "at least partially a function of differential study-related behaviors between high and low test-anxious individuals" (p. 16). Both groups of students completed the Study Habits scale of the Brown-Holtzman Survey of Study Habits and Attitudes and responded to a questionnaire. The results are summarized in Table 19.2.

TABLE 19.2 *Relationship of High and Low Test Anxiety to Various Study Patterns*

Variable	High Test Anxiety		Low Test Anxiety		
	M	SD	M	SD	t
Study habits	37.2	14.8	53.4	14.2	5.42*
Total study hours	21.7	12.7	14.1	7.0	−3.11*
Cramming	4.5	1.4	4.7	1.4	0.57
Missing classes	10.5	7.7	10.7	11.1	0.08
Late exams	0.6	1.1	0.3	0.6	−1.52

*$p < .002$.
Source: Table from R. E. Culler and C. J. Holahan, "Test Anxiety and Academic Performance: The Effect of Study Related Behaviors," in *Journal of Educational Psychology*, vol. 27, p. 18. Copyright © 1980. The American Psychological Association. Reprinted by permission.

The data were consistent with the hypothesis that the study habits of those students with high test anxiety were statistically significantly poorer (at the 0.2 percent level, using a two-tailed test) than those of students with low test anxiety. Also statistically significant were the total study hours, but the difference was in the opposite direction—a good reason for using a two-tailed test! The authors were surprised by this finding and suggested that perhaps the high test–anxious students attempt to compensate for their lower study competence by studying longer. The other comparisons, degree of cramming for tests, number of classes missed, and number of exams missed and made up at a later date, were all statistically nonsignificant.

> ✦ *A t test, which allows us to test the difference between two means for statistical significance, is a commonly used statistical test. It substitutes the t table for the normal probability distribution for more accurate probabilities and uses a formula that provides a more accurate estimate of the standard error.*

Sensitivity, Precision, and Statistical Power

Sensitivity, precision, and statistical power are all names for the same thing, the ability of a statistical test to sense a difference of a size of interest to us. Studies should be designed with appropriate sensitivity if they are to be successful. A study designed as too powerful or too weak wastes money, time, and energy. If the study is not sensitive enough, the researcher risks missing the result that is sought. Since most ways of increasing sensitivity require resources, an overly sensitive study uses resources that could have been put into further studies. (An exception is a study that must be large enough to be intuitively convincing to laypersons or others relatively unsophisticated in research methods.)

Errors of Inference

As we have already noted, when we set a confidence or significance level, we are accepting a certain level of error. With one type of error, we reject the null hypothesis claiming that we have a real difference when in actuality the difference is not real but is due to sampling and chance variation—that is, saying the treatment was effective when it was not. As noted in this chapter's prologue, this kind of error has been labeled a Type I (alpha) error (α). Type I error is always under our direct control as a result of setting significance levels, say, at 5 percent. On the average, when H_o is true, with a 5 percent significance level, 5 times in 100 we will be wrong when we say that there is a real difference.

Such error can be serious when we are relying on a finding as representing the true facts, and not being an atypical result. We want to be sure that a treatment is making a difference, and this is not a chance result. For important decisions, like building special equipment into a classroom building, adding costly computer terminals, or adopting an expensive way of teaching reading, we ought to rely on accumulated evidence rather than on a single study. If we must depend on a single study, however, we reduce Type I error by using a confidence level of 99, or 99.9, or even 99.99 percent. If that is the case, why not always use such stringent confidence levels? Because, for a given set of data, decreasing Type I error causes its opposite, Type II (beta) error (β), to increase. The latter occurs when we miss a real difference and call it chance error; we accept the null hypothesis when we should have rejected it.

As much as we pay special attention to Type I error in validating a finding, we want to attend to Type II error when exploring. When screening cancer cures, we do not want to discard an option by judging the improvement no greater than chance when the treatment was effective. If the effect is too small to be sensed, we run danger of lumping it with chance errors. In exploring, we want a study that is sensitive enough to show any effect of possible interest as statistically significant. Figure 19.8 summarizes these two types of errors.[12]

Figure 19.8 also indicates the probability of occurrence of each of the events. Thus, we define the Type I error as α (say, 5 percent), and this makes the probability of a correct decision when H_0 is true, $1 - \alpha = 95$ percent. Unless we do some estimation ahead of time, we do not usually know the size of β, the Type II error. Whatever it is, however, we know that $1 - \beta$ is the probability of a correct decision where we should reject the null hypothesis. Indeed, because we want correct decisions, $1 - \beta$ indicates their likelihood and therefore the **sensitivity of a statistical test** in a given instance. Hence, we define $1 - \beta$ as the **power of a statistical test,** its sensitivity or precision.

---

[12]Does this look familiar? It should! It reflects exactly the same logic as that illustrated by Figure 19.1. In fact, the prologue introduced this very same logic and pointed out its everyday use. In this sense, the figure shows that correct decisions build trust in a service manager's judgment and incorrect ones lead to distrust. Similarly, correct decisions lead to trust of science by laypersons and incorrect ones lead to distrust. In comparison with laypersons, scientists who understand we are dealing in probabilities continue to trust science. This shows how important it is to educate everyone about the logic of inference!

Decision based on sample data

	Do not reject null hypoth.	Reject null hypoth.
H_o is true	Correct decision $1 - \alpha^*$	Type I error α^*
H_o is false	Type II error β^*	Correct decision $1 - \beta^*$

True state of affairs.

*These are the probabilities of that event occurring.

FIGURE 19.8 Type I and Type II errors and the null hypothesis.

Conventions are not well established for Type II error. If the study is but a small step in the search for knowledge, a Type II error of 10 percent, 20 percent, or even larger may be acceptable. A large Type II error seems better tolerated than a large Type I. This bias reflects the preference of most scientists to miss a possible real effect rather than to be publicly embarrassed by a false knowledge claim that cannot be replicated. Missing a finding is regrettable, but since negative-result studies are rarely published, it is a private matter, and nobody is the wiser. Further, if it is not published, it won't foreclose the work of someone else who might study it with sufficient sensitivity to obtain a statistically significant finding.

✦ *Type I (alpha) errors occur when we decide that an observed value is atypical and not the result of sampling and chance error when it really is. Type I errors are particularly serious when we are attempting to validate a hypothesis that supports an important decision.*
✦ *Type II (beta) errors occur when we decide that an observed value is not atypical and therefore not statistically significant when in fact it results from a real effect. Type II errors occur when a study's sensitivity is insufficient so that a real effect does not cross the threshold of statistical significance. They are especially serious in screening treatments when a beneficial effect may not only be missed but therefore also possibly be excluded from further research.*

Ways to Increase Statistical Power

How can a researcher increase statistical power? Usually increasing sample size comes to our mind first, but once we understand how size affects the standard error formula, we can see other ways as well.

Statistical Power and Sample Size. When we see a poll that indicates a candidate is winning, we want to know "What was the sample size?" A poll based on 50 cases is not nearly as reliable as one based on 500 or 5,000 cases. Intuitively, this makes good sense because the larger sample is more likely to be representative of the population (unless there is a sampling bias, as in selecting all the cases from only one social class). However, there is a statistical reason as well: The standard error decreases with sample size, as shown in Figure 19.9.

Attend especially to the size of the standard errors. Although it is clear that the curves become more peaked and narrower, it is a bit difficult to judge the standard error change from the shape. If we start with a standard deviation of 10,

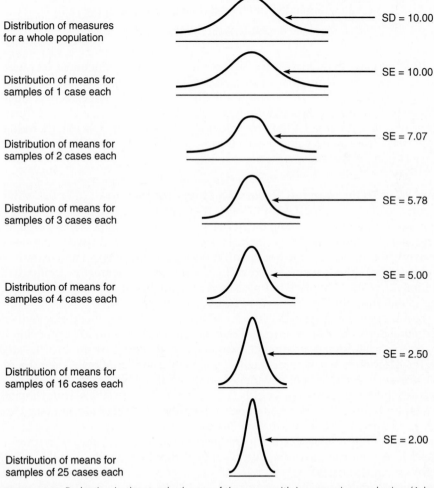

FIGURE 19.9 Reduction in the standard error of the mean with increases in sample size. (Adaptation of a figure from E. F. Lindquist, "A First Course in Statistics." Copyright © 1942 by Houghton Mifflin Company. Used with permission.)

with samples of size 1 the standard error is still 10. Doubling sample size reduces it only to 7.07. To cut it in half, we must quadruple the sample size. Similarly, to cut this in half, we must go to 16 cases. Reductions occur as a function of the square of the change in sample size. To cut the standard error by a third, we must have 9 times the cases; by a fifth, 25 times the cases; and so on. With each halving in the chart, the drop in the size of the standard error is smaller and the number of cases needed to bring it about is substantially larger.

We can see how sample size reduces the standard error if we look at a simplified version of the *t* test of a difference between two means, as shown in the following formula:

$$t = \frac{\text{The difference between two sample means}}{\sqrt{\dfrac{\text{A value dependent on the } \textit{sizes of the variances} \text{ of the samples}}{\text{A value dependent on the } \textit{sizes} \text{ of the samples}}}}$$

By increasing the sample sizes, we increase the "value dependent on the *sizes* of the samples" which in turn, reduces the value of the fraction under the square root sign. This means we are dividing the difference between means by a smaller value, which, in turn, yields a larger value for *t*. Therefore, with a given difference between means, the smaller the denominator, the more likely it is that the value of *t* will exceed the tabled value we need for statistical significance and the greater the sensitivity of the statistical test.

Other Ways to Increase the Power of a Statistical Test. The larger the value of *t*, the more likely it will exceed the value required for statistical significance. We can make it larger by increasing the numerator or by decreasing the denominator. Increasing the numerator requires increasing the difference between the means: increasing the strength of the treatment, choosing for both control and experimental groups individuals who are especially susceptible to the treatment, increasing the motivation of the subjects, administering the treatment over a longer period of time so that the cumulative effect is greater, and similar efforts.

Besides increasing sample size, we can decrease the denominator by reducing the "value dependent on the sizes of the variances of the samples": choosing homogeneous samples, eliminating all extraneous distractions by moving the study into the laboratory, masking distracting noises, and similar efforts. There are also statistics, such as analysis of covariance and partial correlation, which would reduce variability by removing the effect of contaminating variables. Unfortunately, they typically do not work as intended where they are most needed (see Cronbach and Furby, 1970; Cronbach et al., 1976).

Using highly reliable tests also reduces variability and unreliable ones increases it. As an example of the latter, suppose that in trying to find the average height of women, we fail to give two data gatherers instructions on how to measure height. Sometimes they mash down subjects' hair; sometimes they don't. Sometimes they ask subjects to step out of their shoes; sometimes they don't. (To make clear that this is a matter of reliability, consider this comparable to equivalence reliability of two test forms or two clerks interpreting a scoring key differently.) Plainly, this inconsistency will increase the variability of the samples so that the numerator under the square root will be larger and the value of *t* smaller.

We have already noted that a directional hypothesis with its one-tailed test increases statistical power, but we can also change the level of significance. Moving the significance level from 1 percent in the direction of 5 percent increases sensitivity as well.

Finally, some statistical tests are more powerful than others under certain conditions. In general, tests based on interval or ratio scale data are more sensitive than those based on ranked (ordinal) or categorical (nominal) data simply because moving from interval to ranked or categorical scales discards information. However, there are special conditions, such as those in sampling from nonnormal distributions—for example, the Wilcoxon signed-ranks test (May, Masson, and Hunter, 1990, pp. 491–494)—when using ranked data is more powerful than using the *t* test (Blair and Higgins, 1980, 1985). Exploring such special conditions is beyond the scope of this book.

With these many ways of changing sensitivity, researchers clearly will want to do a "statistical power analysis" during the design of a study, if at all possible. For example, with the *t* test, our analysis would involve estimating values for all the variables in the formula except the sample sizes. This includes finding the *t* value for the level of significance we desire with the one- or two-tailed test we plan to use. If we assume the sample sizes are equal, we have a formula with one unknown that we can solve for the proper sample size. A study we design to that size or a bit larger for good measure will sense an effect of the size as statistically significant if it appears; we will have designed the study at an appropriate sensitivity level.

Cohen (1988) gives a detailed description of how to do a power analysis for a variety of statistics. Both Cohen (1988) and Lipsey (1990) include information to allow estimation of the size of sample required and discuss the variables involved. This approach enables researchers to select a sample size that will provide a sufficiently powerful test to suit their purposes. This is the one-and-only answer to the question "When is the sample big enough"?

+ *The power of a statistical test (1 – β) is its ability to avoid Type II error.*
+ *Increasing the statistical power (precision, sensitivity) of the test makes a statistically significant result more likely if a nonchance effect is present.*
+ *We can increase statistical power by increasing the size of the effect (a stronger treatment), reducing variability (moving from field into laboratory or using more reliable tests), or other ways of reducing the standard error (such as increasing sample size).*
+ *A power analysis shows the sample size needed for adequate sensitivity and is the only way to determine what constitutes a "big enough" sample.*

Showing Two Statistics Are the Same

There are instances where we wish to show whether two statistics or distributions are the same rather than different. For instance, a strong alternative explanation of some polling results is that our sample is older than the town's average age. We test the difference between the mean of the sample and the average age given by the latest census data and find that it is not statistically significant. We never accept the null hypothesis as meaning the difference is really zero; we merely fail to reject it; that is, it could be zero or too close to it to be sensed as atypical.

How close it must be to be judged typical depends on the sensitivity of our statistical test. This is an instance in which we cannot escape making a judgment. We must decide what age difference between the sample and the population is big enough to say our sample is atypical. Then, with a statistical power analysis, we can determine whether the existing study is sensitive enough to detect such a difference or we can design one that is. Only then can we say that the particular sample does not differ significantly from the population of which it is representative. Failure to follow this logic is a common error. Cohen (1990, p. 1309), however, notes that in most instances, especially where we are required to sense a very small difference, a power analysis will demonstrate that an impractically large sample size is necessary and that showing similarity with considerable precision may be difficult.

The Level of Significance to Report

The logic so far described assumes that we are testing the truth of the null hypothesis to determine whether the alternate (the research hypothesis we are gathering data about) escapes disconfirmation. The fact that any just barely significant value was missed (as in the hearing impairment examples), is not taken into account. Did you note that the Culler and Holahan study on page 477 reported statistical significance at the 0.2 level, considerably less than the conventional 1 or 5 percent? Authors use significance levels like this to indicate that the finding was not borderline.[13] Indeed, it is common journal practice not just to indicate whether a result is or is not statistically significant but also to tell how rare it is. Thus, instead of the traditional 5 or 1 percent, we find more exact probabilities like 6 percent, 10 percent, .003 percent, or even .00004 percent.

Trying to interpret probabilities, however, can lead to misconceptions since the level of significance depends on a study's sensitivity—and the sensitivity of studies varies so greatly. It is difficult to compare intuitively the results of one study based on 10 cases that is barely significant at the 5 percent level with another

---

[13]Although there are accepted conventions, all research and statistical practices are not cut and dried. Indeed, mathematical statisticians recognize two points of view regarding inference: Fisher's and Neyman and Pearson's. Fisher's concentrates on rejecting the null hypothesis and uses predetermined levels of significance (often 5 percent) and confidence intervals. Decisions are presumably based on a body of studies, and the goal is understanding. Neyman and Pearson give the alternate hypothesis equal importance with the null hypothesis, and are concerned with Type II errors as well as Type I. Their goal is decision making between the null and the alternative hypothesis. This distinction may seem minor as May, Masson, and Hunter (1989) note. In practice, however, the two views often merge—studies follow the logic of a 5 percent significance level but then report whatever level is achieved. Indeed, this chapter is Fisherian in the discussion of the logic of inference, and Neyman-Pearsonian in its discussion of power analyses. For more, see May, Masson, and Hunter (1990, Chapter 7).

of 100 cases that yields a probability of 1 in 10,000. Using samples of 1,000,000 you can produce statistical significance for the most infinitesimal of differences.

Repeated borderline results are probably due to more than chance, however, and deserve to be so interpreted rather than dichotomously as significant or nonsignificant. We can do this by combining study results; aggregating several borderline nonsignificant studies can so increase sensitivity that we have a statistically significant result and are more certain of the appropriate interpretation. As we will see in Chapter 21, meta-analysis is the process we use to combine results. Reporting the exact probability facilitates meta-analysis.

Statistical and Practical Significance

The discussion so far makes it clear that it is possible to so increase a study's sensitivity that any difference, no matter how small, can be made statistically significant. Not all statistically significant findings, however, have **practical significance.** Let's consider an experimental group receiving a $10,000-per-pupil reading treatment to get only a one-point gain in achievement. This difference might be statistically significant and, from the point of view of a researcher, might lead to further useful research. From the school's standpoint, however, such expenditure for so little gain completely lacks practical significance. Thus, practical significance is a function of the purpose for which the results are to be used. What is practically significant is a judgment of the value of the results in a particular context; for example, the school might be willing to add $300 to per-pupil costs for a 10-point gain.

♦ *It is possible to increase the sensitivity of a study to the point where, if there is any effect at all no matter how infinitesimal, it can be made statistically significant. However, whether it is practically significant is another matter entirely, a judgment based on the value of the result in particular contexts.*

Proof of a Proposition Versus Its Escaping Disconfirmation

Suppose a study shows a statistically significant effect in the expected direction. Have we proved the proposition? Don't we wish it! In Section One of this book we noted that all knowledge is not permanently true but must be held as tentatively true until new knowledge modifies or replaces it. Beyond this limitation, however, the logic of statistical inference is such that we are never sure a given finding is not the result of error and chance variation. Positive results simply increase the odds of saying that the results are real; that is, they increase our confidence in our assertion. In any given instance, we can merely say that a proposition has escaped disconfirmation.

Popper (1959) and others have argued that the job of the researcher is to subject each proposition to tests of disconfirmation, to try actively to disconfirm it! Then each escape from disconfirmation creates added confidence about its validity. Unfortunately, we are not as prone in the social and behavioral sciences to attempt disconfirmations as we are confirmations in new circumstances. If the data support the proposition in a new context or an extension of the old one, we feel increasingly confident about its validity. Eventually, it crosses the threshold of what we are willing to accept as knowledge—still tentative but firm enough to act on. However, if we design a sufficiently sensitive study and the result does not appear or a different result appears and we cannot otherwise explain it, we must go back to the now disconfirmed study to find the error.

> ✦ *A statistically significant result proves not that the hypothesis is true but that it has escaped disconfirmation in this instance. Each such instance contributes to confidence that the proposition is valid. With such evidence, a proposition becomes accepted as knowledge that, though tentatively held as true, is considered firm enough to act on.*

Violation of the Assumptions of Statistical Tests

All statistical tests begin with certain assumptions that, together with the laws of probability, enable statisticians to develop the tables we use to determine statistical significance—for example, tables for the normal distribution, t, chi-square, and F. A common underlying assumption of statistical tests used with interval or ratio scale data is random sampling. Many statistical tests further assume that sampling is from normally distributed populations and that where two or more samples are involved, their variances differ by no more than would be "typical." Such statistical tests, called parametric tests, are the focus of most texts and computer programs and are the most widely used and understood.

Nonparametric statistics are based on ranked or categorical data. They ask whether the patterning of the data is typically random or atypically regular. For example, when the merged scores from an experimental and a control group are ordered by size, if nothing is at work, we expect a random alternation between experimental and control as we proceed from the highest to the lowest score. But if most of the experimental group's scores are in the highest ranks and those of the control group at the lowest, then the ordering is atypical and something is at work. Such departures trigger statistical significance in nonparametric tests. Whereas with parametric statistics random sampling provides the chance element that statisticians assume to estimate probabilities (as in t tables), with nonparametric statistics, they assume random ordering or patterning.[14]

---

[14]For both parametric and nonparametric statistics, random sampling supports generalizability of findings by, on average, providing samples representative of the population.

With nonparametric tests, as with parametric ones, however, what appears to be atypical may not be. A pattern actually created by chance may seem too regular to be "typically" random; after all, on average, even ten pennies will come up all heads about once in 1,000 times. Thus, the same inferential logic applies to both kinds of tests and Types I and II errors must be considered. The Mann-Whitney *U* test discussed earlier and the chi-square test, discussed later in this chapter, are nonparametric statistics. Other commonly used ones are the sign test, rank test, run test, and Wilcoxon signed-rank test for matched samples.

Though parametric statistics are the norm, few studies use random samples. What is the justification for violating this assumption? May, Masson, and Hunter (1990) state that in most situations, since parametric statistics approximate the nonparametric results, parametrics result in meaningful and useful interpretations without random sampling. They also suggest, however, that nonparametric statistics assumptions are more appropriate for most behavioral science studies. But, where we are concerned with building a consensus around the interpretation of data and developing credibility with a statistically unsophisticated audience, using unfamiliar nonparametric statistics can create problems. In situations where parametric assumptions are seriously violated, clearly, nonparametric statistics are more appropriate. As long as useful interpretations result, however, parametric statistics will continue to be the major tools.

An important assumption of tests of differences between means (*t* tests, analysis of variance) that is not always understood is that although the means may be affected by a treatment, the variability of the distribution is not. It is assumed the treatment adds or subtracts a constant from all scores but does not affect them differentially so as to increase the variance. The sample's variability is the basis for estimating the standard error used to determine statistical significance. This is a problem, however, only if a treatment strongly affects subjects differentially.

We say that a statistic is **robust** if we can interpret it meaningfully even when one of its assumptions has been violated. Fortunately, many parametric statistics have proven surprisingly robust in the face of sampling from skewed rather than normal distributions or when having unequal variances (for example, the *t* test and analysis of variance merely require using a 1 percent instead of the 5 percent significance level, Hays, 1973). In a situation where assumptions have been violated, and no evidence on the robustness of the statistic is available, it may be desirable to use a nonparametric test.

❖ *Assumptions allow statisticians to use probability theory to develop the tables we use to determine statistical significance.*

❖ *Parametric statistics such as those discussed in this chapter assume random sampling. Sometimes they also assume sampling of normally distributed populations with equal variances unaffected by treatment.*

❖ *Nonparametric statistics using the same logic of inference do not assume random sampling. They assume that random ordering is at work and examine rankings and categorizations for regularity that is atypical and nonrandom.*

✦ Even without random sampling, parametric statistics lead to useful results—perhaps because their results parallel nonparametric statistics, which do not assume random sampling.

✦ A robust statistical test is one that permits accurate interpretation of the data even when an assumption on which the test is based has been violated. Most parametric tests are fairly robust in the face of minor violations and even with major violations can often be used with adjustments, usually in the probability level (for example, with a 1 percent instead of the 5 percent level).

Two Additional Common Inferential Statistics

The last statistics discussed in this chapter are two commonly used ones: chi-square, a nonparametric test that examines patterns of frequency counts, and analysis of variance, which goes beyond the *t* test to handle differences between multiple means, as well as complex designs.

Chi-Square

Chi-square handles only categorical (nominal) data, frequencies, or figures based on them like percentages or probabilities. Besides eliminating the alternate explanation of sampling and chance error, chi-square can

- Test a hypothesis about whether one variable is related to another
- Test whether the data fit a particular model or distribution (for example, were the data normally distributed?)
- Combine probabilities derived from independent samples in a single study or across studies into a single probability (another way of doing a meta-analysis).

The formula for chi-square (χ^2) is simple. It involves finding the difference between the observed frequency and the frequency that would be expected by chance, squaring it, dividing it by the expected frequency, and summing these over all the observed data:[15]

$$\chi^2 = \sum \frac{(f_0 - f_e)^2}{f_e}$$

where f_0 is the observed frequency found in the data, f_e is the expected frequency, and Σ indicates that the fractions are to be summed.

A Chi-Square Example. Let's consider, for example, whether political party affiliation is related to gender. Answers to the question "Are you registered to vote as

---

[15]If one or more expected frequency is less than 10 for a 2 x 2 table, we must use Yates's correction for continuity. We subtract 0.5 from observed frequencies greater than expected and add 0.5 to those lower than expected.

TABLE 19.3 *Responses to the Question "Are You Registered to Vote as a Democrat or a Republican?" Tabulated by Gender*

Gender	Actual Frequencies		Expected Frequencies		Row Totals
	Democrat	Republican	Democrat	Republican	
Females	42	21	29.96	33.04	63
Males	36	65	48.04	52.96	101
Column totals	78	86	78	86	164

a Democrat or a Republican?" were tabulated for males and females and Table 19.3 was created. The data appear to be a significant deviation from a chance distribution. But are they? Chi-square will tell us.

In Table 19.3 numbers at the left are the actual frequencies; those at the right show us how the frequencies would have been distributed if chance were at work. There are 42 + 21 = 63 females. If this were a chance distribution, since the ratio of Democrats to Republicans for the whole sample is 78 to 86 out of 164 cases, then 78 ÷ 164 or 47.56 percent of the 63 cases would be Democrats and 86 ÷ 164 or 52.44 percent would be Republicans. These data give us the figures 29.96 and 33.04 in the top row of the expected frequency table. We similarly derive the next row. We then insert these figures in the chi-square formula:

$$\chi^2 = \frac{(42-29.96)^2}{29.96} + \frac{(33.04-21)^2}{33.04} + \frac{(48.04-36)^2}{48.04} + \frac{(65-52.96)^2}{52.96} = 14.99$$

We need the number of **degrees of freedom** to find our probabilities in the chi-square table. The concept of degrees of freedom refers to the freedom of the cell data in successive samples to vary once the column and row totals are fixed. In 2 x 2 tables, once we determine one cell entry, we can determine the rest as well. Thus, such tables have only one degree of freedom.[16] In general, chi-square tables have $(r-1)(c-1)$ degrees of freedom, where r is the number of rows and c the number of columns. Looking in any chi-square table (such as May, Masson and Hunter, 1990, p. 556) under the 5 percent significance level and one degree of freedom, we find that anything larger than 3.84 is atypical. Since the chi-square of 14.99 is clearly atypical, with a likelihood of being wrong 1 time in 20, we can say that we cannot account for this distribution of males and females into political parties by sampling and chance error. Females are more likely Democrats, and males Republicans.

---

[16]Try this yourself; put a new frequency, 63 or lower, in the top left cell and you can find the other three entries using the column and row totals.

Analysis of Variance: Testing Differences Among Several Means

Analysis of variance (ANOVA) is widely used for complex experimental designs where more than two groups or where multiple conditions are being compared. For example, we can use ANOVA to study the effect of directive and nondirective counseling (two treatments) under conditions where the counselors are of the same or opposite gender (two conditions). These treatments might apply to teenagers, adults, and the elderly (three categories of subjects) and for males and females (two categories of subjects). This is a 2 x 2 x 3 x 2 design resulting in 24 cells (combinations of the variables) and lends itself to ANOVA.

Analysis of variance allows us to partition the variance of the study to find the part that is attributable to each of the variables. We can test the statistical significance of the contribution to effective counseling of gender of subject, age of subject, counseling treatment (directive or nondirective), and matching counselor gender, as well as test the combined effect of variables (gender of subject combined with counseling treatment, age of subject with matching counselor gender, age of subject with gender of subject with counseling treatment, and so forth). After accounting for these variables and their combinations, the residual variance is a purer measure of sampling and chance error, thus providing for more precise tests of statistical significance. With so many groups and categories, there are many pairs of means to examine with a *t* test. With every 20 pairs, the 5 percent level for Type I errors goes up since, on the average, one of the pairs will be statistically significant just as a result of chance alone. ANOVA avoids the **inflation-of-probabilities** problem and keeps the Type I error at 5 percent by, in essence, making a single simultaneous test of all means; this tells us whether the means are equivalent except for differences traceable to chance variation. If they are not, we find which variables' data are statistically significant.

The logic used by analysis of variance involves deriving two estimates of the population variance: first, an estimate that includes the effect of one or more of the variables (for example, the treatment's), and second, an estimate which is free of it. If there is no effect, on average, the two estimates are equal and the expected value of dividing the first by the second, called an *F* ratio, is one. However, given a possible effect, and, in any event, sampling and chance error, the first of these estimates will typically be the larger, so the ratio will usually be greater than one. We consult an *F* table to determine how much above one to allow for sampling and chance error.

An Analysis of Variance Example. Darley and Batson (1973) examined the reactions of seminary students to a person apparently ill and in need of help. The "ill" person, an accomplice, was stationed on a path that subjects were directed to follow. Seminarians were randomly assigned to one of two conditions: They were given instructions to hurry to an appointment (hurry condition) or sent to speak on the parable of the good Samaritan (message condition). The question was whether these conditions individually or together would influence the seminarians' willingness to stop and help an individual apparently in trouble. Table 19.4 shows the results in terms of ratings of helpfulness.

TABLE 19.4 *Helpfulness Means for Combinations of the Three Levels of Hurry Condition and Two of the Message Condition*

Message	Hurry			Summary over Hurry Conditions
	Low	Medium	High	
Helping relevant	3.8	2.0	1.0	2.3
Task relevant	1.7	1.7	0.5	1.3
Summary over message conditions	3.0	1.8	0.7	

Source: Table from J. M. Darley and C. D. Batson, "From Jerusalem to Jericho: A Study of Situational and Dispositional Variables in Helping Behavior," in *Journal of Personality and Social Psychology*, vol. 27, pp. 100–103. Copyright © 1973 by the American Psychological Association. Reprinted by permission.

ANOVA data are usually presented in a standard format such as that from the Darley-Batson (1973) study shown in Table 19.5. Data in the first two rows show the effect of message and hurry respectively, the third, the effect of their interaction (speech but no hurry, speech and hurry, no speech but hurry, no speech and no hurry).

The row labeled "error" is the measure of sampling and chance error. Entries in the "sum of squares" column are divided by the degrees of freedom (the column labeled "*df*") to yield an estimate of the population variance, labeled "mean square." It is the ratio of the mean square to error which yields the *F* ratios shown in the next column. Those *F* ratios can then be compared with the tabled value for 1 and 34 degrees of freedom for hurry and for 2 and 34 *df* for both message and interaction. These provide the probability values shown in the right-hand column.

Only the probability for the hurry condition is statistically significant at less than the 5 percent level (NS means "not statistically significant"). The interaction condition asks whether some combination of hurry with message (such as low hurry with thinking about the parable) is more effective than hurry or message alone. In this instance, since *F* is less than 1 and since only ratios larger than 1 can be statistically significant, this one is not. We might have expected such an interaction, but it apparently did not occur. We should note that the data for the mes-

TABLE 19.5 *A Typical ANOVA Data Table*

	Sum of Squares	df	Mean Square	F	p
Whether or not the subject was being sent to speak on the parable (message)	7.766	1	7.766	2.65	NS
How much of a hurry the subject was in (hurry)	20.844	2	10.422	3.56	< .05
Hurry by message interaction	5.237	2	2.619	.89	NS
Error	99.633	34	2.930		

Source: Table from J. M. Darley and C. D. Batson, "From Jerusalem to Jericho: A Study of Situational and Dispositional Variables in Helping Behavior," in *Journal of Personality and Social Psychology*, vol. 27, pp. 100–108. Copyright © 1973 by the American Psychological Association. Reprinted by permission.

sage condition are in the hypothesized direction but are not significant. A more powerful design might have avoided what appears now to be a possible Type II error.

> ✦ *Analysis of variance (ANOVA) allows for more precise inference by estimating and removing the variance due to factors built into the design. Therefore, it allows a more accurate estimate of the error variance and a more powerful design.*
> ✦ *It allows the testing of the statistical significance of each variable in the design as well as the combined effect of these variables.*
> ✦ *It avoids the inflation-of-probabilities problem that would result when more than two means are compared. Otherwise, the probability of getting a statistically significant difference by chance increases as more tests are run, and the true Type I error level becomes inflated over the stated level.*

Use of Computerized Statistical Programs

Computerized statistical programs make available a wide range of possibilities, statistics users would not have otherwise considered. The ease of computation makes possible studies so complex that researchers are like laboratory workers who manipulate mechanical hands by remote control from a room outside a sealed data container. With no sense of the data, there is little basis for suspecting an absurd result, and one is at the mercy of the computer printout. Pictures are worth a thousand numbers. We are sensitive to patterns in plots, graphs, and other displays of the kind provided by these same computer programs. It is well worth your while to request them. Make certain that the numbers are congruent with what you intuit from the data plots, and look for other patterns not caught by your planned analyses.

It nearly always pays to play with a sample of the data using either exploratory data analysis techniques like those described in Tukey (1977) or easily computed nonparametric tests. In addition, such exploration is fun! Further, such analyses give us an idea of what to expect so that, if the computer analysis differs, we become aware of a possible error. The popular programs have web-sites for support and interchange of ideas and some trial programs; they can be very helpful.

Possible Future Directions of Inferential Statistics

Just as some researchers within the qualitative tradition are attempting to affect future directions, so also in quantitative. These researchers (for example, Cohen, 1990) suggest we should have a greater interest in effect sizes—showing the range within which the effect lies, finding confidence intervals—in contrast to just determining whether or not an effect exists. Similarly, in place of analysis of variance which yields primarily only statistical significance, we should use statistics which yield the sizes of relationships. All this ties into meta-analysis, the topic of Chapter 21, which emphasizes effect sizes obtained by combining the results of multiple studies. Furthering this trend, increasingly, instead of just listing five or one percent significance levels, published articles give exact probabilities which facilitates their use in meta-analyses. Possibly the eventual primary role of statistics in individual studies will be their contributions to meta-analyses. But, most conventions, having stood the test of time, have an inertia of their own; change will probably not be swift in coming.

SUMMARY

Understanding the logic of inference unlocks the mystery of many inferential statistics; the context of its application differs, but the basic logic doesn't. Estimation with interval or ratio data involves finding ways of determining what would be typical values for a statistic due to random sampling variability and the chance error built into the variables used in the study. From these typical values, given a specified level of confidence, we can form a confidence interval within which lies the parameter value for the population from which the sample statistic came. We can test a sample value to see whether it differs from the typical values in a given distribution (for example, normal hearing). We define "typical" as a confidence interval including nearly all cases, such as 95 percent of them, knowing that the remaining percentage of cases, in that case 5 percent of them, are normally outside that "typical" range. Therefore, sometimes when we call a study's result atypical, we will be wrong in our inference when it is one of that percentage normally outside the range.

The confidence interval is expressed as a range, and a percentage indicates the level of our confidence that the interval contains the population value. These confidence levels are usually 95 percent (odds of 19 to 1) or 99 percent (99 to 1). Their accompanying errors, known as Type I (alpha) errors, are .05 and .01 respectively.

With hypothesis testing, our logic assumes that a given sample statistic—for example, a difference between means—is typical of such differences from samples of those sizes taken from populations with the same mean (the null hypothesis). The alternative hypothesis is that the differences come from a population of differences in which one population mean is larger than the other. We then compare the observed difference between means, with the typical range for differences from populations with the same mean, to determine whether the difference falls within that range. Values lying outside the typical range are likely to have been influenced by something other than sampling and error variability (the alternative hypothesis). Atypical values permit our rejection of the null hypothesis and acceptance of the alternative; that is, that the means of the populations from which the sample means come differ. If we fail to reject the null hypothesis, we cannot accept the alternate hypothesis. If our hypothesis was directional, it will indicate which one is the larger, and we should have used a one-tailed rather than a two-tailed test of significance.

Sometimes we fail to consider a value atypical when it should have been. In this instance, we make a Type II (beta) error. The sensitivity of a study is determined by the extent to which such errors are avoided $(1 - \beta)$. Studies should be designed to appropriate levels of sensitivity by conducting a statistical power analysis in the planning stages. Sensitivity can be made greater by increasing the size of the sample, increasing treatment effect, or decreasing the variability of the measures (as by increasing their reliability).

Chi-square is widely used for nominal or categorical data. Analysis of variance is used to avoid the inflation-of-probabilities problem where multiple *t* tests must be performed. It is particularly useful for complex designs.

A Look Ahead

Now that we have the necessary tools—descriptive statistics, measurement, and an understanding of the logic of inference—in the next chapter we will examine experimentation, a method that makes use of all three of them.

ADDITIONAL READING

Useful statistics texts: Freedman, Pisani and Purves (1997), Guilford and Fruchter (1978), Hays (1973), May, Masson and Hunter (1989), Statistic books minimizing formulas and mathematics: Abelson (1995), Dichter and Roznowski (1996), Jaeger (1983). Exploratory statistical techniques, Tukey (1977). Non-parametric statistics, Siegel and Castellan (1988). Sage statistical advice, Cohen (1990). Comparison of multiple means, Hancock and Klockars (1996). Analysis of pre to post change, Collins and Horn (1991). A primer on multiple regression analysis, path analysis, multi-dimensional scaling, logistic regression, ANOVA, and multiple ANOVA, Grim and Yarnold (1995).

IMPORTANT TERMS

Alpha error
Alpha level
Analysis of variance (ANOVA)
Beta error
Chi-square
Confidence interval
Confidence level
Confidence limits
Degrees of freedom
Estimation
Hypothesis testing
Inferential statistics
Inflation of probabilities
Nonparametric statistics
Null hypothesis

One-tailed test
Parameter
Point estimation
Power of a statistical test
Practical significance
Robust
Sampling distribution of the mean
Sensitivity of a statistical test
Significance level
Standard error of the mean
Statistical significance
Two-tailed test
Type I error
Type II error

APPLICATION PROBLEMS

1. Some researchers were interested in comparing the performance of learners working independently on a computer-assisted instruction program with that of learners working on the computers cooperatively in pairs. They were able to conduct the experiment with 60 eighth-grade students (31 male and 29 female) drawn from several health education classes and randomly assigned to either the individual learning group or the cooperative learning group. The students were given a parallel series of 16 lessons on the topic of sex education. Despite the sensitivity of the subject matter, the investigators predicted that the cooperative method would yield superior performances on a written post-test. How would the logic of inference apply here?

2. A medical researcher was interested in the long-term effects of marijuana on users. She tested the reaction time of a sample of 49 long-term users on a test of automobile braking time and compared the results with the adult population average for her city (previously computed in a series of studies conducted by the local traffic safety board for use in licensing tests). The sample had a mean reaction time of 0.98 second, whereas the population average was 0.90. The standard error for the sample was calculated to be 0.043 seconds with the confidence interval for 95 percent ranging from 0.896 to 1.064 seconds using a two-tailed test and 0.909 seconds for a one-tailed test looking in the lower tail. Given these results, should the researcher accept or reject the null hypothesis that there is no difference between this sample's mean and that of the adult population?

3. Sandra Fayette hypothesized that college students who generated their own questions to a passage of text would demonstrate higher comprehension rates than those who were presented with adjunct questions. She decided to replicate her study with high school students. Her results came very close to showing a statistically significant difference between the two approaches in favor of the generative question hypothesis. When she examined her data, she noticed that the comprehension score for one particular student, who was part of the generative strategy group, was considerably lower than the average scores for that group. She also realized that if she were to discard his score, she would have a statistically significant result. What is her dilemma regarding Type I and Type II error? Is it possible for her to demonstrate statistical significance using her current data without discarding the score?

4. Comment on this statement: "As we change from validation to a discovery orientation, we typically change the level of significance from 10 percent toward .1 percent."

5. Comment on this statement: "If we reject the null hypothesis, we can say that the observed result proves that the proposition we are testing is true."

6. Teresa Wright is the superintendent of a suburban school system. Her director of research tells her that the new curriculum is superior at a statistically significant level to the old curriculum. What questions should she ask the director?

7. Dr. Gerrard Goetz is up for tenure. He wants to be sure that his article shows a significant result so that he can get it published. He is comparing the effectiveness of advanced organizers on learning scientific laws by means of traditionally written end-of-chapter summaries. What might he do in

designing and conducting the study to make it more likely he will get a publishable result.

8. Sally Stoltz has to use a convenience sample of teachers in New York state for a questionnaire, but she would like to show that her group of teachers is like those of the state. She has 25 returns. She runs a statistical test on their ages, years of experience, and grade level and finds that the means of all three are not statistically different at the 5 percent level from those published by the state education department. She concludes that she can generalize her sample to the teachers of the state. Is she justified? Why or why not?

9. The following statements appear in Schmidt (1996, p. 126):

a) If my findings are not significant, then I know that they probably just occurred by chance and the true difference is probably zero.

b) If the result is significant, then I know I have a reliable finding.

c) The level of statistical significance test tells me whether the relationships in my data are large enough to be important or not.

d) I can also determine from the level of statistical significance what the chances are that these findings would replicate if I conducted a new study.

Which of these statements is true and which false? If false, why?

Compare your answers with those following the Application Exercise.

APPLICATION EXERCISE

Consider how you might set up your study with an experimental and a control group (which you will learn more about in the next chapter). How might you apply the logic of inference? What would be the null hypothesis? The alternative hypothesis? Would

a one- or two-tailed test of significance be most appropriate? What would be an appropriate significance level? Why? Are you concerned with statistical or practical significance?

ANSWERS TO THE APPLICATION PROBLEMS

1. It would be used in hypothesis testing. The investigators would be interested in examining the difference between the means of the two groups and, expecting a greater effect for the cooperative learning group, would choose directional testing using a one-tailed test. Thus they might adopt the null hypothesis that the difference between the means of the two groups belongs to a population of differ-

ences with a mean of zero. Any observed difference is due to chance and sampling error, and the two samples actually belong to the same population. If they were able to reject the null hypothesis, they would likely accept the alternative hypothesis that the difference between the means belongs to a population of differences with a mean greater than zero and that there was a significant difference between the instructional treatments in favor of the cooperative treatment.

2. The answer depends on which test the researcher chooses, the one-tailed or the two-tailed t test. The latter includes the population mean within the 95 percent confidence interval; the former does not. Thus the one-tailed test is more sensitive and indicates statistical significance. But is the researcher justified in using it here? It depends on whether or not we would expect the drug to slow or quicken an individual's reaction time. The choice of the one-tailed test is justified if the researcher had a directional hypothesis that marijuana slows an individual's reaction. If it were found to speed it up, however, she would consider that an aberration in the study rather than a finding. (If she could find nothing wrong with the study, she might then switch her hypothesis and replicate the study.)

3. Sandra does not want to reject the null hypothesis and claim an effect that really does not exist—that is, commit a Type I (alpha) error. However, especially given the problem of one extreme value within her sample, she also does not wish to reject the possibility of an effect that is really there despite the statistics—that is, commit a Type II (beta) error. She could strengthen the sensitivity of her study in a number of ways. First, she could, of course, discard the data for the one subject, provided that she can demonstrate a valid reason for doing so (perhaps he was ill that day, or it turned out he was from another country and had weak English skills, for example). She should, of course, report this decision. If she had analyzed the data first using a two-tailed test, she probably would have a valid argument for choosing the more sensitive, one-tailed test with a replication, which, since she is close, might well provide statistical significance. This means she has a directional hypothesis, though recognized only after the study had been completed. If her sample were small, it might be possible to repeat the experiment with a larger group to dampen the variability due to size. Finally, if able to return to the sample, she could increase the treatment time (perhaps test the subjects with more text passages) to attempt to strengthen its effect.

4. With a discovery orientation, such as we have in screening remedial reading programs for one that

works, we don't want to miss a potentially good one. We are willing to tolerate what we call false-positives, findings that look significant but are Type I errors. Thus, we change the confidence level in the opposite direction, from 0.1 percent toward 10 percent. Some of those 10 percent are going to be called statistically significant effects and turn out not to be, but that is all right because we will be less likely to miss those that do validate on replication as significant effects.

5. If that were the case, it would make research much easier! No, all we can say is that the null hypothesis escaped disconfirmation this time. We ought to be putting our propositions to the most rigorous tests we can find. Each time we test a proposition and it is validated, we say that it escaped disconfirmation. After it has escaped enough times that we are confident about our results, we eventually act as though it were a true proposition. But science is the only method of knowing wherein every proposition is held as tentatively true until disconfirmed. Thus any proposition could, in theory at least, be disconfirmed at any time. Of course, this would markedly upset our ideas about the way the world works, but in some respects that is what Einstein did with the theory of relativity.

6. Here we run into the problem of statistical significance versus practical significance. Wright needs to know not only that the effect was statistically significant but also whether it was large enough to be practically significant. Thus, she wants to know how big it is in terms of the gains that children normally show at that grade.

7. Dr. Goetz should conduct a pilot study to find estimates of the standard deviations of his variables, as well as an estimated difference between treatments. When he has these, he can design a study that will be sufficiently sensitive that if that size of effect appears again, it will be statistically significant.

Alternatively, he can devise a design that is as sensitive as possible. To do this, he can change the confidence level from 1 percent toward 5 percent, use a directional hypothesis and a one-tailed test of significance, increase the size of the difference between treatments by writing the advance organizers for maximum effect, comparing the two treatments over many samples of material, giving the two treatments to a bright group that might be more susceptible to the effect of advance organizers, and so on. In addition, he could increase the size of the sample of subjects or decrease the variability. The latter can be done by using more reliable tests or measures, by moving into the laboratory to decrease random noise that would decrease attention, by uniformly motivating the students but ensuring that different trials used the same directions for testing, and similar things.

8. Apparently, the difference between the means for these characteristics in Stoltz's sample and those of the population give sufficient reason to attribute them to sampling error for samples of 25. But that assumes that the sensitivity of the statistical test that she ran was powerful enough to pick up a difference that was practically significant so far as she was concerned. Sally must determine what magnitude of difference means a practically significant difference between her sample and the population. If this turns out to be within the sensitivity of her study as already designed, all is well. If not, then getting a larger sample is probably the easiest way to fix the study.

9. They are all false! Here are the reasons:

a) The true difference is not necessarily zero; you only know that it was too small to sense with the statistical power of that study.

b) It may be a chance rather than a reliable finding. On average, 5 percent of them will be such if that was the level of significance used.

c) The level of statistical significance does not indicate the importance of the finding; that is a value judgment a human makes. It could be a real difference that is too small to be considered practically important.

d) Whether the findings would replicate depends on the statistical sensitivity of the replication. However, an exact duplication of the study would more likely yield statistically significant results than if the first results were not statistically significant.

C H A P T E R **20**

Experimental Methods and Experimental Design

> Despite the creative use of experimental design features from the seventeenth century onward, it was not until the past century or so that experimental design notions became systematized. . . . The advantages of experimental control for inferring causation have to be weighed against the disadvantages that arise because we do not always want to learn about causation in controlled settings.
>
> Thomas D. Cook and Donald T. Campbell, "Quasi-Experimentation"

O V E R V I E W

Some social scientists believe that the strongest chains of reasoning can be built only through experimental design. For them, experimentation is the most effective method for creating a consensus around the existence of a cause-and-effect relationship. This effectiveness, however, depends on several characteristics— good experimental control, the elimination or neutralizing of rival explanations, and the manipulation of the treatment in appropriate patterns that are reflected in the effect. They rarely occur together under natural conditions.

Study of experimental design has led to the identification of common rival explanations besides those of chance and sampling variation described in Chapter 19. Many plague not only experimental studies but *all* methods concerned with causality. Indeed, in the discussion or qualitative analysis (p. 317), you met two of them, mortality and instrument decay. Some weaken internal validity (LP); others restrict external validity (GP).

Experimentalists have developed a variety of designs to take advantage of the control features of experiments in order to provide the strongest internal validity (LP) and the least restrictive external validity (GP), yet to fit the often peculiar conditions of particular studies. We will examine some of these designs and in the process learn something about methods of constructing them in general.

This chapter begins by laying out the basics of experimentation: manipulation of treatment, some simple designs, common rival explanations that must be protected against, and the ways in which even the simplest designs provide this protection. Building on this foundation, we examine common single-treatment designs and multiple-treatment factorial design, followed by the after-the-fact natural experiment (*ex post facto* design). Finally we will discuss how to define experimental and control "treatments" and ensure they are properly administered. Tips for researchers and a list of hallmarks of experimentation provide a summary.

CHAPTER CONTENTS

Introduction

Because experimentation is possibly the most structured of research methods, we might think of it as a cut-and-dried procedure. Not so! As we shall see, there is considerable need for good judgment, pilot studies, and provisional tries, which are all part of normal procedure except with very simple problems. We are unaware of their importance because they are rarely part of the published report.

An experiment's strong chain of reasoning helps link cause to effect. Social scientists who use experimentation, like their natural science counterparts, also see themselves as seeking the laws of nature—in their case, the rules and principles that guide individuals, groups, and cultures.

Experimentation uses the method of differences we discussed in Chapter 7. This requires that two or more situations be exactly alike except for one thing—the presence of a treatment or whatever independent variable we are studying. Typically involved are one or more experimental groups each of which receives a treatment (or contains the independent variable), and a control group which receives either no treatment or a treatment just like the treatment but without the "active ingredient" (or does not contain the independent variable). Although it is true that no two groups can be exactly alike—even the same group is different at a later time—the problem is to make **functionally equivalent groups.** That is, they must function as if they were exactly equivalent for the purposes of this study, because anything relevant to the study is made equivalent. Making the groups functionally equivalent is the purpose of control procedures that are the hallmark of experimentation. Let's consider the six facets of design in the chain of reasoning.

1. *Subjects.* In qualitative research, the people studied are in their natural groups. Although this may be true also in an experiment, experimentalists like to be able to assign individuals to groups and, if possible, to do so randomly so as to equate the groups on all variables.[1]

2. *Situation.* In qualitative research, the situation is determined by the field location of the individuals or group studied. This may be true of a field experiment as well. However, in order to eliminate undesired rival explanations of the effect, researchers often prefer doing the study in a laboratory or other situations less vulnerable to events beyond their influence. (Qualitative researchers, by waiting for a contrasting event or situation to become available can achieve similar results. They may also seek out sites or individuals where the desired contrast is more likely to be present.)

3. *Treatment (independent variables).* In qualitative research, the actions and reactions observed occur naturally as a result of the situation and the individuals in it. Similarly, there are "natural experiments" where the researcher waits in readiness to assess the effects of a naturally occurring event. More often, however, the experimentalist researcher administers a planned cause, the treatment, according to procedures specified in the design.

4. *Observation or measurement.* Whereas qualitative researchers prefer the freedom and flexibility of observations and interviews to measurement, experimentalists prefer the targeted precision of valid measures. Experimenters may use observations if no suitable instrument or measure is available, but even then will more likely use a structured low inference instrument. Where instruments may not be totally convincing to one's audience they may use observation to reinforce their measures as did Zimbardo et al. to assure the presence of paranoia in Chapter 1.

5. *Basis for sensing attributes or changes.* In qualitative research, changes in individuals or groups are observed over time so that the difference in various characteristics of interest can be noted. Comparison of individuals with them-

---

[1]Note, too, that the term *subjects* is an experimentalist term. Qualitative researchers point out that they see the persons studied as "informants" who help the researchers understand a situation rather than as individuals to be studied, treated, and possibly manipulated. However, even in experimental situations subjects can become collaborators, as Mitroff and Kilman (1976) showed in engaging the "subject" in an exploration of how the problem should be defined and investigated. Kruglanski (1976), too, used the postexperimental interview to draw on subjects' self-knowledge to determine how the experimental situation was interpreted and to make suggestions. Perhaps the attitude of the researcher, as much as the method, is the critical variable. Most methods can be used in varying ways to fit the orientation of the user.

selves at different points in time is also the basis of some experiments. In experimentation, treated groups are more often compared with untreated control groups or with groups receiving a competitive procedure.

6. *Procedure.* With qualitative research, the order of investigator actions is determined largely by the individuals or group being studied. Even plans to interview certain individuals are not as extensive as those of experimentation. In an experiment, who will get what treatment, when, and how, as well as who will be observed and measured when, where, and with what, are all generally preplanned.

Note in each of the above, although the preferences of qualitative researchers are contrasted with those who typically hew to experimental methods, this is not to say that experimental design is confined to experimentation. It isn't! Once again, although there are clearly differences between qualitative and quantitative orientations, too much can be made of them. Indeed, qualitative researchers use the same designs as experimentalists where they seek to show a cause and effect relationship, but they typically use only the simpler ones. Having identified a presumed cause and effect relationship, they usually must wait until circumstances create a contrasting control situation where the cause and effect are absent, but the effect appears when the cause appears. Alternatively, by who they choose to observe or interview, and/or where they do it, they increase the likelihood that the circumstances for a design will occur.

However, the experimentalist's control of the administration of the treatment can provide especially strong evidence linking cause to effect. An effect that visibly occurs after a treatment application is very convincing. Credence of the relationship is further enhanced when we can produce the effect on demand, as when its timing follows a table of random numbers or the requests of an unbelieving observer! The causal linkage of an effect that disappears when we remove the cause can be even more strongly convincing, since we can turn it on and off at will (for example, introducing food coloring into a child's food where the coloring is suspected of producing emotionally disturbed behavior). Thus, of all the methods we have available, experimentation is probably the one that most strongly links cause and effect.

Control is present in still another feature, one of the strongest aspects and a major function of experimental design: elimination of plausible rival explanations. Although other methods may also be able to rule these out, the special capability of experimentation to accomplish this for a wide range of alternatives is unique. Although experimental design can eliminate conditions restrictive of generality, its use under laboratory conditions is more often a problem than a strength.

The fact that so many experimental studies are designed as difference type studies contrasting one form or level of treatment with another, is indicative of a relatively primitive-level inquiry. Such studies are still asking "Does this variable make a significant difference?" The next higher level of question is "How strongly and in what way is this variable related to the effect?" Though such designs are more complex, with the information they yield, we are in a much better position to utilize the phenomena constructively and to construct theory.

The future of the social and behavioral sciences lies in going beyond which variables make a difference toward determining effects sizes and the strength and nature of relationships between variables. Movement in this direction requires only that we refocus our thinking about research questions and so design our studies that we obtain the effect size and relationship description. Describing the nature of the relationship between variables or between treatment and effect is possible wherever the strength or nature of the treatment can be measured, otherwise quantified, or is present at several distinguishable levels. Then we can use statistics to show the strength of the relationship, or graphics to portray its nature.

♦ *Experimentation provides one of the strongest chains of reasoning for linking cause to effect.*

♦ *Manipulating the strength and/or timing of the treatment to show that the effect reflects those changes strongly links cause to effect.*

♦ *Experimentation typically involves carefully planning in advance the choices for each of the six links in the design chain: subject, situation, treatment, observations or measures, basis for sensing attributes or changes, and procedure.*

♦ *Careful choice of design provides control for rival explanations and restrictive conditions.*

♦ *The future of the social and behavioral sciences lies in moving our research from the "Which-variables-make-a-difference?" level of inquiry to "What is the effect size and how strong and what is the nature of the relationship?"*

Experimentation: Strong Internal Validity (LP), but Weak External Validity (GP)?

Experimentation clearly can build strong internal validity (LP)—the capacity to link cause to effect. But what about external validity (GP), generality—typically considered its weakness? Lack of generality is reinforced by the large number of experiments using laboratory or artificial situations with little apparent practical application. In their defense, some researchers (for example, Henshel, 1980a, 1980b; and Berkowitz and Donnerstein, 1982) note that the purpose of such studies is simply understanding the phenomenon. Such understanding can build to eventual practical applicability.[2] Further, Henshel (1980b) argues that learning in an artificial situation may enable us to see how we can make the real situation resemble the artificial one. We learn about phenomena "that are capable of existing," permitting "the creation of entirely new social structures and institutions heretofore unknown" (p. 194).[3]

---

[2]Analyzing studies of basic research—research done just for understanding—Mosteller (1981) found a long lead time (often 20 to 30 years) between publication of results and their incorporation into major developments. A substantial portion of research contributing to a given development had no relation to application when the research was done—for example, between 1945 and 1975, 41 percent of the advances in cardiopulmonary medicine and surgery.

[3]Among the examples Henshel cites is the propeller-driven aircraft, which does not exist in nature; indeed, humans have lost their lives trying to imitate the birds.

Experimentation is not confined to artificial settings, however, and it has been used in large-scale trials of social reforms. One of the largest, the Income Maintenance Experiment (guaranteed annual income), was even replicated in different cities. It showed an important policy flaw—not that individuals would become lazy, the expected problem, but that families would break up, an unanticipated side effect (Rossi and Lyall, 1976).

There are also "natural experiments" wherein we study the effect of a "treatment" applied by nature. For example, early studies of how societies cope with disaster (Baker and Chapman, 1962) led to studies following earthquakes, volcano eruptions, floods, fires, transportation accidents, and other catastrophes and to new understandings (Raphael, 1986; Kreps, 1989).[4]

Part of the art of experimental design is choosing study situations that achieve the appropriate balance between internal validity (LP) and external validity (GP).

- ◆ *Experimentation has its greatest control potential in the laboratory study, where strong internal validity (LP) is usually gained at the expense of external validity (GP).*
- ◆ *Natural experiments, which wait for a treatment to occur spontaneously, or experiments in which a treatment is applied under field conditions, gain greater external validity (GP) at the expense of internal validity (LP).*
- ◆ *The researcher's task is to achieve a balance of the two types of validity appropriate to the goal of the study.*
- ◆ *Basic research that aims at understanding phenomena, or at inventing conditions that do not yet exist but might, is often considered a first step toward application.*

The Art of Experimental Design

Experimental design is part deductive reasoning and part art. From the analysis we made of Zimbardo et al. in Chapter 1, the many required design decisions are apparent. In addition, however, the report omitted those involved in prior exploration and pilot studies and indicated only by implication the decisions regarding resource planning and allocation. Researchers must balance many things, and choose among manifold alternatives: They must use available resources to maximize audience credibility in the translation of the hypothesis into a design within the constraints of those resources, institutional limitations, and ethical boundaries. This requires finding the most appropriate choices for all six facets of design: subjects, situation, treatment, observation or measurement, basis for sensing attributes or changes, and procedure. The chosen experimental design must balance internal with external validity—enough statistical power to sense the effect while using persons, situations, measures, and treatments sufficiently representa-

---

[4]The Disaster Research Center at the University of Delaware collects such research.

tive for the desired generality. Creatively combining these decisions is an art in it-self, but add to it, the artfully creative parts, for example, Zimbardo's decisions to use hypnosis, three comparison groups, trained confederates, and audio tapes for instructions.

As might be expected, researchers have found ways to make these decisions easier. Frequently used designs have been analyzed in terms of their strengths and weaknesses. Further, because the design is an operational definition of the hypothesis, we have learned to incorporate certain design features when particu-lar terms appear in the hypothesis or are implied by the description of the treat-ment or intended effect. Some sample terms (left column) typically linked to cer-tain design features (right column) appear in the table below, together with examples in parenthesis of how they might appear in a study.

Terms	*Associated Design Features*
Trend (The posthypnotic suggestion will grow increasingly weaker)	Observations or measures taken at three or more points in time
Change in trend (Although a hyperactive child will learn to attend with reinforcement training, that learning can be accelerated by small dosages of ritalin.)	At least two measures before change and at least one after it, preferably two or more
Curvilinear (Ability to concentrate is curvilinearly related to arousal of the individual)	Observations or measures taken at three or more points in time
Retention versus immediate recall (Retention of reading skills is enhanced over the summer vacation months if the child reads at least three books over that period)	Multiple posttests
Gain measures (Per capita income of welfare recipients will increase following socialization training)	Either pretests and posttests or a control group
Relationship (Hits per website is related to the attractiveness of its graphics)	Measures of two or more variables taken on the same individuals, situations or things
Cumulative effect (Each time individuals are hypnotized, it becomes easier to hypnotize them the next time)	Multiple treatments with testing after each treatment or after selected treatments
Different levels of treatment intensity (Three levels of intensive care will be provided to determine the effect on rate of morbidity)	Multiple experimental groups
Weak treatment (It is anticipated that improvement will appear in only a small proportion of those treated.[5]	Larger sample, increased length of treatment, stratification or blocking, use of subjects sensitive to the treatment, a directional hypothesis, one-tailed test of significance, 5 or 10 percent level of significance rather than 1 percent

---

[5]Abelson (1997) argues, when starting out in a new area, "avoid messing with flimsy phenom-ena. . . . [Pursue those] with characteristically large effect sizes (further enhanced by 'sledgeham-mer' manipulations). . . . Once . . . confident that large effect sizes can be reliably observed, . . . strip the experimental manipulations to their essentials and repeat. If the phenomenon is robust enough, . . . supportive results will still emerge" (p. 14).

> ◆ Design is part science and part art—many choices can be combined in so many ways to protect against the rival explanations deemed most threatening.
> ◆ Design is basically an operational definition of the hypothesis; indeed, certain terms that appear in hypotheses have their design counterparts.

Linking Cause Convincingly to Effect[6]

An essential task of design is to link cause to effect. You can provide several kinds of evidence:

1. Use a theory or a rationale to predict the appearance of the effect. Do so in as much detail as possible, indicating when it will appear, how strongly, how long it will last, and so on. Show the agreement of prediction and results.
2. Make the difference between untreated and treated condition as large as feasible.
3. Show that the effect follows the cause.
4. Vary the treatment, and demonstrate the effect follows the same pattern.

The first of these is not confined to experimentation. Astronomy is not an experimental science. An astronomer can tell you, however, that the sun has just had a massive sun spot display with a resultant disruption in world communications at a particular time. The disruption occurs. It is an impressive evidence of the cause-and-effect linkage. In similar fashion, let's theorize that having skipped a developmental task in choosing a vocation, even individuals who were initially happy with their professional choice will become discontent after a period of about ten years. Comparing the satisfaction of individuals about ten years into their chosen occupation, who can recall having completed that developmental task with those who did not, confirms the prediction. We have strong evidence. The more detailed we can make our predictions, the more compelling the evidence for the expected relationship will be when our prediction is borne out by the data. Using a theory or a rationale to predict the effect in as detailed a fashion as possible is an important way of strengthening the evidence. Qualitative researchers use this technique when, having found a presumed cause and effect relationship in one circumstance they predict what they will find in a similar one.

The second kind of evidence, showing a large effect, is not uncommon in the natural sciences but is rarer in the social sciences. Dramatic results from trials of a medical drug or procedure are front-page news.[7] In the social sciences, however, where strong effects are much rarer, we design studies with sensitivity sufficient to sense weak effects.

The third kind of evidence comes from a condition of cause-and-effect relationships—the effect occurs with or follows the cause. Experiments have an ad-

---

[6]This discussion builds on Chapter 7.
[7]However, see the Rosenthal (1994) reference on p. 557. Do we expect too much in the social sciences?

vantage in those instances in which the treatment is administered since the effect should appear only with the administration of treatment.

The fourth kind of evidence, showing congruence in pattern of cause and effect, is the most convincing. There are so many ways to change the causal pattern. We can change the frequency, strength, and duration of treatment application in steps just large enough to produce measurable results, or in increasing steps (a single unit of strength, twice as strong, three times, and so forth), or in rapidly accelerating fashion (twice as strong, 4 times as strong, 16 times, 256 times). We can cluster treatment administration between testing intervals, and change the pattern of clustering and length of intervals. We can use a random pattern of administration. Any such pattern, when accompanied by a similar pattern in the effect, will convincingly link cause to effect.

Studies involving learning or other effects that change the individual or do not rapidly decay, present special problems, since the "off" period may show little or no loss. The amount of forgetting may not be measurable during the short period of the study. To overcome this, we may use strongly contrasting treatment levels—more practice problems or increased contact time—which are different enough to be reflected in the effect. We should remember, however, there are sometimes learning "plateaus" that do not immediately respond to either strength of treatment or extent of practice.

General Methods of Control

Protection from the effect of a confounding variable, that is an unwanted variable that could affect the study's outcome, is most often obtained in one of three methods: (1) removing and excluding it, (2) measuring and adjusting for it, and (3) spreading its effect across all the groups being compared so that they are equally affected. Of these, removing and excluding is the most desirable where loss of generality is not a problem. Measuring and adjusting is difficult to do properly with available methods. Spreading across comparison groups adds variability which reduces the sensitivity of a statistical test and we usually need all the sensitivity we can get. Nonetheless, spreading the effect is the most common method.

Removing and Excluding

Use of the laboratory, or an area where we can control what goes on, is the usually preferred method of removing and excluding unwanted variation. However, other more practical techniques with less reduction of generalizability often have the same effect and can sometimes be substituted. **Camouflage,** for instance, was used by Kounin (1970), who placed a box on a pedestal in classrooms. Because students and teachers never knew whether the box was empty or held a camera, they soon came to ignore it. Similarly, the participant observer, by participating, seeks to lose the stigma of an outsider and to take on the role of group member.

Masking of one variable with another is sometimes effective. "Landscaped" offices illustrate the principle. Five-foot partitions substitute for walls, and "white noise" is introduced to mask sounds coming over the partitions. In a study of autokinesis as a personality variable, Thurstone (1947) used complete darkness as a mask. After moving a penlight in a designated pattern he placed it in a holder. Subjects were to record their perception of the light's movement. Because the holder was masked by the dark, perceived movement long after the pen was stationary—the autokinetic effect—could be measured.

Compensatory action often allays parents' demand that their children also receive the experimental treatment, as for example when administrators promise that the control group will be treated next or build a waiting list that they use as a control group.

Restricting the range of a variable to be controlled reduces or eliminates its power. For example, using a very bright group in which IQs vary little eliminates its variability so that differences in IQ is not a factor in the effect.

Measuring and Adjusting

Partial correlation and analysis of covariance are the two methods most commonly used for reducing the effect of unwanted variables. Where measurement is valid and accurate, the methods work well (as in controlling for length of practice time). But just as in trimming fat from a piece of meat—not too much nor too little—these methods entail problems with making the proper adjustment in most social science uses. For example, Coleman, Hoffer, and Kilgore (1982), used analysis of covariance to correct for the socioeconomic bias in comparing public with private school achievement. The controversy that erupted over the study indicates the lack of acceptance of these methods (Goldberger and Cain, 1982). Alternatively, we can sometimes build the unwanted variation into the study as an independent variable, as in the factorial designs described later in this chapter.

Spreading the Effect to All Comparison Groups

Making sure the groups compared are alike in all respects except one, the treatment, is the goal of spreading the effect of rival explanations. If giving a pretest is likely to boost the posttest scores, we must be sure that we also pretest the control group. If the recipients of the experimental treatment feel special because the treatment was obtrusive, we must give the control group a placebo treatment devoid of the treatment's "active ingredient" and make them feel special, too. The different ways in which individuals react to the pretest and to obtrusive treatment will add to the variance of the study. Although this added variability will increase the minimum effect size needed for a statistically significant effect, it is part of the trade-off for the control of these variables.

How can we be sure that groups are exactly alike except for the treatment variable? They won't be exactly alike; but they must be sufficiently alike with respect to plausible alternative causes of the effect to eliminate them as possibilities. An experimental group that both starts and ends at a higher level than the control baffles us; we can't infer which is the cause, the treatment, or a prior achievement.

Randomization. **Random assignment** is the statistician's preferred way of ensuring that groups are comparable and of avoiding bias in assigning treatments. It involves random assignment of individuals to groups by a flip of a coin or a random number table, and then the assignment of groups to treatment(s) and control by a similar process. Where it is not known which treatment is most effective, random assignment gives participants an equal chance of being in a treatment or control group, whichever has more favorable results. Most important, on average, random assignment of individuals makes groups comparable in all variables—even length of toenails and size of belly button. On average, it equates variables we anticipate might present problems *but also unanticipated ones that were important.* Randomization buys a lot for little!

Campbell and Stanley (1963) thought random assignment contributed so much to internal validity that they applied the term "true experimental designs" to those using random assignment, naming other designs "quasi-experimental." Unfortunately, this terminology sounds as though "true" experimental designs protect against all rival hypotheses—which, of course, they do not. For example, obtrusive random assignment alerts subjects to their participation in an experiment and may result in "on stage" behavior.

Researchers tend intuitively to resist random assignment both because failure of chance to equate a key variable may ruin the study and because so rarely are people assigned randomly under normal conditions that it is difficult to do unobtrusively. Countering this resistance is Boruch, McSweeney, and Soderstrom's (1978) bibliography of some 300 field tests showing random assignment's use, even in delicate situations. Similarly, Boruch and Wothke (1985, Appendix 1) list ten additional such studies and describe eight social experiments to show how random assignment can be used to study important policy matters in areas as different as: welfare versus work incentive programs, arrest and nonarrest in domestic assault cases, treatment of depression, use of mediation in judicial litigation, and hospital versus community treatment of the chronically mentally ill. They make a strong case for our considering it even where we might think it impossible.[8]

Although random assignment equates all variables "on average," this is cold comfort when it fails to equate a very plausible rival cause. Random assignment within blocks ("strata" become "blocks" in experimental design terms), like random sampling within strata in stratified sampling, ensures representativeness of the **blocking** (stratifying) variable yet provides the randomizing element. Especially with small groups, where unequated outliers could be devastating, some form of stratification is important. For example, to control for socioeconomic status, we would sort individuals into high-, middle-, and low-socioeconomic blocks and randomly assign individuals within each socioeconomic class block to experimental and control groups. Matching individuals and randomly assigning to groups is the extreme of blocking: every pair constitutes a block. When randomly assigning individuals, blocking provides us cheap insurance and, as with stratification, we will lose only the labor we have spent if no gain results.

---

[8]Appendix 2 in Boruch and Wothke (1985) lists six objections to random assignment with counterarguments, and the book's final chapter describes strategies for increasing the chances of making randomization feasible through advance planning.

♦ *Random assignment of individuals to groups and groups to treatment protects not only from the effects of variables identified as potential rival explanations but also from those that have not even been so considered.*

♦ *So-called true experimental designs are those in which the groups are equated by random assignment. Despite the name's connotation, these designs are not immune from all rival explanations.*

♦ *Random assignment of individuals to groups from within blocks (strata) is a preferred way of equating groups. It provides a guarantee of representativeness through stratification, as well as an unbiased equating of groups through randomness.*

How Simple Experimental Designs Control Rival Explanations

To provide a basis for understanding how designs protect against rival explanations, let us look at six simple single-treatment designs. Each successive design has an advantage over the previous and thus illustrates both some desirable design characteristics and the way designs evolve.

Let's take a simple case. Ms. Kimball, a first-grade teacher in the inner city, is concerned about her children's progress. She has heard that the University of Chicago's School Mathematics Curriculum has been highly successful. She gives it a four-month trial and then tests the children on the Stanford Achievement Test. In comparison with the test's norms, it appears that her group's score, though still below what should be expected, is better than it might have been.

How do we describe her design? A standard notation for such depiction, developed by Campbell and Stanley (1963), uses X to indicate a treatment and O to indicate an observation or measurement. Events are sequenced in time from left to right, and each group occupies a separate line. To describe the teacher's experiment, with but one group, we need only one line:

Design 1: Case study X O

This indicates that the curriculum was applied (X) and then the students were measured with the Stanford Achievement Test (O for observed). It is the case study design.

You may sense that this is not the strongest of designs. Although the teacher believes the students are ahead of where they might be, the basis on which she determines change occurred is a comparison with the test's norms. If the characteristics of the students in this year's class differ from those students on whom the test was normed, the norms may not be applicable. But had the teacher known where the students started, she would not have had to depend on the norms to show change. They might actually have started as high as they ended; we can't tell from the case study design. Thus, a stronger design in this respect would have tested them both before and after the treatment:

Design 2: One-group pretest-posttest design O X O

This **one-group pretest-posttest design** will at least show change: the students are being used as their own control group—compared with themselves at an earlier point in time.

The mention of a control group suggests that the teacher might have used one in her study, but the control group must be just like the experimental group. How can she get one? She might use another teacher's class, a preformed group that might be comparable to hers. A preformed group is one formed for purposes other than the experiment. Since such groups are not formed by random assignment, we do not know their comparability to one another. This potential lack of comparability is indicated by a line between the rows in design 3, the **nonequivalent control group design.**

$$\text{Design 3: Nonequivalent control group design} \quad \frac{O\ X\ O}{O\ C\ O}$$

The *C* indicates a control treatment, just as the *X* indicates the treatment with the "active ingredient." Though there is no change in curriculum for the control group, the "traditional" curriculum is, nevertheless, a treatment.

The control treatment is often a placebo treatment, one just like the experimental except for the "active ingredient." Suppose we were studying the effect of caffeine on hyperactive children. It may be that, instead of the caffeine, the *expectation* of an effect from the pill is really the "active ingredient"—the **placebo effect.**[9] Unless we also give a placebo pill to the control group, we cannot tell whether the placebo effect or caffeine caused the change.

Establishing groups specifically for the study can ensure, on average, that the groups will be comparable. By the flip of a coin, individuals from a pool of subjects are randomly assigned to either the control or the treatment group. Once one group is full, the rest go into the other. If, at the beginning of the year, children were assigned by the flip of a coin to either Ms. Kimball's or Mr. Johnson's class, the classes, on average, will be equivalent. Then, again by the flip of a coin, one of the two teachers is assigned to administer the treatment. Random assignment of subjects and treatment to groups is designated by the *R* in a square. The pretest in this **pretest-posttest control group design** ensures that randomization, on average, equated the groups.

$$\text{Design 4: Pretest-posttest control group design} \quad \boxed{R}\ \begin{matrix} O\ X\ O \\ O\ C\ O \end{matrix}$$

Trusting randomization to make groups really comparable eliminates the need for pretest. A **posttest-only control group design** simply compares them at the posttest:

---

[9]In medical research, an unmedicated pill given to the control subjects in place of the experimental medicine is called a placebo.

Design 5: Posttest-only control group design $\boxed{R}$ $\begin{matrix} X\,O \\ C\,O \end{matrix}$

To make sure randomization worked; let's combine the last two into a single design, the **Solomon four-group design:**

Design 6: Solomon four-group design $\boxed{R}$ $\begin{matrix} O\,X\,O \\ O\,C\,O \\ X\,O \\ C\,O \end{matrix}$

In design 6, subjects from a pool are assigned to one of four groups: two experimental (one pretested and one not) and two control (one pretested and one not). Though it requires more subjects and treatments, such a design has the combined advantages of designs 4 and 5, as we shall see.

Each design was successively adapted to provide protection from a specific rival explanation—a rival hypothesis to the one being tested. However, these adaptations also provided protection from additional rival explanations. To show this, we need to examine some of the common ones from which we seek protection. Then we can illustrate how well these six designs eliminate alternative explanations or, in some cases, fail to do so.

Common Rival Explanations, and Threats to Validity

The term *rival explanation* also appears in the literature as *rival hypothesis,* as *alternative explanation* and, because it can affect internal and external validity, as ***threat to validity.*** All these terms refer to the same thing, a condition that is confounded with the effect being studied. **Confounding** occurs when two conditions (for instance, the treatment and a condition that could be a rival explanation) are present at the same time. Then we cannot tell which might have been the cause of whatever effect occurred—or whether both contributed. Unless we can rule out rivals by the design of the study, they present alternative explanations of the intended one and can threaten the internal validity (LP) and the external validity (GP) of the study.

Campbell and Stanley (1963) and later Cook and Campbell (1979) named and described a variety of common rival explanations to which Bracht and Glass's (1968) discussion of external validity added. Although studies often have additional rival explanations which must be ferreted out and considered, these authors have provided a very useful list. In the next section, we discuss these rival explanations and the means available for their control. *Beware not to take their names literally.* For instance, as the name implies, "maturation" includes changes in the individual between measurements due to growth; but it also includes any other charges over time such as becoming more tired, less motivated, or more test-wise. The original names have been kept because they are so referred to in the literature.

Threats to Internal Validity (LP), Common Rival Explanations

Sampling and Chance Error. Let's consider, first, the case study design in which Ms. Kimball applied a treatment to her class and then measured her students' achievement. She reports that their average score, "though still below what should be expected, is better than it might have been." We have to wonder whether there really was an effect. After all, merely taking different samples of subjects—sampling error—as well as measurement error would bounce the mean around. There could have been an upward bounce with no treatment effect—a reasonable rival explanation. By using inferential statistics, we determine whether this is a chance bounce or the difference between the class's level and the norms is statistically significant. The study must have been designed with sufficient statistical power (see p. 478), sometimes a problem with field experiments.

> ✦ *Sampling and chance error as a rival explanation can be made improbable by inferential statistics but the study must have been designed with adequate statistical power.*

Testing. Ms. Kimball improved her design by adding a pretest, a one-group pretest-posttest design. She shows a statistically significant gain. Now what? Maybe students did better on the second testing because they were more comfortable, knew what to expect, or had thought about and were more ready for the questions. Crane and Heim (1950) showed that students gained 3 to 5 IQ points solely as a result of retaking the test. Retests of personality measures typically increase apparent "adjustment" (Windle, 1954); sensitized subjects have increased awareness of socially approved answers.

The effect of retesting, called simply **testing,** is a reasonable rival explanation with a one-group, pre- and posttest design. To control it, we eliminate or spread the effect. We eliminate the pretest by using the posttest-only control group or the Solomon four-group, which includes posttest only groups. To spread the effect to a control group, we can use the nonequivalent control group or the pretest-posttest control group design in which both control and experimental groups are retested.

> ✦ *Testing, as a rival hypothesis, occurs whenever two or more testings occur with the same or closely related instruments, since the experience of having been tested earlier may affect later tests.*

Regression. Wherever you find a retest of a group originally split off as a high or low section of a parent group, suspect one of the most subtle rival hypotheses, **re-**

gression. Suppose Ms. Kimball had used the Stanford Achievement Test as a pretest to select the lowest quarter of the students for treatment with the new curriculum. This is group A, the group to the left of the cut score in Figure 20.1. When she retested them, *even if her treatment were totally ineffective,* she would have observed an improvement in scores due to the effect of regression! You may be able to recall studies where just this kind of claim occurred: a remedial group was retested and the treatment was proclaimed a success. Alternatively, an especially able group, group B in Figure 20.1, was selected for accelerated instruction. On retest, students in this group would be found to have gained little, *perhaps even to have lost.* Because of the effect of regression the treatment would be deemed ineffective, perhaps incorrectly.

Regression causes the mean of the split-off section to "regress," or move toward the mean of the parent group, on retest. As shown in Figure 20.2 for group A, it moves higher in low or remedial groups, showing an apparent gain. Any treatment effect looks better than it should because it is added to the regression effect. In high-scoring groups (typically accelerated or enriched groups), group B in the same figure, regression moves the mean lower, showing an apparent loss. Since, for high-scoring groups, regression and treatment effect typically work in opposite directions, the *apparent* treatment effect will be less than the *actual* effect—when regression exceeds treatment effect, subjects will appear to have lost after the pretest.

This kind of regression results from a less-than-perfect correlation between any two tests—in pretest-posttest designs, the unreliability of the test. Greater unreliability results in larger regression. Retesting with the same test involves stability reliability (see p. 438). Retesting with an alternative test form involves both instability and any lack of equivalence between forms.

How does unreliability cause regression? If not perfectly reliable, any individual's score will vary from testing to testing. Think of an individual as having a true score. Suppose you test her an infinite number of times with the same test, each time hypnotizing her and giving her the posthypnotic suggestion to forget having taken it earlier. Her scores would form a normal, bell-shaped curve with its mean

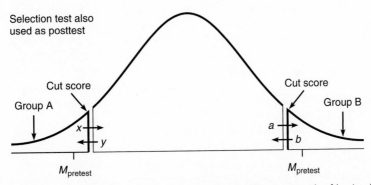

FIGURE 20.1 Groups A and B are subject to the regression effect as a result of having been separated from the whole group by means of a selection test later used to measure treatment effect.

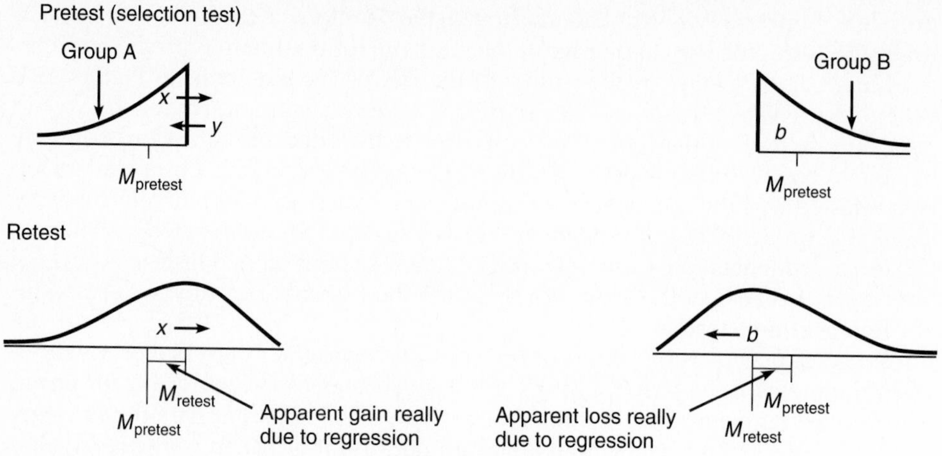

FIGURE 20.2 Regression effect in the selected groups at retest.

as her true score. At any testing, her score will be any one from this distribution. As a result of unreliability, like the spread of shots from an unreliable gun (Figure 18.1, p. 435), sometimes her score will be too high; at other times, too low.

Now, consider just the cases labeled *x* and *y* adjacent to the cut score for group A in the earlier figure (Figure 20.1). The position of the letters *x* and *y* indicates their scores on the pretest. But suppose *x*'s true score is above the cutoff; he is in the remedial group because of measurement error. On retest, his score is likely to be closer to his true score and be higher. The situation for *y* is just the opposite. With a true score below the cut score, on retest, her score is likely to become closer to her true score and therefore to be lower. The movement of scores from pretest to retest is indicated by the arrows. If the groups were not split apart, on retest these scores around the cut score would merely change places within the distribution, leaving the overall shape unchanged. However, when the big middle segment of the parent distribution is removed, *y* is no longer part of the remedial group. Thus, only the effect of *x* appears in the retest.

This effect is shown in Figure 20.2, where the distributions of scores for the tails alone are shown at retest. Concentrate on the lower tail. When the low group is separated from the rest, *x*'s retest score—being closer to its true score—moves above the cut score as shown by the arrow. As others—also misclassified—follow this pattern, their scores form the tail extending to the right above the cut score. Since there are no scores above the cut score to move down to maintain the balance—they were not assigned to either remediation or enrichment—the mean of group A moves higher on retest.

If you concentrate instead on the upper tail, the exact reverse process occurs. Persons with true scores lower than the cut score (they did not belong in the enrichment group) are trapped in the upper tail (like score *b*). When that group is removed for enrichment treatment and then retested, with no treatment effect and only regression operating, their scores move down. With no scores from the big middle not assigned to either remediation or enrichment to counterbalance, they form a tail to the left, downward, and the isolated segment's mean moves lower. A supposedly "enriching" treatment shows no gain (treatment and regression are equal), an underestimated gain (treatment is stronger), or even a loss (regression is stronger or there is no treatment effect).

Since retested control groups are also affected by regression, any mean treatment-control posttest difference in means indicates true treatment effect; control groups provide protection. An alternative control for regression retests the selected group before treatment and averages the two for a pretest score. Retesting provides a larger and thus more reliable sample of the subject's behavior—scores of individuals that are too high, drop, and ones that are too low, rise.

Another instance of regression results from instigating a remedial treatment when an effect is at its peak and would move toward the mean without intervention. For example, critiquing a study comparing the arrest records before and after treatment of 365 delinquents, McCleary, Gordon, McDowall, and Maltz and colleagues (1979) noted "in each case the time of intervention . . . [was] selected apparently, as a reaction to a particularly high rate of arrest" (p. 633). Put another way, the arrest rate for these delinquents was at a peak in comparison with both their own personal record of arrests and the pool in general. This example illustrates the difficulty of assessing a remedial program's effectiveness without a control group or preintervention trend measure. Remediation is unlikely to begin before the problem is sufficiently serious for ameliorating societal mechanisms to come into play.

- ✦ *Regression is a rival explanation wherever an extremely high or low group is selected for treatment (remediation, enrichment, or special treatment) when researchers use a pretest-posttest design with no control group.*
- ✦ *Regression may also be found where a remedial treatment is employed at the height of a problem that in time would subside without treatment.*
- ✦ *Since a control group will also be affected by regression, comparison of control and experimental means controls for this problem.*

Local History. It is possible Ms. Kimball's Stanford Achievement Test scores are higher because many of her students were watching a television program that, to illustrate the power of mathematics to the layperson, happened to be giving practice on the kinds of problems the test emphasized. Such alternative events that could have caused the target effect are called **local history** or just history. If there is a comparable control group, we have reason to believe those children will also watch the television program and so also gain on the posttest. Thus, a comparable control group protects against local history.

- ✦ *Local history is a threat to validity whenever events occur before the posttest that might also cause the effect. A control group that is also subject to those events is an effective control for this problem.*

Mortality. Mortality, introduced in the discussion of qualitative research p. 317), would be a rival hypothesis if Ms. Kimball's lowest-achieving students were absent when the posttest was given—not unlikely, such students often have the poorest attendance records. Such selective dropout from the effect measure would have raised the average considerably and is always suggestive of the rival hypothesis of mortality. As before, a comparable control group would be affected by absenteeism and protect against mortality. However, as here, if those remaining in the control and experimental groups after dropout differ in relevant characteristics from the target group to which we hope to generalize, external validity (GP) may be diminished.

> ✦ *Mortality is a rival explanation wherever individuals leave an experimental group prior to completion of the study. The danger is that the composition of the group is changed by the loss. Consequently, the measure of effect may differ because of this change. A control group with loss of individuals comparable to those in the treated group in both proportion and nature protects against this problem for internal but not external validity.*

Maturation. **Maturation** includes "all those biological and psychological processes which systematically vary with the passage of time independent of specific external events" (Campbell and Stanley, 1963, pp. 177–178). Thus, between observations, students might have grown older, more tired, bored, capable of more mature reasoning, or more serious about getting an education, as well as biologically and socially more advanced. Because Ms. Kimball's treatment lasted only four months, biological growth is an unlikely factor. Nor would such factors as growing bored or tired have persisted over four months. Thus, maturation seems an unlikely alternative in our particular example. However, in a longitudinal study lasting several years or a two-hour study in which prekindergarten children were expected to sit quietly, maturation might well be an issue. Once again, a control group would presumably be affected by maturation in the same way as the experimental group is affected and so would protect against it.

> ✦ *Maturation is a rival hypothesis whenever there is growth or change in the individuals that would affect the measured effect. The term applies not only to natural growth patterns but also to changes such as growing bored, tired, hungry, or other characteristics that might change with the passage of time. A control group provides protection.*

Instrument Decay. As also described in the discussion of qualitative research (pp. 317–318), instrument decay refers to changes in the measurement or observation process in ways that might account for the observed effect. This problem is especially likely if the instrument is relatively unstructured and is a high-inference measure. In qualitative research, where the observer is the instrument, the observer is less attuned to notice the unusual, has more realistic expectations, and becomes more sympathetic with unusual behavior seen as a rational response, as the setting grows more familiar. Similarly, teachers' expectations are highest and marks lowest for the first essay examination papers they read, and become more realistic for later ones.

CHAPTER 20: Experimental Methods and Experimental Design

Instrument decay is understandably rare with multiple-choice tests and less likely with tightly structured observation devices in which coding is clear and unambiguous. Even with the latter, however, observers may become more skilled in using it, create different rules for new situations, or change rules to make observation easier. Interviewers may become more comfortable with an interview schedule or more skilled in eliciting responses. Any of these and similar instances can account for an effect. Therefore, train observers in the use of high-inference instruments or use low-inference measures to reduce or eliminate instrument decay. Throughout the study, compare observers on training videotapes to ensure their continued calibration. Share experiences on new problems so that agreed-upon procedures are used by all.

Another source of instrument decay involves changing the scale between pre- and posttest due to ceiling or floor effects. A measure which spreads the group across the scale at pretest, because of growth, may be too easy on posttest. Grades are limited by the top score and the mean is lower than it should be—a ceiling effect. Too difficult a measure, for example, at pretest, creates a pileup at the opposite end—a floor effect. Frequency distributions reveal both as scores pile up against "floor" or "ceiling." Avoid this problem by using instruments that differentiate across the entire range. A control group measured or observed in comparable ways and at comparable times provides a basis for sensing change and strengthening internal validity (LP). Nevertheless, you can only accurately estimate the size of the change after eliminating the floor or ceiling effect.

> ✦ Instrument decay refers to changes in the way an instrument is used during the study, as in reinterpreting the meaning of categories of an observation instrument or moderating the strictness of grading on an essay test. Decay may occur from different usage over time or from differences in usage between observers.
> ✦ Ceiling and floor effects occur when tests are, respectively, too easy or too difficult and result in group means that are too low or too high in comparison with appropriate measures.

Selection. **Selection** occurs when a factor that determines group membership also affects the outcome of treatment. When unrecognized, it can lead to wrong conclusions. For example, judging from the bottles washed up on a beach, we would conclude that all bottles are discarded in the ocean with their caps on. Of course, we see only the survivors; the others sank. Similarly, some of the groups we study—seniors in high school, college, and graduate students—are survivors.

Commonly, we use groups formed by a regularly occurring process such as subjects' availability in a certain time block, subjects' choice, or an institutional scheduling procedure. But unrecognized selection factors are often at work—especially when student choice is involved. A student's interest in a subject, a group of friends, or an easy-grading teacher may be the selective factor and thus a rival explanation for an effect. The use of preformed instead of randomly sampled and assigned groups is always open to suspicion.

A common example of selection is the use of volunteers to constitute the experimental group, and nonvolunteers the control group. From Rosenthal and

Rosnow's (1975) review of the literature, we know, in contrast to nonvolunteers, volunteers have many positive characteristics. They are more intelligent, better educated, higher in social status, more sociable, higher in need for social approval, more likely to be female (except for physically demanding or stressful situations, where males are more likely to volunteer), more likely to be interested in arousal-seeking situations, and to be somewhat unconventional. Volunteers tend to be less authoritarian, and are more likely to be Jewish than Protestant and Protestant than Catholic.[10]

Is it any wonder studies using volunteer experimental and nonvolunteer control groups are suspect? This range of characteristics is so broad as to affect all but a few studies. Establishment of a control group similarly affected by selection strengthens internal validity (LP), but external validity (GP) is impaired since we can only generalize to those similarly selected.

> ✦ *Selection is a rival explanation when choice of subjects includes a selective factor that affects the measure of treatment outcome. A common example is the use of volunteers for the experimental group but nonvolunteers for the control. Volunteers differ from nonvolunteers on a wide variety of characteristics.*
> ✦ *Random assignment to groups usually avoids the selection effect.*

Base Rate Problems. When we attribute the frequency of an effect to a presumed cause which does not take into account the frequency of that cause (its **base rate**), the base rate may be a serious rival explanation. Changing frequencies to a percentage by dividing the frequency of the effect by the frequency of the cause avoids this problem. Here is an example: Baron and Ransberger (1978) examining 102 major riots in the United States between 1967 and 1971, found a curvilinear relationship between the number of riots and the day's average temperature. This finding contrasted with conventional wisdom that riots are sparked by very hot weather. Carlsmith, Merrill, and Anderson (1979) believed that base rate explained this finding—the number of very hot days that would have provided riot conditions were relatively few. When they adjusted for temperature base rate by dividing the number of riots at a given mean temperature, for example 90°, by the number of days that temperature was the mean temperature, this percentage increased linearly with mean temperature. The probability of a riot did increase with hot weather.

Treatment Interactions. **Interaction** effects occur when the treatment effect is inappropriately strengthened or weakened by a characteristic of another treatment, the situation, or the individuals in it. In **instrument decay by treatment interaction,** an observer reacting to a treatment issues harsher or more lenient judgments than otherwise. For instance, an observer, studying democratic and authoritarian-

---

[10]This listing includes only findings Rosenthal and Rosnow (1975) believed were supported by enough research to merit considerable confidence. They list other differences, with less evidence, that could be important under particular circumstances.

led groups and pleased by the democratic group's collaboration, focuses on its positive attributes. Conversely, reacting to the stifling authoritarian milieu, he is especially sensitive to negative aspects. Clearly, this bias makes democracy look better, authoritarianism worse, and their difference greater than appropriate. A structured instrument combined with training might be the best antidote.

Another example, **selection-maturation interaction,** occurs when a selection factor causes the effect by creating groups with widely differing maturation levels. Suppose, because of a scheduling conflict, an unusually high proportion of senior students enrolled in an experimental physical education section, a situation that naturally depleted such students from the section used as the control. Seniors might differ sufficiently in skills and motivation from freshmen to create a between-groups difference that could inappropriately be interpreted as due solely to the experimental curriculum. As before, random assignment to control and experimental groups can control for this.

♦ *Interaction effects can make a treatment appear more or less effective than it should. Examples are instrument decay by treatment interaction and selection-maturation interaction.*

Threats to External Validity (GP), Common Restrictive Explanations (Conditions)

Rival explanations do not affect internal validity (LP) alone (a few, such as selection, can affect both), but some also strongly affect external validity (GP). They are restrictive conditions limiting generality to situations and conditions similar to those of the study. All six facets of design can be subject to restrictive conditions on generality:

- *Subjects:* An unusually intelligent sample volunteered.
- *Situation:* Treatment and data collection took place in a laboratory.
- *Treatment:* Experimenters administering the treatment received expensive training for a year.
- *Observation or measure:* The operational definition of creativity consisted solely of written verbal responses, a limited measure of creativity.
- *Basis for sensing characteristics or changes:* The control group considered itself in competition with the experimental group.
- *Procedure:* A pretest sensitized the experimental group to essential aspects of the treatment; pretesting is not a normal part of treatment.

Bracht and Glass (1968), discussing external validity, categorized studies allowing generalization to target subjects as having *population validity,* and those to target situations as showing *ecological validity.* The following describes selected common restrictive conditions.

Obtrusiveness and Reactivity. The term **reactivity** covers effects resulting when procedures are sufficiently obtrusive that individuals realize they are the subjects of study. Such **obtrusiveness** can cause a variety of effects:

- "I'm special!" or the **Hawthorne effect** was named after an experiment at the Hawthorne plant of the Western Electric Company by Roethlisberger and Dickson (1939). Intended to show that improvement of a department's working conditions resulted in increased production, the study found that production also increased following negative changes such as reduced lighting. They concluded that the real cause was the effect of giving special attention.[11]

- "What does she expect from me? I'd like to please her!" **Hypothesis guessing** by subjects is common. Reacting to what is perceived as wanted, subjects seek to facilitate the effect to get researchers to think well of them. Especially where a status difference exists, a researcher who might somehow later be of help finds eager-to-please behavior—for example, instructors using their advisees as subjects. Correct guesses enhance treatment effect. Such expectancies are part of a study's demand characteristics (more on that topic later in the chapter).

- "I don't want to be a guinea pig!" In that case, the treatment is perceived to be aversive or dangerous or the research site is too frequently used (for example, laboratory schools). May reduce or sabotage treatment effect.

- "I want my child to get that special treatment!" Placating administrators provide compensatory treatment to the control, decreasing apparent treatment effectiveness.

- "I don't want my group disadvantaged because the flip of a coin made it the control group!" "Compensatory rivalry" results when conscientious teachers work hard to offset experimental benefit. Also called the "John Henry effect," after the legendary railroad worker who pitted his skill against a steam railroad spike driver, it decreases apparent treatment effect (for example, see Zdep and Irvine, 1970).

- "That's new and interesting: I like it!"—the novelty effect. Extra work required by a new curriculum is met with enthusiasm the first time, maybe even the second, but the gusto wears off, and treatment effectiveness decreases.

- "We can't compete with that special help! Why try? Let's quit." Demoralization and feelings of dismay may lower the effect measure in the comparison group, making the treatment look better.

- "Have you heard about the easy new way we are learning long division?" **Diffusion,** where a treatment is communicated (for example, during recess) may occur without reactivity, but is more likely under nonroutine conditions. It decreases the apparent treatment effect.

---

[11]Adair, Sharpe, and Huynh (1989) examined the 86 studies they believe are the body of Hawthorne effect studies involving use of control groups. They classified control treatments as alternate activity, special attention, or awareness of being studied. Attention had the largest effect but was not statistically significant. Since 86 studies did not find it, they concluded that Hawthorne effect, as currently operationally defined, is too small to be of significance. On the other hand, Hawthorne effect is not so dissimilar from placebo effect, which has been confirmed as real even to the point of being able to show physiological changes (see p. 541). The difference may be that the nature of expected effect is usually clear with placebo but often considerably less so with Hawthorne.

- "I'm especially pleased he's studying me." In one-to-one situations, a close emotional bond may develop between the subject and investigator. If the treatment is always so administered, reactivity is part of treatment. But findings clearly may not generalize to larger group situations.

Obviously, the best way to reduce reactivity is through **unobtrusiveness**—unless the treatment itself is too novel, have the regular program staff (for example, the teacher) simply routinely work measures and treatment into the day's ordinary activities. You can try presenting novel treatments simply as program improvements, noting but not stressing beneficial aspects. As with qualitative methods, concealed observations (or unconcealed after accommodation) reduce or eliminate obtrusiveness. Two-way mirrors fool few subjects but are usually forgotten, especially with the realization they are not always in use. Webb and colleagues (1981) provide a very useful treatment of unobtrusive measurement and offer suggestions. If other steps fail, obtrusive treatment of control groups spreads its effect to both groups.

✦ *The reactions to the special circumstances of being observed or part of a research study are termed reactivity. Obtrusive study procedures increase it, whereas unobtrusive methods of treatment, observation, or measurement reduce it. Obtrusively treated control groups provide a measure of its impact.*

Researcher Expectancy Effects. "Did the mouse find the target? Since he stuck his nose in the box, I'll count it." Especially if "success" is open to interpretation, researchers are more likely to perceive events in the desired direction. Also called the Pygmalion effect, after George Bernard Shaw's play, Rosenthal (1969, 1976) named it the **researcher expectancy effect.** Researchers may inadvertently tip the scales in a variety of ways—verbally (for example, with encouragement and clues) and nonverbally (smiling for right answers or frowning for wrong ones).

Rosenthal and Rubin (1980) examined 345 interpersonal expectancy effects studies—for example, experimenters with "especially able" mice, teachers with "unusually capable" children. Though randomly chosen, mice and children showed expectancy effects. Only 2 of 9 reaction time studies showed these effects, but 11 of 15 animal studies did so.

Unintended expectancy effect may be as large as the many intended treatment effects. It is controlled by using **double-blind procedures**—neither researchers nor subjects can distinguish the groups. No one involved with treatment administration (administrators or recipients) nor anyone observing effects can tell which is the control group and which the experimental group. All subjects believe they may be receiving treatment (or no one believes they are)—they are kept "blind." The control treatment is often called a placebo or placebo treatment. Subjects or groups are coded so that an uninvolved party can tell them apart.

Double-blind procedures *cannot* be used in certain circumstances:

- When knowing you are being treated is part of the treatment itself.

- When it is obvious which treatment is to be favored from merely observing the treatment or being exposed to it.
- If the treatment can readily be identified from side effects.
- If withholding a more favorable treatment would have ethical consequences.
- If the effectiveness of treatment is reduced by the elimination of clues that would reveal which treatment is experimental. Sacrificing therapeutic knowledge to methodological precision can demoralize both professionals and subjects.

To eliminate the expectancy effect, unless treatment and side effects are obvious, use independent judges who, kept "blind," are called in only to assess results. All others can be fully aware (Guy, Gross, and Dennis, 1967).

Even after every effort, were those who administer the treatment or evaluate its effects really blind? Did shrewd guesses defeat these efforts? With multiple judges, this is an empirical question. Ask them to identify the experimental treatment or subjects and compare their guesses with chance. If you get a statistically significant result, expectancy effect may have affected the results so you must interpret the data conservatively (Kazdin, 1980).

- ✦ *Researcher expectancy effects may appear when those responsible for giving the treatment or assessing its effects can identify the experimental treatment, experimental subjects, or intended effect.*
- ✦ *Unintended expectancy effects can be as large or larger than some intended experimental effects.*
- ✦ *Keeping observers, measurers, treatment administrators, and subjects blind to which groups are experimental and the nature of the treatment (or having independent evaluators who are) may eliminate these effects.*
- ✦ *Whether such efforts are successful is an empirical question which should be checked where feasible.*

Various Treatment Interaction Effects. The effect of prior treatment(s) may affect later ones to intensify or weaken them. Such **multiple-treatment interaction** makes generalization to a treatment administered on its own, difficult. For instance, halfway through the school year, having found the University of Chicago program only moderately successful, Ms. Kimball switches to a new curriculum by the Southwest Educational Laboratory and finds it more effective. Because of possible multiple-treatment interaction, however, these findings are limited to situations where the Southwest follows the Chicago curriculum, a restrictive condition on external validity (GP). She realizes this limitation when, beginning with Southwest alone the next fall, it is no more effective than the Chicago program. Prior learning from the Chicago program increased the effectiveness of the Southwest curriculum.

To estimate this effect, establish as many groups as there are treatments, and rotate each treatment into the first position.[12] You can find any sequencing effect

---

[12]If you are interested in any possible interaction among multiple treatments, use as many groups as there are possible treatment arrangements.

on the treatment's singular effectiveness by comparison with the sample in which it was given first. Called counterbalancing, these are **counterbalanced designs.**

Testing-treatment interaction occurs when a pretest sensitizes individuals to parts of the treatment similar to pretest problems, perhaps motivating them to better learn these parts. Such pretests are likely to increase treatment effectiveness.[13] Research findings apply only to treatment with a pretest, a restrictive condition on generality. Testing-treatment interaction may be present in any pretest-posttest design but is eliminated by the posttest-only design and the Solomon four-group design. The latter provides an estimate of its size.

Selection by treatment interaction occurs when people attracted to or with a special need for treatment (especially therapeutic ones) seek entrance, and are accepted into the experimental group. Conversely, individuals may avoid an aversive treatment. In either case, the true effect of the treatment is masked.

In another scenario, when you seek institutions for study, all but a few may turn you down because of treatment characteristics—it disrupts the schedule, is not compatible with their orientation, and so on. Are those that welcome you representative? Not likely. Compare them to individual volunteers. Creating both treatment and control groups from volunteers, the usual remedy, strengthens internal validity (LP) but weakens external validity (GP).

Mortality by treatment interaction would have taken place in Ms. Kimball's class if children had high absenteeism because they disliked the curriculum—the interaction between treatment and the absent subjects. This may artificially raise average score. Though difficult, obtaining data from all the initial group membership provides evidence with more generality.

♦ *Multiple-treatment interaction occurs when the residual effects of one treatment influence a later one such that its apparent effect is different from the one without the residual influence. Putting the treatment into first position provides an estimate of its effectiveness alone.*

♦ *Testing-treatment interaction occurs when the treatment effect is strengthened or weakened as a result of pretesting.*

♦ *Selection by treatment interaction may be present when the treatment affects those who are selected (or are self-selected) for the experimental or control group or both.*

♦ *Mortality by treatment interaction occurs when individuals selectively drop out of the treated group in reaction to the treatment.*

The Demand Characteristics of a Study. Any study may have rival explanations stemming from what psychologists call the study's **demand characteristics.** The researcher expectancy effect and many of the obtrusiveness problems described as restrictive conditions for external validity (GP) are all part of the demand con-

---

[13]Hovland, Lumsdaine, and Sheffield (1949) found interaction, but it was negative; their movies were *less* effective changers of attitude when used with a pretest. So beware, pretests don't always make treatment more effective.

ditions. What subjects perceive the study demands of them may not be what the researcher intended. Determining these perceptions can be important to interpreting findings accurately.

A personal example occurred in a study of two versions of a programmed text. The text consisted of questions students were to answer and then the explanation of the text's answer. Students were randomly assigned to a text in which, as usual, successive questions followed logically, or a text in which questions were randomly scrambled but always keeping question and answer together. Surprisingly, performance on the randomly scrambled material was found *not* to be significantly degraded (Krathwohl, Gordon, and Payne, 1967).

Why did scrambling not have the expected effect? Adding qualitative data to a primarily quantitative study, we found from interviews that the study's demand conditions were not what we intended—students had inadvertently interpreted the scrambled material as a challenging puzzle. Individuals were forced to be active learners—not just reading and passively answering. Students rehearsed parts to remember them as they were fitted together; they analyzed and organized questions to place them in proper sequence. All this facilitated learning. Such explanations become so obvious once discovered that researchers tend to believe they should have been anticipated during the study's design! Of course, hindsight is 20/20, whereas research design never is!

Postexperimental debriefings, stimulated recall techniques (playing back a video or audio recording of the subject's interaction with treatment), or think-aloud procedures can help determine the actual versus the intended demand conditions.

✦ *The demand characteristics of a study are determined by how the subjects perceive the study. This perception may or may not be what the researcher intended, but it can seriously affect results.*

A Summary of Protection Offered by Six Simple Designs

Table 20.1 summarizes the protection potentially offered by the six designs with which this discussion started. Keep in mind that this table cannot be taken too literally. Analyze your situation to make sure the design will work as portrayed. The table compares across various designs the potential for protection (+) or lack of it (–). Question marks indicate that protection may or may not exist depending on the particular circumstances. In the various designs using both pre- and posttest, you can see how the combination of random assignment in addition to a control group confers a great deal of protection. By removing the pretest in whole or in part, the Solomon four-group design and the posttest-only design go one step further since the minus is removed for testing-treatment interaction. In that respect they are very strong designs. However, it may not be feasible to randomly assign, or to find enough subjects for the four groups required by the Solomon design.

TABLE 20.1 *Potential for Protection Against Common Rival Explanations That Is Offered by Six Basic Designs*

Design	History	Maturation	Testing	Instrumentation	Regression	Selection	Mortality	Interaction of Selection and Maturation, etc.	Interaction of Testing and Treatment	Interaction of Selection and Treatment
1. X O	–	–				–	–	–	–	–
2. O X O	–	–	–	–	?	+	+	–	–	?
3. O X O / O C O	+	+	+	+	?	+	+	–	–	?
4. R [O X O / O C O]	+	+	+	+	+	+	+	+	–	?
5. R [X O / C O]	+	+	+	+	+	+	+	+	+	?
6. O X O / R [O C O / X O] / C O	+	+	+	+	+	+	+	+	+	?

NOTE: As explained in the text, the pluses and minuses depend on the study's circumstances and should not be taken too literally.

Source: Adapted from D. T. Campbell and J. C. Stanley, *Experimental and Quasi-experimental Designs for Research*, p. 178. Copyright © 1963 Houghton Mifflin Co.

A Summary of Common Control Problems and Their Elimination

Table 20.2 is an alphabetical summary of common rival explanations affecting internal validity (LP) and external validity (GP) and their methods of control. The column "methods of control" applies the three main control methods (eliminate, measure and adjust, and spread the effect) wherever feasible. The last column describes what is gained or lost by controlling and notes any trade-offs. Chapter 24 further discusses the trade-off problem.

Unique Rival Explanations

Besides the standard rival explanations for studies, alternatives may exist that are unique to the particular study, its setting, or its procedure. For example, Zeigarnik (1927; see also Denmark, 1984) argued that unreleased tension has an effect on memory. She proceeded to illustrate this hypothesis by giving subjects a series of common tasks (such as winding thread), a randomly selected half of which were interrupted when the subjects were thoroughly engaged. The other tasks were completed without interruption. Zeigarnik then asked subjects to recall all the tasks. She found that the interrupted tasks were better remembered.

Critics argued, however, that the impact of being interrupted was what caused the increased memory. To answer this rival explanation, she then arranged that all the tasks were interrupted with a new set of subjects, half of them were then allowed to complete their tasks. Again, the uncompleted tasks were better remembered.

But maybe these tasks were better remembered because they were to be completed later? Thus, Zeigarnik did two more studies with instructions that indicated either the task would be completed later or it would not be worked on anymore. Again, interrupted tasks were better remembered. This cascade of studies to answer new objections not only nicely illustrates the process of science at work but also how alternatives unique to a study arise.

Should the researcher have anticipated these alternatives and designed protections into the original study? The better such predictions, the shorter the route to building a consensus around the interpretation of the data and acceptance as a contribution to knowledge. Sometimes, however, a common rival explanation occurs outside the context in which we have been trained to look for it. Mark (1990) noted such an instance that escaped the careful monitoring of two of the most significant contributors to the literature of social science experimental design. Both were dissertation committee members of Seaver's (1971) ingenious "natural experiment," a study of teacher expectancies. All prior studies had been of artificially manipulated circumstances.

Seaver observed that elder siblings created expectancies in teachers for their younger brothers and sisters. He hypothesized that, depending on whether the elder one had done well or poorly, the siblings would, on the average, achieve more in a like direction than if they had been assigned to a different teacher. The results confirmed the hypothesis. Considerably later, Reichardt (1985) noted that these results might have been due to the students' having been assigned to good or poor teachers. Any two siblings who had the same *good* teacher did well, but the

TABLE 20.2 Summary of Rival Explanations and Their Control

Alternative Explanation, Rival Hypothesis, Threat to Validity[a]	Method of Control	How to Control or Estimate	Gains or Losses (Trade-offs) Resulting from Control
Base rate problems	Measure and adjust.	Determine whether opportunities for the phenomenon to occur were constant or varied in relation to your hypothesis; if the latter, adjust for variation by converting to percentages.	Measuring the base rate determines the extent to which the effect is influenced by changes in the base rate in contrast to the treatment or independent variable.
Demand characteristics	Measure and adjust or redesign study.	Use stimulated recall, think-aloud procedures, or interviews to obtain representative subjects' perceptions of the study as it proceeds.	Obtaining subjects' perceptions determines whether design worked as intended; think-aloud procedures may change the way subjects approach what is asked; recall may not be accurate or may be modified to please the researcher.
Instrument decay	Eliminate.	Train carefully in the use of instruments; use calibration checks during study; use double-blind conditions; hold regular conferences with observers to resolve use and interpretation problems.	Training is expensive; researcher needs a pilot study to tell how much training is sufficient; determining the success of training requires checks on observer reliability.
Local history	Eliminate.	Discard affected cases, such as those interrupted by a fire drill.	Discarding cases decreases power by reducing sample size; researcher may not know all persons exposed. Exposure may have been selective. Replicating the study to recover lost cases is expensive; data may be impossible to reproduce; trades more internal validity (LP) for less external validity (GP).
	Equalize across groups.	Be sure the control group is as likely to be exposed to the same events as the experimental is; keep in as close proximity as possible.[b]	Proximity may result in increased chance of rivalry, other reactivity, and diffusion.

[a] Arranged alphabetically.

[b] Local history is one of the most difficult problems to control because it is impossible to predict what to expect when, or how serious it will be. Keeping close to the groups so that you will know when something untoward occurs is the main line of defense.

Alternative Explanation, Rival Hypothesis, Threat to Validity	Method of Control	How to Control or Estimate	Gains or Losses (Trade-offs) Resulting from Control
Maturation	Measure and adjust.	Use norms to determine growth of comparable groups or measure trend prior to treatment and extrapolate to posttreatment expectation.	Norms on comparable group may not be available; nonlinear growth is hard to extrapolate; growth could be linear prior to treatment and nonlinear after.
	Equalize across groups.	Use randomly assigned and blocked, or matched groups.	Blocking and matching decrease variability and thus increase the sensitivity of the study (unless variable used to stratify is unrelated to cause or effect–then, only loss is the labor of blocking).
Mortality	Eliminate.	Provide incentive for completion of study.	Incentives are likely to be obtrusive; reward becomes part of the treatment; trades more internal validity (LP) for less external validity (GP).
	Measure and adjust.	Discern the kinds of individuals who dropped out and remove equivalent individuals from the other groups.	Loss of cases reduces the statistical power and generality of the study; trades more internal validity (LP) for less external validity (GP).
	Equalize across groups.	Assign to groups randomly and make placebo treatment of the control group as similar to the experimental treatment as possible.	Mortality by treatment interaction may occur if the "effective ingredient" is too unpleasant or difficult; then it trades more internal validity (LP) for less external validity (GP).
Multiple-treatment interaction	Eliminate.	Use a separate group for each treatment.	Separate groups eliminate interaction but require more groups with treatment and measurement for each.
	Equalize.	Assuming interaction is equal among treatments, divide into subgroups—each receiving one of the possible orderings of treatments—and combine data.	Such studies are usually done on one or a few subjects because of the scarcity of such persons or the cost of treatment; trades more internal validity (LP) for less external validity (GP).

TABLE 20.2 *(continued)*

Alternative Explanation, Rival Hypothesis, Threat to Validity	Method of Control	How to Control or Estimate	Gains or Losses (Trade-offs) Resulting from Control
Reactivity	Eliminate.	Use low-obtrusiveness conditions for treatment and measurement or observation; isolate groups from one another.	Groups and situations may not be comparable; local history may cause variation in effects.
	Equalize across groups.	Apply placebo treatment with equal obtrusiveness to a control group.	Obtrusiveness may interact with treatment, potentiating or weakening it over normal use; trades more internal validity (LP) for less external validity (GP).
Regression	Reduce regression effect.	Use the most reliable measure possible; double-test individuals.	Reliable measures and double testing do not correct for the type of regression that occurs when corrective measures are instigated at the peak of a problem that would subside without remediation.
	Equalize across groups.	Use randomly assigned experimental and control groups.	Control group measures gain due to regression.
Researcher expectancy	Eliminate.	Use double-blind procedures—neither treatment nor test administrators, observers nor subjects know which is experimental group.	If clinical knowledge is required of the treatment administrators, observers must be blind, but the rest need not be.
Selection	Eliminate.	Use random assignment with matching and blocking on all relevant variables.	Procedures for special assignment to group may result in obtrusiveness and its effects; may trade more internal validity (LP) for less external validity (GP).
	Measure and adjust.	Use analysis of covariance, partial correlation, or build in as an independent variable.	Elimination may be incomplete, depending on the validity and reliability of the measure.
Testing	Eliminate.	Use posttest only.	Posttest only eliminates testing-treatment interaction; reduces testing cost, and necessitates only one form, but researchers may not be sure the groups were initially equivalent.

T A B L E 2 0 . 2 *(continued)*

Alternative Explanation, Rival Hypothesis, Threat to Validity	Method of Control	How to Control or Estimate	Gains or Losses (Trade-offs) Resulting from Control
	Reduce testing effect.	Use different forms of test or different tests at pretest and posttest.	The more alike the forms are, the greater the comparability of pretest and posttest but the greater the likelihood of a residual testing effect. The latter is reduced with the use of different tests, but so is the comparability of pretest and posttest, a trade-off.
		Use a different group for each testing; use the Solomon four-group design.	Use of extra groups, such as the Solomon design, requires a much larger sample, and groups may not be comparable. It increases the cost of testing but controls for testing-treatment interaction.
	Equalize across groups.	Use the same pattern of observation or testing with experimental and control groups.	Testing by treatment interaction not eliminated; thus trades more internal validity (LP) for less external validity (GP).

younger sibling assigned to a different teacher had a *closer-to-average* teacher and did more poorly, a regression toward the teacher mean. Similarly, any two siblings assigned to a poor teacher did poorly, but the younger sibling assigned to a different teacher also had one closer to the average, in this instance a better one, and thus did better. The usual clues to regression—extreme groups, retesting, and remediation or enrichment groups—are missing. While we may take comfort in the fact that acknowledged experts missed these rival explanations, it is at the same time discomforting to note how subtle these effects can be.

Special Internal Validity (LP) Problems in Field Experiments. Boruch and Gomez (1977) argue the statistical sensitivity adequate to show a treatment effective in a carefully controlled setting may lead us to underestimate the statistical power required of field experiments. For example, adaptation to different conditions may lower treatment fidelity: "Simple indifference among field staff may reduce the treatment's fidelity to 75% of its design value, and natural random variation in staff delivery and in student receipt will reduce the uniformity of treatment as well" (Boruch and Gomez, 1987, p. 412). Boruch and Gomez further note that these effects are multiplicative not just additive, and thus more severely degrade the study.

Standard measures, used so that the results can be easily understood, may poorly match treatment goals. Measures determining success or failure in a policy decision are often corrupted. For example, although a test merely samples a domain to be mastered, teachers "teach to the test"—overly emphasize the tested knowledge and skills at the expense of the untested. In another instance of corrupted measures, Bogdan (1976) found that students were promptly reclassified as special education students when the U.S. Congress decreed that the percentage of special education students in Head Start classes should match the percentage of such persons in the general population. Researchers doing policy studies need to be especially alert to such problems.

Additional Designs

The Nonequivalent Control Group Design

Because of its prevalence, and the fact that we must often use intact groups, the nonequivalent control group design (O X O/O C O, see p. 510) deserves further attention. Much has been written about it, especially by Cook and Campbell (1979), who discuss a number of variations. Bracht and Glass (1968) noted that this design is most interpretable when the experimental group begins below the control and their positions are reversed at posttest (Figure 20.3). Cook and Campbell (1979) point out that such results rule out several rival explanations. An initially lower treatment group might draw even with the control because of a ceiling effect, but it would not draw ahead. The initially lower-scoring group might be expected to regress upward toward the group mean, but it would not overtake it.

The temptation is to assign the lower group at pretest to the experimental treatment and hope it overtakes the control. Cook and Campbell (1979) warn, as possibly indicated by its lower start, that its growth rate may be lower than that of

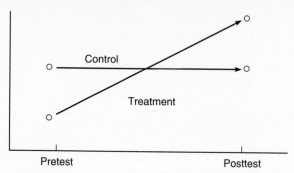

FIGURE 20.3 Outcome of the nonequivalent control group design when the treatment group overtakes the control group.

the control's. If it is, the lines may not cross or, even if they do, they will underestimate the effect, possibly showing no statistically significant difference. We cannot tell whether there was no treatment effect, or an unsensed change due to slow growth rate.

✦ *The nonequivalent control group design is in common use because researchers must often work with preformed groups. The design is interpretable if the experimental group begins below the control group and then overtakes it. Deliberately designing a study in this way, however, may underestimate the effect.*

Time-Series Designs

Time-series designs (O O O X O O O) are especially useful for studies of single subjects, but they can be employed with groups. Longitudinal studies are time-series designs, some with a manipulated treatment, some merely allowing nature to take its course. First, an individual is sufficiently observed that a **baseline** is established (O O O to indicate baseline establishment in the notation of this chapter, but A in time series notation), then a treatment or new variable is introduced (X in this chapter's notation, B in time series) and finally a new baseline is found (A); hence, they are often designated as **ABA designs.**

The protections offered are summarized in Table 20.3. Local history would not be measured without a control group, though single subjects might be questioned if it is suspected. Maturation is automatically built into repeated observations. Testing effect wears off with repeated measurements, as does regression. Testing-treatment interaction and researcher expectancy effect can be a problem. If "blind" conditions can be established for either subjects or researcher, researcher expectancy can be reduced, or, under double-blind conditions, eliminated. Protection from instrument decay would require continued calibration of instruments or observers. Depending on the subject's needs and the procedure's obtrusiveness, there might or might not be selection by treatment interaction (a person who sought treatment) and reactivity. From the foregoing, we can see how

TABLE 20.3 *Potential for Protection Against Common Rival Explanations That Is Offered by Three Additional Designs*

Design	History	Maturation	Testing	Instrumentation	Regression	Selection	Mortality	Interaction of Selection and Maturation	Interaction of Testing and Treatment	Interaction of Selection and Treatment
OOOXOOO	-	+	+	?	+	+	+	+	-	?
OOX₁OOC...	+	+	+	+	+	+	+	+	-	?
R O (X) / X C R O C / C O	+	+	+	+	+	+	+	-	+	+

Source: Adapted from D. T. Campbell and J. C. Stanley, *Experimental and Quasi-experimental Designs for Research*, p. 178. Copyright © 1963 Houghton Mifflin Co.

the circumstances of a particular study modify the protection pluses and minuses of Tables 20.1 and 20.3.

The multiple measurements to establish baseline also sense any trend, whether linear or curvilinear. Extrapolating it provides a prediction of the post baseline without treatment, deviations from which we assume to have resulted from treatment. This variation of the time-series design, called a regression discontinuity design, is discussed extensively in Cook and Campbell (1979).

A much stronger design repeats the treatment as in ABABA, or even ABABABABA. Replication in the effect of a pattern of treatments each of which is successively different from the previous, possibly one or more being control or placebo treatments (e.g., $O\,O\,X_1\,O\,O\,C\,O\,O\,X_2\,O\,O\,X_3\,O$ .... line 2 Figure 20.3), is strong evidence of causation. Only a recurring local history event would be a problem and its timing would have to match that of the treatment's. Unless treatment was repeated unobtrusively, reactivity might be present. Further, if the real treatment is distinguishable from the control treatment, researcher or subject expectancy may be a problem. Depending on the persistence of the effect of treatment, there may be multiple-treatment interaction. Given a nonpersistent effect and unobtrusive and double-blind treatments, adding a control group would provide about as strong evidence of causation as can be obtained.

✦ *Time-series designs provide good control for a number of the common rival explanations and gain especially strong internal validity (LP) with a patterning of the treatment which is reflected in the effect.*

A Patched-up Design

A patched-up design solves particular problems of control with peculiar patterns of groups or of testing. As Campbell and Stanley (1963) note, this approach should be typical of the spirit in which designs are developed. For example, when observation of a group is easier to arrange than its treatment, the simulated before-and-after design (Jahoda, Deutsch, and Cook, 1951) shown below overcomes the common field limitation of using intact groups (school classes, churches, and so forth). It involves pairs of two separate experimental and control groups. The $\boxed{R}$ indicates that the groups are randomly assigned to experimental conditions within the first pair and last pair; thus, the two sets of pairs may not be equivalent. The X in parentheses stands for any treatment that is administered with an obtrusiveness comparable to that of X, the treatment of interest.

$$
\begin{array}{l}
\boxed{R}\ \ O\ \ (X) \\
\phantom{\boxed{R}\ \ O\ \ }X\ \ O \\
\hline
\boxed{R}\ \ O\ \ C \\
\phantom{\boxed{R}\ \ O\ \ }C\ \ O
\end{array}
$$

A "Patched-up" design

Since both of the first pair receive treatments and neither of the second does, reactivity is controlled within each pair. The second pair controls for history, maturation, and mortality. It is possible there is a selection difference between the two sets of pairs (for example, one pair of classes is older and less likely to grow tired than the others). Since selection might interact with time (interaction of selection and maturation), this possibility creates a minus in the selection column in Table 20.3. The lack of a pretest in the experimental group controls for testing and for testing-treatment interaction.

+ *Many designs are "patched-up" designs that use peculiar patterns of groups and measures to fit particular situations. They are so designed as to provide the kind of protection that is important for a given study.*

Factorial Designs

Over the years, studies have increasingly involved more than one variable; they compare two or more treatments or examine the effects of such characteristics as demographic, situational, personality, or ability variables. **Factorial designs** facilitate determination not only of the effects of these variables singly, but also of their interactions in all possible combinations. *Factor* is simply another term for variable that is present in two or more *levels*: gender has two, male and female; a strong, medium, and weak treatment has three. (Factorial design examines the effects of factors; factor analysis helps determine the underlying factors that account for a set of relationships among variables.)

Let's consider a study of ways to control speeding on the New York State Thruway involving three factors: (1) two kinds of police cars—marked and unmarked; (2) five ways of handling a violation: (a) require immediate court appearance, (b) issue a ticket for later court appearance, (c) issue a ticket that can be handled by mail, (d) give a stern warning, (e) do whatever they normally would (control group); (3) two kinds of driver—commuter and noncommuter. (Commuters can be distinguished by the barcoded Thruway pass hanging from their rearview mirror which allows them to pass through the toll gates without stopping; the toll is automatically deducted from their accounts. Although frequent users of the Thruway may also have set up such accounts, the number will be comparatively minimal.)

Factorial designs collect data for each combination of factors which, in this $2 \times 5 \times 2$ design, is 20 sites as diagrammed in Figure 20.4. The "x's" of "site x" would designate each of 20 randomly assigned 5-mile stretches of highway over which we would find the average speed of randomly sampled cars.

By analysis of variance (see pp. 490–492), we can determine (1) whether marking a police car makes a difference, (2) whether violator treatment in general, and certain treatments in particular, reduce speed, and (3) whether commuters react differently from noncommuters to the treatments. In addition, we can determine whether each variable interacts with others to form a more potent or weaker effect in combination than alone. For example, was the mail-in ticket treatment more effective with commuter or noncommuter traffic? With marked or unmarked cars? We can examine whether the three characteristics formed a pattern that together raised or lowered the average speed. Thus, we

Treatment of Violators

	Control		Immediate trial		Delayed trial		Mail		Warning	
	Com-muter	Non-com-muter	Com-muter	Non-com-muter	Com-muter	Non-com-muter	Com-muter	Non-com-muter	Com-muter	Non-com-muter
Marked car	Site x	Site x	Site x	Site x	Site x	Site x	Site x	Site x	Site x	Site x
Unmarked car	Site x	Site x	Site x	Site x	Site x	Site x	Site x	Site x	Site x	Site x

FIGURE 20.4 A 2 x 5 x 2 factorial design for a study of speeding.

can check the effect of each major factor by itself and in all possible combinations. This makes it possible to determine how treatments are affected by context variables.

Nested designs reduce the number of groups to those combinations in which we are particularly interested. Let's suppose, we are convinced that marked cars are more effective in reducing the number of speeding commuters, so we need no further data on that issue, and can collapse this distinction. In the language of experimental design, we allow these two variables to be confounded. We assign marked cars to attend to arresting commuting speeders, the most effective speed reducing combination, and assign unmarked cars to monitor noncommuting speeders. Thus in each column designating a treatment of violator (warning, mail, etc.) there will be two cells: the upper left commuter-marked car cell and the lower right non-commuter-unmarked car cell. This still gives us information on the marked versus unmarked cars in relation to the different treatments of violators as well as commuters versus noncommuters in relation to these violator treatments. However, this nested design has only 10 cells and thus needs only 10 sites.

♦ Factorial designs are popular because they permit estimation of the effect of the treatment and other independent variables singly and in all possible combinations.

♦ We build variables we wish to control into such designs as independent variables (for example, commuting) so that we can determine the extent of their effect. This design can give us information on the effect of context variables.

♦ Where we are not interested in all possible combinations of variables, our use of nested designs reduces the demand for cases and possibly sites as well.

Causal Comparison, *Ex Post Facto* Studies, and After-the-Fact Natural Experiments

The world is such that we can't manipulate many of the phenomena that interest us most. What is the effect of low socioeconomic class on school achievement? Of low spatial visualization on creativity? Manipulating these variables like a treatment is impossible. We must examine them and their consequences as they exist in the world—that is, we must create **after-the-fact natural experiments.** Some call such research *ex post facto* studies, using the Latin form of after-the-fact.[14] Others refer to them as using the "causal comparative method." The title *ex post facto* is more often applied to studies in which data are gathered retrospectively; *causal comparative* where data are gathered from preformed groups and the independent variable is not manipulated as in an experiment.

After-the-fact natural experiments are a common form of research, especially among medical researchers who contrast groups to determine the effects of variables on health—for example, of eating meat by comparing meat eaters with vegetarians and fish eaters, or of the protective effect of certain vitamins and aspirin by comparing those who routinely ingest them with those who don't. An example of the causal comparative method is that by Hollowood, Salisbury, and Rainforth (1995) who contrasted six students with severe disabilities with twelve nondisabled in the use of time in the classroom. Arguing for inclusion of the handicapped in normal class rooms, they found that groups had comparable levels of engaged time and that the disabled did not cause loss of instructional time for the nondisabled.

The term *after-the-fact natural experiments* is nicely descriptive since, like experiments, they contrast two or more groups. These experiments are formed "after-the-fact," however, because the cause, the effect, or both are already present—sometimes in preformed groups, sometimes in specially constructed groups having certain characteristics. They are "natural experiments" in that the "treatment" or the effect of some variable occurs naturally and the effect is observed either after the fact, or as it occurs.

Such studies are used to test a hunch, to extend previous research, or to search for causative variables. For example, we have a hunch that highly creative individuals have higher verbal fluency than less creative ones. Since no known treatment changes verbal fluency, we must find (or create) groups with high and low verbal fluency and determine their difference in creativity, or find (or create) groups with high and low creativity and see if they differ in verbal fluency.

Often, particularly in the health field, the effect of interest has already occurred (for example, individuals with emphysema) and we would gather data on previous activities (for example, smoking) as a potential cause. The problem, after-the-fact and by a combination of logic and luck, is to develop an experiment by creating a functionally equivalent control group (for example, nonemphysema victims). We must either find a pool of individuals on which appropriate data are available, gather data to arbitrarily form such a group, or find an appropriate already formed group. Then we look for the cause (for example, smoking rates) in each group. Because there are rarely "before" data on both groups, the causal relationship is usually analogous to a posttest-only control group design

---

[14]Kerlinger (1973) changed their name to the too inclusive term "nonexperimental studies" in his 1986 edition. Babbie (1992) refers to them as the "elaboration model." None of these names seems satisfactory. Since terminology is nonstandard, it seems wise to use something as descriptive as possible—hence, this discussion uses "after-the-fact natural experiments."

(X O/O). The actual equivalence of the groups is always a nagging question in such studies.

Using the after-the-fact method in exploratory fashion to find what determines creativity, we might find (or constitute) groups of creative and noncreative individuals and search for characteristics that distinguish them (for example, a low fear of failing). Since these might be chance differences, we would then need to cross-validate these results by finding (or creating) samples differing in those characteristics (for example, persons with low and high fear of failing) and those without them and check for a relationship to creativity.

As in all research studies, after-the-fact studies provide convincing evidence of a relationship when: (a) findings are backed by a solid rationale that accurately predicted in advance what to expect (explanation credibility), (b) variables were accurately operationalized (translation fidelity), (c) expectations were confirmed (demonstrated result), (d) findings cannot be otherwise explained (rival explanations eliminated), and (e) findings show consistency with previous results (credible result).

Problems of After-the-Fact Designs

Finding Comparable Groups. We define the experimental group in terms of the cause (treatment or independent variable, for example, smoking) or the effect (dependent variable, for example, lung cancer) or both (smokers with cancer). We must accept such individuals, selected from the natural environment, just as they are. For a basis of comparison, we must provide a functionally equivalent group on all relevant variables. But what variables are relevant? We don't always know! Further, variables like gender, socioeconomic status, and personality, do not act independently; they come in "bundles" or "constellations"—a complicating factor. Consider that smokers' self-selected lifestyle is almost impossible to duplicate in the control group—otherwise, they might also be smokers. It is possible that nonsmokers, health-conscious and self-controlled enough to avoid smoking, have attitudes and personality characteristics that, independent of smoking, relate to low lung cancer incidence. Such constellations make it hard to analyze variables separately as well as to build a strong case.

Relying on Available Data. In retrospective studies, we must make do with what data are available. Often such data were not gathered with the same thoroughness as we would employ if we knew its future use. Frequently, such data also has missing cases or measures at critical points or has outliers for which there may have been a reasonable explanation but which is no longer known. Further, using data based on peoples' recall, which is the nature of much such data, always creates nagging doubts regarding accuracy.

Establishing Precedence of Cause Retrospectively May be Difficult. Without data on prior conditions, order of precedence may be hard to determine. If lung cancer patients both smoke more and are nervous, is the root cause nervousness, which caused smoking, or vice versa?

Having no Control Over the Independent Variable or Treatment. We cannot vary the cause in a particular pattern to show the effect follows it; if natural variation happens to do this, we are very fortunate.

Concentrating on Late Links When Early Links May Be the Cause. After-the-fact experiments may concentrate on late links in the causal chain of events (see pp. 130–131) instead of the critical earlier ones. For example, perhaps the underlying cause was stress which led to nervousness, which triggered smoking, which caused lung cancer.

Despite these problems and the barrages of rival explanations by groups desiring to undercut confidence in the findings (for example, the long battle regarding the effects of smoking), the evidence for many policy decisions rests on after-the-fact studies—arranging existing data so as to examine the effect of some variable. Despite concerns about their accuracy, findings from such studies are often widely embraced when they suggest inexpensive problem solutions (for example, large doses of vitamin E) that could possibly reduce the risk of a costly effect (for example, Alzheimer's disease).

- ✦ *After-the-fact natural experiments provide us with a comparison of a target group of interest possessing either a cause, an effect, or both with a group so constructed as to be comparable in all important ways except for presence of the presumed cause. The intent is to show a causal relation.*
- ✦ *In validation studies, we check the comparison group, comparable in all relevant ways except for the presumed cause, for absence of the effect. Or, alternatively, we start with persons with the effect and show they were exposed to the cause, whereas similar persons without the effect were not.*
- ✦ *For exploration studies, we look for differences between groups with and without the effect but otherwise comparable, seeking potential causes for which we can construct reasonable rationales. We then use these findings to construct validation studies.*
- ✦ *Although they often provide evidence where experimentation is difficult or impossible, after-the-fact studies have many weaknesses. The difficulty of constructing comparable groups that exclude all reasonable rival explanations is especially serious. The accuracy of data gathered retrospectively is often suspect. Precedence of cause may be difficult to establish from existing records. Further, relevant data may be missing from such records or not be as reliable as if they were gathered for research purposes. We cannot manipulate the treatment or independent variable; thus, we cannot obtain strong patterns of evidence (such as the reflection of an on-off-on-off pattern of cause in the effect) unless they occur naturally.*
- ✦ *We can often effectively employ after-the-fact studies to gather evidence for policy decisions where experimentation is impossible.*

Treatment Definition and Fidelity

The unique aspect of experimentation, the treatment, requires careful attention because our task is to link strongly no cause with effect. Let us examine three potential problems:

- Defining the experimental treatment
- Defining the placebo or control treatment, and
- Ensuring treatment fidelity.

Defining the Experimental Treatment

Essential to defining a treatment is the delineation of the "active ingredient" that sets the treatment apart. Since control and experimental treatments must be alike except for that one aspect, they must be conceptualized and operationalized accurately. Understanding the theory or rationale underlying the hypothesis is essential to treatment conceptualization as well as to explanation credibility. It also facilitates finding optimal operationalizations of the hypothesis's constructs to attain treatment fidelity. Sometimes we can reuse the operationalizations of the original study on which we are building.

Let's consider the hypothesis: "The greater students' active participation in the social and academic campus life, the less likely they will become college dropouts." We can operationalize the treatment, "active participation in social and academic life" in many ways. Returning to the original context, we find that Tinto (1987) drew a parallel to Durkheim's analysis of suicide cases, persons too isolated from their society to benefit from its support. He argued that potential college dropouts likely also have isolated themselves from social and academic support. Therefore, we define activity levels of "participation in social and academic life" in terms of their capacity to involve and support students and prevent feelings of isolation and disconnectedness.

> ✦ *Conceptually defining the treatment involves delineating the parts of the treatment that are the "active ingredient." Relating treatment to its conceptual base in an underlying theory or rationale helps both to conceptualize and to find optimal operationalizations of it.*

The Placebo or Control Treatment

The "Swahili syndrome,"[15] involving a comparison of something with nothing, sounds simple on the face of it: One teaches Swahili to the experimental group and not to the control and, lo and behold, the experimental learns more Swahili. Before you consider this example ridiculous, recall that the treatment always has something the control doesn't. It is in the reasonableness of the comparison of the "active ingredient" with the lack of it that the definition of the control treatment

---

[15]I am indebted to Gavriel Solomon for this stark rendition of the problem.

avoids the Swahili syndrome and the placebo treatment gains definition. A placebo has all the characteristics of the experimental treatment except for the "active ingredient," or cause.

Suppose, instead of learning to solve the variety of mathematical problems usually taught, a researcher has found they can be combined into five problem types. These, once learned, allow access to the usual variety. Learning and using the problem types are the "active ingredient." Additional conditions of treatment are: The teacher can devote as much time as she wishes, teach however she pleases, and involve the students in any way and as much or little as she desires, as long as the students learn the problem types above a specified minimum ability to use them. These experimental conditions help to define the placebo treatment, which should devote an equal amount of time to content, follow the same teaching style including involvement of students, and in all other ways be like the teaching in the experimental section. There is only one difference—it should not include the five problem types as such or the test of their use. The teacher might teach solutions to similar problems, but she would teach them as solutions to specific problems rather than as types. By making the placebo a completely parallel treatment, the researcher also eliminates many potential alternative causes: length of instruction, kinds of instruction, involvement of students in active learning, and so on.

◆ *The placebo treatment should be exactly like the experimental treatment or as much like it as possible, except for the characteristic that delineates the treatment itself—the "active" ingredient.*

It has long been recognized that placebos can have an effect, but it was only recently realized that the effect is, in many respects, a genuine organismic response—medical placebos, for example, develop antibodies and in other ways muster the body's therapeutic defenses. In many situations, the placebo effect, the expectation of efficacy of treatment, is an intended part of treatment. Counseling and psychological therapy can be effective only if the client wants to participate in it and has some hope, however small, of benefiting from it. But in many instances we wish to disentangle the placebo from the treatment effect and its interaction with treatment. Ross and colleagues (1962) demonstrated such a design involving two pairs of experimental and control groups. One pair receives treatment obtrusively for placebo effect and the other receives a "silent administration" wherein neither group realizes it was treated (Gottschalk, 1961).

For example, consider an experiment to determine whether adaptation of instruction to the individual is effective or placebo effect makes it appear so—the students' expectancy of improved efficacy because adjusted instruction fits them personally. A new, very flexible set of materials on the history of the U.S. Constitution can be adapted to fit aural, visual-graphic, and visual-text learning styles. You create four randomly selected groups and randomly assign treatments to them. To the first group, you very conspicuously promote this wonderful new approach, which should ensure raising student grades when material is fitted to their learning style. You make changes in the material very obtrusively, posting the unit assignments for each student on a large wall chart for all to see. You make assignments according to your diagnosis of learning style in such a way as to maximize learning (treatment plus placebo expectancy, condition 1).

For condition 2, the placebo treatment, unbeknown to the students, assignments are chosen from a random number table instead of being personally assigned. For condition 3, nothing special is said about the course material; it is just another assignment. But you make individual learning style assignments unobtrusively as you walk around the room interacting with students as you normally would. Condition 4 is like condition 3 except that the assignments for each student are random instead of intentional.

Comparison of conditions 2 and 4 tells whether obtrusively changing the course material increases learning, that is whether there is a placebo effect. Comparison of 3 with 4 shows whether intentional individual assignment results in greater learning than random assignment, that is, whether the treatment is effective. Comparison of conditions 1 and 3 indicates whether the placebo effect strengthens the treatment effect, that is, whether it improves the effectiveness of the individual assignments.

> ✦ *If the treatment can be given without the subjects' being aware they are receiving it (silent administration), the placebo effect can be determined by varying the obtrusiveness of placebo and treatment.*
> ✦ *The placebo effect is often consciously made a part of treatment because subjects are likely, consciously or unconsciously, to render ineffective treatments of no expected benefit to them.*

Ensuring Treatment Fidelity

Treatment fidelity ensures that "treatment administered was treatment intended." This includes three aspects:

- Congruence of operational with conceptual definition (already noted but needing further discussion)
- Representativeness of the intended generality by the operational definition
- Assurance that the administered treatment was the intended treatment.

Operational Definitions of Treatment. *It does not matter what was intended; operationalization defines the treatment.* The complexity that may be involved in judgments of treatment fidelity is often surprising. Although the following examples appear to focus on teaching a topic, substitute your treatment's terms for "teaching," "topic," and similar specific items and you will find that most of these questions have general applicability.

- How much time must be devoted to this topic for treatment to be authentic? Must all the content be covered? If not, how much? Must it be spread over a certain period, or can it be concentrated? If the latter, how much?

- Are some aspects essential, others desirable, others marginal? Must certain ones be included for the treatment to be authentic? Which ones?
- Can other material be included in the teaching of these concepts, or must these be the only things taught in this block?
- What activities constitute teaching? Lecture? How must it be organized and delivered? Discussion? What kinds of questions must be asked? What kinds of answers must be given before continuing to the next lesson? Should questions be drawn from the text or from the work of the class?
- How much must the students be involved in doing problems? What constitutes adequate assignment of problems? What constitutes adequate attempts at solving problems?
- What level of absenteeism constitutes the threshold for noncompletion of treatment?

Some of these items may be nonessentials yet the list is clearly far from exhaustive. That, of course, is the point; we must decide which are the essentials, the "active ingredients," to ensure treatment fidelity. (See Walker and Schaffarzick, 1974)

Availability can snare us into less-than-optimal operational terms: "Full-time students who become members of university-recognized clubs are less likely to become dropouts than those who never join." The university has a definition for "full-time student," and "dropouts." It registers campus clubs; their rules determine membership—all neatly defined! Not so! The treatment's original context included the notion of the individual's feeling supported by being involved, but organizational membership is no guarantee that individuals participated in any activities, much less felt supported by them.

Comparability may be a problem with multitreatment or multisite studies. For example, "active involvement" at a local junior college, where commuting students have little time for student life, may be different from that at a small four-year residential college. Operational definitions need to be appropriate for each situation yet true to their original conceptualization.

As we noted earlier, where there is a possibility of testing-treatment interaction, any pretest becomes part of the treatment's operational definition when we generalize from this evidence, a limiting condition on external validity (GP).

◆ *Treatment fidelity involves translation from the concepts in which treatment is expressed into operational terms.*

◆ *The operational definition is the treatment and inaccurate representation makes fuzzy or misses the study's intent.*

◆ *A judgment must be made about the congruence of operationalization with intended treatment as one aspect of treatment fidelity.*

Representativeness of Treatment. Are we interested in this treatment itself, or in what it represents? The use of the Chicago curriculum by Ms. Kimball might simply be an evaluation of it, but, if the Chicago curriculum is intended to represent curricula built from the same rationale, then it must either be a typical example of it, or, if we seek the boundaries of generality, be one close to a perimeter.[16] For example, in a study of the effectiveness of prewriting outlining in English composition, the treatment should be typical either of the way outlining is usually taught, or, if it can be taught in many ways, of the extremes of those methods.

> ✦ *Where faithfulness of translation of treatment into operations is to have general-ity, treatments selected for study may be typical examples, or, where we seek the boundaries of generality, representative of that range.*

Treatment Administration. Was the treatment really given as intended? The lat-itude exercised in giving the treatment may be so great, that variations in admin-istration may blur treatment definition or constitute an experimental variable in its own right. How do we ensure fidelity of treatment implementation? Usually, we provide detailed structure, instructions, and/or training in its administration and then observe its use with a low-inference observation instrument such as an observation checklist of those "active ingredients." But there are probably limits to the effectiveness of structuring treatments administered by humans instead of by books, machines, or computers. Leonard and Lowery (1979), for example, found that too structured a curriculum was resisted so strongly that its original potency was lost.

Where a treatment requires improvisation, we learn from observation what the variety of changes is, how skilled personnel make the basic structure effective, and how improvisation affects the "active ingredients." Studies of treatments still in the process of adoption will show the extent and fidelity of adoption may vary considerably from site to site. Hall and Loucks' (1977) "levels of use of the innova-tion" scale can be used to control for this variability in these instances.

Since variations in administration probably influence effectiveness, to avoid a restriction on external validity (GP) and generality, that variation should be rep-resented in an effectiveness evaluation. For example, workshop training of treat-ment administrators may decrease treatment variations and increase effectiveness over multisite trials. However, if the treatment will be disseminated in booklet form, implementation from those alone may be quite different and should be part of the study.

Although the need for monitoring the experimental treatment is clear, we of-ten must also monitor any control and placebo treatments to ensure maintenance of the expected contrast. Sometimes the experimental treatment spreads to these

---

[16]Readers familiar with models of analysis of variance will recognize the parallel of the first point to the fixed model, of interest in and of itself; the second to the random model, representa-tive of the typical; and the third to the mixed model, where examples represent a range. There is also some parallel here to two of the three parts of conceptual analysis, first noted on page 263 in qualitative research and again in the discussion of measurement, page 431. Here we are calling for key examples and boundary markers.

groups through diffusion, which we discussed as a rival hypothesis earlier in this chapter.

✦ *Treatment fidelity involves administration of whatever is considered the "active ingredients" of the treatment.*

✦ *Detailed description of the active ingredients and training helps ensure fidelity.*

✦ *Monitoring treatment administration, both experimental and placebo, ensures treatment fidelity as well as maintaining appropriate contrast of treatments.*

✦ *For maximum generality, conditions of treatment administration should be realistically like those under which the treatment is intended to be used. Pretests and special training may limit generality.*

Hallmarks of Experimental Design and Tips on Constructing Them

All of the following are hallmarks of good experimental design. However, some—the tips—are aimed primarily at the developmental process. The others—hallmarks—are characteristics of the published report that can help you judge the product. *Remember also that all the asterisked items in the similar list for qualitative methods (14 of the 19 listed on pages 344–346!) are equally applicable to quantitative methods. Be sure to reread them because they should be considered part of this list as well.*

1. Start with a translation of the hypothesis; then add features to protect against rival explanations likely to be important in the eyes of your intended audience.

2. Experimental designs are often developed through a series of iterations and result in a patched up design (see page 534). Make a provisional try at developing the design. Then, when you see a flaw, fix it. This repair may make apparent either a new rival explanation or one not previously noticed. It, too, will require changes and so it goes. Continue until you are satisfied, but remember that nearly all designs are compromises because of the trade-offs involved.

3. Control undesired variables by eliminating them, if their elimination does not unduly affect whatever external validity (GP) is required (for example, laboratory versus field). If possible, control others by building them into the design as independent variables. As necessary, spread their effect equally among the groups.

4. Describe in your write-up any rival explanations not protected against but of possible concern to your audience; indicate that they were left that way by conscious choice, usually a trade-off compromise, not ignorance. Explain why this design was the best choice.

5. Don't decide on a final design until you have done a pilot study, including gathering qualitative data (see point 17 below). Use its results for a power

analysis to ensure that the study is statistically sensitive enough to detect a finding of interest.

6. Random assignment of treatment to groups and of individuals to experimental groups and a well-constructed placebo control group ensure more protection than any other design feature. Block (stratify) on important variables not otherwise controlled. You lose only your labor if the variable turns out not to be important, but you make the study more sensitive if it is. Using such procedures obtrusively, however, may reduce external validity (GP).

7. Use double-blind methods to control for expectancy effects. (Follow up with point 17 below—the subjects may not have been as blind as you thought!)

8. In learning studies, tests of later retention are often more sensitive to differences in treatment than immediate posttests. This is an easy way to increase the power (sensitivity) of your study.

9. In studies of treatments that do not have residual effects, for maximally convincing results, vary the treatment in an on-off-on-off pattern, possibly at random intervals or in randomly constructed patterns.

10. Besides an on-off pattern, use different levels of treatment or reverse the treatment—its opposite where feasible and ethical. For example, in studying the effect of praise on achievement, vary the frequency of praise or even scold instead of praise. But be sure they are really opposites; for example, extreme praise and extreme punishment may not have opposite effects (see Cook and Campbell, 1979).

11. Where preexisting growth or change might be a plausible rival explanation, multiple observations—at least three for a curvilinear one—will reveal a trend. Use a design of the regression discontinuity type to sense changes in trend resulting from treatment. Compare the equation describing the pretreatment trend with that of the posttreatment. An effective treatment will show the trend has been displaced upward and may also angle upward more sharply (see Cook and Campbell, 1979).

12. Carefully delineate the "active ingredients" in the treatment by a supporting rationale or theory. Build them into the experimental treatment, putting all the treatment's other characteristics in the control (placebo) treatment.

13. Assign a group to each separate combination of independent variables. For ease of analysis, vary them systematically from group to group (for example, use a factorial design).

14. Counterbalance the order of measures or multiple treatments when you expect the order to have an effect (see p. 522).

15. Use unobtrusive measures and administer treatments as unobtrusively as possible for increased external validity (GP).

16. Remember that replication is the ultimate validation. Repeating a study with the same or similar results is very strong evidence.

17. Every experimental study should include an element of qualitative research to help understand the point of view of the subject, the treatment administrator, and the observer or measurer. Interviewing the subjects after the study often reveals that the treatment was perceived quite differently from what

was intended (the demand characteristics of the study) and leads to new and important rival explanations. It also provides anecdotes that help verify the phenomenon being studied and make the statistics more meaningful.

18. Consider that when you subtract an unreliable score that might be too high or too low from another similarly unreliable score, the difference score is still more unreliable than the scores that made it up. Although such scores can be useful, avoid pretest-posttest change scores where feasible, using random assignment with posttest-only designs (see Collins and Horn, 1991 regarding best methods to study change).

19. Where the effect of repeated testing is expected to be significant, establish multiple comparable groups (possibly by splitting experimental and control groups), one for each testing.

20. Evaluate carefully all design changes you made after the pilot study. Let them gestate for 24 hours before acting on them.

21. Conduct data gathering in the least amount of time that is appropriate. Reducing study length decreases the likelihood of local history events; the possibility of selection, mortality, and maturation effects; and personnel costs (usually the largest budgeted item). Remember: Even if your time is not budgeted, you still incur what economists call "opportunity costs," the potential value of using that time in other ways.

22. Although, experimental studies usually test hypotheses, afterward, *explore*! Gathering data is too expensive not to extract all you can out of it. Talk to subjects and co-workers about their experiences. Explore conceptually some "what if's" and gather a bit of information about some of the more promising leads. Explore your data with scatterplots and distributions; try different cross-breaks and look for patterns. It's exciting, fun, and often fruitful! Keep your horizons wide. Your most precious finding may be something other than what you were looking for.

SUMMARY

Experimentation produces one of the strongest chains of reasoning for testing a cause-effect hypothesis. Design is at the heart of experimentation—development of a plan for data collection and analysis providing the strongest possible chain of reasoning. Random or intentionally complex manipulation of the treatment, which is reproduced in the effect, provides especially strong cause-and-effect linkage. Control is also a hallmark of a strong design. Through control, we provide protection against rival explanations (rival hypotheses, threats to validity) and potential weakeners of internal validity (LP), as well as against restrictive explanations or conditions that weaken external validity (GP) and reduce generality. Control by removing the effect of unwanted variables increases statistical

sensitivity more than control by spreading their effect to both control and experimental group. The latter is often more feasible, however.

Although each study may have unique rival explanations or restrictive conditions, Campbell and Stanley, (1963) and others have formulated a useful set of prevalent ones. Though developed in the context of experimentation, many apply equally well to other research methods. A number of common design configurations have been analyzed for their strengths and weaknesses in protecting against rival hypotheses. Where these are not feasible or inadequate, you can use either additional designs described in the additional readings or create a patched-up design. Where the best choice of design does not eliminate possibly important rival explanations, make clear that your choice was intentional, and show why it is the best one.

Experimentation runs the range from laboratory to so-called natural experiments where society or nature are the treatment administrators. In between are treatments applied under field conditions. The laboratory approach offers considerable control over problem variables and hence provides evidence with strong internal validity (LP). Field studies and natural experiments seek greater external validity (GP), at the possible expense of internal validity (LP).

After-the-fact natural experiments involve the comparison of previously gathered, retrospective, or new data gathered from a target group with groups intentionally formed to be comparable in relevant ways. The intent is to show a relationship, ideally a causal one, between variables present in different amounts in the two groups. Many policy studies regarding the effects of drugs, lifestyles, and past educational practices are of this nature. Such studies are subject to a variety of problems, however, because of the limitations of using prior data and the difficulty of eliminating rival explanations.

A Look Ahead

The next chapter shows how the results of multiple quantitative studies can be combined to yield a more stable and more definitive finding regarding the phenomena in question.

In Chapter 24, we will note that often, as we devise the best possible study, a combination of quantitative and qualitative methods may provide the strongest design. The chapter also includes an evaluation of the strengths and weaknesses of a variety of methods of gathering data.

ADDITIONAL READING

Campbell and Stanley (1963) and Cook and Campbell (1979) are excellent materials to read for the detailed analysis of a great many designs. In addition, both contain a variety of examples that make the principles come alive. Except for the material on statistical analysis in Cook and Campbell, both books are quite understandable. The latter also has an excellent section on analysis of causation. Ellsworth (1977) suggests guidelines for choosing natural research settings for experimentation. Cronbach (1982) has useful discussions of treatment, especially Chapter 8. Seligman (1995) uses many of this chapter's design suggestions to evaluate psychotherapy effectiveness. Wortman (1994, p. 102) has an excellent list of common rival hypotheses.

IMPORTANT TERMS

After-the fact natural experiments
Base rate
Camouflage
Confounding
Demand characteristics
Diffusion
Double-blind procedures
Factorial design
Functionally equivalent groups
Hawthorne effect
Hypothesis guessing
Instrument decay by treatment interaction
Interactions
Local History
Masking
Maturation
Mortality by treatment interaction
Multiple-treatment interaction
Nested designs
Nonequivalent control group design

Obtrusiveness
One-group pretest-posttest design
Placebo effect
Posttest-only control group design
Pretest-posttest control group design
Random assignment
Reactivity
Regression
Researcher expectancy effect
Selection
Selection-maturation interaction
Selection by treatment interaction
Solomon four-group design
Testing
Testing-treatment interaction
Threats to validity
Time-series designs
Treatment fidelity
Unobtrusiveness

APPLICATION PROBLEMS

1. As a researcher in science education, you are interested in the role of diagrams in instruction. These are usually combinations of text and arrows to indicate what phenomenon leads to what other one. Examples are the oxygen and water cycles. You wish to investigate whether using small pictures in place of text within the diagrams will facilitate comprehension of the principles and concepts that are taught. To do so, you have developed grade-8 geography units on the water and oxygen cycles that incorporate the liberal use of diagrams. How would you design your study?

2. A state government curriculum team wished to demonstrate the superiority of its new approach to the junior high school level social studies program. Team members selected a sample of teachers from around the state to carry out a one-year pilot study of the new program. All the teachers were volunteers.

   a. Assume that students who were taught using the new approach scored significantly higher on a test of comprehension of key concepts than did comparable students in the regular program. What alternative explanations can you advance to the claim that the new approach was better? How can these be avoided?

   b. Assume that the control (regular curriculum) group scored significantly higher. What could explain this result?

3. A university mathematics instructor has developed and incorporated an extensive computer-assisted instructional (CAI) program into his own course on introductory calculus. Wanting to assess the effectiveness of his approach, he decides he will randomly assign students to each section of the course and compare the mean scores on the final exam at the end of the semester (the posttest-only control group design). He hypothesizes a significant difference between the means in favor of his approach. What rival explanations represent a threat to his design? How can he avoid them?

4. Recall the study (Chap. 2, prob. 1, page 35) in which a group of researchers investigated the interaction between the age of viewers of an instructional film and the gender of the narrator. Subjects in the second and fifth grades were randomly assigned to one of two groups. One group watched a film narrated by an adult female, and the other group viewed the same film narrated by an adult

male. During the film, the investigators measured the children's visual attention to the program. They also tested recall of the story ideas using a multiple-choice test. What research design would these investigators probably have used and why?

5. A nursing graduate student investigated the neurological problem of unilateral neglect (in which a patient is unaware of one side of the body). She decided to compare unilateral neglect patients who also suffered from another, related problem, anosognosia (the inability to recognize that anything is wrong with them), with those who did not. She believed the patients with both unilateral neglect and anosognosia would experience more difficulties with self-care activities. Assuming she had located a reliable measure of self-care, how would she design a study to compare the two groups? Note that these disorders are relatively rare. Take into account, as well, that such medical conditions tend to be unstable; that is, the severity of the symptoms varies with such factors as patient fatigue and stress. In addition, such patients do tend to improve, albeit slowly.

6. A 1986 study by DeBack and Mentkowski attempted to answer the question of whether or not nurses with baccalaureate degree preparation were more competent than those graduating from a hospital-based or two-year diploma program. They hypothesized that baccalaureate graduate nurses would have more nursing competencies than other graduates, as would nurses with more experience regardless of training. They broadly defined these competencies as a set of "generic" abilities that represent the underlying characteristics of nursing performance. The investigators described these in behavioral terms inferred from descriptions of effective and ineffective behaviors on the part of professional nurses.

   To do so, they selected three midwestern health care settings with excellent reputations: an acute-care setting, a long-term care environment, and a community agency. Nursing staff members were asked to cite "outstanding" and "good" nurses; 90 percent of them returned the questionnaire. A group of 45 "outstanding" nurses and 38 "good" nurses equally weighted for education were selected for interview. They were asked to describe three critical incidents in which they believed they were effective and three in which they were ineffective. They also completed a biographical questionnaire. There was no significant relationship between the nominations and either education or experience.

A codebook model of nine generic nursing competencies (conceptualizing, emotional stamina, ego strength, positive expectations, independence, reflective thinking, helping, influencing, and coaching) was developed from the interviews and used to evaluate 502 critical incidents gathered. A 2 x 2 analysis of variance (education x experience) yielded statistically significant results in favor of baccalaureate preparation for six of the nine competencies: independence, ego strength, coaching, helping, conceptualizing, and reflective thinking. Three statistically significant effects favoring the two-year program were also shown (influencing, conceptual-

izing, and helping). There were no significant interaction effects (between education and experience), but level of education was significantly correlated with setting (the community agency had almost all baccalaureate-prepared nurses) and, in the acute-care setting, with supervisory position.

DeBack and Mentkowski concluded from this analysis that nurses with baccalaureate preparation exhibited more competencies than those with associate degrees or diplomas and that such education had long-term benefits. Was this an after-the-fact natural experiment? Are the researchers' conclusions warranted?

Compare your answers with those following the Application Exercise.

APPLICATION EXERCISE

In order to explore the possibilities of using experimentation with your problem, you need some kind of hypothesis and treatment. If these are not normally part of your problem, find an aspect about which enough is known that setting forth a hypothesis is reasonable. What kind of experiment does a translation of the hypothesis lead to? What terms in the hypothesis automatically translate into design features?

How would you define the treatment? Should you check to be sure it is being administered faithfully to what is intended? How would you do that? Are you interested in the treatment per se? Or do you intend it to be representative? If so, of what? What are the implications of this?

How might you administer the treatment so as to have the most convincing evidence of cause and effect? What kind of design does that suggest? Do you need an alternative or a placebo treatment? Of what will it consist? What essential characteristics of

treatment must you exclude from it, and what other characteristics must you include because they go with the treatment but are not really part of it?

What rival explanations are likely to be a threat to the internal validity (LP) of the study? How will you protect against them? Can you protect against the worst threats? If you can't, what would you do? Are there alternative designs among which you could choose? What trade-offs would be involved in selecting one design over another?

Will you be concerned with generality? If so, what restrictive conditions should you be aware of that might limit external validity (GP)? What design considerations might be involved?

Can you examine your problem as an after-the-fact natural experiment? What might be the problems of constructing an adequate comparison group? To what rival explanations might such a group be open? Is there any way of reducing their plausibility or eliminating them?

ANSWERS TO THE APPLICATION PROBLEMS

1. You will be designing a single-variable study and have many options, depending on the availability of subjects and your control over the situation. If you are able to bring the students to a laboratory or otherwise rearrange their natural classroom groupings for the purposes of the study, you may be able to assign your subjects randomly to each treatment. It is unlikely that you could successfully assign different units (with or without the

pictures within the diagrams) on a random basis within each classroom as the students would soon realize the differences and compare materials (the diffusion threat to validity). If you are able to assign subjects randomly (rearrange the classes), the best choice would be the randomized posttest-only control group design, in which the no-pictures group is the control. This would allow you to avoid any testing effect caused by a pretest. Most likely, however, you will have to give each treatment to existing, presumably comparable classes. The time required to cover both units might stretch the cooperation of the school authorities so your design choice would probably be the nonequivalent control group design with two sets of control and experimental groups. For analysis, either combine the oxygen and water data to compare the experimental and control groups or, using analysis of variance, examine differences between both units and treatments. Since this design includes a pretest, you could assign the class with the lower mean to the treatment. But remember, only if the experimental group catches up and outscores the control on the posttest will you have an interpretable result.

2. (a) If the treatment group did score significantly higher, we could point to several rival explanations:

Selection, since all the pilot study teachers were volunteers

Hawthorne effect, since the students would likely have been aware of belonging to an experimental group

Novelty effect, if the approach was substantially different from standard classroom procedure

Researcher expectancy effect, if members of the curriculum team or its supporters were involved in the evaluation of the effect.

(b) A significant result in favor of the control group might have resulted from compensatory rivalry, or the John Henry effect. This is more likely if the teachers using the regular program were opposed to the introduction of the new approach. They may well have made an extra effort to demonstrate that the old approach was equally effective or even more effective.

3. We could argue for several rival explanations: a researcher expectancy effect, a Hawthorne (or novelty) effect, and, if the regular section was superior, the John Henry effect (compensatory rivalry). The instructor could not very well keep the section leaders blind to the treatment, given its obvious inclusion in the course. One way that he could avoid the expectancy and John Henry threats is by gaining the section leaders' support and involving them in the use of the CAI program in their sections. This might reduce, though not entirely eliminate, researcher expectancy, since the section leaders would probably not have the same vested interest in the outcome. Gaining their agreement to use the program themselves would also remove the possibility of their trying to improve the standard approach to compete with the CAI.

Eliminating a Hawthorne (or novelty) effect might be more difficult because of the obvious and unusual nature of the treatment, communication between students, and other factors. One possibility is using a placebo (perhaps a CAI program containing topics not examined) so that all students are exposed to CAI in the course and are kept blind to the actual treatment. Lastly, the researcher could use the nonequivalent control group design by using the CAI with all the introductory calculus students one semester and comparing results with past exam results or with those of a future group not exposed to the treatment.

4. The investigators would probably have used a 2 x 2 x 2 factorial design because they tested children of two different age groups (second and fifth grades) on two variables (recall and attending) to determine the effects of two treatments (a film with a male narrator and the same film with a female narrator). Use of analysis of variance would have allowed them to determine the effect of each factor in turn and also the various possible combinations. In actual fact, Klein and colleagues (1987) did report a combination effect: second graders showed a significant difference on attending in favor of the male narrator.

5. She is restricted in her choice of design for several reasons. The most obvious is that her study is actually observational and not truly experimental. That is, it is a "natural experiment" in which she intends to study the "treatment" applied by nature. In effect, the treatment is the disorder of anosognosia acting in concert with unilateral neglect. So rather than apply a treatment, she would need to locate, in sufficient numbers, two groups of neurological patients: one whose members exhibit unilateral neglect only and another whose members have that disorder and anosognosia. If she considers the disorders to be a form of treatment, she could consider one of the experimental designs, the nonequivalent control group design. She could not, of course, apply a pretest, because she cannot identify ahead of time who will develop the disorders. The randomized posttest-only control group design would be the strongest choice, but she could not randomly assign the subjects to each group, as they have to suffer from each particular disease. In actuality, she would have to conduct a series of case studies.

Consequently, her study would be subject to a variety of threats to internal validity (LP), the most serious of which are selection, local history, and maturation. The first is important because it might be argued that the subjects who volunteered (or whose families agreed to the study) might well differ from those who did not. The second, local history, is a serious threat because the severity of these syndromes varies with such factors as patient stress and fatigue. The third, maturation, is perhaps the biggest threat, as patients do tend to get better. Since the numbers of such patients are small, she may be compelled to assess various subjects in different stages of the progress of disease.

She might be able to control for the threats of local history and maturation by using a variation on the time-series design and conducting several assessments of each of the subjects throughout their convalescence. The problem of selection, however, may be difficult to avoid, since the numbers of such patients are small, and the researcher may have to accept the patients to whom she can gain access.

6. It was an after-the-fact natural experiment. The investigators were unable to control the variable of interest, which was the possession of baccalaureate nursing training. They were, however, able to select a stratified random sample, which provided them with comparable groups in most respects. They could not, however, control for self-selection. This, since they are arguing for baccalaureate preparation for nurses, is an important rival explanation. Perhaps nurses who complete the higher degree have greater ability (for example, intelligence) or are more strongly motivated. It may be that these characteristics are responsible for the difference in these competencies and would display their effect regardless of education.

Also, to agree with their conclusion, one would have to accept DeBack and Mentkowski's definition of nursing competencies. Does their rationale make sense? Does it support their hypotheses? Though not presented in this summary, the investigators did indeed develop their hypotheses from a theoretical basis and from past research evidence. The operationalization of the hypotheses also appears to be sound since the codebook was developed from the subjects' descriptions of effective and ineffective nursing behavior.

CHAPTER 21

Meta-Analysis—Synthesis of Findings

Like the artisans who construct a building . . . , scientists contribute to a common edifice called knowledge. Theorists provide the blueprints and researchers collect the data that are the bricks. . . . researchers are the bricklayers and hodcarriers. . . . It is their job to stack the bricks according to plan and apply the mortar that holds the structure together.

Cooper and Hedges (1994b, p. 4)

Meta-analysis has . . . revealed how little information there typically is in any single study. . . . Any individual study must be considered a data point to be contributed to a future meta-analysis.

Schmidt (1996, p. 127)

OVERVIEW

Any reviewer of literature intends, as accurately as possible, to synthesize research findings to determine the true state of knowledge about the phenomena in question. For years this was strictly a conceptual process resulting in a verbal summary, and usually weakly concluding that more research was needed. Only occasionally did a quantitative literature summary appear. However, such summaries became widespread once it was shown how, with a few assumptions, a variety of findings, including negative ones, could be reduced to an effect size, and the name meta-analysis was coined.[1] The procedure was especially attractive because it brought dramatic resolution to many intensely debated issues. "The aim of meta-analysis . . . [has been] to discipline research synthesis by the same methodological standards that apply to primary research. . . . research reviews should be just as replicable as any other piece of scientific work. . . . Disagree-

---

[1]Meta-analyses are "comprehensive-analyses" from the Greek prefix *meta-*, a meaning of which is transcending or comprehensive. In like manner, meta-evaluations are assessments of evaluations done after they are concluded.

ments among the experts should become more a matter of method than opinion" (Wanner, 1995).

Meta-analysis has evolved into a research method in its own right. As results are cumulated over different contexts and conditions, in the presence of different variables, and involving different strengths of variables, meta-analysis allows us to determine the shape of the relationship (linear, a particular curvilinearity, J shaped and so forth), to ascertain what potentiates or weakens a relationship, the pattern in which that occurs, and where and how the effect is maximized.

The pendulum has swung part-way back toward verbal analyses. Realizing meta-analysis also requires considerable judgment, most researchers add conceptual commentary evaluating the meta-analysis and the studies it includes to give a better perspective on the results.

CHAPTER CONTENTS

Introduction

Conventional literature reviews have sought to evaluate and integrate the body of research relevant to a question or proposition. Since studies are rarely exact replications of previous ones, how can we combine these apples and oranges? Does putting them together make fruit salad? Or garbage? Until recently, such a synthesis was entirely a matter of judgment. A reviewer estimated the contribution of a given study to the synthesis being constructed by weighting such characteristics as centrality to the target phenomenon, sample representativeness and size, tightness of design, control of important moderating conditions such as socioeconomic class or time on task, and validity of instrumentation. Next the reviewer had to assess the combined nature and direction of the studies, bearing in mind the appropriate weighting for large studies, for studies exceptionally well done, for exceptionally representative samples, and for studies with unusually valid instrumentation. Since the human mind can juggle only seven to nine things at a time, this variety of characteristics immediately suggests a very difficult task.

This difficulty and the contrasting advantage of meta-analysis were dramatically shown by Lipsey and Wilson (1995) who, on examining meta-analyses of psychological, educational, and behavioral interventions, found the results overwhelmingly positive! Only 6 of 302 meta-analytic studies showed negative results! Furthermore, 85 percent found treatment strengths such that 55 percent of the treated group would exceed their untreated or placebo-treated controls. Yet, why have the conventional reviews for years concluded that at best these results are equivocal and, more often, that there is insufficient evidence for superiority of the interventions?

The difficulty of conventional syntheses may be part of the reason, but another is the tendency to vote-count—that is, to tabulate study results as positive if statistically significant, and negative, if not. Hedges and Olkin (1985) have shown that vote-counting procedures, especially with small samples, are very likely to miss small effect sizes. Small-sample studies, however, are common. Still another is that reverse effects, for example, when the control group's effect measure is higher than that of the experimental group, seem devastating to conventional reviewers. It is conceptually hard to accept negative results when we expect the intervention to yield positive ones.

Although **meta-analyses** do not replace the judgmental aspects of traditional summaries, their appeal derives from five main considerations:

1. A study's result may align with the hypothesis but, because of insufficient power, may not be statistically significant. Although several such near-misses may seem more than happenstance, by widely accepted statistical logic, near-misses do not count. However, combining such studies in a meta-analysis yields statistical power greater than any one study and may show statistical significance whereas the individual studies did not.

2. In conventional reviews, the tendency is to determine which studies are the best estimate of the effect rather than to consider all results as samples from a population of studies estimating an effect's size. When we sample from such a population, half the findings will be larger than the true effect size and half smaller. If the true effect size is close to zero, *simply due to sampling variability, the range of findings will normally include negative ones.* Verbal summarizers rarely take that point of view so that the subjective feeling given by negative results is: "any is too many."

3. From a single study, it is hard to judge the effect of moderating variables such as personal attributes, characteristics of the context, and the way the study was done. Combining results of studies can help us to target the specific set of circumstances under which an intervention can be most effective.

4. As Hall, Rosenthal, Tickle-Degnen, and Mosteller (1994) point out, combining multiple operationalizations of variables extracts the essence of a construct giving the effect size greater construct validity than does any single study. "For example, to learn about the construct 'anxiety,' we may use a self-report anxiety scale, a coding of observed anxiety behavior, or electrodermal skin response. Through aggregation, meta-analysis extracts the essential anxiety effect, while sloughing off residuals due to instrumentation factors" (p. 20).

5. Meta-analytic techniques are "ideal . . . for confidently answering a question about the generality of an effect . . . [since they provide external validity's] empirical assessment . . . to an extent rarely available to a single primary study" (ibid., p. 20). The reviewer must still judgmentally assess whether the populations of subjects, situations, and procedures involved in the combined

result are adequate representatives for the intended generality. But the effect size indicates the generality over whatever groups were studied.

For all these reasons and more, quantitative literature reviews have rapidly increased in popularity. Meta-analyses now "appear in disciplines from marketing (to synthesize studies of advertising) to meteorology (. . . an overview of 750 cloud-seeding experiments), and from education (. . . studies of class size . . .) to epidemiology (. . . studies of the health effects of power lines)" (Mann, 1990, p. 476).

Actually, as Bangert-Drowns (1986) indicates, such studies have been done for years: "Ghiselli (1949, 1955, 1973) for instance averaged correlation coefficients from numerous studies to estimate the validity of different tests in predicting proficiency in different occupations. Bloom (1964) aggregated correlation coefficients to summarize evidence of stability and change in behavior" (p. 389). Finally, meta-analysis blossomed when Glass (1976) showed how to average results after conversion to a standard metric called **effect size,** coined the term *meta-analysis,* and Smith and Glass's (1977) meta-analysis decisively showed positive results for psychotherapy, a conclusion that researchers had unconvincingly sought since clinical psychology began—what is the effectiveness of "just talking about a problem"?

Glass proposed that effects measured by different operational definitions of the same construct could be compared if they were translated into a standard-score-like form. Routinely used to compare different test results, standard scores remove the contexts of raw scores—number correct on measure A, or number chosen as self-descriptive on measure B—by dividing them by each measure's standard deviation. Standard scores, and therefore also effect sizes, are expressed in standard deviation units. Correlations from various studies may also be averaged and used as the effect size. With certain assumptions, effect sizes can be translated from standard deviation form to correlations and vice versa.

In meta-analysis, it is the score difference between two means, usually the means of the experimental and control groups, that is divided by a standard deviation—but what standard deviation? Glass suggested using either the standard deviation of the control group or an estimate of the population's standard deviation derived from the pooled standard deviations of the samples. The latter are presumed to be uncontaminated by treatment. Given that the effect sizes collected in a study are random samples of a population of effect sizes, the mean estimates the true size of treatment effect.

For example, Smith, Glass, and Miller (1980)—seeking the mean effect size of psychotherapy—found that more than 1,000 studies had been done to convince skeptics. They selected for intensive analysis the 375 studies that had both an untreated and a treated group, even though some were weak designs. These yielded 833 effect sizes from more than 25,000 subjects. Eighty-eight percent of the effect sizes were positive. Although only 12 percent were negative, fully half would have been negative had there been no effect.

An average effect size of 1 would indicate that the average treated person's score exceeded that of an untreated person by one standard deviation. The average effect size over all measures of psychotherapy improvement was .67. What is considered a strong or a weak effect seems relative to the field. Effects of 1 are considered strong in the behavioral sciences; effects of .3 or below, weak. By assuming the sample effect sizes are normally distributed we can translate a gain into percentiles. For example, the average client in the psychotherapy treated group was about two-thirds of a standard deviation better off than the average person in the untreated control—that is, better off than the person at the 75th percentile in that group. Expressing gains in percentiles puts synthesized results into understandable terms.

Rosenthal (1994) raises the question as to whether our expectations are too high in the social sciences. He cites a study of the effects of aspirin in reducing heart attacks which was prematurely ended because "it had become so clear that aspirin prevented heart attacks . . . that it would be unethical to continue to give half the . . . subjects a placebo" (p. 242). What was the magnitude of this dramatic finding, he asks? Was it correlations in the 60's, 70's, or 80's? No, the correlation was .034 and would be considered insignificant in a social science study! However, Rosenthal notes even that low a correlation reflected a 4 percent decrease in heart attacks. Granted, because life and death issues are involved, the stakes are higher. Still, it makes one reconsider whether we are presenting our findings in an appropriately compelling way.

We can determine the dependence of the effect on various factors by categorizing studies in terms of study conditions. For instance, Smith and Glass (1977), coding the studies on overall quality, found no difference in effect size between stronger or weaker studies. This has not always proven true, however; stronger designs often yield larger effects.

- ✦ *Each study yields one or more estimates of a population effect size.*
- ✦ *Just as standard scores translate the scores for an individual from different measures into a common scale, so translation of findings on measures of a construct into effect sizes converts them into such a scale so they may be meaningfully combined into an average effect size.*
- ✦ *We find effect size by dividing the difference between experimental and control group means by the population standard deviation estimated from the pooled sample standard deviations, or by the standard deviation of the control group. We can also average correlation coefficients to obtain an effect size. Effect sizes in standard deviation form can be translated into correlations and vice versa.*
- ✦ *In a meta-analysis, these effect sizes are averaged across studies to get a better population estimate. To make clear the effect of treatment, we can assume the effect sizes are normally distributed and translate them into percentiles of the untreated group.*
- ✦ *Meta-analysis gives a different perspective on a mixture of negative, not statistically significant, and positive results. From that perspective, one realizes that, by chance, half the results will fall above and half below the effect size mean for the population. If that mean is not far from zero, one can expect negative and no effect findings as a matter of course. Therefore, such a mixture of results simply indicates a weak relationship rather than none. The latter is what a conventional reviewer, who did not give consideration to this meta-analytic expectation, would be inclined to conclude.*

✦ *Meta-analysis has evolved as a new research method. As subsets of data provide estimates of effect sizes under contrasting conditions, we are able to determine whether a phenomenon is strengthened or weakened by certain conditions. With enough data, we can map the nature of that relationship.*

Considerations in Meta-Analytic Methodology

Glass included weak studies since, for studies done independently, the weak point of one might be the strong one of another. Thus, they would cancel each other out—like a combination of fishnets where the rips and tears of one are covered by another (Guba and Lincoln, 1985). But, suppose that study A employs multiple measures of a construct, each of which is translated into an effect size. When these estimates are combined with others to estimate the population average, because study A's errors are multiply represented, the estimate if not composed of interdependent appraisals. When Smith and Glass (1977) obtained 833 psychotherapy effect sizes from 375 studies, it was clear that most studies provided two or more effect sizes and so were represented several times in the overall result. For example, were the Zimbardo study of Chapter 1 used in a meta-analysis, it would yield three effect sizes since there were three measures of paranoia. It would thus be represented three times in any average effect size. Flaws in the Zimbardo design would therefore be represented three times in that average, which is clearly a concern.

Further, in general, we would expect larger samples to yield estimates closer to the population value than small studies. Therefore, when a small sample effect is given equal weight in an average with the results from large samples, another question arises (the ratio in sample sizes is sometimes 50 to 1).

Confining the search to published materials probably inflates effect size, since published studies have more positive and larger effects than unpublished—the "file-drawer effect."[2] Including unpublished research reports or dissertations corrects this. Rosenthal (1979) provides a way of estimating a "fail-safe n"—how many "file-drawer studies" would be required to nullify the effect found. An implausibly large number suggests publication bias is not serious.

Nevertheless, we still have an apples-and-oranges problem. If we mix measures of changes in attitude with changes in skills, we find that the effect of psychotherapy is moderated by the kind of effect we are measuring. Should we report each separately or give a combined effect size? Is there a single best measure of psychotherapy—or any other intervention? This is a judgmental issue.

In many instances, enough published data are available that turning data into effect sizes is straightforward. If we want a standardized effect size (d) but have only correlations, we can obtain it from the formula (Rosenthal, 1994, p. 239):

---

[2]Rosenthal assumes that researchers have file drawers bulging with studies showing null results which were never submitted because they were deemed unpublishable.

$$d = \frac{2r}{\sqrt{1 - r^2}}$$

To find d when the *t* value is given: (Rosenthal, 1994, p. 238)

$$d = \frac{t\left(n_1 + n_2\right)}{\sqrt{df}\sqrt{n_1 n_2}}$$

Creating effect sizes from incomplete data requires backward reasoning and some assumptions. For example, given only that a *t* test was statistically significant, but also given the exact level of significance and the size of the samples, we can consult a *t* table to determine what ratio yielded that significance level. This is the effect size. This procedure assumes that the control group standard deviation is close to that used in the denominator of the *t* test, usually a reasonable assumption. If no exact probability is given, we can still estimate a minimum effect size from whatever level was used, for instance the 5 or 1 percent level. Glass, McGaw, and Smith (1981), Hedges and Olkin (1985), Rosenthal (1991, 1994), and Fleiss (1994) provide instructions for translating most statistics into effect sizes. Becker (1994) discusses combining significance levels into a single significance test, and Shadish and Haddock (1994) explain how to combine effect sizes. However, we cannot cover the details here.

Corrections have been developed for small-sample studies (Hedges and Olkin, 1985) and for restricted and unreliable variables (Hunter, Schmidt, and Jackson, 1982). In the former case, the correction is so small that it is rarely of potential significance, and in the latter case it must be used with care. Hauser-Cram (1983) has suggested a number of cautions to observe in synthesizing research studies.

These concerns show that although meta-analysis is a relatively simple idea, it cannot be done perfunctorily. Important judgments regarding procedures must be made. Especially useful in his regard is the nearly 600-page *Handbook of Research Synthesis* (Cooper and Hedges, 1994), as well as a casebook (Cook et al., 1992). Since alternative models of meta-analysis have emerged, meta-analyses of the same data, following different rules, may yield different answers. The holy grail of a single completely objective "right" answer has escaped again!

Some considerations in doing a meta-analysis:
- *Each effect estimation is assumed to be independent of every other. This assumption is violated when more than one estimate from a single study is included in the combined estimate.*
- *Larger samples yield estimates closer to the population value than do smaller ones.*
- *A combination of different kinds of effects (for example, achievement and attitude) may or may not be meaningful; each instance requires a judgment.*

✦ Published data often omit information required to estimate an effect size. Reconstruction of the effect size from what is available will require making reasonable
   assumptions about the data.

✦ If the data are based solely on published studies, average effect sizes are likely to
   be overestimates. Studies not published, dissertations, and studies rejected for
   publication may show smaller effects.

Meta-Analysis Methods

All methods of meta-analysis start with an exact enough definition of the phenomenon to be studied that the body of literature pertaining to it can be located.
With the methods described in Chapter 6, as complete a search is conducted as
feasible, including unpublished federal research reports, convention papers, and
dissertations, as well as published sources. We still often find that the phenomenon of interest is confounded with other variables and we must broaden our
search to include these (see the whole-part learning example later in this chapter).
Next we must decide whether to use all the studies, or some select group of them.
Glass, for example, discarded those without control groups. Then we must decide
how we will synthesize results. Whatever the method, we must translate the results into a common "currency"; votes, effect sizes, and correlations are the most
common. With the latter two, just as we would with any data set, we must make a
distribution of the effect sizes and see if it fits our expectations. Outliers, or deviations from the normal bell-shaped curve usually suggest the influence of one or
more variables additional to the study's focus. It is worth examining the aberrations to see what they are and how they relate to what we are studying.

The Handbook of Research Synthesis (Cooper and Hedges, 1994) describes a variety of ways of synthesizing results, as do Hunter and Schmidt (1990) from the
least sophisticated vote-counting methods on up. The latter, and their chapter in
the *Handbook*, include an excellent analysis of artifacts that may affect individual
study results, their correction and their impact on a meta-analysis if uncorrected.
Let us look at two methods designed to overcome meta-analytic problems considered serious.

Study-Effect Meta-Analysis

Study-effect meta-analysis (SEMA) attacks a number of problems, but especially
that of allowing more than one effect size from a single study to enter the synthesized estimate. SEMA takes the study as the unit of analysis instead of all the individual findings within a study as Glass had done (Bangert-Drowns, 1986). In doing this, however, we throw away valuable information. For example, a study
might show that a curriculum had three positive effects: achievement, attitudinal,
and study skills. We must choose one of these, probably achievement, to represent the study. In addition, SEMA calls for the researcher to exclude outliers,
studies sufficiently deficient as to distort the outcome. Furthermore, studies are
weighted in the overall average in relation to sample size, with more weight being given to larger samples. By limiting the studies to those involving a particular

treatment and a particular kind of outcome, the procedure's conclusions are limited to these variables; they do not paint a broad picture of a research area, such as that of Glass's psychotherapy study (Hunter and Schmidt, 1990).

Variance-Partitioning Meta-Analysis

Ideally, if studies were replications of one another, instead of using the study as the unit, we could pool individual subjects into one huge study. However, since studies are not replications, we can only approximate data pooling. Further, the variability in the results is often so great that the results are clearly the consequence not only of the treatment variable but also of variations in method, instruments, and so on. This broad variability suggested to researchers with a background in analysis of variance, that they could do **variance-partitioning meta-analysis.** They would determine the effects of the various sources of variance and subtract each of them from the total variance so that what remains is more clearly the effect of the independent variable of interest. Hedges (1982) and Rosenthal and Rubin (1982) worked out statistical tests for the homogeneity of effect sizes so as to determine whether they could account for the data with a single variable. If not, then they needed to partition the variance into subgroups on some reasonable basis (by type of outcome measure, by treatment variation, by research quality, etc.) and subtract it until they could show that what remains is homogeneous. Hunter, Schmidt, and Jackson (1982) proposed a similar approach, but instead of using statistical tests for homogeneity, they estimated the sampling error. If it were no greater than 25 percent of the total variance, they assumed that the variance was homogeneous and they could account for it by a single variable.

Hunter and Schmidt (1990, 1994) have taken this procedure a step further. In their psychometric meta-analysis, they make corrections for the unreliability of the instruments, code the studies for a variety of characteristics potentially related to the phenomena under study (such as gender of subjects), and also note any study artifacts that might systematically affect the pool of results (for example, artificial dichotomization of continuous variables or restriction in range). They suggest ways of correcting for these artifacts and for unreliability in the measures in both the cause and effect variables. They then correlate each of the study-characteristic codings with the corrected effect sizes to determine whether there are relationships between effects and these variables and to determine how much of the variance of the effect measures can be accounted for. Thus, they show the presumed causal relationships between study characteristics and effect. Although many assumptions are involved, this method is an attempt to find potential inaccuracies in the estimates and to make allowances for them. For the method to be explanatory, however, substantive theory has to guide both the selection and grouping of the variables to be coded and the manner in which they are employed in the analysis; otherwise, exploration may lead to treating chance relationships as real ones.

✦ *In study-effect meta-analysis we use only one effect size from each study in the combined estimate and weight studies in relation to sample size.*

◆ *In variance-partitioning meta-analysis we group studies on the basis of character-istics that might contribute to the effect size such as the kind of persons in-volved, context factors, and methodology. We correct for the measurement un-reliability of these variables as well as other artifacts and isolate the variance attributable to these characteristics in both cause and effect variables. Finally, we determine how these variables relate to treatment outcomes and how well these corrected effects can be predicted from them.*

Advantages and Disadvantages of Quantitative Literature Summaries

They yield more decisive research summaries. Early on, Cooper and Rosenthal (1980) demonstrated a major advantage of quantitative literature summaries by showing they are more likely to yield a clear-cut answer than conventional ones. They gave seven studies supporting the same hypothesis to 41 judges who were randomly as-signed to prepare either meta-analytic or traditional analyses. Judges were asked to determine whether the studies upheld the proposition. More than twice as many of the traditional reviewers (73 percent) as meta-analytic reviewers (32 percent) found "probably or definitely" no support for the proposition. In commenting on the study, Glass, McGaw, and Smith (1981) note: "The entire set of studies occupied . . . fewer than 56 journal pages. One can imagine how much more pronounced would be the difference between these two approaches with bodies of literature typical of the size that are increasingly being addressed with meta-analytic techniques" (p. 17).

They give more complete understanding of relationships. Meta-analytic re-views help us to understand the phenomena better. For instance, Glass and Smith (1979) and Glass, McGaw, and Smith (1981) plotted class size against achieve-ment. They found that achievement increases only very slightly from huge classes sizes to those in the low teens, and then accelerates rapidly for class sizes below ten to a maximum with size one—tutoring. By plotting the effect sizes against class size, they provided a much clearer idea of the nature of the relationship. In-cidentally, small sample studies with stronger designs yielded larger effect sizes than did comparably sized studies with weaker designs.

They identify the critical features in implementation. Light (1984) notes re-search syntheses can explain which features of a treatment are critical. For exam-ple, Raudenbusch (1984), examining 18 studies of expectancy effect, found only a small effect overall (.11). However, by comparing studies with a strong ex-pectancy effect with those with a weak one, he discovered an important finding: Teachers who met their children *after* they were given information creating the expectancy showed a strong effect. Those who met the children first showed al-most none. Unless a researcher entered a study with this hypothesis, it is unlikely that it would have been determined from a single study. In the same way, using syntheses researchers can demonstrate the robustness of treatment across sites and sometimes explain conflicting results.

Their results depend on the choice of studies included and the way they are combined and contrasted. Light and Pillemer (1984) emphasize as a critical feature of such summaries the decision of what studies to combine and how to combine them. Cordray (1993) notes that the selection of studies often confounds quality of treatment implementation with quality of the research. He constructs a four-fold table of the intersections of well and poorly implemented interventions with strong and weak studies, noting that only well-implemented interventions in strong studies are usually selected for meta-analysis. However, this method limits generality and discards important information. Contrasting strong studies of well with poorly implemented interventions, he notes, "might reveal why program implementation is weak, and corrective actions could be proposed. . . . [It may also indicate] the evidence about the shortfalls or obstacles that could be encountered in other settings. . . . [And it may be interpreted in terms of a dose-response relationship to yield information about the] added value of increasing the strength of the intervention"(p. 83). Most important is how *"out-puts,* or *benefits,* or *effect sizes* vary from one set of circumstances to another . . . [since the meta-analyst] rarely works on a collection of data that can sensibly be described as a probability sample from anything" (Glass, 1995, p. 738, emphasis in the original).

Broadening the inclusion rules may also be important if the target to which we plan to generalize is not well represented by the studies we chose. For example, selecting only sites where the treatment was well implemented may be closer to a convenience than a representative sample, as Crain (1984), for example, showed. He found that studies selected by the National Institute of Education to evaluate the effectiveness of school desegregation differed in important ways from typical practice.

Their results can depend on the classification system used for grouping studies homogeneously. The system used for classifying studies into homogeneous groups is important in determining both what variables are found related to the effect and how well a meta-analysis illuminates the interrelations of independent to dependent variables. Providing a classification system adequate for the variables being studied is critical to the acceptability of the summary.

For example, in a meta-analysis of whole vs. part learning of psychomotor skills LaMura (1987) had to develop a system for classifying the studies in terms of what pattern of whole and part learning was used. Using W for practicing the whole skill, P1 to designate the first part practiced, P2 for the second and so forth, she could describe the variety of possible patterns and classify the studies. One pattern might begin with practicing the whole, concentrate on a part, return to the whole and similarly proceed through all the parts (WP1W, WP2W . . .). Alternatively one might add successive parts: (P1), (P1 + P2), (P1 + P2 + P3) until W is reached. However, examination of the literature showed that these variations of treatment were administered under conditions of massed practice (all at one learning session) or distributed practice (distributed over several sessions), or both. Thus, a second variable was introduced, and studies had to be sorted into the different possible combinations of variations of whole versus part learning with massed versus distributed practice. Developing such a structure from a review of the literature is one of the most important tasks of the meta-analyst. The structure facilitates understanding the field and also shows where research has and has not been done and hence where new research is most needed.

They can inform strategic plans for future research. Neyman (1967) refers to careful design of a study as the tactics of science. By analogy, design of a series to explore and understand a phenomenon is the strategy. Whereas Glass saw a strength of meta-analysis as the synthesis of studies using different methods in which the strengths of one made up for the weaknesses of another, Shadish (1993) suggests that we should use "critical multiplism" to so design a series of studies to achieve this result. Certainly, after completing a meta-analysis, the researcher is in an excellent position to suggest a strategy for future studies such as Shadish recommends.

They show that the consistency of social science findings is comparable to natural science's. We have noted that replication is the ultimate validation of a generalization; meta-analyses bring together the data from replications. We tend to think that results in the social and behavioral sciences are less replicable than those of the physical sciences. Hedges (1987) notes that "essentially identical methods are used to test the consistency of research results in physics and psychology" (p. 443). He compared thirteen exemplary reviews from each domain and found that the results of physical experiments are not strikingly more consistent than those of social or behavioral experiments. This welcome news contradicts a stereotype about the "softness" of behavioral science results. Hedges suggests that "study of the actual cumulativeness found in physical data could inform social scientists about what to expect from replicated experiments under good conditions" (p. 443).

- ✦ *Reviewers using meta-analytic procedures are more likely to give clear-cut answers regarding the existence of a relationship than traditional literature reviewers.*
- ✦ *From meta-analysis data researchers can determine the shape and nature of a relationship as it is affected by other variables.*
- ✦ *Similarly, researchers can find the critical features in implementation.*
- ✦ *Researchers can also find the best strategy for designing future studies of a phenomenon.*
- ✦ *Meta-analysis results depend on the framework used in classifying the studies.*
- ✦ *Judging from meta-analysis results, the consistency of social science findings appears comparable to that of the natural sciences.*

Hallmarks of Meta-Analytic Studies and Tips for Doing Them

A good meta-analytic study should meet the following guidelines; you should:

1. Describe the search pattern used to find studies as well as the criteria for selecting from these.

2. Either enter each study in the meta-analysis only once or, alternatively, show the effect size with and without multiple measures from the same sample.
3. Develop a reasonable framework for classifying the studies that include the variables likely to be found together in that domain.
4. Indicate the characteristics of studies that were selected and how they were coded.
5. Where multiple judges are used in categorizing or classifying studies or their characteristics, indicate the extent of their agreement.
6. Estimate effect size from the best studies as well as the total composite.
7. Compare the composite effect sizes of published studies with unpublished ones such as dissertations and convention papers.
8. Examine the distribution of effect sizes: look for outliers or deviations from the expected bell-shaped curve, and seek their explanation by examining the apparently aberrant studies.
9. Indicate where there are adequate studies for the analysis and where they are lacking.
10. List the studies, their sample sizes, and the effect sizes they contribute (if not published it should be available on request).
11. Trace the sources of variation among studies to variables that might reasonably be considered to account for them; in a variance-partitioning analysis, partition and remove variance until the remainder is homogeneous.
12. Evaluate judgmentally the adequacy of the kinds of studies included. This is especially important if all research in the area is weak, or if weak studies predominate.
13. Discuss any interesting results or side effects discerned in borderline studies that just missed being included in the set analyzed because of the definition of the variables.

Despite the fact that meta-analyses require many judgments, as do also conventional reviews, meta-analytic techniques are here to stay. However, combining them with traditional judgmental qualifications about the strengths and weaknesses of the studies, and their influence on the composite results, is probably the most reasonable course to follow. Slavin (1985) has argued for "best-evidence synthesis," a combination of judgmental and quantitative methods. In the same vein, Light and Pillemer (1984) is still an excellent analysis of problems in both narrative and quantitative reviews.

SUMMARY

Meta-analysis combines the results of studies of a relationship to produce an overall estimate of its size. It provides a perspective on mixtures of positive, zero, and negative effect sizes. The latter two are difficult for conventional reviewers to handle; however, they must be expected in meta-analyses of weak treatments since they are simply the low end in a distribution of effect sizes. Providing a framework within which the studies can be analyzed throws light on the important variables and their interrelationships; it is conducive to theory and model building. Meta-analysis can show the moderating effect of variables, of research methods, and of measures, in addition to estimating the overall treatment effect and its shape in relation to treatment strength (dose-response). It is one of the most important advances in integrating findings and unifying a fragmented field of research results.

A Look Ahead

Having explored research methods that deal with the quantitative approach, we turn to areas where their mixture of methods borrows from both qualitative and quantitative approaches and adds to them as appropriate to devise the best study possible. We turn first to the discipline of history as an example of such research.

ADDITIONAL READING

Glass, McGaw, and Smith (1981) is one of the earliest treatments; it gets across the basic ideas without the complexities of later discussions. Hedges and Olkin (1985) requires statistical knowledge to appreciate what they accomplished but is solid. Hunter and Schmidt (1990) is one of the most readable accounts, as is Hunter, Schmidt, and Jackson (1982), an earlier version. *The Handbook of Research Synthesis* (Cooper and Hedges, 1994) is one of a series of books sponsored by the Russell Sage Foundation staff who, sensing meta-analysis's potential, sought to show how to do it correctly. The chapters vary in their complexity but the *Handbook* is currently the most complete treatment. See Glass (1995) for a review of the *Handbook* and another point of view. Cook and colleagues (1992), another in the series, is a casebook of four meta-analyses that reflect a variety of techniques and includes useful commentaries. Regarding meta-analysis as a research method in its own right, see Shadish (1996). For a well-done example that combines meta-analysis and narrative, see Cooper, Nye, Charlton, Lindsay, and Greathouse (1996).

IMPORTANT TERMS

Effect size
Meta-analysis

Study-effect meta-analysis (SEMA)
Variance-partitioning meta-analysis

APPLICATION PROBLEM

David Ausubel's concept of advance organizers has been heavily studied and thus is a prime candidate for meta-analysis. (Advance organizers, placed at the beginning of material to be studied, convey the concepts of that material in terms that relate it to what the student already knows without using the terms in the material—for example, by analogy). In one such project, Luiten, Ames, and Ackerson (1980) did a study-effect meta-analysis because they believed that advance organizers might have small but consistent treatment effects that might not always show up as statistically significant. For the period from 1960 to 1979, they found 170 published and unpublished studies, including 76 doctoral dissertations. The authors focused on both learning and retention effects. Learning was defined as measured within 24 hours of the treatment. Retention was divided into five periods ranging from 2–6 days to over 22 days. Mean effect sizes ranged from .21 for the aggregate learning scores to .38 for the 22+ periods. Even the lowest effect size of .21 indicated that, with the advance organizer, the average student performed better than 58 percent of those without it. Luiten and colleagues concluded that advance organizers have a facilitative effect on retention.

Luiten and colleagues also considered the effect of advance organizers by grade level, by subject type, and by ability level. For example, for the four years of college, average learning effect size was .28 and retention was .21. For the primary grades 3–8, learning was .17 and retention was .33. They reached a number of conclusions:

a. The studies showed a trend toward increased effect size over time, thus indicating that advance organizers provide a permanent advantage rather than a short-term "warm-up" effect.

b. Advance organizers are effective with individuals of all ability levels and most effective with those of high ability.

c. Advance organizers are useful at all grade levels. However, grade level is an influencing variable since college-age students showed the highest effect for learning but those in the primary grades had the greatest average effect in terms of retention.

d. Since positive average effect sizes were found for all subject groupings, advance organizers facilitate learning and retention in a wide range of subject areas.

Based on the data available to you, do these conclusions seem reasonable? What additional information would you like to have?

Compare your answers with that following the Application Exercise.

APPLICATION EXERCISE

Have enough studies been done on some aspect of your study to mount a meta-analysis? If so, how might the results from such an analysis help in the reformulation of your problem? Which form might such a meta-analysis take? SEMA? Variance partitioning? Vote count? Average all the effect sizes found in the studies?

ANSWERS TO THE APPLICATION PROBLEM

Given that the authors are noting trends, their assumptions appear reasonable. Although we may disagree with the groupings they use to analyze their data, they nevertheless have used a straightforward classification system for dividing the studies into homogeneous groups for analysis and hence for examining the relationship between independent and dependent groups. They have discussed each study only once for a particular conclusion and have included unpublished as well as published sources.

On the other hand, the investigators have not provided any criteria for inclusion of studies. It is implied, but not stated, that they used every study that they could find. Further, they did not indicate whether there was a difference in the average effect sizes between published and unpublished studies, which might indicate whether and to what extent the published studies overestimated the effect. Their conclusions should be interpreted with caution.

Examples of Fields Applying Basic Methods

Many fields of research have no methods that are unique to their discipline. They build on and, as did survey research for the development of questionnaires, add to the basic techniques we have discussed in previous sections. Representative of such fields rather than comprehensive, the chapters in this section are illustrative of the possibilities for employing basic research methods in different research areas. Obviously, many more kinds of studies could have been included, for example, longitudinal studies or single-subject studies. Researchers are constantly inventing new combinations of methods, extending and refining them, and finding new fields of application. The two fields included in this section are:

- Chapter 22 on historical research, which explores how qualitative techniques can be applied to past records and how, in some instances, quantitative techniques can be used as well.
- Chapter 23 on evaluation studies and action research, which describes the ways a range of research methods is employed in evaluation where use of the findings is a key criterion. In evaluation, the audience is sometimes involved in the process to ensure they are privy to, and will use the findings. The audience for the findings actually does the research in action research.

As did the earlier methods chapters, these chapters include sections on hallmarks and tips for skilled application.

C H A P T E R 22

Historical Research

Sometimes historians search for a single fact as when Mosteller and Wallace . . . sought to determine whether Madison or Hamilton wrote the Federalist papers. In other instances, they try to understand the meaning of the past to the living as when the black historian John Hope Franklin tutored the Supreme Court lawyers in the 1954 case that overturned the "separate but equal" doctrine. He demonstrated convincingly " . . . in the view of the framers, the Amendment meant equality . . . and that if they were around today they wouldn't support segregation and discrimination."

J. Starr, "Above All, a Scholar"

Through an understanding of the past many historians seek to contribute to our current knowledge of the human condition. They explain if they do not predict. In this role, they follow the same rules as do other behavioral scientists. For their finding of patterns in the past, historians are to be especially treasured. True, hindsight is on their side. But it is difficult enough to make progress when we can set our own stage for data collection. Making sense of the leavings of a culture is a tough job!

D. R. K.

OVERVIEW

History consists of the discovery, selection, organization, and interpretation of evidence to describe a situation or to answer a question about past events. Free to choose and interpret their data, historians are judged by the intelligence and honesty they bring to the task as they seek to interpret data from a new standpoint. The chapter is titled "historical research" instead of "historical method" because history is distinguished mainly by content rather than method. Its methods include careful and sometimes clever application of logic and the basic social science research techniques we have already covered. It is unique mainly in its emphasis on authentication of evidence.

CHAPTER CONTENTS

Introduction

What is a historical study? There are probably as many definitions as there are historians. Particularly noteworthy, however, is the definition provided by Fischer (1970, p. xv): "A historian is someone (anyone) who asks an open-ended question about past events and answers it with selected facts." He notes that "questions and answers are fitted to each other by a complex pattern of mutual adjustment." Facts teach us how to better formulate the questions; this step leads to a different selection of facts, which in turn requires reformulation of the question. Thus, Fischer sees the logic of history as neither inductive nor deductive. Instead, it is adductive reasoning, where *adducing* means "leading out the answer . . . to specific questions so that a satisfactory explanatory fit" is attained. The result "may take many forms: a statistical generalization, or a narrative, or a causal model, or a motivational model, or . . . maybe even an analogy" (p. xv).

Historical studies serve many purposes. Sometimes they help us to see a parallel between present and past events. Allison (1971) analyzed the Cuban missile crisis in which the United States and the Soviet Union stood toe to toe in a nuclear confrontation with disaster. He points out that a historian's analysis was important: "Kennedy . . . saw how miscalculation . . . could turn this path into a slippery slope. Having recently read Barbara Tuchman's *Guns of August* he mused about the miscalculations . . . within each government [that] allowed them to tumble into war" (pp. 218–219). Allison shows how Kennedy, resisting his own bureaucracy, provided time for the Soviets, to minimize hurrying that might lead to miscalculations.

Sometimes history is used to support theoretical positions. For instance, Laslett (1980), employing Marx's theory of social change, used contrasting groups and time frames. She showed how it explained the 1850–1870 change from the extended family to the small nuclear family structure as a result of the shift from farming for family and local consumption to farming for production purposes.

In other instances, historians give us perspective so that we may better judge progress. Such views may yield unique and useful insights on particular social science problems.

Methods of the Historian

History displays the increasing unity of the behavioral sciences in borrowing techniques from other fields. As all of human experience is the stuff of history, it is natural that historians should search widely for techniques to facilitate their work. They most commonly use the qualitative method's analysis of content. But they also use the statistical analyses associated with experiments and surveys; the analytic techniques of the linguist to determine the authorship of texts; carbon dating and ink chemistry to date various artifacts, especially documents; and the instincts of the detective to track down the obscure records, lost manuscripts, forgotten diaries, and other evidence of the past. Historians have to become adept at authenticating their evidence and determining how it bears on the particular problem they are studying. The good historian is a jack-of-all-trades and the master of as many of them as possible.

Many historians consider themselves "the real interdisciplinarians." Dealing mainly in words, historians, like many scholars in other fields, have voiced concerns about the "number crunchers" (cliometricians). Nevertheless, historians also have succumbed to the siren call of numbers for the same reasons others have: "Correct or not, they speak to us with authority; they have rhetorical force" (Barzun and Graff, 1977, p. 201). Hence, some historians, like Aydelotte, have actively sought to illustrate how quantitative methods contribute to historical understanding (Aydelotte, 1971; Aydelotte, Bogue, and Fogel, 1972). Historians have also borrowed theory from other behavioral sciences. For example, psychohistorians describe their psychological insights into the reasons that public figures acted as they did, as in Mazlish's (1972) study of President Nixon.

History as Selective Interpretation

The match of a strongly developed rationale with carefully selected and organized data to show their congruence is always partly an art. The skills of the writer are critical in all research methods that rely on narration to make their case; qualitative method is a prime example. The best historians are very good writers because they think clearly and logically, and they write the way they think: Words flowing effortlessly through the narrative pique reader interest while they simultaneously drive home the points to be made. Consider Fischer's (1970) description of a local antiquarian:

> In every New England town library, there is likely to be an ancient Puritan virgin, shriveled and dried in the snows of sixty Massachusetts winters and suitably shrouded in black bombazine, who has been at work for the past twenty years on the story of her home town from 1633 to 1933 when Franklin Roosevelt was inaugurated and history came to an end. (pp. 140–141)

For some historians, just as for some qualitative researchers, description is an adequate goal. For many historians, however, there are too many stories to be told; thus, not the story, but generalizations drawn from it are significant. They prefer to select facts and tell stories that provide an explanation or rationale, clarify a principle, or reveal a point of view, thus giving forward-looking usefulness and perspective to their work. Out of this mold have come writers like Toynbee, Spengler, Nietzsche, Malthus, and Voltaire. Probably the great majority of historians are between these two extremes, neither solely telling a story for the story's sake nor explicating some grand theory. More likely, they are using an explanation to throw light on a corner of history not yet illuminated from that angle.

Every research method has its special demands. Clearly, the ability to combine strong storytelling with an organizing rationale is critical to the historical method. Nevins (1975) tells a story of Lincoln Steffens, who on seeing a man bearing a glittering fragment of truth warned Satan "that man has hold of some truth. He could kill you if he tried. . . . 'No danger,' Satan replied. 'He will take that fragment home, chisel it, rub it, dull it until it has no power whatsoever.'" "Not so," says Nevins. "Truth, like the South African diamond, is a dull cloudy pebble when first discovered. Long labor and the nicest art have to be applied to cut it into those well-polished facets that give it scintillating power" (pp. 41–42). That is the work of the historian.

Scientific History

With a longer tradition than other social sciences, historians have watched many views of their role become dominant and then fade. For example, scholars, seeing the success of the methods of the physical sciences, suggested that historians attempt to be completely objective in writing the chronicle of some event or era. Such "scientific history" attempted to re-create what "really" occurred in great detail and resulted in what has been called "dry as dust" history (Barzun and Graff, 1977). Perhaps, some still hold this view. Certainly, the effort to be objective in the sense of accurately interpreting the evidence is a matter of considerable pride to every historian. Still, as with any observation, historians also realize that there can never be a complete picture. Nor, if that were possible, would we want one; all the details are usually not important to what is of most interest.

Interpretive History

Most historians would argue that all history is interpretive; the human mind continually seeks patterns in the events that pass before it. The historian interprets not only in selecting what is important but also in determining how important facts are juxtaposed and organized; the latter implicitly creates relations and imparts ideas. To say that "Franklin D. Roosevelt won the election over the conservative Herbert Hoover" implies, in some way, that conservativeness caused the defeat. How the historian arranges that pattern is at once an important contribution for some observers and, to the extent that another person would arrange it to convey something else, a problem for others.

"The objection that historians select their facts to suit themselves is seen to be no objection but a helpful necessity. They are meant to think and to choose and they are judged by the intelligence and honesty with which they do both" (Barzun and Graff, 1985, p. 190). And, as they indicate, historians must wrestle with the problem of making a single stream of words weave a multidimensional tapestry. It must include the various strands occurring simultaneously at different locations, viewed from whatever perspective the historian has chosen.[1]

Thus, there is the realization that all history is interpretative, that the extent of interpretation varies with the author, the author's purpose, and the reader's perception of the events. This interpretiveness may be particularly apparent when an author is advancing a hypothesis and is marshaling evidence for it, especially if we suspect that he or she is selectively overemphasizing or underemphasizing to make the point. Some people have so criticized Toynbee's (1948) analysis of past civilizations, which contends that their fall was the result not just of external attacks but of internal defects or failures. Where the readers' view of the facts is congruent with that of the historian's, they may perceive the extent of interpretation as relatively minor, as in Tuchman (1962). In retelling the story of World War I, she shows how individuals set in motion events over which they lose control and then repeatedly interpret the evidence selectively to fit their predispositions.

Historians, perhaps more than professionals in other fields, restudy a problem. The outlook and way of thinking of historians are products of the age in which they live. Doing revisionary history, reinterpreting previous accounts, imposing a new explanatory framework, adding new data, and discounting old data are common activities. "The past cannot help but be reconceived by every generation, but the earlier reports upon it are as good and true as they ever were" (Barzun and Graff, 1992, p. 191). The picture is never finished, more recent accounts are not necessarily more true, each "subtracts a little and adds more" (ibid.) Thus, early historians view the Protestant Reformation

> as mainly a theological and military event; in . . . the eighteenth century . . . as a reshaping of the map of Europe, a strengthening of emergent states and a furthering of intellectual freedom. In the nineteenth century [it is seen] . . . as a religious movement with profound social implications; in the twentieth . . . a social and economic revolution with religious and political side effects. (Barzun and Graff, 1977, p. 156)

The authors point out that knowing the full history requires reading successive treatments just as a researcher of an event "seeks out all its witnesses" (ibid.).

When setting forth a generalization, historians employ the same chain of reasoning we have found useful in analyzing other research methods. As earlier, the chain does not describe how they do their work so much as how they present the results. How the historian constructs different parts of the chain will become clearer as the chapter progresses.

 ✦ *Historians seeking generalizations find, assemble, organize, and interpret evidence.*
 ✦ *They may adduce a rationale or an explanation from the evidence or may have developed it in advance and seek to demonstrate its validity.*

---

[1]Notice how well these two paragraphs apply to the report of any qualitative study; they are right on target!

✦ Selectively choosing and organizing the evidence, historians seek to show effectively, yet honestly, the correspondence between it and their proposed explanation.

✦ Historians are judged by the intelligence and the integrity with which they perform this task.

Steps in a Historical Study

Problem Formulation, Problem Modification, and Hypothesis Development

Just as methodologists with new tools seek problems that they can attack with them, the historian may start with a lucky find and work backward to learn what interesting questions to ask of that evidence. Sometimes a new set of papers is given to an institution, formerly confidential papers are declassified, or recently discovered materials are made available by an archivist for study. Often, as in other fields, the initial formulation of a problem is considerably altered by later findings. Then the researcher must recast the whole problem as he learns both what evidence can be found and what questions are appropriate to ask of it. No more than in any other field do historians necessarily conduct their studies in the ordered way that the evidence is reported.

Historians often begin like participant observers, determining the important aspects of the person or event as they proceed, though probably having predetermined notions about where to look—an inductive or emergent problem approach. For them, the design links of the chain of reasoning—persons (subjects), situation, causes (treatments) and effects (independent variable, observation or measurement), basis for sensing the attributes or changes that occurred—are only partly determined at the outset. They emerge more clearly as the historian repeatedly cycles back through the data deciding what is important, finding and examining it, analyzing it, deciding more precisely what is needed next, searching for and finding it, examining it, deciding still again, and so on. Thus, the chain of reasoning evolves as the historian defines the study more clearly.

With a hypothesis dimly in mind, historians' first steps are like those of any other researchers—to see what others have done and to clarify concepts. The main difference lies in the references they will consult; certain topics have their own access routes. For example, historians may get their first hunches from Adams' *Dictionary of American History* (1976–1978), Johnson's *Oxford Companion to American History* (1966), Langer's *Encyclopedia of World History* (1972), the *Harvard Guide to American History* (Friedel and Showman, 1974), and the American Historical Association's series ending in the 1961 *Guide to Historical Literature.*

Just as other researchers have difficulty cutting their problem to fit their time and energy, historians, too, are likely to take on too large an initial problem. Barzun and Graff (1992) define a just-right-sized problem as one where the "group of associated facts and ideas . . . presented . . . leave no questions unanswered WITHIN the presentation, even though questions could be asked OUTSIDE of it" (p. 16).[2] Comparable to the feasibility problem in other research, there is the limitation of whether there are adequate records, artifacts, or other evidence to permit the investigation planned. Such evidence was not often designed to help the historian. It consists of what someone else thought was worth collecting and saving and is nearly always incomplete. It is thin in times of intense action when historians would like a complete and accurate immediate record instead of a self-edited retroactive one. It can be fullest when there is little else to do, during a time of less interest.

Historians cannot manipulate treatment, create new data, or take new measures. Because they are confined to the objects, artifacts, and records left to them by the past, often they must resort to indirect evidence. A classic example of this is the problem of showing the growth of the British bureaucracy in the days before organizational charts. Records of the growth of government procurements of sealing wax very nicely documented the expansion. Failing such evidence, there is little the historical researcher can do if the records are not there. However, a good bit of ingenuity goes into both in divining evidence that might have been kept, and undertaking the detective work of finding it; a good bit of luck helps, too.

Like the lawyer who distrusts hearsay evidence, historians most value firsthand accounts by participants instead of secondary reports of persons who have heard about, read about, or perhaps talked to participants. They seek evidence in official records and reports, minutes of meetings, photographs, recordings, bulletins, catalogs, licenses, certificates, and other documents likely to be generated in the activities they are studying. The author's relation to the event is important. Was it an immediate or a retrospective account? If the latter, how much time elapsed between event and report? Was the event viewed directly, or is the account based on what other people saw?

Oral history has special problems (Vansina, 1965; Davis, Back, and MacLean, 1977; Rosaldo 1980). Just as in interpreting documents, oral statements must be understood as cultural products, and one must learn when to take them literally, figuratively, or in some instances, ironically (for example, do they really mean to "kill the ump" in a baseball game?).

+ *The focus of a historian's study is often emergent as is typical of qualitative research*
+ *Data collection is limited to what a culture left behind and is often thinnest during active periods and vice versa. Indirect evidence must be relied on when direct evidence is missing.*
+ *Firsthand accounts are sought in preference to hearsay evidence.*

---

[2]This is an excellent specification of problem size for any research method, not just history!

Validation of Evidence

How can the researcher be sure that the evidence unearthed is what it purports to be? In a few instances, artifacts may be forgeries, like the Hitler diaries unveiled with much fanfare some years ago. Records may be drafts; an autobiography may really be a biography. Authenticity of dubious historical evidence may be hard to establish. We typically proceed by looking for consistencies in its content, its physical condition, and the context in which it was found. We may examine the dates of other material found with it; may subject ink and paper to chemical analysis, radioactive-carbon, or other dating techniques; examine watermarks and word usage for typicality at the time of presumed production; and look for facts and allusions appropriate for the time as well as ensuring the absence of inappropriate ones. In some instances of disputed authorship, counts of unusual word usages and constructions can be made by computer, and the document can then be analyzed to determine its resemblance to the base rates of the contending authors in other documents. Mosteller and Wallace (1984) used this technique to analyze the Federalist Papers to determine whether Hamilton or Madison authored them. Their evidence strengthened the prevailing opinion favoring Madison.[3]

✦ *Authenticating evidence is one of the unique skills of the historian.*

Accuracy of Account

A document may be genuine in that it was produced at the time and by the person presumed to have produced it but still be an inaccurate account of what is of interest. To evaluate the accomplishments of President Franklin D. Roosevelt, we would not take the campaign speeches of 1942 as accurate. Not only are they deficient because they are campaign speeches but also a war was being fought; so there might be things that could not be revealed at that time. The person, the circumstances under which the document was produced, the purposes it is to serve, and the question we are trying to answer, all affect our estimate of the likelihood of an accurate account. For example, if not a record of accomplishments, Roosevelt's speeches would still document the kinds of anxiety that people in the government felt had to be allayed during those difficult times.

An analysis of the other work of an author or in the records of a clerk may help to establish whether the individual was accurate in instances where there is certainty regarding what occurred. Internally inconsistent reporting destroys the credibility of the reporter. Obvious errors in totals, or apparent inconsistencies in recording data brand a writer as untrustworthy.

The training of the author may be helpful in this regard, particularly if it would provide competency in the field involved and an understanding of the sig-

---

[3]Authentication of artifacts has been called *external criticism,* and the problem of establishing their accuracy or worth, *internal criticism.* For a variety of reasons, these terms seem less used these days; they are noted here in case you come across them.

nificant aspects of a situation. A good television sports commentator points out many aspects of the game a novice would otherwise miss. But knowledge is only part of the story. A professor visiting another professor's classroom may be thoroughly familiar with the subject being taught. But a trained observer who has been observing classrooms might give us a report that we would prefer for its accuracy and its attention to detail regarding teaching methods. Both knowledge of the phenomenon and experience in observing and reporting it on the part of the author increase our confidence in that author's report.

The circumstances under which the report is made also affects its accuracy. We might expect that routine records would generally be kept accurately and without bias. Yet when these are the basis for punitive administrative or other action, they may not represent the facts. For example, the statistics for the New York State narcotics law should show the size of the drug problem. However, faced with the law's mandates for long sentences on conviction, judges may be more reluctant to find the person guilty of that particular crime in the first place, thus biasing the conviction record. Similar pressures may make open letters of reference less reliable than those never intended to be seen by the subject.

Lastly, the purpose for which the report is made is important. A public record is one thing, a private report another. A report to a superior may be written to impress, whereas a staff report, intended for guidance in decision making, may be more objective. Propaganda and advertising contrast with report writing, though the latter, too, may have less obvious but equally distorting hidden agendas. Ascertaining purpose obviously helps us judge the author's motives.

Historians are reconciled to the fact that some truths may never be known where accounts differ. Did President Truman fire Secretary of State James F. Byrnes? Truman's memoirs say he did. Byrnes, in his autobiography, says he didn't. "Barring the presence of an unsuspected witness, . . . precision must often remain an ideal and finality a dream" (Barzun and Graff, 1970, p. 159).

◆ *The historian is responsible not only for finding but also authenticating evidence and then determining its worth and contribution to the problem. Authenticity is a necessary but not sufficient condition that evidence will make a worthwhile contribution.*

Problems of Analysis and Rival Explanations

The relation of constructs to their operationalization, a problem for any researcher, contains a special twist for the historian. Is the meaning of the construct consistent from one time period to another, or does it change in ways that might suggest rival explanations? For example, in considering changes in family size as judged from census data, we must make sure that the meaning of "household size" was constant. We must ask, did a "family" include adult sisters and brothers, in addition to husband, wife, and children living together? Apparently it did at one time. Did it include boarders who ate and lived with the family? The latter, in particular, could have a significant effect on apparent household size but would also constitute a different concept of a household from any usual meaning.

Whereas we usually think of operationalization as moving from construct to evidence, the reverse process is equally important for the historian where the intended purpose of an artifact in a culture is not clear. Consider the many spoofs of how today's toilets might be interpreted by historians of the future as places of religious ritual and sacrifice to unknown gods. The difficulty of inferring the meaning of things in another time and place is readily apparent.

Rival Explanations. Most of the rival explanations listed in Chapter 20 on experimentation apply to historical events as well. Especially prevalent is selection, since we nearly always use intact groups (no mystical figure was out there arranging randomly assigned ones for tomorrow's researchers!). Such groups are almost always subject to some selection pressure, often related to the topic being studied. We are not even free of the problem of volunteers, since many groups are self-selected. For example, were people who immigrated to the United States those who were the most unhappy in their homeland, the most aggressive and proactive in seeking solutions to problems, the misfits and maladjusted, the uneducated? All of these are possible selection factors that might have contributed to the nature of their lives. Differential mortality among immigrants is also a factor in that those who returned disgruntled to their homeland were not a random sample of the original group. Selection was a factor in the representativeness of the army during the U.S. Civil War. Although there was a draft, it was both legal and common practice for wealthy men to hire individuals to take their place.

Just as selection may occur with respect to the individuals involved, it may also occur with respect to the records. Laslett (1980), for example, noted the belief that extended families were the dominant form in preindustrial societies. She wondered whether this belief was a reflection less of commonality than of the fact that wealthier families tended to live in larger and more complex households. Since such families were more likely to create diaries, letters, and other artifacts as well as to preserve these records, the impression may have been more a function of the selective availability of records than of reality.

Society and culture determine what is important to record. The kinds of persons who make and retain records are different from those who don't. Only certain kinds of events are typically recorded. There are, for example, plenty of probate records in precolonial Maryland but no regular methods of recording births and marriages. Exactly the reverse is true of Massachusetts; both reflect what was important in the religion and life of that time. Clearly, knowledge of the culture is essential to correct interpretation.

Many rival explanations can be eliminated if there is a control group. Establishing such groups requires creativity and ingenuity. Briggs (1978), for example, wanted to show how children of Italian immigrants in the United States compared with their non-Italian classmates in achievement. He compared each child with an Italian surname in three Rochester public schools over the years 1910–1924 to the child nearest on the class roll with a non-Italian surname. With this group he could compare age in grade, attendance, and promotion to next grade. Children of Italian immigrants tended to be older but had better attendance and had very slightly less chance of repeating a grade. Briggs was concerned about the middle-class bias of the district as a whole. Therefore, instead of comparing these children with district averages, he sought a comparable working-class control group. His scheme depended, of course, on the assumption that the neighborhood attendance area for a school was relatively homogeneous with respect to socioeconomic class, a not too improbable assumption in that day.

Historians face special problems of analysis, including these:
+ *The necessity for understanding the meaning of constructs in the culture and at the time studied*
+ *The possibility that constructs change in meaning over time*
+ *The difficulty of inferring the meaning of artifacts except as we understand their meaning in the culture*
+ *The fact that society and culture determine what is important to record so that selectivity with respect to records may be an important factor to take into account*
+ *The difficulty of establishing control or contrasting groups in past data; much ingenuity is required*
+ *Historical studies are subject to the same rival explanations as other studies, but selection and mortality may be especially common.*

Inference of Causation

Like other behavioral scientists, historians are very much interested in causation, and the internal validity (LP) of their study. Some work on a grandiose scale, like Marx, who viewed the world in terms of the social forms of production and its consequences. Others are concerned with less cosmic events, such as the cause of a particular war or battle or of the triumph of an individual over circumstances. Causation pervades history.

Nearly all the voluminous writing on the historical method has considered problems of causation. Historians have certain advantages. They can choose selectively among the wide scope of past events to prove their point. They are not caught up with and blinded by the passions of the time studied. They have the advantage of hindsight, of knowing what happened, and they can trace backwards for causes. In spite of the favorable factors, authors agree that the historian's task is formidable, even with the clarity of hindsight. Given, among other problems, faulty and partial records and differing perspectives, people who think deeply about the problem generally believe only "highly plausible connections" can be demonstrated.

But historians want to write forcefully and present a strong case, often doing so dramatically. Many write as though the cause were clear using words like *inevitable*, *unavoidable*, and *inescapable*. Carr (1962), in discussing causation, suggests that we should do without such terms: "Life will be drabber. But let us leave them to the poets and metaphysicians."[4] Barzun and Graff (1992, p. 177) propose using

---

[4]But he is nevertheless partial to vivid writing; on the next page, he asks to be excused for not getting rid of *inevitable* in his own work (p. 126).

the term *conditions* and talk of the "probability of events." These are the exceptions. Just like all other behavioral scientists, historians make the strongest case the evidence permits for each of the internal validity (LP) judgments.

Satisfying the Conditions for Inferring Causation. The rationale or explanation plays the same role in historical studies as in other studies. We show the fit of the rationale to the data and the extent to which changes in causes resulted in changes in effect. If we argue that emigration is a function of economic conditions, the more tightly the rate of emigration follows the gyrations of the economic indicators, the stronger is the presumption of a causative relationship.

One of the most convincing conditions, the production of an effect at will, is denied the historian, who can only pick and choose to illustrate past events and cannot create them. In one important sense, however, there are predictive possibilities: predicting the as yet unknown or undiscovered on the basis of the known. The historian who supplies missing pieces later confirmed by new discoveries is in much the same position as the astronomer who predicts the existence of an unseen planet or moon later shown to be present. Such evidence is very convincing. Sometimes such predictions can be made from one period to another when the data from the other period have not yet been analyzed in that way. This serves exactly the same purpose as a cross-validation sample or replication does in quantitative research.

The presumption of causation is strengthened by showing repeated examples in varying circumstances—Mill's method of agreement applied to historical data. Toynbee, for example, tracing his thesis about the rise and fall of civilizations over a range of cultures, shows that his argument holds under a variety of circumstances.

Demonstrating that cause precedes effect is difficult, if not impossible. Fischer (1970), for instance, disagrees with Potter's (1954) *People of Plenty,* which argues that much of Americanism resulted from affluence. Only recently have people thought of themselves as affluent, says Fischer; "portraits of our ancestors have a lean and hungry look . . . They became American and *then* became affluent" (p. 172). Which came first? Were Americanism and affluence interactive? Have we found an amplifying loop? Precedence as a condition may not be possible to show, nor may it make much sense in this or other historical situations. The large number of historical phenomena that are really relatively self-contained interactive systems makes precedence useful only for analyzing isolated sections of the chain of events.

Multiple Causes. Can historians ever claim to have found the single necessary and sufficient cause of an event? It is true that there are events in history that appear to be the key to what follows? For example, Fischer (1970, p. 173) notes that enemy possession of Confederate General Robert E. Lee's General Order 191 allowed Union General George B. McClellan to anticipate where Lee would mass his troops. It may have been fatal to the loss of Antietam, a defeat that may have cost the South the possibility of European intervention and hence the Civil War.

Others, in return, may build competing chains of events. Which is correct? Perhaps all are! Perhaps the possession of the Confederate order is but one of multiple contributing conditions, which together produced the eventual outcome.

Like all behavioral scientists, historians abstract and simplify. In this pursuit, they are confronted with complex people in biographies, with institutional histories, and with a range of people and institutions in important events and over periods of time. Therefore, historians are much less prone to the highly simplified single-variable descriptions of the psychologist or the more complex pictures painted by many sociologists. Patterns of multiple causation are the norm instead of the exception. With the acceptance of multiple causation, complex social phenomena can be looked at from different points of view, each making good sense.

David Tyack (1976) demonstrates this very nicely in an essay explaining the rise of compulsory schooling as driven by five different intents or causes: (1) as a means of binding students to the nation-state, (2) as a means to satisfy the ethnocentric demands of religious and ethnic groups, (3) as an outgrowth of the developing school bureaucrat, (4) as an investment in human capital, and (5) as a way of reproducing the class structure of American society, a Marxian interpretation. Each explanation is shown to fit the facts, some better at certain periods than others, but all apparently having some validity.

Not only does Tyack's example demonstrate how a single event can be open to multiple understandings but it also indicates the creativity that historians bring to the reinterpretation of events. Often they reconstruct the past from a new angle, bringing a different insight to past explanations. In some instances, such as the Laslett (1978, 1980) example described previously, these grow out of a theory. The Marxist viewpoint is but one model of how all or some part of society functions.

♦ *Historians face the same problems of showing causality as other social scientists. Those who have thought about it seriously doubt that tight cases are possible. Yet historians, like other social scientists, continually attempt to build convincing cases for causality.*

♦ *Historians cannot vary causes and show that effects follow, but they can selectively seek instances where that has occurred naturally.*

♦ *Precedence of cause may be difficult or impossible to prove.*

♦ *With complex phenomena, explanations involving multiple causes are the most common and make the most sense. They open phenomena to multiple useful interpretations. They also result in useful reinterpretations, or revisionist history.*

Hallmarks of Historical Studies

In seeking to build a strong case, the historian will attempt to

1. Conduct a reasonably complete search for sources of evidence.
2. Indicate the sources of information.
3. Use primary sources; where secondary sources were used, this is made clear.
4. Lay out the approach to the evidence in an evenhanded and open fashion.
5. Present a credible rationale or explanation. If it builds on previously available evidence, it extends, clarifies, and revises prior interpretations.

6. Ensure that the evidence presented is appropriate to the constructs employed.
7. Give sufficient instances of evidence so that the reader is able to judge its adequacy.
8. Weigh carefully and present important rival explanations as appropriate or rejected.
9. Show a close correspondence between the rationale and the evidence.
10. Cite evidence from more than one instance where generality is claimed (preferably considerably more, depending on the generality sought).
11. Team up with someone having the appropriate expertise, if venturing into a field or time period that is new.
12. Make clear any biases that might have affected judgments.

SUMMARY

The historian, in advancing a rationale or explanation of an event (or set of them), provides the reasoning that persuades us that the relationship being advanced does exist. The better the match of rationale to events, the more convincing the case. The art and skill of the historian is in the selection and organization of the facts and data to show congruence without distorting either data or theory. Historians range widely, looking for strong and convincing explanations to encompass a set of events. They borrow from all the behavioral sciences the propositions, viewpoints, and research methods that can be applied to retrospective data. Authentication of data is a problem unique to the historical study.

A Look Ahead

The next chapter, concerned with evaluation studies and action research, is another example of a field that borrows from qualitative and quantitative approaches as appropriate while dealing with its own special concerns through its own adaptations of and additions to the methods.

ADDITIONAL READING

Aydelotte, Bogue, and Fogel (1972) presents nine examples of historical studies demonstrating different quantitative approaches. Barzun and Graff (1992) is readable and practical, with much useful detail. Fischer (1970) is a fantastic laundry list of errors of historians, full of lively examples. See also Gottschalk (1956); Nevins (1975).

APPLICATION PROBLEMS

1. Burton (1988) traced the evolution of school discipline in the United States from the mid-nineteenth century until the present. At the heart of her study was the analysis of 475 journal articles from 1940 to 1980 with a specific focus on elementary public schooling. This was supported by a general review of the history of school discipline and an analysis of the social, political, and economic changes in American society based on such social analysts as Galbraith, Henry, and Potter.

Burton delineated three historical periods, indicating what she thought to be the overriding societal philosophy pertaining to school discipline for each, and compared them to the modern era. From the mid- to late-nineteenth century there was a search for a theory of discipline that would "provide self-disciplined citizens and workers for a rapidly growing, industrializing young nation"—a production-oriented society. During the first quarter of the twentieth century, the philosophy of John Dewey, the spirit of social cooperation, and community life dominated—interest was the key to discipline. During the mid-twentieth century, discipline was based on self-control and the recognition of each individual's "responsibilities to the group consonant with good citizenship in a democratic society." In the last half of the twentieth century, two major social changes affected both the purpose and the methods of school discipline. One was a recognition of social diversity and individual rights. The second was a shift from a producer to a consumer society—increased consumption became the cornerstone of democratic and economic security.

On the basis of this analysis, Burton argued that American educators now face unrecognized and therefore unaddressed conflicting social purposes. They are disciplining for the needs of a consumer-oriented society, the purpose of which is instant gratification. This runs counter to traditional American beliefs and standards—"the production-oriented goals of thrift, sobriety, diligence, responsibility, hard work, and delayed gratification are not conducive to, [or] supportive of, a consumer society." The response of educators has been to concentrate on workable methods of immediate control in the classroom without regard to general, long-term, social purpose.

How does Burton demonstrate internal validity (LP) in this study?

2. Laslett (1978) described past and present family structure in American society, how and why it has changed, and its importance in contemporary society. She begins her study with a brief discussion of two contradictory sociological views of family. The first is that the institution is in trouble—that it is "alive but not well," a view predicting its demise and borne out by a steady increase in divorce rates and in family violence. The second view is that the family is "here to stay," contending that society depends on it for the development of personal identity and the satisfaction of personal needs.

Laslett argues the second viewpoint, stating that "changes in household composition, in the demography of kinship, and in the relationship between family and other institutions have contributed to the greater emotional significance of the family through their impact on the socialization process" (p. 477) and have increased its significance for personal identity and emotional gratification. The problems of divorce and violence are the negative result of the intense feelings generated by this increased intimacy.

To make her argument, Laslett attempts to trace the changes over time and compare family in the past to that in the present. Thus household composition of preindustrial society is held to have included others unrelated to the conjugal family unit, such as boarders, lodgers, and employees; today's family rarely does. Further, in the past, adolescence tended to be spent outside the family home (job hunting, apprenticeships, etc.). Today, adolescents tend to remain at home with increased identification of the self based on the particular family. Increased life span and improved means of communication have led to the modern availability of ascendant kin—grandparents, aunts, and uncles—who may elaborate the meaning of kinship.

Finally, the ideology of family living has changed from the Puritan view of family as guardian of the public good to that of the private family and the home as a personal sanctuary where a sense of personal control and intimacy can be found. This has been further accentuated by the separation of home and work and of home and schooling. These historical changes have resulted in an increased weight of meaning attached to the personal relations of the family.

What has Laslett attempted to do in this study? Is her argument convincing?

Compare your answers with those following the Application Exercise.

APPLICATION EXERCISE

How might your problem be examined in historical perspective? What might this add to your understanding of it? How might it give a clearer picture of the causal chain of events? What, if any, might be the problem of obtaining data and records? Of authenticating them?

ANSWERS TO THE APPLICATION PROBLEMS

1. Remember that the basis of the historical method is interpretation, the extent of which varies with the author, the author's purpose, and the reader's own perceptions. Internal validity (LP) is demonstrated by means of a strong organizing rationale, one that effectively shows a correspondence between the explanation (the construct) and the evidence (the data). Burton developed her theme first from historical sources and then supported it with an analysis of an exhaustive series of studies (475) drawn from a 40-year period. She further strengthened her rationale by tying her themes to contemporary social analysis. Her rationale makes sense based on her selective interpretation of the evidence.

2. Laslett has tried to show causality. She has presented a thesis: that the role of the family has changed from preindustrial to modern times and that society is now dependent on it for the development of personal identity and the satisfaction of personal needs. To support her argument, she has tried to demonstrate a pattern of multiple causes all acting together to produce the current situation. To be convincing, she needed to satisfy the conditions for inferring causation. Does her rationale fit the data? Does it make sense? Although insufficient information has been presented in this summary to permit judgment, she seems to have put forward a convincing argument.

C H A P T E R **23**

Evaluation Studies and Action Research

Evaluative investigation is an art. The design must be chosen afresh in each new undertaking and the choices to be made are almost innumerable. Each feature . . . offers particular advantages and entails particular sacrifices.

       Lee J. Cronbach, *Designing Evaluations of Educational and Social Programs*

Conceptualizing an evaluation depends on understanding self-interest: yours and theirs. Useful evaluations put theirs first.

       Michael Quinn Patton, *Qualitative Evaluation Methods*

OVERVIEW

Evaluation borrows its methods from other fields but differs from them by being oriented toward findings that contribute more to decision making than to new knowledge and generalizations. Indeed, the success of an evaluation lies in the utilization of its findings. Action research solves this problem since the evaluation is actually done by those who will use the findings. The evaluators may choose from a variety of approaches to find a best fit to their problems as well as to their predilections about how the evaluation should be done and what it should achieve.

    Evaluations are inherently political when they empower one group rather than another, threatening when the results may have negative consequences, conservative when findings reinforce the status quo, and subject to conflict when sponsors or those with a stake in the outcome are displeased by the findings. Evaluation standards have been developed for the protection of both evaluators and their clients.

CHAPTER CONTENTS

Introduction

Having no methods of its own, evaluation has always borrowed from all the social sciences. Almost anything can be evaluated—a person, a curriculum, a student, a process, a product, a program. Each such evaluation category (for example, personnel evaluation, teaching evaluation, student achievement evaluation) has its own literature and problems. This chapter focuses on the evaluation of social and educational programs and products, for example, curricula, welfare policy reform, a library's new access system, or a change in the highway speed limit.

Evaluation differs from research not by its methods, but by other aspects:

- It is **decision-driven** instead of hypothesis-driven—it is intended to facilitate making a decision about the applicability or worth of something in a situation. Like research, it seeks a consensus around the proper interpretation of data, but the consensus may be limited to two persons—the evaluator and the client. Alternatively, it may be broader as when a congressional committee, a group of decision makers, or people affected by the outcome (**stakeholders**) are involved. Any way we look at it, however, evaluation generally deals with a more targeted audience than research.
- Because it is decision-driven, the value of an evaluation lies in its usefulness in that process. Therefore, **utilization** is a prime criterion. An evaluation that is a nice piece of research but does not create the desired consensus or is not accepted as a basis for decision making has failed its main purpose.
- Because utilization requires trust in the results, the process of evaluation may be as important as the product.
- Policy choice is nearly always made on the basis of incomplete information. The intent of evaluations is to reduce the uncertainty, to provide an informa-

tion-rich decision-making environment. Just as with research, there is no absolute proof, but by providing information that is plausible though not completely certain, evaluations provide a better informed basis for action.

- Because the audience is limited and the goal is usefulness, the form of the evaluation and report of results can and must be tailored to that audience. In order that trust be enhanced in the evaluation, audience members may be involved in the evaluation or be given control over certain parts of the process.

Most action research involves evaluation of, or a comparison of alternative actions, programs, or policies; thus, it is also characterized by the first four aspects listed above. But the last aspect changes in a way that characterizes action research:

- The primary audience is the action researchers themselves who seek the knowledge for their own use. They don't just control the study, they do it. The services of a knowledgeable evaluator or researcher are called for as needed.[1]

The action researcher often is a professional (for example, teacher, librarian, or social worker) seeking improvement of daily practice, or wanting to know the effect of some program or policy change. However, a manager can take on this role as well, as can a group such as a community of stakeholders. Action research, one of several orientations to evaluation we shall explore in this chapter, is the most consumer-based.

Some evaluation studies are oriented primarily toward gathering information that will facilitate improving a program or product—**formative evaluation.** Others, usually of an established project, gather information to help determine its value or worth—**summative evaluation.** Scriven (1991) quotes Robert Stake on the formative/summative distinction: "When the cook tastes the soup, that's formative evaluation; when the guest tastes it, that's summative evaluation" (p. 19). In practice, the distinction is moot since thoughtful consideration of formative findings may lead to project termination just as careful analyses of summative findings often result in redirecting a continuing project.

Examples of Evaluation

Examples come from the full range of social, educational, psychological, and economic problems. In the field of health, for instance, evaluation of the substitution of nurse practitioners for physicians suggested that the substitution was desirable and cost-effective. Because of government reimbursement policies, however, their replacement resulted in loss of income to physicians (Spitzer et al., 1974). Evaluation of the effects of guaranteed annual income on health care (people below a

---

[1]As used in sociology, the term *action research* means *"a systematic collection of information that is designed to bring about social change"* (Bogdan and Biklen, 1992, p. 223, emphasis in the original). The sociologist presents information as objectively as possible from a particular point of view rather than representing both sides of an issue.

minimum receive payments from the government) showed the effects to be more a function of lifestyle than income (Elesh and Lefcowitz, 1977). Evaluation of the benefits of the 55-mile-an-hour speed limit were shown to outweigh the economic cost, although the policy may be a second- or third-best way of achieving such goals as fuel conservation (Clotfelter and Hahn, 1978). A cost analysis of a correctional institution program found a 6 percent reduction in recidivism—but at a cost of $38,000 per inmate (Bloom and Singer, 1979). Many educational programs have been evaluated. For example, the Perry Preschool Program showed the effectiveness of preschool programs such as Head Start when they were carefully developed. Its evaluation extended longitudinally, following the students to age 19 (Berrueta-Clement, Barnett, and Weikart, 1985).

- ✦ *Evaluation studies are used to improve a product, policy, or program or determine its value or worth.*
- ✦ *Formative evaluation is used in the development stage to guide an evolutionary process.*
- ✦ *Summative evaluation determines the worth of a mature program or process. In a sense, however, even this is formative since it usually leads to appropriate program modification.*
- ✦ *Different points of view with respect to the evaluation process emphasize product, process, stakeholder rights, administrator concerns, and client rights and methods.*

Research, Evaluation, and Action Research

How do evaluation and action research differ from the empirical research of the previous chapters? Many evaluations designed, implemented, and reported entirely by an evaluator conform to all the criteria of research, are often published in research journals, and are indistinguishable from action research. But even when identical in form, they differ in intent. Most research is designed to discover or validate a generalization, whereas program and policy evaluations are aimed at helping someone to make a decision. Research findings can sit on the shelf until someone deems them useful; evaluations, by contrast, are intended to be useful from the outset. They are designed to lead to improvement (formative evaluation) or to decisions of whether to continue, to discontinue, or to expand (summative evaluation) a program. An evaluation that fails utilization has not served its purpose.

Program, product, and policy evaluations are most often commissioned by an administrator, an institution, or a policy-shaping community, often pluralistic in interests (for example, a legislature; a consortium of lobbying or interest groups; a professional association). To say that evaluations are to be utilized requires building a consensus around the proper interpretation of the findings among those for whom they are intended. If the evaluation is funded, the sponsor may claim to be the sole client. But this condition may result in the evaluation's being rejected by those affected directly by the program (clients) or indirectly (taxpayers or other supporters).

Moreover, if the client and stakeholders are to have faith in the product of the evaluation, they must have faith in the process that produced it. The knowledge we trust most is that which grows out of our own experience (see p. 48). The greater control we have over the evaluation, the greater our personal identification with the evaluation findings and the more likely we are to accept and use them. As a result, greater attention has been given to involvement of stakeholders, and process has often become as important as product. Indeed, in action research, stakeholders are the evaluators.

How to define the "client," and within what scope the "client" will be involved in the evaluation may be among the evaluator's most important and difficult decisions. Evaluations of federal social programs of the 1970s stimulated diverse points of view on this issue. Because "knowledge is power," these views differed with regard to control of the evaluation and the knowledge obtained from it along a continuum ranging from "these should be the sole prerogative of clients in positions of responsibility" to "control and knowledge should be shared with stakeholders." (In one sense, they are ultimately the clients.)

Evaluation is variously conceived as: a tool for more effective program management vs. a means of empowerment for those affected by programs (House, 1976, 1980; Cronbach, 1982) or an effort to be responsive to the concerns of stakeholders (Stake, 1991); directed by a highly competent professional opinion vs. a transactional endeavor between professionals and stakeholders to seek answers (Rippey, 1973); a means to conclusions and recommendations vs. a process of negotiation with and among stakeholders to produce an agenda for further negotiation (Lincoln and Guba, 1986; Argyris, Putnam, and Smith, 1985).

Analogous to the continuum of qualitative to quantitative, some groups see evaluation as the responsibility of connoisseurial judgments by an area's experts (Eisner, 1981), best done as naturalistic descriptive qualitative research (Stake, 1991) or embedded in measurement and experimentation (Boruch and Wothke, 1985).

Using Worthen and Sanders (1987) organization, these differing views are discussed in detail in the next section as eight commonly recognized evaluation approaches. Action research has been added. Figure 23.1 (next page) displays on the horizontal axis, the nine approaches ordered along the continuum of who controls study and its resulting knowledge. The extent to which control of the evaluation is shared is illustrated in the upper bar by the ratio of the heavily shaded to the lightly shaded area under each type of evaluation. The heavy shading successively decreases from left to right as stakeholders have greater control of the evaluation.[2] The second bar shows that, even though stakeholders gain increasing control along the continuum, except in action research, the evaluator actually does the work.

◆ *Although evaluation uses research methods, it is decision-driven; its results are intended to be used in decision making.*

---

[2]Evaluators may or may not consult stakeholders in preparing their cases for an adversarial evaluation. Since placement on the continuum is therefore arbitrary, it is shown in the middle.

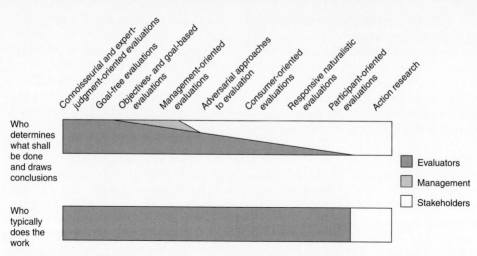

FIGURE 23.1 Depiction, in the top bar, of who controls the study and, in the lower bar, of who does the work in nine approaches to evaluation arranged from left to right in order of increasing stakeholder control.

◆ *Utilization is therefore a prime criterion of success.*

◆ *Having confidence in the evaluation findings sufficient for decision making is another way of saying that one is building a consensus around the proper interpretation of the data.*

◆ *Consensus building among stakeholders requires their having faith in the process by which findings were derived.*

◆ *Process may therefore be as important as the product.*

◆ *Action research is an attractive orientation because the stakeholder becomes the evaluator, and the most trusted knowledge grows out of personal experiences.*

Alternative Evaluation Approaches

Some differences in approaches to evaluation are mainly matters of emphasis, some of method, and some of process. Approaches to evaluation described in this section, except for interchanging the order of goal-based and goal-free evaluations (because their distinction is then easier to explain), move from those done and controlled by the evaluator for the client to increased control by stakeholders who eventually become the evaluators.[3]

---

[3]This discussion is patterned after Worthen and Sanders (1987), a useful treatment of evaluation.

Connoisseurial or Expert-Judgment Evaluation

The **connoisseurial** or **expert-judgment evaluation** (Eisner, 1976, 1981) is the most common and the oldest form of evaluation. It is ubiquitous: personnel promotion, salary raises, award of funding, certification or accreditation, evaluation of essay and oral examinations (including doctoral), and publication of peer reviews. The familiar charges of "cronyism," bias, and unequal standards applied to different people or by different judges all attest to the difficulties of this method. It depends on the wisdom, fairness, integrity, professional knowledge, and judgment of the "expert." It is most widely used where measurement is impossible because of the many "right" answers. For example, a pilot can fly from Chicago to New York in many different ways under a variety of flight conditions. The combinations of possibilities are so numerous that measurement is difficult, if not impossible. In that situation, evaluation by a flight observer is considered the fairest method of assessing such a performance.

What can you do to make judgments less subject to criticism? You can conform to the following five criteria:

1. Structure evaluations in a way all agree is fair: what evidence will be available, what kinds of individuals will judge it, what the criteria will be, and on what cycle the judging will be done—all are clearly stated and understood.
2. State criteria for judgment in written, publicly available form, preferably as close as possible to low-inference criteria and jointly developed by judges and those judged.
3. Involve more than one judge. How many? One is too few; 15, far too many.
4. Make a written report available in some appropriate form to the person who is being evaluated or to some other trusted party who will provide an appropriate summary of the judgment. A person who is being evaluated will have the opportunity to respond, if desired.
5. A group selected as a fair one by both judges and judged should review and approve the evaluation report, any response, and any minutes of meetings.

The public nature of the process and the criteria go a long way toward preventing abuses. More than one evaluator makes it less likely that any one judge's attitude or personality will determine the outcome. A written report may also help to avoid the unreasoning Dr. Fell phenomenon.[4] Opportunity for rebuttal may point out aspects that escaped notice. Lastly, the procedural approval by a review group provides a safety net to catch flaws not otherwise provided for.

◆ *Obtain the judgment of a clinical or connoisseurial expert if there are many ways of achieving a goal, the criteria are complex, or comparable evaluations are not made often enough to warrant developing a low-inference procedure for any one type or style.*

---

[4]This phenomenon was named after the nursery rhyme: "I do not like you, Dr. Fell; the reason why I cannot tell; I only know and know quite well, I do not like you, Dr. Fell."

✦ To minimize charges of bias, structure the evaluations in ways all agree are fair, state criteria in written publicly available form, involve multiple judges, issue a written report with opportunity for response, and provide for a review of the report and procedure.

Objectives- and Goal-Based Evaluation

One of the earliest of modern evaluation points of view, objectives-based evaluation, was advanced by Ralph W. Tyler in the 1930s (Tyler and Waples, 1930; Madaus and Stufflebeam, 1989). Developed in the context of education, it was intended as a means of building a curriculum and evaluating its success. A **goal-based evaluation** requires that the goals or objectives of an intervention be stated in terms of **behavioral objectives**—the behaviors the intervention is to bring about. Covert behaviors, such as "the student should be able to appreciate a painting," are translated into overt behavior that can be recognized: "On studying a painting, the student should be able to describe how the artist used perspective to achieve her purposes."

We can then construct a situation that, if the desired behavior has been learned, would elicit it as an appropriate way of responding. This has typically been considered a measurement-oriented approach, probably because translating the goals into behavioral objectives markedly facilitates construction of measures, and so it is widely used by measurement specialists. Tyler himself, however, clearly indicated that any relevant evidence should be used, not just paper and pencil alone. As evidence of appreciation of painting, we might include library records to see if the student checked out prints from the library's collection of reproductions. If there are records of art gallery attendance, we might note the number of visits.

This approach emphasizes the specification and operationalization of the intervention's goals or objectives. Such specification requires most interveners to think about their program in concrete ways and in detail they have not previously considered. It assumes, however, that we can translate all goals into observable behaviors without losing a wholeness or essence that may be a prime characteristic. However, it is difficult to specify and observe the affective thrill of seeing a painting, a result that may be considered a key goal of art appreciation instruction.

Some critics argue that the effects of objective-based evaluation are not merely finding out what students have achieved but also changing the curriculum. Teachers will "teach to the test" so that their students show up well. If state-by-state comparisons are made, a national curriculum will in effect be established, and the freedom to choose state and local goals will be diminished.

Emphasis on measurement and therefore measurable behaviors may also result in our emphasizing only the simple behaviors that lend themselves to measurement. Further, by using the avowed achievement program goals to guide the evaluation, we may miss important side effects. A boring history curriculum, for example, might teach students to dislike history or to gain considerable skill in avoiding being called upon. Since these results are not included in the intended goals, the evaluation may not pick up such effects.

A key concern of this approach is the question "Who shall specify the evaluation objectives?" The sponsor? Program staff? Stakeholders affected by the intervention? Some policy-shaping community? In a diverse, pluralistic society perceptions may differ. The main goal of a job-training program may be preparing mothers for work, but, program staff may know that, equally importantly, it provides otherwise unaffordable day care and some time away from children. Though not incompatible, providing respite and recovery for mothers could lead to quite different evaluations and findings from the goal of job training.

Rossi and Wright (1986) find goal-based evaluation too restrictive:

> Social programs tend to develop their goals as they proceed; thus to saddle them with evaluations that stress *a priori* goals does an injustice to the evolving nature of most programs. . . . Many potentially innovative social projects are funded with vague goals supposed to be achieved using unspecified procedures. An experimental approach that demands fixed procedures and unchanging goals simply does not work in the "real world" where both goals and procedures are continually being changed in an effort to find something that appears to work. (p. 60)

The investigator has an important role in teasing out the implications of a policy or the dimensions of a program (Cronbach, 1982). For example, an evaluation of most written policies on mainstreaming will show they apply equally well to keeping gifted children as well as the handicapped in the mainstream. That implication may not be acceptable and may call for rethinking what is meant by mainstreaming. Often, the evaluator must assume the additional role of educator.

Similarly, the tasks of identifying and measuring treatment in evaluations are hampered by: (1) vaguely formulated policy—for example, racial integration is operationalized as a program, such as busing, when real racial integration clearly involves much more than that; (2) imperfectly implemented programs—for example, a program begun under one director is taken over by another who does not understand the intended treatment; and (3) programs variously received or delivered at the individual level—for example, tutors "do not spend the same time with each child nor are [they] uniformly enthusiastic, energetic or perceptive with each child" (Boruch and Gomez, 1977, p. 427). By no means a complete list, it nevertheless suggests the evaluator's problems in trying to determine what to include in an evaluation and how to set priorities.

Further, goal-based evaluations may not look at the needs of stakeholders. Needs analyses determine the difference between what is and what ought to be (Witkin, 1984). Using questionnaires or individual or group interviews, they reveal whether proposed solutions address problems important to clients. Surprisingly, some programs address lesser needs and leave untouched the most pressing.

✦ *Goal-based evaluation determines how thoroughly the intended goals of a program, project, or product have been met.*

✦ *A key decision is who determines the goals and how differences in the goals of sponsors, managers, staff, clients, and other stakeholders are taken into account.*

◆ *Vague goals and variations in how treatment is experienced make difficult precise definition of an intervention.*

◆ *Needs analyses determine the gap between present and desired conditions and provide guidance for goal determination, priority setting, resource allocation, and implementation.*

Goal-Free Evaluation

An obvious antidote to some of the problems of goal-based evaluation is **goal-free evaluation** in which the evaluator examines the implementation of the intervention to determine what the real effects have been and thence to infer what goals have been achieved. The evaluator can then compare these results with the goals the program was intended to satisfy. Proposed by Scriven (1972), the evaluator purposely avoids initial awareness of the goals of the project, having minimal contact with the program manager and staff until the achieved outcomes have been determined.

Sometimes unexpected side effects surpass the original goal in importance. The key goal of the toy-lending library, intended to give poor children certain advantages of the middle-class home, was to make available otherwise unaffordable toys. Mothers typically asked for recommendations from the "librarian" who, seizing on this opportunity to teach parenting skills, produced the project's most important outcome. A goal-based evaluation pursued by an internal evaluator—a staff person—and a goal-free evaluation simultaneously conducted by an external evaluator can complement each other.

◆ *Goal-free evaluation examines outcomes and infers the intended goals from these. The evaluator can then compare achieved goals with intended ones.*

Management-Oriented Evaluation

Management-oriented evaluation serves administrators by providing a management information system for continuous evaluation of an intervention—formative evaluation. In addition, intermittent or cyclical evaluations more like summative evaluations may be employed. Stufflebeam's CIPP model (Stufflebeam and Shinkfield, 1985) is a frequently cited management-oriented approach. It consists of four kinds of evaluations corresponding to the initials of its name:

1. *Context* evaluations involve planning decisions such as identifying the target audience and determining the needs to be met by the intervention. As noted, stakeholder mothers may perceive needs different from those perceived by job-training management.
2. *Input* evaluations involve determining the available resources, alternative strategies, and what plan will best meet the needs determined through context evaluation.
3. *Process* evaluations examine how well the plan was implemented, what problems exist, and how they can be solved.

4. *Product* evaluations examine what results were obtained, what needs were met or ameliorated, and what future plans are required.

Rossi and Freeman (1985) list six areas of accountability and assessment with which managers should be concerned. Most evaluations stop with the first but ought to include all.

1. *Impact assessment:* Has the intervention achieved its goals?
2. *Efficiency assessment:* Have program costs been judged in relation to benefits and compared with cost-benefit assessments of alternatives?
3. *Coverage assessment:* What are the numbers and characteristics of those who are served, and their proportion of potential targets (the technical term is *penetration*)? What proportion drop out?
4. *Service delivery assessment* (actual compared to planned delivery): Have all anticipated services been provided? By qualified staff? With expected quality?
5. *Fiscal assessment:* Has appropriate accountability been provided for funds? Judgment of costs per client, per service, marginal cost of serving additional clients, and variations in costs depending on load, program site, and other factors.
6. *Legal assessment:* Have provisions been made for legal and quasi-legal concerns such as "informed consent, protection of privacy, community representation on decision-making boards, equity in provision of services, and cost sharing" (p. 95)?

Although **cost-benefit analysis** procedures are not without controversy, there is some agreement on major steps (Levin, 1983; Wortman, 1984; Yates, 1985). Outcomes must be translated into monetary or some other measure of value so that their relation to costs may be determined. This aspect is often controversial—what is the monetary value of, for instance, learning? Medical procedures may be translated into savings in later medical attention, but inferences so derived are "soft." Since cost figures are often greatly affected by assumptions, analyses are often repeated with different sets (for instance, difficult-to-estimate indirect cost figures such as the expense of physical facilities in different states of repair, or personnel costs of individuals with different levels of qualifications). By measuring outcomes across programs in comparable terms, **cost-effectiveness analysis** allows comparison and ranking of "choices among potential programs according to the magnitudes of their effects relative to their costs" (Rossi and Freeman, 1985, p. 330).

✦ Different evaluation models intended to inform management target different operational aspects and summarize results differently.
✦ Cost-benefit analyses translate benefits into monetary terms to allow for judgments comparing the use of resources for different goals.
✦ Cost-effectiveness analyses make comparisons of different treatments in terms of inputs, outputs, and goals to allow the selection of the most efficient and effective.

Adversarial Evaluation

The model of a law court, continually evaluating cases presented disputatiously by opposing parties, is a ready-made analogy for **adversarial evaluation**. As a model, the strict procedures of the courtroom must be considerably loosened. Wolf (1975, 1979) proposed a judicial evaluation model that included a statement of charges, opposing presenters of the cases who could call witnesses (including experts), a judge or hearings officer, and a jury or panel to render a verdict. Where more than two points of view are dominant, the format may follow the model of a hearing more than that of a trial. The ability of the presenters must be comparable; otherwise, as in legal trials with star lawyers, the case may be swayed more by style than by the evidence. For an example, see the National Institute of Education's trial of minimum competency testing which was recorded and televised. In addition, the two opposing evaluators Popham (1981) and Madaus (1981) presented their cases in print.

As Wolf (1979) makes clear, the object is not so much to win as to provide an insightful examination that educates the audience to the complexity of the issues. The process is expensive and is primarily useful as an alternative way of analyzing and presenting data collected under another evaluation scheme.

> ✦ *Adversarial evaluations, borrowing procedures from courts of law, are useful for educating a public or set of stakeholders regarding the complexity of the problem and the value judgments that are involved.*

Consumer-Oriented Evaluation

If there is a management-oriented evaluation approach, can **consumer-oriented evaluation** be far behind? Consumer-oriented criteria and checklists have been developed for a variety of education products (for example, curricula, textbooks, films, library reference collections). Scriven (1974), the Educational Products Information Exchange (EPIE),[5] and Tyler, Klein, and Associates (1976) have all produced product checklists. Tyler and Klein's standards for educational materials include questions such as:

Is the value of the objectives substantiated?

Is the basis on which the content of the program was selected explained?

Are students given opportunities to practice appropriate skills?

Is evidence available about the effectiveness and efficiency of the materials?

Is evidence available as to unanticipated outcomes?

Is evidence from recent studies on the use of materials reported?[6]

---

[5]Their reports are available from EPIE, 475 Riverside Drive, New York, NY 10027.
[6]L. L. Tyler, M. F. Klein, and Associates, *Evaluating and Choosing Curriculum and Instructional Materials.* Copyright © 1976 Educational Resources Associates. Used by permission.

◆ *Consumer-oriented evaluation has focused on the evaluation of products and the determination of appropriate criteria for judging them.*

Responsive Naturalistic Evaluation

"The responsive approach is an attempt to respond to the natural ways in which people assimilate information and arrive at understanding" (Stake, 1975, p. 23). Researchers engaged in **responsive naturalistic evaluation** gather evidence responsive to the perceived needs of the stakeholder audience. They describe the activities of a program and leave inferences regarding the nature of goals and of success in reaching them to the audience to infer: "We need a reporting procedure for facilitating vicarious experience. We need to portray complexity. We need to convey holistic impression, the mood, even the mystery of the experience" (ibid., p. 23).

These requisites obviously call for qualitative ("naturalistic") data gathering and reporting. One such evaluation included detailed descriptions of science programs totaling well over 1,000 pages (Stake and Easley et al., 1978a, 1978b). Portrayed as case studies of a small sample of persons, such evaluations often emphasize the situation's pluralistic nature and, if the evaluator presents any recommendations, they are presented with alternatives.

The portrayal of individuals in a case study can be the stuff of which headlines are made; thus, presenting the evidence in a "natural" way has its advantages. However, for large-scale projects with clear goals and established procedures, the qualitative approach is likely to yield questionably representative and fuzzy estimates of success.

◆ *Responsive naturalistic evaluation portrays the complexity of situations using qualitative methods and presents findings descriptively so individuals may assimilate the information and arrive at their own understanding.*
◆ *This approach to evaluation has advantages, particularly where the project is small and where goals are not sharply defined. However, it may be less effective with large projects with sharply defined goals.*

Participant-Oriented Evaluation

If we return to the prime assumption that a successful evaluation is one with findings that are used, then clearly one of the most effective ways of getting the evidence used is to involve the stakeholders in as much of the evaluation process as possible—**participant-oriented evaluation**. Rippey (1973) noted that the findings and recommendations of evaluations done by an evaluator and a sponsor, and then delivered to the stakeholders as a *fait accompli*, were often rejected. However, if the stakeholders had a role in the evaluation process, what he called "transactional evaluation," rejection was less likely. Not only did the stakeholders gain ownership in the process and therefore more reason to trust it, but concurrently the process also educated them about the evaluation's problems. Although involvement may make stakeholders more aware of the fallibility and inevitably incomplete nature of the evidence, most likely it will also make them more properly cautious about drawing inferences from it.

Guba and Lincoln (1986) have provoked considerable thought about the stakeholder's role in evaluation:

> The stakeholding audiences are given the opportunity to provide inputs *at every stage* of the evaluation. . . . The inclusion of these divergent views into anything resembling a viable course of action requires extreme political dexterity, persuasiveness, compromise, and let it be noted, integrity. . . . *Evaluation is a social-political process.* (emphasis in the original, Guba and Lincoln, 1986, pp. 78–79)

They espouse naturalistic responsive evaluation and qualitative method in what they call "fourth-generation evaluation," and emphasize, additionally: pluralism, multiple reality, and the involvement of all stakeholders. In contrast to the traditional scientific view that "there is a reality out there to be discovered," they argue that all reality is constructed: "These constructions are made by persons and it is in the minds of persons that one finds them, not 'out there'" (ibid., p. 76).

Because evaluators become both learners and teachers in this model, their role is that of a negotiator: "Once the concept of value-pluralism is admitted and the criterion of fairness is invoked, it becomes plain that fair judgments can be reached only through negotiation, if at all" (ibid., p. 78). The explicitly required power sharing may cause this point of view to be rejected by clients, administrators, and sponsors. Still evolving and not yet widely embraced, nevertheless, this viewpoint has caused some evaluators to consider new options or shifts in emphases.

✦ *The results of participant-oriented evaluations are more likely to be accepted and used by stakeholders since they have a hand in developing them. This parity of roles shifts the responsibilities of the evaluator to those of consultant, teacher, and negotiator. The power sharing that is involved is a stumbling block for some persons.*

Action Research

Action research, research by practitioners to improve practice, carries participant oriented evaluation to its ultimate conclusion—participants do the research. It is the author's personal impression that action research surfaces periodically among practitioners of all professions.[7] It never completely goes away because practition-

---

[7]*Practitioners* here refers not only to front line field-workers—teachers, social workers, librarians, journalists, and so forth—but also to their supervisors and administrators who often are equally frustrated by the gap between academic and practitioner knowledge.

ers want "knowledge that is concrete, timely, prudent and particular to their own circumstances" (Atkin, 1994, p. 105). Contrast this goal with the goals of academic researchers: broadly applicable, abstract propositions, loosely related to specific situations. When does some form of action research come to the fore? When the gap between academic researchers and practitioners becomes uncomfortably large; when reform movements threaten professional practice (they are omnipresent but pressure sometimes peaks); and when a group of proactive professionals can find the time to improve practice.

Like most enthusiasms, action research activity is sporadic rather than sustained. Few busy practitioners have time for structured inquiry; fewer still perceive themselves as masters of it. For most, person-to-person interaction is an all-consuming source of job satisfaction with little left over for reflection and research.

An important appeal of action research is its empowerment of practitioners who, even though they are the prime stakeholders of many evaluations, have so often been made to feel inadequate by academics. The tension between academe and field is endemic; academics, with the responsibility, time, and resources to continually work at improving practice, believe they should always be ahead of the field. To the practitioner, however, their ideas are often impractical, unrealistic, and overly complex; worst of all, despite their confident demeanor, experts are not always right. Action research, controlled and done by practitioners, redresses the balance of power; if and when practitioners need evaluation expertise, they call for it as colleagues.

Many academics have welcomed and encouraged some form of action research as the most effective tool for institutional reform (for example, Hollingsworth and Sockett, 1994; Hargreaves, 1996; Altrichter, Posch, and Somekh, 1993). It follows the dictum: "feed them a fish and you satisfy today's hunger; teach them to fish, and you satisfy a lifetime's."

Action research is "day-to-day reflection made more systematic and intensive" (Altrichter, Posch, and Somekh, 1993, p. 154). It targets successive cycles of reflection, planning, action, and evaluation on a given problem until it is resolved or, more often, on a cascade of evolving problems. Characterized by simple research methods, usually qualitative, it is tailored to what can be achieved without disrupting practice. Sometimes the process is written up as a narrative to share with others facing similar problems.

Such characteristics are illustrated in this account of action research by an elementary school principal who became concerned about extensive fifth-grade discipline problems (Soffer, 1995).[8] Parallel examples can be found in any profession. This principal kept a journal of her thoughts and actions that could be used to reflect on where she had been, where she was, and where she was going. Many action researchers find such journals invaluable as a way of "keeping on the beam." It also facilitates sharing experiences with others.

---

[8]This example is from "The Principal as Action Researcher: A Study of Disciplinary Practice" by E. Soffer in S. E. Noffke and R. B. Stevenson from *Educational Action Research: Becoming Practically Critical.* Copyright © 1995 by Teachers College, Columbia University. Reprinted by permission of Teachers College Press. All rights reserved.

Starting with a reconnaissance of how others perceived her handling of discipline problems, she found "such things as 'a need for more strictness with upper grades,' 'more evenness with application of rules,' 'need for more follow-through with discipline,' and 'need for more consistency'" (p. 117). Agreeing with these comments, she planned to focus on consistency and persistence—beginning with the development and consistent use of a standard form for her disciplinary records and a spreadsheet categorizing incidents so that she could spot trends and patterns.

Although she had to force herself to use these records, "given my distaste for repetitive . . . paperwork" (p. 119), by the end of the first week she realized that patterns were emerging: A small group of boys accounted for many of the incidents that involved disrespect for persons, and her records indicated "she had warned Bob . . ." or "told Ann. . . ." "I did not feel they were learning. . .simply being punished" (ibid.).

How could she make the disciplinary conferences learning experiences? This goal led to a second cycle where, in consulting books on the subject, she found a "responsibility model." She would ask students about their responsibility for the incident, and what they might do to avoid future problems. Her evaluation both on the forms and in her journal noted a marked change: Students got involved and "became more responsive and active in solving their own problems" (p. 120).

In her third cycle, reflecting on her journal notes she noticed that the majority of incidents involved playground aides rather than teachers. Would her occasional presence with the aides enduringly affect student behavior? Her presence three days a week during recreation depressed incident frequency, but it rebounded without her attendance. This discovery made her wonder what she could "do to invest the aides with more authority in the eyes of the students" (p. 121).

In her fourth cycle she noted that even these changes in practice had not affected three fifth-grade boys on whom she had "used almost every approach I knew" (p. 122). After consultation with teachers and parents, she decided to move the two who were followers to separate classrooms, isolating the leader. Then, instead of viewing them "as a triumvirate with the same problems, I was able to see them as individuals with different problems" (ibid.). The two continued to misbehave, running to meet the "'powerful' boy" to brag about their exploits, though— without his friends—he had ceased to be a problem

In her fifth cycle, reflecting on her failure with the two boys, she decided to draw up behavioral contracts with specified consequences of both rewards and punishments. This step reduced the negative behavior! That consequence reminded her of an approach she had read about which varied the disciplinary approach to fit the student. She sought to learn more about it.

During the following school year she continued her research, now keeping several cycles going simultaneously. She found that 54 percent of the school's referrals were to 6 percent of the students, thus narrowing the focus. Further, referrals rose two weeks before a major vacation, information she shared with staff in order to plan appropriate interventions. She took actions at the beginning of the school year designed to reinforce the authority of the aides.

Reflecting on the whole process, however, she realized that changing her role was of limited value; she needed to shift the whole environment, getting teachers to use the responsibility model. However, believing that this course would be manipulating them to her own ends, she decided to discuss the situation openly, to face the tension raised by her role as principal. She also recognized that her journal was "the vehicle that made it possible for my research to be reflective and flexible. [It] . . . captured . . . fleeting but important ideas not reflected in more formal data collection" (p. 123). She resolved to make her journal notes more extensive in the future.

This example captures many of the important characteristics of action research summarized in this box:

+ *Action research provides professionals with a concrete, timely, targeted, pragmatic orientation toward improvement of practice.*
+ *It involves systematic and intensive reflection and is characterized by reflection-planning-acting-evaluation cycles.*
+ *Each cycle provides a better understanding of an evolving cascade of problems.*
+ *Keeping a journal of ongoing reflections and actions helps researchers see where they have been and where they should best go next.*
+ *The simplest data collection methods adequate to the task minimize interruptions of practice.*
+ *Researchers can call for specialized outside expertise as needed.*
+ *Translating the journal into a written narrative helps others.*

In presenting a panorama of evaluation approaches, it must be clear that they overlap one another. Further, in practical terms, any evaluation may, and probably should, borrow from others such aspects as are appropriate to the particular situation. Most evaluators are eclectic in their approach, as are also researchers, a point reinforced in the next chapter. They combine the best of what is available to build the strongest evaluation feasible.

Special Problems of Doing Evaluations

Unlike research, evaluations, especially summative ones, have winners and losers. In that sense, negative findings, even of formative evaluations, can tarnish sponsors as imprudent spenders, administrators as incompetent executives, and staff as candidates for termination. These consequences alone suggest that evaluation harbors problems quite different from routine research, but there are others. This section provides an opportunity to explore some of them.

Evaluations as Afterthoughts

Evaluations are so often afterthoughts: First let's get the program up and running! What then? Oh, yes, we ought to evaluate it—often after the intervention has occurred. For example, we are asked to find a comparison group for children who received Head Start treatment. We might take the group of subjects just above the cutoff point. But they have already had a better start. Thus, if the Head Start group does not equal or surpass them, we won't know whether our results occur because they had a better start or because the program is ineffective. Match them with students in a community without a Head Start program? Are there community and background differences? How do we find a comparable group? With full-coverage programs—every eligible student is already involved. Clearly, we can develop a more satisfactory evaluation if we plan it as part of the project from the outset.

Evaluations as Policy Studies

Many evaluations explore the effectiveness and side effects of certain policies. Examples are the large-scale evaluations of the 1960s and 1970s, which were essentially "true-to-life" field experiments.[9] They demonstrated that such randomized experimentation was logistically and politically feasible, but also very difficult. It was hard to keep the experimental groups uncontaminated over a sufficiently long period for the effects of intervention to develop naturally.

The timing of policy research is often all important. It is usually difficult, if not impossible, to conform study completion to political opportunism, and legislative, budgetary, and administrative deadlines. Initial enthusiasm dissipates— the income maintenance studies took place over six years. If clients are suffering, withholding action until research is complete is not an option. Decision makers, who never have all the needed data, take their chances with what is available, often angering researchers who argue that partial data can be misleading.

Interventions that do not change over the course of the study, like a payment schedule, seem more likely candidates for policy studies than provision of services that evolve in response to conditions and clientele, making it almost impossible to track effects to a cause. Further, evaluations seem more applicable to new programs than ongoing ones with established clientele and strong political connections. Nevertheless, such studies gather useful data about real contexts that policy makers are likely to accept as being indicative of the results if the policy were adopted.

Evaluations as Almost Inevitably Political

Whether formative (designed to improve a program), summative (designed to determine its value), internal (conducted by a staff member), or external (conducted by an outsider)—evaluations are subject to political pressures. Internal formative

---

[9]Such studies include: five negative income tax experiments (Watts and Rees, 1976; Rossi and Lyall, 1976; Moffitt, 1979; Robins et al., 1980); transitional aid to prisoners that provided unemployment compensation to prisoners during time of transition and helped to reduce recidivism (Rossi, Berk, and Lenihan, 1980); and housing allowance that paid subsidies to poor families to permit them to purchase better housing (Struyk and Bendick, 1981; Bradbury and Downs, 1981; Friedman and Weinberg, 1983). Other studies concerned the requirement that the housing purchased conform to certain health standards; the effects of alternative police patrols on crime rates (Kelling et al., 1974); and subsidized medical insurance on consumption of health care (Newhouse et al., 1980).

evaluations may appear less threatening and therefore less likely to stir political winds. However, when negative findings appear, nearly always there are alternative ways to deploy resources and there are frequently strong opinions about the desirability of doing so. Further, although an internal evaluator may find it harder to convey negative findings than an external evaluator does, external summative evaluations usually create the strongest political turmoil. "Programs come into being through political processes, through the rough and tumble of political support, opposition, and bargaining" (Weiss, 1991, p. 214). To gain broad political support, program goals are often unrealistic and fuzzy, designed mainly to placate concerned parties. Their translation into operational goals, either to direct the evaluation or to compare with program achievements, makes transparent what the fuzzy goals concealed, and thus pleases some competing factions and displeases others. It is difficult for an evaluator to be perceived as neutral.

Further, "evaluators take a political stand . . . when they undertake . . . a study. The message is. . . : (1) the program is problematic enough to need evaluating, and (2) the program is a serious enough effort to be worth the time and effort to evaluate. . . . Programs with powerless clientele . . . lack the coalition of support that shields more mainstream groups [from evaluation]" (ibid., pp. 221–222). Further, "while an evaluation is in the field, political forces can alter or undermine it. . . . Legislators cut the budget; . . . the program director resigns . . . and a new director with new ideas is appointed. . . . Some of the things the evaluator was looking at . . . are now no longer relevant; some outcomes now central . . . weren't examined at the start and there are no 'before' data" (ibid., pp. 216–217). Indeed, from the decision to evaluate through all the stages of evaluation, political forces are at work.

The political nature of evaluation also manifests itself whenever there are questions about the concerns of stakeholders with no voice in the evaluation process. Some evaluators argue that evaluation should be used for social justice purposes—to empower the powerless—seek recognition and inclusion of all stakeholders. Although in sponsored evaluations, the employer ultimately determines the role stakeholders will play, the evaluator can often be influential in such discussions. If use of results is considered a prime criterion of a successful evaluation and stakeholders are an important force in marshaling support for or against their implementation, then both sponsor and evaluator must recognize this reality and take into account the goals and priorities of stakeholders. Neither can do solely what they wish. The evaluator as the active agent in the situation becomes the negotiator searching for the "art of the possible" (a phrase often used to define politics!)—finding a mutually satisfying design and procedure (Krathwohl, 1980).

Evaluations as Threats

Countering by Withholding Cooperation. Administrators and staff can make access and data gathering very difficult if they perceive the evaluation as threatening. To overtly deny access is too obvious, but they can defer it well beyond the evaluator's frustration threshold—by holding up scheduling interviews, requiring approval of all instruments by boards or committees, subtly undermining their own requests to teachers or parents to cooperate by the way they are phrased or delivered, informally marshaling the "insiders" to resist the "outsiders," and so on—repeatedly and indefinitely.

Similarly, those being evaluated, if antagonistic to the evaluation, can delay returning questionnaires, leave items blank, change or remove code numbers, give vague responses, and limit observations to favorable times and places. *The whole process is controlled by data givers who have a stake in the outcome.*

Brickell (1978) refers to the needed "instinctive ability of every born evaluator" to "bite the hand that feeds you while seeming to be licking it" (p. 95). Bogdan (1976) argues, "You can only afford to do evaluation if you can afford not to do it" (p. 65). Neither Brickell nor Bogdan imply that evaluations can never be done where there are hostile staff or participants, but there are clearly serious difficulties if they don't want to be evaluated; hence, the considerable interest in making stakeholders participants in the evaluation process.

Pressures for a Favorable Evaluation. The life-or-death stakes for programs undergoing evaluation can lead to pressures for a favorable report. "The view some managers hold about their programs is '*Nil nisi bonum,*' speak nothing but good; it is a phrase usually reserved for the dead" (Weiss, 1991, p. 215). For example, Brickell (1978), evaluating the impact of teacher aides, was warned early. Although Brickell was employed by the board of education, the district superintendents employed the aides and one offered this advice:

> "Okay you evaluators. Let's get one thing straight . . . these paraprofessionals . . . not only . . . help kids learn but . . . link us to the community [not a criterion the evaluator was employed to consider]. We're not looking for a report . . . that will cause any trouble . . . downtown. They've got their reasons . . . we've got ours. . . . We're going to keep our paraprofessionals. Don't make it difficult."
>
> Alerted thus, we made our study. And we were lucky that time. We found that the presence of paraprofessionals did in fact improve pupil achievement. (p. 95)

Here is a second example:

> While serving as the external evaluator of a large-scale program . . . our first submission . . . was a formative evaluation report . . . . Our report was . . . returned . . . and we were told that 100 pages was too much help. . . . He [the sponsor] asked us to shrink the length . . . cut out some of the negative material and try to write with a more balanced viewpoint. Then he could submit a copy of the report to his funding agency. We cut it in half, rethought the negative things we had said, eliminated some, and softened others. (p. 95)

Sponsors may ask to see the report before it is released; they may demand the right to edit the final report. Even if a report is not censored, it can be made unavailable. Coleman (1972) reports that the sponsor perceived his widely discussed *Equality of Educational Opportunity* was damaging the case for programs aiding minorities. Despite wide publicity and interest in the findings, the full report remained largely unavailable during its first year. The right to edit or censor and the availability of the report are some of many conditions that should be agreed on at the outset of an evaluation.

Wide-ranging pre-evaluation interviews can help determine whether a full-scale evaluation will be feasible and useful. They often trigger significant efforts to clarify goals or to improve implementation and delivery systems (Rossi and Freeman, 1993).

Evaluations as Inherently Conservative

Berk and Rossi (1976) argue that evaluation is inherently conservative because it is limited to the politically feasible. The negative income tax experiment was restricted to the narrow range of incentives that Congress might consider instead of the much wider scope that would have contributed to understanding the phenomenon. Further, evaluations focus on the politically dominant view of social problems: the negative income tax on the concern that persons, satisfied with being on public assistance, would withdraw from the workforce. Improved health and enrichment of lives as outcomes were either neglected or downplayed.

Control of the study by a sponsor or manager is an obvious case of evaluation as a conservative force. Employed by a sponsor, the evaluator is perceived as serving the side where the power lies, thus helping maintain the status quo. "Evaluators help political figures remain in power if they supply them with information that other participants in the political process do not possess" (Cronbach, 1982, p. 35). The many voices arguing for the evaluator to negotiate for powerless publics is a reaction to this concern. Evaluators give evidence of personal values by the evaluation opportunities they accept.

The many "close-to-zero effects" and "no-significant-difference" evaluation results conservatively reinforce things the way they are and discourage the search for change. "When 'no significant difference' is interpreted as a program failure, the burden of proof is placed on the innovation" (Cronbach, 1982, p. 33). The problem may lie partly in program execution (no pun intended), that is, the considerable slippage between conceptualization and implementation. The challenge for program designers is to develop programs that are effective over a variety of implementation strategies or have "natural" paths to correct implementation. Alternatively, with trial implementation runs, they can see how and why modifications took place and can determine whether they can be controlled (Fairweather and Tornatzky, 1977; Hamilton, 1979).

Evaluation is seen as conservative when it reinforces the dominant scientific view of the world—focusing on "standard" ways of implementing interventions that permit general conclusions about the best practices. Such critics "believe that probabilistic generalizations are almost worthless, since much of what happens is determined by the specifics of a situation and the perceptions of participants" (ibid., p. 34). They fear authorities who, trusting generalizations, will inappropriately force a program to conform. Such concerns are grounded in fundamental and probably deep-seated differences as to the goals and nature of social science. We alluded to these previously in the discussion of the qualitative method, which, for some, is a point of view in which knowledge is local and context-bound (pp. 235–238 Chapter 11).

Fitting Evaluations to Their Audiences

The widely differing views of the nature of social science have implications for evaluators concerned that their work be used. Society tends to move into administrative positions those individuals who view scientific findings as valuable and who prefer analytic reports. Such individuals will likely view quantitative evidence more favorably than qualitative. However, whereas an administrator may find a statistical report interpretable and useful, an elementary school teacher, librarian, or social worker may find a case study approach describing the impact on specific individuals more meaningful. Evaluators must consider client and stakeholder preferences for certain kinds of research methods and evidence in planning their evaluation process, evidence gathering, and reporting style.

> ◆ *Evaluations initiated as afterthoughts are likely to be weaker than those integrated into program implementation plans.*
> ◆ *Evaluations can usefully explore social policy effectiveness and side effects. The large government studies of the 1960s and 1970s demonstrated the feasibility of large-scale experiments that employed randomization.*
> ◆ *Timing the availability of findings is critical to their use, but it is difficult to coordinate the evaluation process with political moods and deadlines.*
> ◆ *Evaluations almost inevitably stir up political forces, especially when they are perceived as threatening or when a program with political origins is studied. Involvement of stakeholders in evaluation planning and implementation can raise questions of power and program control.*
> ◆ *Individuals who perceive an evaluation as threatening can appear to be cooperating in data collection while subtly sabotaging it since they control the process. There may be pressures for a favorable report from individuals jeopardized by unfavorable results. If utilization is a prime criterion, negotiations to find "the art of the possible" limit evaluations to the politically feasible.*
> ◆ *Evaluations are a conservative force when they reinforce the dominant views in a society and stay within the bounds of the politically feasible. New programs often show too close-to-zero effects to overcome status quo momentum. Sponsor control of evaluations tends to reinforce this conservative bent.*
> ◆ *Evaluators need to take into account the audience's beliefs about the appropriate role of social science, and their preferences for certain kinds of research methods and evidence in planning and implementing an evaluation.*

Evaluation Standards: Protection for Evaluators and Clients

To ameliorate many of the earlier noted problems, evaluators representing interested professional associations developed standards that describe appropriate conduct for both evaluator and client. Like the test standards in Chapter 18, they were a joint project of the interested professional associations (Joint Committee on Standards for Educational Evaluation, 1994). Thirty standards are grouped under the four main concerns of evaluation: utility, feasibility, propriety, and accuracy. Each standard includes an overview of intent, guidelines for application, common pitfalls, caveats (trade-offs where more than one standard applies), and an illustration of the standard's application. Wildemuth (1981) prepared an annotated bibliography addressing each of them.

Although aimed at education projects, the standards have much wider applicability. The standards are particularly useful in the development of a contract between sponsor and evaluator in suggesting some of the potential points of conflict that might evolve out of their relationship as the project progresses. The standards can also be helpful in what has been termed "meta-evaluation," the assessment of how well an evaluation study was done.

Hallmarks and Tips for Evaluation Studies

The following tips for doing evaluations also indicate the hallmarks of a good evaluation.

1. Be sure you want to do the project. Having to work at being nice in continuous contact with protagonists, antagonists, and various stakeholders can be wearing and can reduce your effectiveness. However, if all evaluators were too choosy, only advocates would be available. You should keep a balance.
2. Try to anticipate potential problems and work through the gray areas with the sponsor[10] regarding problem definition and scope, stakeholders' rights in the evaluation, report editing and documentation, the public's right to know, the time schedule, and fiscal details. Be sure they meet your personal and professional standards. Put the agreement in writing.
3. Have a means of modifying the agreement in case sponsor/evaluator negotiations fail; provide for flexibility and accommodation.
4. An advisory group of right-to-know audiences may be helpful in identifying potential "minefields." Depending on your philosophy and that of your sponsor, probe for additional audiences not apparent earlier, and work through their acceptance.
5. Using this group and the sponsor, decide whether a goal-free or targeted evaluation is appropriate, possibly the former preceding the latter. Use such a group for a targeted evaluation to explore what questions are of concern (called the *divergent* phase by Cronbach, 1982). Find those questions important to all, those negotiated as important to enough groups to include, and those with no agreement (Cronbach's *convergent* phase). Allocate resources to the first type of questions and to the second as resources allow.

---

[10]The term sponsor is used as a shorthand for three kinds of persons 1) if an evaluation is requested or contracted for, the person(s) soliciting the evaluation, 2) the person(s) from whom you obtain permission to do the evaluation if it is unsolicited, 3) the person(s) from whom you must get cooperation even though they work for the person who solicited the evaluation or gave permission.

Consider questions of the third type in terms of their intrinsic merit, the powerlessness of the group to get them attended to, resources available, and so on.

6. Act as an institutional resource by bringing appropriate outside research findings to bear and organizing them into a conceptual scheme related to the decisions to be made.

7. Choose methods of investigation appropriate to the questions and to the preferences for kinds of evidence of relevant stakeholders. Remember the importance of the evaluation *process* in instilling trust. "It is . . . of fundamental importance that justice be done, but it should manifestly and undoubtedly be seen to be done" (Stewart, 1924, p. 259).

8. Educate the advisory committee and sponsor regarding trade-offs in the study; have them help in the trade-off decisions.

9. Do not take for granted that a program was implemented as either planned or conceptualized. Reasons for any discrepancy may bear on the feasibility of implementation in a wider sphere.

10. Expect political pressures to increase in the later stages; the study's potential impact is getting closer.

11. Use a format (written or oral report, graphics), style (informal, formal), and wording (technical, nontechnical) that will best communicate with your audience. "Don't expect decision makers to change their style of receiving information just for your evaluation" (Hendricks and Papagiannis, 1990, p. 124).

12. Pace reporting so that it is absorbed. Leak results early in small interim reports dealing with easily understood segments. They can accommodate for negative evidence more comfortably this way. A big report's summary may restore perspective, but the report itself may be mainly archived.

13. Reinforce the limits and constraints of the study to the audience.

14. Separate recommendations and advocacy from interpretation of findings; make clear the judgmental aspects and possible biases. Clarify goal and policy implications.

15. In reporting, remember that audiences reading it will want to know the special competencies of the authors, who sponsored the study and why, what their responsibility was, how well these results match those of comparable studies, and, if the evaluation is controversial, where the response of opposing parties can be found (Hoaglin et al., 1982).

Tips for Doing Action Research

1. Work with one or more colleagues. Not only does this procedure provide motivation over the low spots, but discussion also enhances the reflection critical to all phases of the process.

2. Careful observation and reflection are often the key. Remember others may see things you are oblivious to.

3. Consider a range of solutions. Don't worry about feasibility initially—it is the new perspective that can be most helpful.

4. Diagramming an action strategy is often helpful in seeing how it can be improved.

5. Improved practice resulting from particular actions is very reinforcing. Once you have found something that works, test it under the normal variety of contexts. Increase improvement through successive experiments with changes.

6. Actions in social situations often have unforeseen side effects. Look for them and, where negative, consider the trade-offs.

7. Complex problems may require complex solutions; they are not changed overnight. Since they typically require more than single actions, you must successively adapt strategies over a period of time.

8. Keeping a journal, log or other record will not only force you to reflect on your observations, but reviewing it from time to time will also reinforcingly show how far you have come and provide a rudder guiding future progress. If you decide to share your experiences with others, it gives you a head start.

SUMMARY

Evaluations are typically decision-driven; research is hypothesis-driven. Formative evaluations are intended to help a program improve; summative evaluations are used to determine whether to continue a program or which of several programs is best. Consensus around the interpretation of the data is generally greater within a more targeted group than in research. It may be only the sponsor and evaluator, but more often it includes other stakeholders. Utilization is a prime criterion of its success. If the results are to be utilized, stakeholders must trust the process that produced them. Therefore, the process by which the evaluation was carried out is often as important as the product.

There are various approaches to evaluation:

• *Connoisseurial or expert-judgment approaches*—evaluations employ experts in the field to provide a judgment.

• *Objectives- or goal-based approaches*—the evaluation concentrates on the intended goals of a program. A major question is, whose version of intended goals is used, that of sponsor, administrator, staff, clients, or other stakeholders.

• *Goal-free approaches*—without knowledge of intended goals, the evaluator determines what occurred and compares that with intended changes.

• *Management-oriented approaches*—evaluations are designed to assist managers in the administration of programs. These approaches are often concerned with efficiency and effectiveness.

• *Consumer-oriented approaches*—evaluations are intended to help consumers decide what program to use, what product to buy, and so forth.

• *Adversarial approaches*—evaluators prepare cases to represent the two or more alternative points of view on a problem and present their cases as in a court of law.

• *Responsive naturalistic approaches*—evaluations use qualitative methods to describe what occurred and to seek to be responsive to the stakeholder audience.

• *Participant-oriented approaches*—the stakeholders are involved in determining the evaluation process.

• *Action research*—the evaluation is planned, carried out, and interpreted by those wanting the results for their own decision making. They may prepare a report for colleagues and others like them. Professional evaluators may be used as consultants.

Each approach has certain advantages and disadvantages and is useful under certain circumstances. As the differences among the approaches suggest, the many decision points can lead to quite different evaluations.

Evaluations are almost unavoidably political acts. Evaluations tend to be conservative. Questions of who does the evaluation, who controls the process, and who controls the report are often points of contention. Evaluation standards have been developed to guide both sponsors and evaluators.

A Look Ahead

In the next section, we take the time to step back and seek perspective on the research process. Having studied a variety of approaches to the research process, we now have a whole armory of weapons to conquer problems. The next chapter emphasizes using the best combination of them appropriate for a research study. It notes again the importance to effective research of handling the ever-present trade-offs and reviews the strengths and weaknesses of various means of collecting data.

ADDITIONAL READING

Useful evaluation discussions: Cronbach (1982), House (1980, 1990), Rossi and Freeman (1993), and Rossi and Wright (1986). For particular evaluation approaches: Eisner (1981), Guba and Lincoln (1986), Patton (1980), Rippey (1973), and Stake (1991). For an overview of approaches: Worthen and Sanders (1987). For action research: Altrichter, Posch, and Somekh (1993), Haggerson and Bowman (1992), and Hollingsworth and Sockett (1994).

IMPORTANT TERMS

Action research
Adversarial evaluation
Behavioral objectives
Connoisseurial or expert-judgment evaluation
Consumer-oriented evaluation
Cost-benefit analyses
Cost-effectiveness analysis
Decision-driven
Evaluation

Formative evaluation
Goal-based evaluation
Goal-free evaluation
Management-oriented evaluation
Participant-oriented evaluation
Responsive naturalistic evaluation
Stakeholders
Summative evaluation
Utilization

APPLICATION PROBLEMS

1. The success of the Children's Television Workshop (CTW), especially its best-known program, *Sesame Street*, has been attributed to CTW's unique three-stage program development model, summarized as follows:

a. A long preproduction stage (up to one year)

(1) Instructional designers conduct needs analysis and hammer out detailed behavioral objectives linked to the founder's definition of the educational problem to be solved.

(2) The executive producer and designers agree on the behavioral objectives.

(3) Educational researchers and production staff develop program philosophy and format.

b. Pilot show

(1) Internal, laboratory-style research is done on comprehensibility, and appeal to the viewer population and consequent modification of program segments. Small groups of preschool children are brought to the studios.

(2) A pilot show is produced and used to estimate achievement, audience appeal, and comprehensibility (as measured by

interview, questionnaire, and assessment of eye movement) and to select the best program and features.

    (3) Findings are discussed through informal, supportive teamwork.

  c. Full production: Production takes place with continuing feedback from researchers and subject content experts.

Consider the activities described in stages b and c. Are they research or evaluation? Why? Which of the approaches to evaluation is best represented by this process?

2. Two doctoral candidates at Upstate University were asked to evaluate the Developmental Economic Educational Program (DEEP) run by a local community college. This program was primarily funded by the Joint Council for Economic Education, a private, nonprofit organization, and additional funds came from the state education department. The local DEEP Center was administered by a director and four faculty advisors. It had contracts with 35 school districts, each of which had a resident DEEP coordinator. It ran in-service workshops designed to familiarize the primary and secondary teachers in the districts with the DEEP curriculum (now mandated by the state) and to aid them in developing and implementing their own individual curricula. The director wished to determine if the teachers were really using the DEEP curriculum and if so, to what extent. He wanted to know whether the workshop was successful in helping them to do

so and if it met their expectations. What approach might the evaluators have taken?

3. The superintendent of curriculum of the Fayetteville school board was given the task of developing a teacher evaluation process after the state education department disbanded its inspection system and turned control over to the school boards. What approach would you advise her to take?

4. The directors of a large charity organization in Sandstone City are concerned about the program at their halfway house for teenage girls. The halfway house serves local girls who have no alternative home life and are referred by child care agencies. Most are in legal trouble. At any one time, the home might have between a half-dozen and a dozen residents. The program attempts to teach the girls life skills such as self-care, personal hygiene, home care, and shopping skills. The basis of the program is a behavior modification system in which they earn points to move up level by level and obtain increased privileges. Some of the directors are concerned about the persistent reports that the program is being used to maintain control over the residents and that the point system is merely a means of punishment. They are also alarmed at the high rate of turnover of both staff and residents. They have hired you to evaluate the program. How would you proceed?

Compare your answers with those following the Application Exercise.

APPLICATION EXERCISE

Are there aspects of your problem that are like an evaluation or could be? If there are, consider who will be the stakeholders, who ought therefore to be involved in some way in the evaluation. How should they be involved? What problems might you associate with their involvement? Which kinds or

combinations of evaluation are most appropriate? Which will you most likely utilize? Considering the evaluation standards and the hallmarks of an evaluation, which of them do you think might cause the greatest problems? How might you find your way around them?

ANSWERS TO THE APPLICATION PROBLEMS

1. Although there are elements of research involved here, this is formative evaluation. It is decision-driven, designed to render judgments about what to include in the programs (pedagogical decisions) and whether particular program segments appeal to

and are understood by the intended audience (programming decisions). The emphasis is on in-house teamwork in which a consensus is sought at each stage of development. The purpose is to make production decisions rather than to test hypotheses about the effectiveness of programs as instructional treatments.

2. They would likely have used a management-oriented approach like that of Rossi and Freeman. The intent of this evaluation was to provide information that would improve the administration of the particular intervention, the DEEP program. Their client was the local director, who was interested in assessment of classroom impact, coverage of all the affected teachers in the districts, and the delivery of service. However, since there were many stakeholders, including the program's sponsors (the state education department and the joint council) and the clients of the program (the school districts' administrators and the teachers), whose input might have been important, a qualitative or participant-oriented approach might have been both informative and politically expedient in gathering evidence responsive to their concerns.

3. The evaluation of teaching competency, looked at from the administrators' point of view, requires current knowledge of both teaching practice and curriculum. But since utilization is a prime criterion for an evaluation and since these evaluations will clearly affect stakeholders such as the teachers evaluated, they are of concern to more than the sponsor. Further, they may well be affected by local circumstances of which teachers would be aware (teaching practice certainly being different in a large city from that in a rural setting). Therefore, some kind of evaluation that involved the stakeholders in the development of the evaluation process would be important: teachers, parents, school board, administrators, and experts in the

evaluation of teaching would need to be included (though members of the stakeholder group guiding the evaluation might study the literature to become their own experts).

A common strategy is to develop a standard teacher evaluation procedure with an appeal process. A fair process should take into account the five criteria mentioned in the chapter. Thus, the evaluation should be structured, making clear who will make the judgment, when, and on the basis of what criteria. These criteria should be jointly developed by the stakeholders and be made publicly available in written form. Such evaluations should be conducted by more than one person—for example, by two different school administrators or peers. A written report of the evaluation should be given to the teacher with the opportunity to respond and, if possible (or desired), have the evaluation judged by a review group selected to be fair (again, possibly including peers).

4. Since you want to understand what is truly happening at the home, you would need to collect information that is responsive to the staff and residents as well as the directors. This is, in effect, a case study. In this situation, a naturalistic, or qualitative approach, in which you conduct unstructured interviews or engage in participant observation, would be most informative. Entering with few preconceptions, you may get a better grasp of the differing perceptions of the people involved, understand the pluralistic nature of the situation, and come up with alternative recommendations. Perhaps only by involving the staff and the residents in every stage of the evaluation will you be able to overcome suspicions and resentment and make a viable recommendation.

SECTION EIGHT

The Larger Context of Research

Having studied the tools and methods of research, the two chapters in this section step back to take a longer view, to place the previous material into perspective. Much of what is discussed here has been foreshadowed.

- Chapter 24 examines the advantages of using multiple-method approaches to a problem. Although the discussion of research methods was structured along a continuum, this was not to suggest choice of method was an either/or proposition. Indeed wherever appropriate the complementary nature of the methods was noted. This chapter, in reinforcing that complementarity, explores what can be gained by combining methods. It notes the ever-present trade-offs in both method and design choices. A useful table summarizes the advantages and disadvantages of ways of gathering data.
- Chapter 25 examines the roles of social science research and what is involved in ensuring that it works properly at the individual level, the peer level, and the societal level. It is intended to raise questions for further thought rather than provide answers.

CHAPTER **24**

Optimizing Research Effectiveness Through Multiple Methods

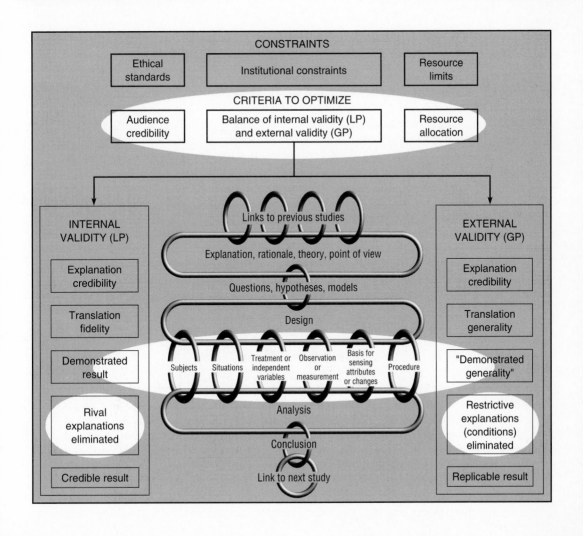

The issue is how we can use the contrast [between quantitative and qualitative methods] to highlight the taken-for-granted practices and perspectives of each approach and how, taken together, they can provide a more textured and productive view of the social phenomena we seek to understand.

Pamela Moss (1996, p. 22)

All quantities are measures of qualities.

Behrens and Smith (1996, p. 947)

Research is a creative act; don't confine your thinking about it to specific approaches. Researchers creatively combine the elements of methods in any way that makes the best sense for the study they want to do. Their only limits are their own imagination and the necessity of presenting their findings convincingly. The research question to be answered really determines the method.

This text, Chapter 2, page 27

OVERVIEW

This chapter emphasizes the strengths to be gained by combining complementary research methods in order to optimally attack a problem. In choosing one method over another, we trade certain strengths for others. This is but one example of the trade-offs that pervade research, however; handling them well is a requirement of research competence. Although replication of findings is the ultimate validation for all methods, evidence from different methods strengthens the cases for causality [internal validity (LP)] and for generality [external validity (GP)].

CHAPTER CONTENTS

Introduction

Having reached this textbook's twenty-fourth chapter, you are well aware that all research methods have both strengths and weaknesses. No single method is research's be-all and end-all. Phillips (1992) notes that from one point of view "there is little difference between qualitative and quantitative inquiry. . . . The good work in both cases . . . has been opened up to criticism, and the reasons and evidence offered in both cases will have withstood serious scrutiny. . . . what is crucial . . . is the critical spirit in which it has been carried out" (p. 78).

Used for an appropriate purpose on the right problem in a suitable context with adequate resources, any method can present a sufficiently convincing case to achieve the consensus that begins the journey to acceptance as knowledge. Good research properly defines a problem so as to encompass all the necessary aspects to understand it as completely as possible, regardless of method (Phillips, 1992). In fact, many problems require more than any one method can deliver; the answer, of course, is a **multiple-method** approach.

In a book devoted to advancing multiple-method approaches, Brewer and Hunter (1989) argue: "Our individual methods may be flawed, but fortunately the flaws are not identical. A diversity of imperfection allows us to combine methods not only to gain their individual strengths but also to compensate for their particular faults and limitations" (pp. 16–17).[1] Indeed, there is a long history of calls for multiple-method approaches as well as many examples in the literature.

Some researchers argue, however, that quantitative methods are incompatible with qualitative methods; the underlying assumptions of each method preclude the use of the other in the same study. For some researchers, qualitative methodologies are a point of view on the nature of the world, one in which all reality is constructed. Since each individual sees the world in his or her own way, multiple realities exist. Quantitative methodologists reject this point of view. Dyed-in-the-wool researchers in either camp can get quite worked up about their differences.

The author of this text agrees with House (1994) that the conflict has been overblown. House notes: "When examined closely [some] quantitative data turn out to be composites of qualitative interpretations" (p. 17). Put another way, quantitative findings compress into summary numbers the trends and tendencies expressed in words in qualitative reports. In many instances, counts of coded qualitative data might have produced data similar to the quantitative summaries. Since qualitative and quantitative methods both offer views of the same world, they may turn up the same findings and usefully reinforce one another. This is but one instance of the many purposes for which the methods can be usefully combined.

Ways Multiple Methods Enhance Research

Researchers have yoked multiple methods for different purposes. Perhaps their most frequent use is to enhance, illustrate, or clarify. For example, qualitative stories are used to make quantitative analyses come alive, as in Clausen's (1993) longitudinal study of the developmental effects of the Depression on children of the 1920s. Though begun when research was technologically primitive—few psychological tests, and no tape recorders or computers—interview, observation, mailed questionnaire, and physical examination data were compiled into abstract numerical analyses that were made real with life story accounts. A book reviewer com-

---

[1]Eisner (1981) notes, "The issue is not qualitative as contrasted with . . . quantitative. . . . With both we can achieve binocular vision. Looking through one eye never did provide much depth of field" (p. 9).

mented: "In a display of methodological virtuosity, Clausen manages to combine longitudinal variable analysis with life histories and the analysis of these histories as narrative. . . . The combination is impressive" (Gerstel, 1993, p. 1157).

Smith, Gabriel, Schott, and Padia's (1976) combination of qualitative and quantitative methods in the evaluation of Outward Bound is another good example. Outward Bound is a voluntary program intended to increase participants' self-confidence and awareness of their dependence on others. Participants train for a wilderness experience that tests their physical, mental, and emotional capacities. Smith provided a qualitative account that conveyed the thoughts and feelings of a participant experiencing it. The qualitative account was accompanied by quantitative evidence of the program's success in achieving its goals.

Perhaps almost as common as supplementing and illustrating is calling upon one method to check the validity of another method's data. We encountered this earlier in the collection of qualitative data to determine whether the demand conditions of a quantitatively measured experiment conformed to what was intended (see p. 523). Similarly, we noted that interviews following the completion of a questionnaire help determine whether queries were interpretable and communicated properly (see p. 372).

As in qualitative research, where we first met this term (see p. 275), *triangulation* using multiple methods corroborates results. It can also increase the accuracy of estimation of an effect size. A problem is approached from different angles, each independent of the other, with the anticipation that congruent answers are free of method bias. For example, the **bracketing model** of Reichardt and Gollob (1987), considers multiple method results as alternative estimates. The trick, then, is to use methods that are biased in opposite directions so that the true value is bracketed. Ideally, the bias is small so that the bracket is narrow and the average is a good estimate. Similarly, Brewer and Hunter's (1989) **complementary multiplism** involves capitalizing on the individual strengths of different methods by using them in complementary roles such that the imperfections of one covers the faults and limitations of another. The strength of the combined evidence is markedly enhanced.

Complementary multiplism may serve many purposes. For example, in the Clausen (1993) study of the children of the Depression, multiple methods were used to build credibility with particular audiences and to enhance the interpretability of the results. Complementary multiplism can provide protection against an alternative explanation as demonstrated in a study by Duffy and Roehler (1990). In their study of the effect of explicit instruction in mental processing on reading, volunteer teachers were randomly assigned to experimental and control treatments. Both sets of teachers were taught ways to improve student engagement on academic tasks. The experimental teachers in addition were taught to provide instruction in mental processing. Both groups were observed seven times during the year to determine the explicitness of the teachers' instruction (qualitative data gathered on process). The researchers also gathered qualitative data through interviews with students in both groups to determine the extent of their awareness of their mental processing. A standardized reading achievement test determined the effect of treatment (quantitative data gathered on product). They were able to use this combination of quantitative and qualitative data to show the success of explicit instruction for low-reading students. Further, they used qualitative methods to assure that mental processing, not rote memory, was occurring.

As indicated in the parenthetical comments in the previous paragraph, multiple methods can be used to investigate different aspects of phenomena; often qualitative methods are used to describe process in studies where quantitative methods evaluate products. This also occurred in the Clausen study of Depression children and the Smith, Gabriel, Schott and Padia (1976) evaluation of Outward Bound.

Multiple methods used sequentially may help decide the next steps in a project. For example, qualitative methods can be used to explore and find effects and then quantitative methods can be used to determine their size. Rossi and Lyall's (1976) income maintenance study combined a field experiment, survey methods, and intensive case studies. Together, these provided the picture that kept a seemingly promising plan for helping low-income families escape poverty from becoming policy. Qualitative case studies caught the family breakup that unexpectedly resulted and also helped the researchers understand why it occurred. Using survey methods, the researchers then determined the size and seriousness of this side effect as well as the intended desirable consequences of income maintenance that they had expected. The combination of three research methods provided evidence of side and main effects, and of relationships, as well as explanatory rationales.

The Rossi and Lyall example reinforces the multiple method suggestion in Chapter 20 that every experimental study should have, formally or informally, an element of the qualitative case study in it. Good researchers stay close to their treatment administration and data collection to learn whether things went according to plan, how subjects viewed the study, what the subjects (informants) were expecting, and how they reacted. Unanticipated events, side effects, or misperceptions can completely alter a study. Demand conditions may convey unplanned perceptions to the subjects. Researchers unaware of such events will completely misinterpret the data. Although assistants may gather data, there is no substitute for the principal investigator gathering some firsthand.

Advocacy of multiple methods is widespread, including, among others, Mark and Shotland (1987), Caracelli and Greene (1993) and Behrens and Smith (1996). This list of multiple method uses could be considerably longer, so let us simply note that multiple methods can enhance a study in ways limited only by the researcher's creativity. *The emphasis, however, should always be on finding the most appropriate methods for a given study. In many cases, only multiple methods can provide the optimal combination required for the powerful development of evidence and explanation that will gain a consensus around the interpretation of the data.*

♦ *Multiple research methods can play many roles in strengthening a study. For example, they may be used in making numeric data come alive, in precisely summarizing narrative data, in checking on the validity of data, in developing rationales, in catching side-effects, in eliminating rival explanations, in determining a study's next steps and in determining the demand conditions. But, this is not a complete listing; their uses are limited only by the researcher's creative imagination.*

Roles of Multiple Methods in Basic, Applied, and Policy Research

Although realistically, the process is not so simple and orderly, consider that sometimes research findings move through basic, applied and policy stages. Findings that originate from a basic research stage, where the researcher is simply seeking knowledge for its own sake, may use laboratory settings. Where it seems likely that the findings could be usefully applied, a second stage of testing in real-world situations determines whether they generalize as expected. A third stage consisting of replications may take place in settings intended to be convincing to policymakers. Each stage has implications for the use of multiple research methods.

In a *basic research study*, we describe a phenomenon and, as tightly as possible, link cause to effect. Such studies emphasize understanding and how variables are related (for example, how different kinds and levels of anxiety are linked to achievement). Strong internal validity (LP) is a key criterion. Audience credibility is almost automatic since the requirements of the audience are typically those basic researchers make of themselves to maximize the descriptive, linking, and explanatory power of a study. Complementary methods that help eliminate alternative explanations, that assure treatment fidelity, that examine demand conditions, that enhance the explanation, and that catch side-effects, markedly strengthen the internal validity of the study.

With *applied studies*, internal validity (LP) is still a consideration, particularly if the previous studies were done in a laboratory. Now, however, we are more concerned with generality—external validity (GP)—to find out whether and how the phenomenon works under real conditions. Much of the target audience for such research is likely to be less sophisticated in research methods, so we may use a combination of well-established instruments and familiar research methods in order to increase understanding and acceptance. In addition, however, we may supplement with complex analyses that better fit the phenomena in order to provide convincing evidence for knowledgeable colleagues. Using multiple methods also helps assure that the effect is not traceable to the use of a particular method in previous studies. Findings that replicate with multiple methods provide evidence of generality [external validity (GP)].

Policy studies are done not only to show the generality of the effects but also to obtain evidence that will convince particular audiences to take action based on the findings. There are usually multiple audiences: the staff of a program, its clients, other people or programs affected by it (including those it might replace), policymakers, and legislators. Often these interests are antagonistic (for example, the various points of view regarding busing to provide racial integration in the schools), but the credibility of the study must be such that as many of the groups as possible—ideally all—will accept its findings. Like evaluations, the process may be as important as the product to be convincing. For acceptance, the process must be public, must involve enough cases, cases must be sufficiently representative, must avoid important flaws and must eliminate important rival explanations. Including evidence targeted to different audiences will facilitate policy adoption and most often calls for multiple methods. Case studies may impress legislators and their constituents; quantitative analyses may be more persuasive to legislative staff members. Field workers may prefer narratives derived from observation, administrators and their staffs, evidence from experimentation.

Each choice of method and design enhancement carries with it implications, including those of cost in time and money, that must be considered. The allocation of resources to achieve the goals of the study through proper choice of single or multiple methods to build the strongest possible chain of reasoning within budget limitations has always been, and will remain, a key skill of a good researcher.

✦ *Basic, applied, and policy research studies may use multiple methods to achieve different purposes: in basic research, to strengthen internal validity (LP); in applied research, to show generality—external validity (GP); and in policy research, to target different audiences.*

Strengths and Weaknesses of Various Data-Gathering Methods

The strengths achieved through the complimentary use of multiple-research methods, is partly a function of the methods themselves and partly that of the nature of their data. Rather than recapitulate the efficacy or lack of it in the methods previously discussed, it will be more useful here to summarize the pros and cons of different ways of gathering data. Metfessel and Michael (1967) summarize the strengths and weaknesses of a variety of data-gathering methods in a useful self-explanatory table, adapted as Table 24.1 (pp. 624–626).

The Power of Replication

In a chapter concerned with multiple-method research, it is important to emphasize that for *all* methods, replication is the ultimate validation. Further, replication using multiple methods is likely to be convincing to a wider array of audiences; it is likely to present a fuller picture of the phenomena, and it will contribute significantly to generality—external validity (GP). Replication using multiple research methods, rules out rival explanations that use of the same research method in all the studies would not.

There is a tendency to associate replication mainly with experimentation, however, since, being under the control of the researcher, experiments can most easily be repeated. What about qualitative research? Because the qualitative researcher may have to wait for events to reoccur, and because the work is so labor intensive, replications are rare. Yet, qualitative research's evidence of replication

TABLE 24.1 *Strengths and Weaknesses of a Variety of Data-Gathering Approaches*

Approach	Strengths	Weaknesses
Data collected by a mechanical device (e.g., audiotape, videotape, lapsed-time photography, galvanic skin response)	• Stays on the job, avoids human fatigue and clerical errors; has infinite patience. • May capture content missed by written records such as voice inflection and nonverbal communication (e.g., posture). • Provides a sufficiently complete record that it can often be reprocessed from a new point of view as new analytic techniques are devised or new insights are gained by further research. (Often what one started out to study is not the most interesting part of the data.) • If the camera is not at the right angle or the lighting is poor, data may be lost.	• Data can be costly to gather and may require special equipment. • Equipment does not make judgments, so it produces an extensive record that must be processed. • Equipment failures can be a problem, especially when failures result in missing vital parts of the data. • Operator error, haste, or insufficient training result in improperly collected data. • Period of acclimation may be necessary, if not concealed, until those observed forget the presence and purpose of the equipment. • Audiotape omits the visual, which could be important. Even videotape catches the action only from one viewpoint. • Visuals of group may have wrong camera angle for some individuals. Good sound recording is often hard to get.
Data collected by an independent observer	• Can be used in natural as well as experimental settings. • Is the most direct measure of behavior. • Experienced, trained, or perceptive observers can pick up subtle occurrences of interactions sometimes not available by other techniques.	• Observer's presence changes the situation, sometimes creating an artificial one. • Record is less complete than when scene is videotaped. • Ambiguities in recording and lack of objectivity in recording by different observers may lead to false interpretations or may cause an inference to be missed.
Written accounts	• May use the critical incident technique which zeroes in on desired situations, eliminating much "chaff." Critical incidents are those that respondents consider critical to triggering the target behavior of the study. Interpretation is kept separate from actual reporting in so far as possible.	• Accounts are difficult to make complete. • Interpretations are often included as though they were factual data (e.g., "Mary kicked John because she was angry with him").
Observation forms (e.g., observation schedules)	• Easy to complete; save time. • Can be objectively scored. • Standardize the observations. • Have built-in point of view regarding what is important to observe. • Analysis is often simultaneous with collection of the data when observer categorizes observations as they are made.	• Forms are not as flexible as written accounts; may lump unlike acts together. • Criteria for ratings are often unspecified. • Researcher may overlook meaningful behavior that is not reflected in the instrument. • Sampling may be inadequate to catch important action (e.g., "categorize and record group action every 90 seconds").

TABLE 24.1 (*continued*)

Approach	Strengths	Weaknesses
Data produced by the subject	• Data can be collected inexpensively that would be very costly to gather by the lengthy observation necessary to learn a person's attitudes, interests, values, and so on. • Data can be collected that is nearly inaccessible by other means (private thoughts, feelings, sensitive topics).	• Accuracy depends on subject's self-perception, which may or may not accurately reflect "objective" judgments of others. • Method requires conditions conducive to honest responses such as nonthreatening situations; may require anonymous responses. • Recall of past events is modified by individual's perceptions of those events rather than accurate memory. This could be a strength if the researcher is interested in perceptions.
Diaries	• Are comprehensive; may give private thoughts and commentaries on activities.	• Can be difficult to analyze; very different from person to person in what is and is not recorded, in accuracy and in point of view.
Checklists, rating scales, and questionnaires	• Are quick and economical to administer. • Are easy to score and summarize.	• If data are collected by mail, it may result in low percentage of returns; nonrespondents may differ from respondents; other than intended respondents may have completed forms or helped answer them. • There is no assurance that respondent correctly understood questions or directions. • Answers may be subject to response sets such as the acquiescence set (a tendency to respond "true" to true-false or "yes" to yes-no queries) and to the halo effect (the tendency to respond to rating scales in terms of a general image of the person rather than rating the specific characteristic requested).
Interviews	• Allow depth of response. • Can ensure individuals understand the questions and follow directions. • Are flexible and adaptable to individuals. • Can capture nonverbal responses that reveal feelings with sensitive interviewer.	• Very costly in time, personnel, and travel. • Require skilled and trained personnel. • Often difficult to analyze and summarize. • Interviewer may influence responses, especially if respondent seeks to please. • Certain responses may be inhibited or encouraged by demeanor or appearance of interviewer (e.g., black middle-class interviewer of white lower-class interviewee). • Confidentiality of response is less certain for interviewee than anonymous response to a questionnaire.

Approach	Strengths	Weaknesses
Sociometry (respondents indicate choices in group of best friend, lab partner, and so on; responses are usually diagrammed using arrows to indicate who chose whom as well as mutual choices)	• Measures a unique aspect of social interaction. • Is easy to score. • Can lead to clinical insights.	• Criteria used in making choices may vary from individual to individual. • Choices of respondents can lead to complex and difficult-to-interpret diagrams. • Method is applicable mainly to small groups.
Projective techniques (Thematic Apperception Test [TAT]; Rorschach; House, Tree, Person Test; etc.)	• Lead to clinical insights. • Allow individual to reveal self without realizing it. • Have no right answers, so responses are largely uncensored. • Are nonthreatening.	• Different clinicians may analyze and interpret the same responses differently. • Reliability and validity of measures are uncertain. • Possible ethical questions may exist in getting individual to reveal self, if not properly used.
Tests	• Are practical—take the place of extensive observation. • Are the most reliable measures available at present. • Can record products and processes of thought.	• Because of availability and ease of use, tests are sometimes used where other data-gathering techniques would be more appropriate.
Tests with constructed responses	• Essay tests allow students to synthesize their knowledge about a topic. • Short-answer and completion tests can be scored reasonably objectively.	• It is difficult to cover a topic intensively with essay tests in a short time. • Essay tests are difficult to score, and students often interpret them in the way they wish rather than in the manner intended. Graders are then uncertain whether this was intentional and should be graded down or whether they should give appropriate credit for excellence of whatever interpretation the testee presents. • Short-answer and completion tests too easily lend themselves to testing trivia.
Supplied-answer, multiple-choice, matching, and ranking tests	• Can be objectively scored. • Can be easily scored. • Usually have high test reliability. • Can be item-analyzed to improve validity and reliability. • Achieve wide coverage of subject matter easily. • Can be easily made diagnostic of errors. • Available as standardized tests in a great variety of fields.	• Problem of validity is always present. • Standardized tests are sometimes used where specially constructed tests would be more appropriate. • Tests of complex problem solving are difficult to construct, so tests tend to concentrate on knowledge, facts, and details. • Apparent precision may result in greater faith in scores than justified.

Source: Adapted from N. S. Metfessel and W. B. Michael, "A Paradigm Involving Multiple Criterion Measures for the Evaluation of the Effectiveness of School Programs," *Educational and Psychological Measurement*, 1961, 27, 937–943.

can be very strong. The more numerous the qualitative replications under different circumstances, the greater the credibility; the more varied the replications, the greater the generality. Consider that as situations and subjects are varied, alternative explanations are ruled out—local history and instrument decay, for example. If the situations and subjects are highly varied, maturation and selection may be eliminated as well. Testing effect is unlikely since tests are rarely used. If the chosen informants are at the top or bottom of a group, regression effect can be a factor; but one may choose a purposive sample so as to rule it out. Mortality and treatment mortality interaction can be a factor, as can reactivity. Having thought of these, however, one can similarly look for them in situations that will rule them out as well. The replicated evidence may take on characteristics of a qualitative meta-analysis with less story-telling of particular instances and more describing the variety of instances and circumstances under which the phenomenon occurs.[2] Clearly, given replication under appropriate conditions of implementation, qualitative research gains strength with replication.

SUMMARY

Good research properly defines a problem so as to encompass all the necessary aspects for us to understand it as completely as possible, regardless of method. For some problems one method may be adequate. However, since the various research methods provide different kinds of evidence about phenomena, by combining methods not only can we compensate for the flaws of one method with the strengths of another, but we can obtain different perspectives, "depth of field," and detail. Using more than one method provides complementary evidence that can reinforce our confidence in the results. It can bracket a phenomenon to reveal its dimensions. Replication of results with a variety of methods under a variety of circumstances is the strongest and ultimate validation of a generalization.

A Look Ahead

In the final chapter, we examine whether the research system works at the individual, peer, and societal levels, raising questions about the process at each level and examining the answers.

ADDITIONAL READING

For multiple research methods generally: Brewer and Hunter (1989), and Fielding and Fielding (1985). Shadish (1993) discusses them in the context of a research strategy. Moss (1996) searches for the common ground in interpretivist and "naturalistic" (read "quantitive") traditions for a "more textured and productive view of . . . social phenomena" (p. 22). In the context of evaluation: Caracelli and Greene (1993); Mark and Shotland (1987, an issue devoted to multiple-method evaluation) and Reichardt and Cook (1979). Sieber (1973) shows how qualitative and survey research complement each other. Behrens and Smith (1996) is an excellent discussion of both quantitative and qualitative data analysis with emphasis on exploratory data analysis and multiple method research.

---

[2]Interestingly enough, this appears to have been the method that such people as Piaget (1952) and others have used in developing and presenting their theories. The evidence they gathered through their observations is, indeed, quite convincing.

IMPORTANT TERMS

Multiple research methods

Bracketing model

Complementary multiplism

APPLICATION PROBLEMS

1. A medical researcher wished to investigate the sensitive topic of incest in American society. Her problem was to find out what incest is and to understand the behavior of the participants. To conduct the study, she had to establish strong rapport with a sample of affected families. Further, to identify a sufficient number of cases, the investigator had to work with an educational treatment agency. "Obtrusive" procedures such as surveys, questionnaires, and psychological tests were actively discouraged by the agency. However, the agency worked with about 500 families. What research method(s) would she have used?

2. Two nursing scholars, Johnson and Lauver (1989), were interested in the relationship between medical patients' ability to cope with stressful experiences and nursing interventions that provided them with information to prepare for each such experience. In particular, they wished to test the predictions of two theories, emotional drive theory and self-regulation theory, which presented alternative hypotheses about how people cope. To do so, they conducted a study using patients suffering from prostate cancer who had to undergo the taxing experience of radiation therapy. The patients were randomly assigned to either a treatment group in which they listened to experimental tape-recorded messages or a control group in which they were visited by a research team member who inquired about their well-being. All patients received the usual care provided by the radiation therapy department. What trade-offs did the investigators make with this design?

3. A group of educational psychologists (Corkhill et al., 1988) were interested in whether or not advance organizers would help learners recall learned material. Normally, advance organizers are introduced ahead of the material to be learned. They are verbal or visual passages written at a more abstract or general level than the material and are intended to help learners relate the material to what they already know. Thus, they aid in encoding the information.

The investigators hypothesized that having learners read the advance organizer for a second time just before a recall test would aid them in retrieving the information.

The researchers conducted a series of six experiments that varied the delays between reading the material to be learned and the recall test from immediately after the reading to two weeks later. Experiments 1–3 and 5 and 6 were conducted using the same materials with samples of university undergraduate education students. They were all laboratory studies, and all students participated for course credit. Experiment 4 was carried out with different materials and a group of grade 7 students in their regular classroom at a university experimental school. Sample sizes varied between 30 for experiment 2, and 98, for experiment 1. Experiments 3–6, those with delays of 24 hours or more between the treatment and the recall test, produced statistically significant results in favor of the investigators' hypothesis. What trade-offs did these researchers make?

4. Cunningham and Stewart (1983) were interested in testing the effectiveness of an innovative counselor training model. Thirty-two masters' level counselor trainees from a large U.S. midwestern university participated in a 10-hour workshop consisting of three sessions spread out over the course of a week. The trainees were randomly assigned to either the treatment group or the control group. Both groups received parallel training and instructional materials, with the exception of the presentation of cognitive material: The experimental group received discrimination training, which emphasized the integration of knowledge of responses to the client with knowledge of the counseling process, while the control group was instructed in another useful counseling skill, the formulation of behavioral objectives for difficult-to-define client problems. Both workshops were conducted concurrently.

Each trainee group was assessed on three measures of counselor effectiveness, a 25-item multiple-choice instrument, 25 free-response questions regarding audiotaped counseling situation descriptions, and a rating of a 10-minute audiotaped counseling interview. Three equivalent forms of each were used. Internal consistency reliability scores for these measures varied between .55 and .95. Each trainee was given a pretest at the first session to check equivalence between the groups and a posttest at the conclusion of the third session. A follow-up testing of 22 trainees who agreed to participate was conducted after six weeks. Statistical analysis revealed significant differences between the experimental and control groups for both the initial and the follow-up studies. What trade-offs did the researchers make concerning choices involving observation and measurement?

5. McKim and Cowen (1987) published a study of young children's school adjustment, which they characterized as multiperspective. The main purpose of the study was "to assess the relationships among five perspectives of young school children's adjustment: teacher, peer, parent, and self-ratings and behavior observations." According to the authors, each of these "five measurement perspectives has its own substantial literature." Secondary purposes were to assess relationships between adjustment and achievement, to compare the adjustment of suburban and urban children, and to compare those children referred for mental health services to those not referred. The investigators studied 462 second- and third-grade children from four urban and two suburban schools. The measures, which were all quantitative, consisted of a series of rating scales completed by teachers, standardized achievement tests, and a classroom observation protocol. The scores obtained on the 27 dependent measures were compared using Pearson product moment correlation coefficients. Analysis of variance was used to test for differences between location and gender.

Is this a multiple-method study in the spirit of what is suggested in this chapter?

Compare your answers with those following the Application Exercise.

APPLICATION EXERCISE

Consider how you might use multiple methods to bolster the study of your problem. Are you doing basic or applied research? If the former, are any aspects of internal validity (LP) not covered by the method you were planning to use? As you considered your problem from the standpoint of different methods, were there some you considered useful? Would a combination of these strengthen the case for your study? If you are doing applied research, what aspects of external validity (GP) need strengthening, and how might other methods facilitate this?

Consider the different enhancements for any tentatively chosen design you may have developed. Examine the trade-offs for those enhancements that might make your design stronger. What are the positive and negative aspects of the enhancements? On balance, do the positives outweigh the negatives? If not, which enhancements would you drop to strengthen the overall picture? Which additional ones might you use?

ANSWERS TO THE APPLICATION PROBLEMS

1. In this basic research study, in which the investigator is interested in understanding and describing the phenomenon of incest, strong internal validity (LP) is the key criterion. This very study was carried out by Patricia Phelan (1987) in San Francisco. She was able to mix qualitative and quantitative methodology in an innovative way to explain the phenomenon. To gain entry, she became involved as an intern counselor in the treatment program and began with an ethnographic study using participant observation. This allowed her to understand the treatment community, including clients and staff, and the treatment model used.

Once accepted, she was able to conduct intensive interviews to reveal the family dynamics involved. Since surveys and other quantitative methods were not permitted and interviews with the large number of families were not feasible, Phelan conducted structured interviews with the counselors to gather detailed descriptions of the incestuous relationships. From this she was able to carry out a numeric analysis and test for statistical significance. Combining the two types of data, numeric and narrative, provided her with a comprehensive picture of the phenomenon.

2. The investigators made trade-offs, in terms of both subjects and situation. First, they chose to study people with a very specific problem, prostate cancer. Thus, the treatment was limited to mostly older men with that disease who had agreed to undergo radiation therapy. This would have helped to ensure that the sample would consist of people coping with a stressful experience who were representative of the target population. They would also presumably be susceptible to the treatment—the coping information. And finally, the group was homogeneous, both in factors such as age and sex and also with respect to various clinical variables related to their disease and medical treatment. These factors all help to strengthen the internal validity (LP). But it would be difficult to generalize beyond such a narrow group to patients with different characteristics or coping with different problems.

Second, even though the theories could be relevant to coping with other aspects of physical illness, such as being diagnosed with a life-threatening disease or having to live with a chronic, debilitating illness, the investigators restricted this to the study of coping with a stressful medical treatment. The situation was a hospital-based treatment program (an acute-care setting). This provided a number of benefits related to greater control such as assurance that treatment preceded effect, more chance of elimination of a number of rival hypotheses (for example, other contacts providing information to help cope), and greater fidelity of the treatment since the stressful experience would also take place at this setting. But, as before, it would be hard to generalize beyond these circumstances.

3. These investigators made choices concerning subjects, situation, and treatment. By conducting several studies with the same materials, they were, in effect, increasing sample size and hence the statistical sensitivity to the effect of the treatment. Since they were able to replicate their results with a different age group and in a more natural environment (the classroom), they were able to increase the generalizability of their results. With that exception, how-

ever, their subjects were a narrow sample: undergraduate university students who had volunteered to gain credits; this decreased generalizability.

All but one of the studies were conducted in the laboratory. This provided the benefits, again, of greater control over treatment. This increased the researchers assurance that treatment preceded effect, eliminated rival hypotheses and random effects contributing to variability of behavior, and provided greater fidelity of treatment since they were able to control its administration. It also helped, presumably, to keep the costs to a minimum. In addition, except for the grade 7 group, institutional restraints were likely minimal. Even then, the children attended a university experimental school. These are typically set up to encourage research and would present fewer constraints than a regular school. Regardless, the study in the school represented a natural use of the treatment and helped increase generality.

One factor helping decrease control was the need to give delayed recall tests. Hence, the subjects would not have been under laboratory control for the duration of the study. There would have been some threat of diffusion as the students would have had the chance to discuss the study. Further, the laboratory situation would have increased the potential for reactivity.

Finally, asking the subjects to read these a second time may have increased the intensity of the treatment and thereby increased the sensitivity of the statistical test. Though unusual, such rereading is not impractical.

4. The investigators used multiple measures of the construct "counselor effectiveness." This would have increased the internal validity (LP) by making it more likely that its essential characteristics were covered. Since they used different testing techniques, method effects would have been minimized. The follow-up tests increased the number of observations and allowed detection of any residual effects, in this case, the retention of the counseling skills training. However, the large number of observations increased the opportunity for instrument decay error and also for testing-treatment interaction

Further, the use of a pretest-and-posttest design had its effects as well. It allowed the investigators to ensure the equivalence of the treatment and control groups and, since they demonstrated the reliability of their measures, to be sure that a change actually took place. Again, the negative aspect was the likelihood of testing and testing treatment interaction.

Finally, the use of volunteers for the follow-up probably inflated that measure of effect because 10 of the original 32—nearly a third—were not followed up. No information is given as to whether the mortality was equal among groups, but if not, that might have compounded the problem.

5. Puzzled about how to respond? Good, you were expected to be! On the one hand, the data is all quantitative, but on the other, clearly it is tapping different perspectives on the individuals' behavior, just as a multiple-method study would be expected to do. It used achievement measures, classroom observations (apparently with a structured, low-inference device), and rating scales completed by teachers—three different points of view and three independent snapshots of behavior.

Is it multiple method in the sense of using both quantitative and qualitative methods? No, it did not use quantitative methods at all. Might they have added something to the mix? Possibly; it depends on the intent and the audience. But, more importantly, is it consistent with the intent and spirit of the chapter? Absolutely! *The whole point of the chapter is that we should use such methods for gathering data as are adequate to encompass our problem and intent* (e.g., convincing policymakers). Combinations of methods, more often than not, will build the strongest study. But what if the study is best implemented solely as a quantitative or qualitative study? Fine—whatever best fits the reality of the situation and the problem posed.

CHAPTER 25

The Macrosystem of Educational and Social Science Research

Few of us realize how short the career of what we know as "science" has been. Three hundred and fifty years ago hardly any one believed in the Copernican planetary theory. . . .The circulation of the blood, the weight of air, the conduction of heat, the laws of motion were unknown; the common pump was inexplicable.

R. Reynolds and Sons, *Some Problems of Philosophy* (1911)

After close to two centuries of passionate struggles, neither science nor faith has succeeded in discrediting its adversary. On the contrary, it becomes obvious that neither can develop normally without the other. And the reason is simple: The same life animates both. Neither in its impetus nor its achievements can science go to its limits without becoming tinged with mysticism and charged with faith.

Pierre Teilhard de Chardin, S. J.

OVERVIEW

This chapter examines the system we call science, starting at the individual researcher level and working successively through the peer to the societal level. Examining problems at each level, it asks whether and how well it works. Lastly, we look at whether, as we have presumed throughout the book, a social science is possible.

CHAPTER CONTENTS

Introduction

A heuristic aids in discovery or encourages inquiry. This chapter is a heuristic that raises questions to which there are not yet satisfactory answers. Indeed, perhaps there never will be since they involve values about which persons differ. The goal is to suggest topics deserving of thought, to raise questions you might otherwise take for granted. Then, because of your greater awareness, perhaps you will pursue deeper analysis of them. Here, however, we can give them only cursory examination.

We will examine whether it is possible to build a social science by examining: Does the system we call science function as intended at the individual, peer, and societal level? We are dealing with a system in which each level depends on the workings of the previous one. Questioning how well the system works is very important because, as a feature article in a recent news magazine stated: "Society is driven by science. The conclusions of researchers answer questions as important to ordinary people as the heritability of alcoholism and the merits of using IQ scores to assign 5-year-olds to 'gifted' school programs. Science, in short, matters" (Begley, 1997, p. 56).

The natural sciences are supported more as a matter of faith; the lay community seldom understands much of what natural scientists do but does see occasional important applications. In contrast,

> the social sciences seldom get full credit . . . because the discoveries, once labeled, are quickly absorbed into conventional wisdom. This is easily demonstrated: note the number of social science concepts common to our vocabulary: human capital, gross national product, identity crisis, span of control, the unconscious, price elasticity, acculturation, political party identification, reference group. (Prewitt, 1981, p. 659)

Furthermore, the content of social and behavioral science is the stuff of everyday life, in which all of us are our own "experts." (Not necessarily correctly, remember the research of Wong, described on page 47!) Nevertheless, such work is judged by everyone. This "transparency" makes it even more important that the social science research process should work as well as possible, since as problems are perceived they tinge its findings with suspicion in the minds of the public.

Does Science Function as Intended at the Individual Level?

There is an amazing amount of trust in the integrity of individual investigators. We tend to think of their reports as containing enough information to judge the study, and in many respects, this appraisal is accurate. But research reports omit much of the detail that is critical to replicating it. If you don't think so, consider the Zimbardo study of Chapter 1, which seems to be reported in detail. Yet, think about all the aspects you would have to supply to replicate it—the method of hypnotism, many of the instruments, and—most surprisingly of all—a time table. How long would you guess the sessions took? Thirty minutes? An hour? A day? Several days? They actually took only about half an hour to an hour, but that information was contained in a newspaper article about the study (Hunt, 1982), not in the study itself.

Fraud in Science

Largely because of contemporary problems in the biomedical field, trust in the individual investigator is being increasingly questioned. Summerlin at Sloan-Kettering painted spots on a mouse (Broad, 1983); Soman at Yale admitted falsifying work; Darsee at Harvard could not produce raw data for his research; and Spector at Cornell used the wrong tracer, a mistake a peer believed could not have been an accident (Broad and Wade, 1983). And in the social sciences, considerable controversy has erupted over charges that Sir Cyril Burt, a famous English psychologist, fabricated some of his data (Mackintosh, 1995). Broad and Wade (1983) trace fraud from the days of Ptolemy (second century, A.D.), arguing that it is more prevalent than supposed, and that it has always been around. They also argue that the response of the scientific community has been inappropriately feeble.

It is unknown, of course, how widespread fraud in science really is. The uncovering of fraud at esteemed institutions in the 1980s caused considerable unease; so much so, in fact, that the federal government stepped in, requiring all institutions receiving federal research moneys to have a procedure in place for dealing with fraud.

The unexpectedness of any fraud at all, combined with the inability to determine how frequently it occurs, raises questions about the whole research enterprise each time an instance is uncovered. Everyone is tainted with the stain. Why does it occur? Pressure to publish, to win research grants, to succeed, and to be first with the significant finding no doubt all contribute. Various studies (among them Katz, 1973; and Tuckman, 1976) have shown that publications in all fields of research contribute significantly to salary increases. Centra (1977) showed that the most important information for tenure, salary, and promotions was the number of articles in quality journals and the excellence of the research as judged by peers. Clearly, these are pressures that every academic researcher feels. No doubt, although specific pressures differ, the situation is similar outside academia. The rush to publish is endemic to the scientist's world. As Price (1963) points out:

> At the root of the matter is the basic difference between creative effort in the sciences and . . . the arts. If Michelangelo or Beethoven had not existed, their works would have been replaced by different contributions. If Copernicus or Fermi had never existed, essentially the same contribution would have had to come from other people. There is, in fact, only one world to discover (p. 69).

The first person to publish is recognized as the discoverer and gets the credit.[1]

It is difficult to convey adequately the excitement of the race to discover. Unfortunately, there are few reports of research competition. One is the story of the unraveling of DNA by Watson and Crick as told by one of those Nobel Prize-winning researchers (Watson, 1968). The intensity of that race is conveyed especially effectively when Watson tells of the laboratory visit of the son of Linus Pauling, who headed a rival team. Watson and Crick's efforts to covertly assess where the two teams stood with respect to the problem solution and their elation at believing they were ahead make fascinating reading.

Another account is that of the marathon between Nobelists Guillemin and Schally to discover the interaction between the brain and the pituitary gland (Wade, 1978). Wade analyzes the way in which the rivalry shaped their approaches, trying to assess whether the competition helped or hindered. Although it certainly interfered with cooperation between the teams, it also " 'stimulated both men to do their very best and check each other's work. They learned from each other' " (Wade quoting Meites, a historian of the field, p. 513). Although neither example is one from the social sciences, the interpersonal relations and team experiences are likely to be similar.

Given these innate features of research, there is no easy solution to the problem of avoiding fraud. As with other ethical problems, we cannot have laboratory police. The responsibility rests with the individual researcher. In the long run, fraud may be uncovered by replications. Meanwhile, however, there is the short-run damage of building new work atop a false foundation.

Researchers must be vigilant to the possibility of fraud. Instead of letting possible incidents pass, we must challenge our peers to guarantee that it is not present. How much fraud is there in the social sciences? Although we are inclined to think very little, we don't know for sure. Any fraud exacts too great a price, for trust once destroyed is very difficult to reestablish.

Can We Trust What We See?

Considerably more prevalent than fraud are the mechanisms likely to bias the interpretation of data. An example of this is the expectancy effect (see p. 521) that Rosenthal and Rubin (1980) showed to be so pervasive—in which, regardless of the facts, results confirm the researcher's expectations.

Remember, "there is a lot more to seeing than meets the eyeball" (Hanson, 1958, p. 7); perception organizes what we see into learned patterns. Phillips (1987) cites research in which playing cards were flashed tachistoscopically—trick cards such as a black six of hearts, were mixed in. Regular cards could be routinely identified; trick cards were either misread or seen as a blur. Moreland

---

[1] Just as hardly anybody remembers vice presidents of the United States, so those who come in second serve the purpose of validating the discovery but are not usually associated with it. This phenomenon may contribute to the lack of replication of research in the social sciences, although the cost in time and energy and forgone opportunity to pioneer are the main reasons.

and Zajonc (1977) flashed abstract designs on a screen at a speed below perception threshold, so fast that the designs were not perceived as seen. Later these designs were mixed with other abstract designs, and the subjects were to indicate how well they liked each design. The designs with which they were familiar as a result of prior subliminal exposure were better liked! Ferris (1981) notes:

> The eye . . . delivers not television pictures to be observed . . . but processed information, much of it . . . hypotheses. . . . And in the dialogue between the eye and the rest of the brain, what we see can become what we expect to see. A field mouse is transformed into a snake to the hiker who fears snakes. (p. 61)

How many such influences are there? How pervasive are they? How much and what effect do they have? We don't know for sure. These, of course, are the very points many qualitative researchers have been trying to stress to their "we-are-unbiased-and-objective" quantitative colleagues! Just as qualitative researchers look inward to become aware of how their actions and reactions affect data gathering, so must all researchers seek the effect of perceptual and expectancy problems on their findings.

Does Science Function as Intended at the Peer Level?

Peer Review

You will recall that peers, usually colleagues, are the first level in the development of a consensus around the interpretation of data. Colleagues can help considerably by correcting misperceptions, calling attention to expectancy effects, and so forth. Other peers are gatekeepers to journals and convention presentations. How well does peer review work? Is peer review a matter of friends taking care of friends instead of attending to the concerns of science? Do people with famous reputations get by with things that lesser-known researchers cannot? Is there a single standard of quality?

Several studies illuminate these issues. First, are reviews really blind, or do reviewers generally know the authors? Studying perceptions among psychologists, Ceci and Peters (1984) found that survey respondents believed, on average, authors were correctly identified about 72 percent of the time. Using six psychology journals from a broad range of areas, however, Ceci and Peters showed that only about a quarter of reviewers were actually able to identify the author of a sufficiently blinded manuscript, about one-third of the commonly suspected rate.

Does blind review make a difference? Tobias and Zibrin (1978), used abstracts submitted for a convention program to examine this question. They compared four evaluations of each proposal—two blind and two with identifying information. They found no differences between these conditions! They also examined the question of the effect of prominence of author. They found that prominent individuals received significantly more favorable evaluations than did others, but they did so under both blind and nonblind conditions. This finding serves as "a kind of validity check on the prominence of the individuals" (p. 16).[2]

Does the importance of the topic and its being a replication make a difference? Fictitious studies incorporating combinations of flawed and unflawed with important and unimportant topics were judged for publication suitability (Wilson, DePaulo, Mook, and Klaaren, 1993). Even though publishability of flawed and unimportant topics was judged low, about a quarter more of those dealing with important instead of unimportant topics were judged methodologically sound. Neuliep and Crandall (1990a, 1990b) found both editors and reviewers prejudiced against publication of replications. Considering the pressure for publication and the rejection rates of some journals—as high as 4 out of 5 submissions—their conclusion is not surprising.

Lastly, do reviewers agree on the criteria of research excellence, and do they agree in their evaluations of articles? The picture is mixed, but with significant problems. For example, in an interesting recounting of the pressures they experienced as editors, Murray and Raths (1996) reported only 36% of their reviewers were in exact agreement, but 79% were within one step of each other's recommendations on a five point scale. Fiske and Fogg (1990), in a careful study of 402 reviews of 153 papers submitted to 12 different psychological journals, found that "reviewers did not . . . disagree on particular points; instead, they wrote about different topics, each making points that were appropriate and accurate. As a consequence, their recommendations about editorial decisions showed hardly any agreement" (p. 591). Intraclass correlation of reviewers' ratings was .20, lower than some other studies. Gottfredson (1978), again with psychological journals, showed that psychologists associated with the decision-making processes of nine journals that covered a range of psychological literature substantially agreed on the desirability of article characteristics. However, even after using scales developed out of the research on desirable characteristics, agreement between judges was quite modest.

Given these data, it is clear that getting comparable reviews for publication is a problem. Robert Rosenthal's experience in publishing his work on expectancy effects (cited on p. 521) presents the problem in its starkest terms: "I recall an especially 'good news-bad news' type of day when a particular piece of work was simultaneously rejected by an APA journal and awarded the American Association for the Advancement of Science (AAAS) Socio-Psychological Prize for 1960" (Shadish and Fuller, 1994, p. 219). This lack of agreement on what points to critique in a peer review is at least partially understandable, however, when we consider the many possible trade-offs and their combinations. These result in a comparison of apples and oranges when we stretch them along a single dimension of

---

[2]The researchers also examined the effect of prominence of reviewer, sex of author, and sex of reviewer. Neither prominence of reviewer nor sex of author interacted with the review process comparing blind and nonblind conditions. Female reviewers gave more favorable ratings to the importance of the problem than male reviewers; but that was the only difference.

quality.[3] Editors, aware of this problem, therefore, generally seek multiple reviews of each submission. They make their accept-reject judgment not just on reviewer ratings, but on a considered evaluation of reviewer comments, synthesizing the aspects to which different reviewers attended into a judgment of the whole.

Conditions for Productive Science

Under what conditions are researchers most productive? Every college administrator and director of a research and development center would like to know the answer, but research results, mostly from the physical and biological sciences, are far from conclusive. Knorr and colleagues (1979), in a book comparing the effectiveness of research groups in six European countries, looked at the effects of quality of leadership and group climate where the latter included dedication, cooperation, and innovativeness. They found the expected positive relationships. Stankiewicz (1979), in the same volume, examined size of research group. He hypothesized that larger groups would be more fruitful because of the greater opportunities to interact, to pursue alternative research strategies in parallel, and to attack different aspects of a complex problem. Beyond a certain point, size would prove counterproductive because of problems of communication. Examining only research groups in Sweden, he found an increase in effectiveness from three to five members and from five to seven, depending on the performance measures used, but a decline in larger groups.

In an excellent comparison of U.S. and Soviet science, Gustafson (1980) observed that the Soviets could concentrate enormous resources on crucial problems in basic research. In that system, senior colleagues were oriented more toward theory than toward experimentation and provided planning and coordination for young researchers. This method was seen, at best, as producing teamwork; at worst, conservatism, deference to superiors, immobility, and going along for the sake of agreement. Conversely, the American belief in individual initiative, tolerance for risk and conflict, and lack of respect for authority were seen as producing a dynamic and competitive system with a zest for "unplanned opportunity" (p. 58). Highly productive, the American system lacks the predictability of support formerly granted in the Soviet system, and there is considerable lack of coordination of governmental support in this country. Gustafson was careful to note that large, block-funded institutions in the United States experienced many of the same problems as the block-funded institutions of the former Soviet Union.

Glaser and Taylor (1973) compared successful applied research projects sponsored by the National Institutes of Mental Health with their less successful ones. They found that the successful projects were characterized by both internal team

---

[3]Buchmann and Floden (1989) note that "in trying to determine how many different ways for doing work in a discipline actually exist—reasoning inductively from some [assumptions] . . . — Schwab (1978) arrived at 2^{20} or 1,048,576 as the number of possible alternative schemes an individual investigator might choose from, on a conservative estimate" (pp. 245–246).

communication and external communication with clients and administrators, especially the latter. Their conclusion is consistent with research on the problem of dissemination, which we shall consider in a moment.

One of the most interesting omissions is the lack of findings that more resources make a difference. It is clear that in the physical and life sciences, expensive equipment is a necessity for certain lines of work. But this is rarely true in the social and behavioral sciences. Indeed, Weick (1984) argues for "small wins," cutting social problems into manageable pieces. "Small wins are like miniature experiments that test implicit theories about resistance and opportunity and uncover both resources and barriers that were invisible before the situation was stirred up" (p. 44). For instance, he notes that the feminist movement failed at the equal rights amendment, but found that sex references in speech were more susceptible to change than had been thought. The opponents were "more dispersed, more stuffy, and less formidable than anticipated" (p. 44). He provides a number of arguments for "small wins" as a strategy.

Obviously, there are many unsolved problems in this area; many are probably context-dependent. Can we learn to maximize conditions for research? It is not at all clear that we can. In contrast to "hard" science, the "soft" social sciences, as must be clear from this textbook, are still evolving standards and goals and improving their methods. But we are getting closer to the target.

The Potential of the Internet

We have typically considered peers to be mainly those in nearby offices, or the colleagues we meet at annual conventions—contacts governed by geography. Electronic forums, listservs and journals are building global cross-institutional peer communities through the Internet. Further, as already noted throughout this text, support groups for substantive fields of research, for methodological problems, for software packages (e.g., statistical and qualitative analysis programs), and for specific instruments and measures can bring expert help to the novice from some of the most knowledgeable persons from anywhere in the world—available to all through the use of automatated agents that search the Web. Electronic journals exist with subscriber bases far too small to be viable in conventional published form. These features have the potential to markedly raise the quality of work in all the sciences, but it is too early to tell the eventual direction and nature of their influence.

One concern arises from the fact that each of us has only so much discretionary time and that devoted to the Internet is not available for journals and books. Further, as Van Alstyne and Brynjolfsson (1996) note, "As quickly as information technology collapses barriers based on geography, it forces us to build new ones based on interest or time. . . . Researchers [may] . . . focus on only those articles and colleagues that really interest them. . . . The same information lens that brings distant colleagues into focus can inadvertently produce tunnel vision and peripheral blindness . . . and narrower scientic interactions. . . . Depending on how this task is managed, the Internet could lead to . . . a balkanization of the global village" (p. 1479).

So far people seem to be tinkering, trying to find the right mix of electronic and ink print. Just as some individuals seek new uses for tools found in other fields, and some have always read widely, so those individuals will no doubt carry those habits to the Web. But with such a deluge of information, they will have to find new ways to explore the margins. It seems likely, however, that those who are slow to use this resource will be left behind. Van Alstyne and Brynjolfsson (1996) already cite one study that suggests those who use information technology "write more papers, earn greater peer recognition and know more colleagues" (ibid.).

Does Science Function as Intended at the Societal Level?

The social sciences as disciplines developed relatively late among the arts and sciences. The University of Chicago's erecting the first building just for the social sciences in the late 1930s was an important act of faith. Although psychology considered itself a discipline and had its own national society, some of its regional societies were still merged with philosophy societies as late as World War II. Emergence of separate departments for each of the social sciences resulted in many changes: for example, better training for new entrants and the development of more sophisticated research methods.

Of course, the literature of social science began centuries before such departments existed. In the past, authors, although they were often the best-educated persons of their period, wrote in the ordinary language of their day. This vernacular made their writing immediately available to educated persons in all fields and it was often widely read. As the social sciences matured, however, the useful shorthand (jargon) that develops within every field, increasingly removed publications from the understanding of the common person. Jargon impedes communication to the general public, increases the problems of dissemination, expands the social distance between researchers and the practitioners who might benefit from their work, and markedly diminishes public support for research.

The use of jargon unique to each field in the social sciences leads to the charge that social scientists write mainly for others like themselves. This may be true, but that is also true for all scientists. When social science findings are translated into the vernacular, however, because of the "obviously-true" problem (p. 47) referred to earlier, public esteem for the enterprise decreases. This attitude denies to social scientists a trust that their work will eventually be of a value at least equivalent to that more freely granted to physical scientists.

The increased distance between professional and practitioner has led to efforts to understand the field of dissemination of findings. Not only has a field of research on knowledge utilization developed, but now a publishing and consulting industry also translates the material of science for the intelligent layperson.

Witness the extensive front section of the journal *Science,* and publications like *Scientific American, Popular Science, Discover,* and others.

Dissemination Research

Dissemination has been extensively researched by persons in the field of agriculture, which had the problem of getting findings adopted by farmers. The agricultural extension agent translated research for the farmer, showed how it applied in a specific situation, and grew demonstration plots to show the results of new practices. These techniques proved effective but expensive. Research showed that individuals could be divided into three classes: early adopters— individuals who were ready and eager to try new things—a middle group, and a late group. The early adopters are important sources of practices for the middle group, who will tend to follow their lead when innovations are successful.

Research has also shown that individuals tend to go through stages of information use in the adoption process (Rogers, 1995):

1. *Awareness* sensitizes them to pay attention when they encounter a demonstration of an innovation or literature about it.
2. *Interest* encourages them to seek information about it.
3. *Evaluation* lets them estimate the chances of its success in their situation.
4. *Trial* involves making a small commitment to the innovation to determine whether it performs as anticipated.
5. *Adoption* is the result of a successful trial.

Characteristics that enable people to predict the probability of successful implementation have also been studied (Rogers, 1995). A first characteristic is the relative advantage of the innovation over alternatives. Thus, cost-effectiveness, especially when it saves time and effort, is important, as is the immediacy of the results. Consider the adoption of wait-time in teaching, which will presumably shift the character of student responses to a much higher level of thinking (Rowe, 1974). It costs the embarrassment of silence following a question and may cause initial discomfort for both teacher and students. The greater thoroughness and depth of discussion that follow adoption, however, have cost little and are easily perceived as much more satisfying to both parties than the classroom climate produced by a bombardment of simple questions.

A second characteristic is compatibility with the existing values, needs, standards, and practices of the adopter. The better the match, the less amount of change needed and the more likely that the innovation will be adopted and integrated into ongoing practice. Wait-time will result in the kinds of responses the teacher values—those much closer to desired standards—and the questioning pattern is not a drastic change from previous practice.

A third aspect is complexity; the simpler, the better. It is a relatively simple matter to extend the time the teacher waits for an answer to a question before modifying it, substituting another, calling on a student, and so on. It may require some thought on the part of the teacher to pose challenging questions.

A fourth property is trialability—the extent to which a small commitment on the part of the adopter will permit a trial that provides sufficient evidence to determine whether to make a complete commitment to the innovation. Certainly, wait-time can easily be given a trial.

A final characteristic is observability, the degree to which the results are apparent to potential adopters. If the research on wait-time is correct, the result should be an immediate change in the quality and level of class discussion.

Key in all the literature on adoption of innovations is administrative support, involvement of adopters in the adoption decision, adaptation to their situations, and their trial of the innovation to obtain evidence firsthand (action research). Administrative support is a necessary but not sufficient condition. Involvement of the adoptee, however, is a sufficient condition if adoption results are sufficiently rewarding in and of themselves. Thus, involvement is stressed in nearly all the literature.

The characteristics that facilitate adoption have implications for how to choose and develop a research idea that will have a practical impact. Let's combine the mentioned principles with an example such as Glass's (1976) development of meta-analysis. Meta-analysis has spread to medicine and many natural science fields and has become widely used in a very short time. Together the characteristics and example suggest a four-step process (references to the facilitating characteristics are indicated in parentheses):

1. In addition to the criteria of a good problem described in Chapter 4, add the criterion of filling an important need. Clearly, Glass did; he chose the long-standing problem of combining quantitative studies to yield a summary overall result.

2. If possible, find a solution that is close to current practice. That means that it can be easily grafted onto it (compatibility). Glass found that quantitative results could be translated into something approximating standard scores, scores that are widely used and understood. It was but a small step to transfer the standard score-like idea to the summary of studies; users would have little problem doing that (lack of complexity and trialability).

3. Use terminology that is self-descriptive, simple, and fits with other terms in the field. Glass called the translated findings *effect sizes,* a simple, and self-descriptive term. Similarly, the name given the process, *meta-analysis,* from the Greek *meta* for *comprehensive* and *analysis,* is self-descriptive. Both terms fit other usage in the field and have been widely adopted and used. (Not a characteristic mentioned in the research literature, but one that markedly facilitates communication about the new item and does reduce complexity and facilitate trialability).

4. Demonstrate the effectiveness of what has been invented or developed. Glass forcefully established the power of meta-analysis by showing the effectiveness of psychotherapy, an area where previous research summaries had yielded only equivocal results (observability and demonstrated advantage).

Thus, research on dissemination provides a basis for researchers to be more effective in getting their innovations adopted. A basic problem, however, is that the involvement of the adopter in the adoption process is costly and time-consuming.[4] Informational materials seem to go only so far. Research is still needed on decreasing the cost of the adoption process and making it more effective.

The Contributions of Science to Policy

Probably the earliest involvement of the social sciences in U.S. policy was the 1832 grant to the Franklin Institute to study the causes of explosions in steamboat boilers. "Professor Bates . . . reported that 'sometimes there is a little carelessness in stoking the fire.' A bursting steam boiler is not just a matter of chemistry and physics; it is also a matter of operator training and human behavior" (Prewitt, 1980, p. 2). Years later, the President's Commission on the Accident at Three Mile Island "similarly concluded that it was 'people-related problems and not equipment problems' that brought the nation so close to a major tragedy" (ibid., p. 3). Repeatedly, government has recognized the importance of the human element in its attempt to regulate and plan.[5]

A tremendous surge in the utilization of social science knowledge in policy decisions came with the use of social science evidence in the federal courts in such cases as the landmark desegregation decision, *Brown* vs. *the Board of Education of Topeka (347 U.S. 483)*; the development of accurate survey samples that provided information regarding the public's view on important policy decisions; the increased use of planning, programming, and budgeting techniques under Robert McNamara in the Defense Department, which spread into management information systems in business and industry as well as across government; and concern over the effectiveness of federal programs by Congress and federal agencies, resulting in many large-scale evaluations. Only relatively recently have studies been undertaken primarily to serve policy purposes. Most past policy decisions based on research findings cited basic research or evaluations done for other purposes.

The increased involvement in policy decisions by researchers resulted in new understandings of themselves. They found that they differed from policymakers in important ways. Their time scales for studies were determined by the problems rather than politics. The problems they chose to work on were the ones of interest to them and easier to study rather than selected on the basis of societal need and resistance to solution. Scientists preferred to hedge and qualify their findings rather than to starkly state preferences. Furthermore, administrators, who had been decisionmakers long before they were responsible for public policy, have nonscientific ways of identifying policy options besides the scientific ones. As a result, researchers have not always found themselves and their work at center stage when they were ready. They have seen their research used for purposes for which it was not intended. They have been forced to try to be useful before they

---

[4]This same issue emerged in Chapter 23 where to get evaluation findings used, the extent and nature of the stakeholder involvement in an evaluation are at issue—an issue solved by action research where the researcher and stakeholder are one and the same.

[5]Plan, that is, in terms of averages and tendencies. The author is reminded of a comment of a historian friend, J. B. Van Hise (personal communciation, February 21, 1989): "Social science always leaves out irrationality: the force of fear, panic, faith, and myth, in causing things to happen." A valid generalization? True, there are exceptions, but . . .

were ready. They have regularly given equivocal opinions when asked for concrete choices. (Politicians are said to prefer one-armed experts rather than those proclaiming "On the one hand . . .") And, in general, they have behaved in ways that, although consistent with their values, lifestyle, and milieu, did not endear them to policymakers.

Researchers have had to learn that timing is extremely important. Policy development goes through stages, and the role of research and the demands on it differ with each stage. At the earliest stage, when policymakers are trying to articulate policy interests and demands, research helps define the problem. At the second stage, which involves the deliberation, modification, and aggregation of support for various proposals, research turns desires into concrete alternatives for action. If there is time, it may pilot them to determine implications. In the priority-setting and allocation-of-resource stages that follow, research helps indicate effect sizes relative to costs of alternative or competing programs. Research is probably more powerful in killing proposals than in improving their chances. The Income Maintenance Experiments, for example, killed this alternative when the side effect of family breakup was discovered.

At the final stage, that of legislative oversight, summative evaluation studies indicate how well the programs are working, formative evaluations show how they might work better, and comparative evaluations show which programs to emphasize and which to downsize or eliminate. Thus, different kinds of research are needed at the different stages. In addition, timing of the research, so that the results are available when decisions must be made, is crucial. Academic researchers, with teaching, advisement, committees, and many other demands on their time, have not been very good at crash research intended to produce results on call. As a result, a large private sector has developed to meet those demands. Time demands are most severe in the early stages, when support is being aggregated for a given policy, and in later stages, when budget deadlines must be met for reauthorization of funding.

Most discouraging to researchers, however, is the apparent politicization as policymakers decide on choices for implementation. It often appears that most policymakers seek out research that fits their point of view and ignore whatever does not. This is going to be increasingly harder for them to do as meta-analysis and research syntheses are developed on policy topics. Other policymakers, however, who are used to making decisions in the absence of complete information, argue that they must take many more things into account than the usually simplified evidence provided them by research. Chelimsky (1991), for example, notes that sometimes politicians are boxed in by events. She notes that, consulted by German leaders during World War I, Max Weber warned that submarine warfare would cause the intervention of the United States and lead to a "sure catastrophe." In that case, "the decision-makers had the information but not the political room to consider . . . a contrary view" (p. 227). She cites the Pentagon Papers during the Vietnam War as a modern example of policymakers' disregard of recommendations made in a study originally requested by them.

Even when policymakers lend a listening ear, inquiry is clearly not ideally suited to policymaking as currently practiced by academic researchers. Whether the private sector will supply the research needs for policy or whether academic researchers will find it in their interest to explore a way to be more responsive remains to be seen. Certainly, much can be done to adjust information needs to the research process and vice versa.

What Are We to Think, Then, of Social Science Research?

Throughout this textbook we pursued the belief that building stronger chains of reasoning is a goal of social science, and we have concentrated on the methodology that would facilitate this. Charles Pierce, an American philosopher writing in 1868, took the chain analogy a step further: "The reasoning should not form a chain which is no stronger than its weakest link, but a cable whose fibers may be so slender, provided they are sufficiently numerous and intimately connected." A good point!

The cable analogy, with its numerous and intimate connections, clearly refers to theory that integrates knowledge—always a higher goal to be sought, as this textbook should have made clear. But consider the fact that two psychological theories as different as cognitive psychology, which views behavior as inwardly controlled, and behavioral psychology, which focuses on its external control, can both coexist and be useful at the same time. This dichotomy says something about the present state of our knowledge. Certainly, we have a long way to go. But how far is the journey? What is the end? Boulding (1968) suggests:

> It is only by the . . . activities of the . . . social sciences that we can hope to understand the social system sufficiently well to be able to control it and to be able to move into a positive image of the future through our own volition and policy. Otherwise we are merely slaves of necessity or victims of chance. (p. 107)

Along these same lines, Asimov (1977) tells of inventing "psychohistory," the mathematical analysis of every kind of sociological trend. We could then predict, with a high degree of accuracy, the social movements of the future. He based his idea on the kinetic theory of gases in which, although trillions and trillions of molecules are moving randomly, we can predict exactly what will happen to a gas if it is heated or compressed. "All the random behavior of the individual molecules ends up by making the gas, as a whole, a completely predictable system" (p. 11).[6] No doubt, this is the dream of many social scientists. Some, however, believe that not even that level of predictability can be achieved, let alone that of the individual's behavior— for example, the prisoner seeking parole or the developmental path of a mentally retarded child. Can we find an intermediate level that is usefully predictable?

Religious persons might ask whether, given God's purposes in the world, such a search for behavioral predictability is an evil act, whether it is more knowl-

---

[6]Does this remind you of Popper's gnats and a cloudlike world?

edge than humans should have. Berger (1961) argues that the scientist must assume that the fundamental integrity in a universe ruled by God is meant to be plumbed. It is an act of faith—an exploration that leads us to understand and appreciate ever more the intricate complexities of our being and to wonder how it all came about.

The insatiable drive of science has been to learn enough about everything so that it would be understandable. It is only very recently that scientists have begun to believe that there are phenomena that are inherently unpredictable. They can be predicted only statistically; the odds of a given condition can be stated:

> According to Cronbach, what frustrates a would-be empiricist social science are complex interactions that make generalization to causal laws *practically* impossible. . . . What is interesting about Cronbach's . . . views is the sense of *déjà vu* one has. For the argument concerning the complexity of educational and social phenomena is precisely the one invoked by John Stuart Mill nearly 140 years ago to explain the paucity of progress in the social sciences! (Ericson and Ellett, 1982, pp. 505–506, emphasis in original)

Although concerns about the progress of social science clearly are not new, Gage (1996) makes a strong case for social science research. He cites examples of useful main effects, not just complex, weak, low-generality interactions that were the concern of Cronbach. For instance, he notes that Walberg (1986), in a synthesis of meta-analyses, turned up nine generalizable findings just examining research on teaching, even though he selected only meta-analyses with 90 percent consistency in the direction of relationship and covering at least twenty studies. Lipsey and Wilson (1993) found 156 meta-analyses of experimental or quasi-experimental studies of mental health treatments, work-setting interventions, and educational methods that met their criteria for lack of bias. They found an average effect size of .47 and about the same results in each of the three categories of interventions. Gage notes: "Such effect sizes betoken a . . . substantial mean-level of effectiveness. . . . whatever the moderating or weakening influences of interaction effects may be, many main effects are consistent and strong enough to allay despair for the behavioral sciences" (p. 11). Furthermore, Gage gives several examples of effect sizes that were considered highly significant medical findings but would have been deemed too small to attract much attention in the social sciences, a point we considered in Chapter 21 on meta-analysis (p. 557).

Many persons believe that social science findings are less consistent than those in the physical sciences. As noted in Chapter 21 (see p. 564), however, Hedges (1987) found them comparable. The social sciences hold their own better than many would have thought.

Furthermore, we do make progress on social issues. The author was struck by a 1992 publication of the Developmental Disabilities Planning Council of New York which compared being a parent of a handicapped child in successive recent decades. In 1942, the parent believes the doctor knows best and is told to put their child in an institution even though it is 150 miles away. Ashamed of their child, parents try to keep the disability secret from co-workers and friends. Rarely is anyone with a disability seen in public and parents don't know other parents in similar situations.

By 1962, the child is attending a day care program but the doctor says he would never be able to function in society. The child has no friends and mainly sits in the living room. The parents are considering purchasing a television to entertain him. The parents are too ashamed to attend a parent group started by the day care center.

By 1982, a congressional act has been passed giving such children the right to attend public school. There is an emphasis on deinstitutionalization and normalization. Nevertheless, preschool children attend segregated programs operated by specialized agencies. Some children have been returned from institutions to community residential settings.

By 1992, preschool programs are mandated by the state with an emphasis on programs integrated with nonhandicapped children. Families are getting support and have an influential role in policy planning, program development, and evaluation of services for people with developmental disabilities.

How many of these changes are due to research? It is difficult to tell. Certainly, parents were central to bringing about change. Yet, it is clear that research played an important role in decisions to deinstitutionalize and normalize the education of children with developmental disabilities. Furthermore, both the earlier discussions of dissemination and Chapter 23 on evaluation and action research, emphasized the importance of involving stakeholders to get findings used. This point is well illustrated by those working in the developmental disabilities fields, where professional societies reporting and discussing research meet simultaneously with the organizations of parents and others concerned with bringing about change. As a result, stakeholders and researchers are aware of each others' work and reinforce each others' efforts. It is a model that is worth considering for other fields

However, advocating for their research is an uncomfortable role for many scientists, who prefer to work on the model of "building a better mousetrap" so that the world will beat a path to their door. Researchers striving hard to keep their work "objective" wonder: "How can we move from gathering facts to telling society how to use them without crossing the line that separates knowledge from values? Once crossed, we find ourselves on the proverbial slippery slope—the one where our more activist colleagues slide as fast and as far as they can in their zeal to cure society's ills" (Howell, 1995, p. 28). But many other researchers argue that all knowledge is value tinged; the choice of what problem to research—for example, the normalization of education for handicapped children—is a value choice in itself. Values determine what we study, may determine how we study it, what we focus on and find surprising or significant in the studying, and what we think is important enough to report as a finding. Which brings us to the need of the social sciences for the humanities.

The Need of the Social Sciences for the Humanities

Ultimately, the answer to how—and how rapidly—the social sciences will develop, is an empirical one that will be increasingly uncovered by you, the future researcher. Whatever your route, however, you can be certain that science alone does not hold all the answers. Frye (1981) notes that there are three different ways in which language can be used. One is the language of science, which seeks to convey information about the world. A second is the language of transcendence, used in philosophy and religion, an "abstract, analogical language that expresses what by definition is really beyond verbal expression" (p. 129). Third, there is the language of immanence, of poetry, where "natural objects can become images of human emotions" (p. 129). It is in the language of transcendence and immanence that the goals of science are found. As Frye (1981) puts it:

> The arts and sciences, . . . for all their obvious differences, have a common origin in social concern. . . . When we think . . . of a world to be remade, we find we need a model or imaginative vision of what we are trying to achieve. . . . The world of dream and fantasy can be a source of models . . . and models are the first product of the chaos of hunch and intuition and guesswork and free association out of which the realities of art and science are made" (pp. 130–131).

We have been studying the processes of science with the intent of improving the quality of our journey through life. But it is to the humanities that we must turn to understand our goals, what "quality" means, and where the journey leads.

Dr. Clifford Erickson, then Dean of the College of Education of Michigan State University addressing the College's faculty in 1961, closed with this still relevant statement, which seems a fitting way to close this book:

> We are grateful for this opportunity to serve mankind during the most critical period in all history. Grant us the courage and the wisdom to play our parts effectively. Forgive us if we falter and seem to hesitate, for the problems are very complex. Strengthen us in our resolve to join hands with our colleagues in doing together, what we cannot do alone. Provide us the stimulation needed to venture into the unknown. Keep us from being divisive, trivial or lacking in faith in each other. For the only things we have to fear are timidity and mediocrity.

ADDITIONAL READING

See Collins and Pinch's discussion of physical science as produced by social factors (1993) and a review of the book by Segerstråle (1994). On public understanding of science, see Collins and Pinch (1993) and Tuomey (1996). On defense of the behavioral sciences, see Gage (1996), particularly against Gergen (1994). Also see Medawar (1984).

Writing a Research Proposal

OVERVIEW

This appendix, building on the material covered in the text, will assist you in developing a proposal such as that usually required for a doctoral dissertation or, in some instances, for a master's thesis.[1] It begins with an unusual definition of a proposal, the implications of which are important to bear in mind as you prepare your own. Discussing the sections of the proposal in sequence, it describes their ideal characteristics and offers tips for writing their subsections. Because certain kinds of proposals with emergent problems pose unique challenges, a section discusses these aspects. The chapter closes with a description and illustration of some writing conventions you will be expected to follow in this and other academic writing.

APPENDIX CONTENTS

---

[1]The section dealing with proposal development is excerpted and condensed from material being prepared for D. R. Krathwohl and N. L. Smith, *How to Prepare a Dissertation Proposal,* © David R. Krathwohl 1997. It is expected to be distributed by Syracuse University Press in 1998. For more detail on proposal preparation see the book, or D. R. Krathwohl, *How to Prepare a Research Proposal,* Syracuse, NY: Syracuse University Press, 1988. The latter not only provides help for proposals that will be submitted for funding but also has a section for graduate students.

Definition of a Research Proposal

What is a proposal? It is an opportunity for you to present your idea and proposed actions for consideration in a shared decision-making situation. You, with all the integrity at your command, are helping those responsible for approving your proposal to see how you view the situation, how the idea fills a need, how it builds on what has been done before, how it will proceed, how you will avoid pitfalls, why pitfalls you have not avoided are not a serious threat, what the study's consequences are likely to be, and what significance they are likely to have. It is not a sales job but a carefully prepared, enthusiastic, interestingly written, skilled presentation. Your presentation displays your ability to assemble the foregoing materials into an internally consistent chain of reasoning.

The write-up of the proposal follows a logical, deductive sequence of presentation. The process of doing research work may, or may not, also follow a similar sequence. This differentiation of work sequence from presentation format is particularly true of qualitative or exploratory research, what we call emergent research projects, where the nature of the research problem is not known at the outset—it emerges from the research work. The discussion of the proposal in the following sections is directly relevant to all researchers who think they know their problem focus and are seeking some kind of generalization. Preparation of proposals for qualitative, emergent, or descriptive research also will markedly benefit from the following material, though it may require some adaptation. A discussion devoted to unique aspects of emergent studies appears later in a separate section.

Relation to the Chain-of-Reasoning Model

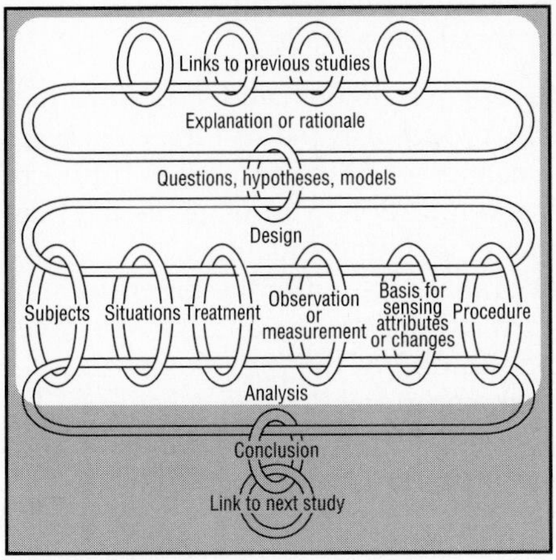

In so far as you can anticipate the nature of the study before beginning the actual dissertation data collection, the proposal encompasses the upper part of the chain of reasoning (see pp. 63–67), all the way down through the six rings of the study's design and analysis, as shown in the inset illustration. Build the problem statement so that the project's hypotheses, questions, or models flow logically from it. The statement of objectives and method of attack should build upon and move beyond the review of past research, showing how this study will add to prior accomplishments, and remedy past failures. These, in turn, will suggest the population and sample and the rest of the research design. The data gathered will determine what analysis, statistical, qualitative or other, is appropriate.

A strong proposal intended to demonstrate or validate a generalization reflects this chain by the plan of its structure, by its internal logical consistency, and by the appropriate development of each section. Each section reflects the previous material and carries it, in a consistent way, a step further. Always make sure that ends are not dropped, objectives slighted, data collected but not included in the analysis plan, and the like. Allocate resources properly to strengthen weak aspects, and make appropriate design trade-offs.

Proposal Format

If you plan a career in research or higher education, prepare your proposal in typical proposal sequence, as outlined in the following sections. Preparing a proposal is excellent practice, since part of such a role is seeking resources and a proposal is the usual method of requesting them. The sequence of sections described in this material is typical of that used by most funding organizations or expected by foundations. To submit for funding, in addition to what is described here, the proposal requires a budget, a description of the other needed resources, a vita for yourself and for those working with you, and other indications of competence and institutional support.

If you are not planning to enter academia or a research institution, and do not expect to do research again, you may wish to consider a proposal that is basically the first three chapters of a conventional dissertation. Some faculty request this format. It consists of:

Chapter 1—Introduction and statement of the problem placing it in perspective to its field

Chapter 2—Review of literature bearing on the problems

Chapter 3—Description of the design of the study and the procedure to be followed, together with a justification for the choices made

With this structure, if the findings of the research do not call for a reformulation of the problem, you may be able to use the proposal as the first three chapters of your dissertation with little more than a change of verb tense from future to past and such touch-ups as are required by modifications you made as the plan was implemented. This format will save considerable time and effort.[2]

We will start the discussion of proposal preparation with: the description of the problem, its basis in the literature, how it relates to theory, and the objectives of the study. We then move to the operationalization of the previous phase, describing the study's design and procedure. If the proposal is being considered for funding, you would add a third aspect, a discussion of available and needed resources. It is beyond the scope of this Appendix; see Krathwohl (1988).

Statement of the Problem

Your first task is to describe your problem in terms so enticing as to make the reviewer eager to examine the rest of the proposal. This job falls especially to the introduction or problem statement, but it is also shared with the literature review and objectives sections.

The introductory section typically develops understanding of the problem by describing its significance in relation to the large, important problems already of concern to your readers and by showing the problem in the perspective of the field in which it is embedded.

The introduction leads into a section on related research, which further develops problem understanding and appreciation by showing specifically how the problem is solidly grounded in the previous work of the field and how this project will take a significant step beyond that.

Thus, it is possible for you, at the end of the literature review, to restate your problem in a more precise and detailed fashion with greater understanding. And from that problem statement you can tease out the research questions, hypotheses or, if you know enough of the causal factors, describe a model of how the phenomenon occurs. This will lead to the development of the objectives and goals of the study. You can then describe the problem statement and goals in such a way that their translation into the procedure, the topic of the second part of the proposal, is natural and easy.

---

[2]Sometimes, you will encounter something so interesting, perhaps a side issue or unexpected side effect, or the situation turns out to be so different from what you anticipated, that your topic must be modified—sometimes a little, sometimes so much it is a different study. In that instance, the proposal no longer describes the study. Few if any committees, however, require a new proposal. After all, whatever learning you might experience by redoing the proposal you will encounter in writing the thesis or dissertation.

Introduction and Initial Problem Statement

First impressions are important! Your opening sentences suggest to the reader whether your proposal will be creative and interesting or just routine. Return to your opening after you have a complete draft and rework it so that it invites the reviewer to read further.

Tips on Developing the Introductory Statement.

- *Show the problem's importance.* The opening statement should convince the reviewer that the project is important. For example:

  Just as Japanese adaptations of the United States' social-psychological discoveries have contributed to their industrial success, so our failure to use that knowledge has compounded our problems in competing with them. This project seeks modifications in Japanese uses of this knowledge that will be effective in our culture. The modifications . . .

- *Show the problem in the perspective of the larger field in which it is embedded.* For example, "show our management practices as a part of our lagging in international economic competition, accounting procedures as a facet of making government intervention effective."
- *Show the problem's generality.* For many, the dissertation's place in the graduate program has become primarily that of a learning experience. As originally conceived, it is at the same time a contribution to knowledge. Many dissertations are still expected to be. Therefore *indicate the generality of the problem and the generalizability of the research.* A good way of doing this is to point to the project's contribution to theory and new knowledge. Indicate how the project builds on previous theory or contributes to new theory. Relate it to the large, important problems of the field. If you can, describe the value of some concrete applications of the knowledge as well as the potential importance of these applications.
- *Foreshadow what is to come.* Save details for the procedure section, but provide enough in the introduction that the reader can see where the project leads. For example, a generalizable project does not necessarily require a national sample. Therefore, very briefly outline here the basic characteristics of the intended sample, situation, and procedure, so it will be possible to infer to whom findings might transfer.
- *Limit the problem.* Learning to focus a study is a skill. Novices often believe that only by encompassing large pieces of a problem can they avoid triviality. Dissertation proposals are often rejected three or four times as a project is successively reduced in scope. However, it is only by focusing on the manageable, on the critically important aspects of problems, that you can successfully complete a project.
- *Don't dwell on the obvious.* The author recently read a proposal that used its first eight pages to convince the reviewer that research in the field was necessary. If reviewers are not already aware of this, they would not have been

asked to be a reviewer, or should not have agreed to be, if asked. Assume interest in research in the area.

- *Find the balance between completeness and brevity.* Some researchers are too brief, taking too much for granted concerning the reviewer's knowledge of the topic (for example, knowledge of a new complex statistical procedure). Conversely, some may make this section extra long on the assumption that if they can sell the reviewer on the importance of the project, the reviewer may overlook flaws in the remainder of the proposal in order to get something going in this field. This is not likely. In this section, as in others, find the balance between completeness and brevity; adjust the length of this section to correspond to the way the rest of the proposal is developed.

- *Give the reader perspective on the whole proposal.* As part of the foreshadowing in the introduction, describe the approach you are planning to use with a two- or three-sentence sketch. Also briefly point out the merit of this approach.

- *Set the frame of reference.* The problem section establishes the frame of reference and the set of expectations that the reviewer will carry throughout the proposal; be sure it is the correct one.

Related Research

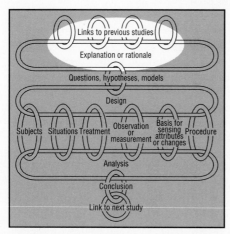

This section builds further understanding of the problem by showing that it is solidly anchored in past work yet moves beyond that work in important ways. *It is an excellent place for you to give an indication of your scholarly competence.* Writing this section well is a sign of professional maturity; it indicates your grasp of the field, your methodological sophistication in critiquing others' research, and the breadth and depth of your reading. In the chain of reasoning, this section is the drawing together of the rings representing the findings of prior research into the statement of the rationale or explanation for whatever phenomenon you are examining.

Qualitative dissertations may differ in the way they handle the literature review from what is described here, particularly if oriented toward "I don't want to be contaminated by the past literature until I know what is of significance in the situation I want to study." Although you may be approaching your dissertation from this point of view, you will still find the discussion below of value, since you will do a review of the literature for your dissertation write-up—if not for your proposal—and the same rules will apply.

No project starts de novo. A conscientious researcher shows the proposed project as building upon what has already been done and as contributing to the forward movement of the field in some significant manner. The section on related research provides such an opportunity. Use the many library indexing, abstracting and reference tools described in Chapter 6 to find the most appropriate literature.

Don't forget to include the Internet and the access it provides to expert help and resources beyond those provided by your library (as well as possibly your own library's home page which may make references easily accessible).

Survey a select group of studies that provide a foundation for the proposed project, discuss these studies in detail sufficient to provide an understanding of their relevance, describe how they contribute to this study, and indicate how this study moves beyond them. Obviously, the review should encompass the most recent literature in *both* content and method; an outdated review hardly adds to the impression of scholarliness. Similarly, dependence on some secondary sources such as other literature reviews may be appropriate, but as a scholar you will usually want to *check some of the original literature* yourself.

Too often this section is an afterthought. After you have developed the "fresh, new idea" into a project, you go to the library to complete the sole remaining section, that on related research. This often makes it difficult to reconcile past research with the "new" project. If you take past studies into account during the planning stage, the project is much stronger.

Tips for the Related-Research Section.

- *Point out any technical flaws in the studies you discuss.* Show how you will avoid these pitfalls. If possible, revise the findings of studies that were incorrectly interpreted by the authors and show how the study's findings should be viewed to fit the study proposed.
- *Describe the theoretical base for your study.* Science is a systematically accumulated body of knowledge. Theories interrelate individual findings and permit greater generalization. This section is an excellent place to convey your grasp of how theory is currently being developed and tested in your area and to critique the solidity of the structure your field is erecting. Emergent studies may not initially have such a base, but, with the completion of pilot studies that indicate future directions, developing such a foundation for your study becomes not only possible, but also important to determining how best to shape its directions.
- *Be highly selective, citing only those studies that form the base from which your study is building.* More is not necessarily better. The most common error is including too many references and commenting too little on them. Proposals are often submitted with lengthy bibliographies on the research topic. Such a comprehensive list does little to convince the reader that the researcher has anything other than the ability to use an index. It is what you do with the references that is the basis for judging this section. The skill shown in selection, the technical competence used in evaluating contributions, and, above all, the originality displayed in realistically and constructively synthesizing conceptual bases of past and proposed work in relation to the proposed problem, are what will impress readers.
- *Become aware of literature bearing on your problem from disciplines other than your own.* Review research in related disciplines using bibliographic sources that extend broadly, such as *Social Science Citation Index*. Discuss your proposal with colleagues from other disciplines to provide a broader perspective on it as well as to provide a fresh point of view. Such contacts alert you to the jar-

gon these fields use to discuss your problem, which can help you use the journal indexes much more successfully.

- *Include studies currently underway that are likely to overlap your project.* Knowing what is currently being investigated in your field is another sign of competence. Show how this project differs from such studies or meshes with them in a constructive way. Many government agencies have web sites on the Internet on which they list newly funded projects. Large foundation grants are listed in *The Chronicle of Philanthropy.* Skim the most recent convention programs of professional associations in your area for related work (now also often posted on their web sites) and contact their authors for a copy of their paper or more information. Use forums, bulletin boards, and listservs to find the invisible college of individuals who are working in your area and determine how their work parallels or reinforces yours.

- *If you state that "no prior research bearing on the problem exists," cite the closest research you found and show how it falls short.* Also indicate under what headings and in which references you made checks.

   Researchers naturally want to claim their ideas as original, unrelated to what others have done. All too often when readers encounter the statement that "nothing has been written that bears on the problem," it becomes a challenge! They know that few projects start from scratch. Challenged to search their memories for relevant studies, if they find some, they are inclined to question the thoroughness of your scholarship and, perhaps, your technical competence as an investigator. Your description of your search shows where you tried and may result in suggestions of untried sources from reviewers.

- *Conclude your literature review with a restatement of the problem as it is informed by past work and indicate how your attack on the problem avoids the mistakes of the past and benefits from prior advances.*

Questions, Hypotheses, Models, and the Goals of the Study

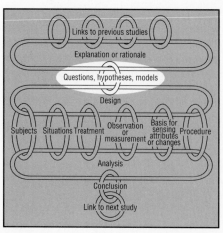

Thus far in the problem statement, you have described the problem in general terms, shown its importance, and set it in a larger context. In the related-research section, you have described what previous work has been done and alluded to how you are going to build on it: going beyond previous accomplishments, opening new territory, redoing a study a new and better way, possibly replicating a study to show the generality of its findings, and so forth. The section that follows, further shows the study emerging from the background of previous thinking and theory. In the chain of reasoning it is the link that joins the problem statement to the design.

Like each successive link in the chain of reasoning, this section forms a basis for judging the remainder of the proposal. It sets the stage for showing how you intend to solve or contribute to the solution of the problem sketched out in the first sections. Just how specific this section can be depends on what you have said in the previous sections, and what turned up in your review of literature:

- The less you have found out about the area, the more likely you are to devote this section to questions.
- If you have a good idea about how at least certain aspects work, you may have hunches to test to see if they are true. This section will set forth those hunches as hypotheses.
- If you have a good idea about how things work, you may be able to construct a model of how various variables are related to each other. This section will describe the model you would like to test.

Because this section comes early in the proposal, you may, still in an expansive I'm-going-to-show-the-world! frame of mind, claim more in this section than you find possible once you flesh out the details of the procedure section. Therefore, one of the first things to do once the proposal is completed, is to reread it to make sure that this section flows neatly from the problem statement and that the procedure section that follows adequately encompasses all that you cover in this section.

The most frequent error made in writing this section is that it becomes a set of vague generalities rather than clear-cut criteria against which the rest of the project can be judged.

Another error is that, instead of having a section in which the research objectives are clearly set forth, they are embedded in a running description of the project, and usually by implication rather than explicit statement. Your readers must then tease out the objectives as best they can, trying to infer what you have implied and placing such emphasis on different objectives as they can "guesstimate" from the contextual clues. Obviously, the readers' accuracy in doing this is critical. Rather than run the risk of misinterpretation, most writers will fare better by developing this material in this section, making the objectives clear and explicit.

The final common error, as already noted, is to include material that is not developed in the procedure section. If the proposal is to be an integrated chain of reasoning, everything should be appropriately followed up in successive sections.

Tips for a Questions Section.

- *Use questions instead of hypotheses where the problem is emergent, the research is exploratory, or a descriptive study or a survey seeks certain facts.* The specificity of the questions shows how carefully you have thought through the problem. For example, consider a study of the effects of female teachers on male students. Instead of merely asking "What is the effect of the female teacher on male students?" a researcher will much more convincingly demonstrate competence by rephrasing the question to "Which of these is the dominant effect of female teachers on male students?" If a listing of the possible dominant effects and explanations follows, it is clear that he has thought through the possible alternatives and is prepared to investigate at least these particular ones.

Where such specific questions might be expected, and you prefer to look at the phenomenon with a fresh eye rather than possibly to bias your search with prior expectations, be sure to explain your approach. If you are eschewing reading previous research, as do some qualitative researchers in order to come to their own conclusions about what is significant, then you will mainly state questions in this section. You will indicate what kinds of questions will initially guide your observations or your inquiries, and why you are starting with these instead of other possibilities. If you are a "purist" about starting *de novo* in the situation, this will be a very short section.

- *Indicate why your questions are the important ones to ask.*
- *Develop the implications for the field of addressing and possibly answering these particular questions.*
- *Explain why other reasonable questions that might be asked in the situation are not of interest and will not be addressed.*

Tips for a Hypotheses Section.

- *Relate hypotheses to their theoretical base if at all possible.* If you have not introduced the theoretical base in the previous sections, state it succinctly (showing how the objectives are derived from it), refine it, and extend it—carefully building the bridge from theory to study so that the relation is clear. For instance, a study of the effects of a vocational education program would be strengthened if the choices that the student must make in the program were related to developing theory on why and how students go through stages of vocational choice.
- *State hypotheses as objectives in such a way that they are testable,* that they can be translated into research operations that will give supporting or disconfirming evidence.
- *Do not state objectives as value judgments* (for example, "All sixth-grade boys should learn to play a musical instrument"). Research can indicate the extent of popular support for such a value statement (such as "Seventy-five percent of our town believe that all sixth-grade boys . . ."); or it can indicate the consequences of an action (such as "If all sixth-grade boys play musical instruments . . ."); but humans must judge how much value to attach to these consequences or to the extent of popular support.
- *Use directional hypotheses wherever there is a basis for prediction.* There will be a basis for predicted outcomes and findings if the study has a theoretical underpinning. (Remember, if you are looking for statistical significance, this is an easy way to increase the sensitivity of a study, see p. 483.)
- *State hypotheses as succinct predictions of the expected outcomes rather than in the null form.* For instance: "Students who receive the experimental treatment will show greater and more differentiated interests than those who do not," rather than "There will be no difference in interest patterns between the experimental and control groups." The latter statement is a part of the logic of the statistical test, but it does not belong in the objectives section and will likely make an amateurish impression on experienced researchers.

Tips for a Models Section.

- *Construct a model when you are concerned with a larger picture than the relationship between two variables, and can reasonably hypothesize the interrelationships among a set of variables.* Using previous research and synthesizing disparate pieces of a larger picture, construct a picture of how each variable influences or is influenced by other variables. Usually, this step results in the construction of a diagram with arrows indicating the direction of influence.
- *Show how the study will provide evidence that the relationships exist, confirm the directions of influence, and estimate their size.* Most such diagrams are relatively simple, since our knowledge of phenomena and our ability to confirm complex ones, without the kind of large-scale studies unlikely to be undertaken in a dissertation, is in its infancy.
- *If not done previously, indicate where you will have gone beyond previous work and how this study contributes new knowledge to the field.*
- *Include the basis in previous research for the proposed model in the literature review section of the proposal.*
- *Describe the model both graphically and verbally, and indicate the parts of it which are well confirmed by previous research, and those that are more tenuous.* If there are alternative conceptualizations of the relationships, indicate those, and give the basis for each. If you believe that one is more likely to be supported by the data, indicate that as well.

Design and Procedure: General Considerations

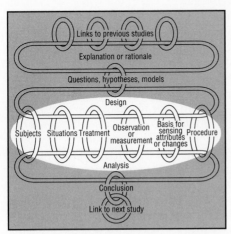

The design and procedure section is concerned with translating the just discussed problem section into project activities. *This is usually the most carefully read section of the whole proposal.* Up to this point, you may have told, in glowing terms and appealing generalities, what you hope to do and what this will mean to your field. The section on procedure brings your problem down to earth in operational terms. Proposals that sound as though they will revolutionize a field frequently appear much more mundane in the procedure section; the techniques proposed for attacking the problem may fall far short of what had earlier been claimed.

This discussion of the procedure section first covers general points to take into consideration in developing and describing procedures. The following sections are detailed discussions of each of the subsections that, together, usually make up the procedure: population and sample, design, instrumentation and data collection, analysis, and work plan (charts showing the sequence of events and the time required for their completion). Adapt this section to fit your study and show it in the best light possible. Most proposals will cover all these topics, if not in this order, in an order more appropriate to what is important to feature first.

An Iterative Process

As you operationalize the terms with which you described your problem, you often come to a different understanding of the study from when you initially conceived it. Terms take on new meaning, and often you have to sharpen and modify your initial conceptualization as you better understand the problem.

Suppose that you start out to study the relation of per pupil expenditures to achievement across a set of public school districts. In operationally defining— that is, determining the dollar value of per pupil expenditures—you find that different districts include different costs. In an effort to get comparable data across districts, you adjust each district to include a common set of costs. But at that point, the study begins changing. There is not much variability in these costs across districts—the variability is in the amount of discretionary money available to the school's principal to improve instruction. Thus, that becomes the focus of the study, forcing you to change the whole front end of the proposal to fit this new conceptualization of the problem. Some researchers argue that you come to a real understanding of the problem only when undertaking operationalization of the study.

Operationalization may never be completely satisfactory, especially when you are dealing with constructs that you cannot concretize in a way that satisfies everyone (for example, certain personality characteristics such as likableness, or monetary estimates of the value of good health). Remember this limitation if you are dissatisfied with your study, or the redevelopment of the procedure section seems never-ending. A compromise operationalization may be the source of your dissatisfaction, but it may be the only way to study your problem.

Sometimes, when the hypotheses of a study are given operational translations, it becomes immediately apparent that the problem is too large or too complex. In the per pupil expenditure example above, an attempt to estimate *all* the resources available in a given classroom might put the project beyond the realm of feasibility (parent volunteer time, laptop computers brought into the class by students, and so forth). Yet these might be important inputs to the classroom in certain circumstances. First attempts at problem definition are particularly susceptible to having to be reduced in scope where the researcher does not want to just go through an exercise but wants to "do something significant" and starts too ambitiously.

Refocusing and limiting the problem to restore feasibility are the answers. Sometimes, however, certain requirements may still be too great. Consider whether these may be handled by alternative design choices. For example, if there are too few cases to establish both a control and an experimental group, you might use the subjects as their own control, with pre- and posttests.

Development of the procedures and design of a study is an iterative process. The researcher sets an initial set of pieces in place; then, finding that one must be changed, sets off an entire cycle of changes that may in turn result in a further reconceptualization, further changes, and so on, until all the pieces fit together and are feasible. The treatment becomes unmanageable, so it must be cut down. This step requires the size of the sample to be increased in order to detect a weaker treatment. The increase results in having to use subjects with characteristics that interact with the treatment and that therefore must be controlled. And so it goes. Often you must go all the way back to the beginning and plan the procedure and design on a different basis. Many cycles may take place before you reach a satisfactory solution. (You don't realize how typical such iterations are because they don't appear in the write-ups.)

Key Sections for Your Research Method

A typical proposal may involve the following subsections: (1) population and sample; (2) design; (3) data and instrumentation; (4) analysis; and (5) work plan. Successful use of a particular method is often dependent on how well certain of these aspects are described. These should, therefore, be given special attention in proposal development. Some examples:

- For a sample survey, develop carefully the population and sample, the instrumentation sections, and the handling of the nonrespondent problem.
- For an experimental study, the experimental design section and what alternative explanations it will and will not control.
- For a study using new analytic techniques, the analysis section.
- For a longitudinal study, population and sample, data and instrumentation, and work plan. Depending on the kind of longitudinal sample (see p. 354), describe plans for replacing lost cases.

Because choice of design is still part art, reasonable persons may differ about the best design for a given problem. Your initial choice of design may not be that which springs to the mind of your readers and reviewers. However, they may be thinking in stereotypes, and your approach may indeed be the best. To minimize the impact of such differences of opinion, help them to follow your line of reasoning so that they, too, can see the rationale for your design choices. *Make clear your design choices, your reasons for so choosing, and why you preferred this choice over alternatives.* There is more on this point in the material that follows.

Limits and Constraints

With your first consideration of the procedure section, you must make tentative decisions:

- What level of resource use is both possible and practical, including your own time?
- What ethical considerations are involved?

- What access and cooperation can you expect from your own institution, from other institutions, from subjects, and so forth?

These estimates are important for making methodological decisions: the possible number of subjects, location of study settings, and so on. Indeed, the limits may rule out certain methods that take too long, such as a longitudinal study. The most desirable and cooperative institutions may be far too distant. Some of the limits are easy to estimate, others more difficult; but you must make some reasonable determination for all of them if development of procedures is to proceed realistically. Further, just as you iteratively develop other parts of the design, so you may have to successively reexamine initial limits and adjust them as your plan develops.

Resource Limits. As soon as you begin to translate the study into operational terms, the question immediately arises, "How big shall I make it?" Although you need not answer this precisely at the outset, you must set some working limits. Include the sensitivity analysis mentioned on page 483 for inferential statistics if you plan on the use of such statistics.

Ethical Limits. Recall that every institution receiving federal moneys is required to have a Committee on the Protection of Human Subjects, which is concerned with the ethical implications of your research plan. Nearly every university extends the federal requirement to all research carried on at the institution, including dissertations. Most institutions have procedures for expeditious approval, but you will do well to look into this aspect early so it will not be a barrier to your collecting data when you are ready.

Institutional Limits. When other institutions or agencies are involved, either as collaborators, as sources of data collection, and so forth, be sure you consider your requests to them from their perspective to ensure they are reasonable. Most institutions have not only limited funds but also limited availability of subjects, facilities, equipment, and personnel. Institutions tend to resist changes in their routines that interfere with "business as usual." It is important to ensure that the sites you expect to use are amenable to your plans. Some universities and funding agencies expect letters to accompany the proposal from the sites you plan to use indicating that access will be granted.

Time Limits on Proposal Development. Although it seems that you ought to able to control your timetable, pressures to get your degree in a reasonable time, to gather data before certain natural breaks in institutional calendars, faculty trips, sabbaticals, or other scheduling difficulties may impinge on it. These problems may, for example, shorten the time you have to get your proposal developed and approved, enforce a particular schedule on data collection, require data collection before you are comfortably ready or at inconvenient times, necessitate the use of nonpreferred sites, or inadequately involve personnel vital to the study in proposal development. It is important to delineate those things that you can do satisfactorily in the time available for proposal development from those that are unwise to attempt or, perhaps, you cannot do even if you try.

Consider the trade-offs involved in rushing to meet the immediate deadline versus waiting until a later time when you could more successfully resolve some of these problems. A several-month delay in proposal approval might pay handsome dividends in more cooperative site conditions as the staff of other institutions and agencies are given a chance to contribute to the research plan and feel it is partly theirs. Considering that this delay may provide better and more convenient working conditions over the period of the study as well as better data, it may be worthwhile. But other considerations, such as the availability of your own or a key person's time, may be overriding.

One thing is certain, however: Trying to do too much in the available proposal development period usually results in a proposal that shows it, as does similar haste in data collection and analysis in the research report. As in sewing, "find a pattern that fits the cloth available" or as in sports, "find a league in which you can comfortably play."

Organization and Adaptation of the Design and Procedure Section

The organization described below, though organized differently from that of the chain of reasoning, was chosen because it is typical of the outline requested by many funding agencies and is one commonly followed in dissertations. As in many things, there are established conventions you may be expected to follow. However, except when your chair, committee or a prospective funding agency decrees that a certain outline must be followed, and many do, if your study is better fit otherwise, *organize this section to fit your study*. The only problem you encounter when you challenge convention is disturbing expectations, and if your presentation is better for having done so, there is no problem. On the other hand, if it isn't, your advisor may ask you to rewrite it in conventional form; that is the risk you take.

The topics in the design and procedure sections differ from the six rings forming design in the chain of reasoning. Established as convention long before the chain of reasoning was described, the topic headings confusingly use the term *design* both in the title for the section (Design and Procedure) and as a subsection heading under it. Similarly, *procedure* multiply appears: in the title for the section, as a topic under the design subsection, and as the major focus of the work plan subsection.

However, the six design rings of the chain of reasoning easily translate into this pattern, which simply repackages the material. Which of the six rings is discussed in each subsection is indicated both in the graphic of the chain of reasoning at the beginning of the subsection's discussion and in parentheses in the following:

1. Population and sample (subjects and, sometimes, situation)
2. Design (situation, if not previously covered, treatment or independent variable, and, sometimes, basis for sensing attributes or changes, and procedure)
3. Data and instrumentation (observation and measurement)

4. Analysis (if not covered earlier, basis for sensing attributes or changes)
5. Work plan (procedure)

Subsections Describing Design and Procedure

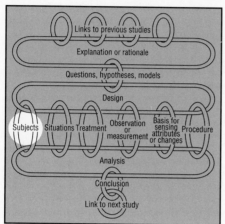

Begin the write-up of the procedure section with a one-paragraph summary or overview that foreshadows the procedure you will use. The discussion which follows describes each subsection, provides suggestions for writing each, and descriptions of some of the common, or most serious, errors.

Population and Sample

The description of population and sample determines the generality of the findings. Obviously this generality should be consistent with the generality claimed in the problem statement and objectives sections. The characteristics of the population define the group to whom the study's results may be expected to transfer. The more representative the sample, the more confidently you can generalize from the sample to the population. However, see pp. 177–178 re-using convenience samples for universal propositions.

Tips for the Population and Sample Section.

- *Describe the sampling plan in detail.* Give a rationale for why that plan is the best of those available.
- *Indicate the variables that will be used as the basis for ensuring representativeness—for example, the basis of stratified and cluster sampling. Show the significance of those variables for the study and why you chose these over others.* Also describe where you will obtain the data on these variables. If there is any reason to think some of the units might be misclassified into strata or clusters, give an indication of the anticipated error's extent, size, and likely impact.
- *Give a worthy rationale for the sample size. For studies with inferential statistics, this step clearly calls for a power or sensitivity analysis to ensure that a real difference is not mistaken for a chance one.* If, because of insufficient sample size, you write in your dissertation "the results are in the predicted direction, but there is no significant difference," reviewers will suspect that the hypothesis should have been supported. Since with a power analysis you can avoid this situation, you should.

Design

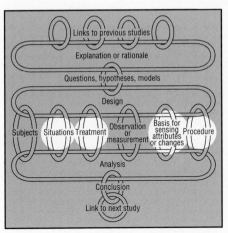

The term *design* in most proposals is used to describe the structure of the study: how subjects or situations will be studied; how groups will be organized; if there is a treatment, when and how it will be administered; when observations will be made—of whom, when, and, if known, of what; and how rival explanations will be eliminated. Of all the subsections of procedure, the design subsection varies most with the methodology. Although we will cover the procedure here, we will also see it in time perspective later in the work plan.

A major purpose of the design subsection is to show how you will structure the situation so that you can gather data with the least contamination by factors providing rival explanations. Whether experimental, qualitative, survey, or other, if the design does not ensure the integrity of the study's chain of reasoning against rival explanations, you will have compromised the case for whatever generalization you may be advancing.

What is an example of a rival explanation such as we are considering here? For example, in a study of the effect of two different curricula, the researcher should be concerned with any initial differences in the groups that might be reflected in their after-treatment performance. Any apparent differential posttreatment effect might be attributed as well to the initial differences as to the effect of the curricula. In this situation, the researcher might be expected to control such potentially contaminating factors as the beginning level of competence or achievement, general academic ability, or motivation.

The term *design* seems to go with *experimental,* as in *experimental design.* You might be tempted to assume that this section is of little importance to other than experimental studies, to a qualitative study, for example. Nothing could be further from the truth! A qualitative study observer, for example, must protect against a variety of rival explanations: the possible effect of the observer's prevailing attitudes and values as they affect observations; the possible choice of individuals and times to observe as "atypical" samples; the possible effect of "dropouts"—persons present at the start of the observations but not as they progress; and the possibility of going "native" and perceiving things differently as observations progress—to name just a few. Describing how these will be avoided both strengthens your proposal and shows your competence with your chosen method.

Tips for the Design Section.

- *Identify potentially serious rival explanations and discuss which ones to control and how to control them.* Having determined the possible rival explanations, you must decide which ones are the most serious threats to the study, then determine the ways you can control each, and decide how you can combine controls of the set of most serious threats into a design. Finally, you must determine whether the design is feasible, and, if not, redesign it until it is.

- Ask such questions as:
  How likely is each of these sources of contamination to occur?
  As you consider confounding variables one at a time, how likely is each to have its expected effect?
  In your estimation, therefore, how critical is it that you control for each rival explanation?
  How would you prioritize them?
  Are your reviewers and intended audience likely to agree with your priorities? Will they see these as "long shots" or real possibilities?
  Taking your own and these other opinions into account, how will you prioritize their claim on resources?
  Which design best controls the top-priority rival explanations?
  Is that design feasible? If not, how can you modify it so that it is?
  Given the other claims on resources, which design is preferable?
- *Convincingly indicate the nature and basis of the particular compromise being proposed and the reasons for accepting it.* Unfortunately, not all judges will weight the desirability of controlling possible contaminating factors the same way. Their "most acceptable compromise" may differ from yours. Once again, this is a place to demonstrate your mastery of the problem. If you have wrestled with the focus of your study and done pilot studies, nobody knows better than you the multiple sources of contamination that might affect it and how best to control them.
- *State clearly the reasons for choosing to control the variables you have selected and for ignoring certain others.*
- *Show how the design realistically controls the critical variables without sacrificing the integrity of the study.*

Data and Instrumentation

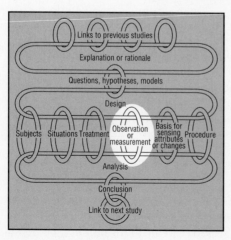

Many studies go awry in the leap from describing what is intended to what is actually done. The translation from the concepts in which the theory and background of the study are described to the actual gathering of data or translating those concepts into instruments is critical to the study's success. The congruence of data and what it is intended to represent is at issue. This is usually less of a problem with qualitative studies, although it can be if the examples the researcher pulls from the data to represent the concept are not what the reviewers and audiences consider the concept to be. It is in the translation into instrumentation, however, that so many quantitative studies fail. Therefore, this section needs to provide satisfactory evidence that instrumentation is not a problem.

Tips for the Data and Instrumentation Section.

- Provide the best possible evidence of validity and reliability of all instruments with which your audience is likely to be unfamiliar.
- Where you have used observation scales, choose low-inference scales, or provide evidence for the greater appropriateness of the ones you have chosen.
- Observe unobtrusively. If you cannot, indicate the steps you have taken to allow for accommodation to being observed.
- Provide evidence of appropriate self-analysis of your observation processes, possibly from pilot studies or prior similar work.

Analysis

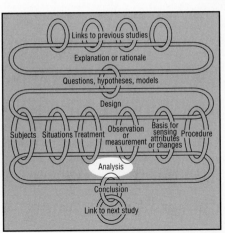

It is not always possible to completely anticipate the nature of the analysis that you will use; it may depend on the data you have collected. This is especially true of qualitative analysis procedures, but it may also be true of statistical methods.

Tips for the Analysis Section.

- *Reveal the depths to which you have anticipated analysis problems by describing projected solutions in sufficient detail to clearly convey their nature. At the same time, show awareness of where departures from plan are more likely to occur. As you must realize by now, anticipating the concerns of the audience and answering their questions even before they think of them are consistent strategies throughout the proposal!*
- *Keep the method of analysis consistent with the objectives and design.* For instance, in a study with quantitative data, when the study calls for finding the extent of a relationship, some kind of correlation coefficient is in order instead of a comparison of high and low groups with a difference statistic such as a *t*test. A statistically significant *t*test would indicate that, had a correlation been computed, it would be statistically significantly different from zero. But statistical significance does not tell the size of the relationship; the correlation could be so low as to be practically insignificant.
- *Statistics should match the level of data* (for example, nonparametric statistics for categorical data) or a rationale for the exception provided.
- *Assumptions of the statistics should fit the data.* If they seem not to do so, tell what corrections you can make. For instance, analysis of variance assumes

normally distributed populations, but you can make corrections in the level of significance for nonnormal data.

- *Carefully describe new statistical techniques, computer programs, or other unfamiliar analytic tools and indicate their advantages over current methods* so that the reader is assured of their appropriateness as well as their reliability.
- In complex multi-factor designs involving analysis of variance, show awareness of the appropriate error term and describe how missing data or unequal cell frequencies are to be handled.
- Qualitative studies with enough pilot studies to have identified the focus of the emergent problem, should be able to *indicate the nature of the analysis problem, describe what analytic progress has been made, and project future directions.* You will not necessarily be held to these projections. However, as in so much of the proposal, they indicate your competence as investigator to handle these problems when divergence from anticipated directions is necessary.

Work Plan

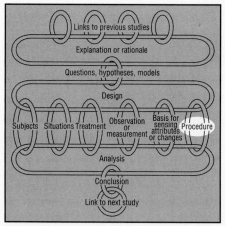

The work plan, or time schedule, basically translates the procedure into a time scale showing what events precede what others, which events can be concomitant, and how they progressively result in the study's findings. The plan can take different forms depending on the complexity of the study.

The work plan is another sign of how carefully and realistically you have developed the project. Some readers turn to it first to get an overall perspective on the activities. In other instances, a reader who is having difficulty understanding the flow of the procedure turns to the time schedule for the first real understanding of what the researcher intends to do. These uses at critical points in understanding the project indicate the importance of the work schedule as a clear, sequential statement of the operations to be performed.

It follows, of course, that the work schedule should present a *consistent and comprehensive representation of the material preceding it.* Omission of segments of the study makes projections of its length unreliable at best and indicates either carelessness, sloppiness, or disorganization. None of these are conducive to a favorable impression.

Depending on the complexity of the project, you can use various means to describe the work plan. A simple time schedule with a list of dates for completion of various activities in the order in which you will do them is one way. A more complete plan lists the dates on which activities will begin and end. You can show the latter thermometer style against a calendar scale. Figure A.1 is such a chart.

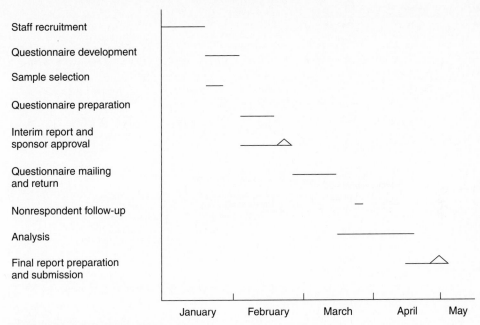

FIGURE A.1 A simple time line chart for a sample survey project (from Krathwohl, 1988. Copyright © 1988, David R. Krathwohl).

The length of the lines indicates both when and for how long the activity will take place. The triangles mark what are called milestones, events marking the completion of a phase or the production of some product.

More often, however, researchers lay out the work plan graphically in flowcharts or diagrams. Especially for complex projects, these are a better way than a list of events and dates for indicating the sequence of work. Figure A.2 (next page) is such a flowchart which can be created by software such as *MacProject*.

Note that the flowchart shows instances where two or more activities can be carried on at the same time, making it possible to shorten the total length of the project. The figures at the top of each box indicate the number of days that activity is expected to require; the dates below it are its actual time period. In place of the triangles of Figure A.1, rounded boxes indicate milestones.

Such detailed flowcharts make it possible to show the interrelationships among the different parts of the study, to reveal activities that can be carried on concomitantly, and to demonstrate more clearly the relative length of various phases. Their advantages are these:

1. They require an estimate of the time required to meet all criteria appropriate for each activity (for instance, how long will it take to get a 65 percent questionnaire return?).
2. They force an exploration of the interrelationships between activities.
3. They require that each step be analyzed in sufficient detail (very helpful for the procedure section!) so that difficulties are uncovered that might have re-

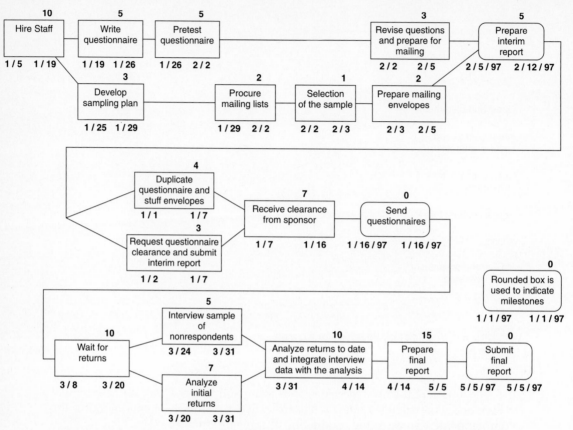

FIGURE A.2 A flowchart of the same sample survey project as the work plan of Figure A.1 (from Krathwohl, 1988. Copyright © 1988, David R. Krathwohl).

mained hidden in a less clearly specified proposal (only to arise later and bedevil the researcher when the proposal is approved).

4. They serve as a basis for resource allocation of personnel time to various parts of the proposal.
5. They provide a basis for administrative control of the project.
6. By maintaining an overall perspective, they provide a better foundation for making informed change decisions when those are required, since they promote clearer inferences regarding the implications of each change for the total operation.

If the work schedule is laid out well, the reader will have little question about what is planned, and the major concerns will be problem significance and strength of design.

There are a number of ways of diagramming the schedule of work, each of which has a jargon of its own. They require some sophisticated common sense and, in the more complex methods, some statistics and computerization to the tasks of planning and controlling progress and resource allocation. Computer programs are now available that markedly facilitate preparation of the work plan.[3] Two such programs for IBM-compatible personal computers are *SuperProject* and *Microsoft Project. MacProject Pro* and *Fast Track Schedule* are such programs for the MacIntosh computer.

The choice of available charts varies with the program. Most such programs provide some form of flow diagram, a project or activity table that lists the various activities and their time and resource requirements, and/or a task timeline that shows the tasks and their expected time requirements.

A Final Check and Review

At last! The draft is finished! Now you can check to ensure that the proposal is a consistent chain of reasoning. Each section should reflect the previous material and carry it a step further in a consistent and coherent way. Make sure that you have not dropped ends—slighted objectives, planned for data but overlooked analysis plan, and so on.

As was suggested earlier, now that you have developed your proposal, it is a good time to return to the opening statement and rework it so that it invites the reader to read further.

Be sure to use a word processor if at all possible; it makes rewriting text and editing so very much easier. Universally available word processing, however, has also raised expectations and lowered tolerance of poorly prepared text. You should use spelling and grammar checkers as necessary to get rid of gaffs. Remember that word processing's best dictionaries will not pick up typographical errors that form a correctly spelled word. These are the worst kind of errors, since they may make enough sense that they are not immediately spotted as typos, and the reader must stop to decipher your meaning. They are eliminated only by time-consuming, careful proofreading. Be aware also that grammar checkers don't allow for style and can make inappropriate suggestions.

Even the best writers benefit from having someone not familiar with the write-up criticize it. Don't be embarrassed to ask one or more friends to read it. Choose those who will be frank, but only if that is what you *honestly* want. If you have the time,

---

[3]Should you decide to submit the proposal for funding, the work plan gives a tremendous boost toward figuring the budget. With most computerized planning software, as you insert steps into the plan, you estimate the costs of the step as well. A test of the adequacy of a work plan is whether the budget is derived easily from it. Use of computer software that ties together the budget figures and the work plan charts makes it possible to generate several kinds of displays to help the researcher focus on different aspects (personnel, equipment, supplies, travel, etc.). You can then explore the effects of various trade-offs between project duration and cost. Since programs use calendars for specific years, you can even anticipate the effect of holidays, vacations, and other problems. *MacProject Pro,* for example, provides tables for each task, its costs allocated across each person or budget category, a table showing the costs for each resource used for each task, a resource timeline showing resources used each week, a week-by-week cash flow table, and a project table with tasks, dates, costs, income, and their accumulation. Interconnections provide for changes to be reflected immediately in all linkages.

put the draft aside and then return to it afresh after a long enough period to look at it in perspective. You will be amazed at what you will find.

It is always helpful to examine previously approved proposals. There may be a file of them in your department, or a faculty member may provide one from a former student. In addition, an annotated proposal appears in Locke, Spirduso, and Silverman (1993) and several will appear in Krathwohl and Smith 1997; see footnote 1). Krathwohl (1988 p. 275–6) has a list of published successfully funded proposals.

Preparing the Final Copy

How important is the appearance of the proposal? Some researchers do a very careful and complete job of preparing the proposal in especially attractive form. Readers may very well be impressed by this. Notwithstanding, your major effort should be on legibility, lucidity, and clarity of presentation. If it is a long or complex proposal, it may help to use tabs or colored paper to convey the structure and make sections accessible; tabs more readily convey the organization. When using colored paper to distinguish sections, place the coding key in a prominent and accessible place (front cover, table of contents, or first pages). Don't put text on dark-colored paper that makes reading difficult.

Other than the time required for assurances, clearances, and letters of support, the place where the writer is most likely to underbudget time is that required for careful, accurate, final review. Though word processing and rapid duplication services have cut the required time for many preparation steps, careful proofreading is extremely time-consuming. Most of us who read a lot are so used to skipping past errors, particularly in familiar material like our own writing, that we are terrible proofreaders. If possible, find someone who is good at it and treasure that person. In fact, the less familiar the proofreader is with the proposal, the better.

Qualitative Method and Other Emergent Problem Proposals

It may seem a contradiction in terms to suppose that a study, the focus of which is expected to emerge from data collection, could be the subject of a proposal. Preparing a proposal for qualitative methods studies (including participant observation and ethnographic studies) requires more than just describing the method you will use. However, if you want to begin your entry into the study situation with a clean slate, a proposal anticipating your objectives seems to violate a basic premise of the method. However, for dissertations, to satisfy reviewers that you have a viable topic and the know-how to do it, for need-to-know gatekeepers who control your entry to their institutions, for funders, in case you seek subsidy, and, for yourself, to get clear in your own mind what you are talking about, a proposal is indeed in order.

As Miles and Huberman (1994) note:

> At the proposal stage: many design decisions are being made—some explicitly and precisely, some implicitly, some unknowingly and some by default. . . . design decisions can . . . be seen as . . . a sort of *anticipatory data reduction*—because they constrain later analysis by ruling out certain variables and relationships and attending to others. Design decisions also permit and support later analysis; they prefigure your analytic moves. (p. 16, emphasis in original)

Qualitative proposals can range from the lightly structured proposal that is basically a hunting license, to the structured and detailed proposal that matches a quantitative study in its anticipatory nature. Just how much structure is required depends on a variety of factors: the caliber of the proposer's previous qualitative research experience, the trust the reviewers have in the proposer, the persuasiveness of the rationale for the study, and the case that can be made that pilot studies are unnecessary or impossible. For those with little qualitative research experience, a pilot study is essential.

Although it is possible to discuss the rationale and related literature sections of the proposal without having considered the findings of pilot studies, the remaining sections of the proposal usually require a pilot study for their accurate formulation. As well, the rationale and related literature sections also benefit from prior pilot work. Pilot studies help define the dimensions of the problem, the sample of persons and sites to be used, the instruments (if any) beside the observer(s) to be involved, the behaviors to be targeted, the sources and availability of records or others' data, the protections against reasonable alternative explanations, and the likely ethical problems to be encountered. Once the pilot study is complete, writing the proposal is markedly simplified.

As we discussed in Chapter 15, one of the criteria of a good study is provision for an "audit trail," a record of the study's methods and procedures detailed enough that someone else can follow it. It will be of help to those who must approve your study as well as any other researchers (possibly fellow students) who would like to either build on your findings or try to replicate them. Make sure to include provision for such a trail in your proposal.

Fully aside from the fact that you will need to clear the ethical aspects of your study with whatever human subjects protection apparatus exists in your institution, you will also have to deal with ethical problems that occur in the field. True, you will not be able to anticipate many of these situations, but some you can. Foreseeing such situations, describe them in your proposal and indicate your proposed solutions. Here again, a pilot study is of special value, since the ethical problems you are likely to encounter are often apparent from events during the pilot stage even if they don't appear full-blown.

We have already discussed the necessity of providing for the elimination of alternative explanations in general or justifying why you could not eliminate them. Because, as the researcher, you are the data collection instrument, qualitative studies have the additional burden of ensuring that your need to have the study come out in a certain way was not the reason that it did. Providing some assurance that predilections, biases, attitudes, likes, and dislikes will minimally affect data collection or, where they are expected to do so, indicating and anticipating the consequences is important. Try to provide "neutrality and reasonable freedom from unacknowledged researcher biases—at the minimum, explicitness about the inevitable biases that exist" (Miles and Huberman, 1994, p. 278). Lillian Rubin (1981) puts it differently, "the quest should not be for the fool's gold of objectivity but for the real gold of self-awareness" (p. 101).

Writing Formats

As long ago as 1660, the Royal Society of London discouraged authors of scientific literature from reports full of emotion and colorful adjectives that were advertisements for their findings, and encouraged them to seek an unbiased and unemotional tone. Such advice continues to be the convention today. That does not mean that your proposal has to be dull, but it does mean that it should be, as indicated by the initial definition of a proposal, "a carefully prepared, enthusiastic, interestingly written, workmanlike presentation." For example, omit personal details of your travails irrelevant to process or result. Use of the first person is still discouraged in most quarters but increasingly tolerated.

Ideally, writers expect that reviewers will give their proposals as much time as necessary to adequately comprehend and evaluate them; as, for that matter, do those responsible for reviewing them. But it is always safest to assume that your proposal might have to be reviewed under time pressures or where there are distractions (for example, reading during committee meetings, or at the end of the semester when everything and everyone clamors for attention).

Depending on the field, the conventions used in writing will typically follow the APA style (American Psychological Association, 1994), the University of Chicago style, or the MLA style (Modern Language Association). Use of the APA style appears to be increasing and is the basic style used in this book.

Format of Headings

We can cover here only two of the stylistic conventions: headings and references. Headings are important because they convey the organization of your writing. APA style consists of five levels for complex, long articles. For shorter articles, use the lower levels: two levels, use 2 and 4; three levels, add level 5; four levels, add level 3. The five levels are:

LEVEL 1: CENTERED ALL UPPERCASE
Level 2: Centered, Upper- and Lowercase
<u>Level 3: Centered, Underlined, Upper- and Lowercase</u>
<u>Level 4: Flush left, Underlined, Upper- and Lowercase</u>
<u>Level 5: Indented, Underlined, Upper-and Lowercase That Ends With a Period.</u>

Since most word processors apply style sheet formatting by the paragraph, level 5 is typically the most difficult to handle since formatting applies only to the first sentence rather than the whole paragraph. Italics may be substituted for underlining.

Format of References

References are troublesome because they vary with the kind of reference. The following provide illustrations of APA style for most of the reference types you are likely to encounter (underlining may be substituted for italics). They are taken from the reference section of this book which follows APA style.

Book

Taylor, S., & Bogdan, R. (1984). *Introduction to qualitative research methods: The search for meanings* (2nd ed.). New York: Wiley.

Book, Edited

Baker, G., & Chapman, D. (Eds.). (1962). *Man and society in disaster.* New York: Basic Books.

Book Chapter, In a Series

Atkin, J. M. (1994). Teacher research to change policy: An illustration. In S. Hollingsworth & H. Sokett (Eds.), *Teacher research and educational reform* (pp. 103–120). Ninety-third Yearbook of the National Society for the Study of Education, Part I. Chicago: University of Chicago Press.

Book, Translation

Schweitzer, A. (1990). *Out of my life and thought: An autobiography* (A. B. Lemke, Trans.). New York: Holt, Rinehart and Winston. (Original work published 1933)

Book Review

Glass, G. V. (1995). The next-to-last word on meta-analysis [Review of *Handbook of Research Synthesis*]. *Contemporary Psychology, 40,* 736–738.

Journal Article

Adair, J. D., Sharpe, D., & Huynh, C. (1989). Hawthorne control procedures in education experiments: A reconsideration of their use and effectiveness. *Review of Educational Research, 59,* 215–228.

ERIC Reference

Centra, J. A. (1977). *How universities evalute faculty performance: A survey of department heads* (Report BRED-75-5bR). Princeton, NJ: Graduate Record Examinations Board. (ERIC Document Reproduction Service No. ED 157 445)

Dissertation

Florio, S. E. (1978). Learning how to go to school: An ethnography of interaction in a kindergarten first grade classroom. *Dissertation Abstracts International, 39,* 3239A. (University Microfilms No. 78-23, 676).

Unpublished Paper

Guba, E. G., & Lincoln, Y. S. (1982). *Causality vs. plausibility: Alternative stances for inquiry into human behavior.* Unpublished paper presented at the Annual Meeting of the American Educational Research Association, New York, NY.

Computer Program

Padilla, R. (1993). *HyperQual 2 for qualitative analysis and theory development* [Computer program]. Chandler, AZ: the author. (Distributed by Qualitative Research Management, 73425 Hilltop Rd., Desert Hot Springs, CA 92240)

You can find style reference manuals at almost any library reference desk. Consult them, or purchase one if you do much writing. The APA manual is liberally illustrated with examples. In a chapter, "Writing in APA Style," Austin and Calderon (1996, pp. 272–281) provide a "dummy" article in APA style into which you could insert your own text.

Tips on Good Writing

Good writing, like good acting, uses both verbal emphases and nonverbal gestures to facilitate communication.

- *Be generous in your use of headings to help the reader sense the organization of the material.* Use headings to break up long sections, to signal the important points, to pilot the reader conceptually through the structure, and, through assigning heading levels appropriately, to provide a continuous sense of where in the structure the piece being read fits.
- *Signal upcoming content with topic sentences at the beginning of paragraphs.*
- *Use foreshadowing of what is to come throughout the proposal to integrate it.*
- *Use diagrams, flowcharts, tables, and other graphic devices.* Employ them to present overviews of content, to put details into perspective, to provide a succinct summary of important aspects, to show the sequence of a process, and to provide a road map of the important concepts and their relationships.

In sections that tend to be lengthy and unbroken by headings or subsections, it is especially important to:

- *Help the reader to easily find essential substance within certain parts of the proposal.* For example, place a succinct statement of the purpose of the research in an obvious position in the problem section. Similarly, list the objectives in order of importance in the objectives section. Summarize the points being made. Underlining, paragraphing, and summary boxes are especially useful

- *Use punctuation, underlining, bullets, listings, indenting (as here), spacing, paragraphing, and the like to command the reader's eye as to what is important.*

The circular pattern that newspapers use is a good one to adopt. Paint in broad strokes, then go over it again filling in the details. Finally, summarize and pull it together.

- *Work the definitions of unfamiliar terms, or words used in unusual ways, into the presentation early and prominently.* The reader learns them from the beginning and they cease to be a continual stumbling block to understanding. Better still, find a way to avoid their use!
- *Test your structure by skimming your proposal.* Read it very rapidly, jumping from topic sentence to topic sentence. Does it convey what you intend?

Avoid jazzing the copy with jargon or with more gesture than sense. Remember, research is essentially a scholarly activity.

Glossary

The number following each entry indicates the page in the text where the term is first discussed. Consult the glossary regarding the meaning of key terms when reviewing material as well as when studying. The necessarily succinct statements in the glossary may pull together the material in ways that are helpful. For a few terms, you may find the most complete discussion occurs later in the book than their first mention. Use the index to find additional places in the book where the term is discussed. With a few exceptions these terms were boldfaced where they first appeared.

ABA design A time-series design in which a control phase called the baseline (A) usually precedes a treatment phase (B). 532

Acceptance In qualitative research, willingness to be observed and/or accommodation to being observed so that behavior appears to return to normal. 255

Action research Research which is done by the consumers of the research to obtain knowledge for their own use. May be written up later for others. 600

Adversarial evaluation Evaluation teams prepare cases for opposite sides of an issue and present them to judges or a jury in a quasi-judicial proceeding. 598

After-the-fact natural experiments Studies in which the data are assembled after the presumed cause and effect occurred in an attempt to demonstrate a causal relationship. Also called *ex post facto* studies and causal comparative studies. 537

Agreement (method of) If two situations of a phenomenon under investigation have only one circumstance in common, the instance in which they agree is presumed to be causally related to the phenomenon. 150

Alpha error See *Type I error*. 457

Alpha level The percentage of instances, on the average, that a researcher will conclude that a value is atypical (there is a statistically significant difference) when in fact it is not (there is none). 468

Alpha reliability coefficient A measure of internal consistency reliability. 437

Alternative explanations See *rival explanations*. 147

Analysis of covariance A statistical technique for adjusting the means of groups for the effect of an unwanted or control variable. 482

Analysis of variance (ANOVA) Estimates of the population variance are made from the variability between groups (which is presumed to be affected by the intervention or independent variable of interest) and from the within-group variability (which is not so influenced). Comparison of estimates from these two sources shows whether the former is larger than the latter by a ratio (F ratio) which is larger than would be expected by the influence of random sampling and chance error alone. 490

Analytic induction   Finding commonalities and regularities in qualitative data, seeking their explanation, and finding other situations in which to test the generality of that explanation. 260

Audience credibility   Judgment on the part of the audience of the credibility they are willing to grant the researcher for having made appropriate judgments in the design and implementation of the study, especially for aspects not directly described in the report. 190

Audit trail   A record of the data gathering and analysis processes kept by the researcher so that another researcher could judge the appropriateness of those processes or possibly use the record to replicate the study. 316

Authenticity of evidence   Reassurance that the evidence is what it purports to be—for example, that a test score represents a sample of a particular individual's behavior and not someone else's. 145

Authority   A figure who believably asserts that something is true either without explanation or rationale (*dogmatic authority*) or with it (*reasoning authority*). 49

Base rate   The rate at which an event occurs naturally. When not taken into account, the base rate may affect study outcomes in ways that are confounded with treatment. 518

Baseline   The phase of a time-series design during which the natural state of the subject is determined before the intervention is applied. 532

Basis for sensing attributes or change   The basis on which we can determine whether an attribute is present or there was a change in the dependent variable as a result of the independent variable or treatment. 66

Behavioral objectives   Objectives stated in terms of the behavior to be learned or acquired with respect to specified content. 594

Beta error   See *Type II error*. 457

Bias   In sampling, an influence that systematically prevents obtaining a representative sample. 166

Blocking   Grouping individuals with a similar level on a characteristic perceived to be related to the effect. See also *stratified sampling*. 508

Borderline cases   Cases used in conceptual analysis to help define the boundaries of the term being analyzed. 261

Bracketing model   The use of multiple research methods such that, although one method may overestimate the effect, another may underestimate it with the result that the true effect is bracketed. 620

Buckley amendment   A federal law that protects the privacy of information held by an educational institution regarding an individual until it is released by the individual or his or her guardian. 216

Camouflage   A method of control whereby a characteristic that is otherwise prominent is made to become part of the background. 506

Case study   A careful, in-depth study of an individual or a situation usually using qualitative research methods; in quantitative research, an application of treatment followed by observation and measurement. 332

Causal chain   The sequence of events that results in an effect. 130

Chain of reasoning   The steps in the presentation of a logical argument in support of a knowledge claim. 63

Chain referral sampling   See *snowball sampling*. 173

Chi-square   A statistic that helps determine whether the pattern of frequencies found in data assigned to categories is likely due to chance or is atypical. Also used to compare data with a model to determine whether the data's fit is within the typical range of sampling and chance error. Also used to combine the results of independently conducted studies to determine overall statistical significance. 488

Citation indexing   Indexing of all references during a given time period that cited a given journal article including when and where and by whom cited. 116

Clocklike world   Causation is presumed to result from tightly coupled events, such as the meshing of a train of gears. 132

Cloudlike world Causation is presumed to result from loosely coupled events such as a cloud of gnats always maintaining a cloud rather than dispersing. 132

Cluster sampling Random samples are taken from cells in a geographic grid placed over a map, or random samples are taken from units organized on some prior basis such as schoolrooms. 170

Code of ethics A set of rules for ethical behavior; usually drawn up by a professional organization for the guidance of its members. 211

Coding Recurring facts, themes, comments, and the like are selected from fieldnotes and organized into categories expected to help explain a situation of interest. Descriptive names of the categories become the codes which are assigned to new fieldnotes as appropriate. 307

Cohort studies Studies of change over time using a constant population but taking new samples during each data-gathering period. 355

Common ownership of information A norm of science that states that information is owned by all and is to be shared freely. Researchers have an obligation to share their findings through universally available publications. Data should be shared on request once the researcher is finished using it. Supporting data for knowledge claims should be open to examination by others. 53

Complementary multiplism The use of complementary research methods such that the weaknesses of one are covered by the strengths of another and the body of work as a whole is strengthened. 620

Computer-assisted telephone interviewing (CATI) Random-digit dialing is usually used to select a sample randomly from among telephone subscribers for interviews. The computer is programmed to determine whether respondent fits the quota sample, what questions to ask, and in what order. Responses entered directly into the computer are checked immediately for consistency and errors so interviewer can take appropriate action. 359

Computer searches Use of a computer to find specific terms in relevant sections of a computer-readable version of an abstracting or indexing source or to search an entire multivolume source for those terms—an impractical task with the printed version. 109

Concealed observation Observation behind two-way mirrors, from hidden position or concealed cameras. 251

Conceptual analysis A process for finding the characteristics that define a term. Especially useful for defining constructs and concepts. 263

Concomitant variation (method of) Phenomena that consistently vary together are presumed to be connected to one another, directly or indirectly, through a causal relationship. 151

Concurrent validity A test correlates with a criterion measure obtained at the same time as the test was administered. 432

Confidence interval An interval constructed around an observed value such as a test score or a mean within which the true value is believed to lie with a confidence expressed by certain odds. The longer the odds (for example, 19 to 1 instead of 2 to 1) and the less reliable the test, the wider the confidence interval. 450, 461

Confidence level The odds we are willing to accept that express our confidence that the population value is contained with the confidence interval. 461

Confidence limits The end points on a confidence interval. With a specified level of confidence, we can say the population value falls between them. 461

Confidentiality Assurance is given that, without the subject's permission, none other than persons working on the study will have access to data gathered during research or obtained for other purposes but made available for research purposes. Typically, identifying information is destroyed as soon as it is no longer needed for research purposes. 215

Confounding Two or more variables that might have caused an effect were simultaneously present, so that we do not know to which to attribute the effect. 511

Congruence of explanation and evidence Evidence that an effect occurred agrees with the explanation advanced for the cause-and-effect relationship; a condition strengthening the inference of causation. 145

Connoisseurial evaluation See *expertise-oriented evaluation.* 593

Consensus The agreement of individuals making separate knowing judgments. 40

Constant comparison method Fieldnotes are coded as the study progresses, and new instances of a dimension or a concept of interest are sought until no more is being learned about it. These concepts are linked with others to develop a theory or an explanation that is constantly compared with new data from the field. Discrepancies call for modification or additions that increase understanding. 260

Construct A concept of which we have a mental image but that has no direct physical referents; an abstract noun. 263

Construct validity A test or measure behaves as the definition of the construct predicts that it should. 426

Consumer-oriented evaluation An evaluation intended to serve the information needs of consumers; contrasts with management-oriented approaches. 598

Contact summary report A one-page record prepared by a qualitative researcher after each interview or other contact which summarizes what was important, information obtained, information still needed, and next steps. 305

Content validity Comparison of the items of a test with the test's table of specifications or blueprint to determine if the items representatively sample the behaviors and content of the subject matter the test is intended to cover. Also called *curricular validity.* 428

Controlled vocabulary The dictionary or thesaurus that lists the stable set of subject-matter terms used to describe abstracts or index entries. 113

Correction for attenuation A formula for correcting a correlation coefficient for unreliability of measurement and estimating the size of the relationship if the reliability were perfect. 454

Correlation See *Pearson product-moment correlation.* 406

Cost-benefit analysis Determination of the costs of achieving certain benefits. 597

Cost-effectiveness analysis Determination of the costs of achieving certain benefits in relation to other ways of obtaining the same benefits. 597

Counterbalanced designs Studies designed such that if two or more treatments are administered in sequence, the treatments are administered in all possible sequences so as to reveal and eliminate the effect of the order of administration. 523

Counterbalancing In equivalence reliability, eliminating the effect of the order in which two tests were taken by giving half the group one order and the other half the reverse order and analyzing the combined results. 437

Covert participant observation An observation method whereby the observer becomes part of the situation by doing what other group members are so that individuals are not as aware they are being observed. 250

Creativity Bringing a new or unique element to research not seen before through researching a new problem; describing or organizing phenomena in new ways; or investigating combinations of persons, situations, treatments, times, operationalizations of constructs, or research methods, one or more of which are new. 32

Credible result A summary judgment of the conceptual and empirical evidence for internal validity (LP) together with a judgment of the consistency of the evidence with prior studies, which results in a determination of the internal validity (LP) of the study. 148

Criterion A measure generally accepted as valid; a measure to be predicted; a standard to be attained. 431

Criterion-referenced tests Tests whose scoring is based on meeting the mastery requirements of a content area rather than placing the score in the context of a reference group like norm-referenced tests. 438

Criterion-related validity See *concurrent validity* and *predictive validity.* 431

Cronbach's alpha See *alpha coefficient.* 437

Cross-break See *cross-tabulation.* 371

Cross-references   Alternative terms that might also be used to describe a particular word or phrase to which the reader is referred by an abstracting or indexing service. 114

Cross-sectional studies   Studies of change that compare current individuals of different age or experience on the variable of interest rather than waiting for change over time. 354

Cross-tabulations   Tabulations of data in terms of two or more variables. For example, respondents' choices of each of five possible answers to a question are tabulated; the tabulations for each response are then categorized by another variable, such as gender. Results would be displayed in a 2 (male, female) x 5 (the five possible responses) table with the frequency of responses displayed in each cell. 371

Data reduction   The analysis process whereby raw data is reduced to manageable and interpretable form. Analysis of qualitative data usually involves selecting, categorizing and organizing; of quantitative data, usually graphing and/or descriptive and inferential statistics. 304

Database   The computer readable form of data, for example, the electronic form of the text of a reference work such as an on-line library catalog, an abstracting service, or an encyclopedia. It may also consist of research data. 108

Debriefing   Informing an individual who has been deceived in an experiment of that fact and assuaging any unfortunate consequences. 205

Deception of subjects   Involvement in an experiment in which subjects are told that one thing is occurring when the point of interest is really something else. 214

Decision-driven evaluation   An evaluation used to help in the making of a decision, thus influencing both development and implementation of the evaluation. 588

Degrees of freedom   The number of data entries free to vary when their total is fixed. 489

Demand characteristics   Responses that subjects perceive as required by the study. 523

"Demonstrated generality"   Evidence that the effect appeared in instances where it was expected within the limits of generality provided by the study and did not show where it should not have. It is in quotation marks since generality can only be inferred from illustrations of it. 180

Demonstrated result   Evidence that four conditions were met: (1) the evidence was accepted as authentic, (2) cause preceded or was concomitant with effect, (3) an effect occurred and was sensed—if sensed by inferential statistics, these were correctly applied and interpreted—and (4) the effect was congruent with the expectations created by the explanation, hypothesis, prediction, or model. 145

Dependent variable   A variable presumed to be affected by a treatment or by an independent variable. 25

Derived score   Standard scores in which the mean and the standard deviation have been changed to numbers chosen for ease of interpretation or computation. Also called *scaled scores*. 403

Description   The perception, naming, organizing, and verbally portraying of a situation, person(s), culture or behavior to highlight its important features, to put those features in context, and to show the interrelations among them. Often gives access to phenomena readers are unlikely to directly experience. 32

Design   A translation of questions, hypotheses, or models into choices of subjects, situations, treatments, observation or measurement, basis for sensing attributes or changes, and procedure so that greater understanding or validation of the former results. 23

Differences (method of)   A situation in which a phenomenon occurs and one in which it does not occur are exactly alike save for one circumstance in the former. The circumstance in which they differ is presumed to be causally related to the phenomenon. 150

Diffusion   Spread of a treatment to the control group, a rival explanation; spread of a finding to the people who can make use of it. 520

Disconfirmation   The process of trying to invalidate a proposition. Causal relations can never be proved; there may always be some as yet untested circumstances under which the relationship does not hold. With each successful test, the relation is said to have escaped disconfirmation. 132

Disinterestedness   Ignoring personal advantage when interpreting data. 54

Dogmatic authority See *authority*. 50

Double-barreled questions Two questions rolled into one, making it impossible to determine to which the respondents formulated their answers. 366

Double-blind procedures Neither the subject nor the treatment administrator knows whether the treatment being given is a placebo or the actual treatment. 521

Effect size The size of an effect in standard deviation units. The average of the effect sizes or correlations in a meta-analysis. 556

Elite bias The tendency of a data gatherer to chose sources such as individuals in an organization in positions of authority, persons who are better dressed in a shopping mall, those living in safe and non threatening areas and the like. 264

Emergent study The focus of the study emerges during the course of working on it instead of being known and targeted from the outset. 238

Emic view The view of a qualitative researcher seeking to see and understand the world as it appears and is understood by those being studied. That view often differs significantly from the etic view, the "reality" as seen by an independent observer. 235

Empirical keying How each answer is scored is determined by which answers given by some criterion group discriminate group members from non-members. 441

Equivalence reliability Evidence that a test measures consistently across different but equivalent forms. 436

Estimation The process in statistical inference whereby a confidence interval is constructed around an observed value within which the population value is presumed to lie with a confidence expressed by odds (such as 19 to 1). 460

Ethical standards Rules that set limits on what can be done in good faith in a study; one of three constraints on research (see also *code of ethics*). 197

Ex post facto **studies** See *after-the-fact natural experiments*. 537

Evaluation Determination of the worth or value of something in order to decide whether to continue it, how to improve it, or how to adjust it to the needs of a certain clientele or management. 588

Expert-judgment evaluation Judgments by experts of the value or worth of something. 593

Explanation (rationale, theory, or point of view) As detailed a description of a phenomenon as current knowledge permits that indicates the relationship among variables. Causal and moderating roles are attributed to variables or to a sequence of events that lead to a result or effect. A description of a part of the causal chain that resulted in the appearance of a behavior or phenomena—usually its most immediate links. 64

Explanation credibility The plausibility of the explanation advanced for a phenomenon. 139

Explanation generality The generality that is claimed, implied, or must be inferred from the study's problem statement. 176

Exploration Exploration may take place in the search for a problem, probing different aspects of a phenomenon to find aspects not previously studied. It may also occur in the later stages of a study where the data is probed to find what else it can tell us beyond the findings originally sought. 32

External validity The capacity of a study to support inferences on the applicability of the findings to other persons, situations, measures, and times. 137

External validity (GP) The generalizing power (GP) of a study; the power of a study to permit inferences regarding the generality of the findings. 137

Face validity The appearance of being a valid test for a particular purpose. 428

Factor analysis Clustering the variables most highly correlated with each other in a table intercorrelating tests, persons, or situations with each other, into homogeneous groups called "factors." Then making inferences regarding the nature of the constructs measured by the factors from the variables that are central to a factor's statistical composition. 430

Factorial design A design in which every combination of variables in the study is provided a separate group from which data on their effect can be gathered. 535

Fieldnotes   The observer's records of what has been observed. 266

Fish-scale analogy   Knowing judgments made by each person in sequence extending from the researcher to laypersons. Each, being less expert than the previous person, looks at the evidence presented by previous judges and determines whether to accept their judgment. 44

Focus group   A panel, selected to be representative of a population, interviewed on a topic of interest. Probes determine the popularity of various comments and points of view and the depth of feeling toward them. There may also be trials of material to determine how the panel's reactions could be changed. 295

Focused interview   Interview in which the respondent is allowed to set the initial course but is increasingly focused on the researcher's agenda as the interview progresses. 291

Formative evaluation   Evaluation intended to provide information that can be used during the development of a project to guide progress toward its goals. 589

Framing of questions   Stating a question in such a way that the respondent understands and reacts to the question exactly as intended. 367

Frequency distribution   A graphic portraying the frequency with which each score occurred in a set of data, the scores being arranged in order from low to high. 392

Functionally equivalent groups   Groups that function as though they were identical to each other in every way that is relevant to the experiment. 500

Funnel-sequenced questionnaire   A questionnaire that, like the focused interview, begins broadly and narrows to the target of interest. 364

Gaining entry   Obtaining permission to observe a situation from the people in authority as well as from the people to be observed. 252

Gatekeepers   Individuals who give approval to conduct a study, such as institution administrators, school boards, and department heads. Also persons who approve the presentation of a study to an audience, such as editors and convention scheduling committees. 51, 253

Generality   The ability to generalize to subjects, situations, treatments, measures, times, study designs, and procedures other than those used in a given study. 160

Generalization   A statement of the relationship between two or more variables that holds across a variety of persons, places, times, measures or procedures. 71, 137

Goal-based evaluation   Use of the goals of the project as a basis for evaluation and for determining whether they have been met. 594

Goal-free evaluation   Inferring the goals of a project from observations and measures of what has occurred as a result of the project. These goals, and the success with which they have been achieved, are compared with the intended goals. 596

Going native   Researchers physically and emotionally cease being detached observers and actively join the community being studied. 318

Grounded theory   An explanation of phenomena based on (grounded in) observations of it and accounting for the events observed. 260

Hawthorne effect   The subject's perceived feeling of being special as a result of being part of an experiment and the resulting impact on the effectiveness of treatment. A rival explanation. 520

Hypothesis   A hunch or guess about a phenomenon or relationship that may or may not be true but which, as it is operationalized, serves as the basis for a study. Usually it is an extension of previous research or observation. 4

Hypothesis guessing   Subjects' guessing what response from them the researcher expects and reacting accordingly. 520

Hypothesis testing   The process in statistical inference whereby the likelihood that an observed value, such as a difference between means, is typical of what might be expected as a result of random sampling variation and chance error (at certain odds, such as 19 to 1, the Type I error we allow) or is atypically larger and therefore the result of some other influence. 465

Independent variable   A variable believed to be a cause; normally used to designate a variable that cannot be manipulated through treatment. 25

Inferential statistics   Statistics that allow us to estimate population values and to test hypotheses that the results of a study differ from the population value only by amounts typical of random sampling variation and chance error. 455

Inflation of probabilities   Inflation occurs with multiple tests of statistical significance. Without steps to prevent it, the more statistical tests that are made on a set of data, the greater the likelihood one or more tests will be significant due solely to chance. Therefore, the actual significance level is inflated over the stated significance level. 490

Informants   Persons selected for their sensitivity, knowledge, and insights into their situation, their willingness to talk about it, and their ability to provide access to new situations. 264

Informed consent   Consent freely given by an individual who has been informed of the nature of the study, understands its procedures, knows who to contact if harmed, and understands he or she can withdraw at any time without malice. 208

Institutional constraints   Constraints imposed on a research study by institutions cooperating with the study's requirements while either keeping their regular program going or interrupting it minimally. 198

Institutional review boards   Boards established by institutions receiving federal research funds that are responsible for ensuring either that individuals involved in the research will not suffer any harmful consequences or that if the possibility of some risk is involved, the benefits outweigh the risks. 206

Instrument decay   A change in the way a measure or observation schedule is used or scored over the course of a study that might provide an explanation for a phenomenon other than the one proposed. In qualitative studies, a change over time in observational point of view or attitude toward the people observed that affects the nature of one's observation in ways one would be concerned about if aware of it. Written about in memos when suspected. 317

Instrumentation decay by treatment interaction   Treatment-induced change in the way an instrument, measure, or observation schedule is used over the course of a study. 518

Interaction   Potentiation or weakening of the effects of an independent variable or treatment due to the presence of another variable or condition. 135

Internal consistency reliability   Evidence that the items of a test are homogeneous, measure a single construct, and correlate highly with one another. A requirement for a score to be interpretable. 436

Internal validity   "The capacity of a study to link [its] operational definitions of cause and effect" (Campbell and Stanley, 1963). 137

Internal validity (LP)   The power of a study to link the variables in a relationship—linking power (LP). 138

Internal validity (LP) and external validity (GP), relative weighting of   Balancing the study's capacity to link cause and effect with its capacity to show the generality of the relationship. Internal validity (LP), linking cause and effect, can be strengthened by tight controls and/or using a laboratory. These characteristics decrease external validity (GP), generality, which is strengthened by using natural—usually field—conditions. 194

Interrater reliability   A measure of how closely two raters of the same phenomena agree. It is better measured by an intraclass correlation rather than a Pearson product-moment correlation. 340

Interval scale   A scale whose units are presumed to be equal (for example, the difference between a score of 8 and 9 is the same as that between 20 and 21). 390

Invisible college   A group of researchers interested in the same problem who communicate regularly with one another by exchanging drafts of articles, corresponding or phoning regarding problems, or participating in an electronic bulletin board. 41

Item analysis   A method of improving a test by correlating the items with either the total score or a criterion measure. Reliability is improved by correlating with the total score, keeping only items that correlate highly with it and changing others to be like those kept. Validity is improved by a similar process, except that a valid measure (criterion) is used instead of the total score. 440

Item difficulty index   An index indicating how hard a test item is; usually the percentage of students correctly answering a test item. 440

Item discrimination index   An index indicating the correlation between the item score (say 1 for correct, 0 for wrong) and some criterion. To improve validity, the criterion is some index of success outside the test; to improve internal consistency reliability, the total test score is used. 441

Judgmental sampling   Samples chosen nonrandomly in such a way as to be representative. 172

Keyword indexing   Indexing with a controlled vocabulary descriptive of a field. The target is found by determining the references at intersection of two or more keywords descriptive of it. 114

Knowing judgment   Each individual's judgment of the acceptability of a knowledge claim, or in the case of the original research, a judgment about the appropriate interpretation of the data. 40

Kuder-Richardson reliability   A measure of internal consistency reliability. 437

Letter of transmittal   The letter accompanying a questionnaire that is intended to motivate the respondent to complete and return it. 368

Linear relationship   A relationship between two variables best described by a straight line; that is, as one variable increases, the other consistently either increases or decreases proportionately. Also called a *straight-line relationship*. 411

Local history   An event that occurs during the course of a treatment that could have the same effect as the treatment. A rival explanation. 515

Longitudinal studies   Studies of change in a particular individual or group over time. 354

Management-oriented evaluation   An evaluation intended to serve the information needs of management in contrast to serving the needs of all stakeholders in a project. 596

Masking   A form of control whereby an unwanted variable's effect is mitigated by a stronger variable that blocks the unwanted one from perception by subjects. 506

Matrix   A display in row and column form that facilitates the analysis of qualitative research data by showing the relationship between two categorical variables. For example, the display might have sites across the top, roles of persons down the side, and relevant information from persons in those roles at each of the sites in the cells of the matrix. 314

Maturation   Changes that occur in subjects over the course of a study that, because they could also have caused the effect, are confounded with it; includes such changes as growing tired or bored as well as taller and heavier. A rival explanation. 516

Mean   The arithmetic average of a set of scores. 397

Median   The middle score of a set of scores; also, the second quartile. 396

Member checking   A qualitative researcher asks one or more individuals being studied to read and give reactions to the researcher's interpretations of data on that group. 340

Memos   Notes written by a qualitative-method observer to record some insight or some aspect of a process that may be helpful in the interpretation of the data. 272

Meta-analysis   Combining the statistical results of studies of the same question into a single result to enhance statistical power, to find the average size of the effect, to determine the nature of the relationship, and to find how the relationship is affected by other variables. 555

Mode   The most frequently occurring score in a set of scores. 396

Mortality   Changes in the composition of the sample due to individuals dropping out of the study before its completion that could also have caused the effect and are confounded with it. A rival explanation. 317

Mortality by treatment interaction   Changes in the composition of the sample due to reactions to treatment that caused some individuals to drop out of the study before its completion. A rival explanation. (See also *mortality*.) 523

Multi-measure, multiple-method procedure (also **multi-trait, multi-method evidence**)   Measurement or observation of the same phenomenon or attribute with different measures each of which uses different methods of assessment. This triangulation determines whether characteristics of the measure or of the method of measuring or observation are affecting the result. 143, 431

Multiple research methods   The use of multiple research methods to study a problem by taking advantage of the particular strengths of each method and using those that complement each other. 619

Multiple-treatment interaction   Earlier treatments effect later ones. A rival explanation. 522

Multi-site studies   Studies of the same phenomena at different research sites which are usually chosen so as to strengthen assertions of generality. 343

Naturalistic evaluation   Use of the qualitative approach in evaluation to determine the goals of the project as in goal-free evaluation as well as to assess the needs and expectations of the stakeholders in the projects. Sometimes called *responsive evaluation* because it is intended to respond to the information needs of the latter. 599

Necessary condition   Conditions that must be present for an effect to occur. 131

Negative cases   In qualitative research, the search for cases that allow one to find the boundary within which a generalization holds from where it does not. Once the boundary is determined, it is often possible to modify the generalization to increase its generality. 261

Nested designs   Factorial designs that reduce the number of groups to the combinations in which one is particularly interested and allow confounding of variables in the remainder. 536

Nominal level (of measurement)   The grouping of like individuals or units (such as institutions) into categories. 390

Nondirective approach   The interviewer rephrases and reflects the interviewee's responses, especially to draw out the underlying feelings and central significance of each response. 292

Nonequivalent control group design   Experimental design in which individuals are not randomly assigned to groups so there is no assurance that they are equivalent. Usually uses preformed groups such as schoolrooms. 510

Nonlinear relationship   A relationship between two variables best described by other than a straight line; as one variable increases, the other does not consistently either increase or decrease, or if it does, it does not do so proportionately (for example, a distribution best described by a U or J). 412

Nonparametric statistics   Inferential statistics that assume random assignment or random categorization as a basis for determining probabilities rather than random sampling. 486

Nonparticipant observation   An observer is present in the research situation and is known by those present to be there to observe. 252

Nonprobability sampling   Any sampling procedure that does not involve random sampling at some stage. 163

Nonrespondents   A person who does not return questionnaires or other instruments and must be recontacted to obtain a large enough sample and to determine whether such persons' responses differ from those whose responses have been received. 373

Norm-referenced tests   Tests on which performance is interpreted in the context of the performance of a group with whom it is reasonable to compare the individual (for example, achieving at the 3.4 grade level). 438

Normal frequency distribution   A frequency distribution with a particular shape produced by the action of probability in a chance event over an infinite number of trials. Often used as an approximation or model for test score distributions. 402

Null hypothesis   The observed value is the result of randomness and chance error; that is, there is a null (no) difference between the value and what typically results from chance error; the value derived from a sample is typical of those in its sampling distribution for samples of that size. 466

Objectivity   The similarity with which two or more judges would evaluate or record a test performance or observation. 340, 442

Observation and measures   The means by which the effect is sensed, assurance is gained that the treatment was given as intended, or the nature of variables that may have a moderating impact on the effect is sensed. 67

Obtrusiveness   The change in a typical pattern of events, schedule, or situation such that it has the same effect as the treatment or independent variable and is perceived as sufficiently significant by subjects as to affect their actions (e.g., an unfamiliar adult visiting a kindergarten class). A rival explanation. 519

One-group pretest-posttest design   Experimental design in which a group is measured, treated, and then remeasured to determine change. 510

One-tailed test   A test on which all Type I errors are assumed to be in one tail of the sampling distribution; a directional hypothesis forecasts the direction of the expected effect (for example, the experimental group mean greater than the control group mean). 470

Operational definition   The definition of a construct formed by the operations of measurement or by the conditions brought about by the situation or treatment. 138, 425

Order of questions   Sequence in which the respondent is to respond to items in a questionnaire. Important, because prior questions can affect later responses. 364

Ordinal level (of measurement)   Individuals or units (such as institutions) are ranked in order on some characteristic. 390

Organized skepticism   The process whereby new knowledge claims in science are routinely challenged by other researchers to determine their validity. 54

Oversampling   Taking more samples from a stratum than its proportional share of the sample. 168

Panel sample   A panel chosen so as to be representative of a population; often used in order to study change over time. 355

Parameter   A statistic descriptive of some aspect of a population, such as the mean or the standard deviation. 460

Parsimony, principle of   Using the simplest of the several equally possible explanations for a phenomenon. 55

Participant observation   Circumstances wherein individuals are aware that they are being observed, but the observer, by participating in the situation as normally as he or she can, tries to become as unobtrusive as possible. 251

Participant-oriented evaluation   Involvement of the stakeholders in the evaluation in a range of roles extending from advisors to the process to having them actually carry out the evaluation, the evaluator acting as teacher and consultant. 599

Pearson product-moment correlation   A number between −1.00 and +1.00 indicative of the strength of relationship between two variables where zero indicates no relation. Positive correlations indicate the variables vary directly; negative ones, inversely. At ±1 they vary perfectly proportionally; between ±1.00 and zero, they vary increasingly imperfectly as zero is approached. 406

Peer checking   Others recode to check coding consistency. 340

Percentile   The percentage of cases in a frequency distribution that fall below that score (for example, the median is the 50th percentile because 50% of cases have lower scores than the median). 404

Permuterm indexing   Using the important words in journal article titles to form an index that displays these words in all possible pairs. 114

Pilot testing   Trying out an instrument or a procedure to determine problems before the actual study is begun. 372

Placebo   A treatment that is just like the actual treatment but lacks the active ingredient. It produces a placebo effect which in some instances may be both real and strong. 510

Point estimation   Estimation of a population characteristic as a specific value such as the mean in contrast to giving an interval within which the population value lies at a certain confidence level. 462

Population   The total group to whom a researcher expects to be able to generalize and which is to be represented in a sample. 160

Posttest-only control group design   Experimental design in which individuals are randomly assigned to experimental and control groups, treated, and then measured to determine effect. 510

Power of a statistical test   The capacity of a statistical test to avoid a Type II error; to avoid missing statistical significance when a more sensitive test would find it. 479

Practical significance   A difference large enough to cause some practical consequence, in contrast to *statistical significance*, which may be so small it has no practical consequences. 485

Precedence of cause   Evidence that a cause precedes or occurs simultaneously with an effect. 145

Predictive validity   Evidence that a test correlates with a criterion obtained at an earlier time, before a selection decision or choice was made. 432

Presence of an effect   A necessary condition for inferring causation; the fact that an effect did indeed occur as indicated by one's measures or observations; often determined by inferential statistics. 145

Pretest-posttest control group design   Experimental design in which individuals are randomly assigned to experimental and control groups, measured before treatment, treated, and remeasured. 510

Primary sources   The original sources of data, facts, findings, theory; the publications of the original authors rather than quotation, summary, or paraphrase of the material by other authors. 106

Privacy   Individuals' right to restrict inquiries about themselves to those areas in which they knowingly and willingly provide access. 215

Probability sampling   A sampling procedure that involves random sampling at some stage. 163

Probe   A question or comment designed to cause the respondent to amplify a response or to jog the respondent's memory. 298

Procedure   The determination of who is administered what treatment as well as who is observed or measured and when and where all this is done. 67

Projective techniques   Techniques used to indirectly measure; what is being measured is not apparent. For instance, individuals may merely be asked to respond to the stimulus by telling what is seen, telling a story about it, or giving the first response that comes to mind. 364

Proportional stratified sampling   A method wherein the percentage of cases randomly selected from a strata is the same as the percentage that the strata represents in the population. 167

Purposive sampling   Samples assembled by intentionally seeking individuals or situations likely to yield new instances and greater understanding of a dimension or concept of interest. Also used to test the generality of a coding category, finding, or principle. Employed in analytic induction. 172

Qualitative point of view   The observer takes the stance of trying to learn how the people being observed see their situation, how they understand it, what it means to them. Also called the *phenomenological point of view*. 235

Qualitative research   Research that describes phenomena in words instead of numbers or measures and usually uses induction to ascertain what is important in phenomena. 5

Quantitative research   Research that describes phenomena in numbers and measures instead of words; the focus of the research is usually predetermined and deduced from prior research. 5

Quartile   The point below which one-quarter of a set of scores fall (first quartile, or Q_1), half the scores fall (second quartile, median, or Q_2), or three-quarters of the scores fall (third quartile, or Q_3). 400

Question, hypothesis, model   The link in the chain of reasoning that is forged out of the rationale, theory, or point of view. It focuses the direction of the study in a quantitative study and emerges from the data in a qualitative study. Whether a question, a hypothesis, or a model emerges depends on the extent of the information available. 65

Quota sampling   Using the frequency distribution of characteristics in the population to choose a sample such that those characteristics are in the same proportion in the sample as they are in the population. 172

Random assignment Assigning individuals to control and experimental groups, or assigning groups to control and experimental treatments, by a random process. 507

Random sampling Choosing samples by chance in such a way that every sample has an equal chance of being selected each time a sample is drawn. 164

Range The distance from the lowest to the highest score. 400

Ratio scales Interval scales with a true zero point that represents the complete lack of what is being measured. 390

Reactivity Change in individuals' behavior due to their perception that they are part of an experimental study. 519

Reasoning authorities See *authority*. 50

Regression The prediction of one variable from another variable. Alternatively, scores of individuals selected into a group, with a less than perfectly reliable measure, on the basis of being low (or high) on a characteristic will, on average, move closer to the mean of the original group from which they were selected, on retesting. Also, a phenomenon measured at a peak will appear to have declined on remeasure (or rebounded if first measured at a trough). 413, 513

Reliability Evidence of consistency of measurement over items, over tests, or over time. 435

Replicable result A judgment as to whether the result would be replicable with new choices of any or all the facets of the study design or whether the results are dependent on some or all of the design choices, thus limiting generality. 181

Replication Repeating a study, ideally with different: research methods, investigators, situations, and samples of persons, to see whether the original findings reappear. 42

Researcher expectancy effect Researchers or judges, knowing what to expect, believe they perceive it. 521

Residuals (method of) Subtract from any situation all aspects known to be the cause only of phenomena other than the one of interest, and the cause of the phenomenon of interest is in the residual. 151

Resource allocation The allocation of resources to achieve the purposes of a study, especially to achieve the appropriate balance of internal validity (LP) to external validity (GP) and to build a strong chain of reasoning. 195

Resource limits The limits on resources available for a study, especially limits on the researchers' time and energy, a constraint. 199

Response sets Tendency of respondents to answer questions in certain directions (such as "yes" or "true") regardless of the actual question. 376

Responsive evaluation See *naturalistic evaluation*. 599

Restriction of range If the range of values on which a correlation coefficient is based is restricted in comparison with the typical situation of which it is intended to be an estimate, the estimate will be too low. 410

Restrictive explanations (conditions) eliminated Conditions of the study that restrict the generality that may be inferred from the evidence. In the interests of greater generality, it is desirable that these be eliminated in the study's design. 180

Rival explanations eliminated Explanations other than the intended one proposed to explain the phenomenon or effect under study. A major purpose of experimental design is their elimination. 147

Robust Describes a statistical test that can be accurately interpreted even when the conditions of its use violate certain of its assumptions. Alternatively an effect strong enough to appear under a variety of conditions. 487

Sample A means by which cases are taken from a population in such a way as to accurately represent the variables of interest in that population; thus a study of the sample may economically be substituted for a study of the entire population. 160

Sample surveys The gathering of questionnaire or interview data from a sample drawn so as to be representative of a population of interest. 353

Sampling distribution of the mean   The frequency distribution of means formed from the means of repeated samples from a population. 460

Sampling frame   An enumeration of all the units in the population or in a cluster from which the sample is to be drawn. 163

Sampling unit   The units that make up the population and are chosen in a sampling procedure. 165

Saturated   Describes a situation in qualitative research where so many examples of a dimension or concept of interest have been gathered that nothing new is expected to be learned from additional ones. 260

Scaled score   See *derived score*. 403

Scatterplot   The plot of scores developed when one variable is measured on the vertical axis (usually the dependent variable) and the other on the horizontal axis. Also known as a *scatter diagram* or *scattergram*. 406

Secondary sources   Quotation, paraphrase, or summary of data, facts, findings, or theory by other than the original authors. 43, 105

Selection   Assignment of individuals to groups in such a way that any characteristic that could have caused the effect is not equated between the groups and is therefore confounded with treatment. A rival explanation. 517

Selection by treatment interaction   Assignment of individuals to groups (often self-selection) because of the attractiveness or repulsiveness of the treatment in such a way that a characteristic that could have caused the effect is not equated between the groups and is therefore confounded with treatment. A rival explanation. 523

Selection-maturation interaction   A rival explanation wherein subjects selected for study are also likely to be more subject to change with time (grow more tired, anxious, taller, heavier, and so forth) and together the selection and susceptibility create an effect confounded with the treatment. A rival explanation. 519

Semi-interquartile range   Half the distance from the first quartile to the third quartile. 400

Sensitivity of a statistical test   See *power of a statistical test*. 479

Sequential sampling   Taking successive samples until the required precision of measurement and stability of the data across samples is attained. 174

Significance level   The frequency or probability (e.g., 1 time in 19, or 5%) with which one is willing to be wrong in saying that a value is atypical and not due to chance error (i.e., statistically significant) when it *is* the result of chance error. 468

Situation   The situation wherein the data are collected; often determined by where the subjects are. 66

Skewness   A deviation of the frequency distribution from symmetry. Positive skewness has a long tail to the right toward the high scores; negative skewness, the opposite. 397

Snowball sampling   The identification of the members of a group by asking individuals who would be expected to know the members to identify them, continuing until no new information is being obtained. Also called *chain-referral sampling*. 173

Social consequences of research   This is an increased concern in all research. It is reflected in qualitative work in some researchers' desire to empower those studied, leave them better off as a result of the study and avoid harming them in any way. In quantitative research it is reflected in the balancing of the positive and negative consequences of testing. It is expected to be included in the current revision of the test standards. 344

Solomon four-group design   A combination of the pretest-posttest experimental and control group design with the posttest-only experimental and control group design. 511

Spearman-Brown formula   A formula for estimating the reliability of a test if it were lengthened or shortened (for example, doubled in length or halved). It is used with split-half reliabilities to estimate the reliability of the full test from the intercorrelation of the halves. 452

Stability and equivalence reliability   The consistency of scores from testing on one form of an instrument with a later testing on an alternate form of the instrument. 438

Stability reliability   Evidence that a test measures consistently over time. 436

Stakeholders   Individuals who are affected by the outcome of a project and who therefore have a stake in how it is developed, implemented, and evaluated. 588

Standard deviation   A measure of the variability or spread of scores; the square root of the average of the squared deviations of the scores from the mean of the set of scores. 401

Standard error of measurement   A measure of the reliability or consistency of measurement. 450

Standard error of the mean   The standard deviation of the sampling distribution of the mean. 461

Standard score   A raw score divided by its standard deviation. Also known as the *z-score*. 403

Stanine score   A test score (one of a *standard nine*, from whence comes the name). Each stanine score is a half deviation wide, and nine of them cover the score range since the top and bottom scores are open-ended. 405

Statistical significance   Evidence that a value is atypical in a sampling distribution, that it would not typically result from the operation of random sampling variation and chance error and that it would appear with a rarity expressed by long odds such as 19 to 1 or 100 to 1. 469

Stem-and-leaf diagram   Tabulation of score in small score intervals down a vertical line. See Figure 19.1. 392

Stimulated recall   Audio- or videotaping the respondent during a session and later playing back the tape, stopping it, and asking the respondent to explain his or her thoughts and feeling at that time. 266

Stratified sampling   Dividing a population into groups (strata) on the basis of some variable such that the groups are more homogeneous on the variable of interest than in a simple random sample. Units are randomly sampled from within strata, usually proportionally to the size of a stratum in relation to the total sample. 166

Structured interview   An interview in which the questions and their order are predetermined. 288

Study-effect meta-analysis (SEMA)   A meta-analysis in which each study is allowed to contribute only one result to the combination determining average effect size. Studies are weighted in relation to sample size in computing the mean. 560

Subjects   The units (usually individuals, but can be classes, groups, or institutions) that are the subject of investigation. 66

Sufficient conditions   All those conditions, in the presence of which the effect occurs. 131

Summative evaluation   Evaluation intended to determine the value or worth of something. 589

Systematic sampling   Choosing every *n*th unit (for example, every tenth person) from the sampling frame. 168

Table of specifications   A matrix (row and column) display of the specifications for an instrument, test, or measure. Desired behaviors or actions are usually listed across the top, and content, or sites down the side. Cell entries are the test items or measures which assess the combinations of the actions or behaviors with the content or sites. The number of items in a cell indicates the relative emphasis to be given that combination in the total instrument. 362

Tailored tests   Tests that are adjusted to the appropriate level of difficulty for each subject by having each subject who passes an item branched to a more difficult item and each who fails branched to an easier one. Also called *adaptive tests*. 444

Tandem interviewing   Conducting an interview as a team of two. 294

Testing   Changes in scores resulting from familiarity with a test taken two or more times; the resulting higher scores are confounded with treatment. A rival explanation. 512

Testing-treatment interaction   Changes in the scores of individuals resulting from individuals having been sensitized to aspects of treatment by a pretest subsequently paying greater attention to those aspects during treatment and thus scoring differently on retest than they otherwise would. A rival explanation. 523

Theory-based studies   The questions, hypotheses, model, explanation, rationale, or point of view on which the study is based grow out of a theory which is set forth as the explanation for some phenomenon. 55

Threats to validity   See *rival explanations* eliminated. 147, 511

Time-series designs   Experimental designs that follow subjects through time, treating and remeasuring them to determine changes. 532

Trade-off   A gain in one aspect of a study at the cost of loss in another (for example, breadth versus depth–a general achievement test does a good job of assessing overall achievement in an area, but a poor job of diagnosing specific weakness in it). 69

Translation fidelity   The faithfulness with which the terms in the question, hypothesis, or model are translated into the six facets of design. 141

Translation generality   A judgment of the extent to which the translation of the question, hypothesis, or model into the six design facets provide data to support the generality claimed or implied by the problem statement. 177

Treatment   A potential cause controlled by the investigator. Also may be called the independent variable. 24, 66

Treatment fidelity   Evidence that the treatment was administered as it was intended to be administered. 542

Trend studies   Studies of changes over time. 354

Triangulation   Determining the consistency of evidence gathered from different sources of data across time, space, or persons, by different investigators or different research methods. 275

Trustworthiness   The judged credibility of a qualitative research study based upon the appropriateness of the data gathering and analytic processes and their resulting interpretations. 337

Two-tailed test   A test in which Type I error may be found in either tail of the distribution; we do not have a directional hypothesis; we expect an effect but do not know its direction. 470

Type I error   The mistake of erroneously indicating that an effect is statistically significant when in fact it is the result of random sampling variation and chance error. 457

Type II error   The error of indicating that a given value is due to sampling variation and chance error when it is not. 457

Uncertainty reduction   The reduction that progressively occurs as a proposition is sufficiently validated that we can accept it as knowledge or act as though it were true. 47

Universal standards   Criteria governing research quality that apply to all researchers regardless of status, personal characteristics or institutional affiliation. 53

Unobtrusiveness   Administration of treatment or measures in such a way that they appear to be part of the situation normally expected by the subjects. 521

Unstructured interview   Interview in which the interviewers, taking their cue from previous responses, formulate and order questions on the spot to obtain the desired information. 288

Utilization   The use of evaluation or research results in an applied setting. 588

Validation   Data assembled in support of a hypothesis. Alternatively, a showing that an instrument measures what it is intended to measure. 4, 33

Validity   Evidence-based judgment that a test measures what it is intended to measure. 427

Variance   A measure of the variability of the scores in a frequency distribution; more specifically, the square of the standard deviation. 401

Variance-partitioning meta-analysis   A meta-analysis in which the variance of the effect is partitioned, as in analysis of variance, to determine the contribution of different variables to the effect. 561

References

Abelson, R. P. (1995). *Statistics as principled argument.* Hillsdale, NJ: Lawrence Erlbaum Associates.

Adair, J. D., Sharpe, D., & Huynh, C. (1989). Hawthorne control procedures in education experiments. A reconsideration of their use and effectiveness. *Review of Educational Research, 59,* 215–228.

Adams, J. T. (1976–78). *Dictionary of American history* (Vol. 8, rev. ed.). New York: Scribner.

Alberts, B., & Shine, K. (1994). Scientists and the integrity of research. *Science, 266,* 1660–1661.

Allen, M. S. (1962). *Allen Morphologizer.* Englewood Cliffs, NJ: Prentice-Hall.

Allison, G. T. (1971). *Essence of decision: Explaining the Cuban missile crisis.* Boston: Little, Brown.

Altrichter, H., Posch, P., & Somekh, B. (1993). *Teachers investigate their work.* London: Routledge.

American Council on Education. (1995). *Guidelines for computerized-adaptive test development and use in education.* Washington, DC: American Council on Education.

American Educational Research Association, American Psychological Association, National Council on Measurement in Education. (1985). *Standards for educational and psychological testing.* Washington, DC: American Psychological Association.

American Historical Association. (1961). *Guide to historical literature.* New York: Macmillan.

American Psychological Association, Committee on Ethical Standards for Psychology. (1951). Ethical standards in research. *American Psychologist, 6,* 436–443.

American Psychological Association. (1973). *Ethical principles in the conduct of research with human participants.* Washington, DC: American Psychological Association, Ad hoc Committee on Ethical Standards in Psychological Research.

American Psychological Association. (1987). *Casebook on ethical principles of psychologists.* Washington, DC: American Psychological Association.

American Psychological Association. (1982). *Ethical principles in the conduct of research with human participants.* Washington, DC: American Psychological Association.

American Psychological Association. (1994). *Publication manual of the American Psychological Association* (4th ed.). Washington, DC: American Psychological Association.

Anastasi, A., & Urbina, S. (1997). *Psychological testing* (7th ed.). Upper Saddle River, NJ: Prentice-Hall.

Anderson, L. W., & Sosniak, L. A. (Eds.). (1994). *Bloom's taxonomy: A forty-year retrospective.* Ninety-third Yearbook of the National Society for the Study of Education, Part II. Chicago: University of Chicago Press.

Anscombe, F. J. (1973). Graphs in statistical analysis. *American Statistician, 27*(1), 17–21.

Argyris, C., Putnam, R., & Smith, D. M. (1985). *Action science, concepts, methods and skills for research and intervention* (1st ed.). San Francisco: Jossey-Bass.

Aronow, E. Reznikoff, M., & Moreland, K. (1994). *The Rorschach technique: Perceptual basics, content interpretation, and applications.* Des Moines, IA: Longwood Division, Allyn & Bacon.

Asimov, I. (1977). The future of futurism. *American Way, 10*(4), 11–12.

Atkin, J. M. (1994). Teacher research to change policy: An illustration. In S. Hollingsworth & H. Sockett (Eds.), *Teacher research and educational reform* (pp. 103–120). Ninety-third Yearbook of the National Society for the Study of Education, Part I. Chicago: University of Chicago Press.

Atkins, T. V., & Ostrow, R. (Ed.). (1989). *Cross reference index: A guide to search terms.* New York: R. R. Bowker.

Austin, J. T., & Calderón, R. F. (1996). Writing APA Style. In F. T. L. Leong, & J. T. Austin (Eds.). *The psychology research handbook: A guide for graduate students and research assistants* (pp. 265–281). Thousand Oaks, CA: Sage.

Aydelotte, W. O. (1971). *Quantification in history.* Reading, MA: Addison-Wesley.

Aydelotte, W. O., Bogue, A. G., & Fogel, R. W. (1972). *The dimensions of quantitative research in history.* Princeton, NJ: Princeton University Press.

Babbie, E. R. (1992). *The practice of social research* (6th ed.). Belmont, CA: Wadsworth.

Bailey, K. B. (1994). *Typologies and taxonomies.* Belmont, CA: Sage.

Baker, G., & Chapman, D. (Eds.). (1962). *Man and society in disaster.* New York: Basic Books.

Balay, R. (Ed.). (1992) *Guide to reference books* (supplement to 10th ed.). Chicago: American Library Association.

Bandura, A. (1978). The self system in reciprocal determinism. *American Psychologist, 33,* 344–358.

Bangert-Drowns, R. L. (1986). Review of developments in meta-analytic method. *Psychological Bulletin, 99,* 388–399.

Baron, R. A., & Ransberger, V. M. (1978). Ambient temperature and the occurrence of collective violence: The long hot summer revisited. *Journal of Personality and Social Psychology, 36,* 351–360.

Barzun, J., & Graff, H. F. (1970, 1977, 1985, 1992). *The modern researcher* (2nd, 3rd, 4th, & 5th ed.). New York: Harcourt Brace Jovanovich.

Baumrind, D. (1985). Research using intentional deception: Ethical issues revisited. *American Psychologist, 40,* 165–174.

Baxter, P. M. (1993). *Psychology: A guide to reference and information sources.* Littleton, CO. Libraries Unlimited.

Becker, B. J. (1994). Combining significance levels. In H. Cooper and L. Hedges (Eds.), *The handbook of research synthesis* (pp. 215–230). New York: Russell Sage Foundation.

Becker, F. D. et al. (1973). College classroom ecology. *Sociometry, 36,* 514–525.

Becker, H. S. (1961). *Boys in white.* Chicago: University of Chicago Press.

Becker, H. S. (1963). *Outsiders: Studies in the sociology of deviance.* New York: Free Press.

Becker, H. S., Geer, B., & Hughes, E. C. (1968). *Making the grade: The academic side of college life.* New York: Wiley.

Begley, S. (1997). The science wars. *Newsweek* (April 21), 54–57.

Behrens, J. T., & Smith, M. L. (1996). Data and data analysis. In D. C. Berliner, & R. C. Calfee (Eds.). *Handbook of Educational Psychology* (pp. 945–989). NY: Simon & Schuster Macmillan.

Bellak, L. (1993). *The TAT, CAT, and SAT in clinical use* (5th ed.). Des Moines, IA: Longwood Division, Allyn & Bacon.

Bereiter, C. (1994). Implications of postmodernism for science, or science as progressive discourse. *Educational Psychologist, 29,* 3–12.

Berger, P. (1961). *The voice of solemn assemblies.* Garden City, NY: Doubleday.

Berk, R. A. (Ed.). (1986). *A guide to criterion-referenced test construction.* Baltimore, MD: Johns Hopkins University Press.

Berk, R. A., & Rossi, P. H. (1976). Doing good or worse: Evaluation research politically re-examined. *Social problems, 23* (Feb.), 337–349.

Berkowitz, L., & Donnerstein, E. (1982). External validity is more than skin deep. *American Psychologist, 37*(3), 245–257.

Bernstein, R. J. (1986). *Philosophical profiles.* Philadelphia: University of Pennsylvania Press.

Berrueta-Clement, J. R., Barnett, W. S., & Weikart, D. P. (1985). Changed lives—The effects of the Perry Preschool Program on youths through age 19. In L. H. Aiken & B. H. Kehrer (Eds.), *Evaluation Studies Review Annual* (Vol. 10, pp. 257–279). Beverly Hills, CA: Sage.

Bersoff, D. N. (1995). *Ethical conflicts in psychology.* Washington, DC: American Psychological Association.

Biernacki, P., & Waldorf, D. (1981). Snowball sampling, problem and technique of chain referral sampling. *Sociological Method and Research, 10*(12), 141–163.

Binet, A. (1912). *A method of measuring the development of the intelligence of young children.* Lincoln, IL: Courier.

Blair, R. C., & Higgins, J. J. (1980). A comparison of the power of Wilcoxon's rank-sum statistic to that of student's *t* statistic under various nonnormal distributions. *Journal of Educational Statistics, 5*(4), 309–335.

Blair, R. C., & Higgins, J. J. (1985). Comparison of the power of the paired samples *t* test to that of Wilcoxon's signed-rank test under various population shapes. *Psychological Bulletin, 97*(1), 119–128.

Bloom, B. S. (1954). The thought processes of students in discussion. In S. French (Ed.), *Accent on teaching: Experiments in general education.* New York: Harper.

Bloom, B. S. (1964). *Stability and change in human characteristics.* New York: Wiley.

Bloom, B. S. (Ed.). (1956). *Taxonomy of educational objectives: The cognitive domain.* New York: Longman.

Bloom, H. S., & Singer, N. M. (1979). Determining the cost-effectiveness of correctional programs: The case of Patuxent Institution. In L. Sechrest, S. G. West, M. A. Phillips, R. Redner, W. Yeaton (Eds.), *Evaluation Studies Review Annual* (Vol. 4). Beverly Hills, CA: Sage.

Bluebond-Langer, M. (1980). *The private worlds of dying children.* Princeton, NJ: Princeton University Press.

Bogdan, R. (1976). Conducting evaluation research—integrity intact. *Sociological Focus, 9,* 63–72.

Bogdan, R. C., & Biklen, S. K. (1982, 1992). *Qualitative research for education: An introduction to theory and methods* (1st & 2nd ed.). Boston: Allyn & Bacon.

Bogdan, R., Brown, M. A., & Foster, S. B. (1982). Be honest, but not cruel: Staff-parent conversation on a neonatal unit. *Human Organization, 4*(1), 6–16.

Borman, K. M., & O'Reilly, P. (1987). Learning gender roles in three urban U. S. kindergarten classrooms. *Child and Youth Services, 8,* 43–66.

Boruch, R. F., & Gomez, H. (1977). Sensitivity, bias, and theory in impact evaluations. *Professional Psychology, 9,* 411–434.

Boruch, R. F., McSweeney, A. J., & Soderstrom, E. J. (1978). Bibliography: Illustrative randomized field experiments for program planning, development, and evaluation: An illustrative bibliography. *Evaluation Quarterly, 2*(4), 655–695.

Boruch, R. F., & Wothke, W. (Eds.). (1985). *Randomization and field experimentation.* New Directions for Program Evaluation, No. 28. San Francisco: Jossey-Bass.

Bosk, C. L. (1979). *Forgive and remember: Managing medical failure.* Chicago: University of Chicago Press.

Bouchard, Jr., T. J. (1976). Field research methods: Interviewing, questionnaires, participant observation, systematic observation, unobtrusive measures. In M. D. Dunnette (Ed.), *Handbook of industrial and organizational psychology* (pp. 363–413). Chicago: Rand McNally.

Boulding, K. E. (1968). *Beyond economics.* Ann Arbor: University of Michigan Press.

Bracht, G. H., & Glass, G. V. (1968). The external validity of experiments. *American Educational Research Journal, 5*(4), 437–474.

Bradbury, K. L., & Downs, A. (Eds.). (1981). *Do housing allowances work?* Washington, DC: Brookings Institution.

Breland, H. (1987). *Assessing writing skill.* New York: College Board Publications, College Entrance Examination Board.

Brennan, R. L. (1992). *Element of generalizability theory* (rev. ed.). Iowa City: American College Testing.

Brewer, J., & Hunter, A. (1989). *Multimethod research: A synthesis of styles.* Newbury Park, CA: Sage.

Brewer, J. G. (1978). *The literature of geography: A guide to its organisation and use* (2nd ed.). London: Clive Bingley.

Brickell, H. M. (1978). The influence of external political factors on the role and methodology of evaluation. In T. P. Cook, M. L. Del Rosario, K. M. Hennigan, M. M. Mark, & W. M. Trochim (Eds.), *Evaluation Studies Review Annual* (Vol. 3, pp. 94–98). Beverly Hills, CA: Sage.

Briggs, J. W. (1978). *An Italian passage: Immigrants to three American cities, 1890–1930.* New Haven, CT: Yale University Press.

Brinberg, D., & McGrath, J. E. (1985). *Validity and the research process.* Beverly Hills, CA: Sage.

Broad, W. (1983). Frauds from 1960 to the present. In B. K. Kilbourne (Ed.), *The dark side of science: Proceedings of the annual meeting of the Pacific Division.* American Association for the Advancement of Science, Vol. 1, Part 2. San Francisco. (ERIC ED 245 917.)

Broad, W., & Wade, N. (1983). *Betrayers of the truth.* New York: Simon and Schuster.

Bronfenbrenner, U. (1977). Toward an experimental ecology of human development. *American Psychologist, 32,* 513–531.

Buchmann, M., & Floden, R. E. (1989). Research traditions, diversity and progress. *Review of Educational Research, 59,* 241–248.

Burks, B. S., Jensen, D. W., & Terman, L. M. (1930). *The promise of youth: Follow-up studies of 1000 gifted children,* Vol. 3. Stanford, CA: Stanford University Press.

Burton, M. A. B. (1988). School discipline: Have we lost our sense of purpose in our search for good method? (ERIC Document Reproduction Service No. ED 291 686.)

Cahalan, D. T. (1968–69). Correlates of respondent accuracy in the Denver validity survey. *Public Opinion Quarterly, 32,* 607–721.

Campbell, D. T. (1969). Definitional versus multiple operationism. *Et Al., 2,* 14–17. Also reprinted in E. S. Overman (Ed.) (1988), *Methodology and epistemology for social science: Selected papers Donald T. Campbell* (pp. 31–36). Chicago: University of Chicago Press.

Campbell, D. T. (1988). Descriptive epistemology: psychological, sociological and evolutionary. In E. S. Overman (Ed.), *Methodology and epistemology for social science: Selected papers Donald T. Campbell* (pp. 435–486). Chicago: University of Chicago Press.

Campbell, D. T., & Stanley, J. C. (1963). Experimental designs for research on teaching. In N. L. Gage (Ed.), *Handbook of research on teaching* (pp. 171–246). Chicago: Rand McNally.

Cannell, C. F. (1985a). Overview: Response bias and interviewer variability in surveys. In T. W. Beed & R. J. Stimson (Eds.), *Survey interviewing: Theory and techniques.* North Sydney, Australia: George, Allen and Unwin.

Cannell, C. F. (1985b). Experiments in the improvement of response accuracy. In T. W. Beed & R. J. Stimson (Eds.), *Survey interviewing: Theory and techniques.* North Sydney, Australia: George, Allen and Unwin.

Caracelli, V. J., & Greene, J. C. (1993). Data analysis strategies for mixed-method evaluation designs. *Educational Evaluation Policy Analysis, 15,* 195–207.

Carifio, J., & Biron, R. (1982). Collecting data anonymously: Further findings on the CDRGP technique. *Journal of Alcohol and Drug Education, 27*(2), 38–70.

Carlsmith, L., Merrill, J., & Anderson, C. A. (1979). Ambient temperature and the occurrence of collective violence: A new perspective. *Journal of Personality and Social Psychology, 37,* 337–344.

Carney, T. F. (1990). *Collaborative inquiry methodology.* Windsor, Ontario, Canada: University of Windsor, Department of Instructional Technology.

Carr, E. H. (1962). *What is history?* New York: Knopf.

Carr, W., & Kemmis, S. (1986). *Becoming critical: Education, knowledge and action research.* London: Falmer.

Casey, K. (1995). The new narrative research in education. In M. J. Apple (Ed.), *Review of Research in Education* (Vol. 21, pp. 211–253). Washington, DC: American Educational Research Association.

Casti, J. L. (1992). *Searching for certainty: What scientists can know about the future.* New York: Morrow.

Ceci, S. J., & Peters, D. (1984). How blind is blind review? *American Psychologist, 39,* 1491–1494.

Centra, J. A. (1977). *How universities evaluate faculty performance: A survey of department heads* (Report BRED–75–5bR). Princeton, NJ: Graduate Record Examinations Board. (ERIC Document Reproduction Service No. ED 157 445.)

Chase, W. G., & Simon, H. A. (1973). Perception in chess. *Cognitive Psychology, 4,* 55–81.

Chelimsky, E. (1991). On the social science contribution to governmental decision-making. *Science, 254,* 226–231.

Chen, P. T. (1996). Conducting telephone surveys. In F. T. L. Leong, & J. T. Austin (Eds.). *The psychology research handbook: A guide for graduate students and research assistants.* (pp. 139–154). Thousand Oaks, CA: Sage.

Cialdini, R. B., Borden, R. J., Thorne, A., Walker, M. R., Freeman, S., & Sloan, L. R. (1976). Basking in reflected glory: Three (football) field studies. *Journal of Personality and Social Psychology, 34,* 335–359.

Clausen, J. A. (1993). *American Lives: Looking back at the children of the Great Depression.* New York: Free Press (Macmillan).

Clotfelter, C. T., & Hahn, J. C. (1978). Assessing the national 55 m.p.h. speed limit. *Policy Sciences, 9,* 281–294.

Cohen, J. (1988). *Statistical power analysis for the behavioral sciences* (2nd ed.). New York: Academic Press.

Cohen, J. (1990). Things I have learned (so far). *American Psychologist, 45,* 1304–1312.

Cohen, M. R., & Nagel, E. (1934). *An introduction to logic and scientific method.* New York: Harcourt Brace.

Coleman, J. S. (1972). *Policy research in the social sciences.* Morristown, NJ: General Learning Press.

Coleman, J. S., Hoffer, T., & Kilgore, S. (1982). *High school achievement: Public, Catholic and private schools compared.* New York: Basic Books.

Collins, H., & Pinch, T. (1993). The golem: What everyone should know about science. New York: Cambridge University Press.

Collins, L. M., & Horn, J. L. (1991). *Best methods for analysis of change: Recent advances, unanswered questions, future directions.* Washington, DC: American Psychological Association.

Converse, J. M., & Presser, S. (1986). *Survey questions: Handcrafting the standardized questionnaire.* Quantitative Applications in the Social Sciences, No. 63. Beverly Hills, CA: Sage.

Cook, T. D., et al. (1992). *Meta-analysis for explanation: A casebook.* New York: Russell Sage Foundation.

Cook, T. D., & Campbell, D. T. (1979). *Quasi-experimentation: Design and analysis issues for field settings.* Chicago: Rand McNally.

Coombs, C. H., Dawes, R. M., & Tversky, A. (1981). *Mathematical psychology: An elementary introduction.* Englewood Cliffs, NJ: Prentice-Hall.

Cooper, H. M. (1985). Literature searching strategies of integrative research reviews. *American Psychologist, 40*(11), 1267–1269.

Cooper, H., & Hedges, L. V. (Eds.). (1994a). *The handbook of research synthesis.* New York: Russell Sage Foundation.

Cooper, H., & Hedges, L. V. (1994b). Research synthesis as a scientific enterprise. In H. Cooper & L. V. Hedges (Eds.), *The handbook of research synthesis* (pp. 3–14). New York: Russell Sage Foundation.

Cooper, H., Nye, B., Charlton, K., Lindsay, J., & Greathouse, S. (1996). The effects of summer vacation on achievement test scores: A narrative and meta-analytic review. *Review of Educational Research, 66,* 227–268.

Cooper, H., & Rosenthal, R. (1980). Statistical versus traditional procedures for summarizing research findings. *Psychological Bulletin, 87*(3), 442–449.

Corday, D. S. (1993). Strengthening causal interpretations of nonexperimental data: The role of meta-analysis. In L. Sechrest (Ed.). *Program evaluation: A pluralistic enterprise* (pp. 59–96). New Directions for Program Evaluation, No. 60. San Francisco: Jossey-Bass.

Corkhill, A. J., Bruning, R. H., Glover, J. A., & Krug, D. (1988). Advance organizers: Retrieval context hypotheses. *Journal of Educational Psychology, 80*(3), 304–311.

Coscarelli, W. C., & Stonewater, J. K. (1979). Understanding psychological styles in instructional development consultation. *Journal of Instructional Development, 3*(2), 16–22.

Cosper, R. (1972). Interviewer effect in a survey of drinking practices. *Sociological Quarterly, 13*(2), 228–236.

Cox, C. M. (1926). *The early mental traits of three hundred geniuses* (Vol. 2). Stanford, CA: Stanford University Press.

Coyne, J. A. (1995). Dobzhansky revisited. *Science, 269,* 991–992.

Crain, R. L. (1984). *Is nineteen really better than ninety-three?* Washingon, DC: National Institute of Education.

Crane, V. R., & Heim, A. W. (1950). The effects of repeatedly testing the same group on the same intelligence test. Part III, further experiments and general conclusions. *Quarterly Journal of Experimental Psychology, 2,* 82–197.

Crocker, L. and Algina, J. (1986). Introduction to Classical and Modern Test Theory. Orlando, FL: Harcourt Brace.

Crocker, L., Llabre, M., & Miller, M. D. (1988). The generalizability of content validity ratings. *Journal of Educational Measurement, 25,* 287–299.

Cronbach, L. J. (1975). Beyond the two disciplines of scientific psychology. *American Psychologist 30,* 116–127.

Cronbach, L. J. (1982). *Designing evaluations of educational and social programs* (1st ed.). San Francisco: Jossey-Bass.

Cronbach, L. J. (1990). *Essentials of psychological testing* (5th ed.). New York: Harper Collins.

Cronbach, L. J., & Furby, L. (1970). How we should measure "change"—or should we? *Psychological Bulletin, 74*(1), 68–80.

Cronbach, L. J., Gleser, G. C., Nanda, H., & Rajaratnam, N. (1972). *The dependability of behavioral measurements: Theory of generalizability of scores and profiles.* New York: Wiley.

Cronbach, L. J., Rogosa, D., Floden, R., & Price, G. G. (1976). *Analysis of covariance in nonrandomized experiments: Factors affecting bias.* Occasional papers, Stanford Evaluation Consortium. Stanford, CA: Stanford University, School of Education.

Cronbach, L. J., & Suppes, P. (1955). Construct validity in psychological tests. *Psychological Bulletin, 52,* 281–302.

Cronbach, L. J., & Suppes, P. (1969). *Research for tomorrow's schools: Disciplined inquiry for education.* New York: Macmillan.

Cronbach, L. J., et al. (1980). *Toward reform of program evaluation: Aims, methods and institutional arrangements.* San Francisco: Jossey-Bass.

Culler, R. E., & Holahan, C. J. (1980). Test anxiety and academic performance: The effects of study related behaviors. *Journal of Educational Psychology, 72*(1), 16–20.

Cunningham, N. J., & Stewart, N. R. (1983). Effects of discrimination training on counselor trainee response choice. *Counselor Education and Supervision, 23*(1), 46–61.

Cusick, P. A. (1980). Personal communication.

Dalton, M. (1959). *Men who manage: Fusions of feelings and theory in administration.* New York: Wiley.

Dalton, M. (1967). Preconceptions and methods of men who manage. In P. E. Hammond (Ed.), *Sociologists at work: Essay on the craft of social research* (pp. 50–95). New York: Basic Books.

Daniels, A. K. (1983). Self-deception and self-discovery in fieldwork. *Qualitative Sociology, 6*(3), 195–214.

Darley, J. M., & Batson, C. D. (1973). From Jerusalem to Jericho: A study of situational and dispositional variables in helping behavior. *Journal of Personality and Social Psychology, 27,* 100–108.

Davis, C., Back, K., & MacLean, K. (1977). *Oral history: From tape to type.* Chicago: American Library Association.

Davis, J. A. (1985). *The logic of causal order.* Quantitative Applications in the Social Sciences, No. 55. Beverly Hills, CA: Sage.

DeAngelis, T. (1988). Gerontologists lament practice-research gap. *The APA Monitor, 19*(2), 9.

DeBack, V., & Mentkowski, M. (1986). Does the baccalaureate make a difference: Differentiating nurse performance by education and experience. *Journal of Nursing Education, 25*(No. 7, September), 275–285.

Denmark, F. L. (1984). Zeigarnik effect. In R. J. Corsini (Ed.), *Encyclopedia of Psychology* (Vol. 3, pp. 484–485). New York: John Wiley.

Denzin, N. K. (1978). *The research act: A theoretical introduction to sociological methods* (2nd ed.). New York: McGraw-Hill.

Denzin, N. K., & Lincoln, Y. S. (Eds.). (1994). *Handbook of qualitative research.* Thousand Oaks: Sage.

Dichter, D. N. and Roznowski, M. (1996). Basic statistical analysis. In F. T. L. Leong, & J. T. Austin (Eds.). *The psychology research handbook: A guide for graduate students and research assistants* (pp. 208–218). Thousand Oaks, CA: Sage.

Dillman, D. A., Gallegos, J. G., & Frey, J. H. (1978). Reducing refusal rates for telephone interviews. *Public Opinion Quarterly 40,* 66–78.

Dispatch Case. (1986, April 16). *Chronicle of Higher Education,* p. 42.

Dollard, J., & Doob, L. W. (1939). *Frustration and aggression.* New Haven, CT: Yale University Press.

Duffy, G., & Roehler, L. (1990). The tension between information giving and instructional explanation and teacher change. In J. Brophy (Ed.), *Advances in research on teaching: Vol. 1, Teaching for meaningful understanding and self-regulated learning.* Greenwich, CT: JAI Press.

Duncan, O. D. (1984). *Notes on social measurement: Historical and critical.* New York: Russell Sage Foundation.

Edwards, J. A., & Lampert, M. D. (Eds.). (1993). *Talking data: Transcription and coding in discourse research.* Hillsdale, NJ: Erlbaum.

Einhorn, H. J., & Hogarth, R. M. (1986). Judging probable cause. *American Psychologist, 99,* 3–19.

Einstein, A., & Infeld, L. (1938). *The evolution of physics.* New York: Simon and Schuster.

Eisner, E. W. (1976). Educational connoisseurship and criticism: Their form and function in educational evaluation. *Journal of Aesthetic Education, 10*(3–4), 135–150.

Eisner, E. W. (1981). On the differences between scientific and artistic approaches to qualitative research. *Educational Researcher, 10* (April), 5–9.

Elesh, D., & Lefcowitz, M. J. (1977). The effects of the New Jersey-Pennsylvania negative income tax experiment on health and health care utilization. *Journal of Health and Social Behavior, 18*(4), 391–405.

Ellsworth, P. D. (1977). From abstract ideas to concrete instances: Some guidelines for choosing natural research settings. *American Psychologist, 32*(8), 604–615.

Elstein, A. S., Shulman, L. S., & Sprafka, S. A. (1978). *Medical problem solving: An analysis of clinical reasoning.* Cambridge, MA: Harvard University Press.

Elstein, A. S., Shulman, L. S., & Sprafka, S. A. (1990). Medical problem solving: A ten-year retrospective. *Evaluation & the Health Professions, 13,* 5–36.

Ely, M. (1991). *Doing qualitative research: Circles in circles.* Philadelphia: Falmer Press.

Emerson, J. D., & Hoaglin, D. C. (1983). Stem-and-leaf display. In D. C. Hoaglin, F. Mosteller, & J. W. Tukey (Eds.), *Understanding robust and exploratory data analysis.* New York: Wiley.

Erdos, P. L. (1970). *Professional mail surveys.* New York: McGraw-Hill.

Erickson, F. (1986). Qualitative methods of research on teaching. In M. Wittrock (Ed.), *Handbook of Research on Teaching* (3rd ed., pp. 119–161). New York: Macmillan.

Erickson, F., & Schultz, J. (1982). *The counselor as gatekeeper: Social interaction in interviews.* New York: Academic Press.

Ericson, D. P., & Ellett, F. S., Jr. (1982). Interpretation, understanding and educational research. *Teachers College Record, 83,* 497–513.

Everhart, R. B. (1977). Between stranger and friend: Some consequences of "long term" field work in schools. *American Educational Research Journal, 14*(1), 1–15.

Exner, J. E. (1986). *The Rorschach: A comprehensive system* (2nd ed.). New York: Wiley.

Fairweather, G. W., & Tornatzky, L. G. (1977). *Experimental method for social policy research* (1st ed.). New York: Pergamon.

Feldt, L. S., & Brennan, R. L. (1989). Reliability. In R. L. Linn (Ed.), *Educational Measurement* (3rd ed., pp. 105–146). New York: American Council on Education/Macmillan.

Ferber, R., & Verdoorn, P. J. (1962). *Research methods in economics and business.* New York: Macmillan.

Ferris, T. (1981). The spectral messenger. *Science, 81,* 2(Oct.), 66–71.

Fetterman, D. M. (1989). *Ethnography: Step by step.* Newbury Park, CA: Sage.

Fielding, N. G., & Fielding, J. L. (1985). *Linking data.* Qualitative Research Methods Series, Vol. 4. Beverly Hills, CA: Sage.

Fillenbaum, S. (1966). Prior deception and subsequent experimental performance: The "faithful" subject. *Journal of Personality and Social Psychology, 4,* 532–537.

Firestone, W. A. (1993). Alternative arguments for generalizing from data as applied to qualitative research. *Educational Researcher, 22*(4), 16–23.

Fischer, D. H. (1970). *Historian's fallacies: Toward a logic of historical thought* (1st ed.). New York: Harper & Row.

Fiske, D. W., & Fogg, L. (1990). But the reviewers are making different criticisms of my paper! *American Psychologist, 45,* 591–598.

Fitzsimmons, S. J., Herriott, R. E., Kidder, S. J., Miller, P. S., & Muse, D. N. (1973). The role of the on-site researcher in Project Rural. In S. J. Fitzsimmons, R. E. Herriott, S. J. Kidder, P. S. Miller, & D. N. Muse (Eds.), *Evaluation and documentation of experimental schools projects in small schools serving rural areas, Phase II plan* (Vol. 2–appendix, draft). Cambridge, MA: Abt Associates.

Flanders, N. A. (1970). *Analyzing teacher behavior.* Reading, MA: Addison Wesley.

Fleiss, J. L. (1994). Measures of effect size for categorical data. In H. Cooper & L. Hedges (Eds.), *The handbook of research synthesis* (pp. 245–260). New York: Russell Sage Foundation.

Florio, S. E. (1978). Learning how to go to school: An ethnography of interaction in a kindergarten first grade classroom. *Dissertation Abstracts International, 39,* 3239A. (University Microfilms No. 78–23, 676).

Foddy, W. (1993). *Constructing questions for interviews and questionnaires: Theory and practice in social research.* Cambridge, UK: Cambridge University Press.

Fontana, A., & Frey, J. (1994). Interviewing: The art of science. In N. Denzin & Y. Lincoln (Eds.), *Handbook of qualitative research* (pp. 361–376). Thousand Oaks, CA: Sage.

Frederiksen, N., Glaser, R., Lesgold, A., & Shafto, M. G. (Eds.). (1990). *Diagnostic monitoring of skill and knowledge acquisition.* Hillsdale, NJ: Erlbaum.

Freed, M. N. (Ed.), Hess, R. K., & Ryan, J. M. (1989). *The educator's desk reference: A sourcebook of educational information and research.* New York: Macmillan.

Freedman, D., Pisani, R. & Purves, R. (1997). *Statistics* (3rd ed.). New York: Norton.

Freire, P. (1970). *Pedagogy of the oppressed.* NY: Seabury.

Frey, J. H. (1989). *Survey research by telephone* (2nd ed.). Newbury Park, CA: Sage.

Friedel, F., & Showman, R. K. (Eds.). (1974). *Harvard Guide to American History* (Vol. 2, rev. ed.). Cambridge, MA: Belknap Press of Harvard University.

Friedman, J., & Weinberg, D. (Eds.). (1983). *The great housing experiment.* Beverly Hills, CA: Sage.

Frye, N. (1981). The bridge of language. *Science, 212,* 127–132.

Gable, R. K., & Keilty, M. B. W. (1994). *Instrument development in the affective domain: Measuring attitudes and values in corporate and school settings.* Hingham, MA: Kluwer Academic Publishers.

Gage, N. L. (1996). Confronting counsels of despair for the behavioral sciences. *Educational Researcher, 25,* (April), 5–15, 22.

Gale Research Company. (1983–). *Surveys, polls, censuses and forecasts directory.* Detroit, MI: Gale Research Co.

Gans, H. J. (1962). *The urban villagers: Groups and class in the life of Italian-Americans.* New York: Free Press of Glencoe.

Garvey, W. D., Lin, N., & Nelson, C. (1970). Communication in the physical and social sciences. *Science, 170,* 1166–1173.

Geertz, C. (1973). Thick description: Toward an interpretive theory of culture. In C. Geertz (Ed.), *The interpretation of cultures: Selected essays.* New York: Basic Books.

Gerberich, J. R. (1956). *Specimen objective test items: A guide to achievement test construction.* New York: Longmans, Green.

Gergen, K. J. (1994). *Toward transformation of social knowledge* (2nd ed.). Thousand Oaks, CA: Sage.

Gerstel, N. (1993). The life voyage. [Review of *American lives: Looking back at children of the Great Depression.*] *Science, 260,* 1157, 1159–1161.

Gesell, A., Ilg, F. L., Learned, J., & Ames, L. B. (1943). *Infant and child in the culture of today: The guidance of development in the home and nursery school.* New York: Harper.

Getzels, J. W. (1982). The problem of the problem. In R. M. Hogarth, (Ed.), *Question framing and response consistency.* New Directions for Methodology of Social and Behavioral Science, No. 11. San Francisco: Jossey-Bass.

Getzels, J. W., & Csikszentmihalyi, M. (1976). *The creative vision: A longitudinal study of problem findings in art.* New York: John Wiley.

Ghiselli, E. E. (1949). The validity of commonly employed occupational tests. *University of California Publications in Psychology, 5,* 253–258.

Ghiselli, E. E. (1955). The measurement of occupational aptitude. *University of California Publications in Psychology, 8,* 101–216.

Ghiselli, E. E. (1973). The validity of aptitude tests in personnel selection. *Personnel Psychology, 26*(4), 461–477.

Gladwin, C. H. (1989). *Ethnographic decision tree modeling.* Newbury Park: *Sage.*

Glaser, B., & Strauss, A. (1967). *The discovery of grounded theory: Strategies for qualitative research.* Chicago: Aldine Publishing.

Glaser, E. M., & Taylor, S. H. (1973). Factors influencing the success of applied research. *American Psychologist, 28,* 140–149.

Glass, G. V. (1976). Primary, secondary, and meta-analysis research. *Educational Researcher, 5*(10), 3–8.

Glass, G. V. (1995). The next-to-last word on meta-analysis [Review of *Handbook of Research Synthesis*]. *Contemporary Psychology, 40,* 736–738.

Glass, G. V., McGaw, B., & Smith, M. L. (1981). *Meta-analysis in social research.* Beverly Hills, CA: Sage.

Glass, G. V., & Smith, M. L. (1979). Meta-Analysis of research on class size and achievement. *Educational Evaluation and Policy Analysis, 1*(1), 2–16.

Glavin, J., & Quay, H. (1969). Behavior disorders. *Review of Educational Research, 39,* 83–102.

Glesne, C., & Peshkin, A. (1992). *Becoming qualitative researchers: An introduction.* White Plains, NY: Longman.

Goetz, J., & LeCompte, M. (1984). *Ethnography and qualitative design in educational research.* Orlando, FL: Academic Press.

Goffman, E. (1983). The interaction order. *American Sociological Review, 48,* 1–17.

Goldberger, A. S., & Cain, G. G. (1982). The causal analysis of cognitive outcomes in the Coleman, Hoffer and Kilgore Report. *Sociology of Education, 55*(2–3), 103–122.

Goldstein, J. H., & Arms, R. L. (1971). Effects of observing athletic contests. *Sociometry, 34,* 83–90.

Good, T., & Brophy, J. (1977). *Educational psychology: A realistic approach.* New York: Holt, Rinehart and Winston.

Gottfredson, S. D. (1978). Evaluating psychological research reports: Dimensions, reliability, and correlates of quality judgments. *American Psychologist, 33,* 920–934.

Gottschalk, L. A. (1956). *Understanding history.* New York: Knopf.

Gottschalk, L. A. (1961). The use of drugs in interrogation. In A. B. Biderman & H. Zimmer (Eds.), *The manipulation of human behavior* (pp. 96–141). New York: Wiley.

Gouldner, A. W. (1954). *Patterns of industrial bureaucracy.* Glencoe, IL: The Free Press.

Gove, P. P. (Ed.). (1976). *Webster's third new international dictionary of the English language* (unabridged). Springfield, MA: G. & C. Merriam Co.

Grant, G. P. (1979). *On competence: A critical analysis of competence-based reforms in higher education* (1st ed.). San Francisco: Jossey-Bass.

Grant, R. (1986). Advice to dissertation writers. *PS, 19*(1), 64–65.

Green, T. F. (1971). *The activities of teaching.* New York: McGraw-Hill.

Griffin, L., & Ragin, C. C. (1994). Some observations on formal methods of qualitative analysis. *Sociological Methods and Research, 23,* 4–21.

Grim, L. G., & Yarnold, P. R. (1995). *Reading and understanding multivariate statistics.* Washington, DC: American Psychological Association.

Groves, R. M. (1990). Theories and methods of telephone surveys. In W. R. Scott (Ed.), *Annual Review of Sociology,* Vol. 16 (pp. 221–240). Palo Alto: Annual Reviews.

Groves, R. M., & Magilavy, L. J. (1981). Increasing response rates to telephone surveys: A door in the face or foot-in-the-door? *Public Opinion Quarterly, 45*(3), 346–358.

Grunder, T. M. (1983). DHHS Human subjects protection: The new regulations revisited. *Health Matrix, 1*(2), 37–41.

Grunder, T. M. (1986). *Informed consent: A tutorial.* Owings Mills, MD: National Health Publishing.

Guba, E. G., & Lincoln, Y. S. (1982a, April). *Causality vs. plausibility: Alternative stances for inquiry into human behavior.* Unpublished paper presented at the Annual Meeting of the American Educational Research Association, 1982.

Guba, E. G., & Lincoln, Y. S. (1982b). Epistemological and methodological bases of naturalistic inquiry. *EC & TJ (Educational Communications and Technology Journal), 30,* 233–252.

Guba, E. G., & Lincoln, Y. S. (1985). *Naturalistic Inquiry.* Beverly Hills, CA: Sage.

Guba, E. G., & Lincoln, Y. S. (1986). The countenances of fourth-generation evaluation: Description, judgment, and negotiation. In D. S. Cordray & M. W. Lipsey (Eds.), *Evaluation studies review annual* (Vol. 11). Newbury Park, CA: Sage.

Guba, E. G., & Lincoln, Y. S. (1989). *Fourth generation evaluation.* Newbury Park, CA: Sage.

Guenzel, P. J., Berckmans, T. R., & Cannell, C. F. (1983). *General interviewing techniques: A self-instructional workbook for telephone and personal interviewer training.* Ann Arbor, MI: Survey Research Center, Institute for Social Research, University of Michigan.

Guilford, J. P., & Fruchter, B. (1978). *Fundamental statistics in psychology and education* (6th ed.). New York: McGraw-Hill.

Gulliksen, H. (1986). Perspective on educational measurement. *Applied Psychological Measurement, 10,* 109–132.

Gustafson, T. (1980). Why doesn't Soviet science do better than it does? In L. L. Lubrano & S. G. Grossman (Eds.), *The social context of Soviet science* (pp. 31–68). Boulder, CO: Westview Press.

Guy, W., Gross, M., & Dennis, H. (1967). An alternative to double-blind procedure. *American Journal of Psychiatry, 123*(12), 1505–1512.

Habermas, J. (1984). *Theory of communicative action: Vol. 1. Reason and the rationalization of society.* Boston: Beacon Press.

Hage, J., & Meeker, B. F. (1988). *Social Causality.* Contemporary Social Research Series, No. 16. Boston: Unwin Hyman.

Hagen, R. L. (1997). In praise of the null hypothesis statistical test. *American Psychologist, 52,* 15–24.

Haggerson, N. L., & Bowman, A. C. (1992). *Informing educational policy and practice through interpretive inquiry.* Lancaster, PA: Technomic Publishing Co.

Haladyna, T. M. (1994). *Developing and validating multiple-choice items.* Hillsdale, NJ: Erlbaum.

Hall, G. F., & Loucks, S. F. (1977). A developmental model for determining whether the treatment is actually implemented. *American Educational Research Journal, 14*(3), 263–276.

Hall, J. A., Rosenthal, R., Tickle-Degnen, L., & Mosteller, F. (1994). Hypotheses and problems in research synthesis. In H. Cooper and L. Hedges (Eds.), *The handbook of research synthesis* (pp. 17–28). New York: Russell Sage Foundation.

Hambleton, R. K. (1989). Principles and selected applications of item response theory. In R. L. Linn (Ed.), *Educational Measurement* (3rd ed., pp. 147–200). New York: American Council on Education/Macmillan.

Hamilton, W. L. (1979). *A social experiment in program administration: The housing allowance administrative agency experiment.* Cambridge, MA: Abt. Books.

Hammersley, M., & Atkinson, P. (1983, 1995). *Ethnography: Principles in practice* (2nd ed.). London: Tavistock Publications.

Hancock, G. R., & Klockars, A. J. (1996). The quest for α: Developments in multiple comparison procedures in the quarter century since Games (1971). *Review of Educational Research, 66,* 269–306.

Hansen, R. A., & Robinson, L. M. (1980). Testing the effectiveness of alternative foot-in-the-door manipulations. *Journal of Marketing Research, 17*(3), 359–364.

Hanson, N. R. (1958). *Patterns of discovery.* Cambridge: Cambridge University Press.

Hare, P., & Bates, R. (1963). Seating position and small group interaction. *Sociometry, 26,* 480–487.

Hargreaves, A. (1996). Transforming knowledge: Blurring the boundaries between research, policy and practice. *Educational Evaluation and Policy Analysis, 18,* 105–122.

Hauser-Cram, P. (1983). Some cautions in synthesizing research studies. *Educational Evaluation and Policy Analysis, 5*(2), 155–162.

Hays, W. L. (1973, 1981). *Statistics for the social sciences* (3rd ed.). New York: Holt, Rinehart and Winston.

Hedges, L. V. (1982). Estimation of effect size from a series of independent experiments. *Psychological Bulletin, 92*(2), 490–499.

Hedges, L. V. (1987). How hard is hard science, How soft is soft science? *American Psychologist, 42,* 443–455.

Hedges, L. V., & Olkin, I. (1985). *Statistical methods for meta-analysis.* Orlando, FL: Academic Press.

Hendricks, M., & Papagiannis, M. (1990). Do's and dont's for offering effective recommendations. *Evaluation Practice, 11,* 121–125.

Henry, G. T. (Ed.). (1997). *Creating effective graphs: Solutions for a variety of evaluation data.* New Directions for Evaluation, No. 73. San Francisco: Jossey-Bass.

Henshel, R. L. (1980a). Seeking inoperative laws: Toward the deliberate use of unnatural experimentation. In L. Freese (Ed.), *Theoretical methods in sociology: Seven essays* (pp. 175–199). Pittsburgh: University of Pittsburgh Press.

Henshel, R. L. (1980b). The purposes of laboratory experimentation and the virtues of deliberate artificiality. *Journal of Social Psychology, 16,* 406–478.

Hewett, F., & Blake, P. (1973). Teaching the emotionally disturbed. In R. M. W. Travers (Ed.), *Handbook of Research on Teaching* (2nd ed., pp. 657–688). New York: Macmillan.

Hillard, J. (1991). *Where to find what: A handbook to reference service* (2nd ed.). New York: Scarecrow Press.

Himmelfarb, S., & Edgell, S. E. (1980). Additive constants model: A randomized response technique for eliminating evasiveness to quantitative response questions. *Psychological Bulletin, 87*(3), 525–530.

Hinkle, D., Wiersma, W., & Jurs, S. (1979). *Applied statistics for the behavioral sciences* (1st ed.). Boston: Houghton Mifflin.

Hoaglin, D. C., Light, R. J., McPeek, B., Mosteller, F., & Stoto, M. A. (1982). *Data for decisions: Information strategies for policymakers.* Cambridge, MA: Abt Books.

Hoffman, J. E. (1980). Problems of access in the study of social elites and boards of directors. In W. B. Shaffir, R. A. Stebbins, & A. Turowitz (Eds.), *Fieldwork experience: Qualitative approaches to social research.* New York: St. Martin's Press.

Hoffman-Riem, C. (1986). Adoptive parenting and the norm of family emotionality. *Qualitative Sociology, 9,* 162–177.

Hollingsworth, S., & Sockett, H. (Eds.). (1994). *Teacher research and educational reform.*

Ninety-third Yearbook of the National Society for the Study of Education, Part I. Chicago: University of Chicago Press.

Hollowood, T. M., Salisbury, C. L., & Rainforth, B. (1995). Use of instructional time in classrooms serving students with and without severe disabilities. *Exceptional Children, 61,* 242–252.

Hopkins, K. D., Stanley, J. C., & Hopkins, B. R. (1990). *Educational and psychological measurement and evaluation* (7th ed.). Englewood Cliffs, NJ: Prentice-Hall.

House, E. R. (1976). Justice in evaluation. In G. V. Glass (Ed.), *Evaluation Studies Review Annual* (Vol. 1, pp. 75–100). Beverly Hills, CA: Sage.

House, E. R. (1980). *Evaluating with validity.* Beverly Hills, CA: Sage.

House, E. R. (1990). Trends in evaluation. *Educational Researcher, 19*(3), 24–27.

House, E. R. (1994). Integrating the quantitative and qualitative. In C. S. Reichardt & S. F. Rallis (Eds.), *The qualitative-quantitative debate: New perspectives* (pp. 13–22). New Directions for Program Evaluation, No. 61. San Francisco: Jossey-Bass.

Hovland, C. I., Lumsdaine, A. A., & Sheffield, F. D. (1949). *Experiments on mass communication.* Princeton, NJ: Princeton University Press.

Howell, W. (1995). We can "build" data but will they come? *American Psychological Association Monitor, 26,* 28.

Huff, D. (1954). *How to lie with statistics* (1st ed.). New York: Norton.

Hughes, E. C. (1971). *The sociological eye.* Chicago: Aldine.

Hume, D. (1902). *Enquiry concerning human understanding.* (L. A. Selby-Bigge, Ed., 2nd ed.) Oxford, England: Clarendon. (Originally published 1748)

Humphreys, L. (1975). *The tearoom trade: Impersonal sex in public places* (2nd ed.). Chicago: Aldine.

Hunt, M. (1982). Research through deception. *New York Times Magazine 66* (Sept. 12), 138–144.

Hunter, J. E., & Schmidt, F. L. (1990). *Methods of meta-analysis.* Newbury Park, CA: Sage.

Hunter, J. E., & Schmidt, F. L. (1994). Correcting for sources of artificial variation across studies. In H. Cooper & L. Hedges (Eds.), *The handbook of research synthesis* (pp. 323–336). New York: Russell Sage Foundation.

Hunter, J. E., Schmidt, F. L., & Jackson, G. B. (1982). *Meta-analysis: Cumulating research findings across studies.* Beverly Hills, CA: Sage.

Huxley, E. (1982). *The flame trees of Thika: Memories of an African childhood.* London: Chatto and Windus.

Hyman, H. H. (1954). *Interviewing in social research.* Chicago: University of Chicago Press.

Jaeger, R. M. (1990). *Statistics: A spectator sport* (2nd ed.). Beverly Hills, CA: Sage.

Jaeger, R. M. (1984). *Sampling in education and the social sciences.* New York: Longman.

Jahoda, M., Deutsch, M., & Cook, S. W. (1951). *Research methods in social relations with especial reference to prejudice.* New York: Dryden Press.

Johnson, J. E., & Lauver, D. R. (1989). Alternative explanations of coping with stressful experiences associated with physical illness. *Advances in Nursing Science, 11*(2), 39–52.

Johnson, J. M. (1975). *Doing field research.* New York: Free Press.

Johnson, R. H. (1978). Individual styles of decision-making: A theoretical model for counseling. *The Personnel and Guidance Journal, 56*(9), 530–536.

Johnson, T. H. (1966). *Oxford companion to American history.* New York: Oxford University Press.

Joint Committee on Standards for Educational Evaluation. (1981). *Standards for evaluations of educational programs, projects, and materials.* New York: McGraw-Hill.

Jonassen, D. H. (1987). Assessing cognitive structure: Verifying a method using pattern notes. *Journal of Research and Development in Education, 20*(3), 1–14.

Jones, L. V., & Appelbaum, M. I. (1990). Psychometric methods. In M. R. Rosenzweig & L. W. Porter (Eds.), *Annual Review of Psychology* (Vol. 40, pp. 23–44). Palo Alto, CA: Annual Reviews.

Judson, H. F. (1980). *The search for solutions.* New York: Holt, Rinehart and Winston.

Jung, C. G. (1971). Psychological types. In *Collected works of C. G. Jung* (2nd ed., Vol. 6). Princeton, NJ: Princeton University Press.

Kagan, N., Krathwohl, D. R., & Farquhar, W. (1965). *IPR-interpersonal process recall by video-tape in exploratory studies of counseling and teaching-learning.* East Lansing, MI: College of Education, Michigan State University. ERIC Document No. 003 230 and 017 946.

Kagan, N., Krathwohl, D. R., & Miller, R. (1963). Stimulated recall in therapy using video-tape: A case study. *Journal of Counseling Psychology, 10*(3), 237–243.

Kagen, J., Rosman, B. L., Kay, D., Albert, J., & Phillips, W. (1964). Information processing in the child: Significance of analytic and reflective attitudes. *Psychological Monographs: General and Applied, 78*(1, Whole No. 578).

Kaplan, A. (1964). *The conduct of inquiry: Methodology for behavioral science.* San Francisco: Chandler.

Katz, J. (1973). A new conception of service: Principles and strategies. In J. Katz (Ed.)., *Services for students* (pp. 127–139). New Directions for Higher Education, No. 3. San Francisco: Jossey-Bass.

Kazdin, A. E. (1980). *Research design in clinical psychology.* New York: Harper and Row.

Kelley-Milburn, D., & Milburn, M. A. (1995). CYBERPSYCH: Resources for psychologists on the internet. *Psychological Science, 6*, 203–211.

Kelling, G. L., Pate, T., Dieckman, D., & Brown, C. E. (1974). *The Kansas City preventive patrol experiment: A technical report.* Washington, DC: Police Foundation.

Kerlinger, F. N. (1973, 1986). *Foundations of behavioral research* (2nd & 3rd ed.). New York: Holt, Rinehart and Winston.

Kidder, L. H. (1981). Qualitative research and quasi-experimental frameworks. In M. B. Brewer & Barry E. Collins (Eds.), *Scientific Inquiry and the Social Sciences.* San Francisco: Jossey-Bass.

Kincaid, H. V., & Bright, M. (1957). The tandem interview. *Public Opinion Quarterly, 21*(2), 304–312.

Kipnis, D. (1997). Ghosts, taxonomies, and social psychology. *American Psychologist, 52*, 205–211.

Kirk, R. E. (1995). *Experimental design: Procedures for the behavioral sciences* (3rd ed.). Pacific Grove, CA: Brooks/Cole.

Kish, L. (1965). *Survey sampling.* New York: Wiley.

Klein, J. D., Voss, D. R., Reiser, R. A., & Gardner, G. N. (1987). The effect of age of viewer and gender of the narrator on children's visual attention and recall of story ideas. *Educational Communication and Technology Journal, 35*, 231–238.

Knapp, T. R. (1990). Treating ordinal scales as interval scales: An attempt to resolve the controversy. *Nursing Research, 39*, 121–123.

Knorr, D. D., Mittermeir, R., Aichholzer, G., & Waller, G. (1979). Leadership and group performance: A positive relationship in academic research units. In F. M. Andrews (Ed.), *Scientific productivity: The effectiveness of research groups in six countries* (pp. 95–120). Cambridge: Cambridge University Press.

Köbben, Andre J. F. (1973). Cause and intention. In R. Naroll & R. Cohen (Eds.), *A Handbook of method in cultural anthropology* (pp. 89–98). New York: Columbia University Press.

Kounin, J. S. (1970). *Discipline and group management in classrooms.* New York: Holt, Rinehart and Winston.

Kounin, J. S., Friesen, W. V., & Norton, A. E. (1966). Managing emotionally disturbed children in regular classrooms. *Journal of Educational Psychology, 57*(1), 1–13.

Kounin, J. S., & Obradovic, S. (1968). Managing emotionally disturbed children in regular classrooms: A replication and extension. *Journal of Special Education, 2*(2), 129–135.

Krathwohl, D. R. (1980). The evaluator as negotiator. *Educational Evaluation and Policy Analysis, 2*(2), 25–34.

Krathwohl, D. R. (1985). *Social and behavioral science research: A new framework for conceptualizing, implementing, and evaluating research studies.* San Francisco: Jossey-Bass.

Krathwohl, D. R. (1988). *How to prepare a research proposal: suggestions for funding and dissertations in the social and behavioral sciences* (3rd ed.). Syracuse, NY: Syracuse University Press.

Krathwohl, D. R., Bloom, B. D., & Masia, B. (1964). *Taxonomy of educational objectives: The affective domain.* New York: David McKay.

Krathwohl, D. R., Gordon, J., & Payne, D. (1967). The effect of sequence on programmed instruction. *American Educational Research Journal, 7,* 125–132.

Kreps, G. A. (Ed.). (1989). *Social structure and disaster.* Newark: University of Delaware Press.

Krueger, R. A. (1994). *Focus groups: A practical guide to applied research* (2nd ed.). Thousand Oaks, CA: Sage.

Kruglanski, A. W. (1976). On the paradigmatic objections to experimental psychology. *American Psychologist, 31,* 655–663.

Kruglanski, A. W., & Kroy, M. (1976). Outcome validity in experimental research: A reconceptualization. *Representative Research in Social Psychology, 7,* 166–178.

Kvale, S. (Ed.). (1989). *Issues of validity in qualitative research.* Lund, Sweden: Studentlitteratur.

LaMura, L. M. (1987). Whole vs. part practice for the acquisition of gross motor skills: A meta-analysis. Unpublished manuscript, Syracuse University, School of Education, Syracuse, NY.

Lancy, D. F. (1993). *Qualitative research in education: An introduction to the major traditions.* New York: Longman.

Lancy, D. F., & Zupsic, A. B. (1991, May). *A case study of running start.* Paper presented at a conference on Family and School Support for Early Literacy, Toledo, Ohio

Lane, S. (1991). Implications of cognitive psychology for measurement and testing: Assessing students' knowledge structures. *Educational Measurement: Issues and Practice, 10,* 31–33, 36.

Lang, K., & Lang, G. E. (1960). Decisions for Christ: Billy Graham in New York City. In M. Stein, A. J. Vidich, & D. M. White (Eds.), *Identity and anxiety: survival of the person in mass society* (pp. 415–434). Glencoe: Free Press.

Langer, W. L. (Ed.). (1972). *An encyclopedia of world history: ancient, medieval and modern chronologically arranged* (5th ed.). Boston: Houghton Mifflin.

Lansing, J., Withey, S., & Wolfe, A. (1971). *Working papers on survey research in poverty areas.* Ann Arbor, MI: Survey Research Center, University of Michigan.

Laslett, B. (1978). Family membership, past and present. *Social Problems, 25,* 476–490.

Laslett, B. (1980). Beyond methodology: The place of theory in quantitative historical research. *American Sociological Review, 45*(2), 214–228.

Lavrakas, P. J. (1993). *Telephone survey methods: Sampling, selection, and supervision* (2nd ed.). Applied Social Research Methods Series, Vol. 7. Newbury Park, CA: Sage.

LeCompte, M. D., Millroy, W. L., & Preissle, J. (Eds.). (1992). *Handbook of qualitative research in education.* San Diego: Academic Press.

Lee, R. M. (1993). *Doing research on sensitive topics.* Newbury Park, CA: Sage.

Leinhardt, G. (1989). Math lessons: A contrast of novice and expert competence. *Journal of Research in Mathematics Education, 20*(1), 52–75.

Leinhardt, G., & Leinhardt, S. (1980). Exploratory data analysis: New tools for the analysis of empirical data. In D. C. Berliner (Ed.), *Review of Research in Education* (pp. 85–157). Washington, DC: American Educational Research Association.

Lengenfelder, H. (1988). *Libraries, information centers, and databases in science and technology: A world guide* (2nd ed.). New York: K. G. Sauer.

Leonard, W. H., & Lowery, L. R. (1979). Was there really an experiment? A quantitative procedure for verifying treatments in educational research. *Educational Researcher, 8*(6), 4–7.

Leong, F. T. L., & Pfaltzgraff, R. E. (1996). Finding a research topic. In F. T. L. Leong and J. T. Austin (Eds.), *The psychology research handbook: A guide for graduate students and research assistants* (pp. 3–16). Thousand Oaks, CA: Sage.

Levin, H. M. (1983). *Cost-effectiveness: A primer.* New Perspectives in Evaluation, No. 4. Beverly Hills, CA: Sage.

Levine, H. G. (1985). Principles of data storage and retrieval for use in qualitative evaluations. *Educational Evaluation and Policy Analysis, 7*(2), 169–186.

Lewis, D. (1983). Causal explanation. In D. Lewis (Ed.), *Philosophical Papers* (Vol. 2). Oxford: Oxford University Press.

Liebow, E. (1967). *Talley's corner: A study of negro street corner men* (1st ed.). Boston: Little, Brown.

Light, R. J. (1984). Six evaluation issues that synthesis can resolve better than single studies. In W. H. Yeaton & P. M. Wortman (Eds.), *Issues in data synthesis* (pp. 57–73). New Directions for Program Evaluation, No. 24. San Francisco, CA: Jossey-Bass.

Light, R. J., & Pillemer, D. (1984). *Summing up: The science of reviewing research.* Cambridge, MA: Harvard University Press.

Lincoln, Y. S. (1995, April). *Emerging criteria for quality in qualitative and interpretive research.* Paper presented at the convention of the American Educational Research Association, San Francisco.

Lincoln, Y. S., & Guba, E. G. (1986). But is it rigorous? Trustworthiness and authenticity in naturalistic evaluation. In D. D. Williams (Ed.), *Naturalistic evaluation* (pp. 73–84). New Directions for Program Evaluation, No. 30. San Francisco: Jossey-Bass.

Linn, R. L. (Ed.). (1989). *Educational measurement* (3rd ed.). New York: American Council on Education/Macmillan.

Lipsey, M. W. (1990). Design sensitivity: Statistical power for experimental research. Newbury Park, CA: Sage.

Lipsey, M. W., & Wilson, D. B. (1993). The efficacy of psychological, educational, and behavioral treatment: Confirmation from meta-analysis. *American Psychologist, 48,* 1181–1209.

Locke, L. F., Spirduso, W. W., & Silverman, S. J. (1993). *Proposals that work: A guide for planning dissertation and grant proposals* (3rd ed.). Thousand Oaks, CA: Sage.

Lofland, J. (1971). *Analyzing social settings: A guide to qualitative observation and analysis.* Belmont, CA: Wadsworth.

Lofland, J. (1974). Styles of reporting qualitative field research. *American Sociologist, 9,* 101–111.

Lofland, J. (1995). Analytic ethnography: Features, failings, and futures. *Journal of Contemporary Ethnography, 24,* 30–67.

Lord Stewart. (1924). Rex vs. Sussex Justices, Nov. 9, 1923. *Kings Bench Reports, i,* 259.

Lord, F. (1968). *Statistical theories of mental test scores.* Reading, MA: Addison-Wesley.

Luiten, J., Ames, W., & Ackerson, G. (1980). A meta-analysis of the effects of advance organizers on learning and retention. *American Educational Research Journal, 17,* 211–218.

Lynd, R. S., & Lynd, H. M. (1929). *Middletown: A study in contemporary American culture.* New York: Harcourt Brace.

Mackie, J. L. (1965). Causes and conditions. *American Philosophical Quarterly, 2*(4), 245–264.

Mackie, J. L. (1974). *The cement of the universe: A study of causation.* Oxford: Clarendon Press.

Mackintosh, N. J. (Ed.). (1995). *Cyril Burt: Fraud or framed?* Oxford, England: Oxford University Press.

Madaus, G. F. (1981). NIE clarification hearing: The negative team's case. *Phi Delta Kappan, 63*(2), 92–94.

Madaus, G. F., & Stufflebeam, D. (1989). *Educational evaluation: Classic works of Ralph W. Tyler.* Boston: Kluwer.

Madigan, R., Linton, P., & Johnson, S. (1996). APA style: Quo vadis? *American Psychologist, 51,* 653–655.

Mann, C. (1990). Meta-analysis in the breech. *Science, 249,* 476–480.

Mann, T. (1994). Informed consent for psychological research: Do subjects comprehend consent forms and understand their legal rights? *Psychological Science, 5,* 140–143.

Mark, M. M. (1983). Treatment implementation, statistical power, and internal validity. *Evaluation Review, 7,* 543–549.

Mark, M. M. (1990). Methodological training: Dispensation from logic, blinders, or what? On using your head in evaluation. In C. Rinne (Ed.), *Proceedings of the 1990 Edward F. Kelly evaluation conference* (pp. 1–12). Albany, NY: The Evaluation Consortium at Albany School of Education, State University of New York at Albany.

Mark, M. M., & Shotland, R. L. (1987). Alternative models for the use of multiple methods. In M. M. Mark & R. L. Shotland (Eds.), *Multiple methods in program evaluation* (pp. 95–100). New Directions for Program Evaluation, No. 35. San Francisco: Jossey-Bass.

Marshall, S. P. (1990). Generating good items for diagnostic tests. In N. Frederiksen, R. Glaser, A. Lesgold, & M. G. Shafto (Eds.), *Diagnostic monitoring of skill and knowledge acquisition.* Hillsdale, NJ: Erlbaum.

Mathison, S. (1988). Why triangulate? *Educational Researcher, 17*(2), 13–17.

May, R. B., Masson, M. E. J., & Hunter, M. A. (1990). *Application of statistics in behavioral research.* New York: Harper & Row.

Mazlish, B. (1972). *In Search of Nixon: A psychological inquiry.* New York: Basic Books.

McCall, W. A. (1923). *How to experiment in education.* New York: Macmillan.

McCleary, R., Gordon, A. C., McDowall, D., & Maltz, M. D. (1979). How a regression effect can make any delinquency intervention look effective. In L. Sechrest, S. G. West, M. A. Phillips, R. Redner, & W. Yeaton (Eds.), *Evaluation Studies Review Annual* (Vol. 4, pp. 626–652). Beverly Hills, CA: Sage.

McKim, B. J., & Cowen, E. L. (1987). Multiperspective assessment of young children's school adjustment. *School Psychology Review, 16*(3), 370–381.

Mead, M. (1928). *Coming of age in Samoa: A psychological study of primitive youth for western civilization.* New York: W. Morrow & Company.

Medawar, P. B. (1984). *The limits of science.* New York: Harper & Row.

Meehl, P. E. (1974). The place of theory in educational research. *Educational Researcher, 3*(6), 3–10.

Mehrens, W. A., & Lehman, I. J. (1991). *Measurement and Evaluation in Education and Psychology.* Fort Worth, TX: Holt, Rinehart and Winston.

Merton, R. K. (1959). Notes on problem-finding in sociology. In R. K. Merton, L. Broom, & L. Cotrell (Eds.), *Sociology today: Problems and prospects* (pp. ix–xxxiv). New York: Basic Books.

Merton, R. K. (1968). *Social theory and social structure.* New York: Free Press.

Merton, R. K., Fiske, M., & Kendall, P. L. (1956). *The focused interview: A manual of problems and procedures.* Glencoe, IL: Free Press.

Messick, S. (1989). Validity. In R. L. Linn (Ed.), *Educational measurement* (3rd ed., pp. 13–104). New York: American Council on Education/Macmillan.

Messick, S. (1995). Validity of psychological assessment: Validation of inferences from persons' responses and performances as scientific inquiry into score meaning. *American Psychologist, 50,* 741–749.

Metfessel, N. S., & Michael, W. B. (1967). A paradigm involving multiple criterion measures for the evaluation of the effectiveness of school programs. *Educational and Psychological Measurement, 27*(4, pt. 2), 931–943.

Metz, M. H. (1983). What can be learned from educational ethnography? *Urban Education, 17,* 391–418.

Miles, M. B., & Huberman, A. M. (1984). *Qualitative data analysis: A sourcebook of new methods.* Beverly Hills, CA: Sage.

Miles, M. B., & Huberman, A. M. (1994). *Qualitative data analysis: An expanded sourcebook* (2nd ed.). Thousand Oaks, CA: Sage.

Milgram, S. (1963). Behavioral study of obedience. *Journal of Abnormal and Social Psychology, 67,* 371–378.

Milgram, S. (1974). *Obedience to authority: An experimental viewpoint.* New York: Harper & Row.

Milgram, S. (1977). Ethical issues in the study of obedience. In S. Milgram (Ed.), *The individual in a social world* (pp. 188–199). Reading, MA: Addison-Wesley.

Milgram, S., Sabini, J., & Silver, M. (Eds.) *The individual in the social world: Essays and experiments* (2nd ed.). New York: McGraw-Hill.

Mill, J. S. (1868). *System of logic: Ratiocinative and inductive: Being a connected view of evidence and the methods of scientific investigation* (7th ed.). London: Longman, Green, Reader and Dyer.

Miller, G. A. (1978). *Spontaneous apprentices: Children and language.* New York: Seabury Press.

Miller, J. D. (1984). A new survey technique for studying deviant behavior. *Dissertation Abstracts International, 45,* 319A. (University Microfilms No. DA84–10–488).

Miller, R. G., Jr. (1993). *Secrecy and fieldwork.* Qualitative Research Methods, Vol. 29. Newbury Park: Sage.

Mills, J. (1976). A procedure for explaining experiments involving deception. *Personality and Social Psychology Bulletin, 2,* 3–13.

Mitchell, R. G., Jr. (1994). *Secrecy and fieldwork.* Qualitative Research Methods, No. 29. Newbury Park, CA: Sage.

Mitroff, I. I., & Kilmann, R. H. (1976). On organizational stories: An approach to the design and analysis of organizations through myths and stories. In R. Kilmann, L. Pondy, & D. Slevin (Eds.), *The management of organization design.* Amsterdam, Netherlands: North Holland.

Moffitt, R. A. (1979). The labor supply response in the Gary experiment. *Journal of Human Resources, 14*(4), 477–487.

Moreland, R. L., & Zajonc, R. B. (1977). Is stimulus recognition a necessary condition for the occurrence of exposure effects? *Journal of Personality and Social Psychology, 35,* 191–199.

Morgan, D. L. (1997a). *Focus groups as qualitative research* (2nd ed.). Qualitative Research Methods, Vol. 16. Thousand Oaks, CA: Sage.

Morgan, D. L. (1997b). *The focus group guidebook.* Focus Group Kit, Vol. 1. Thousand Oaks, CA: Sage.

Moses, L. E. (1986). Think and explain with statistics. Reading, MA: Addison Wesley.

Moss, P. A. (1996). Enlarging the dialogue in educational measurement: Voices from interpretive research traditions. *Educational Researcher, 25*(Jan.–Feb.), 20–28, 43.

Mosteller, F. (1981). Innovation and evaluation. *Science, 211,* 881–886.

Mosteller, F. K., & Wallace, D. L. (1984). *Applied Bayesian and classical inference: The case of the Federalist papers* (2nd ed.). New York: Springer-Verlag.

Muhr, T. (1993). *ATLAS/ti: Computer aided text interpretation and theory building. User's Manual.* [Computer program] Berlin: Author. (Distributed by Qualitative Research Management, 73425 Hilltop Road, Desert Hot Springs, CA 92240.)

Murray, F. B., & Raths, J. (1996). Factors in the peer review of reviews. *Review of Educational Research, 66,* 417–421.

Nelkin, D. (1984). *Science as intellectual property: Who controls research?* New York: Macmillan.

Neuliep, J. W., & Crandall, R. (1990a). Editorial bias against replication research. *Journal of Social Behavior and Personality, 5,* 5–90.

Neuliep, J. W., & Crandall, R. (1990b). Reviewer bias against replication research. *Journal of Social Behavior and Personality, 8,* 22–29.

Nevins, A. (1975). *Allen Nevins on history.* New York: Scribner.

Newhouse, J. P., Rolph, J. E., Mori, B., & Murphy, M. (1980). The effects of deductibles on the demand for medical care services. *Journal of the American Statistical Association, 75*(371), 525–533.

Neyman, J. (1967). R. A. Fisher (1890–1962): An appreciation. *Science, 156,* 1456–1462.

Noblit, G. W., & Hare, R. W. (1989). Meta-ethnography: Synthesizing qualitative studies. *Contemporary Sociology, 18*(6), 962–963.

Nolan, K. L. (1983–). *Gale Directory of Online Databases.* New York: Gale Research.

Oppenheim, A. N. (1966). *Questionnaire design and attitude measurement.* New York: Basic Books.

Ornstein, A., & Phillips, W. R. (1978). *Understanding social research: An introduction.* Boston: Allyn & Bacon.

Osborn, A. (1959). *Creative imagination: Applied imagination principles and procedures of creative thinking.* New York: Charles Scribners.

Padilla, R. (1993). *HyperQual 2 for qualitative analysis and theory development* [Computer program]. Chandler, AZ: the author. (Distributed by Qualitative Research Management, 73425 Hilltop Rd., Desert Hot Springs, CA 92240.)

Page, M. M. (1973). On detecting demand awareness by post-experimental questionnaire. *Journal of Social Psychology, 91,* 305–323.

Parnes, H. S. (1967). *Creative behavior workbook.* New York: Scribners.

Patten, S. C. (1977). Milgram's shocking experiments. *Philosophy, 52,* 425–440.

Patton, M. Q. (1980). *Qualitative evaluation methods.* Beverly Hills, CA: Sage.

Payne, S. L. (1951). *The art of asking questions.* Princeton, NJ: Princeton University Press.

Peters, V., and Wester, F. (1990). *Qualitative analysis in practice: Including user's guide, Kwalitan version 2* [Computer program]. Nijmegen, the Netherlands: University of Nijmegen, Social Science Faculty, Department of Research Methodology.

Phelan, P. (1987). Compatibility of qualitative and quantitative methods: Studying child abuse in America. *Education and Urban Society, 29*(1), 35–41.

Phillips, D. C. (1987). *Philosophy, science and social inquiry.* Oxford: Pergamon Press.

Phillips, D. C. (1992). *The social scientists' bestiary.* Oxford: Pergamon Press.

Phillips, D. C. (Ed.). (1994). Epistemological Perspectives on Educational Psychology. *Educational Psychologist, 29,* 1–55.

Phillips, D. L. (1971). *Knowledge from what: Theories and methods in social research.* Chicago: Rand McNally.

Piaget, J. (1952). *Origins of intelligence in children.* New York: International Universities Press.

Piel, G. (1986). The social process of science. *Science, 231,* 201.

Piliavin, J. A., & Piliavin, I. M. (1972). Effect of blood on reactions to a victim. *Journal of Personality and Social Psychology, 23,* 353–361.

Platt, J. R. (1964). Strong inference. *Science, 146,* 347–353.

Pletz, A. (1965). Psychology of the scientist: XI Lotka's Law and Research Visibility. *Psychological Reports, 16*(2), 566–568.

Poincare, H. (1913). *The foundations of science: Sciences and hypothesis, the value of science, science and method.* New York: Science Press.

Popham, W. J. (1981). The case for minimum competency testing. *Phi Delta Kappan, 63*(2), 89–91.

Popper, K. R. (1959). *The logic of scientific discovery* (1st ed.). New York: Basic Books.

Popper, K. R. (1972). Of Clouds and clocks: An approach to the problem of rationality and the freedom of man. In K. R. Popper (Ed.), *Objective knowledge: An evolutionary approach.* Oxford: Clarendon Press.

Potter, D. M. (1954). *People of plenty: Economic abundance and the American character.* Chicago: University of Chicago Press.

Powers, D. E., Fowles, M. E., Farnum, M., & Ramsey, P. (1994). Will they think less of my handwritten essay if others word-process theirs? Effects on essay scores of intermingling handwritten and word-processed essays. *Journal of Educational Measurement, 31,* 220–233.

Prewitt, K. (1980). Kenneth Prewitt, Frederick Mosteller, and Herbert A. Simon testify at National Science Foundation hearings. *Items, 34,* 1–7.

Prewitt, K. (1981). Usefulness of the social sciences. *Science, 211,* 659.

Price, D. J. D. (1963). *Little science, big science.* New York: Columbia University Press.

Qualitative Solutions and Research Pty. Ltd. (1997). *NUD•IST 4.0* [Computer program]. Distributed in U.S. and Canada by Sage Publications.

Radnofsky, M. L. (1995). *CHROMACODE: A conceptual and pedagogical tool in qualitative data analysis.* ERIC Document Reproduction Service No. ED 390 936.

Ragin, C. C. (1987). *The comparative method: Moving beyond qualitative and quantitative strategies.* Berkeley, CA: University of California Press.

Ragin, C. C. (1993). An introduction to qualitative comparative analysis. In T. Janowski and A. Hicks (Eds.), *The Comparative Political Economy of the Welfare State* (pp. 299–314). New York: Cambridge University Press.

Ragsdale, R. G. (1992). Observations on using the laptop in data recording. *Evaluation Practice, 13,* 211–213.

RAND Corporation. (1969). *A million random digits with 100,000 normal deviates.* Santa Monica, CA: The RAND Corporation.

Raphael, B. (1986). *When disaster strikes: How individuals and communities cope with catastrophe.* New York: Basic Books.

Raudenbusch, S. W. (1984). Magnitude of teacher expectancy's effects on pupil IQ as a function of credibility of expectancy induction: A synthesis of findings from 18 experiments. *Journal of Educational Psychology, 76*(1), 85–97.

Raudsepp, E. (1977). Daydream a little. *American Way, 10*(April), 27.

Redfield, R. (1955). *The little community.* Chicago: University of Chicago Press.

Reed, J. G., & Baxter, P. M. (1992). *Library use: A handbook for psychology* (2nd ed.). Washington, DC: American Psychology Association.

Reichardt, C. S. (1985). Reinterpreting Seaver's (1973) study of teacher expectancies as a regression artifact. *Journal of Educational Psychology, 77,* 231–236.

Reichardt, C. S., & Cook, T. D. (1979). *Qualitative and quantitative methods in evaluation research.* Beverly Hills, CA: Sage.

Reichardt, C. S., & Gollob, H. F. (1987). Taking uncertainty into account when estimating effects. In M. M. Mark & R. L. Shotland (Eds.), *Multiple methods in program evaluation* (pp. 7–22). New Directions for Program Evaluation, No. 35. San Francisco: Jossey-Bass.

Reissman, C. K. (1993). *Narrative analysis.* Newbury Park, CA: Sage.

Rippey, R. M. (Ed.). (1973). *Studies in transactional evaluation.* Berkeley, CA: McCutcheon.

Rist, R. (1977). *The invisible children: School instruction in American society.* Cambridge, MA: Harvard University Press.

Robins, P. K., Spiegelman, R. G., Weiner, S., & Bell, J. G. (Eds.). (1980). *A guaranteed annual income: Evidence from a social experiment.* New York: Academic Press.

Roethlisberger, F. J., & Dickson, W. J. (1939). *Management and the worker.* Cambridge, MA: Harvard University Press.

Rogers, E. M. (1995). *Diffusion of innovations* (4th ed.). New York: Free Press.

Rosaldo, R. (1980). Doing oral history. *Social Analysis, 4,* 89–99.

Rosengarten, T. (1981). Stepping over cockleburs: Conversations with Ned Cobb. In M. Pachter (Ed.), *Telling lives: The biographer's art* (pp. 104–131). Philadelphia: University of Pennsylvania Press.

Rosenthal, R. (1969). Interpersonal expectations: Effects on experimenters' hypothesis. In R. Rosenthal & R. L. Rosnow (Eds.), *Artifact in behavioral research* (pp. 181–277). New York: Academic Press.

Rosenthal, R. (1976a). *Experimenter effects in behavioral research* (enlarged ed.). New York: Irvington.

Rosenthal, R. (1976b). Interpersonal expectancy effects: A follow-up. In R. Rosenthal, *Experimenter effects in behavioral research.* New York: Irvington.

Rosenthal, R. (1979). The "file drawer" problem and tolerance for negative results. *Psychological Bulletin, 86*(3), 638–641.

Rosenthal, R. (1991). *Meta-analysis procedures for social research* (rev. ed.). Beverly Hills, CA: Sage.

Rosenthal, R. (1994). Parametric measures of effect size. In H. Cooper and L. Hedges (Eds.), *The handbook of research synthesis* (pp. 231–244). New York: Russell Sage Foundation.

Rosenthal, R., & Rosnow, R. L. (1975). *The volunteer subject.* New York: John Wiley.

Rosenthal, R., & Rubin, D. (1980). Summarizing 345 studies of interpersonal expectancy effects. In R. Rosenthal (Ed.), *Quantitative assessment of research domains.* New Directions for Methodology of Social and Behavioral Science, No. 5. San Francisco: Jossey-Bass.

Rosenthal, R., & Rubin, D. (1982). Comparing effect sizes of independent studies. *Psychological Bulletin, 92*(2), 500–504.

Rosner, S., & Abt, L. (1970). *The creative experience.* New York: Grossman.

Ross, S., Krugman, A., Lyerly, S. B., & Clyde, D. J. (1962). Drugs and placebos: A model design. *Psychological Reports, 10,* 383–392.

Rossi, P. H., & Freeman, H. E. (1985, 1993). *Evaluation: A systematic approach* (3rd and 5th ed.). Newbury Park, CA: Sage.

Rossi, P. H., Berk, R. A., & Lenihan, K. (1980). *Money, work, and crime: Experimental evidence.* New York: Academic Press.

Rossi, P. H., & Lyall, K. (1976). *Reforming public welfare: A critique of the negative income tax experiments.* New York: Russell Sage Foundation.

Rossi, P. H., & Wright, J. D. (1986). Evaluation research: An assessment. In D. S. Cordray & M. W. Lipsey (Eds.), *Evaluation studies review annual* (Vol. 11, pp. 48–69). Beverly Hills, CA: Sage.

Rothman, B. K. (1986). Reflection: On hard work. *Qualitative Sociology, 9,* 48–53.

Rowe, M. B. (1974). Relation of wait-time and rewards to the development of language, logic and fate control: Part I, wait-time. *Journal of Research in Science Teaching, 11,* 81–94.

Royce, J. M., Lazar, I., & Darlington, R. B. (1983). Minority families, early education, and later life chance. *American Journal of Orthopsychiatry, 53*(4), 706–720.

Rubin, L. B. (1976). *Worlds of pain: Life in the working class family.* New York: Basic Books.

Rubin, L. B. (1981) Sociological research: The subjective dimension. *Symbolic Interaction, 4,* (1), 103.

Russell, B. (1953). On the notion of cause, with applications to the free-will problem. In H. Feigl & M. Brodbeck (Eds.), *Readings in the philosophy of Science* (pp. 387–407). New York: Appleton.

Ryan, K., & Phillips, D. (1982). Teacher characteristics. In H. Mitzel (Ed.), *Encyclopedia of Educational Research* (5th ed., pp. 1869–1875). New York: Free Press.

Sadler, D. R. (1981). Intuitive data processing as a potential source of bias in naturalistic evaluations. *Educational Evaluation and Policy Analysis, 3*(4), 25–31.

Salomon, G. (1981). *Communication and education: Social and psychological interactions.* Beverly Hills, CA: Sage.

Sanjek, R. (Ed.). (1990). *Fieldnotes: The makings of anthropology.* Ithaca, NY: Cornell University Press.

Sasz, T. S. (1974). *Ceremonial chemistry: The ritual persecution of drugs, addicts, and the pushers.* Garden City, NY: Doubleday.

Scheerer, M. (1963). Problem solving. *Scientific American, 208*(4), 118–128.

Schmidt, F. L. (1996). Statistical significance testing and cumulative knowledge in Psychology: Implications for training of researchers. *Psychological Methods, 1,* 115–129.

Schmidt, L. D. & Meara, N. M. (1996). Applying for approval to conduct research with human participants. In F. T. L. Leong, & J. T. Austin (Eds.). *The psychology research handbook: A guide for graduate students and research assistants* (pp. 113–126). Thousand Oaks, CA: Sage.

Schneider, J. W., & Conrad, P. (1985). *Having epilepsy: The experience and control of illness.* Philadelphia: Temple University Press.

Schuler, H. (1982). *Ethical problems in psychological research* (M. S. Woodruff and R. A. Wicklund, Trans.). New York: Academic Press.

Schuman, H., & Converse, J. (1971). The effects of black and white interviewers on black responses in 1968. *Public Opinion Quarterly, 35*(1), 44–68.

Schuman, H., & Kalton, G. (1985). Survey methods. In G. Lindzey & E. Aronson (Eds.), *The handbook of social psychology* (3rd ed., pp. 635–698). New York: Random House.

Schwab, J. J. (1978). Education and the structure of disciplines. In I. Westbury and N. J. Wilkof (Eds.), *Joseph J. Schwab: Science, curriculum and liberal education* (pp. 229–274). Chicago: University of Chicago Press.

Schwarz, N., & Sudman, S. (Eds.) (1996). *Answering questions: Methodology for determining cognitive and communicative processes in survey research.* San Francisco: Jossey-Bass.

Schweinhart, L. J., & Weikart, D. P. (1985). Evidence that early childhood programs work. *Phi Delta Kappan, 66,* 545–551.

Schweitzer, A. (1990). *Out of my life and thought: An autobiography* (A. B. Lemke, Trans.). New York: Holt, Rinehart and Winston. (Original work published 1933)

Scriven, M. (1972). Prose and cons about goal-free evaluation. *Evaluation Comment, 3,* 1–4. Reprinted in *Evaluation Practice, 12,* 55–62.

Scriven, M. (1974). Standards for the evaluation of educational programs and products. In Gary D. Borich (Ed.), *Evaluating educational programs and products.* Englewood Cliffs, NJ: Educational Technology Publication.

Scriven, M. (1991). Beyond formative and summative evaluation. In M. W. McLaughlin and D. C. Phillips (Eds.), *Evaluation and education: At quarter century* (pp. 19–64). Ninetieth Yearbook of the National Society for the Study of Education, Part II. Chicago: University of Chicago Press.

Seaver, W. B. (1971). Effects of naturally induced teacher expectancies on the academic performance of pupils in primary grades. (Doctoral dissertation, Northwestern University, 1971.) *Dissertation Abstracts International, 32,* 3426–3427.

Segerstråle, U. (1994). Science by worst cases. *Science, 263,* 837–838.

Seidel, J. V., Kjolseth, R., & Seymour, E. (1988). *The ethnograph* [computer program]. Littleton, CO: Qualis Research Associates.

Seidman, I. E. (1991). *Interviewing as qualitative research.* Thousand Oaks, CA: Sage.

Seligman, E. P. (1995). The effectiveness of psychotherapy. *American Psychologist, 50,* 965–974.

Shadish, W. R. (1993). Critical multiplism: A research strategy and its attendant tactics. In L. Sechrest (Ed.), *Program evaluation: A pluralistic enterprise.* New Directions for Program Evaluation, No. 60. San Francisco: Jossey-Bass.

Shadish, W. R. (1996). Meta-analysis and the exploration of causal processes: A primer of examples, methods and issues. *Psychological Methods, 1,* 47–65.

Shadish, W. R., & Fuller, S. (1994). *The social psychology of science.* New York: Guilford Press.

Shadish, W. R., & Haddock, C. K. (1994). Combining estimates of effect size. In H. Cooper and L. Hedges (Eds.), *The handbook of research synthesis* (pp. 261–281). New York: Russell Sage Foundation.

Shavelson, R. J. (1996). *Statistical reasoning for the behavioral sciences* (3rd ed.). Boston: Allyn & Bacon.

Shavelson, R. J., Webb, N. M., & Rowley, G. L. (1989). Generalizability theory. *American Psychologist, 44,* 922–932.

Sheehy, E. P. (Ed.). (1986). *Guide to reference books* (10th ed.). Chicago: American Library Association.

Sieber, J. E. (1983). Deception in social research III: The nature and limits of debriefing. *IRB: A Review of Human Subjects Research, 5*(3), 1–4.

Sieber, J. E. (1992). *Planning ethically responsible research: A guide for students and internal review boards.* Newbury Park, CA: Sage.

Sieber, J. E., & Stanley, B. (1988). Ethical and professional dimensions of socially sensitive research. *American Psychologist, 43,* 49–55.

Sieber, S. D. (1973). The integration of fieldwork and survey methods. *American Journal of Sociology, 78*(6), 1335–1359.

Siegel, S., and Castellan, N. J. (1988). *Nonparametric statistics for the behavioral sciences* (2nd ed.). New York: McGraw-Hill.

Simon, A., & Boyer, G. E. (1974). *Mirrors for Behavior.* Philadelphia: Communication Materials Center in cooperation with Humanizing Learning Program, Research for Better Schools.

Simon, H. A. (1992). What is an explanation of behavior? *Psychological Science, 3,* 150–161.

Skinner, B. F. (1957). *Verbal behavior.* New York: Appleton-Century Crofts.

Skinner, B. F. (1959). A case history in scientific method. In S. Koch (Ed.), *Psychology: A study of a science, Vol. 2, General systematic formulations, learning, and special processes* (pp. 359–379). New York: McGraw-Hill.

Skipper, J. K., & McCaghy, C. H. (1972). Respondents' intrusion upon the situation: The problem of interviewing subjects with special qualities. *Sociological Quarterly, 13,* 237–243.

Slavin, R. E. (1985). Best evidence synthesis: An alternative to meta-analytic and traditional reviews. *Educational Researcher, 15,* 5–11.

Slovic, P., Fischhoff, B., & Lichtenstein, S. (1982). Response mode, framing, and informa-tion-processing effects in risk assessment. In R. M. Hogarth (Ed.), *Question Framing and Response Consistency*. New Directions for Methodology of Social and Behavioral Sci-ence, No. 11. San Francisco: Jossey-Bass.

Smith, C. (1990). Post training REMs coincident auditory stimulation enhances memory in humans. *Psychiatric Journal of the University of Ottawa, 15,* 85–90.

Smith, M. L., Gabriel, R. Schott, J., & Padia, W. L. (1976). Evaluation Effects of Outward Bound. In G. V. Glass (Ed.), *Evaluation Studies Review Annual* (Vol. 1, pp. 400–421). Bev-erly Hills, CA: Sage.

Smith, M. L., & Glass, G. V. (1977). Meta-analysis of psychotherapy outcome studies. *Amer-ican Psychologist, 32,* 752–760.

Smith, M. L., Glass, G. V., & Miller, T. I. (1980). *Benefits of Psychotherapy.* Baltimore, MD: Johns Hopkins University Press.

Snyder, M., & Cunningham, M. R. (1975). To comply or not comply: Testing the self-per-ception explanation of the "foot-in-the-door" phenomenon. *Journal of Personality and Social Psychology, 31*(1), 64–67.

Soffer, E. (1995). The principal as action researcher: A study of disciplinary practice. In S. E. Noffke & R. B. Stevenson (Eds.), *Educational action research: Becoming practically critical.* New York: Teachers College.

Spitzer, W. O., et al. (1974). The Burlington randomized trial of the nurse practitioner. *New England Journal of Medicine, 290,* 251–256.

Spradley, J. P. (1980). *Participant observation.* New York: Holt, Rinehart and Winston.

Stack, C. (1974). *All our kin: Strategies for survival in a black community.* New York: Harper & Row.

Stake, R. E. (1978). Seeing and measuring. *Journal of Curriculum Studies, 10*(3), 265.

Stake, R. E. (1991). Excerpts from: "Program evaluation, particularly responsive evalua-tions." *Evaluation Practice, 12,* 63–77.

Stake, R. E. (1995). *The art of case study research.* Thousand Oaks, CA: Sage.

Stake, R. E., & Easley, J. A. Jr., et al. (1978a). *Case studies in science education.* Vol. 1. The case reports. Washington, DC: US Government Printing Office.

Stake, R. E., & Easley, J. A. Jr., et al. (1978b). *Case studies in science education.* Vol. 11. Design, overview and general findings. Washington, DC: US Government Printing Office.

Stankiewicz, R. (1979). The size and age of Swedish academic research groups and their scientific performance. In F. M. Andrews (Ed.), *Scientific productivity: The effectiveness of research groups in six countries* (pp. 191–222). Cambridge: Cambridge University Press.

Stanley, B., Sieber, J. E., & Melton, G. B. (1987). Empirical studies of ethical issues in re-search: A research agenda. *American Psychologist, 42,* 735–741.

Starr, J. (1977). Above all, a scholar. *Change, 9,* 27–33.

Steiner, J. (1984). *Notebooks of the mind.* Albuquerque, NM: University of New Mexico Press.

Stevens, S. S. (1946). On the theory of scales of measurement. *Science, 103,* 677–680.

Stevens, S. S. (1951). Mathematics, measurement, and psychophysics. In S. S. Stevens (Ed.), *Handbook of experimental psychology* (pp. 1–49). New York: Wiley.

Stewart, D. W., & Shamdasani, P. N. (1990). *Focus groups: Theory and practice.* Newbury Park, CA: Sage.

Stockdale, M. S., & Kenny, T. (1996). Conducting a literature search. In F. T. L. Leong, & J. T. Austin (Eds.). *The psychology research handbook: A guide for graduate students and re-search assistants* (pp. 29–39). Thousand Oaks, CA: Sage.

Strauss, A. (1987). *Qualitative analysis for social scientists.* Cambridge: Cambridge University Press.

Strauss, A., & Corbin, J. (1990). *The basics of qualitative research: Grounded theory procedures and techniques.* Newbury Park, CA: Sage.

Strong, E. K., Campbell, D. P., & Hansen, J. (1981). *Strong-Campbell Interest Inventory.* Palo Alto, CA: Stanford University Press/Consulting Psychologists Press.

Struyk, R. J., & Bendick, M., Jr. (1981). *Housing vouchers for the poor: Lessons from a national experiment.* Washington, DC: Urban Institute.

Stufflebeam, D. L., & Shinkfield, A. J. (1985). *Systematic evaluation: A self-instruction guide to theory and practice*. Boston: Kluwer Nijhoff.

Subkoviak, M. J. (1988). A practitioner's guide to computation and interpretation of reliability indices for mastery tests. *Journal of Educational Measurement, 25*(1), 47–56.

Sudman, S., & Bradburn, N. M. (1982). *Asking questions: a practical guide to questionnaire design* (1st ed.). San Francisco: Jossey-Bass.

Sullivan, M. A., Queen, S. A., & Patrick, R. C., Jr. (1958). Participant observation as employed in a study of a military training program. *American Sociological Review, 23*, 660–667.

Survey Research Center, Institute for Social Research. (1976). *Interviewer's manual* (rev. ed.). Ann Arbor, MI: Institute for Social Research, University of Michigan.

Taylor, S. (1977). The custodians: Attendants and their work at state institutions for the mentally retarded. (Doctoral dissertation, Syracuse University, 1977) *International Dissertation Abstracts, 39*, 1145–1146.

Taylor, S., & Bogdan, R. (1984). *Introduction to qualitative research methods: The search for meanings* (2nd ed.). New York: Wiley.

Terman, L. M., & Oden, M. M. (1947). *The gifted child grows up. Twenty-five year follow-up of a superior group* (Vol. 4). Stanford, CA: Stanford University Press.

Terman, L. M., & Oden, M. M. (1959). *The gifted group at midlife* (Vol. 5). Stanford, CA: Stanford University Press.

Terman, L. M., et al. (1926). *The mental and physical traits of a thousand gifted children* (Vol. 1). Stanford, CA: Stanford University Press.

Tesch, R. (1990). *Qualitative research: Analysis types & software tools*. New York: Falmer.

Tesser, A. (1990) *Interesting models in Social Psychology: A personal view*. Invited address presented at the meeting of the American Psychological Association, Boston.

Test Collection, Educational Testing Service. (1986). *The ETS test collection catalog, Volume 1: Achievement tests and measurement devices*. Phoenix, AZ: Oryx Press.

Test Collection, Educational Testing Service. (1988). *The ETS test collection catalog, Volume 2: Vocational tests and measurement devices*. Phoenix, AZ: Oryx Press.

Test Collection, Educational Testing Service. (1989). *The ETS test collection catalog, Volume 3: Tests for special populations*. Phoenix, AZ: Oryx Press.

Test Collection, Educational Testing Service. (1991). *The ETS test collection catalog, Volume 4: Cognitive aptitude and intelligence tests*. Phoenix, AZ: Oryx Press.

Thorndike, R. L. (1947). *Research problems and techniques*. AAF Aviation Psychology Research Program Reports, No. 3. Washington, DC: US Government Printing Office.

Thurstone, L. L. (1935). *Vectors of the Mind*. Chicago: University of Chicago Press.

Thurstone, L. L. (1947). *A development and expansion of the vectors of the mind: Multiple factor analysis*. Chicago: University of Chicago Press.

Tinto, V. (1987). *Leaving College: Rethinking the causes and cures of student attrition*. Chicago: University of Chicago Press.

Tobias, S., & Zibrin, M. (1978). Does blind reviewing make a difference? *Educational Researcher, 7*(Jan.), 14–16.

Toynbee, A. J. (1948). *A study of history*. London: Oxford University Press.

Traugott, M. W., Groves, R. M., & Lepkowski, J. M. (1987). Using dual frame designs to reduce nonresponse in telephone surveys. *Public Opinion Quarterly, 51*, 522–539.

Travers, R. M. W. (1961). *Measured needs of teachers and behavior in the classroom*. Salt Lake City, UT: University of Utah, Department of Educational Psychology.

Tripp-Reimer, T. (1983). Retention of a folk-healing practice (matiasma) among four generations of urban Greek immigrants. *Nursing Research, 32*(2), 97–101.

Tuchman, B. (1962). *The guns of August*. New York: Macmillan.

Tuckman, H. P. (1976). *Publication, teaching and the academic reward structure*. Lexington, MA: D. C. Heath.

Tufte, E. R. (1983). *The visual display of quantitative information*. Chesire, CN: Graphics Press.

Tukey, J. W. (1977). *Exploratory data analysis*. Reading, MA: Addison Wesley.

Tuomey, C. P. (1996). *Conjuring science: Scientific symbols and cultural meanings in American life*. New Brunswick, NJ: Rutgers University Press.

Turner, B. A. (1981). Some practical aspects of qualitative data analysis: One way of organizing the cognitive processes associated with the generation of grounded theory. *Quality and Quantity, 15*(3), 225–247.

Tversky, A., & Kahneman, D. (1981). The framing of decisions and the psychology of choice. *Science, 211,* 453–458.

Tyack, D. (1976). Ways of seeing: An essay on the history of compulsory schooling. *Harvard Educational Review, 46*(3), 355–389.

Tyler, L. L., Klein, M. F., & Associates. (1976). *Evaluating and choosing curriculum and instructional materials.* Los Angeles, CA: Educational Resource Associates.

Tyler, R. W., & Waples, D. (1930). *Research methods and teacher's problems: A manual for systematic studies of classroom procedure.* New York: Macmillan.

Valenstein, E. S. (1994). Neuroscience: Paths, detours, and hazards. [Review of *The Neurosciences: Paths of Discovery, 1*]. *Contemporary Psychology, 39,* 140–143.

Van Alystyne, M., & Brynjolfsson, E. (1996). Could the Internet balkanize science? *Science, 274,* 1479–1480.

Vansina, J. (1965). *Oral tradition: A study in historical methodology.* Chicago: Aldine.

von Wright, G. H. (1971). *Explanation and understanding.* London: Routledge and Kegan Paul.

Wade, N. (1978). Guillemin and Schally: A race spurred by rivalry. *Science, 200,* 510–513.

Waksberg, J. (1978). Sampling methods for random digit dialing. *Journal of the American Statistical Association, 73,* 40–46.

Walberg, H. J. (1986). Syntheses of research on teaching. In M. C. Wittrock (Ed.), *Handbook of research on teaching* (3rd ed., pp. 214–229). New York: Macmillan.

Walker, D. F., and Schaffarzick, J. (1974). Comparing Curricula. *Review of Educational Research, 44,* 83–111.

Wallace, P. (1997). *Psychology on-line.* Madison, WI: Browne & Benchmark.

Wanner, E. (1995). Foreword. In T. D. Cook et al., *Meta-analysis for explanation: A casebook.* New York: Russell Sage Foundation.

Warner, S. L. (1965). Randomized response: A survey technique for eliminating evasive answer bias. *Journal of the American Statistical Association , 60,* 63–69.

Watson, J. D. (1968). *The double helix: A personal account of the discovery of the structure of DNA* (1st ed.). New York: Atheneum.

Watts, H. W., & Rees, A. (Eds.). (1976). *The New Jersey income maintenance experiment* (Vol. 2). New York: Academic Press.

Wax, M. L., & Wax, R. H. (1980). Fieldwork and the research process. *Anthropology and Education Quarterly, 11*(1), 29–37.

Wax, R. H. (1971). *Doing fieldwork: Warnings and advice.* Chicago: University of Chicago Press.

Webb, E. J., Campbell, D. T., Schwartz, R. C., & Sechrest, L. (1981). *Nonreactive measures in the social sciences.* (2nd ed.). Boston: Houghton Mifflin.

Webb, W. H., Beals, A. R., & White, C. M. (1986). *Sources of information in the social sciences* (3rd ed.). Chicago: American Library Association.

Weick, K. E. (1984). Small wins: Redefining the scale of social problems. *American Psychologist, 39,* 40–49.

Weiner, B. (1972). *Theories of motivation from mechanism to cognition.* Chicago: Markham.

Weiner, B. (1980a). A cognitive (attribution)-emotion-action model of motivated behavior. An analysis of judgments of help-giving. *Journal of Personality and Social Psychology, 39,* 186–200.

Weiner, B. (1980b). *Human motivation.* New York: Holt, Rinehart and Winston.

Weiss, C. H. (1991). Evaluation research on political context: Sixteen years and four administrations later. In M. W. McLaughlin and D. Phillips (Eds.), *Evaluation and education at Quarter Century* (pp. 211–231). Ninetieth Yearbook of the National Society for the Study of Education, Part II. Chicago: University of Chicago Press.

Weiss, D., & Davison, M. (1981). Test theory and method. *Annual Review of Psychology, 32,* 629–658.

Weiss, R. S. (1994). *Learning from strangers: The art and method of qualitative interview studies.* New York: Free Press.

Weitzman, E. A., & Miles, M. B. (1995). *Computer programs for qualitative data analysis.* Thousand Oaks, CA: Sage.

Wentland, E. J. (1993). *Survey responses: An evaluation of their validity.* San Diego, CA: Academic Press.

Wertheimer, M. (1945). *Productive thinking.* New York: Harper.

Wharton, C. S. (1996). Making people feel good: Worker's constructions of meaning in interactive service jobs. *Qualitative Sociology, 19,* 217–233.

White, H. D. (1994). Scientific communication and literature retrieval. In H. Cooper and L. V. Hedges (Eds.), *The Handbook of research synthesis* (pp. 41–56). New York: Russell Sage Foundation.

White, R. W., & Lippitt, R. (1960). *Autocracy and democracy.* New York: Harper & Brothers.

Whyte, W. F. (1953). Interviewing for organizational research. *Human Organization, 12,* 15–22.

Whyte, W. F. (1984). *Learning from the field.* Beverly Hills, CA: Sage.

Whyte, W. F. (1993). *Street Corner Society: The social structure of an Italian Slum* (2nd ed.). Chicago: University of Chicago Press.

Wildemuth, B. M. (1981). *A bibliography to accompany the joint committee's standards on educational evaluation.* (ERIC, ED 222 512, Report 81). Princeton, NJ: ERIC Clearinghouse on Tests, Measurement, and Evaluation. Educational Testing Service.

Williams, M. E. (Ed.). (1981—). *Computer-readable databases: A directory and data sourcebook.* Chicago: American Library Association.

Wilson, J. (1971). *Thinking with concepts.* Cambridge, UK: University Press.

Wilson, T. D., DePaulo, B. M., Mook, D. G., & Klaaren, K. J. (1993). Scientists' evaluations of research: The biasing effects of the importance of the topic. *Psychological Science, 4,* 322–325.

Windle, C. (1954). Test-retest effect on personality questionnaires. *Educational and Psychological Measurement, 14,* 617–633.

Winne, P. H. (1995). Inherent details in self-regulated learning. *Educational Psychologist, 30,* 173–187.

Witkin, B. R. (1984). *Assessing needs in educational and social programs: Using information to make decisions, set priorities, and allocate resources.* San Francisco: Jossey-Bass.

Wolcott, H. (1973). *The man in the principal's office: An ethnography.* New York: Holt, Rinehart and Winston.

Wolcott, H. (1990). *Writing up qualitative research.* Newbury Park, CA: Sage.

Wolcott, H. (1992). Posturing in qualitative inquiry. In M. D. LeCompte, W. L. Milroy, and J. Preissle (Eds.), *The handbook of qualitative research in education* (pp. 3–52). New York: Academic Press.

Wolcott, H. F. (1995). *The art of fieldwork.* Walnut Creek, CA: AltaMira Press.

Wolf, R. L. (1975). Trial by jury: A new evaluation method. *Phi Delta Kappan, 57*(3), 185–187.

Wolf, R. L. (1979). The use of judicial evaluation methods in the formulation of educational policy. *Evaluation and Policy Analysis, 1*(3), 19–28.

Wong, L. Y. (1995). Research on teaching: Process-product research findings and the feelings of obviousness. *Journal of Educational Psychology, 87,* 504–511.

Woodbury, M. (1985). *Childhood information resources.* Arlington, VA: Information Resources Press.

Worthen, B. R., & Sanders, J. R. (1987). *Educational evaluation: Alternative approaches and practical guidelines.* White Plains, NY: Longman.

Wortman, P. M. (1984). Cost-effectiveness: A review. In R. F. Connor, D. G. Altman, & C. Jackson (Eds.), *Evaluation studies review annual* (Vol. 9, pp. 308–322). Beverly Hills, CA: Sage.

Wulf, K. M. (1977). Relationship of assigned classroom seating area to achievement variables. *Educational Research Quarterly, 2,* 56–62.

Wurman, R. S. (1989). *Information anxiety: What to do when information doesn't tell you what you need to know.* New York: Doubleday.

Wylie, R. C. (1974, 1979). *The self-concept* (1st and rev. ed.). Lincoln: University of Nebraska Press.

Yates, B. T. (1985). Cost-effectiveness analysis and cost-benefit analysis: An introduction. *Behavioral Assessment, 7*(3), 207–234. Also reprinted in D. S. Cordray & M. W. Lipsey (Eds.) (1986). *Evaluation studies review annual* (Vol. 11, pp. 315–342). Beverly Hills, CA: Sage.

Yin, R. K. (1984). *Case study research: Design and methods.* Beverly Hills, CA: Sage.

Youngstrom, N. (1990). Psychologist receives NAMI science award. *The APA Monitor, 21*(September), 7.

Zdep, S. M., & Irvine, S. H. (1970). A reverse Hawthorne effect in educational evaluations. *Journal of School Psychology, 8*(2), 89–95.

Zimbardo, P. G., Anderson, S. M., & Kabat, L. G. (1981). Induced hearing deficit generates experimental paranoia. *Science, 212*(June), 1529–1531.

Zwick, R. (Ed.) (1997). Innovative uses of computers in testing (special issue). *Journal of Educational Measurement, 34,* 1–100.

Zwicky, F. (1969). *Discovery invention & research through the morphological approach.* New York: Macmillan.

Name Index

Subject Index

The abbreviations *t*, *f*, and *n* stand for table, figure, and reference notes, respectively.